Lecture Notes in Computer Science 16307

Founding Editors

Gerhard Goos
Juris Hartmanis

Editorial Board Members

Elisa Bertino, *Purdue University, West Lafayette, IN, USA*
Wen Gao, *Peking University, Beijing, China*
Bernhard Steffen, *TU Dortmund University, Dortmund, Germany*
Moti Yung, *Columbia University, New York, NY, USA*

Editors
Sander Bakkes
Utrecht University
Utrecht, The Netherlands

Francesco Bellotti
University of Genova
Genoa, Italy

Pierpaolo Dondio
Maynooth University
Kildare, Ireland

Manuel Ninaus
University of Graz
Graz, Austria

Vanissa Wanick
University of Southampton
Southampton, UK

Antonio Bucchiarone
University of L'Aquila
L'Aquila, Italy

ISSN 0302-9743   ISSN 1611-3349 (electronic)
Lecture Notes in Computer Science
ISBN 978-3-032-11042-8   ISBN 978-3-032-11043-5 (eBook)
https://doi.org/10.1007/978-3-032-11043-5

Preface

This volume includes contributions from the Games and Learning Alliance (GALA) conference, which is dedicated to the advancement of research into serious game. The fourteenth edition of the GALA conference was held in Utrecht, The Netherlands, November 19thNovember 21st, 2025. This edition was organized by the Serious Games Society (SGS) and Utrecht University.

The fascinating three-day event provided an international discussion forum to advance the theories, technologies, and knowledge that support the design, development, and research of serious games. GALA 2025 received 142 paper submissions from academic researchers and practitioners from over thirty countries. Each paper was reviewed by three Program Committee members. The accepted papers, covering various aspects of serious game theories and applications, were presented in thematically distinct paper sessions and a poster session. Following a double-blind review process with an average of three reviews per submission, of the 142 submissions only 33 were accepted as full papers, and 24 were accepted as short papers. This year's anthology presents a rich variety of research and innovation across five distinct tracks: the *Educational Science* track, the *Game Design* track, the *Media and Cultural Studies* track, the *Technology* track, the finally the *Application* track.

Finally, the *Poster* section addresses a wide range of topics, ranging from research on metacognitive regulation and cognitive load to tangible interfaces, from clinical avatars to participatory design, and from instructional serious games to real-world play research, and indeed, many more valuable research topics at the intersection of game design and methodology, educational sciences, and (cognitive) psychology.

We were delighted to have four prominent keynote speakers: Regan Mandrykin her talk highlighting innovations in social gaming, Hanneke Scholtenadvocating for so-called "hybrid playgrounds", i.e., games as interactive spaces for discovery and identity development, Hannah Boeijkensreflecting on metric and meaning, to the end of combining scientific and experiential knowledge for impactful game design, and Geoff Engelsteinsharing his expertise on the intersection of human psychology and the player experience, particularly in the context of leveraging cognitive biases in game design. We were truly delighted to host such a diverse and expert line-up of keynote speakers for this 2025 edition of GALA.

The conference featured a Game Exhibition and a *"Games for Good"* game competition with the aim of rewarding games that positively impact society, community, and well-being. The game competition received an impressive 46 submissions in the following three categories: business, academic, and student. Based on reviewer feedback, authors of shortlisted games were invited to demo their games at the conference.

As in previous years, the authors of the selected Best Papers presented at the GALA conference will be invited to submit an extended version of their paper for a dedicated special issue of the International Journal of Serious Games, the scientific journal managed by the Serious Games Society, indexed by the Emerging Sources Citation Index (ESCI), in the Web of Science Core Collection since 2015, and by Scopus since 2020.

We thank the authors for submitting many interesting papers and the international Program Committee for their careful and timely review of these papers. We are also thankful to our conference sponsors for their financial support: CAPTRS, the center for Advanced Preparedness and Threat Response Simulation. Finally, we gratefully acknowledge the Serious Games Society and Utrecht University for organizing the conference.

November 2025

Sander Bakkes
Francesco Bellotti
Pierpaolo Dondio
Manuel Ninaus
Vanissa Wanick
Antonio Bucchiarone

The original version of the book has been revised. The fifth editor name has been corrected. A correction to this book can be found at https://doi.org/10.1007/978-3-032-11043-5_58

Organization

General Chair

Sander Bakkes	Utrecht University, The Netherlands

Program Chairs

Antonio Bucchiarone	University of L'Aquila
Pierpaolo Dondio	TU Dublin, Ireland
Manuel Ninaus	University of Graz, Austria
Sander Bakkes	Utrecht University, The Netherlands

Keynotes Chairs

Vanissa Wanick	University of Southampton, UK
Sander Bakkes	Utrecht University, The Netherlands

Competition and Exhibition Chairs

Kristina Risley	University of Southampton, UK
René Röpke	TU Wien, Austria

Publication Chair

Francesco Bellotti	Università degli Studi di Genova, Italy

Administrative and Financial Chair

Francesco Bellotti	Università degli Studi di Genova, Italy

Communication Chair

Brunella Botte   Link Campus University, Italy

Local Chair

Renée Otten   Utrecht University, The Netherlands

Program Committee

Daisy Abbott	Glasgow School of Art, UK
André Almo	Technological University Dublin, Ireland
Vinícius Andrade	Universidade Estadual Paulista "Júlio de Mesquita Filho"
Mohammad Fadhli Asli	Universiti Malaysia Sabah, Malaysia
Roger Azevedo	University of Central Florida, USA
Jannicke Baalsrud Hauge	KTH Royal Institute of Technology, Sweden
Sander Bakkes	Utrecht University, The Netherlands
Simone Bassanelli	Fondazione Bruno Kessler, Italy
Francesco Bellotti	Università degli Studi di Genova, Italy
Pedro Beça	University of Aveiro, Portugal
Federico Bonetti	Fondazione Bruno Kessler, Italy
Antonio Bucchiarone	University of l'Aquila, Italy
Elena Camossi	NATO Science and Technology Organization, CMRE, Italy
Federica Caruso	University of l'Aquila, Italy
Maria B. Carvalho	Tilburg University, The Netherlands
Chiara Eva Catalano	CNR, Italy
Matheus Cezarotto	New Mexico State University, USA
Giuseppe Città	Consiglio Nazionale delle Ricerche, Italy
Elizabeth Cloude	Michigan State University, USA
Kendra M.L. Cooper	Independent Scholar, Canada
Francesca de Rosa	Centre for Advanced Preparedness and Threat Response Simulation, USA
Tania Di Mascio	University of l'Aquila, Italy
Pierpaolo Dondio	Technological University Dublin, Ireland
Nour El Mawas	Université de Lille, France
Georgios Fesakis	University of the Aegean, Greece
Luca Forneris	University of Genoa, Italy
Manuel Gentile	National Research Council, Italy

Ramesh Gorantla	Arizona State University, USA
Ludovic Hamon	Le Mans Université, France
Simon Hoermann	University of Canterbury, New Zealand
Sarah Howard	University of Leeds, UK
Thorsten Händler	Ferdinand Porsche Mobile University of Applied Sciences, Austria
Sinead Impey	Trinity College Dublin, Ireland
Ville Kankainen	Tampere University, Finland
Michael Kickmeier Rust	St.Gallen University of Teacher Education, Switzerland
Antti Koskinen	Tampere University, Finland
Georgios Kritikos	University of the Aegean, Greece
Kevin Körner	California Institute of Technology, USA
Pierre Laforcade	Le Mans Université, France
Bertrand Laforge	Sorbonne Université, France
Luca Lazzaroni	University of Genoa, Italy
Thiemo Leonhardt	Technische Universität Dresden, Germany
George Lepouras	University of the Peloponnese, Greece
Iza Marfisi-Schottman	Le Mans Université, France
Federico Martusciello	University of l'Aquila, Italy
Carlos Marín Lora	Universitat Jaume I, Spain
Nooralisa Mohd Tuah	University Malaysia Sabah, Malaysia
Maho Wielfrid Morie	Institut National Polytechnique Félix Houphouët-Boigny YamoussoukroIvory Coast
Michela Mortara	CNR, Italy
Thierry Nabeth	P-Val Conseil, France
Manuel Ninaus	University of Graz, Austria
Lahcen Oubahssi	Le Mans Université, France
Alessandro Pighetti	University of Genoa, Italy
Catherine Pons	National University Institute Jean-Francois Champollion Albi, France
Maria Popescu	Carol I National Defence University, Romania
Galih Dea Pratama	Universitas Bina Nusantara, Indonesia
Kristina Risley	University of Southampton, UK
Mariana Rocha	Technological University Dublin, Ireland
Alberto Rojas-Salazar	Trinity College Dublin, Ireland
Margarida Romero	Université Côte d'Azur, France
Valentina Rossi	Università Ca'Foscari, Italy
René Röpke	RWTH Aachen University, Germany
Avo Schönbohm	Berlin School of Economics and Law, Germany
Yoones Sekhavat	Tabriz Art University, Iran
Lynsay Shepherd	Abertay University, UK

Contents

Game Design Track

Media and Cultural Studies Track

Technology Track

Application track

Short Papers

Educational Science track

Foundational AI Knowledge Enhances Epistemic Curiosity Development in Game-Based AI Ethics Instruction

Antti Koskinen[✉] [iD]

Research Centre of Gameful Realities, Tampere University, 33100 Tampere, Finland
antti.koskinen@tuni.fi

Abstract. Naive perspectives on AI capabilities can diminish students' epistemic curiosity for exploring AI ethics. While foundational AI knowledge can theoretically enable meaningful knowledge gap recognition, an essential prerequisite for curiosity activation, its effects in AI ethics instruction remain unexplored. This study examines whether foundational AI knowledge affects epistemic curiosity and self-efficacy developmental patterns during game-based AI ethics instruction. A quasi-experimental design compared 148 students (M age = 13.5 years) receiving either AI fundamentals video pre-training followed by game-based AI ethics learning or game-based learning alone. 2x3 mixed repeated measures ANCOVA was used to examine developmental trajectories of in-game epistemic curiosity and self-efficacy measurements while controlling for prior AI ethics knowledge. Results show that students who received pre-training demonstrated significantly different epistemic curiosity patterns, showing growth compared to the game-only condition (d = 0.34 at final measurement). Self-efficacy development remained equivalent between conditions. These findings contribute to AI literacy framework development by providing empirical justification for integrated approaches linking AI fundamentals with AI ethics instruction to support epistemic curiosity sustainability. Additionally, this research offers empirical insights into the design of game-based learning components for AI literacy education.

Keywords: epistemic curiosity · game-based learning · AI ethics · AI literacy

1 Introduction

The proliferation of artificial intelligence systems in educational and societal contexts has generated polarized perspectives among students, ranging from technological solutionism to complete dismissal of AI utility [1]. Such oversimplified viewpoints can diminish the curiosity to explore AI ethics, the benefits, limitations, and societal implications of deploying AI systems [2, 3]. Foundational AI knowledge can dismantle these oversimplified perspectives by revealing AI's basic working mechanisms, their current use, and future developmental trajectories. This study examines whether foundational AI knowledge affects epistemic curiosity and self-efficacy developmental patterns during game-based AI ethics instruction, thus contributing to the instructional practices aiming to equip students with necessary knowledge, skills, and attitudes to thrive in the age of AI, collectively referred to as AI literacy [3].

S. Bakkes et al. (Eds.): GALA 2025, LNCS 16307, pp. 3–12, 2026.
https://doi.org/10.1007/978-3-032-11043-5_1

This aim is grounded in seminal conceptualization of epistemic curiosity, a driving force for exploration initiated by the need for seeking new information to resolve knowledge gaps [4–7]. Theoretical models posit an inverted-U relationship between prior knowledge and epistemic curiosity activation: insufficient knowledge prevents meaningful gap recognition, while excessive knowledge or mis-knowledge can eliminate exploratory motivation [5–7]. When activated, epistemic curiosity can significantly enhance learning outcomes [8], including game-based learning environments [9].

The curiosity-driven exploration depends not only on knowledge gap recognition but also on confidence in ability to bridge these gaps [10]. Self-efficacy, defined as perceived ability and confidence to successfully complete tasks and achieve goals, can serve as an enabler of information-seeking behaviors, allowing students to persist through uncertainty and perceive knowledge gaps as achievable challenges rather than threats [11]. Therefore, scholars have examined self-efficacy with epistemic curiosity to gain more nuanced insights on the effectiveness of educational interventions [10, 12].

Epistemic curiosity manifests as a response to immediate knowledge gaps, naturally dissipating upon gap resolution [13]: curiosity about how an AI system makes biased decisions may diminish once students understand the underlying algorithmic mechanisms. This transient nature renders traditional pre-post measurements inadequate, as they cannot capture the moment-to-moment fluctuations essential to understand how instruction affects curiosity development. Given the importance of preserving the flow of instruction, scholars have suggested that single-item measurements can be applied to reveal the temporal dynamics of emotional and motivational influence of instruction generally [14] and in game-based learning [15]. Such approaches are justified when measuring clearly defined, unidimensional constructs [14], with empirical support for single-item measure of epistemic curiosity [8, 16] and self-efficacy [17].

Game-based learning environments, defined as cyclical challenge-response-evaluation-feedback pattern [18], provide justified context for examining epistemic curiosity and self-efficacy developmental patterns. Game-based learning environments are shown to support epistemic curiosity [9], and self-efficacy development [15], while enabling situated measurement approaches [15]. Moreover, game-based approaches have demonstrated effectiveness for AI ethics instruction [19], where the uncertainty of ethical dilemmas can trigger knowledge gap recognition essential for curiosity activation. Given these methodological and pedagogical advantages, quasi-experimental research was conducted to compare video pre-training of AI fundamentals followed by game-based AI ethics learning versus game-based AI ethics learning alone.

Pre-training, providing foundational understanding before actual learning tasks, a key principle in cognitive–affective theory of learning with media [20], was selected as the experimental manipulation as it theoretically: a) can provide sufficient understanding to activate meaningful knowledge gaps [20], b) establishes prerequisite knowledge without imposing excessive cognitive demands that could interfere with curiosity development [21], and c) offers concrete mastery experiences with AI fundamentals that may enhance domain-specific self-efficacy beliefs, providing the confidence necessary to sustain exploratory engagement with ethical scenarios [11].

Drawing from this foundation, pre-training of foundational AI knowledge may optimize the conditions for epistemic curiosity in AI ethics instruction by enabling knowledge gap recognition while supporting self-efficacy necessary to sustain exploratory engagement. However, the effects of such instructional sequencing on epistemic curiosity and self-efficacy developmental patterns during AI ethics instruction remain unexplored. Addressing this gap can inform AI literacy framework development by providing evidence-based guidance for integrating foundational and ethical AI instruction to support motivational engagement. Two research questions are examined:

RQ1: Do epistemic curiosity developmental patterns differ between students receiving pre-training of AI fundamentals before game-based AI ethics instruction and those receiving game-based AI ethics instruction alone?

RQ2: Do self-efficacy developmental patterns differ between students receiving pre-training of AI fundamentals before game-based AI ethics instruction and those receiving game-based AI ethics instruction alone?

2 Methods

2.1 Participants

The sample consisted of 148 students (103 seventh-grade, 45 eighth-grade; M age = 13.5, SD = 0.59), 83 girls, 63 boys, and 2 students who preferred not to report gender. The study targeted 7th-8th grade students as they may be better able to understand the complex AI ethics issues than primary school students. Ten classes participated, with classroom-level randomization stratified by grade level. Students were assigned to one of two conditions: pre-training followed by game-based learning (PT-GBL; N = 71; 3 seventh-grade and 2 eighth-grade classes) or game-based learning only (GBL; N = 77; 3 seventh-grade and 2 eighth-grade classes). PT-GBL students watched a 14-min video on AI fundamentals before engaging with the MediaWatch – AI ethics learning game, while GBL students engaged only with the game-based learning environment.

The study adhered to Finnish research ethics standards and GDPR compliance requirements. Following institutional approval, study information was distributed to school administrators, parents, and students. Parentals opt-out procedures were established, and students received explicit information regarding voluntary participation and withdrawal rights without academic penalty. While no parental objections were received, 36 students declined data usage consent, resulting in the final analytical sample.

2.2 Stimulus

Game-Based Learning: MediaWatch – AI Ethics
MediaWatch – AI Ethics is a game-based learning platform that develops AI ethics competence through authentic ethical dilemmas. The platform has previously demonstrated effectiveness in AI ethics instruction [19], showing positive learning outcomes with brief engagement periods suitable for examining the effects of combined instructional approaches.

The environment incorporates three core design features: competition, avatar selection, and a feedback system. Students begin by selecting from four-characters and compete to achieve "AI ethics expert" status within a narrative framework. The game comprises nine ethical dilemma tasks relevant to adolescents' interactions with AI. Each task presents a scenario with multiple response options (typically one correct, one partially correct, and one incorrect choice) (Fig. 1, top). For instance, students evaluated whether an AI application tracking children's phone usage constitutes acceptable monitoring given the possible advantages or requires explicit consent protocols and transparency safeguards.

Following each response, students receive immediate feedback from a simulated "grand AI ethics committee" that explicates underlying ethical insights and guides balanced consideration of AI benefits and limitations. This feedback mechanism serves as the primary instructional component, encouraging nuanced evaluation rather than technological extremism (Fig. 1, bottom left). A dynamic scoreboard displays relative performance against virtual competitors, with one competitor calibrated to require approximately 67% accuracy for expert designation. This competitive structure was designed to maintain engagement while providing clear progress indicators (Fig. 1, bottom right).

The game's relatively straightforward design was deliberately selected to isolate the effects of instructional sequencing on motivational development patterns, as overly complex game mechanics could confound the measurement of epistemic curiosity and self-efficacy trajectories.

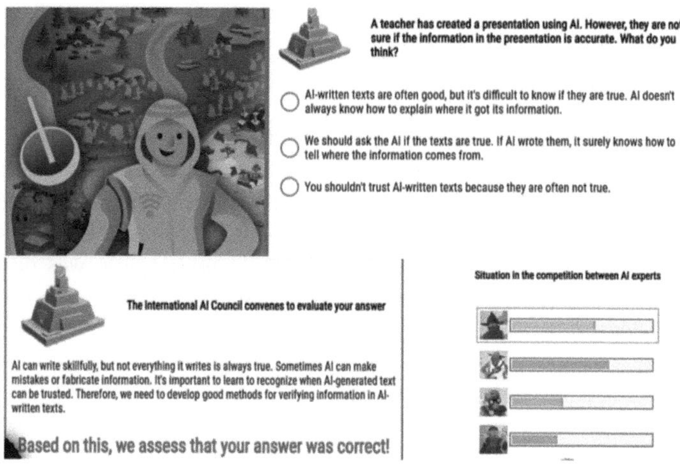

Fig. 1. Task (top), feedback (bottom left), and leaderboard (bottom right).

Instructional Video of AI Fundamentals

A 14-min video presentation was created to deliver foundational AI knowledge. The content was deliberately designed to avoid any discussion of AI ethics to prevent confounding effects with the subsequent game-based AI ethics instruction. The video employed a dual-display format combining slide content with instructor presence (picture-in-picture), replicating traditional classroom instruction. Content delivery utilized developmentally appropriate language with concrete examples and conceptual connections to facilitate comprehension among students. The presentation covered five core themes: AI definitions and terminology, evolution of AI systems from 1956–2024, fundamental components of AI systems, contemporary applications across domains and emerging developmental directions.

2.3 Measurements

Epistemic curiosity and self-efficacy were assessed using situated single-item measures embedded within the game environment. Following established practices for capturing temporal dynamics in game-based learning [15], measurements were administered after similarly difficult tasks 1, 5, and 9 to capture developmental patterns while minimizing gameplay disruption. Items were contextually framed as contributing to an AI ethics committee evaluation to maintain narrative coherence, with students informed that responses would not influence game.

Traditional reliability assessments were not conducted as they are not applicable to single-item measures [14], and test-retest reliability would be inappropriate as epistemic curiosity and self-efficacy are expected to fluctuate across measurements [11, 13].

Epistemic Curiosity was measured using continuous 1–18 scale (completely disagree – completely agree), to capture fine-grained developmental patterns in situated learning contexts with single-item: "My curiosity was aroused, and I would like to know more about the topic", adapted from established epistemic curiosity scales [22]. The item was adapted to specifically capture information-seeking desire, aligning with theoretical conceptualizations of epistemic curiosity as gap-driven exploration [5]. Similar single-item curiosity measures have previously used in capturing moment-to-moment epistemic curiosity fluctuations in instructional contexts [8, 16].

Self-efficacy was measured using continuous 1–18 scale (completely disagree – completely agree), to capture fine-grained developmental patterns in situated learning contexts with single-item: "I will certainly perform well on the following tasks" [15], to capture prospective confidence beliefs, aligning with conceptualization of self-efficacy as future-oriented competence expectations [11]. Similar single-item self-efficacy measures have previously used across educational contexts [15, 17, 23].

Prior AI Ethics Knowledge was assessed prior to the instruction using a 9-item scale adapted from existing AI ethics instruments [e.g., 24], measuring understanding of fundamental AI ethics understanding and practical application competence. Items were rated on a 5-point Likert scale (1 = totally disagree, 5 = totally agree), with good internal consistency (Cronbach's α = .87). Mean scores were used as a covariate in analyses to control for baseline knowledge differences.

2.4 Procedures

The study was conducted during regular school hours in authentic classroom settings. The entire procedure required approximately 50 min and was conducted within a single class period to control for temporal confounding factors. All sessions were administered following a standardized protocol.

Sessions began with standardized orientation covering study objectives, voluntary participation rights, and procedural instructions. Students accessed the game-based learning environment on school laptops using individual login codes and provided demographic information and consent confirmation. Then they concluded AI ethics knowledge assessment.

Following this, PT-GBL condition students viewed the 14-min AI fundamentals video before proceeding to gameplay, while GBL condition students proceeded directly to gameplay. Both conditions received identical game instructions and played without time restrictions. Epistemic curiosity and self-efficacy measurements were embedded within the game after tasks 1, 5, and 9 as previously described. To maintain ethical standards regarding equal educational access, GBL condition students viewed the instructional video after completing the game.

3 Results

3.1 Descriptive Statistics and Condition Equivalence

Table 1 presents sample characteristics and descriptive statistics by condition. Conditions were equivalent on demographic characteristics, with no significant differences in age $(t(146) = 0.69, p = .494)$, prior AI ethics knowledge $(t(146) = -0.97, p = .332)$, or gender distribution $(\chi^2(2) = 5.93, p = .052)$. Examination of epistemic curiosity trajectories revealed that PT-GBL students showed consistent increases across timepoints, while GBL students remained relatively stable with a slight decrease at the final timepoint. Self-efficacy showed increasing patterns in both conditions.

Table 1. Sample Characteristics by Condition, and Curiosity and Self-Efficacy by Condition and Timepoint

	Demographics, M (SD)			Epistemic curiosity, M (SD)			Self-Efficacy, M (SD)		
	Gender (Girl/Boy/NR)	Age	Prior-Knowledge	Task1	Task5	Task9	Task1	Task5	Task9
PT-GBL	45/24/2	13.48 (0.63)	3.72 (0.56)	10.70 (3.95)	11.38 (4.14)	11.70 (4.40)	11.72 (3.21)	12.73 (3.70)	13.39 (3.78)
GBL	38/39/0	13.54 (0.55)	3.61 (0.71)	10.18 (4.07)	10.22 (4.45)	9.97 (4.72)	11.84 (3.42)	12.40 (3.90)	12.79 (3.82)

3.2 RQ1: Epistemic Curiosity Developmental Patterns Between Conditions

A repeated measures ANCOVA was conducted to examine epistemic curiosity developmental patterns across tasks 1, 5, and 9, with condition (PT-GBL vs. GBL) as the between-subjects factor and prior AI ethics knowledge as a covariate. Mauchly's test indicated violation of sphericity (W = .817, p < .001), so Greenhouse-Geisser corrected degrees of freedom were used.

The analysis revealed a significant time × condition interaction (F(1.69, 245.11) = 3.54, p = .038, η^2p = .024), indicating differential epistemic curiosity developmental patterns between conditions (Fig. 2, left). The covariate of prior AI ethics knowledge significantly predicted curiosity levels (F(1, 145) = 23.44, p < .001, η^2p = .139).

Pairwise comparisons at each timepoint showed no significant differences at tasks 1 (p = .643) and 5 (p = .173), but a significant condition difference emerged at task 9 (PT-GBL = 11.57 vs. GBL = 10.09, p = .039, d = 0.34). Within-condition analyses revealed that PT-GBL students showed significant epistemic curiosity increases from task 1 to task 5 (p = .028) and task 1 to task 9 (p = .012), while GBL students showed no significant changes across timepoints (all p > .33).

These results indicate differential epistemic curiosity developmental patterns between conditions, with pre-training facilitating a progressive epistemic curiosity development pattern absent in the game-based learning alone condition.

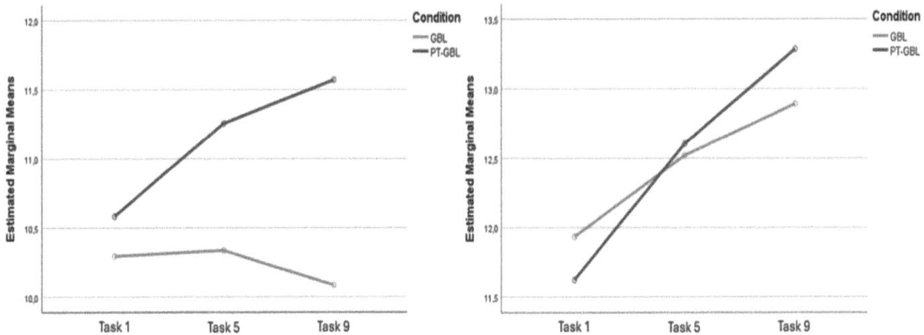

Fig. 2. Epistemic curiosity (left) and self-efficacy (right) developmental patterns by condition during game-based AI ethics learning

3.3 RQ2: Self-Efficacy Developmental Patterns Between Conditions

A repeated measures ANCOVA was conducted to examine self-efficacy developmental patterns across tasks 1, 5, and 9, with condition (PT-GBL vs. GBL) as the between-subjects factor and prior AI ethics knowledge as a covariate. Mauchly's test indicated violation of sphericity (W = .682, p < .001), so Greenhouse-Geisser corrected degrees of freedom were used.

The analysis revealed no significant time × condition interaction (F(1.52, 219.96) = 1.25, p = .283, η^2p = .009), indicating similar self-efficacy developmental patterns between conditions (Fig. 2, right). The covariate of AI ethics knowledge significantly predicted self-efficacy levels (F(1, 145) = 26.49, p < .001, η^2p = .154).

Pairwise comparisons at each timepoint revealed no significant condition differences at task 1 (p = .552), task 5 (p = .884), or task 9 (p = .509). These results indicate that students receiving pre-training of AI fundamentals did not demonstrate significantly different self-efficacy developmental patterns compared to those receiving game-based learning alone.

4 Discussion, Limitations, and Conclusion

This study examined whether students who receive pre-training of AI fundamentals demonstrate different epistemic curiosity and self-efficacy developmental patterns during game-based AI ethics learning compared to those receiving game-based learning alone. The results show that pre-training facilitated epistemic curiosity growth, contrasting curiosity patterns in the game-only condition (final measurement d = 0.34). Self-efficacy development remained unaffected by instructional sequencing.

The observed differential epistemic curiosity development patterns align with propositions suggesting an information gap as a main driver of epistemic curiosity [5–7]: AI fundamental instruction, presumably, enabled meaningful knowledge gap recognition during game-based AI ethics instruction. This process became significant at the end of the game (measurement point 3), where pre-trained students continued their upward epistemic curiosity trend, but students in the game-only condition did not. This finding suggests that sustaining epistemic curiosity in game-based AI ethics instruction is affected by instructional sequencing as theoretically suggested in [20]. Consequently, AI literacy frameworks including game-based learning components, should not only rely on games 'inherent motivational power', but carefully consider how, when and why game-based learning is integrated in the curricular design.

The lack of significant differences in self-efficacy patterns between conditions presents an unexpected finding. The game-based learning environment may have provided sufficient mastery experiences to support self-efficacy development regardless of prior understanding of AI fundamentals. In fact, the opted three-option response format may have restricted designing tasks that were not sufficiently complex to trigger concrete mastery experiences. Because of the same restrictions, the tasks could be successfully completed using general ethical reasoning capabilities rather than requiring AI-specific technical understanding. However, both conditions demonstrated similar upward self-efficacy trajectories.

The contrasting developmental patterns between epistemic curiosity and self-efficacy reveal important insights about their relationship. These differential patterns align with established theoretical propositions that epistemic curiosity and self-efficacy operate through distinct psychological mechanisms [5, 11], extending this understanding to game-based AI ethics instruction. While both groups demonstrated self-efficacy increases from initial to final measurements, only the pre-training condition demonstrated curiosity growth, suggesting that self-efficacy development alone is insufficient for fostering curiosity in game-based AI ethics instruction.

Several limitations constrain the interpretation and generalization of these findings. The absence of learning outcome measures limits assessment of the practical educational significance of the observed motivational patterns. While the findings provide empirically grounded guidelines for AI literacy frameworks and game-based AI ethics design from novel perspective, future studies should establish connections between these motivational patterns and learning gains and examine influence of different feedback mechanisms. The reliance on single-item measures for epistemic curiosity and self-efficacy, while justified for situated assessment in game-based environments, introduces potential measurement error that may compromise the precision of trajectory estimation and reduce sensitivity to differential developmental patterns between conditions. The single-session design constrains understanding of longer-term developmental trajectories. Extended investigations might reveal differential self-efficacy patterns that were undetectable within the current temporal constraints. Third, the sample's restriction to Finnish 7th–8th grade students limits generalizability across developmental stages and cultural contexts. Future research should examine whether the observed effects replicate with different age groups and educational systems.

This study provided empirical evidence that AI fundamentals pre-training facilitated epistemic curiosity growth throughout game-based learning, contrasting with declining curiosity patterns in the game-only condition. Self-efficacy development remained unaffected by instructional sequencing. These findings contribute to AI literacy framework development by providing empirical justification for coherent, integrated approaches linking AI fundamentals with AI ethics instruction to support epistemic curiosity sustainability. The research demonstrates that facilitation of epistemic curiosity may benefit from instructional sequencing rather than isolated game-based approaches. Consequently, these insights inform the development of educational practices that prepare students to engage thoughtfully with ethical complexities inherent in an AI-mediated society.

Acknowledgments. This study was funded by the Strategic Research Council (No. 358250).

Disclosure of Interests. The author has no competing interests to declare.

References

1. Mertala, P., Fagerlund, J.: Finnish 5th and 6th graders' misconceptions about artificial intelligence. Int. J. Child-Comput. Interact. **39**, 100630 (2024)
2. Dabbagh, H., Earp, B.D., Mann, S.P., Plozza, M., Salloch, S., Savulescu, J.: AI ethics should be mandatory for schoolchildren. AI Ethics **5**(1), 87–92 (2025)
3. Ng, D.T.K., Leung, J.K.L., Chu, S.K.W., Qiao, M.S.: Conceptualizing AI literacy: an exploratory review. Comput. Educ. Artif. Intell. **2**, 100041 (2021)
4. Berlyne, D.E.: A theory of human curiosity. Br. J. Psychol. **45**, 180–191 (1954)
5. Loewenstein, G.: The psychology of curiosity: a review and reinterpretation. Psychol. Bull. **116**(1), 75 (1994)
6. Grossnickle, E.M.: Disentangling curiosity: dimensionality, definitions, and distinctions from interest in educational contexts. Educ. Psychol. Rev. **28**(1), 23–60 (2016)
7. Murayama, K., FitzGibbon, L., Sakaki, M.: Process account of curiosity and interest: a reward-learning perspective. Educ. Psychol. Rev. **31**, 875–895 (2019)
8. Kang, M.J., et al.: The wick in the candle of learning: epistemic curiosity activates reward circuitry and enhances memory. Psychol. Sci. **20**(8), 963–973 (2009)
9. Huck, J.T., Day, E.A., Lin, L., Jorgensen, A.G., Westlin, J., Hardy, J.H., III.: The role of epistemic curiosity in game-based learning: distinguishing skill acquisition from adaptation. Simul. Gaming **51**(2), 141–166 (2020)
10. Li, Y., et al.: Functional connectivity mediates the relationship between self-efficacy and curiosity. Neurosci. Lett. **711**, 134442 (2019)
11. Bandura, A.: Self-Efficacy: The Exercise of Control. W.H. Freeman, New York (1997)
12. Shin, D.D.: Curiosity promotes self-regulated learning and achievement in online courses for students with varying self-efficacy levels. Educ. Psychol. **44**(4), 455–474 (2024)

13. Hidi, S.E., Renninger, K.A.: On educating, curiosity, and interest development. Curr. Opin. Behav. Sci. **35**, 99–103 (2020)
14. Allen, M.S., Iliescu, D., Greiff, S.: Single item measures in psychological science. Eur. J. Psychol. Assess. **38**(1), 1–5 (2022)
15. Koskinen, A., McMullen, J., Hannula-Sormunen, M., Ninaus, M., Kiili, K.: The strength and direction of the difficulty adaptation affect situational interest in game-based learning. Comput. Educ. **194**, 104694 (2023)
16. Baranes, A., Oudeyer, P.Y., Gottlieb, J.: Eye movements reveal epistemic curiosity in human observers. Vision. Res. **117**, 81–90 (2015)
17. Hoeppner, B.B., Kelly, J.F., Urbanoski, K.A., Slaymaker, V.: Comparative utility of a single-item versus multiple-item measure of self-efficacy in predicting relapse among young adults. J. Subst. Abuse Treat. **41**(3), 305–312 (2011)
18. Kiili, K.: Digital game-based learning: towards an experiential gaming model. Internet High. Educ. **8**(1), 13–24 (2005)
19. Koskinen, A., Lindstedt, A., Kiili, K.: Game-based learning can enhance students' understanding of AI ethics. In: Schönbohm, A., et al. (eds.) Games and Learning Alliance, GALA 2024. LNCS, vol. 15348, pp. 47–56. Springer, Cham (2025). https://doi.org/10.1007/978-3-031-78269-5_5
20. Moreno, R., Mayer, R.: Interactive multimodal learning environments: special issue on interactive learning environments: contemporary issues and trends. Educ. Psychol. Rev. **19**, 309–326 (2007)
21. Mayer, R.E.: Using multimedia for e-learning. J. Comput. Assist. Learn. **33**(5), 403–423 (2017)
22. Schmidt, H.G., Rotgans, J.I.: Epistemic curiosity and situational interest: distant cousins or identical twins? Educ. Psychol. Rev. **33**, 325–352 (2021)
23. Noreikis, M., Savela, N., Kaakinen, M., Xiao, Y., Oksanen, A.: Effects of gamified augmented reality in public spaces. IEEE Access **7**, 148108–148118 (2019)
24. Ng, D.T.K., Wu, W., Leung, J.K.L., Chu, S.K.W.: Artificial intelligence (AI) literacy questionnaire with confirmatory factor analysis. In: 2023 IEEE International Conference on Advanced Learning Technologies (ICALT), pp. 233–235. IEEE (2023)

Game Over! Exploring the Effects of Playing the Existential Video Game "The Painting"

Raphaela Montera⬛ and Imke Alenka Harbig$^{(\boxtimes)}$ ⬛

University of Klagenfurt, Universitätsstraße 65/67, 9020 Klagenfurt, Austria
{raphaela.montera,imke.harbig}@aau.at

Abstract. Whether to prepare for the loss of a loved one or to reflect on one's own mortality, each of us must eventually confront the reality of death. Scholars exploring death education have long explored how individuals can internalize the transformative effects of facing mortality – even without direct experience. This study investigates how the existential video game (EXG) *The Painting*, which address existential themes such as meaning in life and death, might support such reflection. Using a mixed-methods experimental design, 44 participants were randomly assigned to play either *The Painting* or a neutral game. Attitudes toward death were assessed before and after gameplay using the Death Attitude Profile–Revised (DAP-R), and participants responded to open-ended questions about their emotional and reflective experiences. Results indicate that *The Painting* elicited a range of emotional responses, including sadness, gratitude, and bittersweetness. The game's atmosphere, music, and storytelling elicited thoughtful responses that often touched on the afterlife, acceptance of death, and the emotional consequences of loss. These findings highlight the potential of EXGs as tools for emotionally resonant experiences that support existential reflection. Their narrative and immersive qualities may provide accessible pathways for exploring mortality in therapeutic, educational, or self-reflective contexts.

Keywords: Existential Video Games · Death Education · Experiment · Reflection

1 Introduction

Death. At some point in life, every individual must confront the reality of death - Either through the grief of losing a loved one or through personal reflection on their own existence. Confronting mortality – even without firsthand experience – can bring both anxiety and transformative insights. Death education refers to a range of activities designed to encourage reflection on death, dying, and bereavement. It facilitates the processing of complex and often conflicting emotions by encouraging individuals to contemplate the meaning of life and death, while promoting open dialogue on these subjects [1]. Research has shown that engaging with death education can foster a deeper sense of meaning in life, enhance awareness of life's finiteness [2–4] and reduce death anxiety [5, 6]. It promotes the development of coping strategies for dealing with death and loss, particularly

S. Bakkes et al. (Eds.): GALA 2025, LNCS 16307, pp. 13–23, 2026.
https://doi.org/10.1007/978-3-032-11043-5_2

through emotional recognition and an open discourse about mortality [4, 7] and provides individuals with conceptual and emotional tools that support the navigation of grief [4, 8].

Relying on insights from existential psychology [9], Chittaro and Sioni [10] introduced the concept of Existential Video Games (EXGs), defining them as (serious) games that focus on at least one core existential concern and are specifically designed to encourage players to reflect on them [10, 11]. For instance, *Spiritfarer* (ThunderLotus, 2020) is categorised as an EXG, as it meaningfully engages with themes of death, loss, and interpersonal connection [10]. In *Spiritfarer*, players take on the role of Stella, a ferry master to the deceased, who is responsible for caring for spirits, fulfilling their final wishes, and guiding them to the afterlife. Similarly, *That Dragon, Cancer* (Numinous Games, 2016) is an autobiographical video game that narrates the emotional journey of a family coping with the terminal illness of their young son. The unique aesthetic and soothing soundtracks of these games, facilitate a reflective and compassionate exploration of grief and the human experience [10]. EXGs that focus on death offer an emotionally safe interactive space for engaging with and learning about sensitive topics such as death, palliative care, grief, farewells, and the search for meaning in life [10–15]. They also create space for players to reflect on personal experiences of loss and to confront their own fears surrounding mortality [10, 15–17]. As a form of digital art, EXGs can serve as a powerful medium for knowledge dissemination, challenging cultural taboos around grief and promoting broader public discourse on existential themes [18]. Research examining the effects of EXGs has shown that such games can inspire players to embrace life more fully and to express a deeper appreciation for the enduring emotional impact of lost loved ones [12, 14, 19, 20]. For individuals who have experienced bereavement, EXGs can furthermore prompt a process of reconstructing and reinterpreting those experiences, often leading to the emergence of new personal meanings [12]. Gameplay can also serve as a springboard for confronting autobiographical challenges and fostering deeper emotional reflection, thereby enhancing players' ability to process and cope with loss [12, 13, 19]. Building on this growing body of evidence, this study examines player experience with visual novel *The Painting* (Tymedust Games, 2024).

2 Related Work

Although the field of EXGs has received growing attention in recent years, empirical research focusing on death remains limited. The few experimental investigations conducted to date show promising results, suggesting that such games can effectively foster existential reflection, process grief, and enhance a sense of meaning in life [12, 19, 20].

Chittaro and Sioni [10] were among the first to systematically examine the use of EXGs as a medium for fostering existential reflection. In a laboratory study, they examined the effects of the EXG *Existence*, in which players explore a graveyard and encounter a series of quotes and ideas related to death. The video game successfully prompted reflection on death and mortality, often evoking an increased desire to live life to the fullest, and reflections on personal experiences, and memories of what deceased individuals had given them. While both positive and negative emotions were reported, the negative reactions were generally brief and transient.

In 2023, Eun and Yong [12] conducted a study investigating the effects of the EXGs *Spiritfarer* and *Bear's Restaurant* on individuals experiencing grief. A 7-day gameplay of the two games prompted participants to engage in reflection on their personal experiences of loss, often eliciting positive emotions associated with memories of the deceased and prompting them to re-evaluated their understandings of grief and death. Another recent contribution comes from Khodarkarmi et al. [11], who examined the effects of the EXG *Evergreen*. Using a mixed-methods experimental design, the authors reported a significant change in responses to the Meaning in Life Questionnaire [21], while responses to the Scale for Existential Thinking [22] stayed the same.

While these studies demonstrate the potential of EXGs, the field remains in its early stages. Further empirical research is needed to explore how different games engage players differently. Titles may vary widely in their capacity to evoke specific emotional responses, cognitive shifts, or existential insights. To build a more nuanced understanding of what EXGs can achieve, it is essential to analyse a broader range of games using diverse methodological approaches.

The present study contributes to this growing body of research by investigating the EXG *The Painting*, a visual novel narrated from the perspective of a grieving father. Unlike previous studies that focus on games with metaphorical portrayals of death (e.g., *Spiritfarer*), or on terminal illness and anticipatory grief (e.g. *That Dragon, Cancer*), *The Painting* offers a grounded, realistic narrative centered on mourning and memory. Set ten years after the loss, it shifts the focus from immediate grief to long-term coping, remembrance, and the integration of loss into everyday life. To our knowledge, this is also the first empirical study to investigate an EXG in the form of a visual novel. We explore what kinds of emotional reactions and reflective thoughts *The Painting* elicits, and to what extent it influences participants' attitudes toward death.

3   The Painting

The EXG *The Painting*, created by Tymedust Games in 2022, is a browser-based visual novel that tells the story of Astrid, a young woman who has passed away, as narrated by her father. The narrative unfolds through the exploration of a wall of family photographs, each revealing key moments from Astrid's life. As gentle, melancholic piano music plays, the player's perspective shifts from one photograph to the next, while reading the father's reflections on his daughter's personality, accomplishments, and their shared experiences. He recalls joyful memories, such as winning her first acting contest: *"You held the diploma so high that we almost couldn't see your face behind it. I can only imagine how wide that smile must have been.;"* and expresses regret about time lost: *"Time ... We know that it's our most precious resource, yet we throw it away haphazardly, as if there's no risk of ever running out."* In the final scene, the complete photo wall is revealed with a portrait of Astrid at its center. Marking the passage of time: *"Today, it's been 10 years,"* the father expresses enduring gratitude and gently says goodnight to his daughter.

As a visual novel, *The Painting* does not include branching paths or choices. However, players control the pacing of the experience by clicking through the narrative at their own speed [23]. Centred on death, loss, grief, and memory, *The Painting* exemplifies an EXG that guides players through a deeply personal and emotionally reflective experience and ends on a quiet and hopeful note.

4   Method

To examine the impact of the video game *The Painting* on individuals' attitudes and reflections concerning the topic of death, a mixed-methods experiment was conducted. This design was chosen to capture both the measurable impact on death-related attitudes and the nuanced personal experiences of participants.

4.1   Participants

Aiming for a diverse sample regarding age and educational background, participants were recruited through the email list of the University of Klagenfurt and social networks. Figure 1 outlines the exclusion criteria and resulting sample ($N = 44$). Twenty-one participants were randomly assigned to the experimental group (EG) and 23 to the control group (CG). The EG included 9 men and 12 women, ranging in age from 21 to 55 ($M = 26.66$, $SD = 7.54$), while the CG consisted of 8 men, 14 women, and 1 participant identifying as diverse, aged between 19 and 46 years ($M = 27$, $SD = 7.31$). Most participants' nationalities were Austrian ($n = 26$) and German ($n = 11$). All participants held at least a high school qualification, and about half a university degree. There were no significant differences in video game play frequency between the two groups.

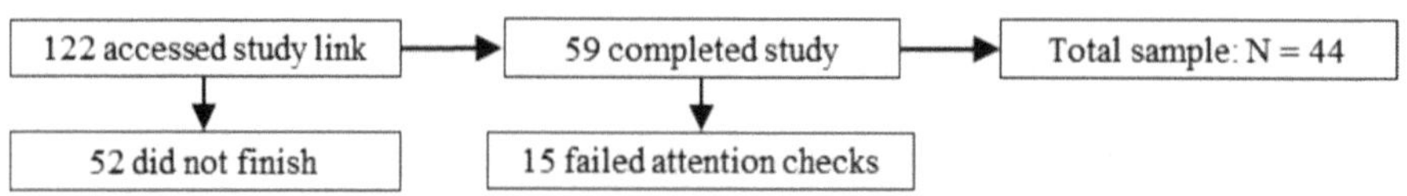

Fig. 1. Flowchart of Sample Selection.

4.2   Procedure

At the start of the study, participants provided demographic information and answered one item from each subscale of the Death Attitude Profile-Revised (DAP-R; [24]): *fear of death, death avoidance and neutral acceptance.* After random assignment, the EG played *The Painting*, while the CG played the puzzle-game *Block Fevrio* (Fevrio, N.D.), a tile-matching puzzle game similar to Tetris. *Block Fevrio* was chosen because it contains neither thematic connections to death nor overlapping gameplay elements with *The Painting.* Both games take approximately 5 to 10 min to complete. Following the gameplay, participants responded to control questions and the remaining DAP-R items. The questionnaire was split between the pre- and post-test phases to minimize potential retest effects caused by participants' memory of the items [25].

Finally, participants were asked two open-ended questions. The first Question was: *What thoughts and emotions did you feel while playing the game? Please describe these emotions during specific moments of the game.* The second question asked: *Did you *feel particular emotions when you were confronted with the topic of death and loss? Please describe them and reflect why you might feel that way.* All participants were fully debriefed and provided with a psychological resource list.

4.3 Analysis

A mixed-methods approach was employed to evaluate the data collected in this study. Participants' open-ended responses were analysed using an inductive coding strategy and following Mayring's qualitative content analysis [26]. This resulted in two code books: one for the EG and one for the CG, which was used to ensure that reflections or emotions observed in the EG were not simply due to general study participation or exposure to the DAP-R items. Between-group differences (EG vs. CG) and within-group changes (pre- vs. post-intervention) in DAP-R were assessed through independent-sample and paired-sample t-tests. When the data violated assumptions of normal distribution, independent and paired Wilcoxon tests were applied.

5 Results

As shown in Table 1, qualitative responses to were categorized into three domains: **Elicited Emotion** (emotional experiences during gameplay), **Evoked Reflection** (thoughts and attitudes towards death) and **Video Game** (comments on the narrative, design, and atmosphere of the game).

Table 1. Summary of categories

Domain	Category	Subcategory	n
Elicited Emotion	Negative emotion	Sadness, Fear of loss, Shock, Regret	18
	Positive emotion	Happiness, Gratitude, Hope, Relief, Curiosity	12
	Bittersweet		10
	Neutral experience	No relation, No reason	5
Evoked reflection	Reflection	General reflection, Effects of loss, Perspective of grieving, Loss is worse than dying, Effects of own death on others, Own mortality, Afterlife, Death acceptance, Wishes	15
	Memories of experiences with loss		3
Video game	Positive aspects of story and plot		6
	Atmosphere and Music		6

(*continued*)

Table 1. (*continued*)

Domain	Category	Subcategory	n
	Negative aspects of story and plot		5

The game successfully elicited a broad range of emotional responses. Ten of the 15 participants, who described emotional experiences, reported both negative and positive feelings and four explicitly highlighted this emotional duality. One participant reflected: *"It was beautiful to play through the father's memories and intentions but also a bit sad."*

Table 2 shows a summary of participants' reflections. The most common theme among these were reflections on mortality, death, and loss. One participant described reflecting on *"thoughtfulness about the time we have with each other,"* while another noted how the game reflected *"the sudden nature of the death of a young person."* Three individuals specifically considered their own experiences with grief while playing: *"It reminded* [me] *of the death of my father and that I also wish that I had spent more time with him and that I had enjoyed it more."*

Many participants also reflected on the emotional consequences of loss and adopted an empathetic perspective toward the grieving process. For instance, one participant wrote: *"I tried to imagine how this must feel. I feel really sad when I'm confronted with a story of someone who lost/loses somebody, but not when it's about dying in general. I think it's human, to feel empathy when confronted with the death of people and the loss of their loved ones."*

Lastly, participants reflected on their own mortality. One participant stated: *"The thought of death is not one I fear, but rather the thought about what will happen to the loved ones we leave behind."* Another participant expressed: *"To prepare accordingly, to find peace of mind and to finish the matters that are most important is one of, if not the ultimate challenge in life. It is a melancholic feeling of something unavoidable further down the road, something that is universal for each of us. It's rather sad, but we have to live with it."*

Table 2. Types of reflections reported by participants

Category	Description	n
General reflection	Participants reflected on the topic of death in general.	6
Effects of loss	Participants reflected on how the inevitable loss affects the bereaved and how difficult it is to accept.	6
Perspective of grieving	Participants theoretically and empathically put themselves in the perspective of the grieving and reflected on it.	3
Loss is worse than dying	Participants expressed that the loss of loved ones is worse than dying themselves.	3
Own mortality	Participants reflected on their own mortality.	3

(*continued*)

Table 2. (*continued*)

Category	Description	n
Afterlife	Participants reflected on life after death or religion.	2
Death acceptance	Participants viewed death as a part of life and therefore did not report strong emotions while playing.	2
Wishes	Participants reflected on wishing they had shared something with the deceased or spent more time with them.	2

In the CG, 17 participants reported positive, eight negative, and five neutral experiences. Positive responses focused on relaxation, joy, and concentration, while negative reflected stress and feeling overwhelmed: *"I felt a bit lost, because I did not know the best strategy for putting pieces"*. All responses of the CG focused on the game's mechanics and none on the themes of death or loss.

To assess whether *The Painting* influenced participants' death-related attitudes, t-tests and Wilcoxon-tests were conducted (see Table 3 for mean scores). Prior to gameplay, the only statistically significant difference between the EG and CG appeared in the death avoidance subscale: $t(42) = 2.54, p = 0.02, d = 0.76$), with the EG avoiding the topic of death more. The EG had higher scores for fear of death $t(42) = 1.14, p = 0.26, d = 0.34$, while the CG had higher scores for neutral acceptance, $V = 204, p = 0.36$). Death avoidance decreased in both groups (EG: $t(20) = 0.92, p = 0.37, d = 0.16$; CG: $t(22) = 1.53, p = 0.14, d = 0.28$), with EG continuing to show higher scores than CG, $t(42) = 2.58, p = 0.01, d = 0.78$). The fear of death subscale scores decreased significantly in both groups (EG: $t(20) = 3.42, p < 0.01, d = 0.43$; CG: $t(22) = 2.46, p = 0.02, d = 0.34$), with EG maintaining to show higher values, $t(41.14) = 1.15, p = 0.26, d = 0.35$). The neutral acceptance subscale scores increased significantly in both groups (EG: $t(20) = 4.32, p < 042.5, d = 0.8$; CG: $V = 42.5, p = 0.02$), with the CG showing higher scores after the video games, $t(42) = 0.81, p = 0.42, d = 0.24$). Finally, individuals with prior experiences of grief demonstrated a tendency toward greater neutral acceptance. However, this association was not statistically significant, $r(19) = 0.29, p = 0.20$.

Table 3. Mean scores and standard deviations of the DAP-R before and after gameplay

	EG M (SD)		CG M (SD)	
	Before	After	Before	After
Death avoidance	5.52 (1.12)	5.31 (1.41)	4.61 (1.27)	4.24 (1.34)
Fear of death	5 (1.48)	4.37 (1.49)	4.43 (1.8)	3.86 (1.41)
Neutral acceptance	1.95 (0.92)	2.65 (0.83)	2.39 (1.41)	2.9 (1.17)

6 Discussion

This study investigated how the Existential Video Game *The Painting* impacts players by examining (1) the emotional reactions and reflective thoughts elicited during gameplay, and (2) the extent to which playing The Painting influences participants' attitudes toward death. Our mixed-methods experimental design provides both qualitative and quantitative insights on how narrative-based serious games can evoke emotional and cognitive engagement with sensitive existential themes.

Our qualitative findings revealed that *The Painting* successfully elicited a broad range of emotional responses, from sadness and fear to happiness and gratitude, and a bittersweet appreciation for life. Participants frequently noted the emotional impact of the game's narrative and music, with several describing the experience as beautiful and authentic. Some expressed frustration with the limited interactivity and slow pacing, showing how player expectations around agency and gameplay shape the reception of EXGs. Cognitive engagement was equally evident. Over half of the EG reported reflecting on death, loss, or grief, connecting the game's story to their own lives, and several expressed a renewed urgency to cherish relationships or reconsider how they spend their time. These findings align with earlier research [10, 13, 16, 17] and support the notion that EXGs can serve as tools for death education by offering accessible, emotionally resonant experiences that prompt introspection.

The quantitative results were more modest but pointed to similar trends. Both groups showed significant decreases in fear of death and increases in neutral acceptance, suggesting that reflection—whether prompted by an emotionally charged game or participation in a study about death—can influence these attitudes. However, the only significant between-group difference observed after gameplay was in death avoidance, where the EG continued to show higher levels. While counterintuitive, this result may be partially explained by the limitations of the study design and the video game itself.

A key limitation of the current study is its focus on immediate, short-term effects. Scholars in the field of death education have noted that death anxiety may initially increase following an intervention, only to decrease over time as the information and elicited thoughts are processed and integrated [3, 27]. This temporal dynamic could mean that some of the attitudinal shifts prompted by *The Painting* may not have fully manifested during the immediate post-test phase. Another limitation is the attrition rate, with 53 out of 113 participants failing to complete the study. Most notably, 12 of 13 participants who dropped out of the EG did so immediately after viewing the content warning. This suggests a self-selection bias, in which individuals most uncomfortable with death opted out. As a result, the effects observed may underestimate the game's potential to influence more avoidant individuals. This also aligns with Chittaro and Sioni's [10] comparisons of the Terror Management (TMT) and Meaning Management Theory (MMT), which suggest that simply being exposed to the topic of death—especially in a passive or non-integrated way—can increase anxiety (TMT), whereas meaningful engagement, such as reflecting on personal values or writing about emotions, can reduce fear and foster existential growth (MMT).

In light of this, EXGs that incorporate more active engagement, such as journaling or branching dialogue, may be more effective than linear visual novels in shifting attitudes toward death. However, the limited agency in *The Painting* also offered a consistent and controlled experience across participants, reducing variability between player journeys and aiding outcome evaluation. Based on this developers tackling topics like death or grief should consider the balance between narrative depth and interactivity. While visual novels provide narrative clarity, they may risk disengagement if players expect more agency. Incorporating reflection tasks or branching dialogue may help sustain engagement while still preserving emotional impact. Developers should also consider player readiness and incorporate tools for emotionally intense moments, such as allowing players to control the pacing as *The Painting* does.

Finally, the findings of our study reinforce the potential of EXGs to serve as emotionally safe, reflective spaces well-suited for educational and therapeutic settings, particularly in death education, grief support or palliative care contexts. Previous studies have also suggested that EXGs can help initiate sensitive conversations and reduce stigma around death and loss [15, 19]. Especially for younger generations, video games can offer a culturally familiar format for engaging with existential concerns and normalizing conversations about death and loss. Future research should continue to examine a wider variety of EXGs to determine which mechanics, genres, and narrative approaches are most effective for fostering reflection, emotional processing, and long-term attitude change. Comparative and longitudinal studies using qualitative, quantitative, and mixed-methods will help establish a more differentiated understanding of how various EXGs function in diverse contexts and populations.

7 Conclusion

This study demonstrates that the EXG The Painting can effectively evoke emotional responses and stimulate personal reflection on death and loss. Participants engaged with the game's narrative on both emotional and cognitive levels, often connecting its themes to their own lives. These findings suggest that EXGs hold promise as tools for death education, grief support, and therapeutic reflection. However, the results also highlight the importance of thoughtful game design and participant readiness. Future research should further explore short- and long-term effects of EXG, which types of EXGs are most impactful, and how they can be integrated into mental health, educational, and community settings to foster deeper engagement with existential topics.

Disclosure of Interests. The authors have no competing interests to declare that are relevant to the content of this article.

References

1. Wass, H.: A perspective on the current state of death education. Death Stud. **28**(4), 289–308 (2004)
2. Durlak, J.A., Riesenberg, L.A.: The impact of death education. Death Stud. **15**(1), 39–58 (1991)
3. Maglio, C.J., Robinson, S.E.: The effects of death education on death anxiety: a meta-analysis. Omega-J. Death Dying **29**(4), 319–335 (1994)

 4. Ronconi, L., Biancalani, G., Medesi, G.A., Orkibi, H., Testoni, I.: Death education for palliative psychology: the impact of a death education course for Italian university students. Behav. Sci. **13**(2), 1–15 (2023)
 5. Chua, J.Y.X., Shorey, S.: Effectiveness of end-of-life educational interventions at improving nurses and nursing students' attitude toward death and care of dying patients: a systematic review and meta-analysis. Nurs. Educ. Today **101**, 104892 (2021)
 6. Menzies, R.E., Zuccala, M., Sharpe, L., Dar-Nimrod, I.: The effects of psychosocial interventions on death anxiety: a meta-analysis and systematic review of randomised controlled trials. J. Anxiety Disord. **59**, 64–73 (2018)
 7. Testoni, I., Tronca, E., Biancalani, G., Ronconi, L., Calapai, G.: Beyond the wall: death education at middle school as suicide prevention. Int. J. Environ. Res. Public Health **17**(7), 2398 (2020)
 8. Dadfar, M., Lester, D.: The effectiveness of 8A model death education on the reduction of death depression: a preliminary study. Nurs. Open **7**(1), 294–298 (2019)
 9. Yalom, I.D.: Existential Psychotherapy. Hachette UK (2020)
10. Chittaro, L., Sioni, R.: Existential video games: proposal and evaluation of an interactive reflection about death. Entertain. Comput. **26**, 59–77 (2018)
11. Khodakarami, F., Sekhavat, Y.A., Alizadeh, F.: Evergreen: an existential video game to increase the indices associated with existential thinking in the audience. Entertain. Comput. **50**, 1–12 (2024)
12. Eum, K., Doh, Y.Y.: A thematic analysis of bereaved adults' meaning-making experience of loss through playing video games. Front. Psychol. **14**, 1154976 (2023)
13. Glaser, N., Jensen, L., Riedy, T., Center, M., Shifflett, J., Griffin, J.: Unlocking the Everdoor: analyzing the serious game Spiritfarer. Educational Tech. Res. Dev. **72**, 1947–1975 (2024)
14. Harrer, S.: Games and Bereavement: how video games represent attachment, loss and grief. Transcript Verlag (2018)
15. Reay, E., Ma, M., Mankee-Williams, A., Pavarini, G., Shaughnessy, N., Bhui, K.: Stones in our pockets: mental health dimensions of grief in contemporary video games (2024). https://doi.org/10.1101/2024.04.23.24306235
16. Boyd, A.: Representation of death in independent videogames: providing a space for meaningful death reflection. Dissertation, University of Central Florida (2024). Stars.library.ucf
17. Correia, G.A., Pereira, V.C., Trevisan, D., Maciel, C.: The art of dying in a digital world: how death is represented in digital art. J. Interact. Syst. **15**(1), 252–264 (2024)
18. Filipović, A.: Phenomenological aspects of video game. Kultura Polisa **21**(2), 98–123 (2024)
19. Austin, H.J., Cooper, L.R.: Feeling the narrative control (ler): casual art games as trauma therapy. Replay. Polish J. Game Stud. **8**(1), 129–143 (2021)
20. Eum, K., Erb, V., Lin, S., Wang, S., Doh, Y.Y.: How the death-themed game Spiritfarer can help players cope with the loss of a loved one. In: Extended Abstracts of the 2021 CHI Conference on Human Factors in Computing Systems, pp. 1–6 (2021). https://doi.org/10.1145/3411763.345160
21. Steger, M.F., Frazier, P., Oishi, S., Kaler, M.: The meaning in life questionnaire: assessing the presence of and search for meaning in life. J. Couns. Psychol. **53**, 80–93 (2006)
22. Allan, B.A., Shearer, B.: The scale for existential thinking. Int. J. Transpers. Stud. **31**(1), 21–37 (2012)
23. Camingue, J., Carstensdottir, E., Melcer, E.F.: What is a visual novel? Proc. ACM Hum. Comput. Interact. **5**, 1–18 (2021)
24. Wong, P.T., Reker, G.T., Gesser, G.: Death Attitude Profile—Revised: a multidimensional measure of attitudes toward death. In: Death Anxiety Handbook: Research, Instrumentation, and Application, pp. 121–148. Taylor & Francis (2015)

25. Schwarz, H., Revilla, M., Weber, W.: Memory effects in repeated survey questions: reviving the empirical investigation of the independent measurements assumption. Surv. Res. Methods **14**(3), 325–344 (2020)
26. Mayring, P.: Qualitative content analysis: theoretical foundation, basic procedures and software solution. Klagenfurt (2014)
27. Whelan, W.M., Warren, W.M.: A death awareness workshop: theory, application and results. OMEGA-J. Death Dying **11**(1), 61–71 (1981)

Cognitive, Affective, and Motivational Effects of Gamified Learning in a Research-Guided Teaching Context

Stefan E. Huber[1]([✉]) [iD], Hanna Rajh-Weber[1] [iD], Elizabeth B. Cloude[2] [iD], Eva Boehlke[1] [iD], Moritz Edlinger[1] [iD], Kristian Kiili[3] [iD], and Manuel Ninaus[1,4] [iD]

[1] Department of Psychology, University of Graz, Graz, Austria
stefan.huber@uni-graz.at
[2] College of Education, Michigan State University, East Lansing, ML, USA
[3] Research Centre of Gameful Realities, Tampere University, Tampere, Finland
[4] LEAD Graduate School and Research Network, University of Tübingen, Tübingen, Germany

Abstract. While evidence accumulates that gamified learning has small to moderate positive overall effects on learning outcomes, these effects may considerably depend on the exact conditions in which learning occurs. This study investigated the effect of embedding a gamified learning task within a homework assignment in a university course on cognitive, motivational, and affective outcomes (in contrast to online and laboratory settings unrelated to specific educational contexts investigated in earlier studies). Fifty students, enrolled in a basic statistics course, completed either a gamified or an equivalent, non-gamified memory task as a homework assignment. Their outcomes were compared with 97 participants not enrolled in the course (overall: $n = 147$). We found that gamified learning had small to medium significant effects on motivation ($d \sim 0.4$–0.6), regardless of enrollment in the course. Effects on affective and cognitive learning outcomes were not significant, ranging from negligible to small effect sizes ($d \leq 0.25$). Juxtaposing our present results with earlier results suggests that, beyond the setting itself, additional contextual features may change the motivational effectiveness of gamified learning in the present, homework assignment setting compared to earlier extra-curricular (online and laboratory) settings. Further research on potential boundary conditions is required.

Keywords: gamified learning · cognition · motivation · affect · context effects

1 Introduction

Gamified learning has been referred to as gamification in the context of learning [1] and defined as the use of game elements to support learning processes and attitudes and further its outcomes [2]. Gamified learning aims to motivate learners by emotionally engaging them more with the learning task [3]. Meta-analyses provide converging evidence for small to medium positive overall effects of gamified learning on different learning outcomes [1, 4, 5]. However, the findings also suggest that effects of gamified

S. Bakkes et al. (Eds.): GALA 2025, LNCS 16307, pp. 24–33, 2026.
https://doi.org/10.1007/978-3-032-11043-5_3

learning on learning outcomes are rather sensitive to contextual aspects like social interaction, research context (school, higher education, informal education), or subject area [1, 4, 5].

Furthermore, the effectiveness of gamified learning may depend on which learning outcomes are under investigation. In some cases, gamified learning shows positive effects on cognitive learning outcomes, yet has no impact on motivational outcomes [1]. Under different circumstances, however, gamified learning had a positive effect on motivation, task behavior, and engagement, but no (net) effect [6, 7] or even a small negative (direct) effect on cognitive learning outcomes [8, 9].

1.1 Theoretical Background

The cognitive theory of multimedia learning (CTML) [10, 11] emphasizes that meaningful learning depends on essential and generative cognitive processing, involving selecting, organizing, and integrating relevant new information. CTML warns against extraneous processing, which involves processing unnecessary task features (like some game elements) that can overload working memory or distract learners from essential content. However, the same distracting features may also give rise to generative processing rooted in the learners' motivation to exert effort in the learning task and facilitating sense-making of the learning material later on [12].

The Integrated Cognitive Affective Model of Learning with Multimedia (ICALM) [13] builds on this foundation by explicitly recognizing the role of motivation and affect in shaping how learners allocate cognitive resources, and by considering the context in which learning occurs. The latter can determine whether game elements are experienced as helpful supports or distractions. Through influencing learners' motivation and affect, game elements can indirectly increase engagement and improve cognitive learning outcomes, partially cancelling any potential negative effects of extraneous processing they might simultaneously introduce [8].

Previous work has consistently shown that effects of gamified learning on cognitive outcomes emerge from an interplay between the costs of increased extraneous processing and the benefits of increasing learners' motivation, both induced by game elements [6, 8]. Recently, however, and aligning with the findings from the meta-analyses considered above, it was found that the positive effect of gamified learning on learners' motivation seems to depend considerably on the conditions in which learning occurs. In particular, while online gamified tasks had a consistent (positive) motivational effect, the motivational effect was absent in a laboratory setting [9], suggesting certain boundary conditions [14] regarding the motivational effectiveness of gamified learning.

1.2 Present Work

Previous research has been conducted in online and laboratory settings [6, 8, 9], two contexts that may be informative for basic research on gamified learning but differ considerably from typical educational environments (e.g., classroom, homework). To address this gap, we investigated the effectiveness of the same gamified learning task used in previous studies embedded in a university course as part of a research-based teaching framework [15]. In particular, we compared learning outcomes for a gamified and a non-gamified associative learning task in the context of a homework assignment for a university statistics course. Data gathered in the framework of the homework assignment were then used in the course to demonstrate the application of basic statistical methods to a real-world dataset with clear, preregistered research hypotheses [16]. To further investigate the role of the educational context, course participants were asked to recruit 1–2 additional participants not partaking in the course (= external participants) to complete the learning tasks. Based on those two participant samples (i.e., course and external participants), we tested the following preregistered hypotheses [16]:

1) On average, learners' motivation is higher for the gamified than the non-gamified learning task (directional hypothesis) regardless of enrollment in the course (i.e., course participants and external participants) for at least one of the following motivational constructs: *intrinsic motivation* (measured with the Situational Motivation Scale [17]), *interest/enjoyment, perceived competence* (both measured with the Short Scale for Intrinsic Motivation [18]), *stimulation*, or *attractivity* (both measured with the User Experience Questionnaire [19]). All five constructs were found to benefit from gamified learning in earlier studies [6, 8], however, to an extent substantially varying between studies.
2) The change in *positive affect* (measured with the Positive and Negative Affect Schedule [20]) from before to after the learning task is higher for the gamified than the non-gamified task version (directional hypothesis).
3) Cognitive learning outcomes (i.e., how much and how fast participants memorized provided learning content) are similar for gamified and non-gamified learning tasks. If outcomes differ, we expect them to be smaller than motivation differences.
4) We expect an interaction between gamified learning (i.e., gamified vs. non-gamified task) and course enrollment (i.e., course vs. external participants) for some of the considered motivational and affective outcomes. In particular, we expect an interaction between the two factors for *stimulation, attractivity, perceived competence*, and the change in *positive affect*. This is because these constructs have been most susceptible to the effects of game elements in earlier studies [6, 8]. Consequently, they offer the greatest scope for a possible influence of contextual factors.
5) We expect no interaction (as in point 4) for cognitive learning outcomes [6, 8].

In addition to the preregistered hypotheses, we explored whether other affective and motivational constructs, not specifically addressed above, are influenced by gamified learning depending on course enrollment (i.e., course and external participants).

2 Methods

Participants. 50 psychology students enrolled at an Austrian university course on statistical methods participated in the study as a mandatory course assignment. For ethical reasons and to ensure voluntariness, students unwilling to participate in the study had the option to submit an alternative assignment with an equivalent workload, but no student took this option. Each student was requested to recruit 1–2 additional adult participants. Overall, 156 people took part in the study. However, data from 8 participants were excluded either for not engaging with the learning task at all or incorrect responses to instructed response items [21]. Hence, $n = 148$ participants remained ($n = 98$ people not enrolled in the course = external participants, 52% female, 48% male, $M_{age} = 22.06$, $SD_{age} = 5.69$, $Range_{age} = 18–63$; $n = 50$ enrolled participants, 92% female, 8% male, $M_{age} = 20.26$, $SD_{age} = 1.05$, $Range_{age} = 18–24$). From the 98 external participants, 59 (60%) were currently enrolled as students (68% not psychology, 5% psychology, rest unclear). The study was approved by the local university's ethics committee.

Procedure. Course participants were provided a URL to complete the homework assignment. Each participant was given 2 weeks (March 2025) to complete the homework (including recruiting 1–2 external participants per course participant). Upon accessing the URL, participants found the study's landing page, where they provided informed consent. Subsequently, they advanced to a questionnaire on demographic information and affect. Next, participants were randomly assigned to 1 of 2 learning task versions (gamified or non-gamified; described in the next section). After completing the task, participants answered additional questionnaires on affect and motivation.

Learning Task. In the associative learning task [8], participants had to learn 20 associations between abstract symbols and numbers, presented on a number line ranging from 0 to 26, over 5 consecutive levels. In each level, all symbols would be presented consecutively in random order in the left upper corner of the screen, see Fig. 1. For a given symbol, participants needed to select a position on the number line (moving a cursor with the arrow keys, confirming the position with the spacebar). After choosing a position, participants would receive corrective feedback highlighting the correct position for the given symbol by a green bar. Participants should then use this information to learn as many associations as possible over the 5 levels of the task.

A non-gamified and a gamified version of the task were prepared (Fig. 1). Each version included a number line, a symbol presentation in random order, interactive movement of the cursor and selection of numbers, corrective feedback upon selection, and a progress bar. Three additional game elements were used in the gamified version (Fig. 1(b)). First, the entire task was embedded within a narrative (a dog taking a stroll in the woods looking for bones). The narrative was supported by appropriate visual aesthetics (scenery, color scheme, a depiction of the dog, and corresponding animations). Lastly, a virtual incentive system was provided for selecting the correct number for a symbol, where the dog would receive a bone and the overall bone count would be visible over the entire current level [left upper corner in Fig. 1(b)]. For further details, see, e.g., Ref. [8].

Learning Outcomes. To measure cognitive learning outcomes, we measured both learning *efficacy* (i.e., how many associations have been learned over the entire course of the task = how much has been learned?) and *efficiency* (i.e., how fast have associations been learned = how efficiently did participants learn?). Learning efficacy is simply given by the number of correctly memorized associations in the last (= fifth) level of the task. Learning *efficiency* was computed as the sum of correct associations across levels 2–5; the faster/slower a learner learns, the higher/lower is this number, representing thus a measure of efficiency.

Affective and motivational outcomes were measured using the Positive and Negative Affect Schedule [20] (administered before and after tasks), the Situational Motivation

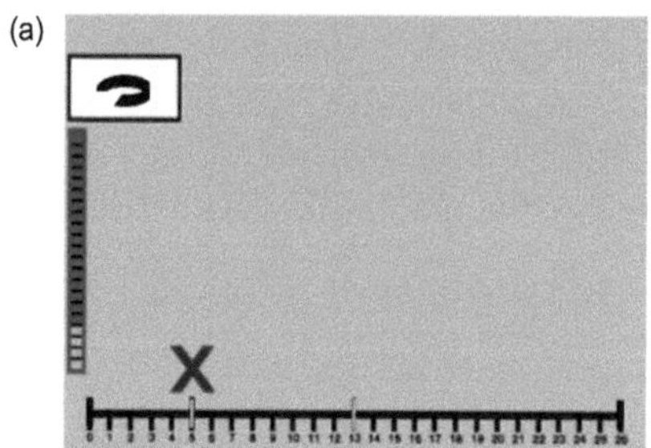 

Fig. 1. Screenshots of the (a) non-gamified and (b) gamified learning task version illustrating corrective feedback if an incorrect number was selected.

Scale (SIMS) [17], the German, short scale adaptation (KIM) [18] of the widely used Intrinsic Motivation Inventory (IMI) [22], and the two subscales *attractivity* and *stimulation* of the User Experience Questionnaire (UEQ) [19] (administered immediately after the task). The two UEQ subscales are closely related to intrinsic motivation [6, 8]. SIMS includes the constructs *intrinsic motivation, identified regulation, external regulation,* and *amotivation*, while KIM (like IMI on which it is based) includes the constructs *interest/enjoyment, perceived competence, perceived choice,* and *pressure/tension*. The reliabilities for *identified regulation* and *amotivation* were satisfactory (Cronbach's α > .7), whereas reliabilities were good to excellent (i.e.,Cronbach's α > .8) for all other considered constructs. Further details are provided at OSF [23].

Data Analysis. Because hypotheses 3 and 5 are statements about similar outcomes in different conditions, we employed Bayes factor analyses and Bayesian estimation in addition to classical null hypothesis testing. Hypotheses 1–3 were tested using two-sample t-tests. Bayes factors are denoted as B_{+0} for one-sided hypotheses, and as B_{10} or $B_{01} = 1/B_{10}$ for two-sided hypotheses. The Bayes factor B_{xy} provides a measure for the ratio of model x being supported more by the given data than model y (conditional on the statistical precision which depends on sample size). For instance, $B_{xy} = 4$ would mean model x is supported 4 times more by the given data than model y. Roughly, Bayes factors $B_{xy} > 3$ and > 10 may be interpreted as moderate and strong evidence for model x, respectively [24]. For effect sizes, we provide 95% credible intervals. Hypotheses 4 and 5 were tested using 2x2 ANOVAs with between-subjects factors for *gamification* (gamified vs. non-gamified learning task) and *population* (course vs. external participants). For confirmatory tests, we used a significance level of .05. Since hypothesis 1 is a composite hypothesis of 5 individual hypotheses, individual tests were performed at a significance level of .01 (i.e., Bonferroni correction). For our exploratory analyses, we used 2x2 ANOVAs to explore the influence of the factors *gamification* and *population* on other affective and motivational constructs not covered by hypotheses 1–5. For exploratory tests a reduced significance level of .005 was used to efficiently limit the false discovery rate even for an elevated base rate of true null hypotheses in the case of theoretically uninformed multiple testing scenarios [25]. All statistical analyses were conducted using R [26] and analysis scripts are openly available at OSF [23].

3   Results

Hypothesis 1. The motivational constructs *interest/enjoyment* [$t(143.51) = 2.63, p = .005$, $B_{+0} = 8.09$, *Mdn* (Cohen's) $d = 0.44$ $(0.11, 0.77)$] and *attractivity* [$t(145.44) = 3.29, p = .001$, $B_{+0} = 44.42$, *Mdn* $d = 0.55$ $(0.22, 0.88)$] were significantly larger in the gamified than in the non-gamified task version. For all other motivational constructs considered in hypothesis 1 (*intrinsic motivation, perceived competence, stimulation*) we found no significant differences between the two task versions, see also Fig. 2.

Hypothesis 2. The change in positive affect from before to after the learning task was not significantly higher for the gamified than the non-gamified task version [$t(135.25) = 1.26, p = .105$, $B_{+0} = 0.66$, *Mdn* $d = 0.21$ $(-0.12, 0.54)$]. Positive affect was reported with similar, intermediate values (on a scale from 1 to 5) before the learning task for both versions ($B_{01} = 4.58$; gamified: $M = 3.02, SD = 0.60$; non-gamified: $M = 2.95$, $SD = 0.59$).

Hypothesis 3. Neither learning efficacy [$t(144.37) = 0.65, p = .741$, $B_{10} = 0.21$, *Mdn* $d = -0.11$ $(-0.43, 0.21)$] nor efficiency [$t(141.89) = 0.51, p = .694$, $B_{10} = 0.20$, *Mdn* $d = -0.08$ $(-0.41, 0.24)$] differed significantly between task versions. Bayes factors provide more support in both cases for the null (i.e., equal means) than the alternative hypothesis (efficacy: $B_{01} = 4.66$; efficiency: $B_{01} = 5.01$). A graphical summary of aggregated learning outcome measures considered in hypotheses 1–3 is provided in Fig. 2 and further details regarding all analyses are provided in the supporting materials at OSF [23].

Hypothesis 4. We obtained no significant interaction between gamified learning (factor *gamification*) and enrollment in the course (factor *population*) for the considered affective-motivational constructs *change in positive affect* [$F(1,144) = 0.06, p = .808$], *stimulation* [$F(1,144) = 0.06, p = .803$], *attractivity* [$F(1,144) < 0.01, p = .981$], and *perceived competence* [$F(1,144) = 2.11, p = .149$]. We obtained a significant main effect of *population* for *attractivity* [$F(1,144) = 4.76, p = .031$] with students in the course ($M = 4.85, SD = 1.14$) rating the task a bit more attractive than external participants ($M = 4.46, SD = 1.30$). For the other affective-motivational constructs, no significant main effect for the factor *population* was obtained.

Hypothesis 5. We obtained no significant interaction between the factors *gamification* and *population* for learning *efficacy* [$F(1,144) = 0.58, p = .449$] and *efficiency* [$F(1,144) = 0.67, p = .414$]. We also obtained no significant main effects for both factors for *efficacy* and *efficiency*.

Influence of Course Enrollment. For the affective-motivational constructs not covered by our preregistered hypotheses, we obtained a significant effect for the factor *population* for *identified regulation* [$F(1,144) = 10.05, p = .002$], and *external regulation* [$F(1,144) = 10.58, p = .001$], while obtaining no significant effect for *gamification* and no significant interaction between those factors for both constructs. *Identified regulation* [$t(115.24) = 3.32, p = .001$, $B_{10} = 15.10$, *Mdn* $d = 0.57$ $(0.24, 0.92)$] and *external regulation* [$t(129.13) = 3.68, p < .001$, $B_{10} = 25.16$, *Mdn* $d = 0.62$ $(0.29, 0.97)$] were significantly larger for participants enrolled in the course than for external participants.

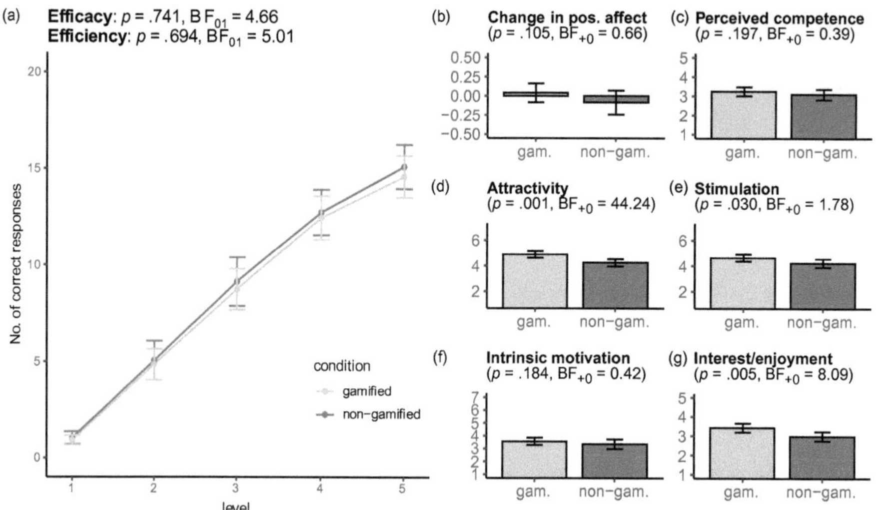

Fig. 2. Aggregated learning outcome measures considered in hypotheses 1–3. Points and bar heights refer to means, error bars refer to two times their standard errors. The abbreviations "gam." and "non-gam." stand for "gamified" and "non-gamified".

Influence of Gamification. For *perceived choice*, we obtained a borderline significant main effect for the factor *gamification* $[F(1,144) = 7.88, p = .006]$, while we obtained no significant main effect for the factor *population* and no significant interaction between those two factors. *Perceived choice* was significantly larger for the gamified than the non-gamified task version $[t(141.43) = 3.07, p = .003, \mathrm{B}_{10} = 12.62, Mdn\ d = 0.51 (0.19, 0.85)]$.

For *amotivation, pressure/tension* and change in *negative affect*, we obtained neither a significant main effect nor a significant interaction between the factors *gamification* and *population*.

4   Discussion and Concluding Remarks

We investigated the effectiveness of a gamified learning task embedded in a university statistics course. We further compared the educational setting with a non-educational setting by recruiting a sample of external participants not enrolled in the university course, besides the sample of students enrolled in the university statistics course.

In line with our first hypothesis, we found a small to medium positive effect of gamification on motivation. Participants reported higher interest and enjoyment ($d = 0.44$) and perceived task attractivity ($d = 0.55$) in the gamified task version. We also found a small, non-significant effect of gamification on the increase in positive affect ($d \sim 0.2$) from before to after the learning task, hence only descriptively supporting our second hypothesis. However, in the previous online setting (without any educational context and using the exact same learning task) [8], a large effect was obtained for motivational constructs ($d > 0.8$) and a medium effect was obtained for positive affect (d

~ 0.5). This suggests that in the current, educational setting both affective-motivational outcomes were smaller by a similar amount in comparison with the previous online setting [8], yet were noticeably higher than in our previous laboratory setting ($d \sim 0$) [9]. In line with our third hypothesis, we obtained negligible effects of gamified learning on cognitive learning outcomes. This supports the suggestion repeatedly made in earlier work [6, 8, 9] that game elements can indirectly increase cognitive learning outcomes via improving motivation while simultaneously impeding learning by inducing extraneous processing [12], resulting overall in a (partial) cancellation of beneficial and detrimental effects, in line with the interrelatedness of cognitive and affective-motivational processes suggested by the ICALM [13].

However, we note that this finding (i.e., some motivational, but no cognitive effect of gamification) may depend on the choice of design elements. In the present study, the latter were specifically chosen not to alter the essential cognitive processes involved for task completion, yet to be capable of affecting learners motivationally [6–9]. However, if, for instance, design elements were used that, in addition to the visual channel, would also tap into the auditory processing channel by allowing acoustic localization of correct responses, different results could be expected regarding cognitive learning outcomes. Future studies could investigate how these expected cognitive effects interact with the known motivational ones.

Interestingly, our results suggest that it is not the educational context in which data were collected that drives the apparent reduction in affective-motivational effectiveness of gamified learning in comparison to the previously studied online setting [8]. In particular, we found (in contrast to our fourth and in line with our fifth hypothesis) no interaction between gamified learning and course enrollment for all considered learning outcomes. Although students enrolled in the course rated both the gamified and the non-gamified task's attractivity somewhat higher than external participants, the cognitive, affective, and motivational effects of gamification did not significantly depend on course enrollment. At the same time, the two groups were significantly different with respect to identified and external regulation (besides differences with respect to gender and age, which, however, had a negligible influence on our effects when considered explicitly, see our supplementary analyses [23]). That suggests that participants from those two populations may have had different reasons to engage with the learning task in the first place. However, this appears not to substantially affect the effectiveness of gamified learning on the considered outcomes. One reason for this apparently absent consequence of slightly different motivational starting conditions could be related to aspects of the social situation (e.g., proximity to the experimenter, relationship between recruiter and participant, social power dynamics) known to potentially affect outcomes of experimental manipulations in general [27].

Another factor potentially contributing to the high enjoyment reported by external participants might also be due to the recruitment strategy. It cannot be ruled out that the recruitment of external participants by course participants might have skewed the sample towards individuals with an pre-existing interest in the topic besides their (supposed) affinity with the recruiters. The positive responses regarding self-reported motivation may thus, to some extent, also reflect a pre-existing interest in the subject matter rather than solely the impact of gamification.

In general, research on gamified learning often includes contextual and specifically social determinants, both related to aspects of game-based pedagogy (like experimenter/teacher roles, integration into curriculum or classroom practices) and research practices (recruitment strategies, participation incentives, population selection and accessibility etc.), that might influence the effectiveness of the studied learning method and limit the generalizability of the present findings. As long as these potential boundary conditions [14] of gamified learning are not identified, no qualified suggestions can be made about how the affective-motivational effectiveness of a gamified learning task may turn out in a specific educational context. A difficult but perhaps necessary path towards an educationally sufficient understanding of how gamification "works" may simply lie in the systematic investigation of such possible contextual and structural influencing factors.

Disclosure of Interests.   The authors have no competing interests to declare.

References

1. Sailer, M., Homner, L.: The gamification of learning: a meta-analysis. Educ. Psychol. Rev. **32**, 77–112 (2020). https://doi.org/10.1007/s10648-019-09498-w
2. Landers, R.N.: Developing a theory of gamified learning: linking serious games and gamification of learning. Simul. Gaming **45**, 752–768 (2014). https://doi.org/10.1177/1046878114563660
3. Schlag, R., Sailer, M., Tolks, D., Ninaus, M., Sailer, M.: Effectiveness of gamification in education. In: Gegenfurtner, A., Kollar, I. (eds.) Designing Effective Digital Learning Environments, pp. 143–159. Routledge, Milton Park (2024)
4. Huang, R., et al.: The impact of gamification in educational settings on student learning outcomes: a meta-analysis. Education Tech. Research Dev. **68**, 1875–1901 (2020). https://doi.org/10.1007/s11423-020-09807-z
5. Ritzhaupt, A.D., et al.: A meta-analysis on the influence of gamification in formal educational settings on affective and behavioral outcomes. Education Tech. Research Dev. **69**, 2493–2522 (2021). https://doi.org/10.1007/s11423-021-10036-1
6. Huber, S.E., Cortez, R., Kiili, K., Lindstedt, A., Ninaus, M.: Game elements enhance engagement and mitigate attrition in online learning tasks. Comput. Hum. Behav. **149**, 107948 (2023). https://doi.org/10.1016/j.chb.2023.107948
7. Ninaus, M., et al.: The added value of game elements: better training performance but comparable learning gains. Education Tech. Research Dev. **71**, 1917–1939 (2023). https://doi.org/10.1007/s11423-023-10263-8
8. Huber, S.E., Edlinger, M., Lindstedt, A., Kiili, K., Ninaus, M.: Game elements improve affect and motivation in a learning task. IJSG. **11**, 103–126 (2024). https://doi.org/10.17083/ijsg.v11i4.769
9. Huber, S.E., et al.: Addressing boundary conditions of cognitive and motivational effects of gamified learning. Frontline Learn. Res. **13**, 53–82 (2025). https://doi.org/10.14786/flr.v13i3.1653
10. Mayer, R.E.: Applying the Science of Learning. Pearson, Upper Saddle River (2011)
11. Mayer, R.E.: Cognitive theory of multimedia learning. In: Mayer, R.E. (ed.) The Cambridge Handbook of Multimedia Learning, pp. 43–71. Cambridge University Press, Cambridge (2014). https://doi.org/10.1017/CBO9781139547369.005

12. Mayer, R.E.: Computer games in education. Annu. Rev. Psychol. **70**, 531–549 (2019). https://doi.org/10.1146/annurev-psych-010418-102744
13. Plass, J.L., Kaplan, U.: Emotional design in digital media for learning. In: Emotions, Technology, Design, and Learning, pp. 131–161. Elsevier (2016). https://doi.org/10.1016/B978-0-12-801856-9.00007-4
14. Mayer, R.E.: The past, present, and future of the cognitive theory of multimedia learning. Educ. Psychol. Rev. **36**, 8 (2024). https://doi.org/10.1007/s10648-023-09842-1
15. Healey, M., Jenkins, A.: Developing undergraduate research and inquiry. The Higher Education Academy (2009)
16. Huber, S.E.: Cognitive, affective, and motivational effects of game elements in a learning task in a research-guided teaching context: Preregistration (2025). https://osf.io/mj7y2
17. Guay, F., Vallerand, R.J., Blanchard, C.: On the assessment of situational intrinsic and extrinsic motivation: the Situational Motivation Scale (SIMS). Motiv. Emot. **24**, 175–213 (2000). https://doi.org/10.1023/A:1005614228250
18. Wilde, M., Bätz, K., Kovaleva, A., Urhahne, D.: Überprüfung einer Kurzskala intrinsischer Motivation (KIM). Zeitschrift für Didaktik der Naturwissenschaften: ZfDN **15**, 31–45 (2009). https://doi.org/10.25656/01:31663
19. Schrepp, M., Hinderks, A., Thomaschewski, J.: Die UX KPI - Wunsch und Wirklichkeit (2017). https://doi.org/10.18420/MUC2017-UP-0100
20. Breyer, B., Bluemke, M.: Deutsche Version der Positive and Negative Affect Schedule PANAS (GESIS Panel). Zusammenstellung sozialwissenschaftlicher Items und Skalen (ZIS). (2016). https://doi.org/10.6102/ZIS242
21. Meade, A.W., Craig, S.B.: Identifying careless responses in survey data. Psychol. Methods **17**, 437–455 (2012). https://doi.org/10.1037/a0028085
22. Ryan, R.M.: Control and information in the intrapersonal sphere: an extension of cognitive evaluation theory. J. Pers. Soc. Psychol. **43**, 450–461 (1982). https://doi.org/10.1037/0022-3514.43.3.450
23. Huber, S.E.: Cognitive, affective, and motivational effects of game elements in a learning task in a research-guided teaching context: Data and analyses (2025). https://osf.io/8rth2
24. Lee, M.D., Wagenmakers, E.-J.: Bayesian Cognitive Modeling: A Practical Course. Cambridge University Press, Cambridge (2013)
25. Benjamin, D.J., et al.: Redefine statistical significance. Nat. Hum. Behav. **2**, 6–10 (2017). https://doi.org/10.1038/s41562-017-0189-z
26. R Core Team: R: A language and environment for statistical computing (2022). https://www.R-project.org
27. Rosenthal, R., Rosnow, R.L.: Essentials of Behavioral Research: Methods and Data Analysis. McGraw-Hill, New York (2008)

Supporting Adolescents' Skills to Interpret Misleading Graphs Through Game-Based Learning: Did Signaling of Visual Manipulations Matter?

Helka Hirvonen[1]([⊠]) [iD], Manuel Ninaus[2] [iD], Carita Kiili[1] [iD], and Kristian Kiili[1] [iD]

[1] Research Centre of Gameful Realities, Tampere University, 33100 Tampere, Finland
`helka.hirvonen@tuni.fi`
[2] Department of Psychology, University of Graz, 8010 Graz, Austria

Abstract. Graphs are powerful tools for conveying information, yet specific design choices may, intentionally or unintentionally, lead to misinterpretations and mislead readers. We examined the learning effects of MediaWatch, a digital graph-reading game designed to teach students how to interpret misleading graphs. Specifically, we examined how feedback that visually "highlights" (i.e., signaling) misleading elements of graphs influences students' skills in interpreting misleading graphs. In this between-subjects study, secondary school students (N = 201) were assigned to either a signaling condition or a no-signaling condition. Graph comprehension was assessed using pre-, post-, and delayed post-tests and analyzed with linear mixed-effects models. Results showed that students' ability to interpret graphs with a reversed x-axis improved over time, but this improvement was not influenced by the presence of signaling in feedback. Moreover, the improvement was sustained at the delayed post-test. In contrast, students did not improve in interpreting truncated y-axis graphs over time, regardless of feedback type. Overall, the signaling feedback did not yield differential effects on performance for either type of examined misleading graph. Future research should explore how signaling can be more effectively implemented with other instructional supports within the game to strengthen students' resistance to different types of graph manipulations. Moreover, the findings align with the observation that the truncation effect is particularly persistent.

Keywords: game-based learning · graph literacy · misinformation · signaling · elaborated feedback · secondary school

1 Introduction

Imagine two students playing a graph-reading game in which their task is to interpret misleading graphs. During gameplay, both receive feedback explaining the correct answers and the manipulation techniques used in the graphs. But there's a twist! One student's feedback includes visual cues that highlight how the graphs were visually manipulated, while the other receives no visual support. This raises a question: Did the student who received visual cues learn more from the game? In this study, we explore this question. Specifically, we investigate how the addition of visual cues supporting elaborated feedback—an application of the signaling principle [1]—influences students' skills to interpret misleading graphs.

By misleading graphs, we refer to graphs that are based on accurate data but are designed in a way that may distort the reader's interpretation [2, 3]. As an example, Fig. 1 presents two bar graphs displaying the same data that compare the effectiveness of two medicines in treating a specific disease. The graph on the left visually exaggerates the difference between the two medicines due to truncating the y-axis—a distortion known as the truncating effect [3]. Truncating of the y-axis tends to mislead readers, and this effect appears to persist even after they are informed about how truncation can be misleading [3]. Research has shown that raising awareness about common misleading graph elements, such as truncating axes and providing feedback on their interpretation, can help develop critical graph reading skills [2].

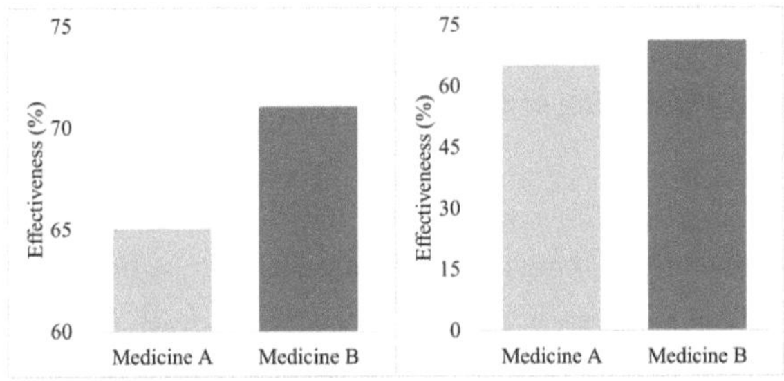

Fig. 1. Truncated bar graph (left) and its non-truncated counterpart (right).

While previous game-based learning research has highlighted the importance of feedback, little is known about the usefulness of signaling in game-based learning environments. This study is significant as it addresses a critical gap in understanding how extending elaborated feedback with visual cues (i.e., applying the signaling principle) influences the effectiveness of feedback given in a graph reading game.

1.1 Interactive Model of Graph Comprehension

Graph comprehension often involves complex cognitive processes. These processes are described in an interactive model of graph comprehension [4]. According to the model, graph comprehension is an iterative, constraint-satisfaction process in which both the characteristics of the graph (e.g., type, scales, labels, and complexity) and the reader (e.g., prior knowledge, cognitive abilities, and familiarity with graphs) influence comprehension [4]. The model explains how individuals interpret graphs through a continuous interaction between bottom-up and top-down processes [5]. When the sensory input of the graph drives bottom-up processing, the top-down processing is driven by the readers' prior knowledge, expectations, and graph literacy skills. Graph readers engage in bottom-up processes by encoding visual elements into meaningful visual chunks, deriving quantitative information or relations from these visual chunks, and finally converting the quantitative information into a conceptual understanding of a graph. Top-down processes affect these bottom-up processes [2].

The initial interaction with a graph helps the reader assess the graph's complexity, guiding whether to rely on intuitive processing or to engage in further interactions for a more coherent understanding. When it comes to reading misleading graphs, it is crucial that readers recognize the graph's complexity and detect visual conflicts with the data to initiate deeper processing. If readers do not recognize these misleading elements, they may process the graph quickly and intuitively, increasing the risk of misinterpretation. For example, in our truncated graph example, readers must recognize that the bars do not accurately represent the quantitative information shown on the y-axis.

A key challenge for educators is to motivate students to engage in deeper processing of graphs to detect potential misleading elements and support accurate comprehension. The use of signaling to guide readers' attention could offer an effective way to promote this deeper engagement and foster the development of graph interpretation skills.

1.2 Signaling and Processing of Feedback

Signaling, grounded in the cognitive theory of multimedia learning [6], is a well-established instructional design principle that can support learning [1]. The signaling principle suggests that highlighting key elements of a multimedia material can help direct learners' attention to relevant information [7], increasing the processing of essential content. The inclusion of signals (e.g., text, arrows, colors) can be particularly beneficial for learners with lower prior knowledge and who face challenges in recognizing essential information on their own. Thus, signaling can also be beneficial to guide readers' attention to the misleading elements of graphs and essential elements of feedback provided. However, as signals can be implemented in various ways, selecting an appropriate signal for a specific context and purpose can be challenging [1].

[8] proposed a five-stage feedback model to assess how learners process critical constructive feedback. According to the model, the effectiveness of feedback depends on engagement across the following stages: 1) noticing, 2) decoding, 3) making sense, 4) acting upon, and 5) using the feedback to make progress. Their study, which examined three feedback signaling conditions, showed that students disengaged at each stage, and only a few ultimately used the feedback to make progress in the game. Notably, the results revealed that one-third of the critical constructive feedback provided in the game was never noticed, and nearly 40% of the feedback that was noticed was never read. These findings highlight that the implementation of feedback and signaling is crucial to achieve the desired benefits. Further, [9] have emphasized that signaling should be used strongly enough to effectively guide learners' attention and support learning.

1.3 Using Games to Support Critical Reading

A systematic literature review on critical reading games identified game-based learning as a promising intervention approach for tackling misinformation [10]. The review revealed that most critical reading games were targeted at adults, focused on misinformation manipulation techniques, and were grounded in inoculation theory. Analogous to medical vaccination, cognitive "inoculation" aims to strengthen individuals' ability to recognize and resist manipulation attacks, making it a useful framework for designing interventions against misinformation [11]. However, none of the game interventions that Kiili and colleagues [10] reviewed focused on graph literacy.

To address this gap, [12] conducted a graph reading intervention using the MediaWatch graph reading game, which is based on inoculation theory. They found that high school students in the game-based condition improved significantly more in interpreting misleading graphs than those in the control group. Further, [13] examined how different types of feedback (results, elaborative, attribution) included in the MediaWatch game affected students' performance in interpreting graphs. The results indicated that, although students' graph interpretation skills improved, the type of feedback had no effect. Although signaling was included as part of feedback in both studies, its specific contribution was not examined. This underlines the need to investigate the role of signaling in game-based graph reading intervention–the focus of the present study.

1.4 Present Study

This study builds on previous research on the MediaWatch graph reading game [12, 13], suggesting that short, game-based interventions can enhance graph comprehension skills. We extend previous research by examining whether the learning effects of the MediaWatch game intervention sustain over time. Specifically, we investigate the impact of signaling designed to highlight visual graph manipulations within the game.

We conducted a short between-subjects intervention in which students were assigned to either a *signaling condition* that provided elaborated feedback with visual cues on graph reading tasks or a *no-signaling condition* that provided only elaborated feedback. The overall aim of the intervention was to raise awareness of misleading graphs and visual manipulation techniques in order to support students' graph interpretation skills.

The key research question is: How did the game version, including elaborated feedback with visual cues, influence the interpretation of misleading graphs (reversed x-axes or truncated y-axes) compared to the version without visual cues?

According to a meta-analytic review [14] instructional support features that help learners select relevant information from educational games enhance learning ($d =$ .46). Although studies specifically examining the effects of signaling in digital game-based learning are scarce, meta-analysis on multimedia learning materials have shown that applying the signaling principle significantly improves learning, with effect sizes varying from small to large [1]. Against this background, *we expected* that students in the signaling condition demonstrate greater improvement in interpreting misleading graphs than those in the no-signaling condition.

2 Methods

2.1 Participants and Design

Participants were 201 students from grades 7 to 9 ($M_{age} =$ 14.03 years, $SD =$ 0.94). Students were recruited from 18 different classrooms across five Finnish secondary schools. Of the participants, 107 identified as girls, 83 as boys, and 11 identified as non-binary or chose not to disclose their gender. Each classroom was randomly assigned to one of two conditions. Permissions for the study were obtained from the school principals. The information letter and privacy notice were sent to both the students and their guardians in advance. Guardians had the right to decline their child's participation, and students were asked to provide informed consent for the use of their data.

2.2 Description of MediaWatch Game and Feedback Conditions

MediaWatch is a digital graph reading game designed to support critical graph-reading skills [12]. A player joins MediaWatch, a fact-checking organization at the fictional island of Sahramao. Problems have arisen as different villages have begun to promote their own interests by producing misleading graphs and news headlines for the media.

The player's job is to review news drafts by interpreting various types of graphs and selecting the headline that best aligns with the data represented. The player completes eight fact-checking assignments, which include both well-crafted and misleading (truncated y-axis, reversed x-axis, and excessively wide y-axis range) graphs. In this paper, we focus on truncated y-axis and reversed x-axis graphs. For each manipulated graph, the player is presented with four headline options: one that accurately reflects the graph (correct option), one that reflects the manipulation, and two that are entirely incorrect. The player receives corrective feedback through experience points, a credibility meter, and a fact-checking ranking system (see [12] for more details). Player's mentor, Guido, provides elaborated feedback on the headline choice (Fig. 2).

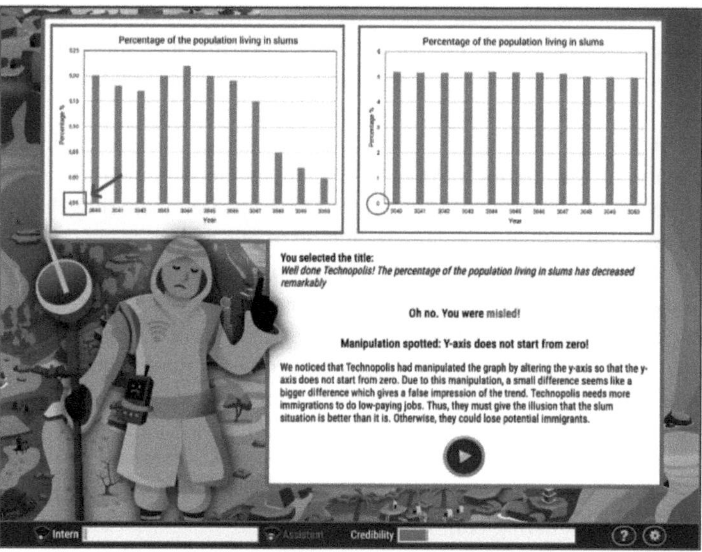

Fig. 2. An example of feedback provided after an unsuccessful task in the signaling condition.

In the no-signaling condition, the interpretation of misleading graphs is supported with visual and textual aids [2]. Guido explains how the graph was manipulated and presents the same visualization without the misleading element, allowing the player to see the difference between misleading and accurate graphs (Fig. 2). **In the signaling condition**, this elaborated feedback is enhanced with visual cues designed to draw the player's attention to the effects of the manipulation and link the given textual explanation to essential elements of the graph (see Fig. 2 in [12] for reversed x-axis graph).

The game design is informed by inoculation theory [11]. The narrative warns players about misleading graphs and the villages' attempts to deceive them. This forewarning aims to encourage players to pay closer attention to the elements of the graphs. Additionally, the game deliberately exposes players to misleading graphs within a safe, fictional environment, highlights when and how they may have been misled, and explains the manipulation techniques involved. The game equips the players to be more sensitive to recognizing and refuting future manipulation attempts.

2.3 Measures

Mathematical fluency was assessed using multiple-choice tasks, including six items. Each item presented a visual comparison question with four answer options (e.g., *How many more white squares are there compared to black circles?*).

Graph comprehension was measured using 11 multiple-choice items (4 well-crafted and 7 misleading graphs including bar and line graphs. The misleading graphs included 4 reversed x-axis and 3 truncated y-axis items (e.g., *How much was the annual rainfall in 2016 compared to 2017?*). To reduce the influence of participants' prior knowledge, detailed titles and labels were anonymized using letters and general terms. Each multiple-choice item for misleading graphs included: (i) the correct answer option aligned with the data; (ii) an incorrect answer option aligned with the visual manipulation (i.e., designed to be appealing if the reader ignores the graph's scales and labels); and (iii) two other entirely incorrect answer options. Students could earn one point for each correct response. The same test was used as a pre-test, post-test, and delayed post-test.

2.4 Procedure

The study was conducted in two sessions during regular school lessons in a classroom setting. In the first session, a researcher introduced the study, explained students' rights, and provided instructions either online or on-site. Then students completed the consent form, the background questionnaire, the math fluency test, and graph comprehension pre-test. Then, students played the MediaWatch game. The mean time on 8 tasks was 4.04 min ($SD = 1.34$) in the no-signaling and 4.56 min ($SD = 1.83$) in the signaling condition. After gameplay, students completed the post-test. In the second session, arranged at least three weeks later, students completed the delayed post-test.

2.5 Statistical Analyses

Linear mixed-effects models were employed to investigate the impact of feedback type and measurement time on students' graph reading performance. Fixed effects included feedback conditions (signaling vs. no signaling), measurement time (pre-test, post-test, delayed post-test), and their interaction. Age, gender (as a binary variable), and math fluency were included as covariates. Individuals were added as a random factor. As the assumptions of normally distributed and homoscedastic errors seemed to be violated after inspection, we obtained heteroskedasticity-corrected standard errors via the HC3 method [15] and used them for inference. As the gender was included as a binary covariate (female, male), the sample size for these analyses was reduced to 190.

3 Results

3.1 Descriptive Statistics and Condition Equivalence

Descriptive performance statistics for the conditions are shown in Table 1. Performance was measured on a scale from 0 to 1 (1 refers to 100%). As shown in the pretest results, students performed better on well-formed graph tasks than on misleading ones.

Table 1. Descriptive statistics for signaling and no-signaling conditions (scale: 0–1).

	Signaling condition		No-signaling condition	
	M	SD	M	SD
Mathematical fluency	0.83	0.19	0.87	0.19
Well-formed graphs (pre-test)	0.90	0.19	0.89	0.19
Reversed X graphs (pre-test)	0.15	0.29	0.11	0.22
Reversed X graphs (post-test)	0.40	0.42	0.43	0.44
Reversed X graphs (delayed test)	0.44	0.44	0.44	0.44
Truncated Y graphs (pre-test)	0.24	0.28	0.27	0.28
Truncated Y graphs (post-test)	0.25	0.32	0.30	0.30
Truncated Y graphs (delayed test)	0.23	0.28	0.28	0.28

As a preliminary analysis, we tested the equivalence of conditions. A Fisher's Exact Test showed no significant association between gender (female, male, other) and condition (signaling vs. no-signaling), $p = .213$. Further, participants in the conditions did not differ on age [$t(168) = -1.936, p = .055$], pre-test score on well-formed graphs [$t(170.64) = 0.193, p = .847$], and math fluency [$t(170.78) = -1.539, p = .126$]. These results suggest that the conditions were comparable in terms of these characteristics.

3.2 Does Signaling Improve the Interpretation of Misleading Graphs?

For reversed X-axis graphs, the model (see Table 2) revealed a statistically significant main effect of time, as students' performance improved from the pre-test to both the post-test ($\beta = .30$) and the delayed post-test ($\beta = .29$). However, there was no significant main effect of feedback condition ($\beta = .03$), and no significant interaction between feedback condition and time (all ps > .440), indicating that the improvement over time did not differ between feedback groups. None of the covariates (age, gender, and math fluency) was a statistically significant predictor. The model explained 11.8% of the variance in performance via fixed effects, and 55.2% when including both fixed and random effects. In sum, while students improved over time in interpreting graphs with reversed x-axes, this improvement was not moderated by the type of feedback received.

Table 2. Results of regression model with reversed X-axis performance as dependent variable

Predictors	Estimates	Robust Std. Error	t-value	p-value
(Intercept)	−.099	0.397	−0.250	.803
Condition	.033	0.039	0.852	.395
Time: Post	**.297**	**0.045**	**6.539**	**< .001**
Time: Delayed	**.291**	**0.049**	**5.984**	**< .001**
Age	.005	0.027	0.176	.860
Gender	−.001	0.047	−0.001	.992
Math	.172	0.104	1.653	.099
Condition x Time: Post	−.045	0.059	−0.771	.441
Condition x Time: Delayed	−.007	0.067	−0.105	.916

Regarding graphs with a truncated Y-axis, the model (see Table 3) showed that there was no significant main effect of time and feedback condition (all ps > .238), indicating that students' performance did not improve over time in either condition. However, there were significant effects for the covariates: age ($\beta = .06$), gender ($\beta = .11$), and math fluency ($\beta = .37$), indicating that older students, boys, and those with higher math fluency performed better in interpreting truncated graphs. The model explained 13.6% of the variance in performance via fixed effects, and 63.7% when including both fixed and random effects. In sum, while individual characteristics such as age, gender, and math fluency were predictive of performance, the intervention and feedback type did not affect students' ability to interpret graphs with truncated y-axes.

Table 3. Results of regression model with truncated Y-axis performance as dependent variable.

Predictors	Estimates	Robust Std. Error	t-value	p-value
(Intercept)	**−.939**	**0.284**	**−3.310**	**<.001**
Condition	.021	0.040	0.528	.598
Time: Post test	.032	0.027	1.178	.239
Time: Delayed test	.020	0.038	0.520	.603
Age	**.058**	**0.020**	**2.896**	**.004**
Gender	**.106**	**0.036**	**2.957**	**.003**
Math	**.373**	**0.074**	**5.070**	**<.001**

(continued)

Table 3. (*continued*)

Predictors	Estimates	Robust Std. Error	t-value	p-value
Condition x Time: Post test	−.020	0.034	−0.586	.558
Condition x Time: Delayed test	−.028	0.046	−0.612	.541

4 Discussion

We examined the effectiveness of visual signaling feedback in the MediaWatch graph reading game. We hypothesized that students in the signaling condition would show greater improvement in interpreting misleading graphs than those in the no-signaling condition. Contrary to expectations, no statistically significant differences were found between the conditions, suggesting that students did not benefit from signaling. However, students' ability to interpret graphs with a reversed x-axis improved significantly over time, regardless of the feedback condition, whereas no such improvement was observed for graphs with a truncated y-axis. Importantly, students' performance on graphs with a reversed x-axis was sustained at the delayed post-test, indicating that the improvement observed from pre- to post-test was retained over time.

The absence of significant effects of signaling is surprising, given that signaling is a well-established instructional principle and is typically beneficial for learners with low prior knowledge [1, 6]—as was the case in this study. Several possible reasons may help explain why students did not benefit from signaling. It is possible that students did not notice, decode or attempt to make sense of the signals—common challenges in processing constructive feedback as emphasized in the five-stage model of feedback processing [8]. In addition to visual signals, students received feedback through multiple channels simultaneously: explanatory text, the facial expressions of the pedagogical agent, and a well-constructed graph besides the manipulated one. Consequently, it is possible that the visual signals were not strong enough to catch students' attention [9], or that students who did notice them were unable to decode the signals accurately [8] or link them to the related explanatory feedback text. Even if decoding occurred, some students may have struggled to make sense of the signals in relation to their graph interpretation strategies and performance.

Notably, the low time on task (approximately 30–34 s per task) suggests that some students may not have engaged deeply with the game tasks and/or the feedback provided. To enhance the effectiveness of signaling in MediaWatch, stronger or animated cues could be implemented to better capture students' attention. Signals could also be integrated into the tasks to ensure they are more deeply processed. Future studies should explore how such enhanced signals influence students' engagement with misleading graphs. Additionally, think-aloud protocols and eye-tracking methods would be valuable to gain deeper insights into how students notice, interpret, and act upon signals during gameplay.

One possible explanation for the differing outcomes is the varying cognitive demands of the examined graph types. With basic elaborated feedback, students may have found it easier to detect and interpret the spatial inconsistency in reversed x-axis graphs. In contrast, identifying truncated y-axes likely required more mathematical reasoning and a shift from intuitive to more analytical thinking, which may have been too demanding after the brief intervention, given the persistent nature of the truncating effect [3]. To conclude, although the intervention did not yield the expected results, the MediaWatch game shows promise, and its development will be continued. Specifically, we aim to develop game mechanics that help students overcome the truncation effect.

Acknowledgements. This study was funded by the Strategic Research Council (grant 358250).

Disclosure of Interests. The authors have no competing interests to declare that are relevant to the content of this article.

References

1. Alpizar, D., Adesope, O.O., Wong, R.M.: A meta-analysis of signaling principle in multimedia learning environments. Educ. Tech. Res. Dev. **68**(5), 2095–2119 (2020)
2. Rho, J., Rau, M.A.: Exploring educational approaches to addressing misleading visualizations. Educ. Psychol. Rev. **37**, 14 (2025)
3. Yang, B.W., Vargas Restrepo, C., Stanley, M.L., Marsh, E.J.: Truncating bar graphs persistently misleads viewers. J. Appl. Res. Mem. Cogn. **10**(2), 298–311 (2021)
4. Shah, P., Freedman, E., Vekiri, I.: The comprehension of quantitative information in graphical displays. In: Shah, P., Miyake, A. (eds.) The Cambridge Handbook of Visuospatial Thinking, pp. 426–476. Cambridge University Press, New York (2005)
5. Shah, P.: Graph comprehension: the role of format, content and individual differences. In: Anderson, M., Meyer, B., Olivier, P. (eds.) Diagrammatic Representation and Reasoning, pp. 199–223. Springer, London (2002)
6. Mayer, R.E.: Cognitive theory of multimedia learning. In: The Cambridge Handbook of Multimedia Learning, pp. 43–71. Cambridge University Press (2014)
7. van Gog, T.: The signaling (or Cueing) principle in multimedia learning. In: The Cambridge Handbook of Multimedia Learning, pp. 263–278. Cambridge University Press (2014)
8. Tärning, B., et al.: Assessing the black box of feedback neglect in a digital educational game for elementary school. J. Learn. Sci. **29**(4–5), 511–549 (2020)
9. Kiili, K., Ketamo, H.: Eye-tracking in educational game design. In: Proceedings of the 4th European Conference on Games-Based Learning: ECGBL2010, pp. 160–167. Academic Conferences Limited (2010)
10. Kiili, K., Siuko, J., Ninaus, M.: Tackling misinformation with games: a systematic literature review. Interactive Learn. Environ. 1–16 (2024)
11. Ecker, U.K.H., et al.: The psychological drivers of misinformation belief and its resistance to correction. Nat. Rev. Psychol. **1**(1), 13–29 (2022)
12. Siuko, J., Cloude, E., Kiili, K.: Improving critical graph reading skills: the potential might lie in game-based learning. In: CEUR Workshop Proceedings, vol. 3669, pp. 79–87 (2024)
13. Cloude, E.B., Kormann, E., Steiner, M., Lindstedt, A., Kiili, K., Ninaus, M.: The role of feedback type and task performance on concurrent emotions and interest during game-based learning. In: Bellotti, F., Ninaus, M., Dondio, P. (eds.) Games and Learning Alliance. LNCS, vol. 15348, pp. 101–111. Springer, Cham (2024)

14. Wouters, P., van Oostendorp, H.: A meta-analytic review of the role of instructional support in game-based learning. Comput. Educ. **60**(1), 412–425 (2013)
15. Zeileis, A., Hothorn, T.: Diagnostic checking in regression relationships. R News **2**(3), 7–10 (2002)

Towards Valid Stealth Assessment: Developing a Novel Assessment Mechanic for a Fraction Learning Game

Antero Lindstedt[1]([envelope]) [iD], Kristian Kiili[1] [iD], and Manuel Ninaus[2,3] [iD]

[1] Research Centre of Gameful Realities, Tampere University, Tampere, Finland
`antero.lindstedt@tuni.fi`
[2] Department of Psychology, University of Graz, Graz, Austria
[3] LEAD Graduate School and Research Network, University of Tübingen, Tübingen, Germany

Abstract. Games hold promise as assessment tools, but the mechanics used must first be validated. Accordingly, we examined a novel implementation of an unbounded number line estimation task to assess students' fraction comparison competence, laying the groundwork for designing a stealth assessment for math games. Sixty-eight Finnish 6th graders played a math game in which they estimated fraction magnitudes on an unbounded number line. Additionally, the students completed a non-game assessment based on a traditional fraction comparison task using the same fractions, as a part of a counterbalanced design. Overall, the results showed many similarities between the assessment conditions, including a typically observed distance effect, a similar correlation with general math achievement, and a moderate positive correlation between the conditions. However, comparison performance was lower in the game assessment. Further, the performance classifications based on whole number ordering consistent and inconsistent comparison tasks showed only a slight agreement between the game and non-game assessments. This suggests that the two approaches may capture different aspects of performance, with the game assessment potentially yielding misleading learning analytics and inappropriate pedagogical decisions. Also, motivational measures suggested challenges with the unbounded tasks, as students' flow experience was significantly lower in the game condition. The results underscore the need to carefully evaluate theoretically informed assessment mechanics and highlight the importance of further research to establish the unbounded number line task as a valid measure of fraction comparison competence.

Keywords: Game-based assessment · Stealth assessment · Unbounded number line estimation task · Fraction · Serious game

1 Introduction

Games' potential use in education extends beyond learning. Research has shown that games can also be used for assessment purposes (e.g. [1–3]). According to Landers and Sanchez [4], game-based assessment refers to digital games designed to assess

S. Bakkes et al. (Eds.): GALA 2025, LNCS 16307, pp. 45–54, 2026.
https://doi.org/10.1007/978-3-032-11043-5_5

individuals' knowledge, skills, abilities, or other characteristics. Game-based assessment leverages learners' interactive gameplay to evaluate their competencies [3] and support learners' and educators' educational goals.

Plass and colleagues [5] have identified three interrelated design mechanics for game-based assessments: learning, assessment, and game mechanics. Learning mechanics refers to core activities designed primarily to promote learning, drawing on principles from the learning sciences. Assessment mechanics focus on activities generating evidence of learning and competencies. Game mechanics work like glue as they define the gameplay actions and are usually informed by learning mechanics, assessment mechanics, or a combination of both, integrating learning and assessment goals. Kim and Shute [3] emphasized that assessment should be integrated into a game in a way that does not disrupt the game's flow and enjoyment—a concept referred to as "stealth assessment [6]. Scholars have suggested that Evidence-Centered Design (ECD) forms the foundation to increase the quality of game-based stealth assessment [6].

Therefore, we use the ECD assessment framework to guide the design of the game-based stealth assessment in the present study [7]. The ECD framework provides a structured approach for developing high-quality assessments by aligning what is measured with how it is measured, and it helps to integrate learning and assessment mechanics with game mechanics. ECD consists of four interconnected models. 1) The competency model defines the target skills or knowledge to be assessed—in our case, understanding fraction magnitude (proper fractions). 2) The evidence model defines the observable behaviors or interactions that serve as indicators of the target competency and outlines how these are scored and linked to the assessed construct. 3) The task model specifies the tasks and specific features of tasks that are designed to elicit the desired evidence to assess the targeted competence. Finally, 4) the assembly model describes the collection of all tasks included in the assessment and how they are sequenced ensuring that sufficient evidence is collected for a valid assessment. Developing these models requires a deep understanding of the cognitive processes involved in the target domain—in our case, conceptual fraction knowledge.

1.1 Conceptual Fraction Knowledge and Common Fraction Tasks

Many children fail to handle simple fraction tasks despite considerable mathematics instruction [8–10]. A common misconception is the whole number bias that originates from the incorrect belief that all whole number properties are shared by fractions [11]. This can lead to an assumption that a larger denominator implies a larger fraction, or that a fraction with larger numerator always has a larger magnitude (e.g., a false belief that 4/9 is larger than 3/5 as numerator 4 is larger than 3 and denominator 9 is larger than 5). A comparison task, in which students have to identify a larger fraction, has been widely used to assess fraction understanding and identify signs of whole number bias [9, 12]. Previous research has shown that fractions consistent with whole number ordering are easier to compare (e.g., which number is larger: 1/2 or 4/5) than fractions inconsistent with whole number ordering (e.g., which number is larger: 1/9 or 1/2) because of the whole number bias [9]. The comparison of fractions is also affected by a phenomenon called the distance effect. This means that fractions with closer magnitudes are more difficult to compare than those that are farther apart [12].

Learning fractions requires a conceptual shift to grasp both the differences and the underlying similarities between fractions and whole numbers. Siegler et al. [8] have emphasized that it is crucial to understand that both whole numbers and fractions represent magnitudes that can be placed on a number line. Accordingly, Number Line Estimation (NLE) tasks have been widely used to assess and develop conceptual fraction knowledge. In a bounded NLE task [13] learners are required to estimate the position of a target number on a number line with a prespecified start point and an endpoint (e.g., where goes ¼ on a bounded number line from 0 to 1). An alternative approach is to use an unbounded number line task, where the endpoint is hidden and an intermediate point is displayed instead. Consequently, the learner needs to use the starting and the intermediate point to estimate the position of the target number. This task has mainly been used on whole number tasks [14], but recent studies have suggested its use also in fraction education [13, 15, 16].

1.2 Present Study and Hypotheses

This study is part of an ongoing design research project in which we are developing a number line-based rational number game environment for math education. We introduce a novel implementation of an unbounded NLE task to assess students' competence in comparing fraction magnitudes, laying the groundwork for designing stealth assessment models for the Number Trace game environment.

Bounded NLE and comparison mechanics have been used in educational games, but these mechanics have typically been implemented as separate tasks [2, 17] or integrated in a way that requires learners to first complete the comparison activity, followed by the number line estimation [18]. Notably, Lindstedt and Kiili [17] have reported that the students tend to prefer the estimation tasks over the comparison tasks. Therefore, we propose a task that seamlessly integrates these task mechanics.

The present study advances previous research in several ways. First, unbounded NLE tasks have primarily been used to teach and assess whole number competencies; in contrast, we examine their applicability to fractions. Second, unlike in unbounded whole number tasks, in our implementation the target number can be smaller than the unit and is not necessarily a multiple of, or divisible by, the given unit (See the Method section for details). Third, while unbounded NLE tasks have previously been used mainly as a learning mechanic in fraction games [13, 15], they have not been examined as an assessment mechanic. Therefore, in this study, we examine the potential and validity of a game-based unbounded NLE task for assessing students' competence in comparing fractions. Accordingly, we conducted a within-subject study comparing assessment metrics from two conditions: 1) game-based assessment using unbounded NLE tasks and 2) non-game assessment using traditional fraction comparison tasks. We formulated six hypotheses, aligned with four types of validity.

Content Validity: We expected to observe similar, general fraction number trends that numerical cognition research has identified, assuming that *(H1a)* students perform better in comparing fractions with larger distances demonstrating a distance effect [12]; *(H1b)* students perform better in comparisons that are consistent with whole number ordering than inconsistent ones [9].

Criterion Validity: We expected that in both conditions *(H2)* fraction magnitude comparison performance would correlate with overall mathematical achievement measured by a previous math grade as shown in previous research [8].

Convergent Construct Validity: We expected that *(H3)* the game would yield comparable results to traditional comparison tasks in terms of overall fraction comparison performance. Specifically, we anticipated a very strong correlation between overall comparison performance across the two conditions.

Consequential Validity: We expected that game and non-game assessment would *(H4a)* yield comparable classification outcomes, demonstrating strong agreement in identifying students' fraction comparison performance levels; *(H4b)* differ in the level of induced flow experience, with higher flow expected in the game condition.

2 Method

2.1 Participants and Research Design

Ninety-six sixth graders from two schools in Finland participated in the study, of whom 13 did not provide consent. The study was approved by the city's ethical board. Informed consent was obtained from both the students and their parents. Fifteen students were excluded from analyses due to poor performance on the onboarding tasks, which were designed to familiarize players with the game controls and game mechanics. The final sample consisted of sixty-eight students (33 females and 35 males; $M_{age} = 12.3$ years, $SD = 0.50$ years). Students completed both the game and non-game assessments in a counterbalanced design (half starting in the game, half in the non-game condition).

2.2 Description of Assessment Conditions

Game Assessment Condition: For this study, we implemented a simplified version of the Number Trace [15] game that included only the core game and assessment mechanics, consisting of unbounded NLE tasks (task model). An unbounded NLE task differs from the bounded one in that the endpoint (in our case always value two) was not visible but instead an intermediate point was provided as a reference. Figure 1 shows an example in which students were asked to locate (estimate) the target fraction, 3/4, on the number line. Students had to make this estimation based on the start point (always zero) and an intermediate point shown as a fraction number, 1/3 in our example. While students perceived these tasks simply as unbounded NLE exercises, the game system assessed whether they could correctly compare the value of the target fraction to the value of the intermediate point. The evidence model of our game system determined the correctness of the comparisons – a comparison was considered correct if the student placed the target fraction on the correct side of the intermediate point (left means smaller; right means larger). Students did not receive any direct feedback on fraction comparison, but they did receive feedback on their estimation accuracy. Students earned points based on estimation accuracy, the dog provided emotional feedback, and the green marker indicated the correct location of the target fraction. The marker and emotional feedback

Fig. 1. *Left*: A starting point of the unbounded NLE task. *Right*: The student has completed the task and received positive feedback as the estimation accuracy was high enough (over 92%).

provided indirect cues on the magnitudes of the target fraction and intermediate point. The game was controlled with a keyboard or virtual directional pad.

Non-game Assessment Condition: The tasks of the non-game assessment were based on a traditional fraction comparison task. Two fractions were shown to students, and they had to click the one with the larger value. After each answer, the student was given simple textual feedback ("Correct" or "Incorrect").

Both conditions included four blocks (levels) of comparison tasks, each consisting of seven tasks, for a total of 28 tasks. The game condition also included two onboarding tasks that used whole numbers and included instructions on how to complete them.

2.3 Measures

Comparison performance was measured by logging the comparison correctness from both assessment conditions. The same fraction values were used in both, drawn from the study by [2]. Based on the task model, the tasks included fraction pairs consistent and inconsistent with the whole number ordering in a combination with small and large value distances. Both conditions included a total of 28 fraction comparison items, of which 14 were consistent and 14 were inconsistent with whole number ordering. Only proper fractions were included, and the comparison pairs were distance-controlled. Small-distance category pairs had distances below 0.3, while large-distance pairs exceeded 0.3 (see more details in [2]). Further, our assembly model ensured that the tasks were balanced so that consistent/inconsistent and small/large distance comparison items were distributed evenly across the four blocks.

Performance classification was conducted to evaluate consequential validity. We defined classification rules based on the performance in both consistent and inconsistent fraction comparison tasks. *High performers* were defined as students who answered at least 11 out of 14 tasks correctly in both consistent and inconsistent comparisons. *Low performers* were those who answered at most 7 out of 14 tasks correctly in both types of comparisons. Students were classified as *showing signs of possible whole number bias* if they demonstrated high performance (at least 11/14 correct) on consistent comparisons but low performance (at most 7/14 correct) on inconsistent comparisons, where whole number reasoning leads to incorrect answers. Students who did not meet the criteria for any of these categories were classified in *the satisfactory-performing* category. The classes created reflect our ECD [7] based competence model, and demonstrate low-level learning analytics that could be provided, for example, to a teacher to differentiate instruction in the classroom.

Flow experience was measured using the flow short scale [19]. Students rated the nine flow items on a 1 (strongly disagree) to 7 (strongly agree) scale. The original items were changed to the past tense, and they were slightly modified to fit the conditions.

Math grade was taken from the student's previous school semester report. It uses the Finnish grading scale ranging from 4 to 10, with 10 being the highest.

2.4 Procedure

A researcher conducted the study during a 45-min lesson. He explained the procedure of the study, informed students of their rights, and gave instructions. Students used Chromebooks to access the materials in a web-based assessment system. First, the students completed a background questionnaire. The system then assigned the student to either the game or the non-game assessment (predefined order). After completing the first assessment condition, the students filled out a flow questionnaire. Next, they completed the second assessment condition, followed again by the flow questionnaire.

2.5 Statistical Analyses

Internal consistency of fraction comparison measures and flow experience items were evaluated using Cronbach's alpha coefficient. We computed mean correctness for fraction comparisons and mean flow scores for both conditions. The normality of the data was assessed based on skewness and kurtosis values, using ± 1 as the threshold. Due to violations of normality, non-parametric tests were used: Spearman's rank-order correlations and the Wilcoxon signed-rank tests. Finally, we used Cohen's Kappa to assess the agreement in a fraction comparison competence classification for the game condition. Statistical analysis software Jamovi (v. 2.6.44.0) was used to conduct the analyses.

3 Results

3.1 Descriptive Statistics and Condition Equivalence

Descriptive statistics for the assessment conditions are shown in Table 1. Students' math grade (M = 8.4, SD = 1.0) was also collected. Cronbach's alpha indicated satisfactory reliability for the game (.75) and non-game (.85) tasks, and good reliability for the flow short scale in both conditions (game: .85; non-game: .88). Conditions were not equivalent in terms of positive feedback given, as students got significantly less positive feedback in the game condition (*Mdn* = 41.1%) compared to non-game condition (*Mdn* = 92.9%), $W = 2346, p < .001$, with a large effect size ($r_{\mathrm{rb}} = 1.00$).

Table 1. Descriptive statistics. All units in percents, except Flow experience is on a 1–7 scale

	Game			Non-game		
	Mean	SD	Mdn	Mean	SD	Mdn
Comparison correctness	68.9	15.9	69.9	87.8	13.7	92.9
With consistent	79.0	14.3	78.6	86.7	11.8	85.7
With inconsistent	58.8	23.8	57.1	89.0	21.7	100
With small distance	64.3	16.5	64.3	85.1	14.2	92.9
With large distance	73.5	19.0	78.6	90.5	14.7	96.4
Flow experience	4.18	1.19	4.22	5.18	1.18	5.44
Estimation correctness	47.0	21.4	41.1	–	–	–

3.2   Evaluating the Validity of Game-Based Assessment

To evaluate the validity of the game assessment, we used the validated non-game assessment as a benchmark. We focused on content, criterion, and convergent construct validity to assess how well the conditions capture the same construct. We also considered consequential validity to explore the potential impact of the game-based assessment in educational settings.

To consider **content validity**, we examined the presence of effects and characteristics typically associated with conceptual fraction knowledge. In line with *Hypothesis 1a*, a Wilcoxon signed-rank test indicated that students performed significantly better on comparison pairs with a large numerical distance ($Mdn = 78.6\%$) than on those with a small distance ($Mdn = 64.3\%$) in the game condition, $W = 1423, p < .001$, with a large effect size ($r_{rb} = .61$). The analyses of non-game assessment condition data confirmed the presence of the expected distance effect. Students in the non-game condition performed significantly better on comparison pairs with a large numerical distance ($Mdn = 96.4\%$) than on those with a small distance ($Mdn = 92.9\%$), $W = 688$, p $< .001$, with a large effect size ($r_{rb} = .76$).

In line with *Hypothesis 1b*, a Wilcoxon signed-rank test indicated that in the game condition, students performed significantly better on consistent comparison tasks ($Mdn = 78.6\%$) than on inconsistent comparison tasks ($Mdn = 57.1\%$), $W = 1726, p < .001$, with a large effect size ($r_{rb} = 83$). However, as some studies have shown that this effect does not always exist due to different whole number ordering-based comparison strategies, we examined this also in the non-game assessment condition to confirm the reliability of the found effect. A Wilcoxon signed-rank test indicated that in the non-game assessment condition this effect was reversed as students performed significantly better on inconsistent comparison tasks ($Mdn = 100\%$) than on inconsistent comparison tasks ($Mdn = 85.7\%$), $W = 430, p < .017$, with a moderate effect size ($r_{rb} = 38$).

In terms of **criterion validity**, we compared the students' previous math grades with their performance on the comparison task. In line with our *Hypothesis 2*, the correlation between the previous math grade and comparison performance was moderate in the game ($r = .52, p < .001$) and small in the non-game ($r = .34, p = .005$) conditions.

To evaluate ***convergent construct validity***, we examined the comparability of the game and non-game assessment conditions. Regarding *Hypothesis 3*, we expected that both assessment approaches would yield similar results in terms of students' fraction comparison performance. As expected, we found a statistically significant moderate correlation between the overall game-based comparison performance ($Mdn = 69.6\%$) and the traditional comparison performance ($Mdn = 92.9\%$), $r = .56$, $p < .001$. This provides preliminary evidence of convergent construct validity. However, the moderate strength of the correlation and difference in medians suggests that the game-based format may also reflect additional or different processes beyond those captured by the traditional comparison task mechanic. The correlation of .56 indicates that approximately 31% of the variance in students' game-based comparison performance can be explained by their non-game comparison performance. This shared variance supports only partial construct validity, while a substantial portion of the variance remains unaccounted for, indicating potential influences unique to the game assessment condition.

To evaluate ***consequential validity***, we examined whether the game and non-game assessment approaches identified the same students as high-performing, satisfactory-performing, low-performing, or exhibiting clear signs of whole number bias. We used Cohen's Kappa to assess the agreement in classification decisions across the two assessment approaches, allowing us to evaluate whether the game-based assessment supports reliable student-level learning analytics and educational decision-making. Although the observed agreement between the game and the non-game assessment approaches was 40%, the Kappa coefficient was only 0.130 ($p = .021$), indicating only slight agreement beyond chance and providing limited support for *Hypothesis 4a*.

To evaluate consequential validity from the perspective of students' experiences, a Wilcoxon signed-rank test was conducted to compare flow experience in game and non-game assessment conditions. There was a statistically significant difference in flow scores between the two conditions, $W = 106$, $p < .001$, with a large effect size ($r_{rb} = -.90$). But contrary to *Hypothesis 4b*, participants reported significantly higher flow in the non-game condition ($Mdn = 5.44$) compared to the game condition ($Mdn = 4.22$).

4   Discussion and Conclusion

The present study examined the extent to which an unbounded Number Line Estimation (NLE) task mechanic can be used to assess students' competence in comparing fractions. To do this, we developed a game-based assessment informed by evidence-centered design framework [7]. We compared the proposed game-based assessment to a traditional, non-game assessment, which was based on a widely used fraction comparison task [8, 9, 12]. The results indicate that both the game and non-game assessment conditions exhibited similarities, particularly in replicating the distance effect commonly observed in traditional fraction comparison tasks [12], suggesting content validity. Further, performance in both assessment conditions showed a similarly positive correlation with math achievement, providing initial evidence of criterion validity. However, comparison performance in the game and the non-game assessments showed only a moderate correlation, indicating that each version may measure different aspects of fraction understanding, supporting only partial convergent construct validity.

Given the relatively low level of convergent construct validity observed, we examined the game assessment's consequential validity to provide an additional perspective on its practical usefulness and overall validity. In line with this concern, the classification of students into different competence levels showed an unsatisfactory overlap between the game and non-game assessments. Given that traditional fraction comparison tasks are often used to identify students who may need support in overcoming whole number bias, the proposed game assessment could provide teachers with misleading information about students' competencies, potentially leading to inappropriate pedagogical decisions or missed opportunities for targeted support.

Furthermore, contrary to our expectations and assumption of stealth assessment [3] and previous study [2] the students reported significantly lower flow experience in the game condition compared to non-game condition. This aligns with the performance data, which showed that students performed substantially better on traditional fraction comparison tasks than on unbounded NLE tasks—resulting in approximately twice as much negative feedback in the game condition. This may partly explain the differences in flow experience, and it further suggests that some students may have had problems understanding the unbounded NLE mechanic. Consequently, they may have relied on strategies better suited to common bounded number line tasks, which may not accurately reflect their conceptual fraction knowledge. This further highlights that students may have engaged in different cognitive processes when solving game-based unbounded NLE tasks compared to traditional fraction comparison tasks.

Unfortunately, the onboarding phase in the game assessment was very limited and did not adequately ensure that students understood the game and its mechanics. To mitigate this, we excluded students who were unable to correctly solve a simple tutorial task involving unbounded NLE with whole numbers. However, future studies should include a more comprehensive onboarding phase as emphasized in [17] to be able to better determine the extent to which the game assessment mechanics reflect the targeted competencies. To conclude, further research is necessary to establish the unbounded NLE task as a valid assessment mechanic for fraction comparison competence. Think-aloud protocols and eye-tracking methods could provide valuable insights into how students approach unbounded NLE tasks with fractions, which is crucial for developing valid stealth assessment mechanics and models.

Acknowledgments. This study was funded by the Research Council of Finland (No. 361832).

Disclosure of Interests. The authors have no competing interests to declare.

References

1. Shute, V.J., Wang, L., Greiff, S., Zhao, W., Moore, G.: Measuring problem solving skills via stealth assessment in an engaging video game. Comput. Hum. Behav. **63**, 106–117 (2016)
2. Kiili, K., Ketamo, H.: Evaluating cognitive and affective outcomes of a digital game-based math test. IEEE Trans. Learn. Technol. **11**(2), 255–263 (2018)
3. Kim, Y.J., Shute, V.J.: The interplay of game elements with psychometric qualities, learning, and enjoyment in game-based assessment. Comput. Educ. **87**, 340–356 (2015)

4. Landers, R.N., Sanchez, D.R.: Game-based, gamified, and gamefully designed assessments for employee selection: definitions, distinctions, design, and validation. Int. J. Sel. Assess. **30**(1), 1–13 (2022)

5. Plass, J.L., Homer, B.D., Kinzer, C.K., Chang, Y.K., Frye, J., Perlin, K.: Metrics in simulations and games for learning. In: Seif El-Nasr, K., Drachen, A., Canossa A. (eds.), Game Analytics: Maximizing the Value of Player Data, pp. 697–729. Springer (2013)

6. Shute, V., Ventura, M.: Stealth Assessment: Measuring and Supporting Learning in Video Games. MIT Press (2013)

7. Rahimi, S., Almond, R.G., Shute, V.J., Sun, C.: Getting the first and second decimals right: psychometrics of stealth assessment. In: Games as Stealth Assessments, pp. 125–153. IGI Global (2023)

8. Siegler, R.S., Thompson, C.A., Schneider, M.: An integrated theory of whole number and fractions development. Cogn. Psychol. **62**(4), 273–296 (2011)

9. Van Hoof, J., Verschaffel, L., Van Dooren, W.: Inappropriately applying natural number properties in rational number tasks: characterizing the development of the natural number bias through primary and secondary education. Educ. Stud. Math. **90**, 39–56 (2015)

10. Stafylidou, S., Vosniadou, S.: The development of students' understanding of the numerical value of fractions. Learn. Instr. **14**(5), 503–518 (2004)

11. Ni, Y., Zhou, Y.D.: Teaching and learning fraction and rational numbers: the origins and implications of whole number bias. Educ. Psychol. **40**(1), 27–52 (2005)

12. DeWolf, M., Vosniadou, S.: The representation of fraction magnitudes and the whole number bias reconsidered. Learn. Instr. **37**, 39–49 (2015)

13. Demedts, F., et al.: The effectiveness of explanatory adaptive feedback within a digital educational game to enhance fraction understanding. Learn. Instr. **94**, 101976 (2024)

14. Reinert, R.M., Moeller, K.: The new unbounded number line estimation task: a systematic literature review. Acta Physiol (Oxf.) **219**, 103366 (2021)

15. McMullen, J., et al.: A game-based approach to promoting adaptive rational number knowledge. Mathematical Thinking Learn. **26**(4), 411–427 (2024)

16. Koskinen, A., McMullen, J., Ninaus, M., Kiili, K.: Does the emotional design of scaffolds enhance learning and motivational outcomes in game-based learning? J. Comput. Assist. Learn. **39**(1), 77–93 (2023)

17. Lindstedt, A., Kiili, K.: Evaluating playing experience and adoption of a math learning game. In: 1st International GamiFIN Conference Proceedings on CEUR Workshop Proceedings, vol. 1857, pp. 39–46 (2017)

18. Kiili, K., Koskinen, A., Lindstedt, A., Ninaus, M.: Extending a digital fraction game piece by piece with physical manipulatives. In: Gentile, M., Allegra M., Söbke, H. (eds.) Games and Learning Alliance: GALA 2018. Lecture Notes in Computer Science, pp. 157–166. Springer (2018)

19. Martin, A.J., Jackson, S.A.: Brief approaches to assessing task absorption and enhanced subjective experience: examining 'short' and 'core' flow in diverse performance domains. Motiv. Emot. **32**(3), 141–157 (2008)

Gaming the System or Learning? Understanding Self-Regulation Through Learning Processes and Outcomes in Game-Based Learning

Cameron Marano[1]([⊠]) [iD], Megan Wiedbusch[1] [iD], Annamarie Brosnihan[1] [iD], Milouni Patel[1] [iD], James Lester[2] [iD], and Roger Azevedo[1] [iD]

[1] University of Central Florida, Orlando, FL, USA
`cameron.marano@ucf.edu`
[2] North Carolina State University, Raleigh, NC, USA

Abstract. Game-based learning environments (GBLEs) are educational platforms created to promote and scaffold learners' self-regulated learning (SRL) strategies while learning complex STEM topics. However, learners can still abuse the intended purposes of GBLEs and engage in 'gaming the system', deliberate behaviors employed to forgo the learning process while still completing the task at hand. 'Gaming the system' is often investigated within intelligent tutoring systems (ITSs), yet these behaviors have been the subject of limited investigation in narrative-based GBLEs. Thus, this study identified two 'gaming the system' behaviors from undergraduate students' ($N = 93$) gameplay during the narrative-based GBLE, Crystal Island, and examined how their prior knowledge of microbiology and two agency conditions influenced their frequencies of gaming behaviors and their learning outcomes. Results indicated that students with high prior knowledge engaged in significantly more 'trial-and-error' gaming behaviors than those with lower prior knowledge. Moreover, we found that students with partial agency engaged in significantly more "trial-and-error' gaming behaviors than those will full agency; whereas those will full agency engaged in more 'guessing' gaming behaviors than those with full agency. These results indicate the importance for identifying contextually driven gaming behaviors, as well as future GBLE scaffolds to adopt real-time, adaptive scaffolding methods based on learner's active gameplay and SRL (in)efficiency.

Keywords: Gaming the System · Self-Regulated Learning · STEM · Learning Outcomes · Log Files

1 Introduction

Self-regulation is a multifaceted skill essential for learners to implement during learning processes, especially while learning complex STEM topics with advanced learning technologies such as game-based simulation environments (GBLEs) [1]. However, the process of self-regulation is relatively difficult to correctly and continuously engage in throughout a learning task [2]. To address this problem, GBLEs have been developed

S. Bakkes et al. (Eds.): GALA 2025, LNCS 16307, pp. 55–64, 2026.
https://doi.org/10.1007/978-3-032-11043-5_6

to promote and facilitate learning by carefully balancing elements of gameplay with educational content through embedded game mechanics [3] Learning mechanics are repeated patterns of interaction within GBLEs that operationalize pedagogical theories into concrete gameplay tasks, whereas assessment mechanics are diagnostic actions that elicit and record learner behaviors for (in)valid inferences about knowledge and skills [4]. Through these embedded game mechanics, STEM-based GBLEs foster essential self-regulated learning (SRL) skills such as problem-solving and inquiry-based reasoning through active gameplay [3]. When core game mechanics are tightly aligned with rich learning activities and seamless assessments, they serve a dual purpose of maintaining player engagement through meaningful interactions while simultaneously promoting deep learning and providing real-time insights into learner progress [5]. As such, GBLEs foster a structured environment where students are guided throughout learning and SRL engagement, while maintaining agency to explore within the games' constraints. Nevertheless, even well-scaffolded SRL processes in GBLEs can be exploited as learners may engage in 'gaming-the-system' behaviors to expedite or completely bypass the learning process [6].

2 Background

'Gaming-the-system' is a widely researched phenomenon defined by learners exhibiting systematic behaviors in an educational learning environment to artificially succeed in a task without gaining any knowledge [6]. A common example of these 'gaming-the-system' behaviors is where learners repeatedly seek out help from the system, where after a certain number of requests, the answer is ultimately given to the user. Such behaviors require little effort for the learner to get to the correct answer without any actual domain learning. These behaviors are prevalent in intelligent tutoring systems (ITSs), where the system is designed with scaffolding features to help learners if they are struggling (e.g., Cognitive Tutor, [7]). While the intentions behind these features are pedagogically grounded, many players take advantage of the scaffolding tools to engage in 'gaming-the-system'. Students may engage in 'gaming-the-system' because of low motivation, boredom, confusion or frustration (see [8, 9] for details). Additionally, being unfamiliar with the systems' domain content may cause students to feel overwhelmed, causing them to avoid genuine attempts at self-regulation and learning. Research has also found that learners with low prior knowledge display more 'gaming-the-system' behaviors than their peers with higher prior knowledge [6]. Few studies have investigated gaming behaviors in learning environments with game elements (Decimal Point, [10]); however, there is an absence of research investigating gaming behaviors in narrative-based GBLEs such as Crystal Island [5, 11].

Narrative-based GBLEs are learning environments that situate learners into the game's storyline, allowing for rich and immersive learning interactions [12, 13]. Research with these environments tends to focus on SRL behaviors, such as monitoring, regulating, and reflecting on one's cognitive and metacognitive processes, goals and actions, and their relation to learning as a process and outcome [11, 14]. The deployment of SRL behaviors has been shown to be imperative to learners' success in GBLEs [15, 16]. Several studies have found that the relevancy [17], temporal deployment [18], and complexity [5, 19] of SRL behaviors specifically in the GBLE Crystal Island, are related to their learning outcomes, as well as their sense of agency [11, 18]. These player actions are often analyzed in descriptive terms based on the quantity of their actions and the underlying patterns in relation to specific learning processes. That is, these studies infer a learners' SRL processes based on their game behaviors (i.e., interactions with the foundational game mechanics, such as reading informational texts and testing hypotheses; [5]); yet they tend to follow a "click to construct" paradigm [20]. That is, actions, or a "click" (e.g., talking to a non-player character) are categorized as a particular psychological construct (e.g., information gathering during scientific reasoning). However, this methodological approach can often exclude context about what a learner has previously done prior to the "click" or what information they have previously encountered leading to that "click". Additionally, these approaches have yet to identify 'gaming-the-system' processes within these clickstream data.

Although these previous works have contributed to the foundational understandings of SRL in GBLEs, the literature on narrative-based GBLEs fails to account for the context and the quality of the learners' self-regulatory behaviors (or lack thereof). By diving deeper into these self-regulatory behaviors, potential patterns of 'gaming-the-system' may appear and contribute to an entirely different narrative that has yet to be investigated in open-ended, narrative-based GBLEs.

3 Current Study

This study intends to identify behaviors of 'gaming-the-system' in Crystal Island, a narrative-based GBLE that promotes learning about microbiology while fostering scientific reasoning and thinking through active gameplay. While previous studies have examined gaming behaviors in learning environments with game elements, there has yet to be research investigating these behaviors in a narrative-based learning environment. This study intends to expand prior literature on 'gaming-the-system' and SRL through identifying how learners' prior knowledge and game condition impacts gaming behaviors in Crystal Island and how these behaviors relate to learning outcomes.

4 Methodology

4.1 Crystal Island

Crystal Island is a first-person, narrative GBLE where players adopt the role of a medical detective to investigate an unknown illness outbreak on a remote island [12]. To do so, players interact with the game environment, a research station based on Crystal Island, while enacting various SRL processes, scientific reasoning, and problem-solving skills [11]. The environment consists of multiple locations (e.g., infirmary, living quarters, dining hall, lead scientist's residence, and the laboratory), where players can engage in conversations with non-player characters (NPCs) that inhabit the island (e.g., sick scientists, Kim the nurse, Quinten the chef; see Fig. 1A and B) and gather empirical evidence about various infections through reading research articles, posters, and books (see Fig. 1C). The knowledge obtained by interacting with specific embedded game components (e.g., reading posters to find symptoms of a viral infection) is necessary to identify the mysterious illness, the contamination source, and a treatment plan for the island's occupants. However, not all the information within the environment is relevant to the final diagnosis (e.g., symptoms of mutagens and carcinogens).

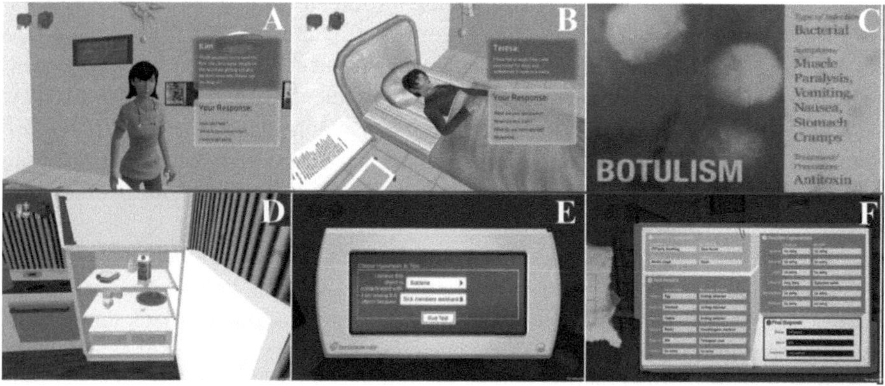

Fig. 1. Screenshots of Crystal Island Game Environment. (A) Receiving information about the illness from Kim, the island's nurse; (B) Talking to patient and finding out what symptoms they are experiencing and what food they ate; (C) Example of information found on poster; (D) Example of food found throughout the island; (E) Entering information into the scanner machine; (F) Diagnosis worksheet.

As players gather information, they can generate hypotheses about the illness, its contamination source, and a treatment plan in the embedded diagnosis worksheet. Players have access to a diagnosis worksheet throughout gameplay, where information can be documented (e.g., symptoms of patients, test results, and final diagnosis) and used to create hypotheses at any time (see Fig. 1F). To identify the illnesses contamination source, players must use the acquired information gathered throughout gameplay to hypothesize through collecting various food items in the game environment (see Fig. 1D). Once collected, players can bring the food item(s) to the laboratory to scan (see Fig. 1E). Food items can only be scanned after answering why the food item was chosen (i.e., sick members ate/drank it, sick members touched it, it wasn't stored properly, it looked dirty, or it often carries disease) and what kind of illness is believed to be present (i.e., mutagen, carcinogen, bacteria, or virus). The scanner will then confirm whether the food item is positive or negative for the previously hypothesized illness, and the player may (but is not required to) document their findings in the diagnosis worksheet. The game design assumes if the learner is using efficient SRL strategies, they would only test items that the NPCs reportedly ate/drank for diseases that match the symptoms the islanders reported and based on the information found in instructional text they read (i.e., articles, books, and posters). However, the game does not require this, meaning a learner could choose to 'game the system' by testing random objects for unfamiliar diseases that may or may not match the symptoms described by NPCs.

Once players believe they have accurately determined (1) the mysterious illness, (2) its contamination source, and (3) a treatment plan for inhabitants, the information must be presented to Kim, the infirmary nurse. If the information presented to Kim is incorrect, she will provide the player with tailored feedback based on the presented hypothesis. If the player identifies the correct illness, contamination source, and treatment plan, the task is complete and the game ends.

4.2　Participants, Experimental Conditions, and Procedure

Undergraduate students ($N = 93$, $M_{age} = 20.07$) from a large North American University were recruited to engage in a learning session with Crystal Island, a narrative GBLE.

Students were randomly assigned to one of two experimental conditions: full agency ($M = 55$) or partial agency ($M = 38$). The full agency condition allowed for open play, where students were not limited or guided during gameplay. For example, if someone in this condition entered a room in the game, they were able to leave the room without interacting with any of the NPCs or instructional materials. Participants in the partial agency condition had access to the same instructional content as the full agency condition; however, this condition had an embedded scaffolding aspect where they were required to interact with all NPCs and instructional material in each area (i.e., the dining hall, living quarters, laboratory, etc.) before moving on.

Once recruited, given consent, and prior to gameplay, students completed a 21-item multiple choice pre-assessment to determine their baseline knowledge of microbiology. Once oriented to the task, students played Crystal Island for 90 min or until the mystery was solved (see Sect. 4.1). During gameplay, participants' multimodal data was collected including their log files, eye tracking, electrodermal activity, and facial expressions of emotions. In this study, we only analyzed the timestamped logfiles that detail participants' interactions within the game environment. Immediately following gameplay, an equivalent microbiology post-assessment was administered which measured the students' knowledge of various microbiology topics but did not directly measure scientific reasoning abilities. Students were paid \$10/h for their participation.

4.3　Coding and Scoring

Operational Definitions. We have defined two gameplay behaviors as 'gaming-the-system' behaviors that can be exhibited in Crystal Island:

'Trial-and-error' scanning. Indicated by participants repeatedly using the scanner back-to-back (i.e., more than one scan without another player action in between) and altering at least one piece of information (e.g., reason for scanning).

'Guessing' scanning. Indicated by participants using the scanner with information they did not directly encounter during their gameplay up until that scan. For example, a guessing scan behavior would be a participant scanning an egg for bacteria when they have not yet looked at any informational content about bacteria or talked to an NPC that revealed they had eaten eggs recently. However, a participant who talked to Teresa (who reveals that she has recently eaten eggs) and looks at a poster about bacteria would not be gaming the system if they chose to scan the eggs for bacteria. If the participant did not encounter any of the information they were scanning for (i.e., the food item, reason for testing, and what they are testing for), that action was labeled as a guessing scan behavior.

It is important to note that these operational definitions are not mutually exclusive and do not account for participants' prior knowledge (e.g., knowing salmonella often comes from raw chicken), as one of the goals of the game is to acquire knowledge through gameplay. Additionally, we did not measure their prior knowledge about food born illnesses specifically and therefore cannot reasonably assume their prior knowledge for scanning behaviors.

For our analysis, we calculated the ratio of 'gaming-the-system' scans to total scans as a proportional value for our research questions. In doing so, we control the different number of total scans across participants (e.g., 7 'gaming-the-system' scans for a participant with 14 total scans is 50% while it would be 100% for a participant with 7 total scans.

Prior Knowledge and Normalized Learning Gains (NLGs): Before and after the learning task, participants completed a multiple-choice microbiology assessment (see Sect. 4.2). There were four possible answer choices for each question, with one correct answer and three incorrect answers. We scored each assessment separately and used the pre-assessment scores as a baseline for participants' prior knowledge. Using the participants pre- and post-assessment scores, we calculated their normalized learning gains (NLGs) using a series of equations that assesses how much students learned relative to their prior knowledge [21]. We then categorized participants NLGs into "high" and "low" groups based on a median split of the scores, to keep our metrics consistent throughout our analyses (i.e., high/low prior knowledge).

5   Results

For research questions 1, we split the sample into those with high ($N = 46$)- versus low-prior knowledge ($N = 47$) based on a median split of the participants' microbiology assessment pretest scores ($Mdn_{Pre} = 11$). Proportions of 'Trial-and-error' scanning behaviors were not normally distributed (Shapiro-Wilk W $= 0.87$, $p < 0.05$), nor were 'Guessing' scanning behavior proportions (Shapiro-Wilk W $= 0.92$, $p < 0.05$). As such, we used non-parametric tests for research questions 1 and 2. For research question 3, we split the sample into those with high ($N = 47$)- versus low-NLGs ($N = 46$) based on a median split of the participants' normalized learning gains ($Mdn_{NLG} = 0.03$).

RQ1.a Is there a difference in the proportion of 'Trial-and-error' scanning behaviors between participants with high prior knowledge versus those with low prior knowledge? A Mann-Whitney test was conducted to determine whether there was a difference in the proportion of 'trial-and-error' scanning behaviors between participants with high prior knowledge ($N = 46$) versus those with low prior knowledge ($N = 47$). Results indicated that there was a significant difference in the proportion of trial-and-error scanning behaviors between participants with varied prior knowledge (W $= 5037.5$, $p < 0.05$), where participants with low prior knowledge engage in less trial-and-error scanning behaviors ($Mdn_{Proportion} = 0.80$, $Mdn_{Rank} = 41.5$) than participants with high prior knowledge ($Mdn_{Proportion} = 0.86$, $Mdn^{Rank} = 48.5$). In sum, these results indicate that the participant's prior knowledge impacted their trial-and-error scanning behaviors, suggesting that participants with high prior knowledge were more likely to engage in trial-and-error gaming behaviors.

b. Is there a difference in the proportion of 'Guessing' scanning behaviors between participants with high prior knowledge versus those with low prior knowledge? A Mann-Whitney test was conducted to determine whether there was a difference in the proportion of 'guessing' scanning behaviors between participants with high prior knowledge versus those with low prior knowledge. Results indicated that there was not a significant difference in guessing scanning behaviors and prior knowledge ($W = 4369$, $p > 0.05$). In sum, these results indicate that the participant's prior knowledge did not impact their guessing scanning behaviors.

RQ2. a. Is there a difference in the proportion of 'Trial-and-error' scanning behaviors between participants in the Full Agency condition versus those in the Partial Agency condition? A Mann-Whitney test was conducted to determine whether there was a difference in the proportion of 'trial-and-error' scanning behaviors between participants in the full agency condition ($N = 55$) and the partial agency condition ($N = 38$). Results indicated that there was a significant difference in the participants trial-and-error scanning behaviors based on their experimental condition ($W = 825$, $p < .001$), where those in the full agency engaged in less trial-and-error scanning behaviors ($Mdn_{Proportion} = 0.80$, $Mdn_{Rank} = 41.5$) than the participants in the partial agency condition ($Mdn_{Proportion} = 0.89$, $Mdn_{Rank} = 55.5$). Overall, these results suggest that participants without scaffolding—i.e., those in the full agency condition, were less likely to engage in trial-and-error behaviors while testing food items.

b. Is there a difference in the proportion of 'Guessing' scanning behaviors between participants in the Full Agency condition versus those in the Partial Agency condition? A Mann-Whitney test was conducted to determine whether there was a difference in the proportion of 'guessing' scanning behaviors between participants in the full agency condition and the partial agency condition. Results revealed that there was a significant difference in the participants guessing scanning behaviors based on their experimental condition ($W = 110$, $p < .001$; Partial agency $Mdn_{Proportion} = 0.58$, $Mdn_{Rank} = 34.5$; Full agency $Mdn_{Proportion} = 0.80$, $Mdn_{Rank} = 55.5$). Overall, these results show that participants in the full agency condition engaged in more guessing scanning behaviors than those in the partial agency condition.

RQ3.a. Is there a relationship between the proportion of 'Trial and error' scanning behaviors and participants with high NLGs versus those with low NLGs? A point-biserial correlation was conducted to determine if there was a difference in the proportion of 'trial-and-error' scanning behaviors and participants' with high normalized learning gains ($N = 47$) versus participants with low normalized learning gains ($N = 46$). Results did not find a significant relationship between the proportion of trial-and-error scanning behaviors and participants learning gains, $r(91) = 0.2$, $p > 0.05$. These results indicate that there was not a significant relationship between the amount participants learned and their trial-and-error scanning behaviors.

b. Is there a relationship between the proportion of 'Guessing' scanning behaviors and participants with high NLGs versus those with low NLGs? A point-biserial correlation was conducted to determine if there was a difference in the proportion of 'guessing' scanning behaviors and participants' normalized learning gains. Results did not reveal significant relations between the proportion of guessing scanning behaviors and participants learning gains, $r(91) = -0.09$, $p > 0.05$. These results suggest that the proportion of guessing scan behaviors participants complete is not significantly correlated to participants' learning gains.

6 Discussion

To examine both 'gaming-the-system' behaviors, we first examined the potential differences in their proportional frequency between different levels of prior knowledge. While there was no difference in the amount of 'guessing' scanning behaviors, our results indicated that learners with high prior knowledge were more likely to engage in 'trial-and-error' scanning behaviors compared to those with lower prior knowledge. This result contrasts with prior work within ITSs where students with lower prior knowledge tend to game the system more frequently [6]. We interpret this finding to suggest that learners with greater domain knowledge may engage in more strategic forms of hypothesis testing in a rapid iterative fashion as a means of trying to be as efficient as possible. If these learners value beating the game more than acquiring more domain knowledge, then these behaviors could be considered adaptive instead of disengagement or learning avoidant. In this way, these findings support the call to consider more contextual nuances and learner intentions when interpreting gaming behaviors in complex learning environments [22]. Importantly, we did not account for prior knowledge about foodborne illness specifically, which could have affected how participants chose to engage with the scanner, especially those with higher levels of prior knowledge about microbiology in general.

We also examined the impact of other GBLE scaffolds, specifically the role of agency, on 'gaming-the-system' behaviors. While prior knowledge examined learner-level factors that may influence these behaviors, our research question 2 focused on how agency as a scaffold might influence 'gaming-the-system' behaviors. Consistent with previous research that found there is a "sweet spot" for restricting agency to support SRL enactment in GBLEs [11, 18], our study found that participants within the partial agency condition engaged in significantly more 'trial-and-error' behaviors. These learners were required to interact with all available information before changing locations, which could have influenced how they approached their problem solving. In contrast, those in the full agency condition, who were not restricted in how they chose to play the game, engaged in more 'guessing' behaviors. In conjunction with one another, these findings suggest that scaffolding via limiting a learners' agency may encourage learners to become more task-oriented, and compliance driven, relying on brute-force strategies to progress. However, too little scaffolding may encourage learners to be more exploratory, but less informed in their decision making. As such, future GBLE scaffold mechanics should consider adaptive scaffold designs in which learners are supported based on their actions or inferred states rather than imposing blanket constraints.

Finally, we examined the impact of 'gaming-the-system' behaviors on learning outcomes. Surprisingly, neither 'trial-and-error' nor 'guessing' scanning behaviors were significantly related to learning gains, diverging from prior studies in ITSs where these behaviors are negatively correlated with learning outcomes [6, 8]. We argue this may be because of the affordances and structure differences between GBLEs and ITSs. Crystal Island is a highly exploratory game that has a built-in narrative arc. Even when learners 'game-the-system', they may still be acting with partial or semi-relevant information. Furthermore, 96% of participants successfully solved the mystery, suggesting learning gains may not be the only indicator of (in)effective SRL strategy use. These findings raise important questions requiring further examination of how we define "gaming-the-system" behaviors in less structured environments such as GBLEs. Moreover, it prompts further discussion in the field regarding what constitutes (mal)adaptive 'gaming-the-system' behaviors in relation to the goal of the learner (e.g., learning as much as possible or completing the game as quickly/efficiently as possible). As Knight and Shum [20] caution, assigning (meta)cognitive intent to discrete clickstream data may be over-simplifying the dynamic nature of SRL in complex learning environments. Additional contextual data, such as time between and within 'gaming-the-system' behaviors, when the behaviors occur relative to overall game time, and scientific reasoning or problem-solving skills/knowledge may all offer additional insight into when and why learners seem to deviate from theorized "optimal" strategies.

Overall, our findings challenge traditional assumptions about 'gaming-the-system' behaviors and underscore the need for context-sensitive interpretations within open-ended learning environments. As these behaviors continue to be explored and refined within narrative-based GBLEs, we anticipate contributing to the larger discussion of developing pedagogical scaffolds to counteract potential maladaptive behaviors while also identifying behaviors that may not be 'gaming-the-system' within GBLEs.

Acknowledgments. This study was funded by the National Science Foundation (DUE#1761178 and DRL#1661202) and the Social Sciences and Humanities Research Council of Canada (SSHRC 895-2011-1006). The authors would like to thank the SMART Lab at UCF and the IntelliMEDIA Group at NCSU for their contributions.

Disclosure of Interests. The authors do not have any competing interests to declare.

References

1. Azevedo, R., Wiedbusch, M.: Theories of metacognition and pedagogy applied to AIED systems. In: Handbook of Artificial Intelligence in Education, pp. 45–67. Edward Elgar Publishing (2023)
2. Winne, P.H.: Cognition and metacognition within self-regulated learning. In: Handbook of Self-Regulation of Learning and Performance, pp. 36–48. Routledge (2017)
3. Plass, J.L., Mayer, R.E., Homer, B.D.: Handbook of Game-Based Learning. MIT Press (2020)
4. Plass, J.L., Homer, B.D., Kinzer, C., Frye, J., Perlin, K.: Learning mechanics and assessment mechanics for games for learning. G4LI White Paper **1**, 2011 (2011)
5. Dever, D., et al.: From product to process data: game mechanics for science learning. Int. J. Serious Games **11**(4), 127–153 (2024)
6. Baker, R.S., Corbett, A.T., Koedinger, K.R.: Detecting student misuse of intelligent tutoring systems. In: Intelligent Tutoring Systems: 7th International Conference Proceedings 7, pp. 531–540. Springer (2004)
7. Koedinger, K.R., Aleven, V.: An interview reflection on "intelligent tutoring goes to school in the big city." Int. J. Artif. Intell. Educ. **26**, 13–24 (2016)
8. Baker, R.S.d., et al.: Modeling and studying gaming the system with educational data mining. In: International Handbook of Metacognition and Learning Technologies, pp. 97–115 (2013)

 9. Mogessie, M., Elizabeth Richey, J., McLaren, B.M., Andres-Bray, J.M.L., Baker, R.S.: Confrustion and gaming while learning with erroneous examples in a decimals game. In: Artificial Intelligence in Education: 21st International Conference Proceedings, Part II 21, pp. 208–213. Springer (2020)
10. Baker, R.S., et al.: Gaming the system mediates the relationship between gender and learning outcomes in a digital learning game. In: Instructional Science, pp. 1–36 (2024)
11. Taub, M., Sawyer, R., Smith, A., Rowe, J., Azevedo, R., Lester, J.: The agency effect: the impact of student agency on learning, emotions, and problem-solving behaviors in a game-based learning environment. Comput. Educ. **147**, 103781 (2020)
12. Lester, J.C., Spires, H.A., Nietfeld, J.L., Minogue, J., Mott, B.W., Lobene, E.V.: Designing game-based learning environments for elementary science education: a narrative-centered learning perspective. Inf. Sci. **264**, 4–18 (2014)
13. Lester, J., Bansal, M., Biswas, G., Hmelo-Silver, C., Roschelle, J., Rowe, J.: The AI institute for engaged learning. AI Mag. **45**(1), 69–76 (2024)
14. Taub, M., Azevedo, R.: How does prior knowledge influence eye fixations and sequences of cognitive and metacognitive srl processes during learning with an intelligent tutoring system? Int. J. Artif. Intell. Educ. **29**(1), 1–28 (2019)
15. Cloude, E., Carpenter, D., Dever, D., Azevedo, R., Lester, J.: Game-based learning analytics for supporting adolescents' reflection. J. Learn. Analyt. **8**(2) (2021)
16. Nietfeld, J., Sperling, R.: The impact of narrative-based goals in a game-based learning environment. In: ICERI2024 Proceedings, pp. 359–365. IATED (2024)
17. Taub, M., Azevedo, R., Bradbury, A.E., Millar, G.C., Lester, J.: Using sequence mining to reveal the efficiency in scientific reasoning during stem learning with a game-based learning environment. Learn. Instruct. **54**, 93–103 (2018)
18. Dever, D.A., et al.: Identifying the effects of scaffolding on learners' temporal deployment of self-regulated learning operations during game-based learning using multimodal data. Front. Psychol. **14**, 1280566 (2023)
19. Dever, D.A., Wiedbusch, M., Park, S., Llinas, A., Lester, J., Azevedo, R.: Assessing the complexity of gaming mechanics during science learning. In: International Conference on Games and Learning Alliance, pp. 299–308. Springer (2023)
20. Knight, S., Buckingham Shum, S.: Theory and learning analytics. Handb. Learn. Analyt. **1**, 17–22 (2017)
21. Marx, J.D., Cummings, K.: Normalized change. Am. J. Phys. **75**(1), 87–91 (2007)
22. Paquette, L., Baker, R.S.: Comparing machine learning to knowledge engineering for student behavior modeling: a case study in gaming the system. Interact. Learn. Environ. **27**(5–6), 585–597 (2019)

Gravitas: A Simulation-Based Learning Game for Diagnosing Misconceptions in Mechanics

Katharina Richter$^{(\boxtimes)}$, Dominik Tschirky , and Michael D. Kickmeier-Rust

St. Gallen University of Teacher Education, St. Gallen, Switzerland
`{katharina.richter,dominik.tschirky,michael.kickemier}@phsg.ch`

Abstract. Despite ongoing curricular reforms, misconceptions in Newtonian mechanics remain widespread among lower secondary students and often persist after conventional instruction. *Gravitas* is a simulation-based learning game designed to identify and transform such misconceptions through a structured cycle of diagnostic tasks, cognitive conflict, and exploratory interaction. Grounded in Conceptual Change Theory, Self-Determination Theory, and Knowledge Space Theory, the game integrates misconception-oriented items, conflict-inducing animations, and non-evaluative, concept-focused feedback. Each level targets a specific misconception from the Force Concept Inventory and engages learners in a recursive cycle of prediction, conflict, feedback, and reconstruction. Event-level logging of responses, timing, and simulation use enables analysis of learning trajectories and strategies. By combining simulation-based learning with diagnostic logic, *Gravitas* provides a curriculum-aligned tool that supports conceptual change while generating research-grade data. This paper outlines the game's theoretical foundations, instructional architecture, and motivational design, and discusses its potential as both a classroom-ready environment and a research platform for physics education.

Keywords: Serious Games · Conceptual Change · Simulation-Based Learning · Physics Education · Diagnostic Feedback · Knowledge Space Theory

1 Introduction

Despite curricular reforms and technological innovation, deeply rooted misconceptions about fundamental physical concepts—especially in mechanics—remain a major obstacle to effective learning. Students often believe, for example, that gravity is a downward "pushing" force or that there is no gravity in outer space [1–3].

Research has shown that such intuitive, everyday concepts are cognitively stable and are not reliably corrected through formal instruction [4–6]. One central reason is the lack of diagnostic attention: traditional instruction often fails to address these ideas explicitly, allowing them to persist beneath the surface [7]. Moreover, successful conceptual change depends not only on cognitive interventions but also on motivational factors, such as fostering intrinsic motivation and interest—conditions that can be undermined by school requirements or external constraints [8, 9].

S. Bakkes et al. (Eds.): GALA 2025, LNCS 16307, pp. 65–74, 2026.
https://doi.org/10.1007/978-3-032-11043-5_7

Against this background, *Gravitas* was developed—a digital learning game designed to explicitly address common misconceptions in mechanics. Targeting lower secondary school learners, the game was developed within the context of the Swiss education system and its competence-oriented curriculum (*Lehrplan 21*). *Gravitas* integrates simulation-based exploration, concept-diagnostic tasks, and non-evaluative feedback. In addition to its cognitive dimension, the game also captures motivational variables (e.g., goal orientations) and allows for their systematic analysis in follow-up evaluation. The present work extends existing research in three respects. First, it introduces an instructional architecture that operationalizes conditions for conceptual change in a structured microcycle of diagnosis, conflict, feedback, and simulation. Second, it demonstrates a systematic alignment of game levels with well-documented misconceptions in Newtonian mechanics, thereby linking theoretical insights to concrete task design. Third, it positions *Gravitas* as both a classroom-ready tool and a research platform by embedding event-level logging that enables the analysis of learning trajectories and strategies. Taken together, these elements move beyond prior demonstrations of gamification in science education by offering a replicable and data-rich environment that explicitly addresses the epistemic structure of student misconceptions.

The following sections present the theoretical foundations, didactic design, diagnostic principles, simulation elements, and empirical potential of *Gravitas*.

2 Related Work

The development of *Gravitas* intersects three core domains: (1) digital game-based learning in science education, (2) conceptual change in physics education, and (3) cognitive diagnostic assessment. Each has contributed substantially, yet their integration into a unified, theory-driven, and curriculum-aligned design remains rare.

Existing systems such as *Newton's Playground* [10] and the *Go-Lab* inquiry environment [11] offer valuable platforms for exploratory learning, yet they generally lack structured diagnostic routines that systematically address validated misconceptions. Neither system aligns its instructional design with instruments like the Force Concept Inventory (FCI) [1], a robust instrument for identifying persistent misconceptions. *Gravitas* closes this gap by mapping each level to FCI-based misconceptions and embedding them in a recursive diagnostic–feedback–simulation loop guided by conceptual change theory [12, 13]. Simulation environments like *PhET* [14] are widely used but often presuppose instructional scaffolding and lack embedded diagnostic logic. *Gravitas* extends this paradigm by integrating simulation into a closed instructional cycle—linking diagnosis, conflict, feedback, and application—and thus functions as both a learning tool and a research-grade diagnostic platform. While many designs cite conceptual-change principles, few operationalize them. *Gravitas* does so via structured distractors, conflict triggers, and non-evaluative feedback within a motivation-sensitive architecture (cf. [4, 13]). In cognitive diagnosis, *Gravitas* builds on Knowledge Space Theory [15] but embeds it in a dynamic system generating high-resolution interaction data. Unlike static assessments, it supports real-time profiling of conceptual development and strategy use. In contrast to gamified tools focused on extrinsic incentives (e.g., badges, leaderboards

[16]), *Gravitas* employs an intrinsically structured, SDT-based design. Feedback is neutral, errors productive, pacing self-regulated—fostering autonomy without sacrificing conceptual depth.

3   Theoretical Framework

The development of *Gravitas* follows an integrated design approach, which we define as the systematic integration of multiple theoretical perspectives into a coherent didactic concept. This approach combines conceptual change theory, structured models of cognitive diagnosis, and motivational psychology. The aim is not only to convey factual knowledge in physics but to initiate restructuring processes in learners' thinking, foster conceptual coherence, and create the motivational conditions for sustainable learning—especially for students using the game as part of a compulsory school setting.

3.1   Conceptual Change and Cognitive Conflict

Persistent misconceptions in mechanics are well documented and often resist traditional instruction [4, 5]. According to conceptual change theory [12], restructuring occurs only when prior conceptions are recognized as inadequate and alternatives appear plausible, intelligible, and fruitful. *Gravitas* operationalizes these conditions through two conflict-inducing mechanisms: (1) simulations following incorrect responses that visually contradict learners' intuitions (e.g., equal fall rates of a hammer and feather in a vacuum), and (2) context-rich anchor questions that activate intuitive beliefs and trigger epistemic dissonance. This design aligns with the principle of cognitively optimal conflict [13], which emphasizes productive irritation over correction—within a non-punitive environment fostering exploration and reflection.

3.2   Diagnosis and Conceptual Modeling

To not only address but systematically make misconceptions visible, *Gravitas* employs a cognitive diagnosis model with a structured task logic. The tasks are based on concepts and distractors from the Force Concept Inventory [1] and target common conceptual difficulties related to free fall, gravitation, or weight. The instructional format follows a recursive diagnostic–conflict–feedback–simulation cycle (see Sect. 5.1). Feedback is predefined, concept-targeted, and non-punitive. In line with findings from learning psychology [4], such feedback supports both conceptual correction through belief revision and metacognitive reflection—especially when learners recognize contradictions between their prior knowledge and new information. Response data, task durations, patterns of exploration, and selected explorer profiles are recorded eventwise. The task architecture is formalized according to Knowledge Space Theory [15], which allows inferences about latent knowledge states based on response patterns. This structure-oriented model enables rule-based concept diagnosis and forms the foundation for potential future extensions using probabilistic inference methods (e.g., DINA, G-DINA).

3.3 Motivation and Goal Orientation

A key design objective of *Gravitas* was to reflect the motivational realities of classroom learning, addressing not only intrinsically engaged learners but also externally regulated or hesitant users. The motivational architecture draws on two complementary theories: Self-Determination Theory (SDT) [8] informs autonomy-supportive features (e.g., user-controlled simulations), fosters competence through non-evaluative feedback, and, to a limited extent, supports relatedness via narrative elements. Achievement Goal Theory (AGT) [17] is reflected in the initial selection of an "Explorer Profile" (e.g., "Scientist" or "Tinkerer"), which represents one of four motivational orientations. While this profile does not influence gameplay progression, it enables post-hoc analysis of motivational patterns in relation to learning behavior. In future versions, these profiles could be leveraged to optionally adjust feedback density, task formats, or simulation flexibility according to learners' goal orientation—without compromising the principles of autonomy and self-regulation.

4 Motivation-Sensitive Design

Building on the motivational design principles outlined in the previous section, *Gravitas* translates Self-Determination Theory and Achievement Goal Theory into concrete gameplay mechanics. The environment is designed to support autonomy and reach learners who may lack intrinsic motivation or confidence in physics. In classroom settings, such users often experience pressure, low self-efficacy, or fear of failure—factors known to undermine engagement, particularly under conditions of low autonomy [8]. Rather than relying on adaptive personalization, *Gravitas* employs a structurally relieving architecture. It avoids time pressure and normative evaluation, allows self-directed repetition, and provides feedback that is neutral in tone, concept-focused, and explicitly tied to content. Score and time data are shown solely for self-monitoring. Errors are framed not as deficits but as natural entry points for conceptual reflection—reducing performance anxiety and supporting self-regulated learning. Although learner profiles (e.g., "Scientist," "Tinkerer") currently serve analytic purposes only, future iterations may use them to vary feedback density or task format—while preserving autonomy and consistency with SDT principles. Feedback in *Gravitas* is linguistically neutral, content-specific, and avoids evaluative judgments. It aims to highlight conceptual gaps without assigning failure, thereby supporting learners who are sensitive to academic evaluation. This design reinforces a sense of competence and epistemic agency, in line with SDT principles. Although *Gravitas* does not implement adaptive steering, its linear structure, user-controlled simulations, and repeatable tasks create an environment navigable even for less engaged learners; simplified simulations and non-evaluative feedback aim to prevent overload and sustain engagement [18, 19].

5 Game Structure and Level Design

Gravitas is designed as a linear, scenario-based learning game and consists of six content-focused levels, each addressing a specific common misconception in mechanics. Every level follows a consistent didactic structure that integrates diagnostic elements, targeted conflict induction, simulation-based exploration, and formative feedback. The level

architecture deliberately avoids extrinsic control and standardized evaluation: learners
are confronted with their own conceptions without being penalized—an approach that
offers particular motivational and didactic benefits for extrinsically motivated players.
In addition, the core simulations were deliberately implemented in a two-dimensional
interaction space. This reduction minimizes extraneous cognitive load and keeps causal
relations between parameters and motion transparent, while still allowing teachers to
prompt transfer to three-dimensional contexts.

5.1 Microstructure of a Level

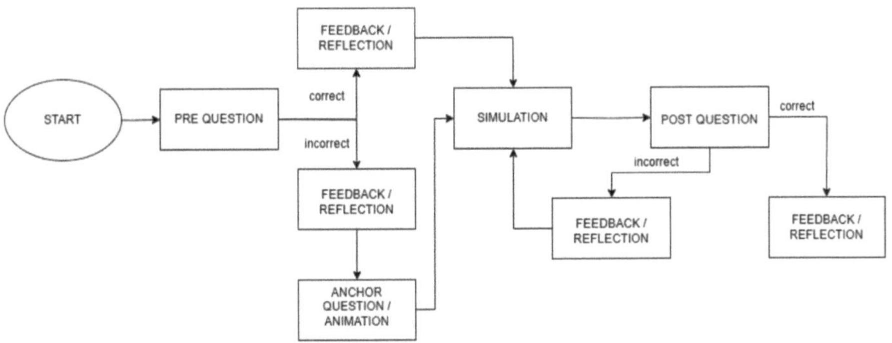

Fig. 1. Recursive learning cycle in *Gravitas* combining diagnosis, conflict induction, simulation,
and feedback.

Each level implements this cycle through five concrete phases (Fig. 1), ranging from
the activation of prior knowledge to post-questioning and repetition:

1. **Pre-question:** A multiple-choice item activates prior knowledge and elicits misconceptions using FCI-based distractors.
2. **Conflict Induction:** A narrative anchor or animation confronts learners with intuitive
   but incorrect beliefs, triggering epistemic dissonance.
3. **Feedback:** Immediate, concept-specific feedback addresses the misconception without evaluative language.
4. **Simulation:** Learners explore simplified, interactive environments by manipulating
   physical parameters to test revised hypotheses.
5. **Post-question & Repetition:** A follow-up item checks conceptual revision. Learners
   may revisit the simulation, enabling self-paced, cyclic progression.

5.2 Overview of the Six Levels

The content of the six levels is based on misconceptions documented in the Force Concept
Inventory [1] and on research into intuitive thinking in physics education [2, 3, 20].
Each level is dedicated to a specific misconception, aiming to uncover, disrupt, and
conceptually reconstruct it through cognitive conflict. Table 1 provides an overview of
the misconceptions addressed and the conceptual shifts targeted in each level.

This mapping ensures that learners encounter not generic physics content but precisely those conceptual obstacles that are most resistant to conventional instruction. In contrast to earlier serious games that addressed physics topics broadly, *Gravitas* embeds misconceptions as the central design unit.

Table 1. Overview of targeted misconceptions and conceptual focal points across *Gravitas* levels.

Misconception	Conceptual Focus
1. Gravity results from atmospheric pressure	Gravity as an attractive force (vacuum vs. air)
2. Heavier objects fall faster	Mass-independence of gravitational acceleration
3. Gravity ceases in space	Gravitational continuity in orbital environments
4. Astronauts are weightless because gravity is absent	Weightlessness as free fall in a gravitational field
5. Jump force is equal across planets	Weight variation due to planetary gravity
6. Rockets need air to function	Action–reaction (Newton's third law) in a vacuum

These six levels form a didactically sequenced learning pathway: they diagnose misconceptions, provoke cognitive conflict, enable exploratory model-building, and provide iterative consolidation. *Gravitas* thus operationalizes core principles of Conceptual Change Theory [12] in a simulation-based learning architecture. While the first four levels focus on diagnostic elicitation, conflict induction, and simulation-supported conceptual revision, Levels 5 and 6 introduce an additional gameplay layer (Fig. 3): learners actively apply the reconstructed concept in an embedded microgame. In Level 5, gravitational differences across planetary bodies are experienced through a platform-style jump-and-run scenario. In Level 6, Newton's third law is explored via the navigation and propulsion of a space shuttle in a zero-gravity environment, where learners must orient and steer the spacecraft using reactive thrust while simultaneously targeting and destroying asteroids in real time. Although the shooting mechanic does not implement physical recoil, it serves as a motivational extension of the simulation, demanding continuous coordination between propulsion-based control and action-based engagement. Thus, conceptual understanding is not only tested through reflection and manipulation but also enacted under dynamic, game-like conditions that promote spatial reasoning, timing, and transfer of physics-based control strategies. These final segments transform conceptual understanding into sensorimotor gameplay, requiring learners to embody physical principles in real-time tasks. The physical laws themselves define the game rules—thus reinforcing learning through epistemically grounded mechanics.

This integration of simulation and real-time enactment reflects *Gravitas*' core design principle: that conceptual learning is best fostered when abstract principles are not only

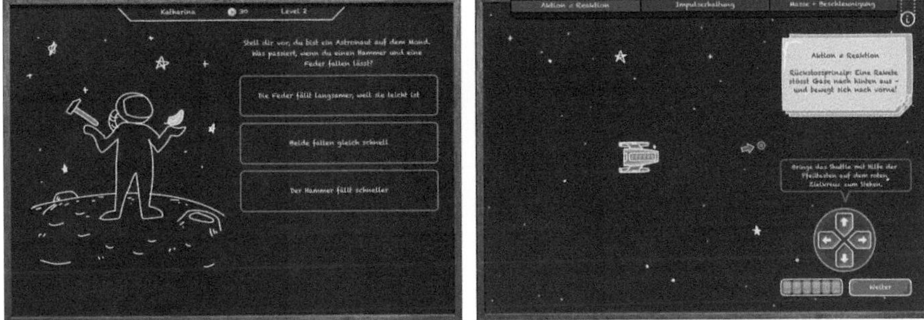

Fig. 2. *Left:* Anchor question from Level 2 addressing the misconception that heavier objects fall faster. *Right:* Simulation from Level 6 illustrating Newton's third law in a vacuum through directional thrust control.

visualized, but enacted through systems whose interaction rules are defined by physical law itself.

5.3 Progress Feedback and Transparency

At the end of the game, learners receive feedback on the number of correct answers and the time spent. This information serves self-monitoring purposes only, not assessment. *Gravitas* deliberately avoids high scores, leaderboards, or time pressure—in favor of an exploratory, non-competitive learning environment. Progress through the levels is linear. Although no adaptive path control is implemented, the free use of simulations and repeatable tasks offers a degree of autonomy that is particularly relieving for extrinsically motivated learners. Responsibility for depth, pace, and revision frequency remains with the learner—a key feature of motivation-sensitive design.

5.4 Game Mechanics and Core Gameplay Loop

Although *Gravitas* avoids superficial gamification elements such as points or leaderboards, it implements a structured gameplay mechanic that defines its identity as a serious learning game. At its core is a recursive cognitive loop—diagnosis, conflict induction, feedback, simulation, and reassessment—designed to guide learners through iterative conceptual reconstruction. Players actively navigate epistemically uncertain scenarios, test hypotheses, and revise mental models, distinguishing *Gravitas* from static quiz tools with media enhancements. From a ludological perspective, the system follows a rule-based progression driven by cognitive conditions rather than performance metrics. Actions such as modifying physical parameters produce epistemic consequences, and errors are reframed as productive failure moments aligned with research on error-tolerant learning. Learners determine when to repeat, explore, or advance, supporting autonomy and metacognitive control. This mechanic—visualized in Fig. 2 and consistent across all levels—translates the core conditions of conceptual change [13] into interactive learning dynamics. Rather than validating correct responses, *Gravitas* embeds each answer in a feedback loop that fosters reflection, model testing, and theory refinement.

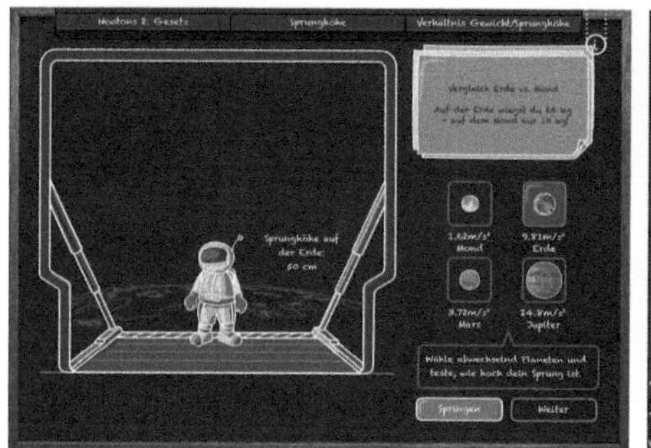

Fig. 3. *Left:* Guided simulation of gravitational variation across celestial bodies; learners compare jump height by modifying planetary conditions. *Right:* Jump-and-run environment for real-time application of gravitational understanding.

6 Teacher Role and Reflective Orchestration

Gravitas is designed for flexible use both inside and outside the classroom. As a stand-alone tool, it enables learners to explore mechanics concepts independently, repeating levels at their own pace and testing alternative explanations without evaluative pressure. This mode allows engagement with physics content beyond school hours and supports the iterative refinement of conceptions. At the same time, *Gravitas* can serve as complementary classroom material. Teachers may use the game to introduce or deepen specific topics, highlight common misconceptions, and make abstract phenomena experientially accessible. Gameplay can be followed by discussion, short reflective writing, or small-scale experiments that reconnect the digital experience with hands-on inquiry. Such activities are optional and adaptable to local teaching practices, but they help learners consolidate revised conceptions and identify persisting difficulties.

In this way, *Gravitas* supports both autonomous exploration and teacher-mediated reflection, ensuring that misconceptions confronted in the simulation can be further reconstructed through dialogue and metacognitive awareness.

7 Diagnostics and Learning Analytics

Gravitas is designed not only to initiate conceptual learning but also to diagnose and trace learner trajectories through structured, task-based interaction logging. Rather than relying on automated inference models, the system employs pre- and post-items derived from the Force Concept Inventory [1], with misconception-oriented distractors revealing both response accuracy and conceptual depth. All interactions—including answer choices, response times, repetitions, simulation use, navigation behavior, and engagement with explanatory elements—are logged event-wise and timestamped. This fine-grained data enables analyses of strategy profiles, persistence of misconceptions, timing–understanding correlations, and the role of motivational orientation. As such, *Gravitas* serves not only as a learning environment but as a research-grade platform for studying conceptual change, epistemic agency, and exploratory behavior in physics education.

8   Outlook and Conclusion

Gravitas integrates simulation-based instruction, cognitive diagnostics, and motivation-sensitive design into a curriculum-aligned platform that combines instructional utility with empirical data generation. Planned extensions include: (1) a dynamic feedback system that adjusts to learner behavior and misconception patterns; (2) motivational profiles to modulate task formats or feedback without compromising autonomy; (3) a web-based dashboard for privacy-compliant classroom analytics; and (4) longitudinal studies on retention and transfer of conceptual change. The long-term aim is to establish *Gravitas* as both a teaching tool and a research-grade environment for conceptual learning in physics education. While cognitive conflict in *Gravitas* is mainly induced through the contrast between prediction and simulation, the interactive design also has an enactive dimension. Learners manipulate parameters such as thrust or air resistance and immediately experience the consequences—for example, a rocket drifting under insufficient thrust or objects falling at the same rate in a vacuum. These interactions make conflict situations enacted rather than merely observed. Future development could extend this principle by incorporating more immersive or physically engaging modalities (e.g., motion-based input or integration with classroom experiments), strengthening the link between conceptual conflict and embodied experience and supporting deeper, more durable conceptual change.

Gravitas demonstrates how a simulation-based game environment can translate conceptual change theory into instructional and diagnostic mechanics tailored to persistent misconceptions in mechanics. The game offers a coherent, curriculum-aligned solution for secondary school physics education. The strengths of the system lie in its clear task architecture, its consistent alignment with empirically documented misconceptions, and the comprehensive logging of interaction and simulation behavior. As such, *Gravitas* functions not only as an instructional tool but also as a data-driven research platform that can inform theoretical models of exploratory learning, epistemic agency, and misconception persistence. It serves as a model for a genre of educationally grounded serious games in which instruction, diagnostics, and research are conceived not as opposites but as integrated components of a learning-effective design. *Gravitas* is thus not only compatible with current international research but also concretely applicable within competency-based physics curricula such as *Lehrplan 21*.

Acknowledgments. The research presented in this paper was funded by the Swiss National Fund (SNF) under grant number 100014_207864.

References

1. Hestenes, D., Wells, M., Swackhamer, G.: Force concept inventory. Phys. Teach. **30**(3), 141–158 (1992)
2. McCloskey, M., Washburn, A., Felch, L.: Intuitive physics: the straight-down belief and its origin. J. Exp. Psychol. Learn. Mem. Cogn. **9**(4), 636–649 (1983)
3. Viennot, L.: Spontaneous reasoning in elementary dynamics. Eur. J. Sci. Educ. **1**(2), 205–221 (1979)

4. Chi, M.T.H.: Three types of conceptual change: Belief revision, mental model transformation, and categorical shift. In: Vosniadou, S. (ed.) Handbook of Research on Conceptual Change, pp. 61–82. Erlbaum, Hillsdale (2008)

5. Halloun, I.A., Hestenes, D.: The initial knowledge state of college physics students. Am. J. Phys. **53**(11), 1043–1055 (1985)

6. Planinić, M., Boone, W.J., Krsnik, R., Beilfuss, M.: Exploring alternative conceptions from Newtonian dynamics and simple DC circuits: links between item difficulty and item confidence. J. Res. Sci. Teach. **43**(2), 150–171 (2006)

7. Vosniadou, S.: Conceptual change in learning and instruction: the framework theory approach. In: Vosniadou, S. (ed.) International Handbook of Research on Conceptual Change, 2nd edn., pp. 11–30. Taylor and Francis, New York (2013)

8. Ryan, R.M., Deci, E.L.: Intrinsic and extrinsic motivations: classic definitions and new directions. Contemp. Educ. Psychol. **25**(1), 54–67 (2000)

9. Hidi, S., Renninger, K.A.: The four-phase model of interest development. Educ. Psychol. **41**(2), 111–127 (2006)

10. Shute, V.J., Ventura, M., Kim, Y.J.: Assessment and learning of qualitative physics in Newton's playground. J. Educ. Res. **106**(6), 423–430 (2013)

11. de Jong, T., Sotiriou, S., Gillet, D.: Innovations in STEM education: the Go-Lab federation of online labs. Smart Learn. Environ. **1**, 3 (2014). https://doi.org/10.1186/s40561-014-0003-6

12. Posner, G.J., Strike, K.A., Hewson, P.W., Gertzog, W.A.: Accommodation of a scientific conception: toward a theory of conceptual change. Sci. Educ. **66**, 211–227 (1982)

13. Limón, M.: On the cognitive conflict as an instructional strategy for conceptual change: a critical appraisal. Learn. Instr. **11**(4–5), 357–380 (2001)

14. Wieman, C.E., Adams, W.K., Perkins, K.K.: PhET: simulations that enhance learning. Science **322**(5902), 682–683 (2008)

15. Doignon, J.-P., Falmagne, J.-C.: Spaces for the assessment of knowledge. Int. J. Man-Mach. Stud. **23**(2), 175–196 (1985)

16. Hamari, J., Shernoff, D.J., et al.: Challenging games help students learn: an empirical study on engagement and immersion. Comput. Hum. Behav. **54**, 170–179 (2016)

17. Elliot, A.J., McGregor, H.A.: A 2×2 achievement goal framework. J. Pers. Soc. Psychol. **80**(3), 501–519 (2001)

18. Sweller, J.: Cognitive load theory, learning difficulty, and instructional design. Learn. Instr. **4**(4), 295–312 (1994)

19. Wouters, P., van Nimwegen, C., van Oostendorp, H., van der Spek, E.D.: A meta-analysis of the cognitive and motivational effects of serious games. J. Educ. Psychol. **105**(2), 249–265 (2013)

20. Clement, J.J., Brown, D.E., Zietsman, A.: Not all preconceptions are misconceptions: finding anchoring conceptions for grounding instruction on students' intuitions. Int. J. Sci. Educ. **11**(5), 554–565 (1989)

Efficiency or Effectiveness in Game-Based Learning: Is Engagement Enough?

Maral Karimi[1]([⊠]) [iD], Megan Wiedbusch[1] [iD], Natalie Blaize[1] [iD], James Lester[2] [iD], and Roger Azevedo[1] [iD]

[1] University of Central Florida, School of Modeling, Simulation, and Training, Orlando, FL, USA
{maral.karimi,Megan.Wiedbusch,natalie.blaize,
Roger.Azevedo}@ucf.edu
[2] North Carolina State University, Raleigh, NC, USA
lester@ncsu.edu

Abstract. In STEM education, game-based learning environments (GBLEs) have become prominent platforms to scaffold students' self-regulated learning (SRL) strategies. This study challenges the assumption that all engagement in GBLEs is equally beneficial by distinguishing cognitive from behavioral engagement within the Integrative Model of Multidimensional SRL Engagement (IMMSE). We analyzed data from 227 high-school students playing Crystal Island, a narrative-centered microbiology GBLE, to examine how these engagement types during the forethought and performance SRL phases predict learning gains and problem-solving accuracy. Overall, results showed that cognitive engagement significantly predicts learning gains, whereas behavioral engagement does not. This result supports IMMSE's distinction between surface-level actions and deeper processing, indicating that meaningful learning depends on strategic cognitive engagement. We discuss implications for designing adaptive scaffolds that dynamically balance engagement dimensions across early SRL phases to optimize both efficiency and effectiveness.

Keywords: Engagement · Self-Regulated Learning · Game-based Learning Environments · STEM · Log Files

1   Introduction

Game-based learning environments (GBLEs) are increasingly used to develop students' complex cognitive and metacognitive STEM skills [1]. These environments are often recognized for their capacity to engage learners through immersive narrative-centered stories, interactive problem-solving, and instant feedback [2]. While engagement is frequently seen as a key factor in successful learning, studies show that it comprises different types (i.e., cognitive, affective, behavioral, and agentic), and that not all are equally helpful; moreover, time spent actively "engaged" may not always lead to meaningful learning improvements [3, 4]. As researchers and designers work on designing GBLEs,

S. Bakkes et al. (Eds.): GALA 2025, LNCS 16307, pp. 75–84, 2026.
https://doi.org/10.1007/978-3-032-11043-5_8

it becomes important to ask whether increasing engagement alone is enough or if it needs to be balanced with other learning goals such as efficiency (e.g., optimal time-on-task, strategy use) and effectiveness (e.g., learning improvements, transfer of learning). Finding this balance is essential for designing thoughtful GBLEs that are truly effective in education [5]. This paper investigates whether learners who appear highly cognitively and behaviorally engaged within GBLEs are also learning effectively. Drawing from research in GBLEs, self-regulated learning (SRL) and engagement, we argue that optimal learning in GBLEs requires more than sustained interaction; it requires learners to strategically allocate cognitive resources and to adaptively engage both cognitively and behaviorally with tasks throughout the different SRL phases, supporting both efficient and effective learning.

2 Prior Work

Self-regulated learning (SRL) is learners' ability to actively monitor and regulate their own cognitive, affective, metacognitive, and motivational processes to achieve a goal across three phases (i.e., forethought, performance, and self-reflection) [6–10]. Researchers have designed GBLEs [1] to foster effective SRL using a range of game features that influence learners' engagement and interest in learning, by leveraging diverse data sources such as self-report surveys, log traces, and facial expressions [11–14]. Their work highlights that engagement is a multifaceted psychological construct (e.g., behavioral, emotional, agentic, (meta)cognitive) that is difficult to define, measure, and scaffold due to lack of concrete definition and its multiple dimensions [7, 15]. Additionally, while increased SRL engagement is inherently cognitively demanding for learners [16] and difficult to define, measure, and scaffold, it is even more challenging in GBLEs, where immersive game mechanics can disrupt effective self-regulation. GBLEs are open-ended environments, allowing learners to explore freely, but at the expense of scaffolded SRL support [11], underscoring the need for adaptive scaffolds especially early within the SRL phases. While many GBLEs incorporate scaffolding for domain knowledge acquisition [11], few learning environments incorporate scaffolding techniques intended to enhance individual learners' multidimensional engagement during SRL phases that are grounded in theory and data driven [15]. Several studies highlight the impact of early interventions in GBLEs on learners' engagement and efficient learning, showing that learners who are more cognitively engaged during the forethought and performance phases are more likely to set meaningful goals, develop effective plans, and allocate mental effort efficiently [8, 9, 14]. For example, Wiggins et al. [14] found that learners' behaviors and affective states in the tutorial phase explain most variance in engagement and mental demand, marking these early moments as optimal intervention points. Li and Lajoie [17] argue that learners require adaptive scaffolding that helps them strategically manage the different dimensions of engagement, especially across early SRL phases, to optimize learning outcomes [17]. Despite the theoretical and conceptual understanding that supporting engagement within GBLEs should result in more effective and efficient learning, additional research is needed to understand how different phases of SRL (specifically forethought and performance phases), and the multiple dimensions of engagement interact to enhance efficient and effective learning. As such, this study is grounded in Wiedbusch et al.'s [15] Integrative Model of Multidimensional SRL Engagement (IMMSE), which highlights that engagement is not static but dynamic and cyclical, comprising behavioral, emotional, cognitive, and agentic dimensions [19], and each of these dimensions offers a different lens into learners' engagement behavior in different SRL phases [15]. Specifically we focus on students' cognitive and behavioral engagement during the forethought and performance SRL phases and their relationship to learning gains and problem-solving accuracy while using Crystal Island, a narrative-centered GBLE, to learn high-school microbiology [12], to contribute to the development of intelligent scaffolding systems that support individual learners' needs while maintaining a balance of cognitive and behavioral engagement while optimizing learning efficiency [20].

3   Theoretical Framework: An Overview of the Integrative Model of Multidimensional SRL Engagement (IMMSE)

Because engagement is a complex construct, it has been defined in several ways. SRL and student engagement are distinct but complementary research domains that both seek to understand how students function and perform academically [21]. To deepen our understanding of effective and efficient learning, researchers have explored how SRL phases interact with different dimensions of engagement, rather than viewing one as a subset of the other [17]. Pintrich and de Groot [22] identified cognitive strategies, effort management, and metacognitive strategies as key SRL components that align with cognitive engagement. Cleary and Zimmerman [18] linked SRL to cognitive engagement through a self-regulatory engagement framework. Li and Lajoie [17] advanced this by introducing the Integrative Model of SRL Engagement, which adds strategic and effort planning to the forethought phase for a more nuanced view of cognitive engagement. Building upon their model, the Integrative Model of Multidimensional SRL Engagement (IMMSE) [15] further advances our understanding by integrating emotional and behavioral engagement in addition to cognitive engagement based on the work of Reeve [19]. Wiedbusch et al. [15] propose that engagement is a multidimensional construct, comprising behavioral, emotional, cognitive, and agentic dimensions that all fluctuate dynamically across SRL phases [19]. Within this model, *behavioral engagement* refers to actively using learning strategies and maintaining attention, effort, and persistence to stay on task [23]. *Cognitive engagement* involves strategic thinking and the mental effort invested across a task continuum [17]. *Emotional engagement* captures affective states, like curiosity or anxiety, that influence learning processes [24]. *Agentic engagement* includes learners' proactive contributions, such as asking questions and modifying goals [24]. Moreover, they [15] argue that behavioral engagement, like paying attention or staying on task, must be visible, but this isn't necessarily true for the other dimensions of engagement. For instance, a learner may appear behaviorally engaged; however, this does not necessarily reflect cognitive engagement. The IMMSE model clarifies this difference and separates strategy use from cognitive engagement and argues for the potential regulatory and reciprocal nature between cognitive engagement and behavioral engagement. This model assumes engagement is dynamic across the various SRL phases. Specifically, in the forethought phase, learners initiate task analysis and goal setting, which activates cognitive engagement as they determine strategies and allocate effort. As learners transition to the performance phase, they enact and monitor the strategies they planned. According to the IMMSE, cognitive efficiency is central to effective and efficient learning within GBLEs. Learners must decide how to allocate and sustain mental effort strategically [15]. Thus, sustaining cognitive engagement across the forethought and performance phases is essential for meaningful strategy use during learning. This model also includes a self-reflection phase, in which learners evaluate their performance and progress to inform future learning [15]. We do not examine this phase, focusing instead on the role of engagement in the forethought and performance SRL phases within GBLEs, where instructional interventions can most effectively promote efficient and effective learning [18]. We also exclude agentic and emotional engagement because IMMSE positions cognitive and behavioral dimensions as the primary dimensions for goal setting, strategy execution, and effort maintenance, which affect learning gains and problem-solving performance. Although the IMMSE has not yet been empirically tested, with this study representing one of the first applications, it builds upon and synthesizes empirically supported components of SRL and engagement research.

4   The Present Study

In this study, we investigated whether in-game cognitive and behavioral engagement actions during the forethought and performance SRL phases influence learners' learning gains and problem-solving accuracy (i.e., measures of GBLE effectiveness), and game-solve time (i.e., a measure of GBLE efficiency) in Crystal Island, a narrative based GBLE for high-school microbiology. The following research questions (RQs) guide this study:

RQ1. To what extent does time spent on cognitive and behavioral engagement actions during the forethought and performance phases of self-regulated learning predict participants' learning gains?
RQ2. To what extent does time spent on cognitive and behavioral engagement actions during the forethought and performance phases of self-regulated learning predict participants' problem-solving accuracy?
RQ3. Is there a significant difference in the time spent on cognitive versus behavioral engagement actions during the forethought and performance phases of self-regulated learning?

5   Methodology

5.1   Participants

After excluding 12 participants due to missing data, the final sample included 227 high school students (Mean age = 15 years; 33.5% were female) from southern U.S. schools.

5.2   Measures: Learning Outcomes and Self-Reports

Each student completed 17-item pre- and post-tests on microbiology, with learning measured via normalized learning gains (NLGs). The pre-test included the Achievement Goals Questionnaire [25] and the Junior Metacognitive Awareness Inventory [26], while the post-test included the Intrinsic Motivation Inventory [27] and the Presence Questionnaire [28]. Self-report data were not analyzed.

5.3 Crystal Island Game Environment

Crystal Island is a narrative-centered game-based learning environment developed to support middle school students' scientific reasoning skills in microbiology [12]. This study used the full-agency version, in which learners, as CDC agents, freely explore a first-person simulation to investigate a mysterious research outbreak by identifying the source, diagnosing the illness, and proposing a treatment plan. Players explore island buildings and informational resources, interact with non-playable characters (NPCs), and navigate the environment. Interactive mechanics scaffold problem solving; for example, a diagnosis worksheet enables them to record symptoms. To finish, participants submit the worksheet to the camp nurse. Correct submissions confirm successful mystery resolution; incorrect ones trigger either targeted prompts or more generic feedback when multiple components are wrong, encouraging self-reflective re-exploration. We used the first worksheet submission as a behavioral marker indicating completion of the initial SRL phases (forethought and performance) and transition into the self-reflection phase. We analyzed detailed log files to extract time-based indicators of cognitive and behavioral engagement by aggregating the duration of specific in-game behaviors including reading resources, conversations with NPCs, navigating the island, viewing posters, using the scanner, and reviewing or completing the diagnosis worksheet (see Coding and Scoring; Fig. 1).

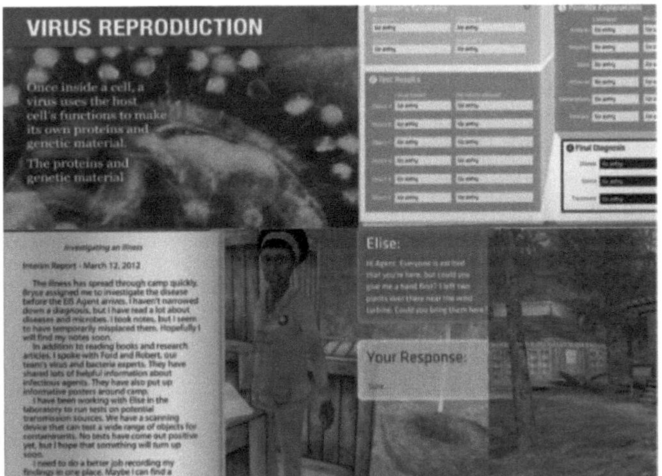

Fig. 1. In-Game Behaviors

6 Procedures

After obtaining parental consent and student assent, the study followed three phases: (1) pre-test, during which students completed the microbiology assessment and self-report measures (see above); (2) a gameplay session of up to 60 min or until mystery completion on Crystal Island; and (3) post-test, during which they took the microbiology assessment and self-report measures (see above). IRB approval was obtained beforehand, and no participant compensation was provided.

7 Coding and Scoring.

7.1 Engagement Actions Gains

We measured participants' engagement during the forethought and performance SRL phases, which occur before participants submit their first worksheet using log files of player actions. Five gameplay behaviors were categorized according to the cognitive and behavioral dimensions of engagement; the proportional duration of each category was calculated by summing all relevant action durations and dividing by the total game time until the first worksheet submission (or the full session if no submission occurred before the end of the time period).

Behavioral engagement actions included movement and conversation. Movement was defined as when a player traveled from one in-game location to another. Conversation referred to interactions between learners with (NPCs), such as scientists or locals on the island.

Cognitive engagement actions included four main actions: reading books and articles refers to opening and engaging with informational texts available within the game, such as scientific guidebooks or educational reading materials, viewing posters by inspecting educational materials like disease charts and pathogen visual guides placed throughout the game., using the worksheet to enter observations, evidence, and hypotheses, and operating the in-game scanner to conduct lab-based analyses by testing suspected contamination sources against pathogens.

7.2 Normalized Learning Gains & Solving the Mystery

Normalized learning gains (NLGs) were calculated using Marx and Cummings's [29] normalized change score equations, which account for prior knowledge when comparing pre- and post-test microbiology quizzes. Participants' NLGs averaged 0.12 (SD $= 0.35$), and 98 of 227 (43%) participants solved the mystery within 60 min.

8 Results

8.1 Research Question 1

A multiple linear regression was conducted to examine whether proportional time spent on cognitive and behavioral engagement (relative to total game time to the first worksheet submission) actions predicted participants' learning gains. The overall model was significant, $F(2, 224) = 8.37, p < 0.001$, R2 $= 0.07$. Time spent on cognitive engagement was a significant positive predictor of learning gains, $\beta = 0.64$, SE $= 0.16, t(224) = 4.09$, $p < 0.001$. Time spent on behavioral engagement did not significantly predict learning gains, $\beta = 0.12$, SE $= 0.12$, $t(224) = 1.01$, $p = 0.32$. That is, holding time spent on behavioral engagement constant, for every one-unit increase in time spent on cognitive engagement, learning gains increase by 0.64 units. This result suggests that enhancing cognitive engagement is more impactful for learning than emphasizing behavioral actions.

8.2 Research Question 2

A binary logistic regression was conducted to examine whether proportional time spent on cognitive and behavioral engagement actions (relative to total game time to the first worksheet submission) during the forethought and performance phases predicted the odds of successfully solving the mystery. The overall model was not significant, $\chi^2(2, N = 227) = 3.64$, p $= .162$ (Nagelkerke R2 $= .012$), indicating that time allocation on cognitive versus behavioral engagement actions did not reliably predict learners' accuracy in solving the mystery. This result highlights the need to investigate additional factors such as strategy effectiveness or contextual task demands to predict problem-solving success.

8.3 Research Question 3

Before conducting the analysis, we tested the assumption of normality for the difference scores (cognitive–behavioral) of the proportional time spent on engagement activities (relative to total game time to the first worksheet submission) using the Shapiro-Wilk test, which revealed a significant departure from normality (p $< .001$). Due to this violation, we used a non-parametric Wilcoxon signed-rank test which revealed a significant difference between cognitive and behavioral engagement times, W $= 9413.0$, p $= .0004$. On average, participants spent more time on cognitive engagement (M $= 0.429$, SD $= 0.149$) than on behavioral engagement (M $= 0.380$, SD $= 0.191$). This suggests that students allocate more of their early gameplay time to cognitively demanding actions, such as reading and analyzing (e.g., evaluating scanner or poster data).

9 Discussion

Our study examined differences in how learners engaged in behavioral and cognitive engagement actions during GBL and their impact on learning and performance outcomes. We found that while time spent on behavioral engagement did not significantly predict learning gains, time spent on cognitive engagement did. However, neither behavior was predictive of solving the mystery. These results provide empirical support of the IMMSE model [15], which distinguishes between the appearance of engagement and its deeper cognitive quality. Although behavioral engagement was visible, it did not significantly predict learning gains, suggesting that surface-level actions are not sufficient for meaningful learning. According to the IMMSE model, impactful engagement arises when cognitive engagement regulates behavioral actions. These findings also highlight that learners have two goals in Crystal Island: understanding microbiology and solving mysteries. While learning might require deeper cognitive engagement with the game, problem-solving performance (i.e., GBLE effectiveness) may hinge less on this requirement and more on strategic efficiency through hypothesis testing or trial-and-error strategies. Some successful students may have relied on intuitive guessing rather than deep conceptual understanding, resulting in solving the mystery but not learning. Less successful learners may have focused heavily on information gathering without effectively applying it, learning more but failing to solve the mystery. Our study also found a difference between time spent on cognitive and behavioral actions, with learners spending more time on cognitive engagement. These findings offer important insight into how learners allocate their limited (meta)cognitive resources during early gameplay. Specifically, it suggests a cognitive trade-off in which learners devote more time to mentally demanding activities, which may result in a reduction of their exploratory or interactive behaviors. From an IMMSE perspective, future research is needed to test the theoretical assumption that engagement dimensions are dynamically regulated. Our study has highlighted that they appear differently within the first two phases of SRL. That is, learners do not simply engage in more or less overall but instead may shift engagement types based on evolving goals, task demands, and available cognitive resources. In open-ended, narrative-driven environments like Crystal Island, learners must choose how to explore, gather, and process information, which can accentuate these trade-offs. For example, spending more time on cognitive engagement during the earlier phases of learning might reflect an intentional focus on the goal of learning science content. Conversely, spending more time on behavioral engagement actions may not have been strategic but instead reflect goal ambiguity or superficial exploration. This would align with prior research that suggests behavioral engagement actions may not promote learning [3, 13]. However, distinguishing cognitive from behavioral engagement using log data alone is challenging, and additional evidence (e.g., eye-tracking to capture attention patterns) may be needed to clarify this differentiation. Our study not only provides empirical evidence for the IMMSE model by finding a distinction between engagement type and strategy use, but it also supports the assumption that one type of engagement may not be better. Ultimately, it is the type, timing, and coordination of engagement dimensions that matter. While our interpretation aligns with IMMSE, other alternative explanations must be considered. For example, learners' prior knowledge may have shaped engagement patterns. Differences in motivation and goal-orientation could also explain variations, with performance-oriented students may have prioritized solving the mystery, while mastery-oriented students invested more time in learning about the content. Additionally, the design of Crystal Island may itself encourage exploratory actions that are not tightly coupled with deeper processing. GBLEs, therefore, should aim to support learners in making strategic decisions about how and when to engage cognitively versus just behaviorally.

10 Future Directions

The future of game-based learning research must move beyond simple engagement metrics and focus on developing validated instruments that can distinguish between cognitive and behavioral engagement with other dimensions of engagement (i.e., affective and agentic) in real-time during gameplay. This will require the integration of multiple sources of data, including well-timed administration of self-reports (e.g., at the beginning, middle, and end of the forethought and performance phases of SRL) with continuous multimodal data in real-time during gameplay. Future research on efficiency and effectiveness in game-based learning should explore the nuanced interplay between cognitive and behavioral engagement and their impact on learning outcomes. Researchers should design studies that distinguish between surface-level behavioral metrics and sophisticated cognitive and metacognitive processes. Another key direction involves developing and testing adaptive GBLEs that dynamically balance efficiency (e.g., time to mastery, reduction of redundant activities) and effectiveness (e.g., conceptual understanding, transfer of skills) using real-time engagement diagnostics. Finally, individual learner characteristics such as prior domain knowledge, metacognitive ability, motivation, and even personality traits must be considered to examine the efficiency-effectiveness-engagement relationship.

Acknowledgements. This study was funded by the National Science Foundation (DUE#1761178 and DRL#1661202) and the Social Sciences and Humanities Research Council of Canada (SSHRC 895-2011-1006). The authors would like to thank the SMART Lab at UCF and the IntelliMEDIA Group at NCSU for their contributions.

Disclosure of Interests. The authors do not have any competing interests to declare.

References

1. Plass, J.L., Homer, B.D., Pawar, S., Brenner, C., MacNamara, A.P.: The effect of adaptive difficulty adjustment on the effectiveness of a game to develop executive function skills for learners of different ages. Cogn. Dev. **49**, 56–67 (2019)
2. Lee, S., Mott, B., Vandenberg, J., Spires, H.A., Lester, J.: Exploring gameplay and learning in a narrative-centered digital game for Elementary Science Education. IEEE Trans. Games **16**, 947–959 (2024)
3. Huber, S.E., Cortez, R., Kiili, K., Lindstedt, A., Ninaus, M.: Game elements enhance engagement and mitigate attrition in online learning tasks. Comput. Hum. Behav. **149**, 107948 (2023)
4. Reeve, J., Basarkod, G., Jang, H.-R., Gargurevich, R., Jang, H., Cheon, S.H.: Specialized purpose of each type of student engagement: a meta-analysis. Educ. Psychol. Rev. **37** (2025)
5. Mayer, R.E.: Computer games in education. Annu. Rev. Psychol. **70**, 531–549 (2019)
6. Winne, P.H., Azevedo, R.: Metacognition and self-regulated learning. In: Sawyer, R.K. (ed.) The Cambridge Handbook of the Learning Sciences, Cambridge Handbooks in Psychology, pp. 93–113. Cambridge University Press (2022)
7. Azevedo, R.: Defining and measuring engagement and learning in science: conceptual, theoretical, methodological, and analytical issues. Educ. Psychol. **50**(1), 84–94 (2015)
8. Taub, M., Azevedo, R., Bradbury, A.E., Millar, G.C., Lester, J.: Using sequence mining to reveal the efficiency in scientific reasoning during STEM learning with a game-based learning environment. Learn. Instr. **54**, 93–103 (2018)
9. Winne, P.H., Hadwin, A.F.: Studying as self-regulated learning. In Hacker, D.J., Dunlosky, J., Graesser, A.C. (eds.) Metacognition in Educational Theory and Practice, pp. 277–304. Lawrence Erlbaum Associates Publishers (1998)
10. Zimmerman, B.J.: Attaining self-regulation: a social cognitive perspective. In: Boekaerts, M., Pintrich, P.R., Zeidner, M. (eds.) Handbook of Self-Regulation, pp. 13–39. Academic Press (2000)
11. Dever, D.A., et al.: Identifying the effects of scaffolding on learners' temporal deployment of self-regulated learning operations during game-based learning using multimodal data. Front. Psychol. **14**, 1280566 (2023)

12. Dever, D.A., Wiedbusch, M., Park, S., Llinas, A., Lester, J., Azevedo, R.: From product to process data: game mechanics for science learning. Int. J. Serious Games **11**(4), 127–153 (2024). https://doi.org/10.17083/ijsg.v11i4.790
13. Taub, M., Sawyer, R., Smith, A., Rowe, J., Azevedo, R., Lester, J.: The agency effect: the impact of student agency on learning, emotions, and problem-solving behaviors in a gamebased learning environment. Comput. Educ. **147**, 103781 (2020)
14. Wiggins, J., et al.: Affect-based early prediction of player mental demand and engagement for educational games. Proc. AAAI Conf. Artif. Intell. Interact. Digit. Entertain. **14**(1), 243–249 (2018)
15. Wiedbusch, M., Dever, D., Li, S., Amon, M.J, Lajoie, S., Azevedo, R.: Measuring multidimensional facets of SRL engagement with multimodal data. In: Kovanovic, V., Azevedo, R., Gibson, D.C., Ifenthaler, D. (eds) Unobtrusive Observations of Learning in Digital Environments. Advances in Analytics for Learning and Teaching. Springer, Cham (2023)
16. Winne, P.H.: Theorizing and researching levels of processing in self-regulated learning. Br. J. Educ. Psychol. **88**, 9–20 (2018)
17. Li, S., Lajoie, S.P., Zheng, J., Wu, H., Cheng, H.: Automated detection of cognitive engagement to inform the art of staying engaged in problem-solving. Comput Educ. **163**, 104114 (2021)
18. Cleary, T.J., Zimmerman, B.J.: A cyclical self-regulatory account of student engagement: theoretical foundations and applications. In: Christenson, S., Reschly, A., Wylie, C. (eds) Handbook of Research on Student Engagement. Springer, Boston, MA (2012)
19. Reeve, J.: A self-determination theory perspective on student engagement. In: Christenson, S., Reschly, A., Wylie, C. (eds) Handbook of Research on Student Engagement. Springer, Boston, MA (2012)
20. Huber, S.E., Edlinger, M., Lindstedt, A., Kiili, K., Ninaus, M.: Game elements improve affect and motivation in a learning task. Int. J. Serious Games **11**(4), 103–126 (2024)
21. Wong, Z.Y., Liem, G.A.D., Chan, M., Datu, J.A.D.: Student engagement and its association with academic achievement and subjective well-being: a systematic review and metaanalysis. J. Educ. Psychol. **116**(1), 48–75 (2024)
22. Pintrich, P.R., De Groot, E.V.: Motivational and self-regulated learning components of classroom academic performance. J. Educ. Psychol. **82**(1), 33–40 (1990)
23. Reeve, J., Cheon, S.H., Jang, H.R.: A teacher-focused intervention to enhance students' classroom engagement. In: Fredricks, J., Reschly, A.L., Christenson, S. (eds.) Handbook of Student Engagement Interventions, pp. 87–102. Academic Press (2019)
24. Reeve, J.: How students create motivationally supportive learning environments for themselves: the concept of agentic engagement. J. Educ. Psychol. **105**(3), 579 (2013)
25. Elliot, A.J., Murayama, K.: On the measurement of achievement goals: critique, illustration, and application. J. Educ. Psychol. **100**, 613–628 (2008)
26. Schraw, G., Dennison, R.S.: Assessing metacognitive awareness. Contemp. Educ. Psychol. **19**(4), 460–475 (1994)
27. Ryan, R.M., Mims, V., Koestner, R.: Relation of reward contingency and interpersonal context to intrinsic motivation: a review and test using cognitive evaluation theory. J. Pers. Soc. Psychol. **45**(4), 736–750 (1983)
28. Witmer, B.G., Singer, M.J.: Measuring presence in virtual environments: a presence questionnaire. Presence Teleoper. Virt. Environ. **7**(3), 225–240 (1998)
29. Marx, J.D., Cummings, K.: Normalized change. Am. J. Phys. **75**, 87–91 (2007)

The European Parliament Virtual Role-Play Game: Results of a Player Study

Martin Sillaots[1](✉) and Mikhail Fiadotau[1,2]

[1] Tallinn University, Tallinn, Estonia
`martins@tlu.ee`
[2] IT University of Copenhagen, Copenhagen, Denmark

Abstract. The paper reports on an evaluation study of the European Parliament Virtual Role-Playing Game, a hybrid multiplayer parliamentary simulation aimed at increasing young people's political interest and understanding of the EU legislative process. The study is based on data from pre- and post-questionnaires collected during a large-scale run of the game (303 players) at a European Youth Event. Results indicate that participants found the game to be engaging and viewed it as a helpful tool for increasing players' political interest and knowledge. At the same time, several areas for improvement were identified, such as the need for more flexible time allocation. These considerations will be addressed in the next version of the game.

Keywords: Parliamentary simulation · Civic education · Player experience

1 Introduction

Governmental institutions have a responsibility not only to govern, but also to make governance understandable to citizens and encourage civic engagement [6]. To this end, political institutions such as parliaments offer a variety of activities for the public, including site visits, youth events, and educational videos. Increasingly, physical and digital games are becoming part of this repertoire; indeed, most national parliaments in Europe use some form of games as part of their educational outreach [10].

The use of game-based learning is not exclusive to national parliaments. The European Parliament is a case in point, offering both a physical and a virtual game to teach players about the legislative process in the EU.

This article focuses on the latter: the European Parliament Virtual Role-Play Game (EP vRPG), a parliamentary simulation in which players take on the roles of members of the European Parliament. The EP vRPG is a hybrid multiplayer game that requires an internet connection to run (the game is controlled by an online backend) but is designed to be played with the players sharing the same

S. Bakkes et al. (Eds.): GALA 2025, LNCS 16307, pp. 85–95, 2026.
https://doi.org/10.1007/978-3-032-11043-5_9

physical location. The game was conceived as an alternative to the existing EP RPG, which is only playable on-site in the EP's Europa Experience visitor centers and which became unavailable during the COVID-19 pandemic. The goal was to create a game that could reach a wider audience, without requiring travel, and would not need much training or resources to set up and play.

The first version of the EP vRPG was developed by ICF NEXT and launched in 2023. Currently, the game is being developed further by Serious Games Interactive (SGI) and the Europa Experience unit of the EP. The next version of the game will be launched in 2026. The goal of this study is to collect feedback from a larger player group in order to evaluate the EP vRPG's ability to meet its objectives, thereby informing the design of the game's next iteration. The main research questions are:

- RQ1: What impact does the EP vRPG have on players' political interest?
- RQ2: How engaging is the EP vRPG for players?
- RQ3: What is the educational potential of the EP vRPG?

2   Background

2.1   Parliamentary Simulation Games

Games and simulations have a long history of use in political and civic education. A predecessor of modern parliamentary simulations, the mock parliament, was played in many schools throughout the Commonwealth of Nations in the late 19th century, where it has been credited with raising girls' interest in politics, foreshadowing the suffrage movement [11]. By the mid-20th century, a variety of tabletop games were available to teachers interested in a game-based approach to political education [2]. This interest in games stems from their ability both to improve learning outcomes and promote attitudinal change [9], which is crucial to tackle the long-standing issue of "the lack of political engagement by young people" [8]. It is not surprising, then, that the use of games for political education has not been limited to formal learning settings: for example, governmental institutions such as parliaments often use digital and non-digital games as part of their educational outreach initiatives [10].

A notable subset of games used in civic education are parliamentary simulation games. In them, players "reenact political processes such as parliamentary sessions," typically in teams representing different political parties, and engage in discussion, negotiation, compromise-seeking, and voting in order to navigate fictional scenarios such as deliberating on a controversial bill [12]. These games can take various forms: from on-site activities for parliament visitors, to digital and tabletop multiplayer games, to browser-based single-player ones, to dedicated international events such as the European Youth Parliament [7,10]. Despite their wide use in education, academic research on parliamentary simulation games is limited. While existing studies suggest that such games are "valuable tools to increase political knowledge and foster democratic attitudes" [12], there is a shortage of empirical research into their effectiveness.

2.2 European Parliament Virtual Role-Play Game

The European Parliament Virtual Role-Play Game (EP vRPG) is a digital parliamentary simulation, in which 16–40 players take on the role of Members of the European Parliament (MEPs). The goal of the game is to teach young players (16–20 years old) about the legislative process and promote democracy. The game is available in 24 EU languages and can be played at https://virtual-role-play-game.digital-journey.europarl.europa.eu/. A single playthrough takes 60–90 minutes [5].

Although it is a digitally mediated game that requires a stable Internet connection, the EP vRPG is designed to be played with all players assembled in a larger space with a game facilitator present. This makes a school classroom an ideal setting for play. The facilitator presents game information on a large screen, and players join and interact with the game via their smartphones (see Fig. 1).

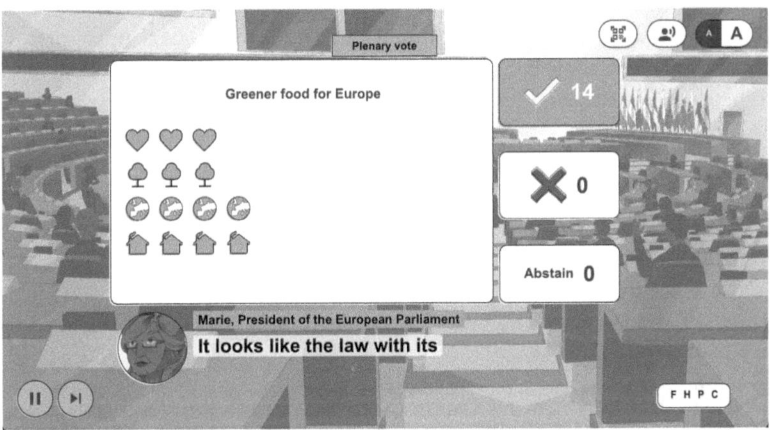

Fig. 1. EP vRPG gameplay: Plenary voting

Structurally, the EP vRPG is similar to a seminar game: a type of umpire-led, discussion-centered game in which groups of players, representing different entities, must navigate a scenario consisting of a set of pre-scripted events [1]. However, unlike traditional seminar games and most parliamentary simulations, it relies on a hybrid design, combining the use of digital technology (video-recorded non-player characters, information delivered on personal devices) with face-to-face player interaction. The scenario in the EP vRPG proceeds as follows [5]:

1. Pre-recorded video introduction (shown on the facilitator's screen): the President of the EP welcomes players as MEPs and explains the need for a new EU law that they are about to work on.

2. Players are randomly divided into four groups symbolizing different kinds of political parties: Tradition, Solidarity, Ecology, and Liberty. Players rearrange their seating so that each group sits together, then use their personal devices to familiarize themselves with their group's manifesto, key stakeholders, and proposed amendments for the new law.

3. Players are regrouped into two inter-group committees. Each committee receives four proposed amendments (out of a total eight), which they must discuss, find a compromise between the political groups' positions, and choose two amendments to go to the plenary session.

4. Players join back with their political groups to discuss the amendments chosen by the committees and decide how to vote during the plenary.

5. All players join the plenary session. A spokesperson from each political group presents their group's views on the new legislation and its amendments. Players then vote first on each individual amendment and then on the legislative proposal as a whole.

6. Breaking news: an unexpected event in the game story changes the needs and public perceptions around the bill, leading the Council of the European Union to propose its own amendments to the law. Players must now rethink their stances and seek compromise again.

7. The plenary continues, and players must decide whether to support the newly proposed amendments, go back to the original proposal, or find a compromise. Voting takes place, at the end of which the law has either been passed or rejected.

8. After the voting results have been announced, various stakeholders (pre-recorded non-player characters) present their views, whether critical or favorable, on the outcome.

9. If players failed to pass the law, they must hold a press conference to respond to the public's concerns.

The EP vRPG Facilitator's Guide contains a more detailed breakdown of the game's structure and rules [5].

3   Methodology

3.1   Context

This study is based on data collected during the European Youth Event (EYE), organized by the European Parliament on June 13–14, 2025 in Strasbourg (https://european-youth-event.europarl.europa.eu/en). The broader event aimed to foster political interest among young people (ages 16–30) and bring them into conversation with Members of the European Parliament, politics experts, activists, and content creators. It attracted around 9,000 participants and featured hundreds of activities to choose from, such as tours, performances, interactive workshops, and games, including an opportunity to play the EP vRPG. In total, the EP vRPG was played by 303 players (all EYE participants) across eight sessions.

3.2   Research Design and Data

This study follows a mixed-methods pre-post intervention evaluation design and is based on a convenience sample: the 303 participants who chose to play the EP vRPG were asked to complete a pre- and post-intervention questionnaire about their experience. To ensure more consistent results, both questionnaires were printed and handed out to the participants before the beginning of the game session as a single document. The original questionnaire had been created by the EP Europa Experience unit to measure the impact of the EP RPG during various play sessions. For the purposes of this study, the questionnaire was adapted for a pre-post intervention design.

The questionnaire contained the following items (the pre-questionnaire only had the first four, while the post-intervention one included all the items):

1. I'm interested in following political news on a regular basis.
2. I am interested in actively influencing decisions, voicing my concerns, and engaging with society.
3. I am interested in EU topics and affairs.
4. I have a good understanding of how the European Parliament works.
5. Time spent interacting with other players was valuable.
6. Discussions with other players were engaging.
7. I had enough time for all the game activities.
8. The game rewarded my ability to make compromises.
9. I enjoyed the game.
10. I enjoyed this as a learning experience.
11. I would recommend this game to friends.
12. I would like to play this game again with another topic.
13. Playing this game made me want to learn more about the European Parliament.
14. If you have any other comments, please add them here.

All of the questions except the last one were presented as a 1–5 scale, and the extreme values for each item were explained depending on the item's wording (e.g., "1 = not interested at all" and "5 = very interested"). The final question was open-ended and intended for freeform feedback.

Following the intervention, questionnaire responses were digitized and subjected to initial data cleaning (e.g., removal of incomplete entries). To assess internal consistency, Cronbach's Alpha was calculated for item clusters corresponding to each of the research questions. Descriptive statistics (means, standard deviations) were computed for all items, and paired t-tests were conducted to evaluate statistically significant pre-post differences. Open-ended responses were analyzed using inductive content analysis [4].

4   Results and Discussion

Out of the 303 players, the pre-intervention questionnaire yielded 267 responses, while the post-questionnaire received 242. The results of the post-questionnaire are presented in Table 1. A comparison between the pre- and post-intervention responses is shown in Table 2. (Differences for each participant were calculated as an additional field in the dataset, and means and standard deviations are based on the resulting numbers.) All the identified differences are statistically significant.

Table 1. Post-intervention questionnaire results

No.	Questionnaire statement	Mean	SD
Q01	I'm interested in following political news on a regular basis	4.40	0.78
Q02	I am interested in actively influencing decisions, voicing my concerns, and engaging with society	4.42	0.74
Q03	I am interested in EU topics and affairs	4.44	0.69
Q04	I have a good understanding of how the European Parliament works	4.19	0.78
Q05	Time spent interacting with other players was valuable	4.27	0.87
Q06	Discussions with other players were engaging	4.12	0.94
Q07	I had enough time for all the game activities	3.49	1.17
Q08	The game rewarded my ability to make compromises	3.87	0.91
Q09	I enjoyed the game	4.50	0.74
Q10	I enjoyed this as a learning experience	4.45	0.78
Q11	I would recommend this game to friends	4.47	0.80
Q12	I would like to play this game again with another topic	4.62	0.71
Q13	Playing this game made me want to learn more about the European Parliament	4.38	0.82

4.1 Political Interest

Questions Q01, Q02, and Q03 correspond to RQ1: "What impact does the EP vRPG have on players' political interest?" Cronbach's Alpha for this cluster of questions is 0.52 (poor) in the pre-questionnaire and 0.65 (questionable) for the post-questionnaire. Reliability could have been improved by including additional questions related to participants' civic activity and political interest; however, it was a conscious decision on the study facilitators' part to keep the questionnaire as short as possible to reduce the participants' cognitive load.

Although no dramatic increase in political interest was expected after a one-hour gameplay session, the results demonstrate some positive change. It is important to note that participants' interest in politics was already high beforehand (as they had chosen to participate in the event in the first place), but still showed a modest increase, at least in the short term, after playing the game. A task for a future study is to determine whether and how playing the game would affect the perceptions of 16–20-year-olds with varying levels of political interest.

4.2   Game Experience

Questions Q05, Q06, Q07, Q08, Q09, Q11, and Q12 relate to RQ2: "How engaging is the EP vRPG for players?" Cronbach's Alpha for this cluster of questions is excellent (0.82).

Table 2. Difference between pre- and post-intervention items

No.	Mean (pre)	SD (pre)	Mean (post)	SD (post)	Mean (diff.)	SD (diff.)	p (t-test)
Q01	4.28	0.83	4.40	0.78	0.11	0.57	0.0018
Q02	4.31	0.76	4.42	0.74	0.13	0.56	0.0002
Q03	4.30	0.80	4.44	0.69	0.13	0.55	0.0001
Q04	3.48	0.89	4.19	0.78	0.68	0.78	0.0000

The results suggest that players found the game to be enjoyable (M = 4.5) and would recommend it to friends (M = 4.47). 34 of the respondents additionally stated in the freeform comment (Q14) that they had a positive experience with the game; two respondents specified that they would recommend the game for school use. Notably, players expressed a strong interest in playing the game again with a different scenario (M = 4.62). This points to the EP vRPG's high replayability and the potential to be expanded with new scenarios that highlight different issues and debates important to the EU. In freeform comments, three participants stated they would in fact like to replay the game with the same scenario, which may imply that the role-playing aspect of the game (the presence of multiple political groups with differing agendas) lends it further replayability.

Players also agreed, if not as strongly, that the time they spent interacting with other players was valuable (M = 4.27)—one respondent wrote in the freeform comment that they "liked making new friends"—and that the discussions they had were engaging (M = 4.12). This suggests that social interaction and discussion, which are a key part of the gameplay, are enjoyable to players but could perhaps be handled in an even more engaging way.

Aspects of the game that the respondents did not feel as unequivocally positive about relate to time management and finding compromise. Q07 ("I had enough time for all the game activities") averaged 3.49 (SD = 1.17), indicating mixed feelings among the players. While 52.2% of the players did moderately or strongly agree with the statement, others pointed out that there was not enough time for some in-game activities, particularly discussions. In the free comments, 21 respondents suggested increasing the amount of time allocated to specific parts of the game (mostly for discussions within political groups and in committees). One player pointed out that the extra time was necessary "to develop our ideas and negotiate and compromise with the other players." Something that the game facilitator manual could suggest more explicitly is that facilitators can increase the amount of time spent on different phases of the game depending on the circumstances. (In our case, however, this was not feasible due to the tight scheduling of the event, with other activities preceding and following the gameplay session.)

Responses to Q08 ("The game rewarded my ability to make compromises") were somewhat more positive (M = 3.87, SD = 0.91). The freeform comments contain some indications as to why players may have found compromise-seeking to be challenging. Two players opined that, at a maximum of 40 players total (20 per committee and 10 per political group), the number of players was too large, making discussion and compromise-seeking difficult. This challenge could be mitigated by allocating more time, as discussed above. Four respondents stated that they found parts of the game (e.g., splitting into committees after the groups had been formed; the content of the amendment itself) to be confusing. This additional cognitive load could also negatively affect the ability to find compromise, as some players may be too busy making sense of the game itself. In retrospect, the wording of the question itself may have been confusing, as it potentially conflates players' compromise-seeking skill with the game's reward mechanics.

Some of the freeform comments contained suggestions on how to improve the player experience and the game itself. One player suggested implementing different difficulty levels for the game, so it could be playable by both younger, novice players as well as more knowledgeable and experienced ones. (While clearly a valuable suggestion, it is beyond the scope of the current project, whose focus is on a specific age group.) There were several helpful technical suggestions, such as making the content of the legislative proposal, as well as the changes proposed by the Council of the EU, available through the players' personal devices, so they could be consulted at any point during gameplay.

4.3   Learning Outcomes

Questions Q04, Q10 and Q11 speak to RQ3: "What is the educational potential of the EP vRPG?" Cronbach's Alpha for this group of questions is 0.56 (poor). Including more items in this cluster could have improved this, but was consciously eschewed in favor of having a shorter questionnaire, potentially increasing the response rate.

Before playing the game, participants provided mixed responses regarding their understanding of how the European Parliament works (M = 3.48). Following the game session, their level of agreement with the statement substantially increased (M = 4.19), with the difference (0.68) being statistically significant (p < 0.0001). While self-reported and lacking a longer-term follow-up, this finding suggests the EP vRPG has high educational potential. This is further supported by players reporting having enjoyed the game as a learning experience (M = 4.45) and expressed a desire to learn more about the EU after playing (M = 4.38). More broadly, this result supports the findings by Cruz-Martínez et al. that "students exposed to role-plays have higher short-term knowledge retention about political systems than those who took traditional lectures" [3].

Overall, the questionnaire data demonstrates that players found the EP vRPG to be an engaging experience, that they felt it helped them learn about the European Parliament, and that the game can increase players' interest in the subject and in EU politics in general.

4.4 Limitations and Future Research

Several important limitations of the study must be acknowledged. While the analysis identified statistically significant differences between pre- and post-test questions, the effect size (other than for Q04) is fairly small, suggesting limited practical significance in terms of the game's ability to influence players' political interest. At the same time, the context in which the game was tested may have to some extent shaped the results. Namely, the European Youth Event, during which the game was played, attracted participants who were already interested in matters such as politics and civic participation, making even a small increase potentially meaningful. Conversely, these findings may not be generalizable to the average secondary school student, who may not have the same level of existing political interest. Furthermore, due to the event participants' broader age range (16–30) compared to the game's target demographic (16–20), the data may not reflect high-schoolers' perceptions. While the present study provides a useful starting point, future research is needed to test the EP vRPG in a classroom setting.

The results presented in the study, including those relating to the game's educational potential, are self-reported. A future study could incorporate a pre- and post-intervention knowledge test to determine whether the game increases players' actual knowledge (and of what specific facts and concepts). Moreover, the post-game questionnaire was administered immediately after playing; a follow-up after a week or a month could provide a more longitudinal perspective and shed some light on knowledge retention after playing the game. Additionally, to increase data consistency and overall study reliability, more questions could be included related to political interest and learning outcomes. Incorporating observation data and complementing the players' perspectives with, for example, interviews with game facilitators could also provide a more nuanced and comprehensive picture.

Since the EP vRPG supports a variety of scenarios, it could also be interesting to test alternative scenarios (based on different legislative proposals) to see if a particular type of proposal or subject matter could influence the players' responses.

5 Conclusion

The aim of this study was to evaluate the European Parliament Virtual Role-Play Game—a hybrid, multiplayer, scenario-based parliamentary simulation—in terms of its ability to increase players' political interest, improve learning outcomes, and provide an engaging player experience. Data was collected using a pre/post-intervention questionnaire administered during an event at which the EP vRPG was played by 303 participants. The findings suggest the game is engaging and can be considered a promising tool to both increase players' political interest and improve their knowledge. Empowering facilitators to be more flexible with time allocation could further enhance player experience, allowing larger and more vocal groups sufficient time to deliberate and find compromises.

Future research should test the game in a more naturalistic classroom setting, incorporate a follow-up questionnaire to track the longer-term impact the game has on player knowledge and political interest, and explore a variety of scenarios.

Acknowledgments. The authors would like to thank the European Parliament Visitors Services Coordination Unit and Europa Experience Unit for their support.

Disclosure of Interests. The authors have no competing interests to declare that are relevant to the content of this article.

References

1. Callaghan, P., Fiadotau, M.: Using Meaningful Choices and Uncertainty to Increase Player Agency in a Cybersecurity Seminar Game. In: Dondio, P., Rocha, M., Brennan, A., Schönbohm, A., De Rosa, F., Koskinen, A., Bellotti, F. (eds.) Games and Learning Alliance, vol. 14475, pp. 23–32. Springer, Cham (2024). https://doi.org/10.1007/978-3-031-49065-1_3
2. Cousins, J.: Simulation Games for Political Education. Simul. Games **8**(3), 361–374 (1977). https://doi.org/10.1177/003755007783004
3. Cruz-Martínez, G., Soto Sainz, O., Benito Sánchez, A.B.: Learning about political systems while playing: Testing short-term knowledge retention through a role-play classroom game. Revista española de ciencia política **60**, 53–83 (2022), https://dialnet.unirioja.es/servlet/articulo?codigo=8679779
4. Elo, S., Kyngäs, H.: The qualitative content analysis process. J. Adv. Nurs. **62**(1), 107–115 (2008). https://doi.org/10.1111/j.1365-2648.2007.04569.x
5. European Parliament: Facilitator's guide to the Virtual Role-Play Game, https://virtual-role-play-game.digital-journey.europarl.europa.eu/docs/guides/A4_Facilitator_Guide_VRPG_EN.pdf
6. Fox, R.: Engagement and Participation: What the Public Want and How our Politicians Need to Respond. Parliam. Aff. **62**(4), 673–685 (Oct2009). 10.1093/pa/gsp027, https://doi.org/10.1093/pa/gsp027
7. Junussova, A., Ayapbekova, A., Byulegenova, B., Nagymzhanova, K., Aykenova, R.: Modern strategies for conceptualising and implementing state youth policy. World Development Perspectives **37**, 100653 (2025). https://doi.org/10.1016/j.wdp.2024.100653
8. Lo, J.C.: Learning to Participate through Role-Play: Understanding Political Simulations in the High School Government Course. PhD thesis, University of Washington, Seattle (2015), http://hdl.handle.net/1773/33766
9. Oberle, M., Leunig, J., Ivens, S.: What do students learn from political simulation games? A mixed-method approach exploring the relation between conceptual and attitudinal changes. European Political Science **19**(3), 367–386 (2020). https://doi.org/10.1057/s41304-020-00261-2

10. Sillaots, M., Fiadotau, M.: Making Legislative Process Understandable: Survey of Parliaments' Serious Games of European Countries. European Conference on Games Based Learning **17**(1), 583–591 (2023). https://doi.org/10.34190/ecgbl.17.1.1533

11. Sunderland, H.: Politics in schoolgirl debating cultures in England, 1886–1914. Hist. J. **63**(4), 935–957 (2020). https://doi.org/10.1017/S0018246X19000414

12. Zamora, P.: Political simulation games in civic education. PhD dissertation, University of Zurich, Zurich (2019). https://doi.org/10.5167/uzh-177747

Enhancing Student Engagement Through AI and Gamification: A Case Study of an Educational Platform

Antonio Bucchiarone[1][(✉)] , Simone Bassanelli[2] , and Tommaso Guidolin[1]

[1] SWEN, Università degli Studi dell'Aquila, 67100 L'Aquila, Italy
antonio.bucchiarone@univaq.it
[2] Fondazione Bruno Kessler (FBK), 38123 Trento, Italy
sbassanelli@fbk.eu

Abstract. Integrating artificial intelligence (AI) and gamification in education opens new opportunities for personalized and engaging learning. This paper presents PolyGloT, an AI-powered platform enhanced with gamified elements to support the motivation and adaptability of learners. The system offers AI feedback and adaptive content in real time to maintain engagement. We outline its rationale, core characteristics and pedagogical foundations and report on an empirical study with 48 students using the UEQ-S questionnaire. The results showed moderately positive impressions, especially in hedonic quality, while pragmatic aspects such as clarity require improvement. Lessons learned stress the need to balance innovation with usability and point to future work on interface refinement, broader evaluation, and deeper analysis of the roles of AI and gamification.

Keywords: AI in Education · Gamification · Adaptive learning · User Experience Evaluation

1 Introduction

In recent years, the integration of Artificial Intelligence (AI) in education has opened new opportunities for personalized and adaptive learning experiences [1,2]. Educational tools powered by artificial intelligence can analyze learners' behaviors, provide real-time feedback, and adjust content to suit individual needs, making learning more efficient and engaging [2]. However, the effectiveness of such systems also depends on their ability to maintain student motivation and foster long-term engagement.

Gamification, the application of game elements in non-game contexts [3], has emerged as a powerful strategy to increase motivation and participation in educational settings [4]. By incorporating elements such as points, levels, achievements, and challenges, gamified systems can transform traditional learning experiences into more dynamic and interactive ones. When combined with AI, gamification has the potential to go beyond one-size-fits-all approaches by tailoring motivational strategies to different learner profiles [5].

S. Bakkes et al. (Eds.): GALA 2025, LNCS 16307, pp. 96–105, 2026.
https://doi.org/10.1007/978-3-032-11043-5_10

This paper presents PolyGloT, an AI-based educational platform enhanced with gamification features designed to support the student's learning paths. The system leverages AI to adapt content and feedback in real time, while its gamified components aim to improve user engagement, persistence, and learning outcomes. We describe the rationale for the design of the tool, its key functionalities, and the pedagogical principles that guided its development. Moreover, we report on an empirical study evaluating the tool's effectiveness in a real educational setting, focusing on user experience. In Sect. 2 we present the background literature regarding the use of AI in educational context. Section 3 describes the tool, the rationale behind its development, and its features. Section 4 report the study and the methods, while Sect. 5 reports the findings. Finally, Sect. 6 concludes the paper, summarizing the results and reporting future work.

2   AI in Education

In the current era of digital transformation, education systems worldwide are being reshaped by rapid advances in Artificial Intelligence (AI). As AI technologies continue to permeate various sectors of society, the need to prepare both educators and learners for an AI-enhanced world becomes increasingly urgent. Artificial intelligence literacy, defined as the ability to understand, critically evaluate, and responsibly use AI, has emerged as a fundamental competency, comparable to traditional literacies such as reading, writing, and mathematics [6,7]. It encompasses not only technical knowledge, but also the capacity for ethical reasoning, critical thinking, and awareness of AI's societal implications [8,9].

Although the integration of AI into educational contexts offers significant transformative potential [10], including more personalized learning pathways, improved assessment practices, and data-informed teaching strategies, its implementation is not without challenges. Studies have highlighted several systemic and pedagogical barriers, such as limited access to AI tools, the absence of AI topics in existing curricula, and the lack of targeted professional development for teachers [11,12]. Educators, particularly in vocational education and training (VET), face additional difficulties in aligning AI literacy with practice-oriented instructional methods and adapting existing frameworks to the hands-on nature of their teaching environments [13].

To address these gaps, educational institutions must reimagine their strategies for building AI competency through both theoretical and practical approaches. In higher education (HE), this involves developing frameworks that support the digital competence of educators and students alike, such as the HeDiCom and SQD2 models [9]. These models provide essential guidance on topics such as digital identity, affective engagement, and AI-enhanced reflective practice, allowing a more holistic integration of AI into pedagogy. At the same time, vocational learners require context-specific tools and methods that emphasize real-world application and environmental responsibility, including exposure to concepts like Green AI.

Given this complex landscape, there is a pressing need for adaptable, collaborative, and user-friendly platforms to support the design and implementation of AI literacy initiatives. Such platforms can empower educators to create engaging and context-aware learning experiences that integrate AI meaningfully into diverse educational settings. By facilitating the co-creation of learning activities aligned with learner profiles, disciplinary goals, and ethical considerations, these environments promote accessibility and relevance.

3   The Tool

In response to evolving educational needs and the demand for personalization, PolyGloT offers a flexible, competency-based framework to support the creation of adaptive, student-centered learning experiences. Rather than imposing a rigid structure, it provides educators with the tools to design modular, pedagogically sound learning pathways. Educators begin by defining specific competencies they wish learners to develop. These competencies are then broken down into modular units, each representing a cluster of related knowledge and skills. From here, educators can construct learning pathways, which are structured sequences of activities designed to guide students through progressively deeper understanding and practice of each competency.

PolyGloT provides an intuitive and visually streamlined interface for managing learning paths. As shown in Fig. 1, educators are presented with a dashboard view in the Learning Paths section. This area enables educators to easily navigate through their personal collections using the `My Learning Paths` tab or explore all available paths. Each entry features a card-based layout that displays the title, contextual tags (e.g., ML, APPLIED), a brief description, and the number of learning activities included. A thumbnail preview of the flow diagram gives immediate visual feedback, while a trash icon allows quick deletion of any entry.

Central to the platform is the visual learning path editor, a powerful graph-based interface where educators can design learning flows by assembling interconnected `learning fragments`. These fragments consist of smaller thematic clusters of activities ranging from videos, coding exercises, and reading tasks to assessments and collaborative challenges. As seen in Fig. 2, each activity is visually represented as a node, which can be easily arranged on the canvas using drag-and-drop interactions. The platform offers a diverse palette of node types, categorized by learning intention and assessment type, organized into different categories (e.g., REMEMBER, UNDERSTAND, APPLY and CREATE). These categories are directly inspired by Blooms Taxonomy [14], a foundational framework in educational psychology that classifies cognitive learning objectives into hierarchical levels. By aligning activity types with Blooms levels, PolyGloT ensures that learning pathways are grounded and progressively structured, from lower-order skills such as remembering and understanding, to higher-order thinking such as applying, analyzing and creating.

Activities are color-coded and icon-marked to convey their cognitive level at a glance, e.g., readings and videos align with REMEMBER, while collaborative

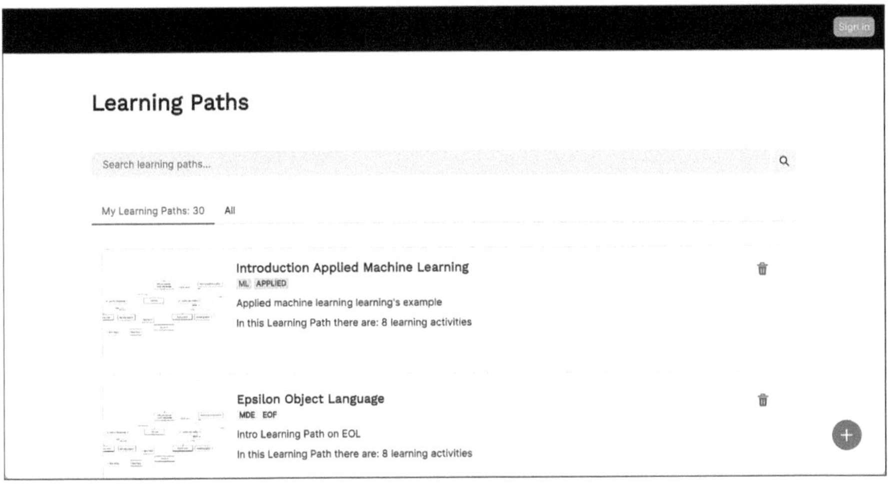

Learning Paths

Search learning paths...

My Learning Paths: 30   All

Introduction Applied Machine Learning
ML   APPLIED

Applied machine learning learning's example

In this Learning Path there are: 8 learning activities

Epsilon Object Language
MDE   EOF

Intro Learning Path on EOL

In this Learning Path there are: 8 learning activities

Fig. 1. PolyGloT dashboard.

projects fall under CREATE. Assessments range from simple quizzes to complex open-ended tasks, helping educators design varied and developmentally balanced pathways. Adaptivity is driven by `Progress Edges`, conditional transitions that guide learners based on performance (e.g., pass / fail, value matches or custom rules), allowing personalized progression through the learning path.

In Fig. 2, a `passFailEdge` directs learners based on task outcomes: success leads to advanced activities, while failure triggers recovery exercises or support material. Other edge types, such as `failDebtEdge` or `manuallyProgressEdge`, add flexibility through retry options or instructor guidance. This rule-based model introduces pedagogical intelligence, enabling personalized paths that adapt to the progress of each learner and supporting differentiated and mastery-based learning.

A notable feature of PolyGloT is its deep integration with Generative AI technologies. Educators can invoke AI support at any stage of the authoring process, from creating activity content and generating assessments to formulating feedback and alternative learning paths. An educator can open the panel of properties of a node and choose `'Create with AI'`, triggering a guided process in which they submit textual material or objectives. Behind the scenes, the platform utilizes models such as GPT-4o[1] of Gemini[2] and integrates with Semantic Kernel APIs[3] to generate relevant and well-aligned educational content on the fly. This AI-driven authoring capability is fully embedded in the visual editor. The flow editor also includes activity suggestions and instant content genera-

---

[1] https://platform.openai.com/docs/overview.

[2] https://ai.google.dev/.

[3] https://learn.microsoft.com/en-us/semantic-kernel/.

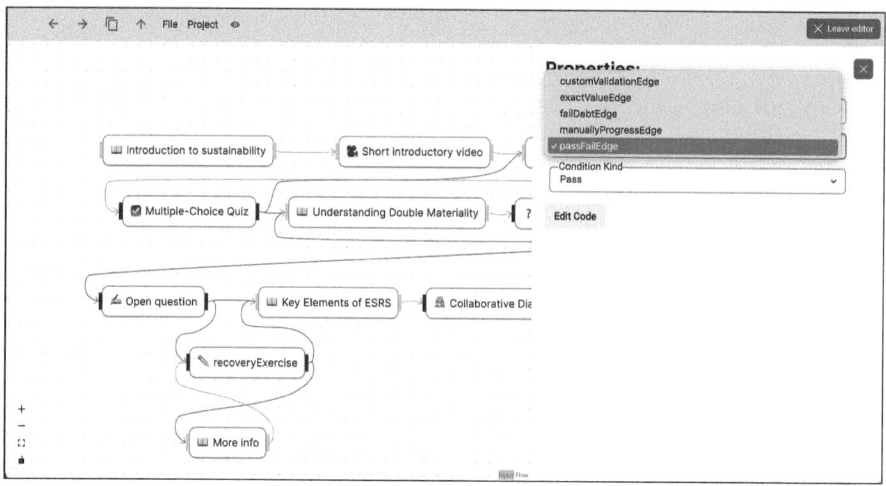

Fig. 2. Visual representation of learning paths and progress edges system.

tion, significantly reducing the manual effort required to design engaging and pedagogically sound experiences.

Once written, learning paths can be deployed across multiple platforms. PolyGloT's execution engine supports integration with tools such as Visual Studio Code, Moodle, Alexa, and WorkAdventure, allowing learners to interact with content in versatile formats: from voice interfaces and live coding notebooks to immersive gamified environments. The system continuously monitors the progress of the learner and dynamically adapts subsequent steps based on real-time performance and engagement metrics. Learning activities vary in type and purpose. Some are AI-generated, while others involve choice, collaboration, or branching paths. Assessments include formative and summative types, and transitions are based on validation logic (e.g., quiz results or submissions). This multipath structure allows learners to be rerouted when needed without interrupting their progress.

To further support motivation and participation, PolyGloT incorporates a set of gamification features designed to maintain the engagement of the learner over time. Educators can define **badges**, **achievements**, and even **interactive quests** that reward learners for reaching milestones, demonstrating persistence, or working with peers. These elements act as tangible markers of progress and foster a sense of achievement while reinforcing the autonomy of the learner. Importantly, the system is not limited to the collection of superficial points: **achievement** can be tied to pedagogical goals (e.g., completing all prerequisite activities, revisiting challenging tasks, or participating in reflective practice), ensuring that rewards remain meaningful in the educational context.

When combined with virtual platforms such as WorkAdventure,[4] Poly-GloT extends these gamified elements into a spatially immersive environment. Students access a **virtual campus** through **avatars**, navigating **rooms** and **interactive areas** assigned to specific learning activities. In this environment, **badges** and **quests** are visually represented (e.g., **unlocking new rooms** after completing certain challenges), reinforcing a sense of **progression** and **discovery**.

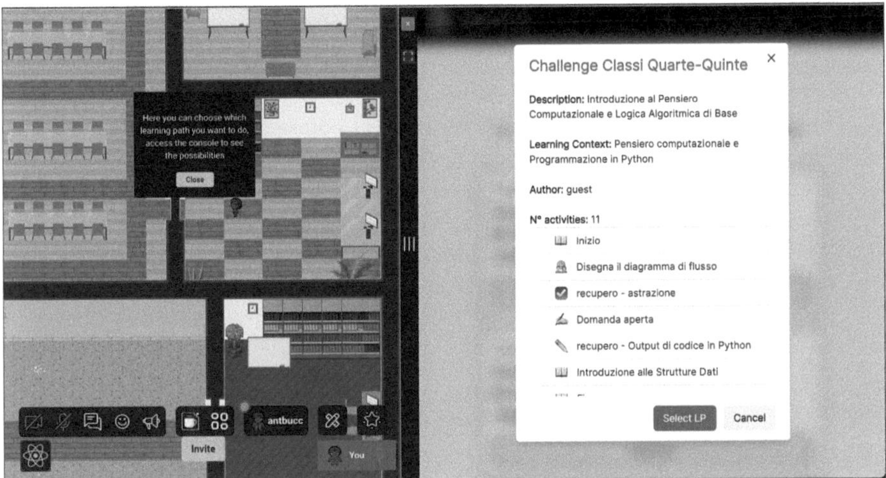

Fig. 3. Challenges in WorkAdventure implementation (text in original language).

The learner **avatar** is shown walking through a simulated educational environment where **gamified prompts** drive interaction. For example, a message on the screen can invite the learner to *"unlock the next quest"* by completing a reading activity or to *"collect a badge"* after submitting a response. Such interactions blend **exploration** with structured **task initiation**, transforming the traditional course list into an **adventure-like navigation system** particularly appealing to younger or gamified learning audiences.

In Fig. 3, after selecting a **learning path**, a pop-up displays the metadata of the flow, including title, description, context, number of activities, and a preview of steps. This smooth transition from playful exploration to structured progression allows learners to connect their **gamified actions (quests, badges, room unlocking)** with concrete educational results, promoting both participation and clarity of purpose.

Through this integration, PolyGloT and WorkAdventure merge **gamified mechanics** with structured, goal-oriented learning, providing a unique approach

---

[4] https://workadventu.re/.

to student engagement. The learners not only consume content, but also **navigate, explore, and interact**, turning the learning process into a **narrative-driven adventure**. Whether accessing a reading, submitting a solution, or progressing to a quiz, each action is embedded in a **fun journey** reinforced by **spatial memory, curiosity**, and **reward mechanisms**.

Quests are defined as sequenced challenges within the learning flow, while learners earn *XP points* for completing activities or overcoming recovery nodes. A shared *leaderboard*, integrated into the WorkAdventure environment, displays updated XP rankings and fosters friendly competition. Together, these features provide concrete mechanisms for motivation and adaptive support, transforming the course into an engaging narrative-driven journey.

At runtime, PolyGloT combines educator-defined branching logic with adaptive support mechanisms. Instructors design competencies, sequences, and assessments, while the system dynamically intervenes when learners face difficulties. For example, *Abstract Node* generates AI-refined learning fragments to revisit unmet concepts, and *MyGym* offers personalized practice with AI-created review content. Rather than replacing the teacher, PolyGloT complements their role by automating recovery materials and providing student-centered remediation. By blending rule-based logic with AI-generated fragments, it delivers a coherent and adaptive learning experience that supports scalability and personalization.

4   Methods

As part of our educational outreach, we organized a `computational thinking` challenge for high school students from different institutions in L'Aquila, divided into two groups based on academic level: first- and second-year students and third- through fifth-year students. Each group followed a custom learning path with an appropriate level of complexity and progression. The learning paths were centered on solving a real-world problem using algorithmic thinking.

After an initial brainstorming session, the students participated in visual modeling activities, where they mapped the problem using flowcharts and abstraction. Then, they participated in collaborative discussions, quizzes, and Python-based coding exercises. The activities were delivered through PolyGloT that included adaptive content, AI-driven feedback and gamified elements, such as quests, XP points, and leaderboards, to support engagement and personalized pace. At the end of the challenge, the top performers in each category received merit certificates personalized with their avatar ID and total XP earned.

We evaluated user experience using the Short User Experience Questionnaire (UEQ-S) [15], a 7-point bipolar semantic differential scale, which was chosen for its efficiency, ease of completion, and robust validation in educational contexts. The UEQ-S measures pragmatic (usability/functionality) and hedonic (affective/aesthetic) qualities and includes built-in heuristics to detect suspicious responses. Data were analyzed using the methodology provided in the official tool guidelines.

5   Results

A total of 53 students answered the online survey. After the first review by the authors and the internal detection methodology of the tool, five (5) responses have been removed, reducing the analyzed data to 48 responses. This sample size is considered adequate according to methodological standards, providing a precision of 0.5 with a probabilistic error of 0.01, thus ensuring that the findings are robust and reliable [15].

Table 1 presents the descriptive statistics for the UEQ-S items, summarizing both the pragmatic and the hedonic dimensions of the user experience. In general, the results indicate a generally positive evaluation, with particularly favorable scores in the hedonic aspect. However, a pragmatic quality item related to clarity appears to be less positively rated, suggesting a potential area for improvement.

Table 1. Overview of the item results, converted in a range from –3 to +3

Item	Mean	Std. Dev.	Negative	Positive	Scale
1	1.1	1.5	Obstructive	supportive	Pragmatic quality
2	0.5	1.6	Complicated	easy	Pragmatic quality
3	1.0	1.7	Inefficient	efficient	Pragmatic quality
4	0.1	1.9	Confusing	clear	Pragmatic quality
5	1.0	1.8	Boring	exciting	Hedonic quality
6	1.5	1.7	Not interesting	interesting	Hedonic quality
7	1.7	1.2	Conventional	inventive	Hedonic quality
8	1.8	1.3	Usual	leading edge	Hedonic quality

The results indicated a mean pragmatic quality score of 0.66 (SD = 1.41), suggesting that the users found the system difficult to use. The hedonic quality score was averaged at 1.48 (SD = 1.26), reflecting moderately positive perceptions about the aesthetic appeal of the system and the pleasure derived from its use. The overall UEQ score was 1.08 (SD = 1.23), suggesting that users have a moderately positive impression of the system (see Fig. 4).

In our study, the consistency of the Short UEQ scale was assessed using Cronbach's α. Both the pragmatic quality and the hedonic quality scales achieved an alpha of 0.86, indicating a high degree of internal consistency. This result confirms that elements that measure usability and efficiency, as well as those that capture the affective and aesthetic dimensions of the user experience, reliably assess the intended constructs.

6   Lessons Learned and Future Directions

An evaluation of PolyGloT, which integrates gamification and artificial intelligence, revealed a moderately positive user experience. Users particularly

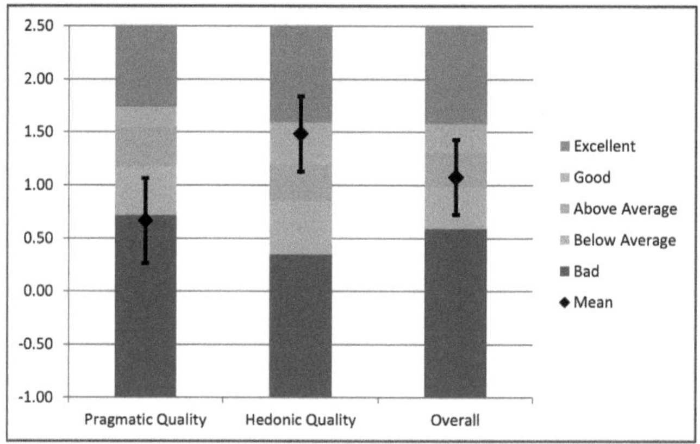

Fig. 4. User results at the UQE-S.

appreciated its aesthetic appeal and engaging qualities, as reflected in higher hedonic quality scores. However, lower ratings in the pragmatic dimension, especially in terms of clarity, highlight usability challenges. This underscores a key lesson: Although AI and gamification can enhance motivation and personalization, they can also introduce complexity that hinders intuitive use.

These findings suggest that future development should focus on improving the interface and interaction flow to effectively balance innovation and usability. Clearer design, more intuitive navigation, and simplified interactions are essential to ensure accessibility without compromising adaptive or motivational features.

The study also revealed limitations that will inform future research. A small geographically limited sample restricts generalizability and the short intervention may not have provided sufficient exposure to all the features of the system. Additionally, relying solely on the UEQ-S provides only a surface-level view of the user experience. Indeed, UEQ-S scores conflate platform usability with pedagogical design; for example, low clarity may reflect interface issues or ambiguous educator-written instructions. This confounding threatens the construct and internal validity and limits causal claims about the effectiveness of the platform. Addressing these issues will require broader studies and qualitative methods to gain deeper insight.

The combined use of AI and gamification requires controlled studies to distinguish their individual effects on user experience and learning outcomes. Future research should also examine long-term participation, measurable learning gains, and adaptive personalization as steps toward scalable, learner-centered technologies. In PolyGloT, future work will deepen the analysis of the integration of generative AI and its technical and pedagogical challenges, with a particular focus on explainability mechanisms, such as dashboards to the learner and transparent justifications, that can improve motivation, trust and intuitive use of the platform.

References

1. Essa, S.G., Celik, T., Human-Hendricks, N.E.: Personalized adaptive learning technologies based on machine learning techniques to identify learning styles: A systematic literature review. IEEE Access **11**, 48392–48409 (2023)
2. Gligorea, I., Cioca, M., Oancea, R., Gorski, A.T., Gorski, H., Tudorache, P.: Adaptive learning using artificial intelligence in e-learning: A literature review. Educ. Sci. **13**(12), 1216 (2023)
3. Deterding, S., Dixon, D., Khaled, R., Nacke, L.: From game design elements to gamefulness: defining" gamification". In: Proceedings of the 15th international academic MindTrek conference: Envisioning future media environments. pp. 9–15 (2011)
4. Bucchiarone, A., Cicchetti, A., Bassanelli, S., Marconi, A.: How to merge gamification efforts for programming and modelling: a tool implementation perspective. In: 2021 ACM/IEEE International Conference on Model Driven Engineering Languages and Systems Companion (MODELS-C). pp. 721–726. IEEE (2021)
5. Suresh Babu, S., Dhakshina Moorthy, A.: Application of artificial intelligence in adaptation of gamification in education: A literature review. Comput. Appl. Eng. Educ. **32**(1), e22683 (2024)
6. Kong, S.C., Cheung, W.M.Y., Zhang, G.: Evaluation of an artificial intelligence literacy course for university students with diverse study backgrounds. Comput. Educ.: Artif. Intell. **2**, 100026 (2021)
7. Santana, M., Díaz-Fernández, M.: Competencies for the artificial intelligence age: visualisation of the state of the art and future perspectives. RMS **17**, 1971–2004 (2023)
8. Ng, D.T.K., Leung, J.K.L., Chu, S.K.W., Qiao, M.S.: Conceptualizing ai literacy: An exploratory review. Comput. Educ.: Artif. Intell. **2**, 100041 (2021)
9. Tondeur, J., Trevisan, O., Howard, S.K., van Braak, J.: Preparing preservice teachers to teach with digital technologies: An update of effective sqd-strategies. Computers & Education p. 105262 (2025)
10. Mogavi, R., Deng, C., Kim, J., Zhou, P., Kwon, Y., Metwally, A., Tlili, A., Bassanelli, S., Bucchiarone, A., Gujar, S., Nacke, L.: Chatgpt in education: A blessing or a curse? a qualitative study exploring early adopters' utilization and perceptions. Comput. Human Behav.: Artif. Humans **2**(1), 100027 (2024)
11. Saputra, I., Astuti, M., Sayuti, M., Kusumastuti, D.: Integration of artificial intelligence in education: Opportunities, challenges, threats and obstacles. a literature review. Indonesian J. Comput. Sci. **12** (2023)
12. Polak, S., Schiavo, G., Zancanaro, M.: Teachers' perspective on artificial intelligence education: An initial investigation. In: CHI Conference on Human Factors in Computing Systems Extended Abstracts. pp. 1–7 (2022)
13. Rosyadi, M.I., Kustiawan, I., Tetehfio, E.O., Joshua, Q.: The role of ai in vocational education: A systematic literature review. J. Vocational Educ. Stud. **6**(2), 244–263 (2023)
14. Krathwohl, D.R.: A revision of bloom's taxonomy: An overview. Theory into practice **41**(4), 212–218 (2002)
15. Schrepp, M., Thomaschewski, J., Hinderks, A.: Design and evaluation of a short version of the user experience questionnaire (ueq-s). Int. J. Interactive Multimedia Artif. Intell. **4**(6), 103–108 (2017)

What Would Your Character Do? Emotional Intelligence, Psychological Safety and Identity in TTRPG Design

Kristina Risley[(✉)][iD], Vanissa Wanick[iD], Richard Gomer[iD], and Christopher Buckingham[iD]

University of Southampton, Southampton, UK
{K.Risley,vwv1n12,R.C.Gomer,C.R.Buckingham}@soton.ac.u

Abstract. This paper explores how Dungeon Masters (DMs) design and facilitate scenarios in Dungeons & Dragons (DnD) that scaffold the practice of emotional intelligence (EI) during play. This study used a qualitative, abductive methodology, drawing on interviews, co-design data and live gameplay recordings to examine how narrative and mechanics engaged players in emotional regulation, empathy and relationship management. DnD is positioned as an immersive environment for leadership learning, where emotionally intelligent behaviours are rehearsed and refined through narrative framing, role negotiation and in-character decision-making under uncertainty. Findings highlight a series of mechanics and design strategies such as soft failure, secret objectives and managed player-versus-player tension that support players in exploring emotional and interpersonal dynamics in character. These moments are deliberately structured to support reflection and interpersonal responsiveness; the construct of 'alibi' enables psychological safety and experimentation, while 'bleed' facilitates personal insight and identity work. This analysis contributes a practice-oriented map of the levers DMs use to design for emotional engagement and identity work, as well as of how players respond in terms of leadership, identity and group dynamics.

Keywords: Serious games · Leadership development · Emotional intelligence · Identity · Social constructionism

1 Introduction

As organisations face progressively complex and unpredictable environments, effective leadership depends on soft skills such as emotional intelligence (EI), ethical reasoning and adaptability [18]. Serious games (SGs) are increasingly recognised as offering psychologically safe environments [9] to develop these competencies, enabling players to rehearse decision-making, navigate interpersonal dynamics and experiment with identity, protected from real-world consequences [6,23]. Many SGs remain tightly structured around predefined choices and outcomes, while TTRPGs allow collaborative storytelling and open-ended

S. Bakkes et al. (Eds.): GALA 2025, LNCS 16307, pp. 106–115, 2026.
https://doi.org/10.1007/978-3-032-11043-5_11

decision-making [22]. From a social constructionist perspective, they function as shared narrative spaces where meaning is produced through interaction [7,14]. By adopting fictional roles and navigating uncertain scenarios, players rehearse ethical reasoning and leadership decision-making [8,11]. These processes also enable emotional expression, perspective-taking and identity exploration [2,19].

Dungeons & Dragons (DnD) is one of the most well-known TTRPGs worldwide and while not traditionally classified as a SG, it aligns well to Gee's conceptualisation of games as systems that immerse players in meaningful problems, offer feedback and enable identity exploration through role-play [11]. The Dungeon Master (DM) acts as storyteller, facilitator and guide, scaffolding emotionally and ethically charged situations where players can explore leadership, identity and group dynamics [5,25,27]. Recent research explores how DMs contribute to scaffolding cognitive, emotional and social learning within gameplay [21], but less is known about how they design scenarios that engage players in leadership dilemmas, identity work and ethical decision-making. There remains a need for a more formal account of DM design practice, particularly in how narrative choices and scenario structures are used to shape leadership, identity and emotional engagement in DnD and related TTRPGs

This work therefore addresses the research question: *How do Dungeon Masters design emotionally engaging scenarios in DnD and how do players respond to these challenges in terms of leadership behaviours, identity and group dynamics?* By focusing on emotional engagement and identity work within leadership development contexts, this research aims to contribute new insights to leadership education, particularly in developing EI through experiential and immersive methods. This also aligns with emerging perspectives in serious game design, such as Wanick et al.'s [26] call for transferable, emotionally resonant systems that emphasise player agency, modularity and contextual adaptability.

2   Background Literature Overview

This study explores how EI is demonstrated and developed during live DnD gameplay. Drawing on Goleman's model of EI as comprising self-awareness, self-regulation, motivation, empathy and social skill [1,12,13], EI is framed as enacted through social interaction. This view emphasises EI as a capacity that develops through social practice rather than as a fixed trait, with implications for leadership education and experiential learning. There is growing evidence that emotional and interpersonal competencies can be strengthened through practice in contexts of risk, ambiguity and negotiation [23]. Role-playing games such as DnD provide such contexts, involving improvised social performances that demand regulation, empathy, relationship management and the concealment of intention [21].

These moments of emotional experimentation are not without risk, with learning processes shaped by psychological safety, defined as shared norms that support trust during interpersonal risk-taking [9]. In TTRPGs, psychological safety is maintained through group agreements, consent-based mechanics and structured facilitation. When present, players are more willing to accept narrative and relational risks, enabling DMs to design scenarios that surface moral ambiguity or identity strain [21]. Meanwhile, the shifting boundary between player identity and character identity adds yet further complexity; concepts of *bleed* and *alibi* explain how emotional experience moves between fiction and real life [2,16]. *Bleed-in* occurs when a player brings their emotional patterns into the character; *bleed-out* occurs when experiences in-game shape out-of-game reflection or response. Meanwhile, the *alibi* of character provides psychological protection: players can engage in ethically risky or emotionally intense behaviour, as the fiction absorbs personal accountability. Both processes create conditions for identity work, as identity is continually constructed and re-constructed through performance and narrative [4,8,19]. From a social constructionist perspective, emotional meaning is produced through these shared performances [7].

Taken together, these elements highlight three recurring dynamics: reflective challenges, where players confront emotional or ethical dilemmas; role-anchored conflict, where identity and responsibility are tested through character play; and the joint performance of agreed reality, where groups co-produce shared fictions through improvisation and social negotiation. While prior research has examined EI in games, identity work through role-play and the conditions that support safety, less is known about how these ingredients combine in practice and how DMs intentionally design scenarios to elicit them. This study addresses that gap, towards supporting the development of leadership capacities not easily addressed in traditional learning formats.

3   Research Design

This study employed am absudctive, qualitative design over three sequential stages. DMs were tasked with designing and managing DnD games involving collaborative challenges, difficult choices and conflict, requiring character-based decision-making and group interaction. Study phases consisted of an unstructured interview with an experienced DM, a co-design workshop with five DMs and two recorded gameplay sessions, each led by participants from the DM design workshop. Insights from the interview informed the workshop design, which in turn shaped the scenarios used in the gameplay sessions.

Participants and data collection centred on DnD gameplay, where a DM describes the world, presents challenges and narrates outcomes. Players assume fictional characters with defined abilities and declare their intended actions, with outcomes resolved through dice rolls ("checks") that determine whether actions succeed or fail. This involved a purposive sample of six experienced DMs (aged 25–54). One male DM contributed a 90-minute unstructured interview focused on narrative design and emotional engagement. Five others (three men, two women) took part in a two-hour co-design workshop. Two of these DMs (one male, one female) then led separate recorded gameplay sessions based on their scenario designs. A total of nine experienced players took part in two four-hour one-shot sessions (four in group 1, five in group 2). Players were gender-balanced, aged 25–44, and had prior experience with DnD campaigns and core mechanics, though they had not met before, allowing group dynamics to develop organically. All sessions were held in person at a board game café in Southampton, UK. All were audio recorded and supplemented with field notes and artefacts (e.g. mind maps, draft scenarios).

Data analysis followed Braun and Clarke's [3] reflexive thematic approach. Interview and workshop transcripts were coded inductively, line by line, to capture how DMs embedded leadership dilemmas and decision-making pressure. These codes guided the analysis of fully transcribed gameplay sessions, which were examined using a distanced coding approach. Codes were applied to dialogue, actions and interaction patterns, with illustrative quotes extracted. Key categories included: emotional regulation, empathy and social awareness, relationship management, leadership expression, identity and role alignment, improvisation under ambiguity. Patterns were compared across sessions and clustered into three overarching themes: (1) identity work and role experimentation, (2) interpersonal complexity and social navigation, alongside (3) emotional regulation and reflective insight.

4 Results

Across three themes of reflective challenges, role-anchored conflict and joint performance of agreed reality, the following examples show how DMs explained their design choices and how players practiced and performed EI [1, 12, 13]. These cases illustrate moments of failure, identity work and collaborative play, demonstrating scaffolding [25] and emotional learning in safe, narrative contexts [27].

4.1 Example 1: Failure as a Narrative Device and Reflective Challenge

The first example centres on emotional self-regulation and adaptive insight, scaffolded through a failure intentionally left open to interpretation [5, 25, 27]. As explained by one DM during interview,

> *"DnD works best when the players fail... that's where the best stories come from ... there's a lot more problem solving and a lot more interaction."*

Failure was framed not as punishment but as a scaffold for emotional development [2], with the DM using psychological safety [9] to let players fail in character without risking their real-life identity. In one session, a druid's repeated inability to transform into a bat was reinterpreted as discovery, with each failed attempt providing new narrative clues.

– DM: *"As you've already tried and seemingly failed four times, can you give me some sort of check to figure out why might you be unable to turn into this specific kind of bat? ...with what you've collected so far the conclusion you've come to is that they might not be a beast?"*

– Player 2: *"...This is what I was saying... their schedule is really strange for a bat and the fact that I can't transform into it tells me that it's not an animal of some kind."*

This moment drew on mechanics including *soft fail*, where setbacks redirect rather than penalise; *clue via failure*, which turns mistakes into new insight; and a *progress clock* that built tension across repeated attempts. The use of *multiple skill attempts* sustained engagement and encouraged players to reconsider their assumptions. Together these features supported *self-awareness*, as the player recognised misjudgements, and *self-management*, as they regulated frustration and adapted their approach.

4.2   Example 2: Role-Anchored Conflict and the Alibi of Role-Play

Conflict between characters is a common and often deliberate part of narrative tension in TTRPGs, but DMs are acutely aware of the emotional risks it carries. As one explained, *"Usually... it's not really that you use DnD to solve actual conflict... but rather if people are playing their characters well there's going to end up with conflict between the characters but the people just kind of laughing and apologising to each other...[SIC]"*. Another stressed *"It's not a personal attack at the player, it's aimed at the character–I am in character."*

This careful distinction between character and player lies at the heart of the concept of *alibi* [2,15]–the protective framing that enables players to act through a character without that behaviour being interpreted as a reflection of their real self. By offering psychological safety [9], this allows emotionally risky actions to unfold in-character while relationships at the table remain intact. An example is shown below, where a player was secretly instructed to sabotage a teammate mid-battle.

– Player 3: *"I just get so enthusiastic, I knock your hand out the way and it misses"*
– Player 2: *"¡laugh¿ You are terrible."*
– DM: *"(Her secret note said) you must fail one of your friends' rolls in the future. It misses instantly... and it's a good time. Had you waited for the beholder you would have been screwed."*
– Player 3: *"That's why I did it now."*

The DM confirmed this was a safe moment for sabotage and the group endorsed the decision. The scene combined *secret objectives*, limited *PvP sabotage* and a timed *reveal trigger*, all within a consent-based system that kept conflict bounded. In this context, players practiced *managing conflict, relationship management* and *empathy* by preserving trust and anticipating others' responses.

4.3   Example 3: Managing Emotions and Joint Performance of Sustained Reality

The third example focuses on sustained deception as an EI act, with players skillfully co-creating a false identity to infiltrate a facility. This introduces concealed intentions as a design theme, supported by multiple interwoven mechanics. As explained by a DM during interview,

> *"...if it's just one evil character... like they're clearing out a bandit camp, but they're doing it for different reasons, so they secretly want to clear out the bandit camp, to put their own bandits in... I will only ever pick players that I know is really experienced, who can pull that sort of stuff off because a lot of players aren't very good at holding stuff in or role-playing stuff that subtly."*

In a gameplay session, players impersonate government inspectors to access a facility. They layer their deception with escalating detail:

- Player 1: *"I am a senior regional manager... and then something with accountant on the end which makes people much more nervous."*
- Player 3: *"I'll latch on to this little illusion that we've got going on and I can be like this, inspector. You know, like the bottle machinery inspector or something stupid."*
- DM: *"As they notice you've entered the building, they'll come towards you and ask–who are you and why are you here?"*
- Player 3: *We're from the city office here to do an inspection."*
- DM: *"What city?"*
- Player 1: *"We assumed that you would have already been told. This is frankly, already rude. Write this down!"*

What unfolds is a coordinated emotional performance where players draw on *illusion magic, charisma-based checks* and *collaborative improvisation* to sustain the deception. Success depends on *emotional regulation, trust* and *social responsiveness*. Each player maintains the fiction under scrutiny, predicting the responses of non-playable characters (NPCs) and adapting to one another. This is not just about persuasion, but also demonstrates *self-management, social awareness* and *relationship management*: staying composed, protecting the group's credibility and maintaining cohesion under pressure. At the same time, this scene illustrates *identity work* [4], as players take on roles far removed from their own, experimenting with new modes of authority and interaction. Through their improvisation, they co-create a believable social order, demonstrating the *social construction of shared reality* [7] through commonly agreed language, cues and context. Emotional intelligence here means *managing expression, anticipating responses* and supporting a shared lie without breaking character.

5   Discussion

This work explored how DMs design scenarios that support EI and how players respond in terms of leadership, identity and group dynamics. Acting as a *mentor-in-play*, DMs scaffolded EI by creating socially and emotionally complex situations that required players to adapt and reflect [5,25,27]. Players engaged through character-led decision-making, practicing empathy, regulation and social responsiveness. Soft failure, deception mechanics, interpersonal sabotage and secret motives emerged as pivotal design tools for EI development; each linked to specific EI domains and player behaviours (see Fig. 1). These findings suggest that TTRPGs enable both DMs and players to develop leadership skills through active, structured experiences.

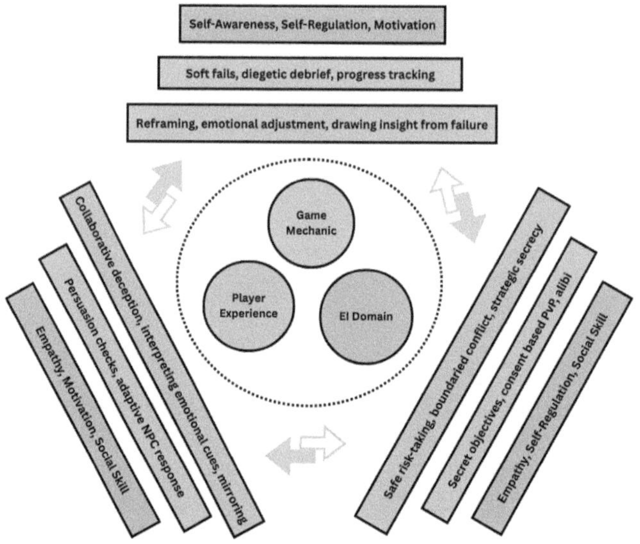

Fig. 1. Mechanics, EI domains, player experiences mapped to design structures

Across the gameplay cases, it is evident EI was not only thematically present in player interactions, but also scaffolded as learning interventions by the DM's design. These mechanics emerged as pivotal design tools deployed to enable emotional regulation, perspective-taking and relational awareness. This emphasis on failure also aligns with the established "play to lose" ethos in role-playing scholarship, where character setbacks are deliberately embraced as a source of drama and emotional depth [2]. In this context, failure operated as both a narrative device and a scaffold for emotional intelligence, requiring players to regulate frustration, adapt their approach and reflect on leadership choices made in character. Players responded to these prompts through in-character decisions as well as engaging metacognitively as part of reframing failure, moderating conflict, co-managing deception and adjusting their social performances in response to feedback. In doing so, they exercised and performed dimensions of Goleman's EI framework [1,12,13] in real time–particularly self-awareness, self-regulation and relationship management. Figure 1 can be understood as a framework for design, showing how mechanics such as soft failure or secret objectives connect to dimensions of emotional intelligence and to specific player behaviours. This synthesis provides a reference point for those seeking to embed leadership and emotional learning into role-play.

These findings align with previous literature on identity work and emotional learning through role-play [2,4,7], but extend it by providing a more practical account of how specific game design choices elicit such behaviours. While earlier work focuses on player experience or group dynamics, this study highlights the intentional strategies DMs use to scaffold moral complexity and social tension. In this sense, the DM operates not only as a narrative facilitator but as a pedagogical designer, shaping experiential learning environments that cultivate affective and interpersonal competencies. A key insight is the function of psychological safety as a design precondition. In all observed cases, the players' willingness to engage emotionally and ethically was underpinned by shared norms and safety mechanisms (e.g., consent-based PvP, character alibi) which preserve trust. This resonates with Edmondson's work on team learning [9] and reinforces the idea that emotional experimentation and leadership risk-taking require carefully scaffolded contexts. The DM's role in sustaining these norms by structuring interpersonal risk, timing reveals and managing tone is central to enabling emotionally rich gameplay without undue relational fallout. Another theme concerns the blurred boundary between identity and role. Emotional performances within the game were often entangled with out-of-game reflection. This supports Bowman's concept of bleed [2,16] and illustrates how emotionally complex play enables identity rehearsal: players not only *act* as leaders but also *feel* like leaders, experiencing the affective and interpersonal costs of their decisions vicariously. The alibi of fiction/character allows for emotionally risky but psychologically safe experimentation, while the shared narrative context invites feedback and reflection.

5.1 Implications for Research and Practice: Collective and Empathy-driven Learning Practices Facilitated by TTRPGs

This analysis highlights two main implications for research and practice:

Expansive and collective learning: TTRPGs can be understood through the lens of expansive learning [10], where knowledge and practice emerge from collaboration and co-creation. Leadership and learning are distributed across the group, with the DM facilitating structures while leaving space for players to shape narratives and exercise agency. For practice, this highlights the value of designing activities that build in collaborative problem-solving, encourage shared authorship and give players opportunities to co-create outcomes, rather than relying on tightly scripted content. This peer-based process strengthens EI domains–such as empathy, social skills and self-regulation through collaborative problem-solving, role-play and mutual support [17].

Learning and wellbeing By engaging in both cognitive and affective empathy, players explore different perspectives and practice emotional regulation [24] in a safe, fictional context. This suggests practical use of TTRPGs not only for leadership education but also for interventions that support emotional resilience and mental health, for example structured role-play workshops or therapeutic groups. Beyond leadership training, TTRPGs can support emotional well-being by offering collective spaces for empathy, reflection and healing, reinforcing their role as tools for both educational and therapeutic use [20].

6 Conclusion and Outlook

In response to the research question: *"How do Dungeon Masters design emotionally and ethically engaging scenarios in DnD, and how do players respond to these challenges in terms of leadership, identity and group dynamics?"*, these findings confirm that unlike traditional case-based learning, TTRPGs offer embodied, improvised and emotionally consequential encounters with ambiguity, allowing for the rehearsal of leadership in a psychologically safe but morally rich sandbox. The analysis offers a framework that links mechanics to dimensions of emotional intelligence and player behaviours, providing a reference for embedding leadership and emotional learning into role-play. However, this study is limited by its small sample and lack of systematic post-session reflections from players, which would provide richer insight into how in-game experiences translated into perceived learning or personal development. Future work could build on this by employing longitudinal designs or integrating physiological or psychometric measures of emotional engagement. Further exploration of DM training, improvisational skill and scenario planning could support the formal development of DM pedagogy as a distinct professional craft within experiential education.

Acknowledgments. This study was funded by the University of Southampton's Sustainability and Resilience Institute (SRI). The team at Board in the City, Southampton is deeply appreciated for the expertise and engaging environment that played a significant role in this research.

References

1. Antonopoulou, H.: The value of emotional intelligence: Self-awareness, self-regulation, motivation, and empathy as key components. Technium Educ. Human. **8**, 78–92 (2024)
2. Bowman, S.: Immersion and Shared Imagination in Role-Playing Games. Routledge (2024)
3. Braun, V., Clarke, V.: Thematic Analysis: A Practical Guide. Sage (2022)
4. Brown, A.D.: Identities and identity work in organizations. Int. J. Manage. Rev. **17**, 20–40 (1 2015)
5. Bruner, J.S.: The Culture of Education. Harvard University Press (1996)
6. Buchanan, J.L.: Leadership development and experiential methodology: the impact on learning leadership. Int. J. Arts and Sci. **10**, 601–608 (2017)
7. Burr, V.: Social Constructionism. Routledge (2015)
8. Deterding, S., Zagal, J.: Role-Playing Game Studies Transmedia Foundations. Routledge (2018)

9. Edmondson, A.C., Lei, Z.: Psychological safety: The history, renaissance, and future of an interpersonal construct. Annu. Rev. Organ. Psych. Organ. Behav. **1**, 23–43 (2014)
10. Engeström, Y., Sannino, A.: Studies of expansive learning: Foundations, findings and future challenges. Introduction to Vygotsky pp. 100–146 (2017)
11. Gee, J.P.: Learning by design: Good video games as learning machines. E-Learning and Digital Media **2**, 5–16 (3 2005)
12. Goleman, D.: Leadership that gets results. HBR **78**, 78–90 (2000)
13. Goleman, D.: Emotional intelligence. Bantam Books, Inc (1995)
14. Gomer, R., et al.: Learning participatory budgeting via collaborative world-building: A case study of empaville. In: Lecture Notes in Computer Science. vol. 15348, pp. 275–284. Springer Science and Business (2025)
15. Hoffman, S.G.: The practical use of other realities: Taking berger and luckmann into the wild. Cult. Sociol. **10**, 109–124 (2016)
16. Hugaas, K.H.: Bleed and identity: A conceptual model of bleed and how bleed-out from role-playing games can affect a player's sense of self. Int. J. Role-Playing pp. 9–35 (6 2024)
17. Khumalo, N., Dumont, K.B., Waldzus, S.: Leaders' influence on collective action: An identity leadership perspective. Leadersh. Q. **33**(4), 101609 (2022)
18. Kubátová, J., et al.: Soft Skills for the 21st Century. Springer Nature (2025)
19. Mackay, D.: The Fantasy Role-Playing Game: A New Performing Art. McFarland (2001)
20. Merrick, A., Li, W.W., Miller, D.J.: A study on the efficacy of the tabletop role-playing game dungeons & dragons for improving mental health and self-concepts in a community sample. Games Health J. **13**(2), 128–133 (2024)
21. Monahan, R., et al.: Learning from ludemes: An inventory of common player actions within tabletop role-playing games (ttrpgs) to inform principled design of game-based learning experiences. Int. J. Role-Playing **15**, 178–210 (2024)
22. Risley, K., Wanick, V., Gomer, R., Gene-Rowe, F., Owen, J.: Collaborative world-building as sustainable problem-solving: The role of tabletop role-playing games. In: Bucchiarone, A., Rossi, V., Wanick, V. (eds.) Engineering Educational Games for a Sustainable Society. Springer (2025)
23. Risley, K., Wanick, V.: Asking the experts: A delphi method investigation into serious games for leadership development. In: Lecture Notes in Computer Science (including subseries Lecture Notes in Artificial Intelligence and Lecture Notes in Bioinformatics). vol. 15348 LNCS, pp. 233–242. Springer Science and Business Media Deutschland GmbH (2025)
24. Thompson, N.M., Van Reekum, C.M., Chakrabarti, B.: Cognitive and affective empathy relate differentially to emotion regulation. Affect. Sci. **3**(1), 118–134 (2022)
25. Vygotsky, L.S.: Mind in Society: The Development of Higher Psychological Processes. Harvard University Press, Cambridge, MA (1978)
26. Wanick, V., Stallwood, J., Xavier, G.: Future Directions in Games for Serious Contexts: A Conversation About Transferability, pp. 137–153. Springer (2023)
27. Whitton, N., Moseley, A. (eds.): Using Games to Enhance Learning and Teaching: A Beginner's Guide. Routledge, New York, NY (2012)

Video Games *Do* Belong in Classrooms: Empirical Insight into Learning with Narrative Video Games

Jaron Müller[(✉)] [iD]

University of Education Freiburg, Kunzenweg 21, 79117 Freiburg Im Breisgau, Germany
`jaron.mueller@ph-freiburg.de`

Abstract. The potential of video games as pedagogical tools for achieving curricular learning objectives remains underexplored, particularly regarding their systematic implementation in classroom contexts. Contributing to recent efforts of making game-based learning and its benefits more accessible for application in educational settings as well as better understandable from an empirical standpoint, this article investigates how game-inherent prompt systems can meet or even surpass external instruction by intrinsically motivating and cognitively activating learners. It provides insight into an empirical study conducted with a sample of 106 students in German Literature classes, focusing on cognitive processes when practicing the participants' competencies of understanding a narrative video game's literary characters. In a mixed-methods approach, results demonstrated superior literary analysis and reflection performance when learners were scaffolded by game-inherent prompts compared to externally provided instructional tasks. The study provides insight into effects of video games as catalysts for cognitive activation, identifies beneficial ludonarrative structures, and discusses practical implications for integrating game-based learning in formal education settings.

Keywords: Games for Learning · Cognitive activation · Ludonarrative scaffolding

1 Introduction: Why Do We Need Empirical Insight into Learning with Games?

In educational innovation, the quest to bridge the gap between traditional learning methods and the engaging potential of interactive digital media remains ever vital. Amidst this evolving landscape, video games have emerged not merely as instruments of entertainment, but also as transformative educational tools capable of fostering deep engagement. But despite their growing prominence in the everyday lives of pupils [14], they still haven't successfully found their way into common classroom settings.

The limited integration of video games as learning media stems from a complex interplay of sociocultural, institutional, and pedagogical factors. Historically, video games have been stigmatized as mere leisure activities or distractions rather than legitimate

S. Bakkes et al. (Eds.): GALA 2025, LNCS 16307, pp. 116–125, 2026.
https://doi.org/10.1007/978-3-032-11043-5_12

educational tools, a perception that reinforces their absence in the repertoire of both current and prospective educators, as well as their trainers. This lack of familiarity and institutional endorsement further diminishes their consideration as viable instructional tools. Unsurprisingly, this stagnation is further compounded by a lack of both pedagogical frameworks for effective implementation and the necessary technical infrastructure in schools [1]. Additionally, school textbooks predominantly examine video games from a critical, often cautionary perspective, reflecting broader societal scepticism toward their pedagogical value.[1] Consequently, despite advances in discovering their potential to enhance engagement, motivation, and interactive learning, video games remain marginalized in formal education. The challenge is to overcome entrenched biases and to in systematically research game-based learning to facilitate its integration into teacher training programs and curricular frameworks and to legitimize their use as effective pedagogical instruments. Without systemic research that lets us explore clearly what works and what doesn't when using games to learn, they will likely continue to be underutilized in classrooms.

To address this, this paper presents an experimental study that investigates the convergence of narrative video games and literature learning, postulating video games as an exceptional medium for cultivating literary competence. It ascertains the value that a narratively driven game holds for effective learning processes by measuring the cognitive activation fostered by the puzzle-video game *A Normal Lost Phone* (2017). Conducted in German literature classes, 106 mid-grade students showed significant positive effects on competence-oriented learning outcomes in a group exploring the digital game guided by its internal prompting structures, while another group received direct instructions as frequently used in established classroom settings. The results show clear implications for how we can and should promote video game use in classrooms, be it for engaging learning processes in general or for differentiation in heterogenous learning environments, as well as how video game design can foster effective learning.

1.1 Advancements and Challenges of Educational Video Game Research

To situate the objectives of this empirical study within the broader landscape of educational game research the specific knowledge gaps within it that the investigation aims to address need to be identified. While existing research has documented games' motivational benefits, uncertainties remain on how well game mechanics interact with cognitive learning processes – a lacuna this study targets through its experimental design.

Documented Motivational Benefits And Inherently Pedagogical Game Structures

In recent years, various efforts have been made to better understand and evaluate games as effective learning tools. As De Freitas [5] summarizes in her broad literature review, the field of so-called "game sciences" [5, p. 74] has made continuously expanding efforts to evaluate games as learning and teaching tools, pointing out findings such as increased motivation and benefits to skill transferability when learning with games. While empirical evidence generally supports the efficacy of games in fostering meaningful learning

---

[1] The absence of concrete teaching materials or structured curricular units incorporating digital games is inherently understandable, given that textbooks cannot assume the widespread accessibility or usability of specific games.

processes, her analysis simultaneously reveals critical gaps in understanding the underlying mechanisms that drive these educational outcomes. This underscores the need for further research to elucidate the specific conditions under which game-based learning achieves optimal pedagogical effectiveness.

Previously, research has established various positive impacts of digital games on key aspects of learning. Among these, the motivational benefits of game-based learning have been particularly well-documented [7, 10, 17]. While studies have demonstrated how heightened learner motivation correlates strongly with improved knowledge acquisition and retention [9, 15], this focus on motivation has become so dominant in game-based learning discourse that it risks creating the misleading impression that it constitutes the sole pedagogical advantage of digital games. Such a narrow perspective overlooks the broader instructional potential inherent in game design.

In fact, digital games have long been recognized in educational research as complex didactic systems that inherently facilitate learning processes - particularly through their interactivity. As Gee and others have argued, the very structure of digital games and their mechanics (e.g., progressive challenges, feedback systems, and problem-solving scenarios) fosters skill development and knowledge construction [4, 8]. This nature of games as structured learning environments suggests that their educational value extends far beyond simple engagement metrics, encompassing deeper cognitive and metacognitive benefits that warrant further exploration in classroom applications. The current challenge for educational research lies in moving beyond the established motivational paradigm to develop a more nuanced understanding of how different game mechanics can be systematically harnessed to support diverse learning objectives.

The Empirical Challenge of Accessing Cognitive Learner Activation

The previously mentioned factors of games as learning tools have been well explored and are becoming consequentially accepted as productive starting points for educational concept development and application. On a different note, an increasingly recognized construct in educational science remains empirically elusive: The cognitive activation of students during the usage and processing of digital learning environments [11, 12]. While video games clearly engage learners, we lack robust methodologies to measure how effectively they activate higher-order thinking processes. This measurement challenge has limited our ability to evaluate games' potential for deep conceptual learning. The present study addresses this gap by proposing a novel assessment framework to approach research of cognitive activation during gameplay-driven learning. This will give us an idea how video games may intrinsically foster cognitive skills – and based on what criteria serious games as well as edutainment games should be designed by programmers and chosen by teachers to be used as educational media with a high potential to successfully engage players in desired learning activities.

To achieve this, the empirical study employs a mixed-methods approach, grounded in the BOLIVE model of literary learning [2], to evaluate as an exemplar how effectively a narrative game fosters students' understanding of literary characters. By statistically analyzing qualitatively coded student outputs (e.g., character analyses), the study tests the hypothesis that exploratory learning through gameplay enhances character understanding more effectively than externally delivered direct instruction via cognitively activating tasks. This dual analysis aims to reveal which game-inherent structures (e.g., gameplay prompts) positively influence specific learning processes, providing evidence for how ludic design can scaffold literary competence.

2 How *a Normal Lost Phone* (2017) Employs Inherent Prompts to Incentivize Deep Learning

"You have just found a phone. Find out the truth." The premise of the narrative serious game *A Normal Lost Phone* – developed by Accidental Queens and published in 2017 by Plug In Digital for PC and mobile platforms – is as simplistic as its title: Players are tasked with investigating the origin of a mysterious smartphone they are said to have found in an unspecified location. The game UI, accordingly, presents itself akin to a rather conventional smartphone user surface in a stylized fashion [see Fig. 1]. Apps like a music player, an email service or a gallery form the structure of its main menu.[2]

Fig. 1. The game's UI mimics a smartphone's interface. From left to right, the simulated applications shown are: Main menu, email service, gallery app.

The game's narrative, then, presents itself to players in a rather unconventional manner: Though mostly text-based, the game doesn't outright spell out to players what happened, but simply tells them to "find out the truth" on its start-up screen. It then starts *in medias res*, letting players uncover the events preceding the smartphone's discovery by reading messages, going through its owner's digital calendar and trying to gradually

---

[2] From a procedural perspective, this already provides a surface level advantage for use in classrooms: Navigating the game doesn't require the adoption of complex new control schemes. For most pupils, the game's contents become accessible simply via the activation of already established scripts of smartphone usage.

unlock more of the phone's features, such as internet access or app profiles. To understand what happened to the story's protagonist, 18-year-old Sam, they need to assemble textual and narrative information from several different sources and combine them into a coherent mental representation of what events led to Sam's eventual disappearance. The core gameplay mechanic in this regard is that to gain access to some apps and features, players need to enter certain codes as "passwords" – a slightly unprecise term given that each prompt only allows for numeric digits to be entered.

The game was selected following a detailed analysis of its ludonarrative design, as its interactive structures demonstrated strong alignment with the target literary competency. Its embedded prompts allowed for adequate translation into equivalent instructional tasks focused on character analysis, which provided the conceptual cornerstone of the study's variation of experimental conditions. This parity between in-game mechanics and external instructions ensured methodological consistency when comparing learning outcomes across conditions, while preserving the game's inherent capacity to scaffold higher-order literary reasoning through experiential problem-solving.

2.1 Game-Inherent Prompts as Cognitively Activating Learning Tools

The game's main didactic potential lies in its use of the previously mentioned inherent prompts: carefully designed gameplay elements that require players to actively apply their knowledge of the narrative's characters, fostering deeper character understanding [see Fig. 2]. These game prompts function as cognitive prompts which are well explored for educational settings [e.g., 19, 21], and at the same time act as implicit scaffolding. To progress, players must engage in processes of selecting relevant information among what knowledge about the characters they have been able to grasp, organizing it into a coherent mental model so that it may be pragmatically applied to the problem at hand and integrating it with activated previous knowledge from long-term memory.

This triad of selecting, organizing and integrating information represents processes central to effective multimedia learning according to frameworks such as Mayer's CTML [13]. For instance, when confronted with a password that is said in an email to correlate with "dates that matter to [Sam]", players are compelled to reactivate, select and organize acquired information about what might qualify as an important date to the character, evaluate its relevance to the problem, and anticipate which solution offers – from their perspective and understanding – the highest chance of success.

Crucially, the game's design ensures that these processes are not ancillary but obligatory: Players cannot advance without deliberating on character-driven analysis and anticipation. By embedding such prompts organically within gameplay mechanics, the system actively encourages players to reflect on characters based on their prior analyses, creating a feedback loop where in-game actions reinforce and refine understanding. If students manage to assess and connect character-related information, they are rewarded with the advancement of the story and more answers to their questions regarding its contents; should they fail to do so, they can try again and are thus encouraged to reassess their previous approach. Here, the ludic structure itself becomes the mediator of cognitive activation, leveraging the interactive nature of games to transform passive reception into active construction of meaning and character understanding.

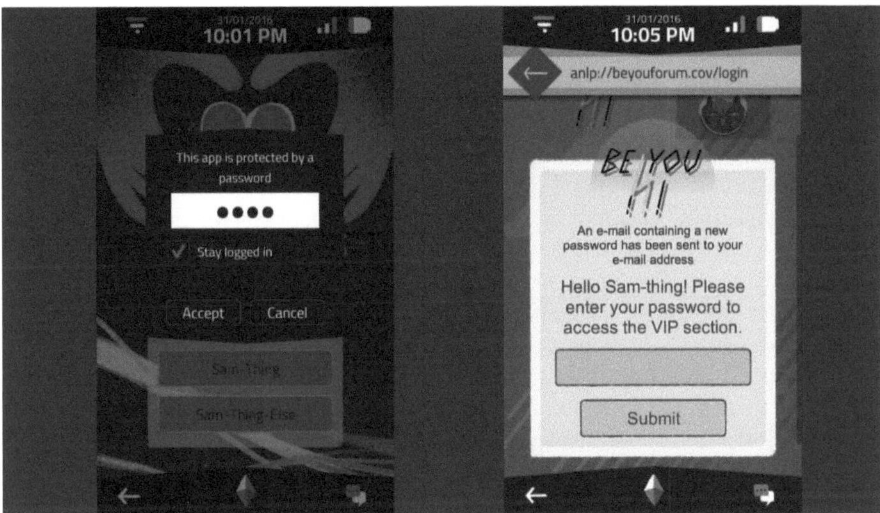

Fig. 2. Several points in the game present players with prompts that request a specific numeric code to be inserted. From left to right: Prompt to unlock a dating app profile, prompt to unlock the VIP section of an online forum

3 Study: How Learners Benefit from *a Normal Lost Phone*'s Inherent Prompts When Engaging in Character Understanding

Empirical observations from the study suggest that using video games to foster learning through their prompt structures not only sustains engagement but also scaffolds it toward discipline-specific thinking. While prior research has broadly examined the educational efficacy of digital games [e.g., 3, 6, 18], this study specifically investigates the effectiveness of ludonarrative video game elements regarding learners' cognitive activation, focusing on how and to what extent game-inherent prompts intrinsically scaffold the application and practice of literary understanding competencies.

3.1 Methodology

The empirical study, informed by the conceptual framework of approaching cognitive processes published recently by Reinhold et al. as CoDiL [16], engaged 106 ninth-grade students from *Realschule* and *Gymnasium* tracks in Germany. Prior to the study, written informed consent was collected from all parents and teachers along with participating students' assent; institutional approval was granted by the school administrations. No identifying information was collected, and all data was immediately pseudonymized, then stored on a password-secured drive. Each class was assigned to either one of two conditions via classroom randomization to prevent treatment diffusion between conditions. When interacting with the game during two separate 90-min interventions, the first group (Exploring condition; $N = 60$) received only minimal guidance via broad gameplay goals (e. g., unlocking a specific app) to scaffold character understanding organically through gameplay and exploratively followed the game's inherent prompt structures. The second group (Instructed condition; $N = 46$) received explicit instructional tasks designed with their potential for cognitive activation [20] in mind to elicit as close to the same type of cognitive activation as possible to the implicit tasks given by the game's prompts. To ensure consistency across all sessions and control for instructor bias, the intervention was conducted by the same researcher in all classrooms, using a standardized protocol with fixed time allocations and scripted instructions. In tandem with video game play, students also used digital learning journals which provided written explicit instructions to Instructed or general goals to Exploring conditions. Fidelity-of-implementation as well as time-on-task and extraneous cognitive load was controlled by the researcher through the script, a timer and a detailed checklist.

To assess depth of character understanding, a competency test measured three hierarchical levels – character identification (Level 1), analysis (Level 2), and reflection (Level 3) – aligned with the empirically validated BOLIVE model of literary understanding [2]. Per level, two items were designed in order to better address and enable different phases of understanding within each level in a nuanced manner. Written student responses were qualitatively coded following a catalogue of criteria based on BOLIVE, then converted into ordinal-scale values representing progressively complex phases of competency attainment within each level. Each phase (1–5, where 1 = basic proficiency and 5 = advanced mastery) is defined in BOLIVE through precise criteria which outline the development of literary understanding from surface level processes to higher levels of abstraction and generalization. Simplified, phases for character identification (Level 1) range from naming explicitly mentioned characters (phase 1) across conceptualizing implicit categories among a narrative's character roster (phase 3) to pointing out changing categories and relations across the whole narrative (phase 5). For character analysis (Level 2), differentiation ranges from reproducing explicitly mentioned characteristics (phase 1) to drawing differentiated conclusions from diverse sources of information (phase 3) and peaks with coherent characterization considering explicit and implicit information (phase 5). Lastly, reflecion (Level 3) codes range from expressing unsubstantiated statements regarding a character (phase 1) to substantiating one's opinion based on diverse information (phase 3) and, finally, reflecting upon a character's design while accounting for their narrative function (phase 5).

An item response such as "Sam / Alice / Melissa / Phil / [Parents]"[3] (Sample Ab18, Item 1) is accordingly coded as identification phase 1, as only explicitly mentioned characters are being named, while a response such as "[Good relationship with Alice, because she accepts Samira]" (Sample Ad7, Item 2) indicates achievement of identification phase 3, categorizing a "good" relationship between characters via the category of "accepting". This assessment framework and the catalogue of criteria adapted from it to match the study format permit accurate distinction between the achieved phases when evaluating student responses. Testing for reliability (sample: 192 items; 15.09% of total), weighted Cohen's kappa shows substantial agreement between two raters with $\kappa = .754$). This mixed-methods approach allowed quantification of competency levels and phases, enabling statistical comparison of learning outcomes between condition, while preserving nuanced cognitive processes evident in open-ended responses.

---

[3] Parts in brackets are translated for this paper from German to English to improve legibility.

3.2 Study Results

Because the data violates the equality of variances assumption, assessed via Levene's test, on the levels of analysis ($p < .001$) and of reflection ($p = .012$), and also is not normally distributed, Shapiro-Wilk revealing $p < .001$ across both conditions and all levels, we reported the Welch's t-test results to ensure robustness of our analysis. Each test was conducted with the alternative hypothesis assuming that the Exploring condition would perform better than the Instructed condition. The study revealed differentiated effects of game-guided vs. instruction-guided learning across hierarchical levels of character understanding.

Firstly, no significant condition effect emerged for character identification, which involves surface-level information processing, specifically the identification of characters and their narrative relationships through increasing abstraction [2, pp. 62–65]. Looking at the learners' maximum values attained, both the Exploring condition ($M = 2.75$, $SD = 0.816$) and the Instructed condition ($M = 2.65$, $SD = .674$) achieved comparable proficiency levels, with no significant impact of condition ($t(103.382) = 0.676$, *Cohen's d* $= 0.131$, $p = 0.250$, *95% CI* $[-0.192, \infty]$).

However, notable advantages were observed for higher-order competencies. The results show significant, medium-to-large effects on character analysis ($t(103.2) = 3.243$, *Cohen's d* $= 0.628$, $p < 0.001$, *95% CI* $[0.296, \infty]$), with the Exploring Condition ($M = 2.400$, $SD = 0.616$) outperforming the Instructed Condition ($M = 2.043$, $SD = 0.515$). This second level of character understanding entails more complex cognitive processes of differentiating and integrating diverse types of information about characters, as well as drawing conclusions regarding the characters' personas [2, pp. 66–68].

Smaller but statistically significant effects were likewise detected for character reflection ($t(103.998) = 2.498$, *Cohen's d* $= 0.481$, $p = 0.007$, $SE = 0.201$, *95% CI* $[0.143, \infty]$; Exploring Condition: $M = 2.433$, $SD = 0.909$; Instructed Condition: $M = 2.043$, $SD = 0.698$), requiring learners to position themselves critically toward characters and evaluate characters' portrayal in relation to their respective narrative functions [2, pp. 69–71]. This result indicates that the game's prompts also enhanced cognitive engagement with the design of its protagonist in light of their narrative function.

Interpretation of Results
These study results suggest that while game mechanics may not outperform traditional instruction for surface-level recognition, their inherent scaffolding more effectively supports complex literary reasoning. It can be concluded, then, that the intervention achieved significant positive effects in the game-guided condition regarding higher-level cognitive processes in analysing and reflecting upon characters, e. g., the analysis and derivation of character traits based on obtained information or the critical evaluation of their narrative construction.

It must be noted that because the empirical study examines a specific facet of literary learning through exemplary game-based scaffolding, its context- and subject-bound design necessitates cautious generalization. The findings are primarily transferable to literary education settings where interactive game elements align closely with curricular goals. Future research should assess whether the identified efficacy of narrative prompts extends to other video game formats and examples, and different learning objectives across subjects. It would also be desirable for future research to be conducted with an additional condition using a digital environment with surface-level and structural equivalence, but no game mechanics (e.g. a specifically developed software variant that doesn't require unlocking certain apps). This would grant further insight accounting for construct equivalence and cognitive load, which the external instructions may have impacted. Such investigations could clarify the boundary conditions of game-guided cognitive activation while advancing evidence for scalable implementation.

4 Conclusion

This article argued that game-based learning offers significant potential for classroom integration due to the inherent structures of digital games, such as their embedded prompt systems. These design features can create engaging, interactive learning environments that established learning media such as print-based content don't inherently provide. For optimal educational impact, careful attention must be paid to ensuring that in-game prompts maintain clear and meaningful connections to the intended learning objectives – a crucial consideration for both educators selecting games and developers designing them for learning purposes. When this alignment is achieved, empirical evidence strongly suggests that digital games can effectively motivate students to explore learning materials and engage in deeper cognitive processing. By doing so, we can sustainably enrich the repertoire of instructional media, offering learners more dynamic and immersive pathways to knowledge acquisition.

Acknowledgments. This study was conducted as part of the Di.ge.LL Graduate College, a collaborative initiative of the Freiburg University of Education, Freiburg University, and the Freiburg Advanced Center of Education (FACE), funded by the Baden-Württemberg Ministerium für Wissenschaft, Forschung und Kunst. It was conceptualized and designed with guidance by the Zentrum für didaktische Computerspielforschung (ZfdC).

References

1. Boelmann, J.M., König, L., Stechel, J.: Warum Computerspiele eine eigene Didaktik brauchen. In: Standke, J. (ed.): Spiele(n) in der Gegenwartskultur. Medien und Praktiken des Spiel(en)s im literatur- und mediendidaktischen Kontext. S, pp. 129–140. Trier (2022)
2. Boelmann, J.M., König, L.: Literarische Kompetenz messen, literarische Bildung fördern. Das BOLIVE-Modell. Empirische Forschung in der Deutschdidaktik Bd. 5, Schneider Hohengehren, Baltmannsweiler (2021)
3. Boelmann, J.M.: Literarisches Verstehen mit narrativen Computerspielen. Eine empirische Studie zu den Potenzialen der Vermittlung von literarischer Bildung und literarischer Kompetenz mit einem schüleraffinen Medium. Medien im Deutschunterricht, Beiträge zur Forschung 13, kopaed, München (2015)
4. Bopp, M.: Immersive Didaktik und Framingprozesse in Computerspielen. Ein handlungstheoretischer Ansatz. In: Neitzel, B., Nohr, R.F. (eds.): Das Spiel mit dem Medium. Partizipation – Immersion – Interaktion, pp. 169–185. Marburg, Schüren (2006) https://doi.org/10.25969/mediarep/14267

5. de Freitas, S.: Are games effective learning tools? a review of educational games. J. Educ. Technol. Soc. **21**(2), 74–84 (2018)

6. Flores-Gallegos, R., Mayer, R.: Learning cognitive skills by playing video games at home: testing the specific transfer of general skills theory. J. Cogn. Enhancement, **6**(4), 485–495 (2022) https://doi.org/10.1007/s41465-022-00253-8

7. Fu, F., Su, R., Yu, S.: EGameFlow: a scale to measure learners' enjoyment of e-learning games. Comput. Educ. **52**(1), 101–112. Elsevier Ltd. (2009) https://doi.org/10.1016/j.com pedu.2008.07.004

8. Gee, J.P.: What Video Games Have to Teach us about Learning and Literacy. Palgrave Macmillan, New York (2003) https://doi.org/10.1145/950566.9505953

9. Hattie, J.: Visible learning. The sequel. a synthesis of over 2,100 meta-analyses relating to achievement. First edition. Routledge, Tayler & Francis Group, London/New York (2023) https://doi.org/10.4324/9781003380542

10. Ilić, J., Ivanovic, M., Milicevic, A.: Effects of digital game-based learning in STEM education on students' motivation: a systematic literature review. J. Baltic Sci. Educ. **23**(1), 20–36. https://doi.org/10.33225/jbse/24.23.20

11. Klieme, E., Rakoczy, K.: Empirische Unterrichtsforschung und Fachdidaktik. Outcome-orientierte Messung und Prozessqualität des Unterrichts. In: Zeitschrift für Pädagogik, vol. 54, pp. 222–237 (2008) https://doi.org/10.25656/01:4348

12. Leuders, T., Holzäpfel, L.: Kognitive Aktivierung im Mathematikunterricht. Unterrichtswissenschaft **39**, 213–230. Juventa, Weinheim (2011)

13. Mayer, R.E.: Cognitive theory of multimedia learning. In: Mayer, R. E. (ed.): The Cambridge handbook of multimedia learning, pp. 31–48. Cambridge University Press, Cambridge (2005) https://doi.org/10.1017/CBO9780511816819.004

14. Medienpädagogischer Forschungsverbund Südwest: JIM-Studie 2024. Jugend, Information, Medien. Basisuntersuchung zum Medienumgang 12- bis 19-jähriger (2024)

15. Plass, J., Homer, B., Kinzer, C.: Foundations of game-based learning. Educ. Psychol. **50**(4), 258–283 (2015) https://doi.org/10.1080/00461520.2015.1122533

16. Reinhold, F., et al.: Learning mechanisms explaining learning with digital tools in educational settings: a cognitive process framework. Educ. Psychol. Rev. **36**, 14 (2024) https://doi.org/10.1007/s10648-024-09845-6

17. Sabourin, J., Lester, J.: Affect and engagement in game-based learning environments. IEEE Trans Affective Comput. **5**, 45–56 (2014) https://doi.org/10.1109/T-AFFC.2013.27

18. Squire, K.: Video games in education. Comput. Entertainment **2**(1), 49–62 (2003)

19. Tomasek, T.: Critical reading: using reading prompts to promote active engagement with text. Int. J. Teach. Learn. High. Educ. **21**(1), 127–132 (2009)

20. Winkler, I.: Cognitive activation in L1 literature classes: a content-specific framework for the description of teaching quality. L1-Educ. Stud. Lang. Literat. **20**(1), 1–32 (2020) https://doi.org/10.17239/L1ESLL-2020.20.01.03

21. Zeitlhofer, I., Hörmann, S., Mann, B., Hallinger, K., Zumbach, J.: Effects of cognitive and metacognitive prompts on learning performance in digital learning environments. Knowledge **3**(2), 277–292 (2023) https://doi.org/10.3390/knowledge3020019

MLopoly: A Machine Learning "Mod"

Seyed Mahdi Seyedishandiz[1(✉)] [iD], Amirmohammad Dalvand[1] [iD],
Sina Gholami Fashkhami[1] [iD], Amirali Hoseinnatajaghamaleki[1] [iD],
Chiara Eva Catalano[2] [iD], and Francesco Bellotti[1] [iD]

[1] Department of Electrical, Electronic and Telecommunication Engineering (DITEN),
University of Genova, Genova, Italy
mahdiseyyedi98@gmail.com

[2] Istituto di Matematica Applicata e Tecnologie Informatiche (CNR IMATI) – Genova, Genova,
Italy

Abstract. As machine learning (ML) instruction is dramatically widened its audience, new tools and methods are needed to allow an effective comprehension also by students without a strong mathematic/programming background, who may have more difficulty in districting among the fundamental theoretical concepts. To address this gap, we propose MLopoly, a Monopoly-inspired serious game designed to support interactive and experiential learning of core ML topics. The game maps decision-making challenges across realistic scenarios (e.g., restaurant, farm, bank) where players iteratively build, tune, and evaluate ML models. Game mechanics such as property upgrades, rent calculations, and challenge cards are directly tied to players' performance on ML tasks. We discuss game design, gameplay dynamics and implementation issues, A preliminary validation study has been carried out conducting a 20-item questionnaire based on Bloom's Taxonomy and Attention, Relevance, Confidence, and Satisfaction (ARCS) Motivation Model to assess learning and motivation. Results indicate that MLopoly offers an engaging, low-barrier environment for understanding and applying ML, also encouraging disciplinary deepening of the covered topics.

Keywords: Serious game design · Machine Learning teaching Decision Trees · Monopoly · Hyperparameter Tuning

1 Introduction

As Machine Learning (ML) has become a highly-valued and attractive academic discipline, state of the art gaming technologies offer an opportunity to motivate, introduce and support students, complementing instructional tools and methods [1, 2]. An abstract and technical approach to fundamental concepts (e.g., classification, model training, overfitting, and hyperparameter tuning) may be overwhelming for beginners and discourage engagement, forming a barrier to the discipline.

By embedding gameplay elements such as challenges, feedback, choice, and immersion into the learning process, serious games create an experiential and motivating context for grasping complex ideas [3]. This approach is valuable for STEM disciplines,

S. Bakkes et al. (Eds.): GALA 2025, LNCS 16307, pp. 126–135, 2026.
https://doi.org/10.1007/978-3-032-11043-5_13

as learners benefit from safe, iterative experimentation and the ability to visualize and manipulate key concepts in action.

We introduce MLopoly, a Monopoly-inspired serious board game designed to teach fundamental ML concepts, the first release focuses on the Decision Tree algorithm - through interactive gameplay. MLopoly aims to become a pleasant tool, useful for students by allowing them to directly engage with fundamental, abstract concepts like model complexity, data splitting, overfitting, and hyperparameter tuning in a playful and intuitive environment. To advance in the game, players are called to manage a thorough machine learning workflow process, progressing through data collection, training, validation, and testing phases, tuning their models and observing performance across various application scenarios.

MLopoly uses tangible metaphors to make abstract ML concepts concretely applicable and meaningful. For example, players acquire and upgrade model "properties", use Decision Cards to adjust model parameters, and earn performance scores as feedback. In this way, the game leverages the motivational and cognitive benefits of game-based learning to improve understanding and retention of ML concepts. In the following, we present the design rationale, implementation, and evaluation of MLopoly. Submitting a questionnaire based on Bloom's Taxonomy and Attention, Relevance, Confidence, and Satisfaction (ARCS) Motivation Model, we assessed the game effectiveness in helping players internalize key ML principles through structured gameplay and compelling decision-making.

2 Related Work

Typical ML education - often lecture- or code-based – may be too abstract and difficult, particularly for students without strong programming or math backgrounds [1]. To address these limitations, researchers have increasingly explored serious games as engaging alternatives for teaching AI and ML concepts.

One example is the Learn to Machine Learn project by Voulgari et al. [1], which developed ArtBot [4], a narrative-based game that introduces supervised and reinforcement learning to younger students. ArtBot emphasizes algorithmic transparency and student engagement through interactive, visually guided feedback and simplified decision trees.

Other games, like ViPER [5], also aim to foster AI literacy but tend to abstract away algorithmic detail, offering limited direct interaction with parameters or evaluation metrics [1]. As a result, key applied concepts such as hyperparameter tuning, model evaluation (e.g., F1-score, RMSE), or regression/classification strategies remain underexplored in current ML game-based curricula.

Beyond digital platforms, Monopoly-style board games have been adapted to educational settings, such as psychology and finance, to facilitate learning through structured play [6, 7]. Among these, REV-OPOLY [8] stands out for incorporating Augmented Reality and multiplayer elements to enhance engagement and knowledge retention. Students reported high satisfaction and improved outcomes compared to traditional revision methods [7].

Building on these foundations, MLopoly is introduced as a serious board game designed to teach core ML concepts, particularly decision trees, through scenario-based challenges (e.g., restaurant, bank, farm). Unlike prior work, MLopoly integrates active hyperparameter control (e.g., max_depth, min_samples_split), iterative model testing, and domain-specific feedback mechanisms. It distinguishes itself from ArtBot by enabling deeper model tuning, and from REV-OPOLY by embedding evaluation metrics and diagnostic feedback into its gameplay loop. In doing so, MLopoly addresses a critical gap in ML education: providing students not just with conceptual familiarity, but hands-on, structured experience in model development and tuning within an accessible game format.

3 Game Design & Methodology

3.1 Game Structure and Metaphor

Each side of the board is explicitly linked to a specific business domain (restaurants, farms, supermarkets, banks) (See Fig. 1), and each domain is directly associated with both a machine learning task and the tuning of a particular hyperparameter. For example, the restaurant side involves a regression task where the key focus is adjusting the max_depth parameter of a decision tree.

This mapping was designed to provide players with concrete challenges while simultaneously linking gameplay to the effect of hyperparameters on different ML tasks. In this way, each business context serves not just as a thematic setting, but as an accessible metaphor to illustrate how changes in model configuration impact performance outcomes. All sides with their machine learning task and particular hyperparameter are listed below:

- Regression with max_depth (restaurants)
- Classification with max_depth (farms)
- Regression with min_samples_split (supermarkets)
- Classification with min_samples_split (banks)

The ownership and upgrade systems are directly tied to how well the player understands and applies machine learning concepts. Performance is not based on luck or capital alone, but on measurable understanding and practical modeling decisions.

MLopoly simulates a machine learning workflow, embedding regression and classification tasks into the different domain-themed tiles. When landing on a tile, players are presented with a structured ML problem relevant to the domain, either a regression (e.g., predicting customer return frequency based on features) or classification task (e.g., predicting crop success based on soil and rainfall conditions).

Each challenge prompts players to build and tune a Decision Tree model (See Fig. 2), initially with default hyperparameters (e.g., max_depth = 2). Based on their decisions, the game provides immediate feedback using performance metrics relevant to the task type, such as RMSE for regression or F1-score/confusion matrix for classification. (Fig. 3).

This feedback guides players to iterate on their model design by adjusting hyperparameters like max_depth or min_samples_split.

Performance improvements (e.g., a reduced RMSE or improved recall) unlock in-game rewards, including model upgrades, property enhancements, or rent multiplier, mechanically linking model quality with economic advantage in gameplay. In parallel,

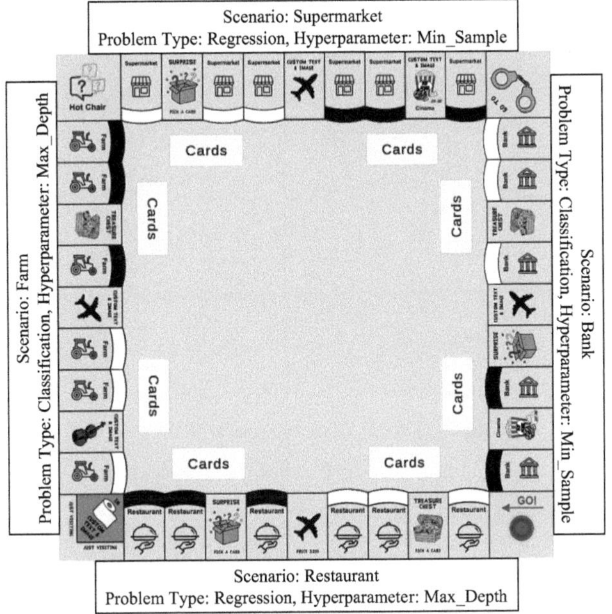

Fig. 1. The MLopoly board

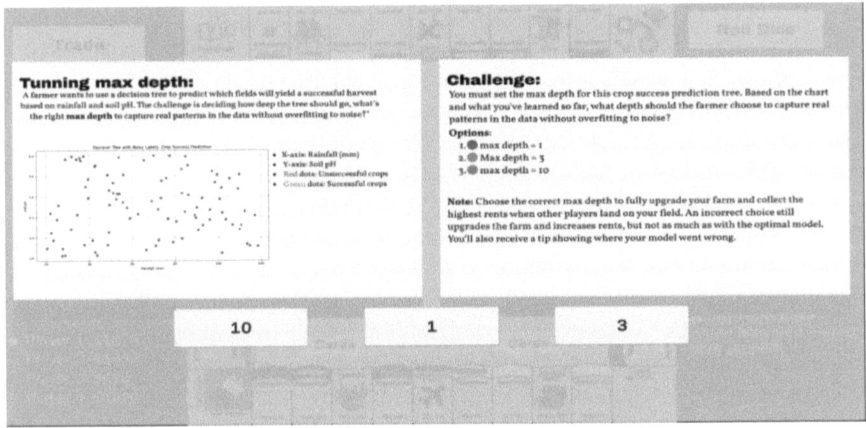

Fig. 2. Tuning hyperparameters through Q&A

short conceptual challenges (e.g., multiple-choice questions on evaluation metrics) allow players to consolidate understanding and earn strategic bonuses.

The game structure encourages experimental learning, where players iteratively refine models and observe the trade-offs involved in ML design decisions, such as overfitting due to excessive depth or misclassification caused by shallow models. These mechanics make abstract concepts like generalization and metric-based optimization more tangible and retainable through repeated play.

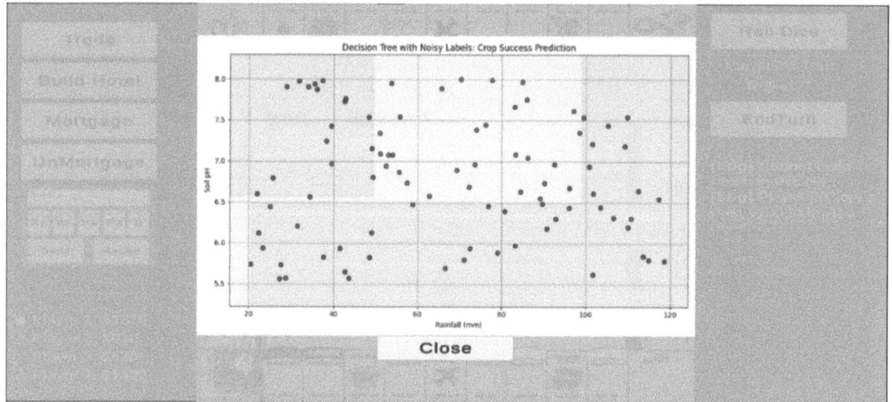

Fig. 3. Feedback on the player's choices

3.2   Learning Approach and Content

The core educational content centers on the Decision Tree algorithm, selected for its interpretability and pedagogical accessibility. Within the game, players engage with the structure and logic of decision trees, including the role of nodes, splits, and leaf predictions—as they iteratively build models on regression and classification problems.

A major instructional focus is placed on hyperparameter tuning, especially max_depth and min_samples_split, as these directly influence the trade-off between model complexity and generalization. Players are required to make tuning decisions based on the behavior of their model on simulated validation data, thereby experiencing firsthand the bias-variance trade-off in action. For example, increasing max_depth may improve performance on training data, but risks overfitting, a tension visualized through changing game outcomes such as fluctuating rent values.

Model evaluation metrics are embedded contextually: players working with regression tasks (e.g., restaurant or supermarket scenarios) are introduced to RMSE, MSE, and R2, while those addressing classification problems (e.g., farms or banks) engage with confusion matrices, precision, recall, and F1-score. Each domain emphasizes metrics aligned with realistic concerns, for example, high recall in crop prediction (to avoid missing a productive yield) or precision in banking (to avoid false loan approvals).

The overarching pedagogical objectives of MLopoly include:

- Enabling learners to understand how decision trees generate predictions.
- Differentiating between regression and classification tasks via gameplay.
- Experimenting with hyperparameter values and observing their impact.
- Applying evaluation metrics appropriately to scenario-driven challenges.
- Reinforcing understanding through feedback loops and reflective tuning.

The pedagogical design of MLopoly is rooted in constructivist and experiential learning theory [6], which emphasizes learning through doing, reflection, and contextual engagement. This foundation supports a shift from passive absorption of ML theory to active, iterative exploration of models and metrics. One core design element is constructive alignment: the game mechanics are purposefully linked to intended learning outcomes. For instance, when players tune max_depth and observe changes in rent (reflecting model evaluation), they are actively engaging with the concept of overfitting. This alignment ensures that every game action contributes meaningfully to concept acquisition.

To facilitate scaffolded learning, the game deploys a tiered system of "Educational Cards" that gradually increases complexity. Each domain features a series of three cards that introduce core ideas sequentially beginning with model structure, followed by tuning strategies, and culminating in metric-based evaluation. This design supports progressive internalization of ML concepts and allows players to revisit and reinforce earlier material.

Feedback is contextualized through consequences in the game economy and narrative. A poorly tuned model may lead to low rental income or missed opportunities, while strong model performance (quantified via evaluation metrics) unlocks property upgrades and rewards. These mechanics simulate the stakes of real-world ML decisions and embed learning within meaningful game outcomes.

Furthermore, the game encourages learners to compare model performance over time - across different sectors and tuning strategies - promoting reflection on generalization and adaptation. For example, players may notice that deeper trees improve performance in some domains but fail in others, implicitly reinforcing the notion that model effectiveness is context dependent.

3.3   Implementation

We built MLopoly using the Unity game engine (version 2022.3.6f1 LTS) with C# scripting, leveraging Unity built-in UI, animation, and scene management system [9]. Its overall design mirrors a classic Monopoly board: each colored property set corresponds to a specific ML scenario and focuses on tuning a particular decision tree hyperparameter. This familiar board layout provides a structured framework where acquiring properties equates to engaging with different ML tasks.

Gameplay progresses as players move around the board, acquire properties, and tackle ML tasks in each domain. Owning all properties in a color group unlocks a mini ML challenge for that domain. These challenges are dataset-driven problems or multiple-choice quizzes presented through Unity UI system. To simulate model evaluation, the game provides visual feedback with decision tree diagrams and evaluation metrics. Each domain uses a unique dataset, ensuring varied data distributions and problem settings for realism. An interactive trading system is included to preserve strategic decision-making akin to classic Monopoly. Players can trade properties via an in-game menu to negotiate domain coverage. Trades execute automatically to maintain smooth game flow and prevent interruptions to the learning experience.

MLopoly emphasizes clear, consistent visual feedback to reinforce learning. Unity 2D graphics renders the Decision Tree structure and decision boundaries, and illustrates concepts like overfitting, underfitting, or well-tuned models. Gameplay interactions are event-driven using Unity event system, enabling natural actions such as dice rolls, player movement, and property management. During key decisions, context-sensitive pop-up messages explain the underlying ML mechanisms, helping players connect their in-game actions to ML outcomes. An internal simulation module computes the impact of player-selected hyperparameters on synthetic datasets. It generates mock evaluation results (performance scores, model behavior outcomes), which are dynamically shown as visual overlays and directly influence in-game consequences (e.g., adjusting in-game rewards or penalties based on model performance). One particularly engaging feature is the "Hot Chair Challenge," a timed quiz competition between two players. This head-to-head quiz tests recall and decision speed under time pressure, reinforcing key concepts in a funny, competitive way. All quizzes and outcomes are handled through a modular system, making it easy to expand content with new questions or topics.

During the game, ML concepts are introduced gradually through gameplay rather than overwhelming players with mathematical formalism upfront. Each new concept is first presented via a teaching card or scenario-specific example, allowing players to learn incrementally. Hyperparameter tuning, for example, is transformed from an abstract idea into a tangible game mechanic with clear consequences: players see how tuning affects their "model" and game progress, reinforcing its importance through immediate feedback and iterative practice.

4 Experimental Results

To evaluate MLopoly effectiveness we conducted a mixed-methods user study combining in-game behavioral metrics with a post-game questionnaire [3]. The study was grounded in two widely recognized educational frameworks targeting mid-level cognitive skills: Bloom's Revised Taxonomy [10, 11] and the ARCS Motivation Model [12]. We designed a 21-item Likert-scale questionnaire, aimed at assessing perceived learning (Part A) and motivational engagement (Part B). Additionally, three open-ended questions allowed participants to share reflections on the game design, usability, and educational impact. The full list of questions is shown in Table 1. Also, all the questions and results are accessible through [13].

The study involved university students, with various academic backgrounds. In total, 24 participants took part in the study (10 females, 14 males), with an average age of 27 years. While all had basic math knowledge, their prior exposure to ML varied, allowing us to observe how MLopoly performs across different levels of experience.

Before each session, participants received a short introduction to ML concepts (e.g., decision trees, terminology of training/validation/test data) to ensure a smoother start with the game.

Results (Fig. 4) show strong alignment between the game objectives and self-reported learning. For instance, 83% of participants agreed or strongly agreed that they could recall key ML concepts about Decision Trees (Q1). Over 75% of the respondents reported better understanding of hyperparameter distinctions (Q2) and data partitioning (Q7). Around 70% stated they could now explain the effect of decision tree hyperparameters like max_depth and min_samples_split (Q8) and identify issues like overfitting and underfitting (Q4). These outcomes were supported by qualitative comments such as: "I now understand how depth affects accuracy," and "The decisions I made in the game helped me see how models learn."

ARCS-related items showed high engagement. Over 80% of participants agreed that the game was enjoyable and maintained their attention (Q11, Q12). Around 70% found the content relevant and felt satisfied with their progress (Q13, Q17, Q18). Most felt

Table 1. Questionnaire

ID	Text
Q 1	I can recall key concepts about decision trees after playing the game.
Q 2	The game helped me understand the difference between parameters and hyperparameters.
Q 3	I was able to apply the knowledge from the game to real-world examples.
Q 4	I can identify whether a model is underfitting, overfitting, or well-fitted.
Q 5	I feel confident evaluating the performance of a machine learning model.
Q 6	I feel able to build a basic decision tree with the knowledge I gained.
Q 7	The game helped me recognize the purpose of training, validation, and test data.
Q 8	I can explain the effect of hyperparameters like max_depth and min_samples_split.
Q 9	I now understand how machine learning can be used in different domains.
Q 10	I was able to reason about how the model made decisions during the game.
Q 11	The game grabbed my attention and kept me focused.
Q 12	The game content was interesting and enjoyable.
Q 13	I found the game's content relevant to my learning goals.
Q 14	I saw a clear connection between game mechanics and machine learning concepts.
Q 15	I felt capable of completing the game tasks.
Q 16	The difficulty level of the game was appropriate for my skills.
Q 17	I was satisfied with what I learned through the game.
Q 18	I felt a sense of accomplishment after finishing the game.
Q 19	I would be interested in learning other topics through similar games.
Q 20	This game encouraged me to explore more about machine learning after the session.
Q 21	I was able to make meaningful choices in the game that affected my learning outcome.

confident completing the tasks (Q15), though some expressed uncertainty in interpreting complex visuals (Q16), highlighting areas for improving the interface.

Open-ended feedback highlighted the usefulness of visual aids, challenge cards, and incremental decision-making. Some participants suggested shortening the overall game duration and introducing a clearer onboarding process, especially for those unfamiliar with ML terminology.

Additional feedback emphasized how MLopoly translated abstract ML topics into compelling contextualized challenges. Many respondents appreciated how challenge cards and sector-specific tasks improved retention. Visual elements such as performance metrics and outcomes of choices were cited as particularly helpful. Some participants

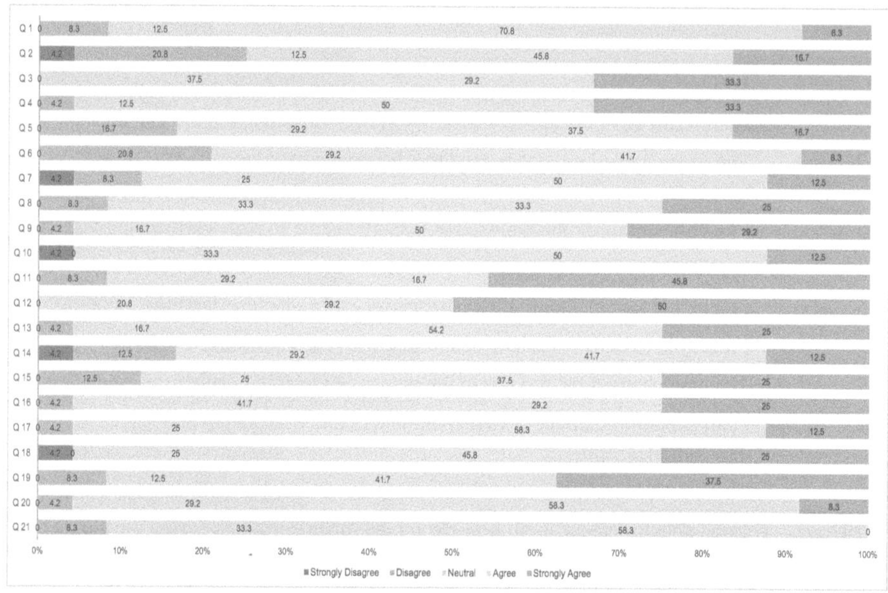

Fig. 4. Break-down of the responses to the questionnaire

also noted the need for better pacing and clearer feedback during tuning tasks, suggesting concrete improvements for future iterations.

Overall, the questionnaire suggests the strong potential of MLopoly as a complementary educational tool. The combination of structured gameplay, visual feedback, and scenario-driven challenges supported both cognitive learning and motivational engagement. While some usability aspects should be refined, the study suggests that MLopoly can support ML instruction by providing a pleasant context where students can play in teams while applying and practicing with disciplinarily rigorous concepts.

5   Conclusion & Future Work

This study explored the potential of game-based learning to address the challenges of teaching foundational machine learning concepts. We introduced MLopoly, a serious game inspired by Monopoly, designed to teach key ML principles through scenario-driven gameplay and interactive decision-making.

Our findings suggest that MLopoly effectively enhances learner engagement and facilitates conceptual understanding, particularly for those with limited prior exposure to machine learning or programming. While our evaluation was limited in scale, both qualitative and quantitative feedback indicate that the game offers a compelling ancillary tool for disciplinary instruction and motivation.

The current implementation of MLopoly was limited to Decision Trees. However, thanks to the modular design, the board and mechanics can be easily reskinned to address additional ML concepts, such as Random Forests and Neural Networks, thus extending the scope of the game.

In addition to broader content coverage, further future directions include increased adaptability to different learner levels (e.g. personalized feedback) and the exploration of AR or web-based versions for easier usage. A more ambitious goal is scaling the game framework to other academic domains beyond machine learning, while improving instruction quality and fun.

References

1. Voulgari, I., Zammit, M., Stouraitis, E., Liapis, A., Yannakakis, G.: Learn to machine learn: designing a game based approach for teaching machine learning to primary and secondary education students. In: Proceedings of the 20th Annual ACM Interaction Design and Children Conference, pp. 593–598. Association for Computing Machinery, New York, NY, USA (2021). https://doi.org/10.1145/3459990.3465176
2. Zammit, M., Voulgari, I., Liapis, A., Yannakakis, G.: Learn to machine learn via games in the classroom. Front. Educ. **7**, 913530 (2022). https://doi.org/10.3389/feduc.2022.913530
3. Gundersen, S.W., Lampropoulos, G.: Using serious games and digital games to improve students' computational thinking and programming skills in K-12 education: a systematic literature review. Technologies **13**, 113 (2025). https://doi.org/10.3390/technologies13030113
4. von Davier, T.S., Larsen, A.J.H., Van Kleek, M., Shadbolt, N.: ArtBot: an exploration into AI's potential for guiding art analysis. In: Proceedings of the Extended Abstracts of the CHI Conference on Human Factors in Computing Systems, pp. 1–11. Association for Computing Machinery, New York, NY, USA (2025). https://doi.org/10.1145/3706599.3720181
5. Aissi, M., Grislain, C., Chetouani, M., Sigaud, O., Soulier, L., Thome, N.: VIPER: Visual Perception and Explainable Reasoning for Sequential Decision-Making (2025). https://doi.org/10.48550/arXiv.2503.15108
6. Schumacher, C.: Cognitive, metacognitive and motivational perspectives on learning analytics: synthesizing self-regulated learning, assessment, and feedback with Learning Analytics. https://madoc.bib.uni-mannheim.de/53712. Accessed 24 July 2025
7. Alam, A.: A digital game based learning approach for effective curriculum transaction for teaching-learning of artificial intelligence and machine learning. In: 2022 International Conference on Sustainable Computing and Data Communication Systems (ICSCDS), pp. 69–74 (2022). https://doi.org/10.1109/ICSCDS53736.2022.9760932
8. Nordin, N., Mohd. Nordin, N.R., Omar, W.: REV-OPOLY: a study on educational board game with web-based augmented reality. AJUE **18**, 81 (2022). https://doi.org/10.24191/ajue.v18i1.17172
9. Borromeo, N.A.: Hands-On Unity 2022 Game Development: Learn to Use the Latest Unity 2022 Features to Create Your First Video Game in the Simplest Way Possible. Packt Publishing Ltd., Birmingham (2022)
10. Gogus, A.: Bloom's taxonomy of learning objectives. In: Seel, N.M. (ed.) Encyclopedia of the Sciences of Learning, pp. 469–473. Springer, Boston, MA (2012). https://doi.org/10.1007/978-1-4419-1428-6_141
11. Bloom's Taxonomy of Educational Objectives. https://teaching.charlotte.edu/services-programs/teaching-guides/course-design/blooms-educational-objectives/
12. Keller's ARCS Model | EBSCO Research Starters. https://www.ebsco.com/research-starters/social-sciences-and-humanities/kellers-arcs-model
13. SinaGholami/MLOPOLY: This is the Result and questionnaire of MLOPOLY article. https://github.com/SinaGholami/MLOPOLY

Game Design Track

DOZER: A Toy Model of Coastal Hazard Mitigation During a Storm

Eli D. Lazarus$^{(\boxtimes)}$ (iD)

School of Geography and Environmental Science, Environmental Dynamics Lab,
University of Southampton, Southampton, UK
E.D.Lazarus@soton.ac.uk

Abstract. Motivated by observations of emergency road-maintenance crews in coastal settings, DOZER is a video game in which the player uses a bulldozer to clear sand from a beachfront road during a storm. DOZER is also a toy model in a formal sense: a heuristic tool for insight into the dynamics of real-time intervention in the physical processes of a natural hazard. Here, I introduce DOZER as both a game and a numerical model, and demonstrate its utility for exploring divergence between a human-altered environmental system and its natural counterpart. I also situate the mechanics of DOZER in the broader context of game design principles and philosophy. For models of systems in which adaptation is an important dynamic, ceding control of adaptive behaviours to a human player can enable novel model outcomes that random, probabilistic, deterministic, or genetic-programming approaches may not produce.

Keywords: Agent-based model · Rhetoric of failure · Coastal hazard

1 Introduction

Some road crews plow snow; others plow sand. Beachfront roads are vulnerable to disruption from flooding and sediment deposition by coastal storms [1]. Tasked with maintaining the functionality of road networks as critical infrastructure, emergency road crews in low-lying coastal settings will use fleets of heavy machinery–front-end loaders, bulldozers, graders–to clear sediment washed or blown onto roadways [1,2]. Crews may work intensively while a storm is in progress, plowing sediment back into the fronting dune even as water and sediment courses around their vehicles [3]. Such work constitutes a deliberate, enigmatic, and distinctly anthropic process of sediment transport [4]. Mechanised sediment transport during storm events remains unmeasured, and falls outside the scope of leading numerical models used to investigate, simulate, and predict physical change along low-lying coastal landscapes [3].

Plowing sand during a storm makes the intervention a synchronous morphodynamic process. Morphodynamics refers to changes in the physical landscape that develop as a function of feedbacks between fluid flow, topography, erosion,

© The Author(s), under exclusive license to Springer Nature Switzerland AG 2026
S. Bakkes et al. (Eds.): GALA 2025, LNCS 16307, pp. 139–149, 2026.
https://doi.org/10.1007/978-3-032-11043-5_14

and deposition. Topography directs flow, which affects spatial patterns of erosion and deposition, which reshape topography, which redirects flow. Using a bulldozer to intervene in active storm-driven deposition means that the bulldozer and storm-driven flow become morphodynamically coupled: each affects, and is affected by, the pathways and patterns of flow and deposition shaped by the other. Modelling these dynamics are not limited by their physics. Rather, to model a bulldozer as an agent of morphodynamic change requires representing the behavioural agency of a bulldozer operator.

To this end, I introduce DOZER, a single-player video game in which the player guides a bulldozer to plow sand getting washed onto a beachfront road (Fig. 1). Although stylised as a retro arcade game, DOZER is also an exploratory numerical model of deliberate, synchronous intervention into storm-driven coastal processes. DOZER can be typified as a participatory agent-based model [5,6], inasmuch as the model relies on the participation of a human player: rather than affect adaptive agent behaviour through an abstracted genetic algorithm [7,8], the player handles those adaptive mechanisms directly. I use ensemble model results from my own game play to show how DOZER functions both as a game and as a heuristic tool for dynamical insight. While DOZER can be played casually, its intended audience is researchers, practitioners, and students in coastal science or hazard science. I situate DOZER in the broader context of game design principles and philosophy: specifically, rhetoric of failure, sources of uncertainty, persuasive versus serious games, and retro nostalgia. I also speculate on the potential for applying this kind of modelling to other human-altered environmental systems in which adaptive behaviour is an important dynamic.

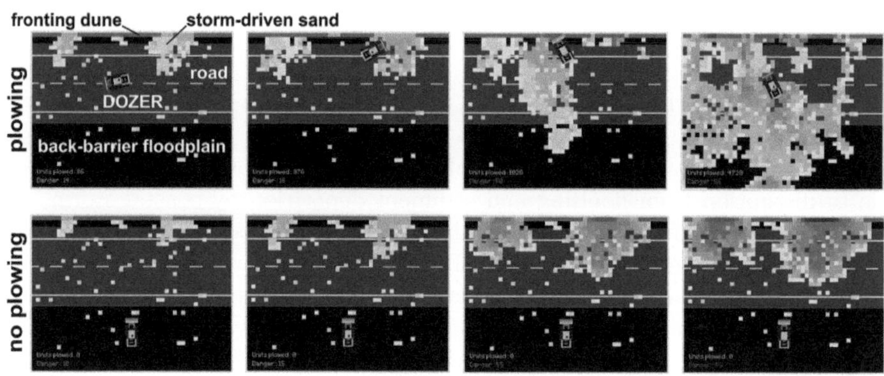

Fig. 1. Screenshots from DOZER. Upper time series shows DOZER plowing back pulses of storm-driven sand. Lower time series illustrates evolution of the game domain under the same forcing conditions without any intervention by the player.

2   Method

2.1   Physical Geographical Context

The setting for DOZER is a sandy coastal barrier. Characterised by a shoreface, beach, dune crest, and back-barrier floodplain, coastal barriers are found all over the world. An essential mechanism by which barrier systems maintain their height and width relative to sea level is a process called overwash [9]. Typically triggered when water is pushed over the barrier during storms, overwash is a shallow cross-shore flow that transports sediment from the beach to the back-barrier floodplain. The sedimentary deposit that overwash leaves behind is called washover. Where washover deposition on a human-altered barrier is deliberately prevented or removed, theory suggests that with sea-level rise the barrier will tend to lose sediment volume over time, becoming more sensitive to storm impacts in the short term and possible drowning in the long term [3]. This tension between dependence upon and vulnerability to extreme weather is intrinsic to the persistence of human-altered barriers, and underpins the premise of DOZER.

2.2   Model Design

Lazarus [10] details how the physical processes of overwash and washover are represented in DOZER. Here, I summarise the mechanics of the model that are most relevant to game play.

Domain. Discretised in a grid, the DOZER domain represents a plan-view reach of back-barrier floodplain. The beach is not modelled, nor is the landward edge of the floodplain. The dune is treated as a "one-line" slice in the alongshore dimension, visible to the player as a single row of coloured cells across the top of the domain. The shade of a cell occupied by sand conveys its relative volume: darker shades of brown represent deeper sand; empty cells are black. The model does not include any explicit dependence on grain size, but the version described here assumes a sandy barrier. A two-lane road spans the upper half of the domain, but is only aesthetic.

Overwash Flow and Washover Deposition. DOZER draws on research indicating that overwash sites may organise into spatial patterns by competing with near neighbours for capture of forcing flow [11,12]. In its initial state, the model has a fronting dune of uniform height alongshore, which overwash punches through. A game typically has three or four overwash sites, spaced at quasi-regular intervals, each associated with a proportion of flow capture. Overwash sites, their relative spacing, and their proportions of flow capture are determined by a subroutine using watersheds of directed random walks [10,13].

Overwash is delivered from the top of the domain to the floodplain in pulses, which occur at randomised intervals every 3–10 s. Each pulse through an overwash site entrains sand, incrementally incising a channel through the fronting dune. Sand in the model is conserved: volume eroded from the dune is transferred to washover on the floodplain. Instead of solving hydrodynamics, the model uses a rule-based flow-routing routine to redistribute and deposit sand [2, 10]. Cumulative deposition evolves the floodplain condition, with each depositional pattern steering the next.

The top row of the screen reflects the relative integrity of the dune, serving as a kind of status bar. Reaches of dune that are intact (at or near their initial height) are a dark brown, indicative of maximum sand volume; the more deeply incised the dune is at a given cell, the redder that cell becomes. A "danger" meter at the bottom left of the domain shows the maximum incision along the dune (as a percentage of initial height). When overwash at a given site fully incises through the dune to the floodplain floor, the game ends.

Bulldozer Agent. When the game begins, DOZER sits idle, centred in the bottom third of the screen. The player controls the actions of the bulldozer using keyboard inputs. The bulldozer can move forward or backward, and rotate in a full circle to the right or left. The player also determines whether the plow blade of the bulldozer is up or down. Player inputs are nonexclusive, so that the bulldozer can travel, turn, and plow simultaneously. If the bulldozer is traveling forward with the blade down and encounters a sandy cell, the volume of sand at that cell is subtracted from the floodplain and added to the plow blade. The blade can collect and push sand up to a maximum volume (i.e., the blade capacity), beyond which the blade stays full but skims over the floodplain surface without picking up any more sand. Sand stays on the blade until the player deposits it by raising (releasing) the plow. The bulldozer cannot push sand off the edges of the domain. The start screen provides instructions for how to operate DOZER, but the player is given no explicit directive or objective. There are no fixed rules of play for bulldozer operation.

Process Coupling. Coupling between overwash flow, washover deposition, and DOZER actions (i.e., morphodynamic coupling) is affected in two ways. The first is expressed on the floodplain. By altering the shape of the washover deposits as they develop, plowing reorients local flow paths of steepest descent, diverting overwash flow and washover deposition into patterns different from those that would form in the absence of plowing. Floodplain coupling occurs as long as the player plows at least part of a washover deposit somewhere in the domain.

A second mode of coupling occurs if the player plows sand back into incised sections of the dune. Where partial infilling of the dune reduces or blocks subsequent overwash, forcing flow is redirected laterally and reapportioned to the nearest neighbouring overwash site (or sites). No new overwash sites are created during a game, but existing sites that DOZER closes can reactivate as the forcing flow gets redistributed. This effectively assumes that freshly infilled sections of the dune are structurally weaker. I refer to this second mode of coupling as "whack-a-mole" dynamics: plugging one incision exacerbates incision elsewhere along the fronting dune. Because the model assumes constant forcing, the storm-driven flow can be redirected but never fully stopped.

Dummy Model for Comparative Analysis. During a game of DOZER, a dummy model of the overwash and washover routines, absent the player, runs in parallel. The dummy model is not visible to the player and does not affect game play, but enables direct quantitative comparison between human-altered versus natural outcomes given the same forcing conditions.

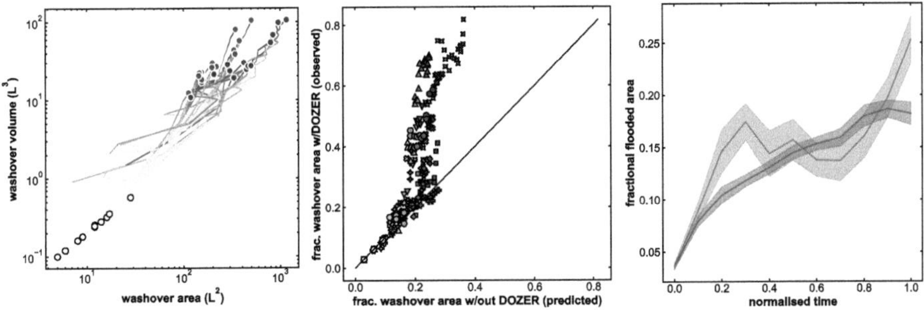

Fig. 2. Examples of analytics compiled from 10 games with different initial conditions. **a** Log-log plot of scaling relationship between washover volume and area for DOZER (red) versus the dummy model (blue). Open/closed circles show initial/final washover morphometry. Trajectories show transient states of allometric growth (see [12]); shade darkens with time elapsed. **b** Observed (DOZER) versus predicted (dummy) total washover area (as fraction of the floodplain); 1:1 reference line indicates perfect correspondence. Symbols denote different games. **c** Ensemble mean ($\pm 1SE$) of fractional flooded area versus normalised game time. Time series demonstrate impact escalation with DOZER intervention (red) relative to the dummy model (blue). (Color figure online)

3 Illustrative Analytics

Even with its rule-based simplifications of physical processes, the numerical model on which DOZER operates yields washover deposits with geometric scaling relationships like those found in real settings and laboratory experiments [2,11,12,14]. For example, washover volume changes as a function of area according to a power law (Fig. 2a). The final geometric characteristics of the deposits, and the allometric trajectories they express as they grow [12], reflect power laws of different slopes for the dummy and DOZER conditions. In the dummy model, allometric growth of deposits reflects a smooth pattern of progressive expansion, while bulldozing affects excursive departures from the expected scaling.

Tracking state variables through time illustrates divergence between what is predicted by the dummy model versus observed in the DOZER condition (Fig. 2b). Perfect correspondence between a variable predicted and observed falls on a 1:1 reference line. Although the dummy model and DOZER begin in perfect correspondence, their floodplain states soon diverge. Some variables reflect more pronounced divergence than others. For example, total depositional area exhibits an abrupt departure from predicted values, with DOZER trials resulting in approximately double the depositional area of the dummy model.

The game also produces a temporal pattern of impact escalation–a dynamical expression of divergence associated with human-altered systems prone to flooding [15, 16]. The basic form of the pattern is that interventions to limit frequent, minor hazard events unintentionally drive the human-altered system toward infrequent, major hazard events. In a real setting, this dynamic of escalation might develop over time scales of many decades or longer; here, DOZER compresses the dynamic within the time scale of a single storm (Fig. 2c).

These signatures of divergence between natural and human-altered cases hold for ensembles of games with different initial conditions (Fig. 2) and for repeat trials of the same initial condition [10]. They are also a product of DOZER being both a numerical model and a game of responsive, adaptive behaviour.

4   Discussion

4.1   Failure as a Premise

With a deliberate nod to classic arcade games like Space Invaders and Tetris, DOZER is unwinnable. The implicit objective–because the player is never given an explicit one–is the "goal of improvement" [17]: play as long as possible before the game ends. At times, DOZER can feel winnable. When two successive pulses of overwash are separated by a long interval, a player might plow enough sand without interruption to stoke the illusory possibility of a winning state. Or a player may discover that plowing sand back into the dune extends the duration of a game–except doing so triggers the "whack-a-mole" dynamics that makes the dune deterioration harder to anticipate and more catastrophic. DOZER thus employs a procedural "rhetoric of failure" [18]: whatever the player chooses to do, or how technically skilled the player is, failure is intrinsic, in that the game has no winning state. Its mechanics guarantee the inevitability of the conclusion.

4.2   Sources of Uncertainty

Within this rhetoric, DOZER leverages five "sources of uncertainty" [19]. The most fundamental is *solver's uncertainty*. Each game has the same basic elements, but the puzzle of any given game–where to plow in order to sustain play for as long as possible–is different. Even when the configuration of the overwash sites is held fixed over repeated games by the same player, subtle differences in plowing actions means that no two floodplain puzzles are exactly the same [10].

Randomness is present in two mechanics of DOZER: the initial configuration of overwash sites at the start of a game, and the time interval between overwash pulses. Neither element is completely random. Over many games, overwash locations reflect a statistical distribution of preferred spacing alongshore, analogous to real settings [11,12], but in any given game the player cannot know where in the dune the breaches will appear. Bounding the interval between successive overwash pulses (3–10 s) helps keeps the game from being metronomic, and from dragging. (A typical game of DOZER lasts just a few minutes.) Randomness in DOZER ensures that each game is different, but does not undercut the logics of game play [19].

Apart from randomness, *hidden information* is embedded in the volume of forcing flow directed through each overwash site. A player does not know *a priori* which overwash site will deliver the most washover, nor does the player get a clear sense of how plowing will affect pathways of overwash flow and washover deposition, or may redistribute forcing flow through the fronting dune.

Contending with this hidden information creates the mechanic of *analytic complexity* in DOZER. If the goal of the player is improvement [17], then analytic complexity comes in operating DOZER in a way that achieves the longest game. By diligently plugging a gap in the dune, the player may make their plowing task more unpredictable and harder. Following Costikyan [19, p. 86], the player has "only a handful of choices, but difficult ones", and is left "uncertain, even as they make a decision, that it is necessarily the correct decision to make".

Counterintuitively, the inevitability that DOZER will be overwhelmed is what sets up *narrative anticipation*. Costikyan [19, p. 95] notes that even when a narrative arc is a well-worn trope, "there is still great uncertainty on a moment-to-moment basis, and the...surprises...keep us interested". In DOZER, the player knows (after a few attempts) how the game will end, but not how or when the ending will arrive. Moment-to-moment narrative anticipation, driven by analytical complexity, builds "micro-tension" [20]: the longer a player postpones the inevitable in DOZER, the stronger the mechanics of uncertainty become.

4.3   DOZER as a Persuasive Game

The rhetoric of failure in DOZER is a contrivance of design, but unwinnability is what turns DOZER from a participatory agent-based model into a "persuasive" game [18,21]. The extent to which this rhetoric of failure might translate to real settings [22] is left for the player to think about, or not: a player can drive DOZER unaware that the game derives from a real phenomenon [3]. In the wider context of climate-driven change on low-lying sandy coastlines, perhaps using bulldozers to intervene in storm impacts is discomfitingly analogous to holding on as long as possible before the game ends [22]. But DOZER itself does not take an explicit position or pass judgement on programmes of hazard intervention, and its meaning is left ambiguous. The player always fails, but the role of failure, and of experimenting with failure, as opportunity for deep learning and critical thinking is a compelling dimension of game design [17,23–25].

In that frame, DOZER can be used as a tool for teaching, learning, and engagement regarding adaptation to climate-driven hazards and management of environmental change [26–28]: the game repository [10] includes an open code notebook of quantitative analytics and data visualisations, including those in Fig. 2, so that formal users can examine ensembles of game outcomes in a variety of ways. However, in this initial release of the game, there is no associated intended-learning outcome or specific guide for user reflection. DOZER thus is not oriented as "serious" in the sense that Abt [29, p. 9] employed: as a game with "an explicit and carefully thought-out educational purpose" or "created under the direct influence and guidance of external institutional goals" [18, p. 55]. Rather, DOZER is intended to be "persuasive" in the way that Bogost [18, p. 59] describes: as a game "whose promise lies in the possibility of using procedural rhetoric to support *or* challenge [emphasis original] our understanding of the way things in the world do or should work".

4.4   Style as Reference

The aesthetic of DOZER as a retro arcade game is both a signifier of its nostalgic "indie-ness" [30], and a reference to a period in the 1980s and early 1990s when a wave of research into nonlinear dynamics was leaning into grid-based models and cellular automata. Much of that work, back to its mainframe roots, became the corpus for models of complex adaptive systems [7,8,31]. Integrated throughout that corpus are games [21]. For example, Holland [7] recounts how at IBM in the early 1950s his then-labmate, Arthur Samuel, taught a prototype computer to play checkers [32]. Checkers, itself, was not the point: Samuel was using checkers as a simple, rule-based system to make inroads into machine learning.

That historical legacy is relevant to DOZER because representing adaptation and learning in model agent systems remains a fundamental challenge [33]. Ideally, the modeller establishes a minimal set of behavioural rules that give bounds to agent interactions but do not script them. One approach to enabling intelligent automata is to give them the mechanics of machine learning: an agent learns from and adapts to its environment (and other agents) by passing information through a genetic algorithm. An alternative approach, such as in DOZER, is to lend the model participatory mechanics [5,6]. From there, the conceptual and procedural transformation from model to game is a step, not a leap [21,34].

5   Future Work

DOZER cannot capture why a player might choose to plow sand in one area versus another, but it can record where the player moved (and when and how much they plowed), providing at least a narrow window into player behaviour [10]. The rationale for a given strategy, if there is one, will be unknown without interviewing the player. In teaching, learning, and engagement settings, the impact of the game on specific aspects of player learning and conceptual insight could be assessed with participant surveys (per ethics approval) before and after a play-centred exercise. DOZER could be used to explore how different players, and groups of players (e.g., naïve players, coastal experts, professional operators), engage with the same model condition, and what their actions collectively reveal about the emergence of strategy from moment-to-moment decisions. A multi-player format of DOZER could be used to examine the dynamics of cooperative strategies. Human players and a machine player could be tasked with a particular target for optimisation, and their approaches compared. For example, what is the most effective means of both keeping the road clear of sand and achieving the longest-possible run time? Do human and machine players converge on the same solution? The openness of the game to different strategies–regardless of what a given strategy achieves–may allow model outcomes that are otherwise inaccessible to random, probabilistic, deterministic, or even machine learning approaches to simulating adaptive behaviour. Extending the design premise of DOZER to examples of other human-altered environmental systems leaves ample room for dynamical surprises.

Acknowledgments. I am grateful to Evan Goldstein, Alida Payson, Dylan McNamara, Darren Page, Chris Cooper, Ben Weeks, Steve Darby, Justin Sheffield, Alvise Finotello, Luca Carniello, Vanissa Wanick, and James Stallwood for helpful discussions, and to Marjorie Lazarus for beta-testing. Web tutorials by Christian Koch for coding in Pygame were immensely instructive [35]. Special thanks to the Department of Geosciences at the University of Padova (Italy) and the "Shaping a World-class University" initiative. This work was supported in part by NERC grant NE/X011496/1. For the purpose of open access, the author has applied a Creative Commons attribution license (CC BY) to any Author Accepted Manuscript version arising from this submission.

Data Availability. Code, analytics, and a detailed model description are at Lazarus [10].

Disclosure of Interests. The author declares no competing interests.

References

1. Nordstrom, K.F.: Beaches and dunes of developed coasts, 2nd edn. Cambridge University Press, Cambridge, UK (2004)
2. Lazarus, E. D., Goldstein, E. B., Taylor, L. A., Williams, H. E.: Comparing patterns of hurricane washover into built and unbuilt environments. Earth's Future **9**(3), e2020EF001818 (2021)
3. Lazarus, E.D., Goldstein, E.B.: Is there a bulldozer in your model? J. Geophys. Res. Earth Surf. **124**(3), 696–699 (2019)
4. Haff, P.K.: Hillslopes, rivers, plows, and trucks: mass transport on Earth's surface by natural and technological processes. Earth Surf. Proc. Land. **35**(10), 1157–1166 (2010)
5. Seidl, R.: A functional-dynamic reflection on participatory processes in modeling projects. Ambio **44**(8), 750–765 (2015). https://doi.org/10.1007/s13280-015-0670-8

6. Schulze, J., Müller, B., Groeneveld, J., Grimm, V.: Agent-based modelling of social-ecological systems: achievements, challenges, and a way forward. J. Artif. Soc. Soc. Simul. **20**(2), 8 (2017)
7. Holland, J.H.: Emergence: From chaos to order. Oxford University Press, Oxford, UK (1998)
8. Miller, J.H., Page, S.E.: Complex adaptive systems. Princeton University Press, Princeton, USA (2007)
9. Donnelly, C., Kraus, N., Larson, M.: State of knowledge on measurement and modeling of coastal overwash. J. Coastal Res. **22**(4), 965–991 (2006)
10. Lazarus, E.D.: DOZER: code and documentation [model]. Zenodo (2025). https://doi.org/10.5281/zenodo.15589917
11. Lazarus, E.D.: Scaling laws for coastal overwash morphology. Geophys. Res. Lett. **43**(23), 12113–12119 (2016)
12. Lazarus, E.D., Davenport, K.L., Matias, A.: Dynamic allometry in coastal overwash morphology. Earth Surf. Dyn. **8**(1), 37–50 (2020)
13. Jögi, P., Sornette, D.: Self-organized critical random directed polymers. Phys. Rev. E **57**(6), 6936–6943 (1998)
14. Lazarus, E. D., Williams, H. E., Goldstein, E. B.: Volume estimation from planform characteristics of washover morphology. Geophys. Res. Lett. **49**(22), e2022GL100098 (2022)
15. Criss, R.E., Shock, E.L.: Flood enhancement through flood control. Geology **29**(10), 875–878 (2001)
16. Werner, B.T., Mcnamara, D.E.: Dynamics of coupled human-landscape systems. Geomorphology **91**(3–4), 393–407 (2007)
17. Juul, J.: The art of failure: An essay on the pain of playing video games. MIT press, Cambridge, USA (2013)
18. Bogost, I.: Persuasive games. MIT Press, Cambridge, USA (2007)
19. Costikyan, G.: Uncertainty in games. MIT Press, Cambridge, USA (2013)
20. Larsen, L. J., Walther, B. K.: Gameplay 2.0: Toward a new theory. Games and Culture 1–21 (2024)
21. van Bilsen, A., Bekebrede, G., Mayer, I.: Understanding complex adaptive systems by playing games. Inf. Educ. **9**(1), 1–18 (2010)
22. McNamara, D.E., Lazarus, E.D., Goldstein, E.B.: Human-coastal coupled systems: Ten questions. Cambridge Prisms: Coastal Futures **1**, e20 (2023)
23. Ruggiero, D., Becker, K.: Games you can't win. Comput. Games J. **4**, 169–186 (2015)
24. Frommel, J., Klarkowski, M., Mandryk, R. L.: The struggle is spiel: On failure and success in games. In: Proceedings of the 16th International Conference on the Foundations of Digital Games, pp. 1–12. Association for Computing Machinery, New York, USA (2021)
25. Foch, C., Kirman, B.: "The game doesn't judge you": Game designers' perspectives on implementing failure in video games. In: Proceedings of the 17th International Conference on the Foundations of Digital Games, pp. 1–13. Association for Computing Machinery, New York, USA (2022)
26. Wu, J.S., Lee, J.J.: Climate change games as tools for education and engagement. Nat. Clim. Chang. **5**(5), 413–418 (2015)
27. Flood, S., Cradock-Henry, N.A., Blackett, P., Edwards, P.: Adaptive and interactive climate futures: systematic review of "serious games" for engagement and decision-making. Environ. Res. Lett. **13**(6), 063005 (2018)

28. Fernández Galeote, D., Rajanen, M., Rajanen, D., et al.: Gamification for climate change engagement: review of corpus and future agenda. Environ. Res. Lett. **16**(6), 063004 (2021)
29. Abt, C.C.: Serious Games. University Press of America, Lanham, USA (1970)
30. Juul, J.: Handmade pixels: Independent video games and the quest for authenticity. MIT Press, Cambridge, USA (2019)
31. Axelrod, R.: The complexity of cooperation: Agent-based models of competition and collaboration. Princeton University Press, Princeton, USA (1997)
32. Samuel, A.L.: Some studies in machine learning using the game of checkers. IBM J. Res. Dev. **3**(3), 210–229 (1959)
33. de Marchi, S., Page, S.E.: Agent-based models. Annu. Rev. Polit. Sci. **17**(1), 1–20 (2014)
34. Szczepanska, T., Antosz, P., Berndt, J.O., et al.: GAM on! Six ways to explore social complexity by combining games and agent-based models. Int. J. Soc. Res. Methodol. **25**(4), 541–555 (2022)
35. Clear Code, https://github.com/clear-code-projects, Last accessed 01/June/25

Go Beyond Atmosphere Rendering: XR-Mediated Script Entertainment

Xinyi Wu[1], Yiming Zhang[1], Yawen Zhang[2], and Ruowei Xiao[1]

[1] School of Design, Southern University of Science and Technology, Shenzhen, China
xiaorw@sustech.edu.cn
[2] Clemson University, Clemson, USA

Abstract. Script Entertainment (SE), originating from murder mystery games, has flourished in China over the past decade. Beyond entertainment, it has gradually evolved into a brand new game genre and a vast industry integrating with education, cultural tourism, commerce and so forth. Against this background, extended reality (XR) has become a key driver for the digital transformation of SE industry. However, the current use of XR technology in SE remains simply enhancing visual and audio effects, with limited interactability and integration into game mechanics. In this Research-through-Design (RtD) study, we explored what aspects and how XR can mediate SE. First, we conducted expert interviews with 10 SE practitioners to gain industrial perspective and initial design insights. Second, we developed an annotated portfolio that comprises a set of game demos co-created with SE industry stakeholders and game creators. As a result, 4 actionable design implications were generated. Grounded in both our designerly practices and industry perspectives, we intend to contribute fresh and in-depth insights for future design and development of XR-mediated SE.

Keywords: Script entertainment · Murder mystery game · Serious game · Extended reality · Research through design

1 Introduction

Murder mystery games (MMGs), which stem from live-action role-playing (LARP) games in the United Kingdom [15], center around a script while incorporating elements like reasoning, role-playing and puzzle-solving. Players primarily interact with each other through collocated social play in real-world venues, guided by a Dungeon Master (DM). During the past decade, it has undergone phenomenal popularity in China and become a new form of social entertainment among young generations, known as the Script Entertainment (SE). With the continuous growth of the market, SE has gradually expanded into a broader and more content-rich game genre, encompassing tabletop games and more hybrid, dynamic forms combining LARP and escape rooms.

S. Bakkes et al. (Eds.): GALA 2025, LNCS 16307, pp. 150–161, 2026.
https://doi.org/10.1007/978-3-032-11043-5_15

Recently, the SE industry has witnessed a growing trend of integrating with extended reality (XR) technology, driven by the emergence of "Script Entertainment+" (SE+) and "Script Entertainment 3.0" (SE 3.0) models. Explicitly, SE+ refers to the cross-industry integration with sectors like education, cultural tourism and so forth. Meanwhile, SE 3.0 emphasizes more realistic settings and immersive gameplay, such as merging script with scenic spots and physical venues. Specifically fueled by the soaring demand from galleries, libraries, archives, museums (GLAM) and other cultural tourism domains, the SE industry started to actively embrace XR technology, including but not limited to virtual reality (VR), augmented reality (AR), and mixed reality (MR). XR-mediated SE has become a key driver of the immersive experience economy. However, its usage remains to be an optional multimedia enhancement, primarily for amplifying the overall atmosphere of the gameplay.

In this study, we aim to address two research questions (RQs). **RQ1**: *What aspects of SE can be potentially mediated by XR technology?* Here, SE refers to not only a general game genre, but also the industry per se. **RQ2**: *How can we use XR technology to mediate SE experience?* This question looks for more practical guidance for the design and development of XR-mediated SE. Therefore, we carried out a Research-through-Design research. First, we conducted semi-structured expert interviews with 10 SE industry practitioners to elicit initial design insights from a practical, industrial perspective. A grounded theory method was adopted to iteratively collect and analyze the interview materials. Second, we conducted co-design workshops with industry stakeholders and game creators to co-create a total of 6 XR-mediated SE game demos, which were analyzed and summarized into an annotated portfolio. Finally, we synergized both the expert interview results and the annotated portfolio into 4 actionable design implications. Notably, these implications are not merely confined to a designerly reflection on the specific SE industry and its related cultural phenomena in a particular country or region. Rather, they can also be generalized and transferred to other serious domains where XR-mediated SE can be potentially applied.

2   Background

SE is a narrative-driven cultural experience emphasizing logical reasoning, combining scripts, mechanical puzzles and immersive real-world venues. A prominent genre, MMGs (known as "Jubensha" in China), originated from LARP in the UK and was introduced to China in 2013, marking the start of SE there. Most SE games involve deduction-based role-playing guided by a DM, and are played in physical venues, with fewer taking place on online platforms [15]. Similar to tabletop role-playing games (TRPGs), SE also emphasizes collocated social play. However, the difference is that SE features fixed plots and roles, while TRPGs typically involve open-ended storytelling, customizable characters and more complex rules.

By 2023, China's SE market reached approximately 19.5 billion RMB. As the industry matures, innovations such as the cross-industry "SE+" model, which integrates sectors like education and cultural tourism, have emerged. Moreover, SE has evolved from "SE 1.0," focused on deduction-based play, to "SE 2.0," involving clue searching in physical venues, and now to "SE 3.0," which further stages immersive role-playing in authentic settings like historical towns and scenic spots.

Current SE literature broadly embraces escape rooms [13], immersive theater [11], LARP [9] and pervasive or location-based games [2]. Some of these have already been applied in contexts such as education and training [11], GLAM[13] and tourism [4]. With the growing demand for immersive and interactive experiences in SE, recent state-of-the-art studies have increasingly tapped into XR technology to enhance player experiences. Although existing studies have proposed design frameworks for specific domains like social play [8], LARP [5] and pervasive games[1], there is still a lack of systematic investigation and practical guidelines tailored for SE.

As for development and authoring tools, existing research has introduced relevant tools and technology stacks to support the creation of XR-mediated SE. For instance, XR storytelling tools like *Jigsaw* [17] and *Story CreatAR* [10] facilitate interactive narrative design. XR (game) development toolkits by Svanæs et al. [12], Zarraonandia et al. [16], Kern et al. [7] and Xiao et al. [14] have been proposed. We adopted the technology stack proposed by Xiao et al. for this study due to: (1) its end-user-oriented design, which facilitates participatory design involving non-technical stakeholders; and (2) its cost efficiency, achieved through the use of lightweight, commercially available devices, such as Cardboard VR and passive Ultra High Frequency (UHF) RFID.

To summarize, although XR-mediated SE remains a niche research field, its industrial scale and phenomenal popularity demonstrate its potential value in fields such as culture, education and commerce.

3   Research Approach

The overall research followed an RtD method [18], and was structured into two phases corresponding to our two RQs respectively. The study was carried out with the approval of the Institutional Review Board (IRB) of the authors' affiliated institution.

For RQ1: *"What aspects of SE can be potentially mediated by XR technology?"*, we conducted semi-structured interviews with 10 experts from different professions within the SE industry, ranging from script creator, publisher, industry association officer, to veteran player. We adopted a grounded theory method[6] to collect and qualitatively analyze the interview materials in an iterative and generative manner. Thus, we managed to familiarize ourselves with the industry landscape and gain preliminary design insights, which guided us to address our RQ2.

For RQ2: *"How can XR technology mediate SE experiences?"*, we followed an annotated portfolio approach [3] and organized two co-design workshops to co-create XR-mediated SE game demos. According to the previous results of expert interviews, the two co-design workshops intentionally featured different participant groups and co-creation themes to generate complementary outcomes. The first workshop spanned 16 weeks with the theme of "fire safety education" to emphasize the applicability of XR-mediated SE in serious application scenarios. It involved 20 students with novice-level game creation skills, with the active engagement of multiple stakeholders from the SE industry and local fire department. In contrast, the second workshop adopted the form of a one-day Game Jam without specified themes, involving 10 professional game creators from a leading game company in China and 15 students with moderate or advanced game creation skills. A total of 6 game demos were generated.

Further, we synthesized industry perspectives from the expert interview analysis and empirical insights from the annotated portfolio into 4 major design implications. Due to the space limitation, detailed expert profiles and the full annotated portfolio are provided in the online supplementary materials (https://bit.ly/4ekzpsj).

4   Expert Interview

In this section, we present the qualitative results derived from our expert interviews. The aim was to identify design opportunities for guiding our next research stage, by emphasizing the difference and similarity between the traditional SE and XR-mediated SE particularly. We adopted an iterative process of collecting, coding, and clustering following the grounded theory method. To ensure inter-coder reliability, the materials were analyzed by 2 to 3 independent coders, with discrepancies resolved through group discussions until a consensus rate over 99% was achieved. The resulting code set included 81 codes, forming 46 themes and 4 major categories. The four major categories each spotlight a different design dimension, further branching into subcategories and their subsidiary design themes. As shown in Fig. 1, they were streamlined and organized in a hierarchical structure, with bracketed numbers denoting each theme's frequency in the raw interview materials.

(1) *Contextualization* explores the sub-genres under XR-mediated SE, and the application scenarios and themes that our expert interviewees identified as more aligned with XR-mediated version compared to its traditional counterpart. It was commonly agreed that XR technology lends itself to application contexts like *Tourism and Attraction, GLAM,* and for themes related to Education and Skill Training.

(2) *Constitution* focuses on the game mechanics, interactables and specifications of XR-mediated SE. Similar to traditional SE, *Social Play* remains the core game mechanic, while *Puzzle Solving, Reasoning* and *Game in a Game* were considered with the highest potential to be integrated with XR's technological affordances through interactables like *Costumes* and *Props.* In addition, the experts suggested that XR-mediated SE should have a shorter average play *Time* than traditional SE due to the concern about the limited wearability of current Head-Mounted Displays (HMD).

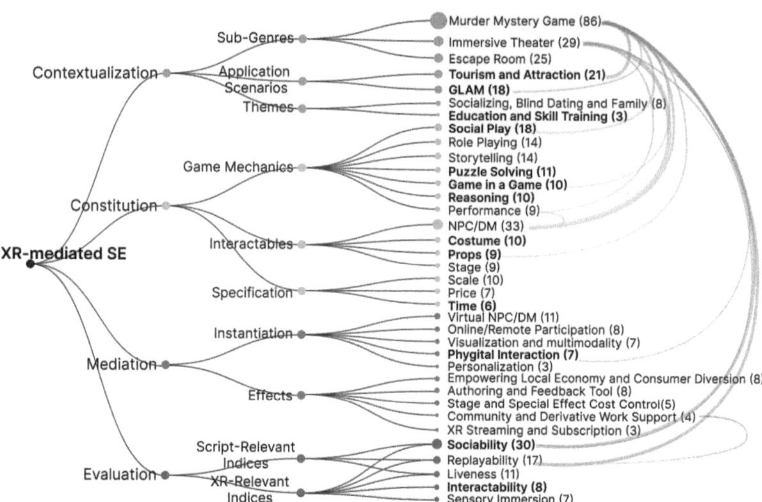

Fig. 1. Design dimensions and subsidiary themes of XR-Mediated SE

(3) *Mediation* investigates the aspect of XR mediation. The typical instantiation of XR mediation includes *Online/Remote Participation, Visualization and Multimodal Enhancement,* both of which are common in traditional SE. *Virtual DMs,* the most mentioned instantiation, were cautioned by experts to be limited to certain scenarios such as GLAM or educational tours, where players primarily seek knowledge, making the demands for DMs' storytelling and improvisational performance less stringent compared to those placed on human counterparts. *Phygital Interaction,* referring to the integration of physical and digital in-game elements, emerged as the most significant theme. We will leave the expected industry effects of XR mediation to Sect. 6.

(4) *Evaluation* proposes metrics for XR-mediated SE experiences along two sub-dimensions: script-relevant and XR-relevant. Given that social play is the core game mechanics, *Sociability* emerges as the most salient index. Followed by *Replayability,* which the experts refer to as the "biggest bottleneck" for most MMGs, while *Liveness* refers to the emergent experience from situational interactions with human NPCs/DMs and game settings, that vary each game session, even following the same script. Many experts agreed that *Interactability* and *Sensory Immersion* are the experiential indices most likely enhanced by XR technology.

Particularly, some design themes, e.g., *Education and Skill Training, Game in a Game, Phygital Interaction,* have inspired and influenced the game design presented in the next section, which are highlighted in bold in Fig. 1.

5   Game Design Overview

This section showcases the four representative game demos from the first workshop, with the remaining two are provided in the supplementary materials. Collectively, these demos presented a rich repertoire of game mechanics, player interactions, XR mediation and educational contents. For technical implementation used, please revisit Sect. 2.

(1) Flame Within

Game Mechanics: In *Flame Within* (Fig. 2a), players **role-play** one of three witnesses to a mysterious fire and enter a virtual post-fire environment to investigate its cause. The game consists of two stages: Evidence gathering and presentation. During evidence gathering, players are given limited action points to investigate virtual objects and collect clues for their **puzzle-solving** and **reasoning**. After several rounds, players must present all collected evidence to establish a complete chain of reasoning (Fig. 2a top right). The game adopts a **non-linear narrative**, with story branches and endings shaped by player's decisions and whether key items are gathered.

XR Mediation: Each player wears a **cardboard VR headset** and interacts with virtual scenes and objects by pressing the headset's button. Notably, this game incorporates **tangible props** with RFID tags as action cards (Fig. 2a bottom left). Scanning an action card consumes one action point to investigate a virtual item, then the card is turned into an evidence card for the later evidence presentation stage.

Player Interaction: The game supports turn-based play for 3 to 4 collocated players who can cooperate or compete. As the story progresses, the player who discovers they are the culprit behind the fire may hide key evidence to conceal their identity, while others may collaborate by sharing or revealing clues to identify the mastermind.

Educational Contents: This game mirrors real fire investigation process, where players are required to learn and apply their knowledge about flammable materials and potential fire risks to identify key items.

(a)   (b)

Fig. 2. Game components and Gameplay of (a) Flame within and (b) Burning time.

(2) Burning Time

Game Mechanics: *Burning Time* (Fig. 2b) is a **narrative** based game featuring time slip. Players from different timelines collaborate to solve a fire investigation case. Based on **reasoning** and **puzzles solving**, players need to figure out the correct event sequence. It also adopts a **plot twist**: the player who appears to be a fire victim is later revealed to be his sibling, a firefighter undergoing post-fire psychological therapy.

XR Mediation: The VR player primarily interacts with virtual scenes and objects using basic cardboard VR functions, e.g. eye gaze and the headset button.

Player Interaction: The game involves two collocated players in different timelines—before and after the fire—who exchange key information and reason together to complete the puzzle and uncover the full picture.

Educational Contents: This game leverages a fictional time-slip story to reflect a real-life issue faced by firefighting personnel—post-traumatic stress disorder or other mental symptoms after major incidents. Through **narrative tricks**, it aims to evoke greater social awareness and understanding toward the firefighting profession.

(3) XFGO

Game Mechanics: *XFGO* (Fig. 3a) divides 4 players into two opposing teams for a competitive firefighting drill: one is tasked with selecting the correct fire extinguisher to put out fires, while the opposing team must identify and ignite flammable or explosive materials. Each team includes an operative and a commander, and characters differ in abilities and parameters like vision range and capture skills, enabling **asymmetric confrontation** and various team strategies to compete for a higher **game score**. Each game lasts for 5 minutes, and the higher-scoring team wins at the end of the countdown.

XR Mediation: Players use the headset button to move or stop their avatars. One team's operative ignites virtual flammable objects by gazing, while the opposing operative wears an RFID-tagged firefighter uniform as a **costume**, with each tag representing a different type of extinguisher. A hand-held RFID reader is used to scan and select the correct extinguisher (Fig. 3a bottom left).

Player Interaction: The game supports collaboration-based competition among 4 collocated players. Each team's commander utilizes a broader vision to deliver critical information—like enemy positions and fire dynamics—to the operative, who follows instructions to act, such as capturing or escaping.

Educational Contents: The game's fire safety knowledge covers: (1) materials and their flammability; (2) fire sources, e.g. fuel-based fires; (3) extinguisher types, e.g. CO_2 and water-based etc. These are tightly interwoven into the game mechanics—for example, igniting less flammable objects requires longer gaze time, increasing the risk of detection and capture, thereby improving the strategic element and educational value.

(4) Back into Fire

Game Mechanics: Two players collaborate in a cross-reality manner to rescue an infant trapped in a burning house, the stage for a VR **escape room**. Player A remotely operates a **firefighting robot** on a physical floor model

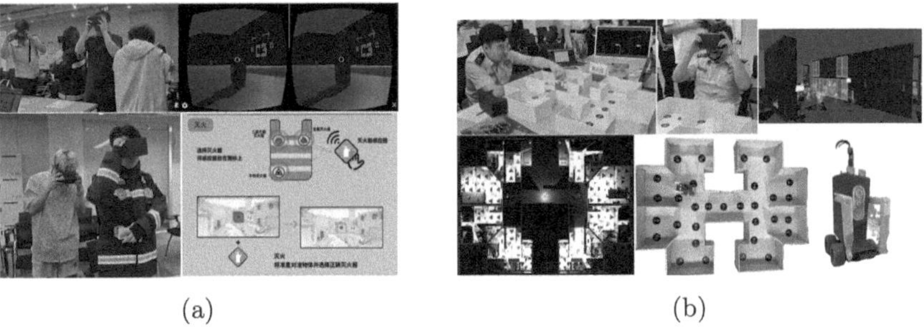

(a)   (b)

Fig. 3. Game components and Gameplay of **a** XFGO; and **b** Back into fire.

(Fig. 3b bottom right), while Player B observes the fire scene in VR from a synchronized perspective with the robot and performs rescue operations. The game features **time-limited tasks** requiring quick responses, e.g. avoiding collapsing building parts, finding safe routes, picking up **collectibles** like fire mask etc.

XR Mediation: To enable cross-reality collaboration, this game relies on **tangible props**, i.e. a firefighting robot and a building floor model. The robot is an assembly of a remote controlled car, a Raspberry Pi with RFID module and a 3D-printed chassis. Multiple RFID tags are attached to the floor model, allowing real-time positioning of the robot. Thus, the other player's perspective in VR will be synchronized accordingly.

Player Interaction: The cooperative social gameplay requires both players to work closely as if they separately shared the robot's vision and mobility functions. For example, When the VR player discovers a blocked path, they must promptly inform the robot operator to replan the robot's route to the destination.

Educational Contents: This game showcases common fire hazards, e.g., low visibility, breathing difficulty and collapse, while promoting safety measures like using fire masks or damp cloth to cover the nose and mouth, and crawling to avoid smoke.

6   Discussion and Conclusion

In this section, we will discuss our four design implications and conclude our contribution of this study. Each implication is discussed with a consistent structure: starting from a general industry perspective (in response to RQ1) and progressively narrowing down to concrete prototypes and actionable design insights (in response to RQ2).

(1) SE's Core Value: A Live Social Experience

All the experts reached the consensus that whether or not technology mediation is involved, the core value of SE experiences always lies in **sociability** and **liveness**. As P4, P9, P8 mentioned, SE is essentially social play, and players value the collocated dynamic social interactions and happenings that emerge improvisationally during each play. It is the interaction with real people in real world that fundamentally distinguishes SE from other games, e.g. multi-player online games. We argue that the engagement of XR mediation, instead of cutting off players' awareness of the outside world, must help establish and maintain the player's connections with other people and the surrounding. As P5 and P9 noted, *"For example, in immersive theater, the use of technology is supposed to make the human performers stand out, rather than replace them."* Similarly, technology should be used to facilitate interactions between players and human NPCs/DMs. In particular social contexts or scenarios, virtual NPCs/DMs can also serve an important function. As P1 noted, *"Virtual NPCs/DMs are particularly suitable in specific contexts such as cultural tourism or GLAM."* (RQ1)

Following the same thread, we believe that aside from sensory appeal and immersion, XR's potential to enhance SE lies in its capability to facilitate the overall social experience and encourage live interactions among on-site players, by supporting various social play modes. Representative game demos include *Burning Time, Western Cowboy Showdown* and *XFGO*. They have respectively demonstrated different social play modes, i.e. cooperation, competition and cooperation-based competition. In practice, AR, MR and projection mapping are some preferable technologies that attend to collocated interactions. (RQ2)

(2) XR as Interfacing Technology Should Go Beyond Atmosphere Rendering

Several experts (P6-P9) mentioned that the current use of XR in SE is largely limited to rendering audiovisual effects to supplement the pre-written script contents, such as using VR or projection mapping to create a non-interactable story backdrop. However, these experts also agree that XR's application is expected to go beyond merely multimedia content enhancement or atmosphere rendering. Some in-game elements in SE can be possibly reformed using XR. For instance, P9 said: *"Virtual avatars may provide more personalized and customizable role-play experience than physical costumes."* Moreover, to address MMGs' replayability issue, P9 further pointed out that: *"XR should engage player community and encourage secondary content creations, so as to improve the overall replayability."* (RQ1)

Despite its constrained use in post-production phase currently, our annotated portfolio shows that XR can be proactively engaged from the beginning in script composition and game mechanics design. An example is *Flame Within*, where RFID technology was tightly merged into the investigation and evidence presentation stages of the game. While in *Back Into Fire*, the spatial mapping between the virtual environment and the physical floor map renders **cross-reality interactability** for the game. It hence entails SE creators to be aware of the technological affordances of XR, as an **interfacing technology** that communicates the virtual and the physical, and make full use of them. To this end, both P8 and P6 suggested: *"For MMGs that involve mechanisms as part of the crime, it would add more realism and persuasiveness, if a 3D exploded or cross-section model can be displayed in VR for players to understand and interact with the key mechanism behind the crime."* P6 also added: *"For tabletop games with physical* *maps and player figurines, it's natural and more fun to blend with AR or MR."* Considering its technical threshold, we believe that end-user development tools and generative AI can help lower the entry barriers for non-technical users to design and develop XR-mediated SE. (RQ2)

(3) Low Tech, Rich Experience

When discussing about the factors hindering full-fledged XR-mediated SE, the concern shared among experts (P1, P4, P8, P10) is the technological limitations and cost: limited wearability, short battery life, motion sickness and fatigue due to prolonged use of heavy headsets etc. On one hand, XR may contribute to a reduced production cost by *"replacing real stages and installations by virtual settings"* (P8). On the other hand, expensive XR equipment will also impose heavy initial investment and maintenance cost on specifically SE store owners (P1, P4, P6, P8). (RQ1) Therefore, **lightweight low-tech solutions** and **moderate use (against full use)** of XR turned out to be among the key principles that most experts agree on. As P4 highlighted, *"By prioritizing end user experience over technical implementation, we've achieved strong market performance."*

Our annotated portfolio aligns with this insight, in the way that we adopted exclusively low-cost, low-tech components such as cardboard VR goggles and passive RFID tags. Notably, in *Wilderness Adventure* and *Western Cowboy Showdown*, everyday objects and crafts like water bottles and LEGO blocks, when attached with RFID tags, immediately turn into instant game controllers that render fun and meaningful bodily play. It again underlines that the adoption of any technology in SE needs to be self-explained and experience-driven. Moreover, by confining the use of XR to only key segments of the gameplay or "game-in-a-game", it can further avoid over-reliance on devices and reduce technical overhead. (RQ2)

(4) SE+: Combination with GLAM, Tourism and More

Currently, the traditional SE industry in China is facing serious bottlenecks due to issues like post-pandemic recession and consumer downgrading. The experts generally agree that stand-alone businesses, e.g. script murder mystery and escape room stores, will struggle to maintain a sustainable business model. As P4, P6 and P7 pointed out, one way for SE to break through is to work hand in hand with the local real economy as a tactic for **traffic attraction** and **consumer diversion**. Many cultural, educational and commercial scenarios can employ XR-mediated SE to improve public engagement. To this end, the technological affordances of XR can empower traditional SE, by intelligently adapting to on-site, context-sensitive settings. Examples include location-aware contents along tour routes, or interactive experience centering physical museum exhibits, which traditional SE may find difficult to achieve alone. (RQ1)

Presumably, to accommodate high user traffic, future XR-mediated SE experience must feature **bite-sized, fast-paced** interactions. It will drastically differ from the traditional SE model, where a single session oftentimes spans from 2 to 8 hours. It will be accompanied by purposes beyond entertainment, including but not limited to education, cultural promotion, or commercial advertising.

Consequently, SE creators need to always consider how to deliver the knowledge or information in a way that is seamlessly interwoven into the script and game mechanics, contributing to an experiential continuum. The first four game demos have set up some modest examples for future discussions. Meanwhile, for XR-mediated SE deployed in GLAM, scenic spots and similar application domains, we propose to further incorporate GPS- or beacon-based positioning to expand SE into a wider activity range. (RQ2)

7   Conclusions

This study intends to explore the technological affordances of XR and their potential impact on both future SE game experience and the industry per se. Our work did not cover the full spectrum of XR-mediated SE regarding the sub-genres and application scenarios. Due to practical limitations, we were also not able to traverse all possible XR technical components in our game development. Instead, by carefully scrutinizing available design options and narrowing down to a representative subset, we aimed to explore the research domain and extract transferrable and actionable design insights for facilitating future design and development of XR-mediated SE and beyond.

References

1. Arango-López, J., Gutiérrez Vela, F.L., Collazos, C.A., Gallardo, J., Moreira, F.: Geopgd: methodology for the design and development of geolocated pervasive games. Univ. Access Inf. Soc. **20**(3), 465–477 (2021)
2. Bell, M., Chalmers, M., Barkhuus, L., Hall, M., Sherwood, S., Tennent, P., Brown, B., Rowland, D., Benford, S., Capra, M., Hampshire, A.: Interweaving mobile games with everyday life. In: Proceedings of the SIGCHI Conference on Human Factors in Computing Systems. p. 417–426. Association for Computing Machinery, New York, NY, USA (2006)
3. Bowers, J.: The logic of annotated portfolios: communicating the value of'research through design'. In: Proceedings of the Designing Interactive Systems Conference. pp. 68–77 (2012)
4. Bozdog, M., Galloway, D.: Performing walking sims: from dear esther to inchcolm project. J. Gaming Virtual Worlds **12**(1), 23–47 (2020)
5. Buruk, O.O., Isbister, K., Tanenbaum, T.J.: A design framework for playful wearables. In: Proceedings of the 14th International Conference on the Foundations of Digital Games. New York, NY, USA (2019)
6. Charmaz, K.: Grounded theory. Qualitative psychology: A practical guide to research methods **3**, 53–84 (2015)
7. Kern, F., Latoschik, M.E.: Reality stack i/o: A versatile and modular framework for simplifying and unifying xr applications and research. In: 2023 IEEE International Symposium on Mixed and Augmented Reality Adjunct (ISMAR-Adjunct). pp. 74–76. IEEE (2023)
8. Segura, E.M., Isbister, K.: Enabling co-located physical social play: A framework for design and evaluation. In: Game user experience evaluation, pp. 209–238. Springer (2015)

9. Segura, E.M., Fey, J., Dagan, E., Jhaveri, S.N., Pettitt, J., Flores, M., Isbister, K.: Designing Future Social Wearables with Live Action Role Play (Larp) Designers. In: Human Factors in Computing Systems. p. 462. ACM (Apr 2018)

10. Singh, A., Kaur, R., Haltner, P., Peachey, M., Gonzalez-Franco, M., Malloch, J., Reilly, D.: Story creatar: a toolkit for spatially-adaptive augmented reality storytelling. In: 2021 IEEE Virtual Reality and 3D User Interfaces (VR). pp. 713–722. IEEE (2021)

11. Skye, E.P., Wagenschutz, H., Steiger, J.A., Kumagai, A.K.: Use of interactive theater and role play to develop medical students' skills in breaking bad news. J. Cancer Educ. **29**(4), 704–708 (2014)

12. Svanæs, D., Scharvet Lyngby, A., Bärnhold, M., Røsand, T., Subramanian, S.: Unity-things: An internet-of-things software framework integrating arduino-enabled remote devices with the unity game engine. In: International Conference on Human-Computer Interaction. pp. 378–388. Springer (2021)

13. Wild, F., Marshall, L., Bernard, J., White, E., Twycross, J.: Unbody: A poetry escape room in augmented reality. Information **12**(8), 295 (2021)

14. Xiao, R., Zhang, R., Buruk, O., Hamari, J., Virkki, J.: Toward next generation mixed reality games: a research through design approach. Virtual Reality **28**(3), 142 (2024)

15. Xiong, S., Wen, R., Zheng, H.: Player category research on murder mystery games. International Journal of Role-Playing **13**, 40–56 (2023)

16. Zarraonandia, T., Díaz, P., Santos, A., Montero, Á., Aedo, I.: A toolkit for creating cross-reality serious games. In: International conference on games and learning Alliance. pp. 297–307. Springer (2018)

17. Zhang, L., Kim, D., Cho, Y., Robinson, A., Tham, Y.J., Vaish, R., Monroy-Hernández, A.: Jigsaw: Authoring immersive storytelling experiences with augmented reality and internet of things. In: Proceedings of the 2024 CHI Conference on Human Factors in Computing Systems. New York, NY, USA (2024)

18. Zimmerman, J., Forlizzi, J., Evenson, S.: Research through design as a method for interaction design research in hci. In: Proceedings of the SIGCHI Conference on Human Factors in Computing Systems. p. 493–502. New York, NY, USA (2007)

Engaging Gen Z in Transformational Games: How Complementary Features Enhance Core Mechanics for Sustainable Mobility–The MOB Tournament Case Study

Domenico Schillaci[✉][iD] and Salvatore Di Dio[iD]

Università degli Studi di Palermo, Palermo 90133, Italy
domenico.schillaci01@unipa.it

Abstract. Generation Z presents unique challenges for serious games designers seeking behavioural change, expecting sophisticated digital interactions beyond traditional core mechanics. This paper introduces the Complementary Features Layer framework, integrating social, creative, and educational elements within transformational games targeting digital-native populations. We present empirical evidence from the MOB Tournament, a large-scale gamified mobility intervention engaging 2,560 Italian Gen Z participants over 10 weeks. The tournament incorporated three novel complementary features: (1) dynamic team formation with institutional matching, (2) user-generated storytelling through MOB Stories, and (3) educational integration via masterclasses and bonus questions. Dynamic team formation achieved 62.1% completion rates while preventing "ghost teams." Educational integration demonstrated measurable knowledge acquisition with 67% accuracy across 2,266 responses. User-generated content sustained creative expression with 78 participants producing stories over 19 days. Phase 3 engagement recovery (12.39 trips per user per week) exceeded Phase 1 levels (10.95), demonstrating complementary features' effectiveness in sustaining motivation. The tournament achieved 33.28% active participation and 6.86 tonnes of CO_2 savings, providing scalable design principles for youth-focused sustainability interventions.

Keywords: Generation Z · Complementary game features · Transformational games · Sustainable mobility · Behavioural change

1 Introduction

Generation Z (born 1997–2012) presents unique challenges for serious games designers seeking behavioural change. Unlike previous generations, Gen Z expects sophisticated digital interactions combining social expression, peer learning, and creative agency within serious gaming experiences [1]. Traditional serious games often fail to sustain engagement with this demographic despite their

S. Bakkes et al. (Eds.): GALA 2025, LNCS 16307, pp. 162–171, 2026.
https://doi.org/10.1007/978-3-032-11043-5_16

environmental awareness, resulting in high dropout rates and limited transformational impact [7].

Current serious games literature focuses primarily on optimising core mechanics—points, leaderboards, and challenges—that drive gameplay [2]. However, emerging evidence suggests that for digital natives, transformational game effectiveness depends equally on **complementary features** [8]: secondary engagement mechanisms that enhance social connection, enable creative expression, and integrate learning opportunities. These features complement core mechanics to address the multifaceted motivational preferences of Gen Z.

Despite recognition of this phenomenon, systematic empirical evidence on how complementary features enhance the effectiveness of serious games for Gen Z remains limited. Most studies examine isolated elements or generic populations, failing to capture the engagement patterns that distinguish younger demographics [4]. This gap is particularly problematic for sustainability interventions requiring sustained engagement for habit formation [5].

This paper addresses this knowledge gap through an analysis of the **MOB Tournament**, a large-scale gamified mobility intervention targeting Italian Gen Z users. Implemented via the MUV (Mobility Urban Values) platform [10] in partnership with Fondazione UNIPOLIS, the tournament engaged **2,560 participants over 10 weeks**, incorporating three novel complementary features alongside traditional competition mechanics:

1. **Dynamic team formation** with institutional matching and temporal constraints
2. **User-generated storytelling** through MOB Stories with social media integration
3. **Educational integration** via masterclasses and bonus questions with academic credit recognition

MUV has deployed gamified mobility interventions across 4,872 participants (2022–2024), achieving consistent 16% corporate penetration rates and 27.12% average CO_2 reduction. Cross-case analysis reveals tournament structures generate 77% higher behavioral intensity than individual challenges.

Unlike controlled laboratory studies, this intervention took place in real-world conditions, with authentic behavioural outcomes—measured CO_2 emission reductions and sustainable mobility adoption. Our analysis reveals that complementary features significantly enhance engagement and learning outcomes beyond those achieved through traditional tournament mechanics alone.

This research contributes to serious games literature by empirically validating complementary features effectiveness with Gen Z users, demonstrating scalable educational-gaming integration, and proposing a framework adaptable across contexts and demographics. The implications extend to educators, policymakers, and designers developing behavioural change interventions for younger generations facing intensifying climate challenges.

2   Related Work

2.1   Generation Z and Transformational Games

Generation Z represents the first digital-native cohort with distinct gaming preferences: shorter attention spans requiring immediate feedback, preference for visual content, and expectation of social integration within digital experiences [6].

Gen Z demonstrates strong preference for microlearning approaches and high expectations for personalisation and user agency [9]. These characteristics significantly impact serious games design for sustained behavioural change interventions.

2.2   Core Mechanics Versus Complementary Features

Traditional serious games design emphasises optimisation of core mechanics—scoring systems, progression mechanics, and reward structures that directly drive engagement. However, emerging research introduces **complementary features**—secondary engagement mechanisms that enhance but do not replace core game mechanics [3]. These typically include social tools (such as sharing, communication, and collaboration), creative expression opportunities (including customisation and user-generated content), and integrated learning experiences (such as tutorials and knowledge challenges). While not directly advancing game objectives, complementary features create richer experiential contexts that significantly impact user retention, particularly for digital-native populations expecting sophisticated interaction paradigms.

2.3   Educational Integration and Social Dynamics

Research on game-based learning demonstrates that educational content must be seamlessly embedded within game mechanics to avoid disrupting flow states and intrinsic motivation. Microlearning approaches—delivering content in small, focused segments—show particular promise for Gen Z, with recent studies showing retention rates of 70-90% compared to 15% with traditional methods, aligning with digital natives' preferences for bite-sized consumption while enabling just-in-time learning [15].

Team formation mechanisms traditionally rely on self-selection or algorithmic matching based on skill levels. However, recent studies on digital learning environments demonstrate that institutional-based matching can generate stronger social bonds while effectively reducing social anxiety, particularly among digital natives experiencing decision fatigue in peer selection processes[14].

User-generated content serves as a powerful engagement mechanism for younger demographics, who view content creation as a fundamental form of digital expression and interaction [13]. In serious games contexts, UGC enhances engagement through creative expression while generating authentic peer-to-peer learning opportunities, often proving more engaging than professionally developed materials.

3   The MOB Tournament Design

3.1   Context and Theoretical Innovation

The MOB Tournament was developed through a strategic partnership between MUV Srl SB and Fondazione UNIPOLIS, targeting Generation Z students across Italian secondary schools, universities, and sports associations. The initiative leveraged MUV's established sport-as-metaphor framework [11], reframing sustainable mobility as athletic participation rather than an environmental obligation, while introducing a novel Complementary Features Layer.

3.2   Dynamic Team Formation

Traditional team formation relies on self-selection or random matching, often resulting in unbalanced participation and organisational fragmentation. The MOB Tournament implemented an institutionally based system that balances organisational coherence with efficient team creation through sophisticated geographic and institutional matching algorithms.

Mechanism: Participants provided hierarchical data (province, municipality, school/organisation), enabling institutional matching. The algorithm checked for existing teams, directing users to join rather than create duplicates. New team founders had 48 hours to recruit five members from their institution.

Quality Control: The temporal constraint prevented "ghost teams" through countdown timers and automated notifications, filtering participants lacking commitment. Teams that failed to meet the minimum requirements were automatically dissolved, maintaining tournament integrity without requiring manual intervention.

This approach leveraged existing social networks while providing leadership opportunities, reduced social anxiety compared to stranger-matching, and ensured teams represented authentic communities with shared contexts essential for sustained engagement.

3.3   MOB Stories: User-Generated Content Integration

Recognising that Gen Z views content creation as fundamental to digital engagement, the tournament integrated "MOB Stories"—a user-generated content system enabling participants to document sustainable mobility experiences within the competitive framework.

Implementation: The system utilised hashtag-based curation on personal social media platforms, aggregated within the MUV application.

Content Strategy: Participants shared diverse content, including photos of sustainable trips, creative videos documenting mobility challenges, before-and-after comparisons, and collaborative team content. Minimal restrictions focused on authenticity rather than production quality, reducing participation barriers while maintaining thematic coherence.

Engagement Functions: User-generated content creates social proof mechanisms, enabling the observation of peer behaviour and the normalisation of sustainable choices. The sharing requirement transformed individual trips into community events, amplifying social validation while aligning with Gen Z communication preferences.

3.4   Educational Integration: Masterclasses and Bonus Questions

Traditional serious games struggle to integrate explicit learning without disrupting gameplay flow. The MOB Tournament addressed this through a distributed educational approach, embedding learning within competitive dynamics rather than treating education as a separate entity.

Masterclass Component: Three online sessions covered: (1) Sustainable Urban Mobility, (2) Game Design for Mobility, (3) Data-Driven Mobility Planning. Sessions were recorded for asynchronous access.

Integration Mechanism: Bonus questions, distributed via a mobile application in the days following each masterclass, tested key concepts while offering additional competitive points. Questions used multiple-choice and short-answer formats optimised for mobile interaction, respecting microlearning principles aligned with Gen Z's attention patterns.

Academic Recognition: For secondary school participants, masterclass attendance qualified for PCTO credits, Italy's mandatory work-related learning program providing tangible academic value while demonstrating institutional recognition of gaming-based learning approaches.

Voluntary Participation: All educational components remained optional, creating differentiated pathways where motivated participants could access additional learning and competitive advantages, while others focused purely on mobility tracking, thereby preventing educational requirements from becoming participation barriers.

3.5   Synergistic Integration

The three complementary features operated synergistically rather than independently. Dynamic team formation facilitated social connections strengthened through collaborative MOB Stories creation. Educational content provided shared knowledge frameworks that teams could apply to optimise mobility strategies. Bonus questions created additional coordination opportunities while reinforcing learning through distributed practice.

This integrated approach transformed the tournament from a simple competition into a comprehensive social learning experience, where participants simultaneously developed sustainable mobility habits, creative expression skills, and domain knowledge while facilitating team coordination and collaborative engagement—a novel framework for enhancing the effectiveness of serious games among digital-native populations, who expect multifaceted engagement opportunities.

4   Implementation and Methodology

4.1   Tournament Structure and Data Collection

The MOB Tournament ran from March 20 to May 29, 2023 (10 weeks), achieving unprecedented scale with 2,560 registered participants across 154 teams. The tournament employed a three-phase structure: Phase 1–Qualification (2 weeks, 154 teams); Phase 2–Group Stage (3 weeks, 128 teams in 32 groups); Phase 3–Playoffs (5 weeks, knockout format with 32 teams).

Data collection captured both quantitative engagement metrics and qualitative behavioural patterns across all complementary features, adhering to GDPR protocols with explicit user consent. Key metrics captured team formation patterns (248 attempts, geographic distribution), educational engagement (masterclass attendance, bonus questions), user-generated content creation (MOB Stories campaign), and mobility behavior (36,221 trips, 233,094 km, 6.86 tonnes CO_2 reduction).

4.2   Comparative Analysis Framework

To evaluate the effectiveness of complementary features, MOB data were compared against previous MUV tournaments [12] that utilised only core mechanics. The MOB Tournament achieved a 33.28% active participation rate (852 of 2,560 registrants) and sustained weekly engagement of 454 active users (17.8% of registrants), substantially exceeding MUV's established corporate benchmarks.

Participants were segmented based on complementary features engagement: MOB Stories creators versus non-contributors, educational content participants versus pure competitors, and successful versus dissolved team formation. This natural experimental design enabled the analysis of how different features influenced the tournament experience and behavioural outcomes, providing multiple analytical lenses for evaluating the specific contributions of each complementary feature to overall success.

5   Results and Analysis

5.1   Overall Tournament Performance

The MOB Tournament demonstrated exceptional scale and engagement, with 852 active participants (33.28% of 2,560 registrants), substantially exceeding typical MUV corporate implementations that achieve 15.7% penetration rates using traditional tournament mechanics alone. Participants achieved an average reduction of 28.10% in CO_2 emissions, with 36,221 validated trips covering 233,094 km, resulting in 6.86 tonnes of CO_2 savings. The modal split reflected the target demographic's characteristics: public transport (81.7%), walking (8.2%), cycling (4.3%), carpooling (3.7%), and e-scooters (2.1%).

5.2 Complementary Features Performance

Of 248 team creation attempts, 154 teams (62.1%) completed formation,[1] while 94 were automatically dissolved. Geographic distribution spanned all Italian regions across diverse institutions. Educational integration achieved 63 masterclass participants and 2,266 bonus question responses (67% accuracy). MOB Stories engaged 78 participants over 19 days (9.15% of active users) with hashtag-compliant content demonstrating sustained creative engagement.

5.3 Engagement Patterns Across Tournament Phases

Tournament engagement varied significantly across competitive phases, revealing the impact of complementary features on sustained motivation. Table 1 presents comprehensive phase-specific metrics.

Table 1. MOB tournament phase trends showing engagement and trip metrics across different competitive phases

(a) Participation Metrics						
Tournament Phase	Duration (weeks)	Teams	RU	IU	Avg AU per week	AU/IU
1. Free ranking	2	154	2,314	1,948	512.50	26.32%
2. Group phase	3	128	2,367	1,846	307.00	16.63%
3. Playoffs	5	32	2,538	1,088	254.60	23.40%
Overall Tournament	10	154	2,560	1,487	321.90	21.64%

(b) Trip Intensity Metrics					
Tournament Phase	Duration (weeks)	Teams	AU/team per week	Trips/AU	Trips/AU per week
1. Free ranking	2	154	3.33	21.91	10.95
2. Group phase	3	128	2.40	25.69	8.56
3. Playoffs	5	32	7.96	61.95	12.39
Overall Tournament	10	154	3.42	109.55	10.95

Note: RU = Registered Users, IU = Involved Users, AU = Active Users

The phase-specific data in Table 1 provides empirical evidence for complementary features' behavioral impact mechanisms. The AU/IU ratio remained relatively stable (16.63–26.32%), indicating that complementary features maintained engagement accessibility across different competitive intensities. More significantly, the trips per AU per week metric reveals the depth of behavioral integration: the Phase 3 intensification (12.39 versus 8.56 in Phase 2) occurred

---

[1] This success rate refers specifically to meeting the minimum team composition requirements within the 48-hour deadline, not to subsequent engagement outcomes.

precisely when traditional tournament mechanics would predict decreased engagement due to team elimination. This counter-pattern demonstrates that educational content (masterclasses and bonus questions) and creative expression opportunities (MOB Stories) activated intrinsic motivation pathways that sustained and even intensified sustainable mobility tracking behaviors independent of competitive outcomes. The sustained trips per AU per week throughout all phases (8.56–12.39 range) contrasts sharply with traditional tournament patterns that show steady decline, providing quantitative evidence that complementary features successfully address Generation Z's need for multifaceted engagement beyond pure competition.

The engagement recovery in Phase 3 (12.39 trips per user per week, exceeding Phase 1 levels at 10.95 trips per user per week) represents a notable deviation from typical tournament patterns, where engagement steadily declines. This pattern suggests complementary features contributed to sustained motivation throughout the extended period.

The engagement fluctuations across tournament phases reveal the specific mechanisms through which complementary features sustained motivation during extended competitive periods. The Phase 1 decline from initial registration excitement (26.32% to 16.63% participation) reflects the natural attrition observed in traditional tournaments. However, the Phase 3 recovery to 23.40% participation and intensification to 12.39 trips per user per week demonstrates the effectiveness of complementary features in counteracting typical tournament fatigue. This recovery pattern suggests that educational integration and social content creation provided alternative motivation pathways when primary competitive pressure decreased. The institutional team formation prevented the dissolution of social connections that typically occurs in elimination phases, while MOB Stories maintained engagement through creative expression even for eliminated participants. The bonus questions provided continued interaction opportunities, creating sustained platform engagement beyond pure competition mechanics.

6   Discussion and Conclusions

6.1   Theoretical Contributions and Scalability

The empirical evidence presented demonstrates that complementary features operate through distinct psychological mechanisms that address Generation Z's specific engagement preferences. The phase-based engagement recovery contradicts established tournament theory, which predicts steady decline in participation intensity. The sustained behavioral intensity (8.56–12.39 trips per user per week) across all tournament phases provides quantitative validation that complementary features create resilient engagement architectures capable of maintaining motivation through varying competitive circumstances.

The tournament's scale (2,560 participants) demonstrates complementary features' scalability. The Phase 3 engagement recovery (12.39 versus 10.95 trips per user per week) shows sustained motivation through extended competitive periods.

6.2 Limitations and Future Research

Several limitations constrain the generalizability. The demographic focus on 16-25-year Italian participants limits transferability to other age groups and cultural contexts. The 10-week duration, while sufficient for observing immediate engagement patterns and short-term behavioral responses, is insufficient to evaluate stable behavioral change or genuine habit formation, which typically requires 6-12 months of sustained practice. The voluntary participation model introduces self-selection bias, which can potentially inflate engagement metrics. The substantial financial incentive structure (€15,000 prizes) may not be replicable across contexts. The voluntary participation model introduces significant self-selection bias, as participants likely represent individuals already predisposed toward sustainable mobility or competitive gaming. Additionally, the substantial financial incentive structure may have influenced participation patterns and engagement intensity, making it difficult to isolate the specific impact of complementary features from extrinsic reward effects. Future research should examine complementary features effectiveness across varying incentive structures to establish their intrinsic motivational value.

The analysis of user-generated content (MOB Stories) remained primarily quantitative, focusing on participation rates rather than content quality or engagement depth. A systematic qualitative coding of participant-created content would provide deeper insights into creative engagement mechanisms and their relationship to sustained behavioral change.

Future research should examine cross-cultural transferability, long-term behavioural sustainability, and alternative incentive structures that maintain effectiveness while reducing resource requirements. The framework's adaptability to various serious game contexts offers a promising area for investigation.

6.3 Conclusions and Implications

This paper demonstrates empirically that complementary features significantly enhance transformational games for Generation Z users.

Key findings: (1) Institutional-based team formation achieved 62.1% completion rates in meeting minimum membership requirements while preventing ghost teams; (2) Voluntary educational integration achieved measurable knowledge retention (67% accuracy) without compromising competitive engagement; (3) User-generated content sustained creative expression when aligned with existing social media practices; (4) Complementary features enabled engagement recovery during extended competitive periods.

Practical implications extend to educators, policymakers, and designers developing behavioural change interventions for younger generations through evidence-based design principles for youth-focused sustainability initiatives.

The Complementary Features Layer framework provides a foundation for developing interventions meeting this generation's sophisticated digital engagement expectations while delivering measurable environmental and educational outcomes—essential capabilities for addressing contemporary sustainability challenges through youth engagement.

References

1. Alruthaya, A., Nguyen, T., Lokuge, S.: The Application of Digital Technology and the Learning Characteristics of Generation Z in Higher Education. arXiv (Cornell University) (2021)
2. Arnab, S., Lim, T., Carvalho, M.B., Bellotti, F., De Freitas, S., Louchart, S., Suttie, N., Berta, R., De Gloria, A.: Mapping learning and game mechanics for serious games analysis. Br. J. Edu. Technol. **46**(2), 391–411 (2015)
3. Toups Dugas, P.O., Kerne, A., Hamilton, W.: Game design principles for engaging cooperative play: Core mechanics and interfaces for non-mimetic simulation of fire emergency response. In: Proceedings of the 2009 ACM SIGGRAPH Symposium on Video Games, pp. 71–78. ACM, New York (2009)
4. Florenthal, B.: Young consumers' motivational drivers of brand engagement behavior on social media sites: A synthesised U&G and TAM framework. J. Res. Interact. Mark. **13**(3), 351–391 (2019)
5. Gardner, B., Rebar, A.L.: Habit formation and behavior change. In: Oxford research encyclopedia of psychology. Oxford University Press (2019)
6. Grigoreva, E.A., Garifova, L.F., Polovkina, E.A.: Consumer behavior in the information economy: Generation Z. International Journal of Financial Research **12**(2), 164–171 (2021)
7. Madani, K., Pierce, T.W., Mirchi, A.: Serious games on environmental management. Sustain. Cities Soc. **29**, 1–11 (2017)
8. O'Connell, T.A., Grantham, J.D., Workman, K.A., Wong, W.: Leveraging game-playing skills, expectations and behaviors of digital natives to improve visual analytic tools. Journal For Virtual Worlds Research **2**(1) (2009)
9. Sutarman, S., Riyanto, S., Lesmana, S.J.: The Role of Microlearning in Lifelong Learning and Its Effectiveness for Generation Z. The International Journal of Education Management and Sociology **4**(1), 23–32 (2025)
10. Di Dio, S., Lissandrello, E., Schillaci, D., Caroleo, B., Vesco, A., D'Hespeel, I.: MUV: A game to encourage sustainable mobility habits. In: Gentile, M., Allegra, M., Söbke, H. (eds.) Games and Learning Alliance, pp. 60–70. Springer (2019). https://doi.org/10.1007/978-3-030-11548-7_6
11. Schillaci, D., Di Dio, S., Filippi, M.: Sustainable Mobility as a Sport. In: Zanella, F. (eds.) Multidisciplinary Aspects of Design. Design! OPEN 2022. Springer Series in Design and Innovation, vol. 37. Springer, Cham (2024). https://doi.org/10.1007/978-3-031-49811-4_70
12. Vesco, A., Di Dio, S., Lissandrello, E., Schillaci, D.: A Gamified Mobility Experience. In: Kurosu, M. (eds.) Human-Computer Interaction. Human Values and Quality of Life. HCII 2020. Lecture Notes in Computer Science, vol. 12183. Springer, Cham (2020). https://doi.org/10.1007/978-3-030-49065-2_45
13. Chang, C. W., & Chang, S. H. (2023). The impact of digital disruption: Influences of digital media and social networks on forming digital natives' attitude. SAGE Open, 13(3). https://doi.org/10.1177/21582440231191741
14. Ifenthaler, D., Cooper, M., Daniela, L., Şahin, M.: Social anxiety in digital learning environments: An international perspective and call to action. Int. J. Educ. Technol. High. Educ. **20**, 50 (2023). https://doi.org/10.1186/s41239-023-00419-0
15. Sutarman, S., Riyanto, S., Lesmana, S.J.: The role of microlearning in lifelong learning and its effectiveness for Generation Z. The International Journal of Education Management and Sociology **4**(1), 23–32 (2025)

Analysis of Students' Collaborative Behaviours in a Virtual Laboratory

Maéva Kurtz[1,2]([envelope]) [ORCID], Luis Alberto Pinos Ullauri[1,2] [ORCID],
Azzeddine Benabbou[1,2] [ORCID], Catherine Pons[1,3] [ORCID], and Julien Broisin[1,2] [ORCID]

[1] Institut de Recherche en Informatique de Toulouse, Toulouse, France
maeva.kurtz@irit.fr
[2] Université de Toulouse, Toulouse, France
[3] Institut National Universitaire Champollion, Albi, France

Abstract. Hands-on laboratories play a crucial role in developing practical and collaborative skills such as teamwork. However, these laboratories are often resource-intensive. Virtual and Remote Laboratories (VRLs) have thus emerged as a viable alternative to address these limitations. To foster collaboration in VRLs, we designed a collaborative virtual environment grounded in principles from Computer-Supported Collaborative Learning. The environment supports group work by assigning learners distinct roles and includes a chat system for exchanging ideas. We conducted an experiment using a two-condition protocol: an Automatic condition, in which role changes were system-driven, and a Manual condition, in which learners could request role changes freely. The results show that the distribution of collaborative behaviours where significantly associated with conditions. The Manual condition had notably different role changes compared to the Automatic condition. Students reported high teamwork quality, although the perceived usability of the system was rated as "OK".

Keywords: Computer-supported collaborative learning · Virtual laboratories · Collaborative behaviour · Chat analysis

1 Introduction

Hands-on laboratories play an important role in education, particularly in STEM (science, technology, engineering and mathematics), as it enables students to learn and better understand theoretical concepts through direct hands-on experience [12]. Additionally, hands-on learning fosters social and teamwork skills [15]. Despite their advantages, conventional hands-on laboratories present several limitations. The growing number of students often exceeds the limited availability of laboratory equipment, leading to organisational constraints [17]. Virtual and Remote Laboratories (VRLs) have thus emerged as a promising alternative. VRLs refer to experimental environments accessible via a web browser [9]. Remote laboratories involve the use of real physical equipment that is accessed and controlled remotely, whereas virtual laboratories simulate experimental setups entirely through software [19]. VRLs have been shown to alleviate a number of issues; however, they have been observed to fail to incorporate the collaborative aspect and associated tools. Nevertheless, integrating collaboration into VRLs is essential, in order to aim for the same skills development as traditional laboratories, but also because the collaborative and community aspects are common mechanisms in gamification [21], which has real potential for performance and learning [24]. Moreover, teachers often express the necessity for students to work in pairs or groups. We designed a VRL aimed at fostering student collaboration, drawing on theoretical principles from Computer-Supported Collaborative Learning (CSCL). The collaborative features of our VRL include shared document editing for reporting task outcomes, a shared experiment screen, and real-time text messaging. To support the development of role-specific competencies, the environment also assigns distinct roles to learners: the *note-taker* is responsible for composing the report of the lab activity, while the *operator* operates the virtual instruments. Two modes are available: in *Automatic* mode, role changes are managed by the system; in the *Manual* mode, students can switch roles at their discretion. The system was experimented in an authentic learning context involving 60 higher education students where two experimental conditions were designed. Our objective was to tackle the following research questions:

- **RQ1: How did students collaborate in the virtual laboratory?**
- **RQ2: What are the differences between the Manual and Automatic conditions in terms of collaboration?**
- **RQ3: What are the differences between the Automatic and Manual conditions in terms of perceived collaboration and usability?**

These questions are motivated by research highlighting high degree of control of role distribution can influence students' collaborative learning processes [8].

2   Related Work

2.1   Importance of Collaboration for Learning in VRLs

In our works, we adhere to the definition of collaboration proposed by Roschelle & Teasley [20] : "*a coordinated, synchronous activity that is the result of a continued attempt to construct and maintain a shared conception of a problem*". Collaboration is a common mechanism in gamification [21] as it has real potential for performance and learning [24]. Several theoretical perspectives underline this point. For instance, the theory of social constructivism and Vygotsky's approach posit that learning occurs through experiential, communicative [14], and social processes [25]. Peer interactions foster explanation, debate, and mutual regulation, all of which contribute to the co-construction of knowledge [6]. Within VRLs, this collaborative dimension is especially relevant as it can yield diverse learning outcomes. For example, it can lead to knowledge acquisition and improved problem-solving abilities during joint tasks [6]. Therefore, embedding collaboration in VRLs is a critical strategy for engaging students and ensuring the effective deployment of this technology. Yet, students working in remote laboratory environments require targeted support to collaborate effectively [3].

2.2   Scripts and Role Assignment in CSCL

The structuring of collaborative learning processes has been identified as an affordance to be taken into consideration [11]. It can take the form of CSCL scripts, which structure collaboration by *"defining sequences of activities, by creating roles within groups and by constraining the mode of interaction among peers or between groups"* [5]. The script theory of guidance delineates four script components: scriptlets, scenes, plays and roles [8]. The term "scriptlets" is used to denote the activities in which individuals engage. Scenes are comprised of a series of scriptlets that are arranged in sequential order for individual performers. Play is composed of scenes, and it describes the objectives of the scenario. Finally, roles can be understood as the distribution of activities across several scenes among individuals [8]. CSCL scripts have the potential to enhance learning outcomes for domain-specific knowledge and collaborative skills when compared to unstructured CSCL [23]. Learning can be derived from the interactions to compensate for the "split" introduced by the script, where resources and roles are divided [7]. Furthermore, some roles provide more cognitive learning opportunities; as a consequence, rotating roles thanks to scripts is a compelling argument to diminish the risk of unequal opportunity for cognitive benefits [22]. Nevertheless, in spite of the aforementioned advantages, it is imperative to exercise due diligence with regard to the monitoring of the risk of overscripting [22]. Overscripting can be defined as a hindrance to the learner's self-regulation through inadequate refinement or superfluous scaffolding by the CSCL script [8]. This has the effect of disrupting learning [8].

2.3   Scripts and Role Assignment in VRLs

The literature reports a variety of tools designed to support collaboration in VRLs, including CSCL scripts. For example, coordination between students is promoted in the COG platform by structuring collaborative activities into pairs and groups of four during computer-based practical work [1]. In some VRLs, such as the one described by [10], access to virtual resources can be coordinated by the instructor, who designates which students may control the laboratory tools at a given time. However, in these studies, the effect of different levels of role distributions in VRLs is not studied. There is, to the best of our knowledge, a lack of detailed analysis regarding the effect of different types of role distributions via CSCL scripts in VRLs. To address this gap, our study aims to compare two distribution of roles within a VRLs environment. In the *Automatic* condition, role changes are managed by the system; in the *Manual* condition, students can switch roles at their discretion. Automatic mode reflects a scripted distribution of roles [22], while Manual mode aligns with emergent role allocation [22].

3   ColLab

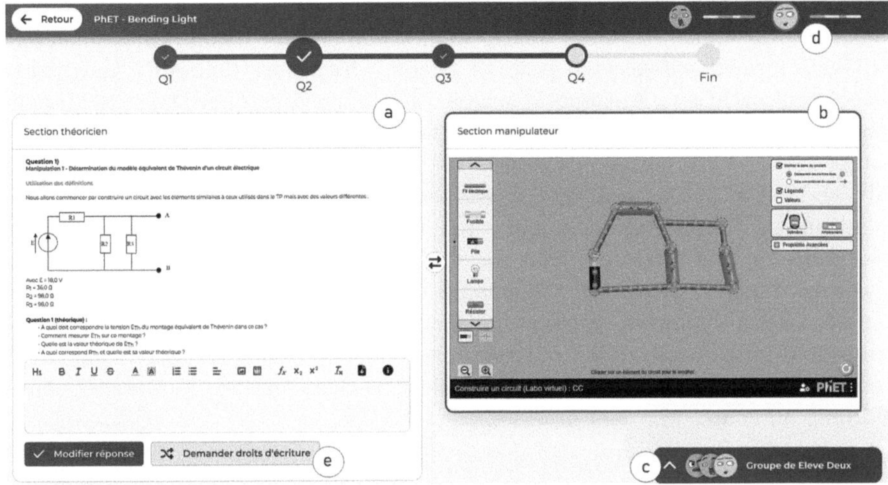

Fig. 1. Virtual laboratory interface. **a** Reporting area. **b** Simulation. **c** Text chat. **d** Role allocation bar. **e** Role change request button.

ColLab is a Node.js application that supports any web-based simulation. It allows groups of learners to collaboratively complete a lab assignment. Its interface has two shared workspaces: (1) a section for teacher-provided instructions and student responses (Fig. 1a) and (2) a simulation area displaying a web-based simulation from a link provided by the teacher, allowing interaction with virtual resources (Fig. 1b). All group members and the teacher can view both areas in real time. User avatars (Fig. 1c and d) show who is online. To facilitate communication, a synchronous text chat is available to students and the teacher. Text chat preserves a record of exchanges and supports reflection after the session. It also simplifies data analysis. The chat window can be expanded or minimised to avoid constant display during tasks (Fig. 1c). A role-based guidance system structures group collaboration. Only the operator interacts with the simulation, while the note-taker(s) complete the report. In triads, one student is the operator and two are note-takers. This structure scaffolds collaboration through assignment of dependent tasks and supports skill development through role rotation. The active workspace is highlighted by a coloured border (e.g., purple for operator, Fig. 1). The teacher decides if roles change automatically or manually. In Automatic mode, the role changes at each question, while in Manual mode a student can request a role change, and the peer receives a notification and can choose whether to accept it or not. A role allocation bar displays each participant's time spent in different roles (Fig. 1d), helping learners monitor and regulate their engagement.

4   Experiment

4.1   Methodology

We conducted an experiment with 60 first-year Chemistry students at a French higher education institution. Participation was voluntary with informed consent. Students formed self-selected pairs or triads, which were randomly assigned to one of two conditions: Automatic, where roles changed automatically, or Manual, where students managed role changes themselves. Groups had three weeks to complete the VRL activity remotely, as preparation for a hands-on electricity lab, and coordinated their own schedules. One week later, students filled out questionnaires on teamwork quality and VRL usability. The following log data was collected and analysed: chat messages, roles assigned after each question, and role change requests—all timestamped. We also collected and analysed self-reported data: teamwork questionnaire (10 items, 5-point Likert scale) from [16], translated into French, filled out per group, and System Usability Scale (SUS) completed individually. We could not collect teachers' grades. As a consequence, learning outcomes were not assessed.

4.2   Data Analysis

Chat Messages Analysis. We detailed the descriptive statistics of the messages per conditions, and compared the number of messages across conditions using a WilcoxonMannWhitney test. Moreover, we used boxplots for visual comparison. Messages were also pre-processed and classified using [4]'s five-category coding scheme: Planning, Contributing, Seeking Input, Reflection/Monitoring, and Social Interaction. Two experts coded the messages. Inter-rater reliability was assessed with Cohen's Kappa. We visualised category distributions via histograms and performed a χ^2 test to detect significant differences between conditions.

Role Changes. As only the Manual condition allowed role changes, we focused on it. We reported total, average and median role changes per group, the variation coefficient, and interquartile range. Then, we performed a MannWhitney test for statistical analysis. We also presented boxplots for a visual representation of the distribution.

Perceived Collaboration and Usability. Teamwork questionnaire responses were analysed using medians. An independent samples t-test assessed differences between conditions. SUS scores were similarly analysed and compared using medians and a t-test to detect usability differences between the two conditions.

4.3   Results

Chat Messages Analysis. We compared the number of messages across conditions using a WilcoxonMannWhitney test, which yielded no significant difference (p = 0.78). The median number of messages was 23 (IQR = 53.5) in Automatic and 19 (IQR = 44) in Manual. Figure 3 presents a visual comparison of the number of messages exchanged across conditions. The number of messages per group ranges from a minimum of 1 in Automatic and 3 in Manual to a maximum of 204 on both conditions. Additionally, the coefficient of variation in both conditions exceeds 100%, indicating a high degree of variability. After the classification of messages, we quantified the agreement of both classifications with Cohen's Kappa, $K = 0.72$, which is considered as 'Substantial', according to [13]. Therefore, we chose one of the raters' classifications, and plotted its distribution, from both the Manual and Automatic conditions, in Fig. 2. It can be seen that *Contributing* was the most frequently manifested behaviour. We also performed a χ^2 statistical test to look for significant associations between the message categories and the experimental condition. We found that the message categories were significantly associated (p < 0.05) with the condition, although this association was weak in intensity (Cramer's V = 0.1).

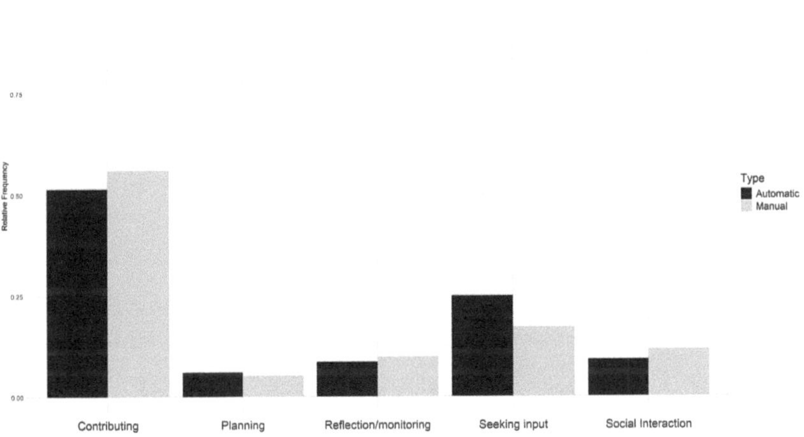

Fig. 2. Comparison of collaborative behaviour distributions across conditions

Role Changes. Table 1 shows a descriptive summary of the number of role changes across conditions and groups, depicting the mean, standard deviation, median, interquartile range and variation coefficient. It can be seen that there is a considerable difference in the number of role changes across conditions. Moreover, a Mann-Whitney test revealed a significant difference, with a p-value smaller than 0.0001. Figure 4 shows a boxplot of the number of role changes in the Manual condition. It can be seen that there is high variability in terms of role changes per groups, with a variation coefficient of 156%.

Table 1. Number of role changes throughout the experiment on both conditions. N_{rc} describes the number of role changes. $\overline{N_{rc}}$ is the average number of role changes per group. $N_{rc50}(IQR)$ describes the median and interquartile range. VC_{Nrc} corresponds to the variation coefficient. The two other indicators respectively describe the minimum and maximum number of role changes per group

Condition	N_{rc}	$\overline{N_{rc}}$ (SD)	$N_{rc50}(IQR)$	VC_{Nrc}	Min_{Nrc}	Max_{Nrc}
Automatic	56	4 (0)	4 (0)	0%	4	4
Manual	24	1.71 (2.67)	1 (2)	156%	0	10

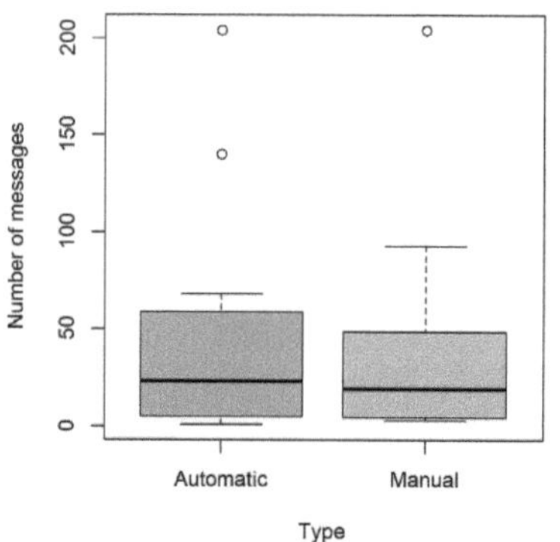

Fig. 3. Boxplot comparison of number of messages across conditions

Fig. 4. Boxplot of the number of role changes

Perceived Collaboration and Usability. We analysed the self-reported data collected through the teamwork quality questionnaire. The overall median score across all groups was 4.00 out of 5. We then compared the responses between the two experimental conditions. The Manual condition yielded a median score of 4.20, while the Automatic condition had a median score of 3.90. An independent samples t-test was conducted to assess the statistical significance of the difference between conditions, revealing no significant effect ($p > 0.05$). We also analysed self-reported data from the System Usability Scale (SUS), completed by 47 students. The overall median SUS score was 55.00. According to [2], this score falls between the categories of 'OK' and 'Good'. A high level of variability was observed, indicating divergent user experiences across participants. We then compared SUS responses between the two experimental conditions. The Manual condition yielded a median score of 60.00, while the Automatic condition produced a median score of 52.50. An independent samples t-test was conducted to evaluate the significance of this difference; however, the result was not statistically significant ($p > 0.05$).

5   Discussion

The type of message was found to be significantly associated with the experimental condition. This variation was particularly evident in the *Seeking Input* category, which predominantly consisted of requests for feedback and assistance, especially in the Automatic condition. Such behaviour can be interpreted positively, as it encourages knowledge sharing among students and promotes engagement with unfamiliar tasks. These findings are consistent with empirical studies demonstrating that scripts can effectively support online collaboration [18]. Conversely, a limited number of messages were transmitted by certain groups of students, a phenomenon that could be attributed to the use of an alternative mode of communication, such as a voice channel. The number of role changes differed significantly between conditions. In Manual, variability in terms of role changes per groups was high. It aligns with [22], who observed uneven role distribution in self-managed settings. Teamwork questionnaire results showed a higher median score in the Manual condition, indicating students felt more positively about collaboration when they controlled role switching. Yet, without learning outcome data, we cannot confirm whether this perception reflected actual effectiveness. SUS scores were generally low, likely due to technical issues (errors when integrating images in reports) and frustration with the text-based chat. The Manual condition again showed higher usability scores, possibly due to reduced frustration with role control. Still, differences in both questionnaires were not statistically significant—likely due to the limited sample size—and should be interpreted cautiously.

These results suggest scripting (e.g., automatic role switching) promotes balanced skill development. However, designers of collaborative virtual labs should consider integrating adaptive role management that responds to group dynamics rather than fixed transitions. Future work should explore links between chat behaviours and role changes to inform adaptive system design. Investigating the academic level of group members may also clarify the role allocation process. Comparing collaborative behaviour with and without the VRL would further illuminate its impact.

The study's main limitations include a small sample size, preventing strong statistical conclusions, and the lack of performance data, as teachers hadn't yet reviewed student work. Additionally, students used a prototype version of the VRL, which still had technical issues (e.g., inserting images in reports).

6   Conclusion

We presented a VRL designed to promote collaborative hands-on learning at a distance. We collected and analysed data from an experiment involving 60 first-year chemistry students at a French higher education institution, following their completion of one practical learning activity. The results indicate that students in the Automatic condition tended to exchange more *Seeking Input* messages. Role changes numbers were significantly different across conditions. Although the differences were not statistically significant, students in the Manual condition perceived the application as more usable and reported higher teamwork quality. These findings are encouraging and suggest that structured role distribution in virtual laboratory environments may influence collaboration dynamics.

Acknowledgements. This work was supported by a French government grant managed by the Agence Nationale de la Recherche as part of the France 2030 program, reference ANR-22-EXEN-0003 (PEPR eNSEMBLE / PILOT).

References

1. Arora, R., Goel, S., Mittal, R.K.: Supporting collaborative software development in academic learning environment: A collaborative pair and quadruple programming based approach. In: 2017 Tenth International Conference on Contemporary Computing. p. 1–7 (2017). https://doi.org/10.1109/IC3.2017.8284330
2. Bangor, A., Kortum, P., Miller, J.: Determining what individual sus scores mean: adding an adjective rating scale. J. Usability Stud. 4(3), 114–123 (2009)
3. Corter, J., Esche, S., Chassapis, C., Ma, J., Nickerson, J.: Process and learning outcomes from remotely-operated, simulated, and hands-on student laboratories. Comput. Educ. 57, 2054–2067 (2011). https://doi.org/10.1016/j.compedu.2011.04.009
4. Curtis, D., Lawson, M.: Exploring collaborative online learning. J. Asynchronous Learn. Netw. 5, 21–34 (2001)
5. Dillenbourg, P., Tchounikine, P.: Flexibility in macro-scripts for computer-supported collaborative learning. J. Comput. Assist. Learn. 23(1), 1–13 (2007). https://doi.org/10.1111/j.1365-2729.2007.00191.x
6. Dillenbourg, P.: What do you mean by collaborative learning? In: Dillenbourg, P. (ed.) Collaborative-learning: Cognitive and Computational Approaches, pp. 1–19. Elsevier, Oxford (1999)
7. Dillenbourg, P., Hong, F.: The mechanics of cscl macro scripts. Int. J. Comput.-Support. Collab. Learn. 3(1), 5–23 (2008). https://doi.org/10.1007/s11412-007-9033-1
8. Fischer, F., Kollar, I., Stegmann, K., Wecker, C.: Toward a script theory of guidance in computer-supported collaborative learning. Educ. Psychol. 48(1), 56–66 (2013). https://doi.org/10.1080/00461520.2012.748005
9. Govaerts, S., Cao, Y., Vozniuk, A., Holzer, A., Zutin, D.G., Ruiz, E.S.C., Bollen, L., Manske, S., Faltin, N., Salzmann, C., Tsourlidaki, E., Gillet, D.: Towards an Online Lab Portal for Inquiry-Based STEM Learning at School. In: Wang, J.-F., Lau, R. (eds.) ICWL 2013. LNCS, vol. 8167, pp. 244–253. Springer, Heidelberg (2013). https://doi.org/10.1007/978-3-642-41175-5_25
10. Jara, C.A., Candelas, F.A., Torres, F., Dormido, S., Esquembre, F.: Synchronous collaboration of virtual and remote laboratories. Comput. Appl. Eng. Educ. 20(1), 124–136 (2012). https://doi.org/10.1002/cae.20380
11. Jeong, H., Hmelo-Silver, C.E.: Seven affordances of computer-supported collaborative learning: How to support collaborative learning? how can technologies help? Educ. Psychol. 51(2), 247–265 (2016). https://doi.org/10.1080/00461520.2016.1158654

12. Jiun, L., Kamarudin, N., Hassan, A., Talib, O.: Inquiry-based learning in laboratory science. In: Graduate Research in Education Conference (GREDUC 2014) (2014)

13. Landis, J.R., Koch, G.G.: The measurement of observer agreement for categorical data. Biometrics **33**(1), 159–174 (1977), http://www.jstor.org/stable/2529310

14. Leinonen, T., Muukkonen, H., Hakkarainen, K., Mielonen, S., Bakhtin, M.: Supporting learning communities in education (01 2000)

15. Ma, J., Nickerson, J.V.: Hands-on, simulated, and remote laboratories: A comparative literature review. ACM Comput. Surv. **38**(3), 7–es (2006). https://doi.org/10.1145/1132960.1132961

16. Meslec, N., Curşeu, P.L.: Are balanced groups better? belbin roles in collaborative learning groups. Learn. Individ. Differ. **39**, 81–88 (2015). https://doi.org/10.1016/j.lindif.2015.03.020, https://www.sciencedirect.com/science/article/pii/S1041608015000783

17. Muchlas, Novianta, M.A.: An online lab for digital electronics course using information technology supports. In: 2015 International Conference on Science in Information Technology (ICSITech). p. 299–302. IEEE, Yogyakarta, Indonesia (2015). https://doi.org/10.1109/ICSITech.2015.7407821

18. Popov, V., Biemans, H.J., Fortuin, K.P., Van Vliet, A.J., Erkens, G., Mulder, M., Jaspers, J., Li, Y.: Effects of an interculturally enriched collaboration script on student attitudes, behavior, and learning performance in a cscl environment. Learn. Cult. Soc. Interact. **21**, 100–123 (2019). https://doi.org/10.1016/j.lcsi.2019.02.004

19. Potkonjak, V., Gardner, M., Callaghan, V., Mattila, P., Guetl, C., Petrovic, V., Jovanovic, K.: Virtual laboratories for education in science, technology, and engineering: A review. Computers & Education **95**, 309–327 (2016). https://doi.org/10.1016/j.compedu.2016.02.002

20. Roschelle, J., Teasley, S.: The construction of shared knowledge in collaborative problem solving. Computer Supported Collaborative Learning (1995). https://doi.org/10.1007/978-3-642-85098-15

21. Santos, L., Sobreira, P., Santiago, L., Abijaude, J., Guemhioui, K., Wahab, O.: Gamification-supported collaborative learning: A systematic literature review. In: IEEE World Conference on Engineering Education (EDUNINE). pp. 1–5 (03 2020). https://doi.org/10.1109/EDUNINE48860.2020.9149543

22. Strijbos, J.W., Weinberger, A.: Emerging and scripted roles in computer-supported collaborative learning. Computers in Human Behavior **26**, 491–494 (07 2010). https://doi.org/10.1016/j.chb.2009.08.006

23. Vogel, F., Wecker, C., Kollar, I., Fischer, F.: Socio-Cognitive Scaffolding with Computer-Supported Collaboration Scripts: a Meta-Analysis. Educ. Psychol. Rev. **29**(3), 477–511 (2016). https://doi.org/10.1007/s10648-016-9361-7

24. Vrugte, J., Lehner, T., Zievinger, D.: Gamified expectation management to foster collaborative learning. In: ISLS Annual Meeting 2023. pp. 245–248 (10 2023). https://doi.org/10.22318/cscl2023.499956

25. Vygotsky, L.S.: Mind in society: The development of higher psychological processes, vol. 86. Harvard university press (1978)

Design and Evaluation of "Sancoro Bingo": an Interactive Game Encouraging Continued Participation Among Older Adults

Sakura Mizobuchi[(✉)] [iD] and Hiroshi Suzuki [iD]

Kanagawa Institute of Technology, Shimoogino, Atsugi 1030, Kanagawa, Japan
`s2485001@cco.kanagawa-it.ac.jp, hsuzuki@ic.kanagawa-it.ac.jp`

Abstract. This study examined the design and effects of cognitive activities that induce older adults' continuous enjoyment and participation. We used "Sancoro Bingo"—a competitive interactive game that combines calculations and bingo. Experience sessions were held from May to July 2025, and evaluations were conducted based on participant attendance and repeat rates, questionnaires measuring subjective changes, game play logs, etc. The results revealed that participants had a positive experience with the game, and improvements were reported in "enjoyment," "concentration," and "self-efficacy." Game performance exhibited a logarithmic improvement, indicating that intuitive controls and explicit rule design fostered rapid mastery. Furthermore, interactions and spontaneous cooperative behavior among participants were observed, confirming that the game promotes social connections. The study indicates that Sancoro Bingo is both psychologically and socially acceptable to older adults and may effectively encourage continuous participation. It provides insights for future development in local communities and application to diverse groups.

Keywords: Game for Older Adults · Game Design Evaluation · Social Connection

1 Introduction

In Japan, older adults (aged 65 and over) accounted for 29.1% of the total population in 2022 [1]. Thus, extension of healthy life expectancy is an urgent issue. Daily cognitive stimulation is recommended as a preventive measure for dementia and frailty [2], and the use of digital games has recently attracted attention [3]. As digital games can also foster interaction and may help alleviate social isolation among older adults [3, 4], their broader adoption is socially valuable. However, the spread of such games in this age group remains limited because of preconceptions that they are "too complicated to operate" or "nothing more than a pastime" [5, 6].

To address this challenge, we developed "Sancoro Bingo"—a game in which players rapidly manipulate a cube-shaped user interface to create arithmetic formulas and achieve bingo [7]. A preliminary study confirmed that the game is easy for older adults to operate and highly acceptable to them, but the effects of continuous play have yet to be verified. Therefore, from May to July 2025 we organized a series of community-based trial sessions, inviting older adults who do not usually play digital games. This study evaluates data from those sessions, focusing on (i) changes in acceptability, (ii) trends in continued participation, and (iii) indications of change in simple cognitive measures. The succeeding section will introduce relevant previous studies.

2 Related Work

Game-based interventions for older adults are valued both for their cognitive benefits and for their capacity to sustain engagement when the play experience is perceived as enjoyable, easy, and socially meaningful. A meta-analysis by Wang et al. [8] showed that digital game training improves processing speed and attention, with competitive or cooperative formats yielding the largest gains. Complementing this, Anguera et al. [9] found that an interactive 3-D game stimulated attention and promoted multitasking while inducing EEG-based plastic changes, and Kuo et al. [10] reported executive-function gains from group card-game sessions underscoring the value of social interaction.

Nevertheless, many studies rely on solitary, screen-based play; research that combines intuitive, body-based controls with real-time competition remains scarce. Such design features are crucial because older adults frequently cite complex controls and vague goals as barriers to participation [5]. Clear interfaces, moderate challenge, and opportunities for social contact foster acceptance and sustained use [4], while the self-determination theory highlights enjoyment, autonomy, and competence as drivers of continued engagement [11]. Together, these findings suggest that cognitively beneficial games for older adults should couple low-friction, physically intuitive interaction with enjoyable social play—an approach our "Sancoro Bingo" system is designed to embody.

3 Sancoro Bingo Design

3.1 Overview of Sancoro Bingo

Sancoro Bingo is an interactive, cognitively engaging game designed for older adults (Fig. 1). Players use cube-shaped controllers marked with numbers and operators and form simple arithmetic expressions, aiming to reach target number displayed on a screen by rotating and arranging the cubes. For instance, the target "8" may be reached using expressions such as [10] [-] [2] or [8] [÷] [1]. The game incorporates both physical and cognitive engagement, encouraging brain activation and social interaction.

The system is implemented using a game system developed by Unity, cube-shaped controllers with NFC tags and readers, and physical buttons, enabling intuitive operation without conventional game controllers with only buttons.

Fig. 1. Sancoro Bingo game system.

3.2 Game Modes and Functions

Sancoro Bingo includes two main gameplay modes and a logging system to track gameplay performance.

Competitive Mode. Two players calculate formulas to obtain numbers displayed on a 5 × 5 bingo card on the screen (placing their own player-colored checkers on the squares) and aim to achieve bingo (placing player-colored checkers in a row). The game's design fosters interaction and conversation through its competitive elements. However, the outcome of the game is influenced by factors such as the opponent's calculation speed and familiarity with the game. Consequently, there are limitations to using it as a measure of individual growth or skill.

Solo Play Mode. To facilitate the analysis of individual performance trends, a solo play mode has been implemented. In this mode, players use cube-shaped controllers to input an equation whose answer matches a target number, like the competitive mode. Instead of filling in the numbers on a bingo sheet, players must create an equation using the specified operators to produce the target number. For instance, challenges such as "Create '17' using addition" are randomly generated each time, with the operator and target number specified. Players have 60 s to resolve as many problems as possible.

Logging System. To record individual performance trends, we distributed personal cards with QR codes to participants and introduced a system that automatically saves scores by linking to a database when the cards are scanned with a QR codes reader. Owing to this system, participants' scores for each session can be managed centrally, which renders it possible to visualize changes in performance on an ongoing basis.

In this study we place our emphasis on how participants accept and continue to engage with the system, rather than on technical specifications. The implementation details are therefore kept brief, and readers interested in a fuller description may refer to our earlier work [7].

4 Study Design and Data Collection

4.1 Experience Session Overview

From May 20 to July 18, 2025, we conducted a seven-session Sancoro Bingo experience event at the citizen exchange facility "Amyu Atsugi" in Atsugi City, Kanagawa Prefecture. The participants included 19 residents aged 75 and older. Participation was open to all, and attendance at each session was left to the individual's schedule. By adopting this flexible format, we are moving closer to a practical operational model that considers real-world implementation.

The flow of each session is as follows. Through weekly sessions, we have observed significant changes in both cognitive and social functions.

1. Paper-Based Math Test: Participants solve math problems for one minute before playing the game once a month.
2. Solo Play Mode: Participants play in solo mode twice to warm up and record their scores.
3. Competitive Mode: Participants play against others with similar skill levels or with friends.

4.2 Data Collection Methods

Questionnaire. A questionnaire was created to assess whether continuous participation in Sancoro Bingo leads to alterations in the psychological acceptance of older individuals. The questionnaire was administered approximately one month after the experience began.

The questionnaire design was informed by research on intrinsic motivational factors considered important in activities in which older adults voluntarily participate on an ongoing basis [11] and research on factors contributing to the continuation of gamification for older adults [12, 13]. These theories and studies indicate that "enjoyment," "self-efficacy," "concentration," and "social relationships" are important psychological factors that promote continued participation.

The questionnaire was designed to evaluate subjective changes in the gaming experience from the following five perspectives: enjoyment, concentration, cognitive reaction speed, confidence, and motivation to continue. These elements are designed to promote sustained engagement and gauge the acceptability and effectiveness of the activity. Based on changes in participants' internal responses, the activity's impact is assessed. In this study, the five questions were categorized into three evaluation axes for analysis: emotional acceptance, cognitive engagement, and self-efficacy. The correspondence between each question and the evaluation axes is presented in Table 1.

Participants responded using a 5-point Likert scale (5 = significantly better than a month ago; 1 = significantly worse than a month ago) to quantify subjective changes. Additionally, a free-response section was included to gather feedback and suggestions regarding the experience and Sancoro Bingo.

Table 1. Questionnaire contents and evaluation axis.

Evaluation Axis		Question Items
Emotional Acceptance	Enjoyment	Q1. Do you find Sancoro Bingo more enjoyable than before?
	Motivation to continue	Q5. Have you become more determined to continue playing Sancoro Bingo?
Cognitive Engagement	Concentration	Q2. Have you been able to concentrate better than before while playing Sancoro Bingo?
	Cognitive reaction speed	Q3. Do you feel that you are quicker than before at coming up with ideas for formulas and deciding which square to get next?
Self-Efficacy	Confidence	Q4. Do you feel that your dislike of math has decreased and that you have become more confident than before?

Play Log Data. This data records play data from each session and stores it in a database linked to ID cards. Specifically, it records the numbers and operators used, the total number of numbers generated, and the average calculation time. The data are utilized to objectively evaluate changes in and improvement trends of individual's calculation skills. This study focused on the date of participation and the number of correct answers in solo play mode.

5   Results

5.1   Acceptability Assessment

Participation in the Experience Session. Each of the seven sessions had between nine and 16 participants. Figure 2 depicts a shift in the number of participants. The participants included individuals who had been with the program from the beginning, as well as those who had joined midway through, having been encouraged by friends or having seen posters of the program. During the seven sessions, the percentage of participants who attended two or more sessions was very high at approximately 89.5%, and the average attendance rate from the first day of participation for individual was approximately 73.0%. This is a high retention rate for a voluntary, face-to-face program for older adults [14], indicating that the program has been well received in terms of continuity.

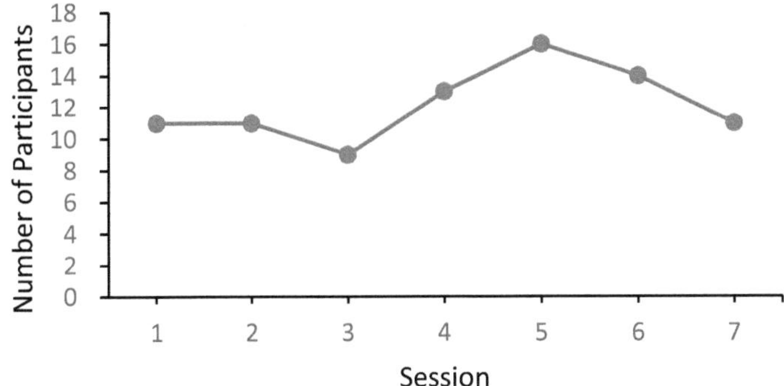

Fig. 2. Change in number of participants in each of the seven sessions.

Results of Questionnaire. A total of 13 participants who had participated in the experience session for over one month were surveyed. All evaluations were conducted using a 5-point Likert scale (5 = significantly better than a month ago; 1 = significantly worse than a month ago). The results of the questionnaire survey are displayed in Fig. 3.

Emotional Acceptance. Regarding the "enjoyment" of Sancoro Bingo in Q1, the average score was 3.85, and regarding the "desire to continue" Sancoro Bingo in Q5, the average score was 4.46. Both had a median of 4, so both received more positive evaluations than one month ago. The willingness to continue was evaluated more favorably, with many positive comments about the experience session, such as "I look forward to meeting various people," "I feel motivated to go to the experience session," and "I spend my time relaxing at home, so I can enjoy the excitement of the experience session."

Cognitive Engagement. Regarding the "concentration" component of the Q2 Sancoro Bingo experience, the average score was 3.77. In Q3, the average score for "insight" and "decision-making" was 3.69. Both components had a median of 4 and were evaluated as having improved compared to one month ago. Free comments included reports such as "I started doing calculations when I look at the calendar" and "I am becoming more interested in numbers and my brain is becoming better at mental arithmetic." The experience session had induced changes in daily life, and participants had undergone a self-motivated change in consciousness, such as doing brain training independently using numbers.

Self-efficacy. In Q4, the average score for "increased confidence" in calculations was 3.69 and its median was 4, indicating an improvement over previous score. In the free response section, comments included, "I am happy that I can experience it on my own because I can understand my own level of understanding, but I am not good at competing with others," and "I want to improve even a little, but I get too nervous and cannot think straight when I try to do it at home." While a few participants reported feelings of inferiority when comparing themselves to others, the sense of personal growth may have contributed to their increased confidence.

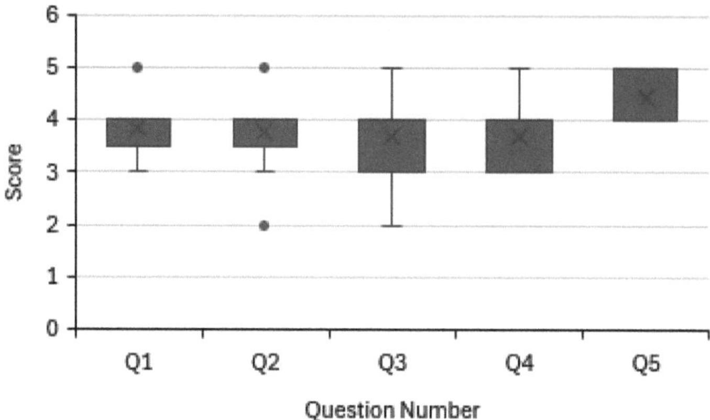

Fig. 3. Results of the questionnaire survey of participants who attended the experience sessions for over one month (n = 13)

5.2 Changes in Scores in Solo Mode

We analyzed the average number of correct answers in solo play mode for eight participants who attended six or more experience sessions. The results are displayed in Fig. 4. The number of correct answers was estimated using the logarithmic function $y = 2.0788\ln(x) + 4.0121$, and the coefficient of determination $R^2 = 0.9649$ confirmed that this model provided a satisfactory fit. This indicates that, after an initial rapid increase in scores, the increase becomes slower but continues to rise over the course of six sessions.

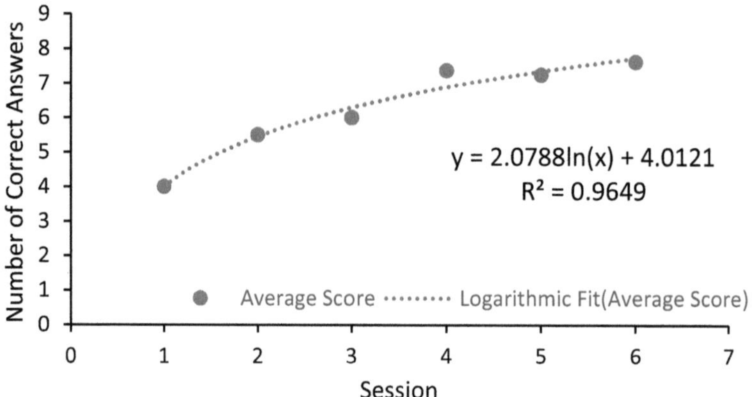

Fig. 4. Average score of number of correct answers (n = 8).

However, in the solo play mode of Sancoro Bingo, it is expected that a score upper limit (number of problems that can be solved in 60 s), and a learning convergence trend (ceiling effect) will appear. Given the theoretical property of the logarithmic function to increase infinitely, it does not accurately reflect the actual situation. In future analyses that include longer-term observations and individual differences, it will be necessary to consider the application of logistic regression or sigmoid curves that assume convergence.

Additionally, the Wilcoxon signed-rank test was performed on the number of correct answers between the first and sixth attempts (see Table 2). The result was $p = 0.014 < 0.05$, indicating a significant improvement in the number of correct answers. This result suggests that engaging in repeated, enjoyable activities may improve one's performance in computational tasks.

Table 2. The Wilcoxon signed-rank test was performed on the number of correct answers between the first and sixth attempts.

	Times		
	1st N = 8[1]	6th N = 8[1]	P-Value[2]
Number of Correct Answers	4.00 ± 1.60 (3.50 [3.00,5.00])	7.62 ± 1.69 (7.50 [6.75,9.00])	0.014

[1] Average ± SD (Median [25%,75%])   [2] The Wilcoxon signed-rank test

6 Discussion

6.1 Change of Psychological Acceptance: Stimulate Enjoyment and Motivation to Continue

The survey results indicated that most participants found Sancoro Bingo to be more enjoyable and motivating compared to a month ago, and that they had a positive experience with the game. Their free comments also revealed that they regarded the experience session as "enjoyable in their daily lives" and "a place to interact with people."

These results suggest that the game design may have satisfied the "intrinsic motivation [9] (enjoyment, curiosity, sense of accomplishment)," indicating that this theory is also effective for older adults. Furthermore, the responses to questions regarding "concentration" and "inspiration" were overwhelmingly positive, indicating that cognitive engagement occurred during the game. Sancoro Bingo is not merely cognitive training; it is a combination of fun and challenge and has been well-received by older adults. It has achieved a certain degree of effectiveness as a design that encourages continued participation.

6.2 Skill Changes: Understanding Rules and Mastering Calculations

Regarding the number of correct answers in the solo play mode, a logarithmic improvement in scores was observed from the first to sixth sessions, and a significant difference was confirmed ($p = 0.014$). This suggests that the learning effects of understanding the rules and mastering the controls in the early stages were evident, confirming that Sancoro Bingo is an intuitive and simple game design that is accessible to older adults.

In this context, the physical game system, which does not require complex operations, is designed to appeal to a wide range of participants, including those unfamiliar with digital games. Additionally, while the cognitive load as a computational task was kept to a minimum, the repeated experience of following rules and performing calculations may have fostered a sense of self-efficacy, such as "I can do it" and "I'm getting used to it." Such mastery of operations and a sense of growth—howsoever minor—are important factors in supporting the motivation of older adults to continue their activities.

6.3 Social Significance and Establishing Participation

In this study, experience sessions were conducted on a voluntary basis with no requirement to continue participation, and data were collected within a realistic framework with a view to actual social implementation. The high attendance and re-participation rates demonstrated the program's seamless integration into daily life without inducing excessive burden.

Additionally, free-response comments included statements such as "Conversations with others increased through the game" and "It became a motivation to attend a tense environment," suggesting that the game promoted social participation. Furthermore, participants taught each other the rules and collaborated to devise solutions, which fostered mutual learning and cooperation. This implies that the game affords cognitive activity as well as a social function as a new means of interaction. Therefore, games such as Sancoro Bingo have the potential to mitigate social isolation among older adults and promote intergenerational exchange.

7 Conclusion

This study used an interactive game called "Sancoro Bingo," which combines calculations and bingo, to conduct ongoing voluntary experience sessions and evaluate the acceptability and effectiveness of the game as an activity that induces older adults' enjoyment and participation. The results demonstrated that a significant number of participants exhibited positive psychological changes in their gaming experience.

Furthermore, results of the questionnaire survey indicated that their enjoyment, motivation to continue, and sense of self-efficacy had increased. It was confirmed that the participants' performance improved as they acquired proficiency in playing the game. It became evident that the rules and adapting to the controls could be effectively taught and learned in a relatively brief period of time.

The high attendance and re-participation rates at the experience sessions indicated that the activity resonated with older adults. Free comments and observations also confirmed the social effects of interaction and cooperation with others, suggesting that games can promote social participation as well as cognitive activity.

These results capture early engagement patterns and suggest that Sancoro Bingo has the potential to stimulate older adults' motivation to participate and to be incorporated naturally into their daily lives as a continuous activity. In the future, it will be necessary to expand the possibilities for implementation in local communities through application to a more diverse range of participants and verification of long-term effects.

Acknowledgments. This work was supported by JSPS KAKENHI Grant-in-Aid for Scientific Research C JP25K15409.

References

1. Cabinet Office, Government of Japan: Annual Report on the Ageing Society (2023). https://www8.cao.go.jp/kourei/whitepaper/w-2024/zenbun/pdf/1s1s_01.pdf. Accessed 22 July 2025
2. World Dementia Council: Dementia Friendly Initiatives—Japan. https://www.worlddementiacouncil.org/sites/default/files/2020-09/DFIs%20-%20Japan_V5.pdf (2020). Accessed 16 Sep 2025
3. Welfare News: Potential of e-sports for older adults: Overcoming digital aversion (2023). https://fukushishimbun.com/topics/29009. Accessed 16 Sep 2025
4. Voida, A., Carpendale, S., Greenberg, S.: The individual and the group in console gaming. In: Proceedings of CSCW 2010, pp. 371–380. ACM, New York (2010)
5. Ijsselsteijn, W.A., Nap, H.H., de Kort, Y.A.W., Poels, K.: Digital game design for elderly users. In: Future Play 2007, pp. 17–22. ACM, New York (2007)
6. De Schutter, B.: Never too old to play: the appeal of digital games to an older audience. Games and Culture **6**(2), 155–170 (2011)
7. Mizobuchi, S., Suzuki, H.: "Sancoro Bingo": a bingo game using dice with dementia prevention in mind. J Digital Contents Information Processing Society of Japan (DCON) **12**(1), 29–39 (2024). [in Japanese]
8. Wang, G., Zhao, M., Yang, F., Cheng, L.J., Lau, Y.: Game-based brain training for improving cognitive function in community-dwelling older adults: a systematic review and meta-regression. Arch. Gerontol. Geriatr. **92**, 104260 (2021)
9. Anguera, J.A., et al.: Video game training enhances cognitive control in older adults. Nature **501**(7465), 97–101 (2013)
10. Kuo, C.-Y., Huang, Y.-M., Yeh, Y.-Y.: Let's play cards: Multi-component cognitive training with social engagement enhances executive control in older adults. Front. Psychol. **9**, 2482 (2018)
11. Ryan, R.M., Deci, E.L.: Self-determination theory and the facilitation of intrinsic motivation, social development, and well-being. Am. Psychol. **55**(1), 68–78 (2000)
12. Johnson, D., Deterding, S., Kuhn, K.-A., Staneva, A., Stoyanov, S.: Gamification for health and wellbeing: a systematic review of the literature. Internet Interv. **6**, 89–106 (2016)
13. Hurmuz, M.Z.M., Jansen-Kosterink, S.M., Hermens, H.J., van Velsen, L.: Game not over: explaining older adults' use and intention to continue using a gamified eHealth service. Health Informatics Journal (2022)
14. Nichols, E.G., Shreffler-Grant, J., Weinert, C.: Where have they gone? recruiting and retaining older rural research participants. Online J. Rural Nurs. Health Care **21**(1), 179–182 (2021)

Toward Prescriptive Design of Educational Games: Mapping Game Mechanics to Learning Elements through Literature and Expert Review

Ilenius Ildephonce[1]([✉]) [iD] and Claudine Allen[2] [iD]

[1] The University of the West Indies–Five Islands, St John's, Antigua and Barbuda
ilenius.ildephonce@uwi.edu
[2] The University of the West Indies–Mona, Kingston, Jamaica
claudine.allen@uwi.edu

Abstract. The effectiveness of educational games (EGs) depends on design strategies that align game mechanics with pedagogical goals. Although research highlights this alignment, findings remain fragmented due to varied, descriptive methodologies. Addressing the need for a prescriptive framework, this study examines how learning elements influence the selection and configuration of game mechanics. A systematic literature review and an expert survey (n = 17, across nine countries) revealed consistent relationships between instructional elements (e.g., Bloom's taxonomy, learning objectives) and game elements (e.g., narrative, environment, feedback). Results show that learning constraints shape game design choices, offering actionable guidance for aligning mechanics with educational intent. This research contributes unified, reusable insights that bridge educational theory and game design practice, enabling the conceptualization and evaluation of EGs with greater coherence and effectiveness.

Keywords: Game dimensions · Learning dimensions · Educational games design · Learning and gaming alignment · Prescriptive design methodology

1 Introduction

In education and training, games and game elements serve different purposes. They can be deployed as tools to demonstrate a concept [23] , as a medium for delivering learning content [9] or as a prescriptive add on to achieve a particular goal such as student motivation [17]. A digital game designed to teach a subject is known as an educational game (EG), typically grounded on sound pedagogical principles [13]. However, EGs are costly and difficult to build [18] and, there are no standardized tools to facilitate their design. A method that works for one successful EG is often not transferable to another [3], leading to an ad hoc design

S. Bakkes et al. (Eds.): GALA 2025, LNCS 16307, pp. 192–202, 2026.
https://doi.org/10.1007/978-3-032-11043-5_19

process that raises barriers to the production and adoption of high-quality EGs [5]. This study aim to inform research on general considerations in selecting the right mechanics for a particular learning element.

The research question addressed in this study is: What are the observed influences of various learning elements on the selection and configuration of game mechanics during the design of effective EGs?

This question can be answered through surveys of educational game design experts or through the literature. This study adopts a systematic literature review approach, given the highly interdisciplinary and multidisciplinary nature of educational game design, which means there are few experts solely dedicated to this field. The systematic literature review was followed by an expert survey targeting EG developers, researchers, EGs' instructional designers and interaction designers. The result revealed that instructional elements and learner characteristics act as constraints when designing game mechanics to ensure the efficacy of EGs. EG designers can benefit from this knowledge when selecting specific game mechanics for given learning constraints, providing a prescriptive approach to choosing game elements for design problems. This paper makes the following contributions:

1. Synthesizes research on learning-game element alignment using a systematic review.
2. Presents empirical evidence from an international expert survey (n = 17).
3. Presents a unified knowledge linking learning constraints to game mechanics.

2   Background

2.1   Effective Educational Games

The literature primarily defines EGs effectiveness by first establishing a positive correlation between learner improvements and the use of EGs [21]. That effectiveness is derived from the EG's capacity to adequately present learning content, as evidenced by quantifiable measures indicating that learners have acquired the intended skills [24]. The second definition of effectiveness pertains to the game's success in attracting and retaining players, typically assessed through the Gameplay Experience Questionnaire (GEQ) [6].

However, these approaches suffer a major challenge; they imply that the effectiveness of EGs can only be determined post-procurement, which poses a high risk of designing ineffective EGs and consequently wasting resources.

Research agrees that a design approach which intentionally integrates learning and game elements to target specific skills is beneficial. The effectiveness of educational games (EGs) stems from deliberate design choices, particularly the careful amalgamation of learning and gameplay, where each game mechanic is purposefully crafted to achieve a specific educational goal.

2.2   EGs' Mechanics

Game mechanics can be defined as the rules, processes, and data at the heart of a game [1]. Some definitions separate game assets and rules from game mechanics; for example, [22] defines game mechanics as methods invoked by agents to interact with the game world. Furthermore, [20] separate mechanics from the contextual meanings generated by interaction with the game system. They associate mechanics with fun, and the game's meaningfulness is associated with connections between players and in-game characters. This study focuses on elements involved in invoking the gameplay's mechanical elements into dynamics that result in the player experiences. These elements range from the rule system, activities, rewards/punishments, environment, context to the player motivation factors etc.

2.3   Learning Elements and EGs' Mechanics Design

Learning is defined as "the ultimate practice of interpreting and evaluating knowledge through one's experiences, which is subsequently translated into skills, values, and comprehension" [2]. In formal training, structuring and delivering learning is crucial. Instructional design techniques such as learning taxonomies and learner-centred approaches have been put forward to formalize how we teach and learn. Research has evolved to study how gaming elements and learning elements align to develop design mechanisms that balance learning and fun [4,7]. These studies have focused on studying the role of learning elements in the design of effective EGs, resulting in specialized conceptual frameworks, software artifacts, and other constructs to develop and assess EGs based on these elements [8,10]. Due to the diversity of constraints, there is no "one size fits all" solution. Many proposed solutions are limited to specific aspects of the game or a few learning elements.

3   Methodology

This study employed a mixed-method approach combining a Systematic Literature Review (SLR) with a follow-up expert survey, aimed at uncovering how learning elements influence the design of game mechanics in educational games (EGs). The methodological details and underlying data from both the literature review and expert survey are openly available at SLR-Survey-Educational-Game-Mechanics

3.1   Systematic Literature Review

The SLR followed the guidelines by [15], suitable for capturing trends across interdisciplinary fields such as EG design [16]. The search was conducted across major academic databases using the Boolean string: *"Game mechanic" OR*

"Game element" AND "learning" NOT "gamification". This formulation deliberately excluded gamification to focus the search on publications discussing integrated learning and game mechanics, rather than motivational features in non-game contexts. The screening process, illustrated in Fig. 1 was guided by the inclusion and exclusion criteria shown in Table 1. This resulted in a final dataset of studies categorized by dimensions of both learning and game elements (see Table 2). Data were synthesized by grouping co-occurring design elements and learning dimensions commonly reported in the literature. The 72 articles were manually coded by one researcher using a hybrid approach: deductive categories from prior frameworks [4] and inductive categories from close reading. Each paper, coded in two passes for consistency, was typically assigned 12 learning dimensions and 23 game mechanics categories.

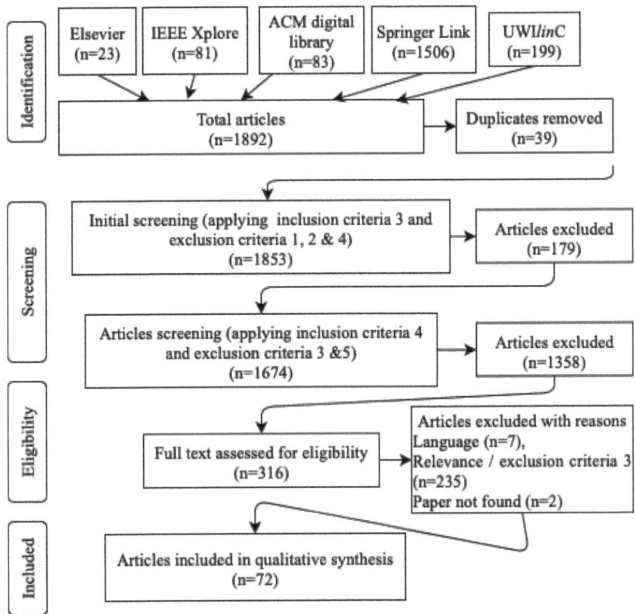

Fig. 1. Stages of the review process

3.2 Expert Survey

Following the SLR, an online questionnaire was administered to collect empirical insights from practitioners. The survey targeted educational game designers, researchers, instructional designers, and interaction designers. It captured professional experience, learner modeling practices (e.g. personality, learning styles, preferences), and the perceived role of instructional elements (e.g. Bloom's taxonomy, learning theories, learning objectives) in game design.

A total of 17 respondents from nine countries participated:

Table 1. Inclusion and exclusion criteria

Inclusion criteria	Exclusion criteria
1. Year between 2014-2020	1. Abstract only
2. Peer-reviewed	2. Books, thesis, editorials
3. Journal papers, conference papers and peer-reviewed book chapters	3. Papers not relevant to study objectives
4. Focuses on elements of designing a digital educational game	4. Extended abstracts or poster papers
	5. Any study focusing on other non-digital games (Physical or Board games)

- 13 game researchers, 3 game designers and 1 interaction designer
- 47% had 10+ years of experience; the remainder ranged from 1 to 10 years

The survey responses complemented the literature findings by validating or extending identified relationships between learning constraints and game mechanics.

4   Results: Observation on Game Elements to Learning Elements Alignment

The results represent a triangulation of evidence from both the systematic literature review (SLR) and the expert survey, rather than a weighted combination of the two. The SLR highlighted uneven coverage in the literature, with frequent emphasis on mechanics such as gameplay and feedback. In contrast, expert responses provided a more balanced perspective, identifying a wider set of learning constraints that influence different game elements. By comparing and cross-validating these sources, areas of convergence were treated as robust evidence, while divergences were noted as important differences between research and practice. The SLR observed mappings are also represented in a heatmap-style matrix (Fig. 2), with darker shades indicating stronger evidence. This visual highlights where learning dimensions most frequently influence game design choices, helping designers prioritize elements during development.

4.1   Summary of Key Mappings

To simplify interpretation, Table 3 presents the consolidated mappings between learning dimensions and their associated game elements, combining the findings of both the SLR and the expert survey.

Table 2. Data categorization and coding

Game dimension	Learning dimension
Gameplay orientation: This covers elements which focus on how mechanics are unfolded during play such as drill and practice, cut scenes, cascading information, time pressure, discovery, ownership, protege effect, pavlovian interaction etc	Learning effectiveness: This includes elements which result in an improved learning experience such as player experience, immersion, engagement, and assessment
Rewards & Feedback: This focuses on rewards elements such as points, leaderboards, status/titles and penalties	Player characteristics: This covers attributes of the target audience such as their age and gender difference, etc
Player character: This is for the character, NPC and character archetypes	Content: This covers content elements such as subject context, content types and scaffolding
Game environment: Covers aesthetics elements such as game content and assets, decorations, music and gravity	Player personality: This focuses on players' intelligence and personality types such as Keirsey's personality classification
Game story: narratives, dialogue tree, and goal setting are collectively represented by the game story dimension	Learning theories and instructional strategies are categorized as learning theories
Game genre: This focuses on play orientation such as simulation, mini-games, action, sports, MMORPG, etc	Skill: This comprised of reported soft, hard and cognitive skills

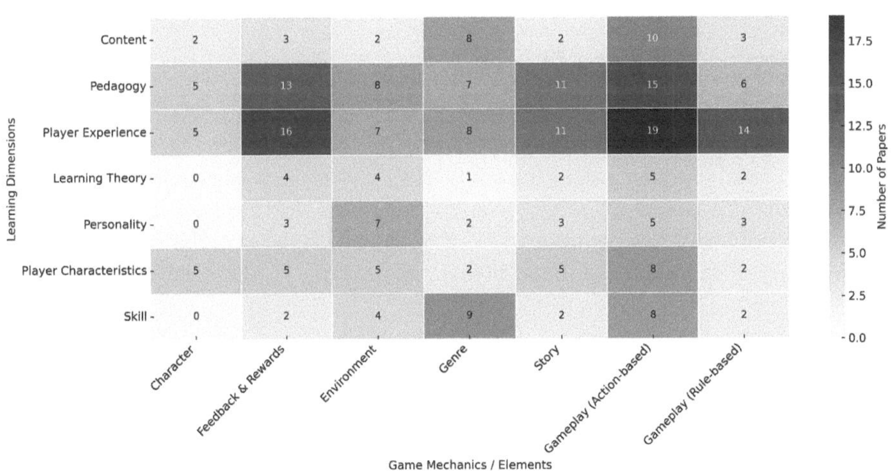

Fig. 2. Heatmap highlighting the studies reporting relationships between learning dimensions and game mechanic dimensions

4.2 Distribution and Emphasis in Literature Versus Practice

The SLR indicated that the reported relationships were not uniformly distributed across the papers, suggesting that some elements have been studied more extensively than others. For example, for game element dimensions, elements of the gameplay (action-based and rule-based) dimension are the most represented, with the action-based subdimension being the most reported. The elements of the gameplay were predominantly associated with the experience of the player, and 26% of the included articles focused on this relationship (see Fig. 2). In contrast, the least number of articles reported elements of character dimension, in contrast to general game studies where character design is a well-explored topic [12]. The expert survey revealed a more balanced picture to complement the systematic literature review. The expert survey confirmed the influence of multiple learning constraints on game design, with respondents highlighting the role of:

– Instructional strategies in shaping gameplay structure and assessment
– Learner characteristics in determining narrative tone, rewards, and visual presentation
– Learning content and objectives as foundational to level design, pacing, and instructional integration

In particular, the survey participants reported less reliance on learning styles, some explicitly stating that such frameworks were outdated or unsupported by evidence.

4.3 Observed Gaps and Divergences

Although both data sources support the alignment of learning and game elements, the SLR tended to underrepresent the influence of learner modeling, personality, and emergent storytelling, which experts saw as crucial to gameplay engagement and pedagogical success. In addition, skill-based mappings, especially soft skills such as collaboration, were more often emphasized in practical applications than in the academic literature.

5 Discussion

This study examined how learning elements influence the design of game mechanics in EGs by synthesizing evidence from a SLR and an expert survey. The findings provide a clearer understanding of how pedagogical intent can be translated into gameplay through specific design choices. The results highlight that instructional design elements, particularly learning objectives and learning content, serve as primary constraints in shaping game mechanics. These elements were most frequently linked to action-based gameplay, game progression, and feedback systems, supporting earlier work that emphasizes goal-driven game design for effective learning outcomes [11]. The expert survey echoed these results, with

Table 3. Key mappings between learning elements and game mechanics design

Learning dimension	Mapped game mechanics/elements
Player Experience	Gameplay elements (e.g., time pressure linked to player performance and competition; cutscenes linked to retention, motivation, repetition, guidance and instruction) ; feedback and reward systems; narrative or story elements linked to motivation and retention
Player Characteristics	Gameplay style (e.g., relaxed versus competitive); environment customization; rewards/feedback; story. Generally, age, gender, culture influence the mechanics design, for example, male players prefers competitive, long games, older gamers prefer relaxed gameplay
Player Preferences	Game genre selection; narrative and thematic alignment; rewards/feedback, asset and level progression design
Player Personality	Simulation, strategy games for planners/achievers; risk-taking and exploratory elements for extroverts; personalization features aligned with personality types (e.g., Bartle taxonomy)
Learning Objectives & Outcomes	Level progression; gameplay scaffolding; game genre; feedback systems; game asset and environment; integration of instruction within story arcs and cutscenes
Learning Theories	Behaviorism linked to drill/practice mechanics; Cognitivism linked to challenge tuning and instructional difficulty; Humanism, Experiential learning, flow theory linked to narrative immersion and visual aesthetics
Learning Content	Mini-games and puzzles for concept delivery; simulation for applied knowledge; environment design linked to content complexity and scaffolding
Skills (Cognitive/Soft)	planning linked to strategy and sports games, Strategic thinking linked to turn-based gameplay; problem solving linked to RPGs and adventure games;

all respondents affirming that learning objectives influence level design, narrative structures, and reward mechanisms. Additionally, learning content was closely tied to mini-games, puzzles, and simulation genres, indicating that content structure directly influences gameplay form.

Notably, both the literature and survey confirmed a strong relationship between game narratives and learning effectiveness. This reinforces the growing consensus that storytelling enhances meaning-making, motivation, and engagement in EGs [14,19,25]. While there was broad agreement across sources, some divergences were evident. Player modeling dimensions—such as personality and preferences—were consistently emphasized by practitioners but underreported in the literature. For example, survey respondents frequently cited Bartle's taxonomy and learner preferences as critical to genre selection, game environment, and cooperative mechanics, yet these were rarely featured in academic studies.

Furthermore, although learning theories are central to instructional design, their influence on game mechanics was only moderately reflected in the literature and expert survey. Only 25% of reviewed papers explored how theories like behaviorism or constructivism map onto game mechanics dimensions (e.g., feedback loops, scaffolding). This suggests a gap between pedagogical theory and its practical implementation in the design of EGs.

The consolidated mappings offer a prescriptive guide for aligning learning elements with EG game design decisions. For example, when the instructional goal emphasizes retention and reinforcement, designers might choose cutscenes, repetition loops, and achievement-based feedback. If the objective is exploration or problem-solving, design strategies may favor open-world mechanics or simulation genres. Importantly, recognizing learner variability, in terms of age, culture, and motivation, enables designers to personalize experiences without compromising instructional integrity. While the use of learning styles was generally discouraged by experts (some explicitly noting its theoretical flaws), elements like learner preferences and play types remain critical to engagement.

6   Conclusion

This study explored how learning elements influence the design of game mechanics in EGs. The results revealed consistent and actionable mappings between instructional elements, such as learning objectives, content, and learner characteristics, and core game elements, including gameplay structure, narrative, environment, and feedback systems. These findings contribute to the development of a prescriptive knowledge base that can guide EG designers in aligning educational intent with interactive gameplay. By consolidating fragmented insights across disciplines, this research offers a unified perspective on how pedagogical constraints can shape design decisions.

However, the study is limited by the relatively small expert sample (n = 17) and the underrepresentation of non-digital game design in the reviewed literature. Despite this, the triangulation of evidence provides a solid foundation for further inquiry. Future work should investigate the contextual application of these mappings across disciplines and learner types, as well as develop practical design tools or frameworks to support the systematic alignment of learning and game elements. Expanding the participant pool to include a more diverse range of practitioners, including non-academic and industry professionals, would also enhance the generalizability and impact of the findings.

Acknowledgments. The authors thank all experts who participated in the survey.

References

1. Adams, E., Dormans, J.: Game mechanics: advanced game design. New Riders (2012)

2. Ahmad, M.: An analysis of educational games design frameworks from software engineering perspective. J. Inf. Commun. Technol. **14**, 123–151 (2020)
3. Arnab, S., Clarke, S.: Towards a trans-disciplinary methodology for a game-based intervention development process. Br. J. Edu. Technol. **48**(2), 279–312 (2017)
4. Arnab, S., Lim, T., Carvalho, M.B., Bellotti, F., De Freitas, S., Louchart, S., Suttie, N., Berta, R., De Gloria, A.: Mapping learning and game mechanics for serious games analysis. Br. J. Edu. Technol. **46**(2), 391–411 (2015)
5. Ávila-Pesántez, D., Rivera, L.A., Alban, M.S.: Approaches for serious game design: A systematic literature review. The ASEE Comput. Educ. (CoED) J. **8**(3) (2017)
6. Braad, E., Žavcer, G., Sandovar, A.: Processes and models for serious game design and development. In: Entertainment computing and serious games, pp. 92–118. Springer (2016)
7. Callaghan, M., Savin-Baden, M., McShane, N., Eguíluz, A.G.: Mapping learning and game mechanics for serious games analysis in engineering education. IEEE Trans. Emerg. Top. Comput. **5**(1), 77–83 (2017)
8. De Freitas, S., Jarvis, S.: A framework for developing serious games to meet learner needs (2006)
9. De Gloria, A., Bellotti, F., Berta, R.: Serious games for education and training. Int. J. Serious Games **1**(1) (2014)
10. De Lope, R.P., Medina-Medina, N., Soldado, R.M., García, A.M., Gutiérrez-Vela, F.L.: Designing educational games: Key elements and methodological approach. In: 2017 9th International Conference on Virtual Worlds and Games for Serious Applications (VS-Games). pp. 63–70. IEEE (2017)
11. De Troyer, O., Van Broeckhoven, F., Vlieghe, J.: Linking serious game narratives with pedagogical theories and pedagogical design strategies. J. Comput. High. Educ. **29**(3), 549–573 (2017). https://doi.org/10.1007/s12528-017-9142-4
12. Gao, K., Zheng, S., Lee, D.L., Lee, D.Y., Huang, H.B.: Design method of the form of fantasy game characters. In: Knowledge Innovation on Design and Culture: Proceedings of the 3rd IEEE International Conference on Knowledge Innovation and Invention 2020 (IEEE ICKII 2020). pp. 113–116. World Scientific (2022)
13. Ildephonce, I., Mugisa, E., Allen, C.: Learning objects in instructional serious game design. In: 2018 IEEE 18th International Conference on Advanced Learning Technologies (ICALT). pp. 119–121. IEEE (2018)
14. Jemmali, C., Bunian, S., Mambretti, A., El-Nasr, M.S.: Educational game design: an empirical study of the effects of narrative. In: Proceedings of the 13th international conference on the foundations of digital games. pp. 1–10 (2018)
15. Kitchenham, B., Brereton, O.P., Budgen, D., Turner, M., Bailey, J., Linkman, S.: Systematic literature reviews in software engineering-a systematic literature review. Inf. Softw. Technol. **51**(1), 7–15 (2009)
16. Kraus, S., Breier, M., Dasí-Rodríguez, S.: The art of crafting a systematic literature review in entrepreneurship research. International Entrepreneurship and Management Journal **16**(3), 1023–1042 (2020). https://doi.org/10.1007/s11365-020-00635-4
17. Majuri, J., Koivisto, J., Hamari, J.: Gamification of education and learning: A review of empirical literature. In: Proceedings of the 2nd international GamiFIN conference, GamiFIN 2018. CEUR-WS (2018)
18. Ravyse, W.S., Blignaut, A.S., Leendertz, V., Woolner, A.: Success factors for serious games to enhance learning: a systematic review. Virtual Reality **21**(1), 31–58 (2017)

19. Recke, M.P., Perna, S.: An emergent narrative system to design conducive educational experiences. In: Universities and Entrepreneurship: Meeting the Educational and Social Challenges. Emerald Publishing Limited (2021)
20. Rogers, R., Woolley, J., Sherrick, B., Bowman, N.D., Oliver, M.B.: Fun versus meaningful video game experiences: A qualitative analysis of user responses. Comput. Games J. **6**(1–2), 63–79 (2017)
21. Serrano-Laguna, Á., Manero, B., Freire, M., Fernández-Manjón, B.: A methodology for assessing the effectiveness of serious games and for inferring player learning outcomes. Multimedia Tools Appl. **77**(2), 2849–2871 (2018)
22. Sicart, M.: Defining game mechanics. Game Studies **8**(2), n (2008)
23. Stefan, I.A., Stefan, A., Gheorghe, A.F.: Using entertainment games in education. In: Proceedings of the 11th international conference on virtual learning ICVL. vol. 7 (2016)
24. Vlachopoulos, D., Makri, A.: The effect of games and simulations on higher education: a systematic literature review. Int. J. Educ. Technol. High. Educ. **14**(1), 1–33 (2017). https://doi.org/10.1186/s41239-017-0062-1
25. Wang, X., Goh, D.H.L.: Components of game experience: An automatic text analysis of online reviews. Entertain. Comput. **33**, 100338 (2020)

Jjodel for Serious Games: A Metamodel-Driven Vision for Assisted Game Design

Antonio Bucchiarone[1]([envelope]) [iD], Francesca de Rosa[2,3] [iD],
and Alfonso Pierantonio[1] [iD]

[1] SWEN, Università degli Studi dell'Aquila, L'Aquila, Italy
{antonio.bucchiarone,alfonso.pierantonio}@univaq.it
[2] Center for Advanced Preparedness and Threat Response Simulation (CAPTRS),
Austin, Texas, USA
francesca.derosa@captrs.org
[3] FDR Strategies, Lerici (La Spezia), Italy

Abstract. Serious games are a powerful way to explore complex problems and promote critical thinking and decision-making in uncertainty. However, designing such games remains a challenge, particularly when integrating real data, modeling domain complexity, and aligning gameplay with learning outcomes. This paper introduces a framework designed to support the structured co-creation of serious games. The co-design process is structured around a formal foundation of interconnected metamodels, each capturing a key dimension of serious game design, such as threats, actors, functional roles, territorial contexts, and event dynamics. These are grouped within a central Megamodel to ensure coherence and traceability throughout the scenario. Although not all aspects are fully implemented, this work lays the groundwork for an assisted design vision, in which AI tools support designers through model validation, reuse of game components, and guided content generation. We outline how the framework, instantiated through the Jjodel platform, can be used to rapidly prototype new game scenarios by adapting and extending a reference game structure across different domains.

Keywords: Serious games · Model-driven engineering · Co-creation · Metamodeling · AI-assisted design · Crisis management

1 Introduction

Serious games are increasingly used to foster critical thinking and decision-making in complex and high-stake situations. In fact, there is a growing attentions towards the use of these techniques in the fields of emergency and crisis management (e.g. [5,10]), public health (e.g., [13]), sustainability (e.g., [2]), safety (e.g., [1]) and security (e.g., [9]). Games are used for learning, to raise awareness or for analytical purposes (e.g, to collect valuable expert knowledge

© The Author(s), under exclusive license to Springer Nature Switzerland AG 2026
S. Bakkes et al. (Eds.): GALA 2025, LNCS 16307, pp. 203–213, 2026.
https://doi.org/10.1007/978-3-032-11043-5_20

used to guide policy making or refine plans) [6]. The design of such serious games presents unique challenges.

They are structured simulations that must convey complex domain knowledge, support reasoning in uncertainty, and reflect dynamic real-world conditions. Their design requires considerable expertise, spanning well beyond the design of game mechanics and ludic elements, to ensure the inclusion of correct underlying scientific theories (e.g., decision-making science) and domain knowledge regarding the operational contexts. This knowledge is wide, spread across several experts, and is often hardly accessible. Furthermore, the process of designing such games remains largely handmade. Game designers often rely on static templates, informal sketches, and disconnected authoring tools to define roles, tasks, and interactions. This lack of structure hinders reuse, makes validation difficult, and limits the scalability of game-based interventions across different domains or learner groups.

To address this gap, we propose a paradigm shift grounded in a principle borrowed from software and systems engineering: model-driven design. In particular, we focus on a technique called *Model-Driven Engineering* (MDE) [4], which emphasizes the explicit modeling of the components, rules, and interactions of a system before any implementation is realized. In MDE, the designer does not work directly with source code or assets but with formal representations, called **models**, of the system being constructed. These models are defined by **metamodels**, which act as grammars specifying the types of elements that can exist and the ways they may be composed. The metamodel defines the elements and rules required to construct a game, a decision flow, or a simulation scenario. The appeal of MDE in serious game design is immediate. If we can express the logic of a game, its narrative, actors, tasks, uncertainties, and consequences as a coherent model, then we can reason about its correctness, adapt it to new contexts, and even generate parts of it automatically.

In this paper, we introduce the proposed general-purpose metamodel that formalizes the structure and semantics for the generation of content and narratives for games focusing on emergency and crisis management. The metamodel is implemented in *Jjodel*,[1] an MDE authoring tool, and is intended to be reusable across various applications domains. Specifically, we discuss the use case for the development of plausible, credible and effective scenarios and game content for the *Reliability Game*, a serious game that focuses on the impact of information and uncertainty on situational awareness and decision-making in potentially high-risk situations [12]. In the next sections, we present the design process, called *Co-Create*, that leverages Jjodel's capabilities to structure and streamline serious game development through modular components and AI-guided support.

2   Jjodel: A Lightweight Platform for Metamodeling

The use of MDE approaches to serious game design has gained increasing attention for their potential to formalize and modularize complex scenario develop-

---

[1] https://www.jjodel.io/.

ment [8,14]. However, traditional MDE tools are notoriously difficult to use, often requiring specialized technical knowledge and offering limited support for participatory or expert-driven modeling in the domain [11]. For educators and designers unfamiliar with software engineering, this can make MDE seem more of a barrier than a solution. *Jjodel* offers a compelling alternative to the web-based on cloud. Jjodel supports the design of both metamodels and models, allowing users to define domain-specific languages and instantiate them through visual and interactive editors. Users can define the structure of their modeling language, modify the way elements are visualized and interacted with, and dynamically evolve both content and syntax without breaking the system. In a traditional environment, the designer might draw boxes and arrows to represent entities and their relationships, but these diagrams often remain informal and ambiguous. In Jjodel, one begins by defining a metamodel: an `entity` class that contains `Attributes`, each with a data type and an optional primary key flag; a `relation` class that connects two entities and specifies multiplicities. Once this abstract structure is defined, users can instantiate specific models. Unlike a static drawing tool, Jjodel ensures that the diagram conforms to the metamodel, supports projectional editing (e.g., directly renaming attributes in place), and validates rules such as every entity must have a primary key. The visual appearance and interaction logic of each model element are not hard-coded. Designers define **syntax viewpoints** that specify how each class in the metamodel is rendered. Furthermore, instead of entities and attributes, one defines actors, tasks, events, data constraints, and game elements (e.g., game cards). Rather than dragging boxes to build a schema, one interacts with cards, timelines, or maps to construct rich, interactive simulations. A persistent challenge in modeling arises when the metamodel evolves, such as when new attributes are introduced, relationships are restructured, or constraints are updated. Jjodel handles these changes through a mechanism of reflective proxies and lossless transformations, which automatically adapt existing models to the updated metamodel. Another essential feature is **event-driven modeling**. In many serious games, the state of the world changes in response to the actions of the player. In Jjodel, such behaviors can be modeled using Event-Condition-Action (ECA) rules [3] that link user interactions to changes in the model. To manage the complexity of interconnected modeling languages and their relationships, Jjodel also supports the notion of a **megamodel** [7], a model that organizes and links multiple metamodels and models, allowing modularity, reuse, and coordinated evolution across different parts of a modeling ecosystem. Finally, Jjodel also supports live validation through **validation viewpoints**. Therefore, Jjodel offers a foundational infrastructure for serious game co-design. It supports a workflow in which domain experts, game designers, and AI assistants can collaboratively construct structured scenarios that are internally coherent, pedagogically effective, analytically rigorous, and adaptable across domains. It replaces disconnected sketches with interoperable models, and informal logic with formal semantics.

3   A Vision for Assisted Game Design

3.1   Use-case: The Reliability Game

The *Reliability Game* is an analytical serious game designed to explore how players interpret uncertain and incomplete information in complex situations. It aims to improve decision-making processes by dissecting how individuals assess situations under pressure. The game has been instantiated in several different domains (i.e., security, public health, global health, food security, and climate shocks) and it has been recently used as part of a simulation exercises at the United Nations World Health Organization (WHO) and in a project founded by the United States U.S. Centers for Disease Control and Prevention (CDC).

In each session, the players are presented with a scenario involving an anomalous event. As new cards are revealed, each presenting fragments of data with varying levels of information source reliability, players must weigh competing hypotheses and reach conclusions based on conflicting, delayed, or ambiguous signals. The design of these scenarios, cards, and hypotheses is non-trivial, requiring deep expertise to ensure plausibility, relevance, and effective reconstruction of the degrees of uncertainty faced in real-world situations.

3.2   The Co-create Framework

To support the structured co-creation of such games, we propose the *Co-Create Framework*, a model-driven approach that decomposes a game scenario and game injects into modular, interoperable components. Rather than crafting each scenario from scratch, designers build on a network of interconnected metamodels, each addressing a specific dimension of game content: actors, territories, functions, threats, and narrative elements. These metamodels are composed through

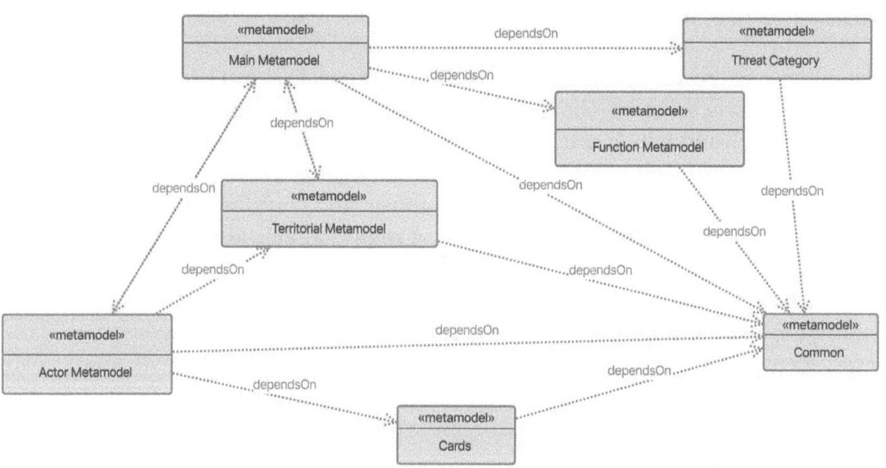

Fig. 1. The central Megamodel and dependencies among Metamodels.

a central *Megamodel* (Fig. 1), which explicitly encodes their dependencies and ensures coherence throughout the overall design of the game.

Due to space limitations, in the following, we present only a representative subset of the metamodels currently implemented in the Co-Create framework, grounded in their application to the *Reliability Game.*

To represent the emergence, evolution, and impact of threats within a scenario, the **Main Metamodel** defines a temporal and causal structure that captures how complex crises unfold. This model enables designers to encode dynamic relationships between trigger conditions, agents, and cascading consequences, making it a foundational layer for scenario plausibility and analytically rigorous gameplay. At the core of this metamodel is the `Threat Situation` class, which acts as the contextual anchor for a crisis scenario. Each threat situation is associated with a specific area (as defined in the **Territorial Metamodel**), a threat actor, and a category that classifies the nature of the threat, such as epidemic, infrastructure failure, or environmental hazard. It also maintains a timeline of all relevant events, enabling fine-grained temporal simulation.

Events themselves are modeled through an abstract `Event` class, which includes semantic descriptions, timestamps, and links to potential consequences. This recursive structure supports both direct cause-effect modeling and more diffuse event propagation. The model distinguishes between initial `Trigger Events`, which initiate a chain of events, and subsequent `Induced Events`, which arise as reactions or side effects. For example, in the pathogen version of the *Reliability Game*, heavy rainfall in a refugee camp might be modeled as a `Trigger Event` that leads to the accumulation of stagnant water. This, in turn, can induce a spike in the mosquito population and ultimately lead to a viral outbreak. This sequence can be directly represented using this metamodel. The nature of the actor responsible for a threat is captured by the `Threat Actor` class and its refinements. A specialized class, `ThreatActorHumanEpidemic`, allows for detailed modeling of epidemics, including attributes for transmission mode, incubation period, threat type, and possible diagnostic confusion. This design reflects real-world complexities where symptoms may be misleading and transmission vectors obscure. In the game, players may be faced with cards reporting patients presenting flu-like symptoms, while other cards suggest an increase in mosquito activity. The metamodel allows such an ambiguity to be coherently encoded and causally traced. Transmission dynamics are handled through the `Vector Dynamics` class, which specifies the movement of an infectious agent between hosts over time Disease progression is captured through the `Disease Spread` abstraction and its associated `Timeline Disease Spread`. This enables the distinction between imported cases and locally transmitted infections, providing critical information for decision-making. In the context of the game, such timelines can help players infer whether the disease is contained, increasing, or misclassified. Lastly, the metamodel includes organizational and spatial dimensions through the `Institution` and `Host` classes. Institutions are modeled as agents operating within specific areas, with roles and functions derived from other metamodels. Hosts, whether human or animal, provide the biological substrate for many threats and are referenced throughout the transmission logic. Taken together, the **Threat** and **Event** aspects provide a detailed and modular framework for constructing rich, temporally structured, and causally coherent crisis scenarios. It allows designers to encode not only what is happening but why it is happening, when, and through whom. In the *Reliability Game*, this metamodel supports scenarios in which players must trace ambiguous and evolving signals across timelines, hypothesize causal chains, and adjust their beliefs as new events unfold, all under conditions of uncertainty and partial information (Fig. 2).

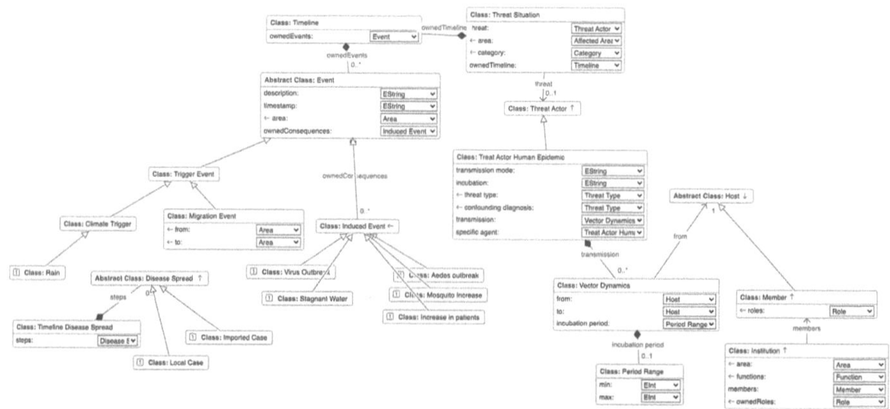

Fig. 2. Overview of the main metamodel.

The **Actor Metamodel** (Fig. 3) defines the taxonomy of agents operating within the scenario, distinguishing among their ontological types, roles, and potential causal relationships with threats. This model provides the foundation for describing interactions in the system, both intentional and unintentional, and supports the design of scenarios in which different agents carry distinct forms of knowledge, responsibility, and influence.

At the highest level, the metamodel introduces an abstract `Actor` class, which branches into several specialized subclasses. One major branch is `Human Actor`, which includes entities like `Patient` and `Human`. These human agents are central to many scenarios in the *Reliability Game*, where decision-making under uncertainty is often modeled through the perceptions and actions of institutional actors, frontline responders, or affected individuals. For instance, a `Patient` class may embody a refugee showing symptoms during a disease outbreak, while the generic `Human` class could represent an unclassified member of the population who contributes observational data or triggers a belief revision during the game.

Another key branch is `Other Actors`, a flexible category that allows the extension of the actor concept beyond humans without predefining their nature. This abstraction is useful for representing agents such as automated systems,

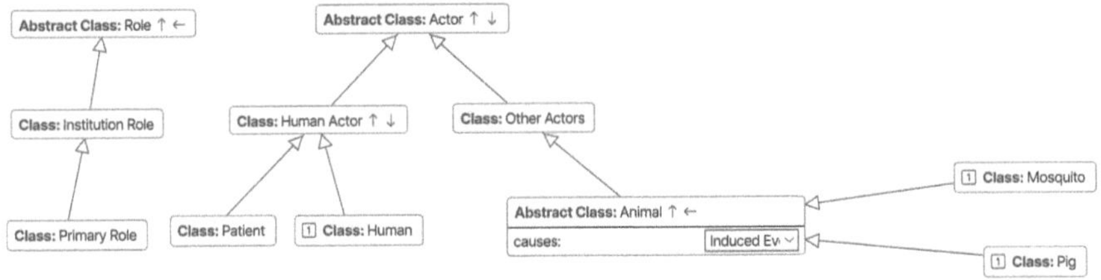

Fig. 3. The actor metamodel.

vehicles, or unknown observers, all of which may play a role in the unfolding of an ambiguous or multivalent scenario.

The metamodel also introduces the abstract concept of `Role`, which encapsulates the functions or responsibilities that actors assume in institutional contexts. The subclass `Institution Role` refines this by modeling formal affiliations or duties within an organization, and `Primary Role` provides further granularity, representing high-level assignments such as "Medical Coordinator" or "Epidemiologist". In the game, these roles are often assigned to players and strongly shape the types of information they can access or interpret. For example, an epidemiologist may receive cards related to vector control or diagnostic test results, while a public security official might only receive behavioral reports.

A particularly important addition is the `Animal` class, which extends the Actor hierarchy to include non-human biological agents. This class allows for the specification of the `causes` attribute, which links animals to `Induced Events`, a connection that is vital in scenarios involving zoonotic transmission. Within this branch, two concrete classes are modeled: `Mosquito` and `Pig`. These are common disease vectors and reservoirs respectively, often appearing in the context of vector-borne disease outbreaks. For example, in a scenario involving an Aedes mosquito outbreak, the `Mosquito` class would be causally linked to increases in patient cases. Likewise, a `Pig` class may serve as a hidden reservoir for viruses that later spill over into the human population, complicating diagnosis and strategic response.

Through this classification of actors, the metamodel enables designers to construct scenarios where agent-based uncertainty, asymmetrical knowledge, and causal ambiguity are meaningfully represented. It becomes possible to simulate, for instance, a situation where human actors observe environmental changes but misattribute causality due to incomplete information about animal presence or unobservable institutional roles.

The **Territorial Metamodel** in Fig. 4 defines the spatial, infrastructural and demographic context within which all other components of the scenario unfold. It models not only the physical layout of areas but also their infrastructural capabilities and the characteristics of their populations. This metamodel is essential for grounding the abstract logic of threats and actors in concrete geographic and logistical constraints.

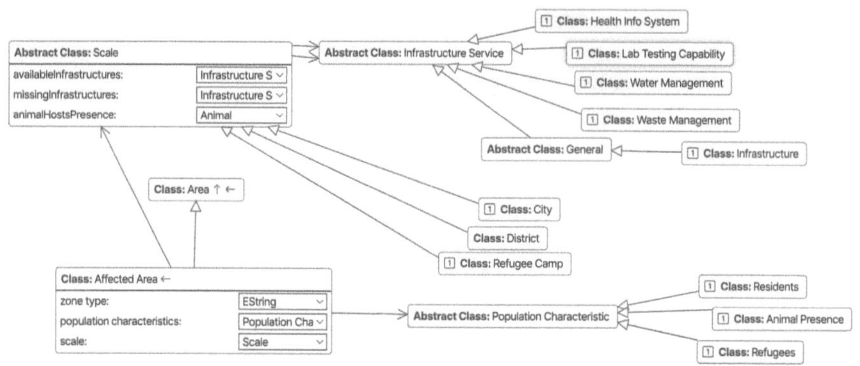

Fig. 4. The territorial metamodel.

At its center is the `Affected Area` class, which represents the spatial entity impacted by a given threat. Each area is characterized by three key attributes: a `zone type` (such as rural, urban, or camp), a set of `population characteristics`, and a `scale` element. These three dimensions allow designers to express how threats may differentially affect small, remote populations versus dense urban centers, or how certain areas may host particularly vulnerable groups. To define the scale and infrastructure of an area, the metamodel introduces the abstract `Scale` class. This class links each area to its available and missing infrastructure elements, as well as to indicators of the presence of the animal host, an important feature for modeling zoonotic risk. For example, an area might lack a functioning waste management system or lack laboratory testing capabilities, both of which could accelerate the spread of disease or alter detection efforts. Similarly, the presence of animals such as pigs or mosquitoes, drawn from the Actor Metamodel, may increase biological vulnerability.

The model provides concrete spatial classes such as `City`, `District`, and `Refugee Camp`, each inheriting from the general `Area` class. These allow designers to distinguish between hierarchical or categorical types of territory, which is especially relevant in games like the *Reliability Game*, where players may receive location-specific reports. For example, the appearance of unusual symptoms in a refugee camp versus a nearby city district may lead to different interpretations, even if both are part of the same scenario timeline.

The population attributes are handled through the `PopulationCharacter` abstraction. This structure accounts for key demographic types that can affect how information is interpreted or how threats propagate. Concrete classes such as `Residents`, `Refugees`, and `Animal Presence` allow designers to incorporate social structure and biological exposure into threat reasoning. In practice, a refugee camp might be modeled as having a high density of `Refugees` and a high probability of `Animal Presence`, contributing to uncertainty when assessing whether a viral outbreak is due to poor sanitation, animal transmission, or deliberate misinformation.

The infrastructure capacity is detailed through the `InfrastructureService` class and its subclasses, which include `HealthInfoSystem`, `WaterManagement`, `WasteManagement`, etc.. These elements describe the operational landscape for institutional actors and influence the plausibility of response strategies. For example, if players in the game receive conflicting cards, one reporting lab results and another noting the absence of testing infrastructure, they must question the source reliability or explore temporal inconsistencies. Infrastructural elements are themselves a subclass of the general `Infrastructure` type, tying the logistical capacity to spatial locations.

4   Research Roadmap

This work introduces the Co-Create Framework and the Jjodel platform as a foundation for the structured, AI-assisted design of serious games. Through reusable and interoperable models, the framework enables an iterative process (Fig. 5): Design, Simulate, Co-evolve and Generate, supported by formal modeling and intelligent automation. This approach shifts game creation from hand-crafted scenarios to a scalable and adaptive pipeline, aligned with the MDE principles.

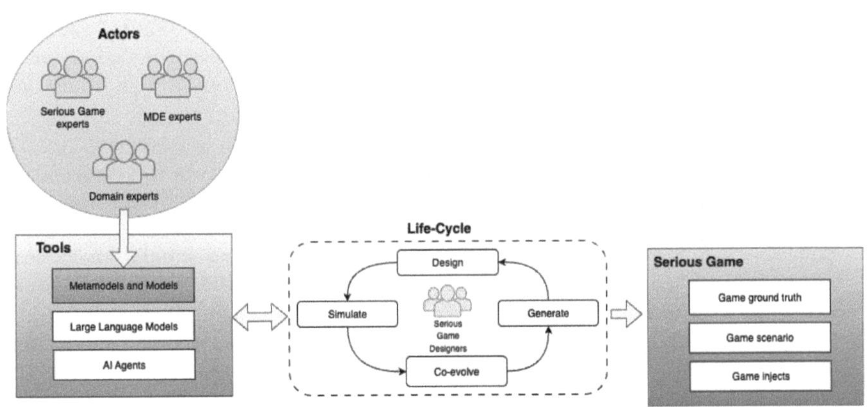

Fig. 5. The co-create process.

To realize this vision, several priorities emerge. First, **expanding the megamodel** to cover narrative structures, player modeling, and uncertainty representation will increase expressiveness and realism. Second, **enhancing Jjodel** with improved simulation support, user interfaces, and AI-driven content generation will streamline co-creation. Third, **evaluating the approach** in real-world domains, such as public health or crisis management, through **empirical validation**, including user studies, pilot demonstrations, and feedback from game designers, will assess its practical effectiveness and usability. Equally important is

refining human-AI collaboration, with explainable co-design workflows and ethical safeguards, and **empowering non-technical designers** to intuitively design and simulate games without advanced expertise. Finally, sustaining this ecosystem requires **building a community of practice**, supported by training materials and studies on how structured modeling influences creativity, collaboration, and scenario quality.

References

1. Ahmadov, T., Karimov, A., Durst, S., Saarela, M., Gerstlberger, W., Wahl, M.F., Karkkainen, T.: Designing serious games for safety education: "learn to brace" versus traditional pictorials for aircraft passengers. IEEE Trans. Vis. Comput. Graphics **22**(5), 1527–1539 (2016)
2. Ahmadov, T., Karimov, A., Durst, S., Saarela, M., Gerstlberger, W., Wahl, M.F., Karkkainen, T.: A two-phase systematic literature review on the use of serious games for sustainable environmental education. Int. J. Serious Games **33**(3), 1945–1966 (2024)
3. Berndtsson, M., Mellin, J.: Eca rules. In: Liu, L., Özsu, M.T. (eds.) Encyclopedia of Database Systems, pp. 959–960. Springer, US, Boston, MA (2009)
4. Brambilla, M., Cabot, J., Wimmer, M.: Model-Driven Software Engineering in Practice: Second Edition. Morgan & Claypool Publishers, 2nd edn. (2017)
5. Di Loreto, I., Mora, S., Divitini, M.: Collaborative serious games for crisis management: An overview. In: 2012 IEEE 21st International Workshop on Enabling Technologies: Infrastructure for Collaborative Enterprises. pp. 352–357 (2012)
6. Djaouti, D., Alvarez, J., Jessel, J.P.: Classifying serious games: the G/P/S model. Handbook of Research on Improving Learning and Motivation through Educational Games: Multidisciplinary Approaches **1**, 118–136 (2011)
7. Gašević, D., Kaviani, N., Hatala, M.: On metamodeling in megamodels. In: Proceedings of the 10th International Conference on Model Driven Engineering Languages and Systems. p. 91–105. MODELS'07, Springer-Verlag, Berlin, Heidelberg (2007)
8. Longstreet, C.S., Cooper, K.: A meta-model for developing simulation games in higher education and professional development training. In: 2012 17th International Conference on Computer Games (CGAMES). pp. 39–44 (2012)
9. Ng, C.Y., Hasan, M.K.B.: Cybersecurity serious games development: A systematic review. Comput. Security **150**, 104307 (2025)
10. Ning, H., Pi, Z., Wang, W., Farha, F., Yang, S.: A review on serious games for disaster relief. In: 2022 4th International Conference on Data Intelligence and Security (ICDIS). pp. 408–414 (2022)
11. Pourali, P., Atlee, J.M.: An empirical investigation to understand the difficulties and challenges of software modellers when using modelling tools. In: Proceedings of the 21th ACM/IEEE International Conference on Model Driven Engineering Languages and Systems. p. 224–234. MODELS '18, Association for Computing Machinery, New York, NY, USA (2018)
12. de Rosa, F., Jousselme, A.L., De Gloria, A.: A Reliability Game for Source Factors and Situational Awareness Experimentation. Int. J. Serious Games **5**(2), 45–64 (2018)
13. de Rosa, F., Escott, M., Walkes, D., Douglas, H., Meyers, L.A.: Transdisciplinarity in serious gaming design for improved crisis preparedness. Int. J. Serious Games **11**(4), 155–172 (2024)

14. Tang, S., Hanneghan, M.: A model-driven framework to support development of serious games for game-based learning. In: 2010 Developments in E-systems Engineering. pp. 95–100 (2010)

Assist Me!—A Smartwatch Mobile Application for Early and Middle-Stage Alzheimer's Care

Damla Cinel, Johanna Pirker, David A. Plecher,
and Christian Eichhorn(✉)

Research Group Augmented Reality, Technical University of Munich,
Munich, Germany
`{damla.cinel,johanna.pirker,david.plecher,christian.eichhorn}@tum.de`

Abstract. Alzheimer's disease affects over 55 million people worldwide, presenting daily challenges for patients and caregivers. This paper introduces *Assist Me!*, a smartwatch-based support system combining multiple assistive modules into a single platform. The application features an AI-powered digital photobook, cognitive games (EuroTest, PAL, Clock Construction), a gamified task-reward loop (Click & Connect), beacon-based medication tracking, and a simplified Mini Mental State Examination (MMSE) interface. All modules are optimized for the Apple Watch and linked to an iOS companion app. An online survey with 24 early and middle-stage Alzheimer's patients and 14 caregivers yielded a combined average System Usability Scale (SUS) score of 78.2, indicating promising usability. Results show strong potential for smartwatch-based tools to enhance autonomy, engagement, and cognitive support in Alzheimer's care.

Keywords: Mobile application · Smartwatch · Bluetooth beacon · Alzheimer's disease · Usability · Gamification · AI integration

1 Introduction

As life expectancy increases and the global population ages, Alzheimer's disease poses rising emotional and economic challenges for caregivers and healthcare systems [15]. Patients face progressive cognitive decline and reduced autonomy, creating a need for scalable, accessible technological solutions that can integrate seamlessly into daily routines.

This paper presents *Assist Me!*, a smartwatch-centred mobile application composed of five complementary modules designed to address the key challenges of Alzheimer's care:

- **AI-generated digital photobook:** Supports memory recall and emotional connection through personalized reminiscence therapy content.

© The Author(s), under exclusive license to Springer Nature Switzerland AG 2026
S. Bakkes et al. (Eds.): GALA 2025, LNCS 16307, pp. 214–224, 2026.
https://doi.org/10.1007/978-3-032-11043-5_21

- **Gamified cognitive assessments:** Includes EuroTest, Paired-Associates Learning, and Clock Construction tasks to provide accessible and engaging cognitive stimulation.
- **Click & Connect reward system:** Reinforces user motivation through immediate visual feedback (e.g., fireworks) and weekly gameplay incentives.
- **Bluetooth-beacon medication tracker:** Facilitates medication adherence by delivering context-aware reminders and logging intake events.
- **Weekly MMSE testing:** Enables lightweight, regular monitoring of cognitive progression through simplified Mini-Mental State Exams.

Our main contributions include: (1) an integrated smartwatch platform combining cognitive stimulation, reminiscence therapy, and beacon-enabled medication tracking; (2) empirical insights from both quantitative and qualitative data on usability acquired from early and middle-stage patients and caregivers; and (3) a set of recommendations for dementia-friendly smartwatch interactions.

The research aims to address the following questions:

- **RQ1**: Does *"Assist Me!"* achieve an acceptable usability level (SUS $\geq$ 70) for its target users?
- **RQ2**: Which application modules are perceived as most engaging and useful by patients and caregivers?
- **RQ3**: How do different age groups influence usability and engagement outcomes?

Table 1. Touchscreen interface design guidelines for older adults with Alzheimer's disease

Design aspect	Guideline/recommendation	Author(s) and Ref.
Touchscreen as preferred input	Touch input is considered the most intuitive for older adults; anything abstract is hard to comprehend	Smith et al. [8]
Button size	Best size for buttons is 22 mm (square); optimal for touch lists between 16.5–19.05 mm	Caprani et al. [5], Phiriyapokanon [12]
Space between buttons	Recommended at least 6 mm inactive distance; 6.35 mm is ideal for lists	IEA (1996), ISO (2000), Phiriyapokanon [12]
Font and layout size	Large fonts make reading easier, but spaces may be broken; thus, efficient layout designs should be chosen	Eichhorn et al. [7], Phiriyapokanon [12]
Familiar metaphors	Using consistent metaphors improves interaction and memory recall	Stüßel [13]

2   Related Work

2.1   Design Guidelines for Older Adults with Alzheimer's Disease

Prior research outlines specific design guidelines for touchscreen interfaces targeting older adults with Alzheimer's disease. These recommendations, summarized in Table 1, cover optimal button dimensions, spacing, font sizes, feedback methods, and layout simplicity. The goal is to maximize usability while accommodating common age-related impairments in vision, memory, and motor control.

2.2   Motivational Design and Existing Applications

Motivational strategies in assistive technologies for older adults often leverage gamification, personalization, and emotional engagement. Features like positive feedback, reward animations, and adaptive difficulty help sustain user interest without overwhelming them [1]. Personalization–such as tailored reminders or content adjustments–further increases relevance and usability. Social elements, including family involvement or communication options, also enhance motivation by fostering emotional connection and routine.

Several mobile and wearable applications already address memory support and caregiving in Alzheimer's care, including *MindMate, Neuromemorize, SmartMind*, and *Alzheimer Assistant*. While some apps emphasize active participation through reminders and games [10,14], others rely on passive sensing for minimal user input [2,9]. Most, however, are smartphone-based and lack dedicated smartwatch integration. Key gaps remain in long-term engagement, accessibility, and wearability.

3   Development

3.1   System Architecture

The support app is written in SwiftUI (Xcode 15.3) and targets patients with early and middle-stage Alzheimer's.

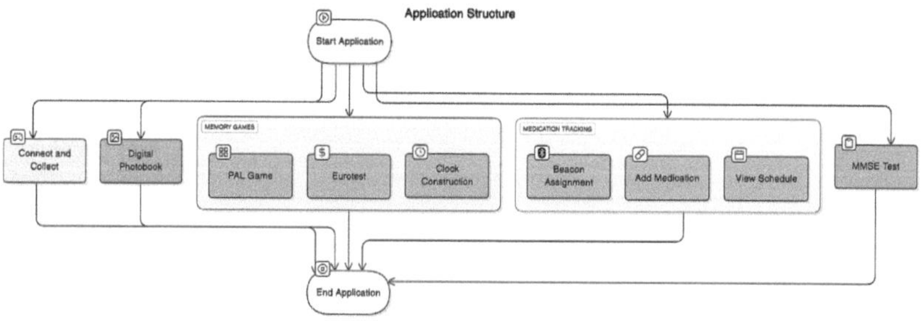

Fig. 1. Application hierarchy and data flow among the six modules

As shown in the Fig. 1, all modules share a common dashboard and exchange data locally on the watch. In the following, each module will be briefly introduced to highlight its purpose and functionality within the system.

3.2 AI-Enhanced Digital Photobook with iOS Companion

The Digital Photobook uses on-device AI to generate personalised short stories from caregiver-selected images, based on three spoken questions asked to the user [18]. This feature promotes memory recall through natural conversation and storytelling.

Workflow

1) **Photo upload:** The caregiver selects an image via the iOS companion app. It is resized, compressed, and sent to the watch using WatchConnectivity.
2) **User input:** The watch displays the image and prompts the user with three questions (e.g., *Who is in the photo?*). Answers are recorded via dictation.
3) **Story generation:** The prompt is sent to GPT-3.5-Turbo, generating a 150-token story.
4) **Playback and storage:** The story is saved locally and read using speech synthesis for accessibility.

iOS Companion Integration. To support older adults who may not be familiar with troubleshooting connectivity issues, the iOS companion app was designed to ensure fully autonomous media transfer. WatchConnectivity handles activation, delivery retries, and error resolution in the background, allowing images selected by caregivers to reliably reach the watch without requiring any manual intervention, even in the case of temporary disconnections [9].

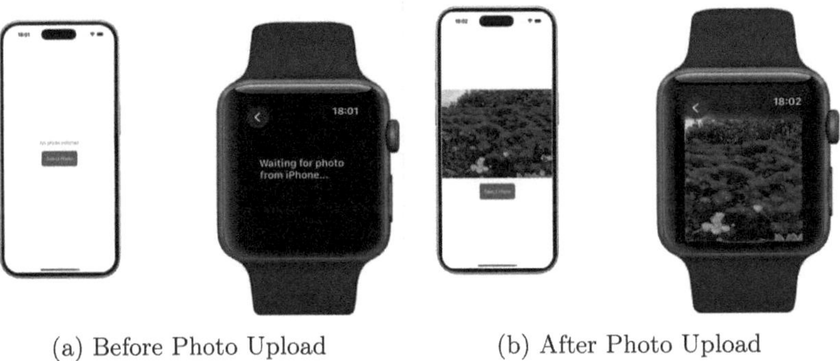

(a) Before Photo Upload   (b) After Photo Upload

Fig. 2. Interaction between Watch and iOS companion applications

3.3   Cognitive Activity Design

To support cognitive engagement, the app includes smartwatch versions of three established neuropsychological tasks: EuroTest, Paired Associates Learning (PAL), and Clock Construction. These tasks are adapted for the small screen with simplified visuals, gesture-based interaction, and progressive difficulty. They assess memory, visuospatial processing, and executive function while logging performance data across sessions [17].

To increase adherence, the tasks are embedded in a gamified weekly challenge system, where successful completion unlocks visual rewards such as firework animations and contributes to the Click & Connect board. This loop fosters regular participation through positive reinforcement.

Given the time and cognitive limitations of our target group, we selected short-form versions of the tests that retain diagnostic value but reduce cognitive load. For example, the EuroTest is reduced to five dynamic multiple-choice currency recognition trials; PAL includes only two object-location pairings per session; and Clock Construction is limited to a single layout task using drag-and-drop hands. These simplifications aim to balance meaningful assessment with accessibility and engagement.

3.4   Adapting MMSE Testing to the Smartwatch

To adapt the Mini Mental State Examination (MMSE) for a small screen, the original 30-item test was condensed to six questions covering orientation, registration/recall, attention, language, and copying [4]. Prompts use speech input, multiple-choice options, and touchscreen gestures to reduce complexity and input errors. Three test versions rotate weekly to limit learning effects, and completions contribute to the Connect & Collect loop.

Shape-Recognition Model. The shape-copying task was redesigned as a single-shape drawing activity using circles, triangles, or squares. A dataset was collected from ten participants, each providing 50 samples per shape via touchscreen input. Mean x and y coordinates were extracted from the touch path as feature vectors to reduce dimensionality. A multi-class logistic regression model was trained in Scikit-learn with an 80/20 train-test split, achieving 96% accuracy. The final model was converted using Core ML Tools and runs entirely on-device.

3.5   Task and Reward System

To motivate users and create a sense of accomplishment, the application introduces a lightweight task and reward system based on familiar game mechanics.

Connect and Collect: The app turns weekly tasks into a 4 × 4 "Connect Four" board (see Fig. 3): every completed memory game, medication log, or photobook interaction yields a colored disk; collecting eight disks enables a quick

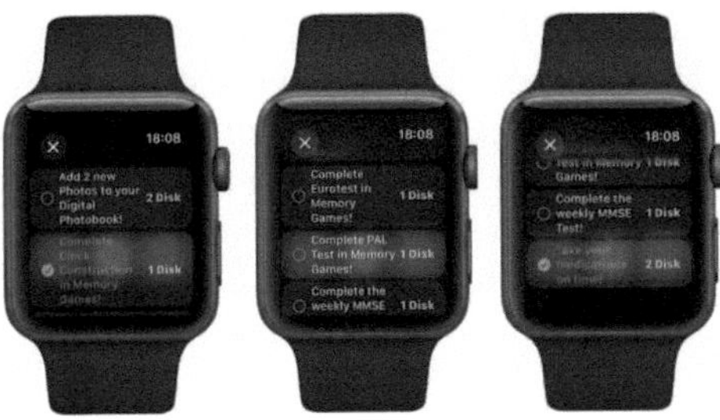

Fig. 3. Task screen

match against the computer. The final reward is pre-agreed with the caregiver, strengthening social ties and sustaining motivation [7].

Visual Feedback: Color-coding (e.g., green/black) gives at-a-glance progress without resulting in extra memory load, while immediate haptic feedback and on-screen confirmation reinforce success [17].

Persistence with Core Data: Task status is stored locally using Apple's Core Data framework, chosen over UserDefaults, SQLite, and CloudKit for its automatic change tracking, offline support, and built-in encryption [12]. At week-start, a background routine resets the achievements, ensuring the reward loop is restarted [16].

3.6   User Interface Standards

The interface of *Assist Me!* was designed to provide a consistent and clear navigation experience, in line with the watchOS Human Interface Guidelines. To accommodate users with cognitive impairments such as Alzheimer's disease, the layout emphasizes simplicity, accessible touch areas, and visual clarity. Key interactions–like tapping or selecting options–are reinforced with intuitive visual feedback, ensuring users understand when actions are successfully completed. Additionally, task guidance is supported by animated instructions that mirror real user gestures, offering non-intrusive support without causing cognitive overload. These design principles collectively ensure that the app remains approachable and usable for older adults with varying levels of familiarity with smart technology.

3.7   Beacon-Based Medication Tracking System

This module enables real-time medication adherence tracking by using Bluetooth Low Energy (BLE) beacons with motion sensors attached to pillboxes. It ensures that users receive timely intake reminders and that all interactions–such as box openings–are accurately recorded. Through local notifications and caregiver alerts, the system supports both independent use and remote monitoring. All schedules and interactions are managed and stored locally, ensuring reliability even without constant internet access.

Beacon Connectivity and Detection. To enable medication tracking, Bluetooth Low Energy (BLE) beacons with integrated accelerometers were affixed to medication boxes [6,19]. These beacons continuously broadcast unique identifiers (UUIDs) and motion data. Accelerometer integration allows for distinguishing between intentional usage and incidental motion; a threshold value of 128 was empirically determined to minimize false positives. This adaptive design aligns with prior smart home monitoring studies [3].

A major UI limitation on the smartwatch was visual clutter from multiple nearby beacons. To overcome this, an RSSI filter was applied with a cutoff of -55 dBm, ensuring only proximal beacons were displayed [5]. Beacon assignment and management were handled via the Core Bluetooth framework and stored persistently through `UserDefaults`, enabling flexible reconfiguration and continuity across sessions.

Medication Schedule and Alerts. Users define a medication schedule by assigning specific times to beacon-tagged boxes. At scheduled times, the app issues local notifications prompting medication intake. If the assigned box is not opened within the time window, a global alert is triggered and forwarded to caregivers via a companion iPhone app [5,7]. This ensures real-time intervention in case of missed or incorrect doses.

Accelerometer readings are used to confirm box opening in real-time. If a box unrelated to the current schedule is opened, the app alerts the user and notifies caregivers. This dual-layered feedback–local cues for the user and remote alerts for caregivers–prevents medication errors and ensures adherence [11].

4   Evaluation

The *Assist Me!* app was evaluated through an online survey conducted using the "Google Forms" platform to assess usability, functionality, and accessibility for early and middle-stage Alzheimer's patients and caregivers. The online initial survey has been performed for ethical reasons to prevent the involvement of patients in the early development. Two online groups for nursing of Alzheimer's patients were recruited. Participants signed an informed consent. Then, a short explanatory video presented the app's core features, including the AI-generated photobook, beacon-based medication tracking, cognitive and MMSE tests, visual feedback, the Click & Connect reward system, and the help module. Image-supported survey questions followed the video, enabling participants to assess each module clearly. Additionally, usability was measured via the System Usability Scale (SUS) alongside custom feature-specific questions.

4.1   Results

A total of 38 participants completed the evaluation: 24 patients with Alzheimer's (aged 60 and above) and 14 caregivers (under 60). The overall mean SUS score was **78.2 (SD = 9.6)**, which corresponds to the usability between "Good" and

"Excellent". This indicates that the interface and interaction design meet and surpass the minimum standards of acceptability for cognitive-assistive technology.

Group Analysis: To assess usability differences between caregivers and patients, a Mann-Whitney U test was conducted due to the unequal sample sizes. The results showed no statistically significant difference in SUS scores between caregivers (M = 76.8, SD = 10.1) and patients (M = 79.4, SD = 9.3). This suggests both groups found the app similarly usable.

Age-Specific Analysis: Within the older adult group, a further comparison was made between participants aged 60–75 and those over 75. A Mann-Whitney U test revealed a significant difference in SUS scores, with users aged 60–75 (M = 81.2, SD = 7.5) reporting higher usability than those over 75 (M = 72.9, SD = 10.8). This supports the assumption that age-related cognitive and motor decline may affect interaction ease.

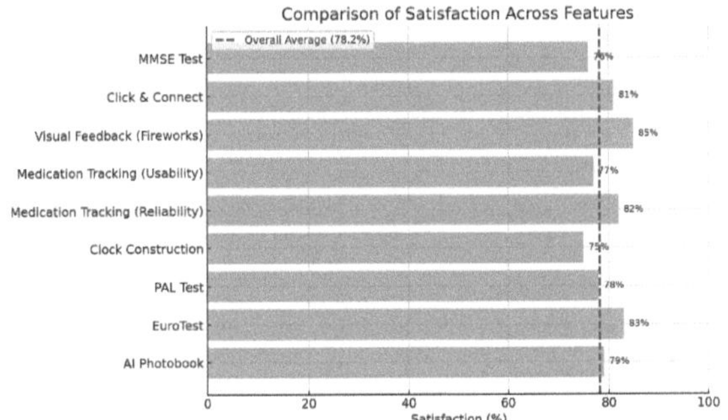

Fig. 4. Satisfaction across features (0–100% ranking interval)

As shown in Fig. 4, satisfaction levels were consistently high across modules, including cognitive games, MMSE, medication tracking, the photobook, visual feedback, and the reward system. The global average satisfaction was 78.2%, and most of the features scored above this mark. While the smartwatch interface slightly trailed the iOS companion app in perceived ease of use, users praised its accessibility and ergonomic layout.

4.2 Discussion

RQ1–Acceptable usability level: The evaluation confirms that Assist Me! achieves a promising level of perceived usability for its target users. The overall SUS score was 78.2 (SD = 9.6), which surpasses the widely accepted usability threshold of 70. This positions the app between "Good" and "Excellent" according to standard benchmarks, indicating that both the smartwatch interface and the iOS companion app are well-designed. These results suggest that the application is accessible and intuitive, even for users with mild cognitive decline.

RQ2–Most engaging and useful modules: Participants consistently rated the AI-generated photobook, cognitive games, and the Click & Connect module as the most engaging and useful components. The photobook was described as intuitive and emotionally meaningful by both caregivers and patients, especially reminiscence and storytelling. Cognitive games like EuroTest and PAL were praised for being "simple to follow" and "motivating," while the gamified reward loop in Click & Connect increased user motivation throughout the week. These modules received the highest satisfaction scores in the feature-specific evaluation.

RQ3–Influence of age: The SUS scores showed differences across age groups and prior experience. Older adults (60+) reported slightly higher average SUS scores (M = 79.4) compared to caregivers (M = 76.8), though the difference was not statistically significant ($p = 0.084$). Within the elderly group, those aged 60–75 rated usability significantly higher than those aged 75+, reflecting expected declines due to age-related cognitive and motor changes. Additionally, participants with prior smartwatch experience reported smoother navigation and higher confidence. This highlights the importance of adaptive onboarding processes tailored to users' digital literacy and cognitive status.

5   Limitations and Future Work

While the evaluation showed overall positive results, several limitations were identified. The main limitation was the inability to test directly with Alzheimer's patients with the first iteration of the app due to ethical constraints. Instead, caregivers and early and middle-stage Alzheimer's patients participated through an online survey, which does not represent real-world cognitive load during extended use. The feedback given is used for refinements, and in the future, a long-term study to confirm the effectiveness of the features will be necessary. Furthermore, a clinician will be involved to review the AI-generated content, making sure it meets the sensitive needs of dementia patients.

To further improve the system, several directions are proposed:

- *Multilingual and Cultural Adaptation:* Adding language options and cultural personalization can increase accessibility and relevance for diverse user groups.
- *Centralized and Voice-Guided Help:* Users requested a unified help hub or voice-based guidance to complement modular help screens and onboarding.
- *Multi-Device Beacon Syncing:* Enabling multiple caregiver devices to sync with beacon data would improve monitoring flexibility in shared care settings.
- *Secure MMSE Data Sharing:* Encrypted sharing of MMSE results with professionals would support remote care and early intervention more effectively.
- *Enhanced Customization:* Options for text size, audio alerts, and haptic feedback to improve usability for users with sensory or cognitive impairments.

6   Conclusion

The study demonstrates that smartwatches, when carefully designed with cognitive and motor limitations in mind, can serve as a viable assistive platform for early to middle-stage Alzheimer's patients. The high usability score (SUS: 78.2) and positive qualitative feedback from both patients and caregivers suggest strong potential for supporting memory, routine, and engagement. While some limitations remain–particularly for late-stage users–the results indicate that wearable technology can play an active role in digital dementia care.

References

1. Adlakha, S., Chhabra, D., Shukla, P.: Effectiveness of gamification for the rehabilitation of neurodegenerative disorders. Chaos Solitons Fract. **140** (2020)
2. Aljojo, N., et al.: Alzheimer assistant: a mobile application using machine learning. Revista Română de Informatică si Automatică **30** (12 2020)
3. Amiribesheli, M., Bouchachia, H.: A tailored smart home for dementia care. J. Ambient. Intell. Humaniz. Comput. **9**(6), 1755–1782 (2017). https://doi.org/10.1007/s12652-017-0645-7
4. Arevalo-Rodriguez, I., et al.: Mini-mental state examination (mmse) for the detection of alzheimer's disease and other dementias in people with mild cognitive impairment (mci). Cochrane Database of Systematic Reviews (3) (2015)
5. Caprani, N., O'Connor, N.E., Gurrin, C.: Touch screens for the older user. In: Assistive Technologies, pp. 95–120. IntechOpen (2012)
6. Coppola, J.F., et al.: Applying mobile application development to help dementia and alzheimer patients. Wilson Center for Social Entrepreneurship (16) (2013)
7. Eichhorn, C., et al.: Innovative game concepts for alzheimer patients. In: HCII. pp. 526–545 (2018)
8. Eichhorn, C., et al.: Combining motivating strategies with design concepts for mobile apps to increase usability for the elderly and alzheimer patients. In: HCII (2020)
9. Lam, K.Y., et al.: Activity tracking and monitoring of patients with alzheimer's disease. Multimedia Tools Appl. **76**(1), 489–521 (2017)
10. McGoldrick, C.: MindMate: A Single Case Experimental Design Study of a Reminder System for People with Dementia. Ph.D. thesis, University of Glasgow (2017), https://theses.gla.ac.uk/8400/
11. Mendez, M.F., et al.: Neurological assessment in alzheimer's disease: Behavioral and cognitive changes. Neurology **40**(3, Part 1), 439–445 (1989)
12. Phiriyapokanon, T.: Is a big button interface enough for elderly users? Towards user interface guidelines for elderly users. Master's thesis, Mälardalen University (2011), https://www.diva-portal.org/smash/get/diva2:416488/FULLTEXT01.pdf
13. Po-Chan, Y.: Cognitive assessment tools in alzheimer's disease research. Multidisciplinary Digital Publishing Institute (MDPI) **3**(3), 35 (2019)
14. Presswala, A., et al.: Neuromemorize—mobile application for alzheimer's patients using ai-based face recognition. In: Data Intelligence and Cognitive Informatics. pp. 363–377. Springer Singapore (2021)
15. Qiu, C.: The abc of alzheimer's disease: Behavioral symptoms and their treatment. Dialogues Clin. Neurosci. **11**(2), 123–125 (2009)

16. Trouva, E.: The Mobile Phone as a Platform for Assisting the Independent Living of Aging People. Master's thesis, Athens University of Economics and Business (2009), https://mm.aueb.gr/research/archangel/theses/Trouva-thesis-09.pdf
17. Wong, D., et al.: Multimodal feedback in alzheimer's disease: Exploring the connections between neuroimaging and cognitive assessments. Neuropsychol, Rev (2023)
18. Xu, L., et al.: Reminiscence and digital storytelling to improve the social and emotional well-being of older adults with alzheimer's disease and related dementias: Protocol for a mixed methods study design and a randomized controlled trial. JMIR Research Protocols **12**, e49752 (2023)
19. Zhang, S., et al.: Decision support for alzheimer's patients in smart homes. In: IEEE CBMS. pp. 236–241 (2008)

Designing Cultural Heritage Serious Games with Generative AI: From Structured Frameworks to Playable Prototypes

Vittorio Murtas(✉) and Vincenzo Lombardo

Department of Computer Science, University of Turin, Turin, Italy
{vittorio.murtas,vincenzo.lombardo}@unito.it

Abstract. Subject Matter Experts (SMEs) are essential in serious games for cultural heritage, where their input ensures accuracy and ethical integrity. Designers must collaborate closely with SMEs to encode cultural content into game components, often relying on structured frameworks to support and formalize this process. However, such collaboration is time-consuming, costly, and often out of reach for small or underfunded cultural projects—especially those focused on niche topics with limited audiences. This study explores the extent to which generative AI can reduce this dependency. Using ChatGPT within the Co.Lab framework, we developed Edgar à GoGo, a prototype inspired by Varèse's Poème Électronique, combining AI-generated content with a human-authored game structure. The experiment examines how general knowledge, enhanced by selected project-specific materials, can partially substitute the traditional SME–designer dialogue. The prototype was reviewed by three SMEs familiar with the heritage item, offering insights into the coherence and completeness of the AI output. Findings suggest a hybrid workflow with AI aiding human design. While not a replacement for expert insight, generative AI may serve as a catalyst for ideation and discussion, especially in low-resource settings.

Keywords: Generative AI · Game design · Serious games · Cultural heritage

1 Introduction

Serious games are increasingly used in the cultural heritage sector to promote tourism and engage the public with both tangible and intangible heritage [5]. Their design typically involves collaboration between game designers and Subject Matter Experts (SMEs), who provide the contextual knowledge needed to translate heritage content into interactive experiences [10]. Frameworks often help map cultural content to mechanics [3].

However, such collaboration is difficult to sustain in small or underfunded projects [11]. Limited expert access, scarce or unpublished documentation—especially from older projects—and the cognitive effort needed for mutual understanding make SME–designer interactions costly.

S. Bakkes et al. (Eds.): GALA 2025, LNCS 16307, pp. 225–234, 2026.
https://doi.org/10.1007/978-3-032-11043-5_22

Generative AI is increasingly explored as a tool for creative and design processes [8]. Although these models offer general knowledge and flexible content generation, their potential to substitute domain expertise in structured design processes—especially within cultural game development—remains largely unexplored.

This study examines whether LLMs can partially replicate the collaborative functions typically fulfilled by SMEs and designers. We focus on their application within the Co.Lab framework [3], investigating how game design components—such as learning goals, mechanics, and feedback—can be generated through AI, guided by both general knowledge and project-specific input.

Our case study is Edgar à Gogo, based on Varèse's Poème Électronique (1958). This electroacoustic work is known for its spatialized sound and integration with architecture and visuals [2]. The experiment builds on the Virtual Electronic Poem (VEP) project [4], which digitally reconstructed the pavilion that hosted the piece and segmented the original soundtrack into spatialized sound "routes."

We prompted ChatGPT with selected VEP materials to complete each Co.-Lab component, aiming to generate a coherent design without expert involvement.

The process followed three phases:

1. *Concept generation*: ChatGPT completed Co.Lab components using structured prompts and curated VEP inputs.
2. *Technical prototyping*: The concept was implemented in Unity through follow-up prompts resolving ambiguities.
3. *Expert evaluation*: Cultural heritage experts reviewed the prototype's coherence and representational accuracy.

This study evaluates the potential of generative AI to partially automate design processes in low-resource heritage contexts. Rather than replacing human insight, we position AI as a support tool—one that helps structure, interpret, and convey cultural knowledge when traditional collaboration is not viable.

2   Related Works

In cultural heritage serious games, collaboration between SMEs and designers is key to ensuring accuracy, ethical integrity, and accessibility. Unlike entertainment games [10], this dialogue is central: early development meetings help define what aspects of heritage to prioritize and how to translate them into gameplay. Notable examples include *Assassin's Creed: Discovery Tour* (2018), created with input from historians and archaeologists, and *Never Alone* (E-Line Media, 2014), where Iñupiat community members directly shaped the game's narrative and visuals.

Several frameworks and authoring tools support structured planning and documentation while facilitating SME–designer collaboration. Among these, Co.Lab stands out as a validated modular framework that divides the design process into 21 components, from problem definition to evaluation. Co.Lab is designed to assist multidisciplinary teams (such as SMEs, designers, and producers), thanks to its step-by-step structure and online collaborative platform. Although not originally tailored for cultural heritage, its modular and systemic approach makes it a strong candidate for integrating cultural content in a structured way. Final implementation typically follows through coding and iterative playtesting [10].

Although collaboration between SMEs and designers can play an important role in cultural heritage communication, it often encounters significant obstacles in peripheral or resource-poor contexts. These projects commonly lack institutional support, rely on limited or informal documentation, and have reduced access to expert knowledge [11]. When sources are fragmentary or highly local, designers must often invest considerable effort just to grasp the cultural context. These structural barriers highlight the need for alternative methodologies that reduce dependencies on large teams or high budgets while still preserving cultural integrity and significance.

Recent advances in generative AI—especially Large Language Models (LLMs) like ChatGPT—support various stages of game design, from procedural content generation (e.g., *MarioGPT* [7]) to ideation and prototyping [8]. Most of these works use a co-creative model where AI supports human designers, who retain control over core decisions. Yet this presumes access to skilled professionals—often unavailable in low-resource heritage contexts. In such cases, LLMs can act as semi-autonomous design agents: with structured prompts and minimal targeted input, they may generate viable concepts otherwise out of reach.

This study explores whether generative AI can effectively substitute for both SME input and creative design in heritage serious games—a question especially relevant in low-resource contexts with limited documentation, expertise, and funding. Our aim is twofold: to assess if AI can generate meaningful game concepts for underfunded settings (e.g., local museums) and to test whether it can partially take over roles typically filled by SMEs and designers. In our model, humans structure prompts and implement the prototype, while AI provides and distributes cultural content within a predefined design framework. This setup serves as a testbed for rethinking workflows where creative and expert input are scarce.

3   A Serious Game on the *Poème Électronique*

To explore AI's role in heritage game design, we focused on a case study centered on the musical dimension of Edgard Varèse's *Poème Électronique*, within the context of the VEP Project. This work represents a niche heritage item from an older research initiative. Composed for the Philips Pavilion at the 1958 Brussels World's Fair—an early multimedia environment designed by Le Corbusier and Xenakis—the piece integrated architecture, sound, and imagery. The pavilion acted as a resonant instrument, with over 350 speakers embedded in its structure to spatialize Varèse's electronic sounds. Although spatial control documentation is incomplete, the VEP Project reconstructed the experience using archival materials and digital tools. The piece is built from a precise sequence of "sound objects" distributed across three mono tapes, categorized by Varèse and Philips engineers using onomatopoeic labels referencing original recordings [2]. The VEP project produced a taxonomy of 142 sound fragments, including their duration and spatial "routes".[1]

Our methodology uses ChatGPT—4o to generate a concept document for a serious game based on the *Poème Électronique*, guided by structured prompts aligned with the Co.Lab framework and informed by VEP Project materials (Phase 1). In this phase, the authors provide the VEP knowledge (the already discussed taxonomy) and act as producers (via project constraints), while the LLM functions as SME (drawing on its embedded knowledge and the provided knowledge) and as game designer (filling up Co.Lab components and generating the concept document). After concept generation, follow-up prompts refine specific design elements for prototyping in Unity (Phase 2), with the authors as programmers and the AI as designer and visual artist. Finally, three SMEs evaluate the prototype, assessing the representation of heritage content and the strengths and limits of the approach. The next sections outline each experimental phase in detail.

3.1   Experimental Design

Our experimental design follows a role-based interaction model between Chat-GPT and the authors, inspired by Tyni et al. [9]. To guide the model's behavior, we used *personas*—fictional professional profiles simulating design roles. In Phase 1, ChatGPT focused on core components like mechanics, interactions, and feedback. In Phase 2, its role shifted toward visual and aesthetic decisions, resembling that of a visual designer—an essential step to support prototype implementation and maintain coherence with the conceptual vision.

Phase 1 – Concept Generation Phase 1 focused on generating a complete game concept by systematically applying the Co.Lab framework through structured, modular prompts. Instead of open-ended dialogue, we used a consistent role-based instruction: *"Act as a professional game designer working within the Co.Lab framework for serious games. Each prompt will restrict your task to defining components of the Co.Lab framework."* To standardize interactions, each prompt included the following core components:

- **Step:** The Co.Lab component to be generated (e.g., Context, Game Universe), defining the prompt's focus.
- **Example:** A short sample from another project to illustrate tone and detail level.
- **Definition:** The official Co.Lab description clarifying purpose and scope.

---

[1] Available here: https://docs.google.com/spreadsheets/d/17o58f_CTaxmRDNg05Z66 StbWxty7MkB2/edit?usp=sharing&ouid=102381116949791592518&rtpof=true&sd= true.

- **Guidelines:** Instructions that steer content and reduce ambiguity.
- **Key Questions:** Focused prompts to guide the model's reasoning.
- **Given Knowledge:** Project-specific information replacing assumptions.

All prompts and responses were systematically recorded[2] to guarantee transparency and replicability. It is worth noting that the "Given Knowledge" field was used only in the initial "Context" step, where the authors provided the taxonomy of sound fragments derived from the VEP project, along with relevant design constraints. Although the VEP also reconstructed the "sound routes" of the composition, we chose to exclude this information, as it was more directly linked to the spatial configuration of the Philips Pavilion than to the intrinsic features of the musical work itself. We deliberately omitted the "Pedagogical Scenario" component, since the game was not intended for use in formal educational settings. Once the Co.Lab components were completed, six illustrative storyboards were generated to simulate the user experience.

Phase 2–Technical Prototyping. Phase 2 focused on developing a functional prototype in Unity, as suggested by ChatGPT during concept generation. The goal was to implement a minimal version of the game that could showcase core mechanics and be evaluated by experts. This process followed an approach similar to Anjum et al. [1], using iterative prompting with ChatGPT to address implementation-specific tasks. The model was provided with the Phase 1 concept document and the sound taxonomy to ensure design continuity.

While Co.Lab structures concept generation, its abstractions don't always suffice for implementation [3]. To address this, we introduced a process called *gap mapping*, aimed at identifying missing or unclear technical specifications in the concept outputs. Each Co.Lab section was reviewed for implementation readiness; when key details (e.g., camera position) were absent, clarification prompts were submitted to ChatGPT. All resulting questions were mapped back to their respective Co.Lab components and compiled into a checklist.[3]

Phase 3–Expert Evaluation. In the final phase, the prototype was evaluated by three domain experts in musicology, sound design, and heritage, all familiar with the *Poème Électronique*. Each expert interacted individually with the prototype, followed by a group discussion guided by two questions:

- Which aspects of the original work are meaningfully represented?
- Which aspects of the original work are missing or underdeveloped?

These open-ended prompts aimed to assess both fidelity to the source and the prototype's interpretive and communicative potential.

---

[2] Available at: https://docs.google.com/presentation/d/1OXLZMKMFrdeSeLnaUV 4Ow_X7kkEjT87bKPWqiH_0KBI/edit?usp=sharing.

[3] Available at: https://docs.google.com/spreadsheets/d/17o58f_CTaxmRDNg05Z66 StbWxty7MkB2/edit?usp=sharing.

4   Results

4.1   Analysis of the Concept Document

The prototype, titled *Edgar à Gogo*, is a short interactive experience introducing players to the sonic world of Varèse's *Poème Électronique*. Players explore a "world of sound" across four levels: (1) discovering and unlocking floating sound objects in a dark and abstract environment; (2) manipulating selected sounds (e.g., changing pitch, volume, panning, and reverb); (3) composing a personal version of the *Poème*; and (4) engaging in a multiplayer, turn-based version of level 3, with sharing features.

The game aims to deepen understanding of key musical features—such as texture, spatialization, and experimental electronic techniques—by letting users interact with and manipulate sonic fragments. Players are expected to grasp how sound is organized in space and how different sonic elements interact within a three-dimensional environment. On a practical level, the game enables users to interact with and manipulate sonic fragments through digital tools, guiding them toward the creation of short compositions and the resolution of sound-based puzzles.

Mechanically, the game combines basic point-and-click interaction with simple puzzle solving and auditory recognition. For example, in level 1, players are tasked with classifying sounds, understanding the provenience of a sound source, and matching sound fragments to a given target sound. Puzzles are available only in the first level: interacting with at least 5 fragments grants access to level 2. Solving puzzles unlocks manipulation tools useful in level 2 (panning and reverb). Manipulating at least 5 fragments grants access to level 3. The game ends when a composition (in level 3) at least 30 seconds long is produced. Level 4 has not been implemented yet. Feedback is provided through color-coded cues and progression through levels. Although the game lacks explicit scoring or time-based challenges, it encourages attentive listening and curiosity-driven exploration.

4.2   Analysis of the Technical Specifications

This phase refined several ambiguous or incomplete elements from the concept document. Key aspects—such as level progression, puzzle structure, camera placement, and player interaction—required clarification before implementation.

The game sound space was populated by physical objects, each linked to a sound fragment from the *Poème Électronique*. Spatialization was implemented through FMOD, using positional stereo panning to simulate distance and direction referring to the game space. Poème Electronique spatialization was addressed in other works [4]. To minimize authorial bias, even fragment selection was handled by ChatGPT, which made visual and behavioral choices based on the onomatopoeic nature of the names found in the taxonomy. From 142 fragments, the model selected 12 and defined their appearance and interaction—for instance, "WBlock" became a jagged, vibrating tetrahedron, likely inspired by its percussive sound (that ChatGPT assumed by the fragment name, "WBlock" as

"Wooden Block"). The model also introduced a distinction between "dormant" sounds (triggered by interaction and then looping) and "active" ones (looping from the start), clarifying the idea of sound "unlocking."

Figure 1 compares the storyboard (Phase 1) and prototype. The final version uses a first-person camera and color-coded 3D objects with varied shapes, contrasting with the simpler geometric forms used in the storyboard.

Fig. 1. A storyboard and its implementation in the prototype

4.3 Expert Feedback

Expert evaluation confirmed the prototype's fidelity to some key features of the *Poème Électronique*, such as its segmentation into sound fragments and spatial diffusion of those single fragments. At the same time, critiques revealed aspects of the original work that were missing or underdeveloped.

First, experts emphasized the need to distinguish original sounds from their gamified versions. They suggested adding a "reset" function to restore (after manipulation) each fragment to its unaltered form, preserving the integrity of the source material.

Second, they highlighted the absence of temporal context. The *Poème* is not merely a collection of sounds but a structured narrative. The prototype treats fragments as isolated units, overlooking sequencing. Experts proposed visualizing neighboring or repeated elements to reflect their original order.

Third, the abstract "sound space" metaphor drew mixed reactions. While its dark palette and pulsing lights evoked the Philips Pavilion, its spatial logic was unclear. Sound sources were too dense, causing auditory clutter. Alternative layouts based on perceptual criteria (e.g., timbre, duration) were recommended.

A notable suggestion was to ground the experience in historical metaphors-such as a 1950s tape studio-to reflect original production conditions and enhance cultural depth.

Lastly, in the composition phase, experts asked for better alignment between fragment visuals and their timeline representations, as well as clearer playback indicators like active highlights and duration markers.

5   Discussion

The experiment demonstrates that generative AI, when guided by structured design frameworks such as Co.Lab, can effectively contribute to designing cultural heritage serious games. ChatGPT produced internally consistent outputs across the various Co.Lab components, with few contradictions or misalignments. This suggests that, with appropriate structuring, LLMs can reliably operate within design frameworks—potentially extending beyond the cultural heritage domain to other genres and contexts.

However, the main limitation of the resulting concept lies in its generic nature. Without in-depth understanding of the musical work or clear guidance on which aspects to highlight, ChatGPT focused on broad features of electronic music and signal processing. This reflects a typical behavior of large language models: generating the most statistically probable (and often safest) answer. This tendency toward generic answers led to less specific outcomes in our case.

Due to this lack of specificity, the concept required a substantial *gap-mapping* phase. Many prompts revealed content omissions or ambiguities, which the AI attempted to resolve with plausible but unfounded inferences. For instance, ChatGPT interpreted sound fragment filenames as semantic cues, translating them into visual or spatial attributes such as color, shape, and vertical position. Percussive-sounding names led to angular forms, while lighter or more abstract names were associated with smaller, floating objects.

Interestingly, this absence of cultural depth became one of the experiment's most revealing elements. It was precisely the concept's inability to convey certain aspects—such as the compositional logic or historical symbolism of the original piece—that triggered the most insightful expert feedback. Experts could identify what was missing because the gaps were made explicit. In this sense, the prototype, though based on a limited concept, functioned not only as a playable artifact but also as a discursive tool: it prompted reflection, critique, and clarification through its limitations.

That said, this discursive potential does not necessarily make the system suitable for niche cultural contexts or institutions lacking SME access. The experiment shows that, in low-resource settings, human expertise is still critical—particularly for identifying what is worth preserving or highlighting in a heritage item. Without this interpretive input, AI tends to default to generic patterns or construct shallow metaphors that fail to respect the complexity of cultural artifacts.

So, is this approach ready for contexts with limited resources? Not yet. While AI can assist in structuring and populating a design framework, the absence of expert insight still results in generic or culturally incomplete outcomes. This is especially problematic when the training data of the AI does not include detailed knowledge of the heritage item.

Nonetheless, the experiment yielded an engaging and thought-provoking prototype. Experts responded positively to the idea of exploring a physical space of sounds and appreciated its potential for stimulating curiosity and playful engagement. Although the AI could not replace cultural interpretation, it did contribute to creating a starting point for design. In this sense, the method may be best suited not for replacing expert collaboration but for supporting early-stage prototyping and discussion in low-resource environments. The exploratory nature of this case study also limits the generalizability of its findings. Broader investigations across multiple cultural domains would be necessary to capture the range of strengths and shortcomings of LLM-based design support.

6   Conclusions

This study examined the feasibility of using generative AI, specifically ChatGPT, to support the design of serious games for cultural heritage, with a focus on low-resource contexts. Through a structured application of the Co.Lab framework, the AI was able to produce a coherent game concept based on a niche cultural artifact—Varèse's Poème Électronique—and assist in the development of a playable prototype. The results highlight both the potential and the limitations of such an approach.

On the one hand, the experiment confirmed that generative AI can operate effectively within structured workflows, producing design elements that are logically consistent and actionable. The resulting prototype was well received in terms of engagement and exploratory potential, demonstrating that AI can lower the entry barrier to concept generation and early prototyping.

On the other hand, the absence of cultural depth and interpretive nuance exposed the limits of relying solely on AI. While the system could simulate coherence, it struggled to represent the symbolic and historical richness of the source material without explicit human input. This reinforces the idea that AI cannot yet replace SME involvement—particularly in heritage domains where meaning is deeply contextual and often undocumented.

Future research should extend this approach to additional case studies, testing different heritage contexts and evaluating how hybrid human–AI workflows adapt across domains. Currently we are working on extending the method to a game on silent movie locations [6] and historical landscape visualization. In summary, the use of generative AI in heritage game design shows promise as a support tool, especially for ideation and structuring tasks. However, its effectiveness depends on the availability of curated knowledge and expert validation. Future work should explore hybrid workflows in which AI augments, rather than substitutes, human expertise—especially in collaborative settings involving small institutions or underrepresented heritage topics.

References

1. Anjum, A., Li, Y., Law, N., Charity, M., Togelius, J.: The Ink Splotch Effect: A Case Study on ChatGPT as a Co-Creative Game Designer. In: Proceedings of the 19th International Conference on the Foundations of Digital Games. pp. 1–15. ACM, New York, NY, USA (5 2024). https://doi.org/10.1145/3649921.3650010, https://dl.acm.org/doi/10.1145/3649921.3650010
2. Dobson, R., Fitch, J., Tazelaar, K., Valle, A., Lombardo, V.: Varèse's poème Électronique regained: Evidence from the vep project. International Computer Music Conference Proceedings **2005** (2005), http://hdl.handle.net/2027/spo.bbp2372.2005.164
3. Jaccard, D., Suppan, L., Sanchez, E., Huguenin, A., Laurent, M.: The co.LAB Generic Framework for Collaborative Design of Serious Games: Development Study. JMIR Serious Games **9**(3), e28674 (7 2021). https://doi.org/10.2196/28674, https://games.jmir.org/2021/3/e28674
4. Lombardo, V., Valle, A., Nunnari, F., Giordana, F., Arghinenti, A.: Archeology of multimedia. In: Proceedings of the 14th ACM International Conference on Multimedia. pp. 269–278. MM '06, Association for Computing Machinery, New York, NY, USA (2006). https://doi.org/10.1145/1180639.1180706
5. Mortara, M., Catalano, C.E., Bellotti, F., Fiucci, G., Houry-Panchetti, M., Petridis, P.: Learning cultural heritage by serious games. J. Cult. Herit. **15**(3), 318–325 (2014)
6. Nasi, A., Magro, D., Lombardo, V., et al.: Ontological representation of narrative places for cinema archives. In: Proceedings of the 3rd Workshop on Artificial Intelligence for Cultural Heritage (IAI4CH 2024) co-located with the 23rd International Conference of the Italian Association for Artificial Intelligence (AIxIA 2024). vol. 3865, pp. 56–65. CEUR-WS (2024)
7. Sudhakaran, S., González-Duque, M., Freiberger, M., Glanois, C., Najarro, E., Risi, S.: MarioGPT: Open-Ended Text2Level Generation through Large Language Models. Adv. Neural Inf. Process. Syst. **36** (2 2023), https://arxiv.org/pdf/2302.05981
8. Sweetser, P.: Large Language Models and Video Games: A Preliminary Scoping Review. In: ACM Conversational User Interfaces 2024. pp. 1–8. ACM, New York, NY, USA (7 2024). https://doi.org/10.1145/3640794.3665582, https://dl.acm.org/doi/10.1145/3640794.3665582
9. Tyni, J., Turunen, A., Kahila, J., Bednarik, R., Tedre, M.: Can ChatGPT Match the Experts? A Feedback Comparison for Serious Game Development. International Journal of Serious Games **11**(2), 87–106 (6 2024). https://doi.org/10.17083/ijsg.v11i2.744, https://journal.seriousgamessociety.org/index.php/IJSG/article/view/744
10. Van Roessel, L., Van Mastrigt-Ide, J.: Collaboration and Team Composition in Applied Game Creation Processes. DiGRA Digital Library **2011**(1) (1 2011). https://doi.org/10.26503/dl.v2011i1.599, https://dl.digra.org/index.php/dl/article/view/599
11. Wu, C.H., Chao, Y.L., Xiong, J.T., Luh, D.B.: Gamification of culture: A strategy for cultural preservation and local sustainable development. Sustainability **15**(1) (2023). https://doi.org/10.3390/su15010650, https://www.mdpi.com/2071-1050/15/1/650

Media and Cultural Studies Track

Decolonizing Gaming

Thomas Widlok[(✉)] [iD]

University of Cologne, Albertus-Magnus-Platz, 50923 Köln, Germany
thomas.widlok@uni-koeln.de

Abstract. Decolonizing gaming is not only about including more participants from the Global South to increase diversity among gamers and game designers. It is also about overcoming limitations that a colonial mindset continues to hold with regard to mainstream gaming and game design. This contribution explores new opportunities that arise from a decolonial revision of key aspects of gaming: Enriching the dominant hero's quest by including ambivalent trickster characters, replacing the logic of conquest, extraction and accumulation by exploring a logic of sharing, diversifying game environments by including ways of playful imagination and practice that are hitherto marginalized. In this process serious games play a particularly important role as they can have a decolonizing impact on gaming grounded in social science research on playfulness beyond "the West".

Keywords: Decolonization · Sharing · Trickster

1   Introduction: Why Gaming Needs Decolonizing

"Relooted" is a new game "against colonialism" in which "Blacks plan their heists into Western museums in order to steal back artefacts" (Drebenstedt 2025). The game was developed and produced in Africa and it seems to successfully invert the colonial logic of exploration, exploitation, conquest and occupation by settlers that is the backdrop of many other games. Developed by Nyamakop Studios, Johannesburg, it features a group of African superheroes taking violent action to speed up the slow response of many museums faced with African demands to return their artefacts, many of which were looted during colonial times. While this inversion can be considered a first step towards decolonizing mainstream commercial gaming, I claim that more serious steps can be undertaken in decolonizing gaming. Impact games and other serious games - which have more freedom to depart from entrenched narratives and consumer expectations - have great potential for pioneering decolonizing in much more fundamental ways than "Relooted". This contribution argues that by decolonizing serious gaming in three concrete ways we may advance the decolonizing efforts of game developers more generally. Firstly, decolonizing through the diversification of game contents beyond the cultural expectations of the Global North promises to enrich gaming ideas and practices. Secondly, making digital games accessible to a wider circle of users and developers is likely to have a positive effect not only on those currently excluded or marginalized but also on those who are currently shaping the field at large. Thirdly, there are some

S. Bakkes et al. (Eds.): GALA 2025, LNCS 16307, pp. 237–246, 2026.
https://doi.org/10.1007/978-3-032-11043-5_23

very concrete features in today's game designs that are limiting the way we think about games. This is due to often implicit biases that can be uncovered through a decolonizing critique. In this contribution I shall focus on the last-mentioned aspect of decolonizing gaming but a few remarks on the first two aspects are also in order.

For as long as access to gadgets and internet infrastructure is globally unequal there will be a degree of exclusion and marginalization affecting those who lack easy access to electricity and the internet, including digital games. The initial hope that the internet and the growing spread of electronic hand-held devices would function as a great equalizer did not materialize. Access to the internet is much more "spiky" (unequal) than what many users want it to be, or assume it to be (see Friedman 2005, Florida 2005): Having worked in African countries over the last four decades I have seen rapid growth in the use of computers, mobile phones and web services for some privileged quarters of the population in those countries. At the same time, many of my local collaborators from underprivileged groups continue to struggle very hard to get connected and to stay connected. Obstacles are wide ranging, including frequent power cuts, the costs of purchasing technology, software and airtime. For many, the inclusion into global markets but also the threat of subsequent disconnection from global markets is tantamount to less opportunities to influence gaming. Ferguson (2001) and others have labelled this experience of being socio-culturally and economically disconnected "abjection". This is one of the first paradoxes when considering gaming through the lens of (de)colonization: There is ample anthropological evidence that pre-colonial and pre-capitalist societies were extremely rich in terms of their ludic capacities and potentials. Take hunter-gatherer societies as an example. While initially thought to be societies at the verge of permanent starvation and therefore devoid of any culture beyond necessity, it soon emerged that in fact humans living under these conditions worked less hours and spend more time on play than workers in the industrial age or their immediate predecessors, the pre-industrial agriculturalists (see Sahlins 1988). Not only was there more time for play, the ludic element also penetrated many fields of life that are now considered to be categorically distinct from leisure. Practicing skills for hunting, gathering, fishing etc. has as much a ludic dimension as a practical-utilitarian dimension. The same holds for story telling and the whole context that has been called serious, "holy play", namely ritual performance (see Lang 1998). In contradistinction to popular assumptions of ritual being necessarily a rigid and somber procedure very unlike games, ritual studies have shown the great dynamic potential of rituals, with room for maneuver and for playfully tampering with rules and authorities (see Chaniotis 2010, Grimes et al. 2011, Brosius et al. 2013). In other words, the current gaming industry, being based largely on Global North ideas and practices of gaming is currently largely disconnected from what arguably could be seen as the strongest traditions of human ludic ideas and practices in the Global South. The "Global North" in this context includes not only "the West" but also the technology-driven gaming industries of Japan, South Korea or India.

It should be clear by now that "decolonizing" gaming does not mean including more ethnic colouring when designing game characters or to design gaming scenes beyond the conventional cosmopolitan urban or rural imagery. It is also not simply a matter of giving other people elsewhere better access to these games (although this is a point of concern, too). Rather, decolonizing could shape the whole gaming enterprise, including serious games, in a number of fundamental ways. Trammell (2023) has argued that the very notion of play as "fun" needs to be decolonized in the light of experience of Black Americans - for whom play is often toxic - since limiting play to fun is another means to erase them from public social life. He demands nothing less than a recasting of game as intellectual repairing or even healing instead of a power tool of subjugation: "Repairing play means tending to the painful as well as the pleasurable aspects of play" (Trammell 2023, 18). Gaming here is no exception from the more general realization that many of the features that we assumed to be universally human turn out to be rather special and Eurocentric, reflecting only experiences of some quarters of humanity, often those who colonized, dominated and subjugate others. More precisely, psychologists and cognitive scientists have labelled the bias as that of the W.E.I.R.D. people (Henrich, Heine, Norenzayan 2010). W.E.I.R.D stands for "Western Educated Industrial Rich Democratic". Even though one can argue critically about each of these labels (see also Widlok 2014) the bottom line of this realization is still valid: Much of what we think we know of humans who were tested in their cognitive or economic (or indeed gaming) behaviour is limited to a rather small circle of people, often university students in the Global North with very peculiar backgrounds when considering a wider comparative perspective. This extends all the way to the manner in which we perceive things in our environment, for instance basic graphical conventions that we find in almost any game. For example, the Müller-Lyer "illusion" according to which all humans always think that a line between outward pointing arrows < -- > is longer than the same line between inward pointing arrows > -- < turns out to be limited to humans who happened to have grown up in a "carpentered" environment of ninety-degree joints. And what is true for spatial perception has also been demonstrated for concepts of time and causality (see Widlok 2017 for an overview): Most of what we find in globalized entertainment culture is a rather limited selection of a much wider human repertoire. This means that the games designed in the mainstream gaming industry may be read, understood and played in many more ways than we currently anticipate. In other words, there are enormous unexplored game worlds out there because we have so far not taken seriously the whole cultural repertoire of how humans have played games.

2   Decolonizing Playful Minds

This takes me to the central argument of my contribution. Decolonizing gaming is not only about being globally more inclusive, lowering thresholds that are continually raised by the industry through developing software that continuously requires us to buy new gadgets, as it needs more memory, greater bandwidth, more and continuous power and connectivity - assets that many people do not have. Decolonizing gaming is, beyond that, also all about exploring new ways of thinking about games, of setting up games differently. It is also about gaming that has so far been limited by a colonial heritage that narrows down the set of human cultural traditions included in the dominant global industry. Decolonizing gaming in this sense is not directed at some marginalized group at the fringes but at the ways in which the majority of us engage with games. At the same time, the segment of serious games, in particular impact games, can become the forerunner for changes in gaming more generally. I am using the label impact games for those games that do not have entertainment as their main goal (and therefore are part of serious games) but that rather have a distinct critical and political agenda such as that of decolonization. I maintain that ultimately all games have a role to play in decolonization and that they all stand to benefit from this process.

It is a wide-spread misunderstanding that "decolonization" is an issue that is by nature of primary or sole relevance to people living in previously colonized countries, the argument being that colonial structures of dependency, domination and marginalization continue to be effective long after European colonialism has ended with the independence of most formerly colonized territories. But colonization also affects the colonizers and their descendants, their mental states, imageries and social practices as much as it affects the colonized and their descendants. This has been convincingly shown by Heinz (2023) for Western ways of conceptualizing the mind and for dealing with mental processes including mental disorders. Heinz argues that the dominant medical understanding of cognition as being governed by a cerebral center (the brain) and a subservient body is largely informed by the way in which colonizers (and their descendants) have become used to think about the global order, the dynamics of empires, and the global division of labour into the "civilizing" centers on the one hand and the countries in which manual labour and the provision of raw materials are situated on the other hand. Independently of the question as to whether our mind-body dichotomy is a direct product of colonial history, it is convincing that the (post)colonial set-up of the world at large has deeply entrenched the ways in which we consider our own bodies, minds and personhood - and continues to do so. It has taken the cognitive and the educational sciences long to realize that "learning" does not take place in isolated brains but is a matter of embodied minds and performative agency. Digital games in particular had to come a long way from being biased towards seemingly "disembodied" operations of signs to the realization that cognition (in gaming and learning, too) is distributed across minds, bodies, tools etc. This process began with early research on "distributed cognition" (see Hutchins 1986) and has now reached applied work on embodied game experience (see Freyermuth et al. 2013). There is now considerable literature (too much to cover here) that seeks to diversify gaming contents and gaming formats. The emergence and promotion of collaborative games are a case in point (see Berland and Lee 2011, Zagal et al. 2006). But decolonizing is more specific than developing alternatives to the dominant competitive gaming formats. "Decolonizing the mind" involves no longer characterizing receiving units and entities as "slaves" and the sending entities as "masters" both in computer communication (modems of the past) and in game settings (e.g. in the case of multiple digital command controllers of toy trains equipped with decoders). But there are more fundamental changes at stake than getting rid of colonial labels, as I would like to illustrate in what follows.

3 Decolonized Play Characters

The main characters of most games - digital or analogue, serious or non-serious - are "heroes". Typical contents taught to people wanting to delve into game design is to teach them the script of "the quest" ("*Heldenreise*", hero's adventure, see Campbell 1949). It is someone venturing out to carry out adventures, solve tasks etc. and to return with riches - or at least with good stories to tell. It is easy to see here how this is merged with - and mutually amplified by - the imagery and practice of colonial empires that send out explorers to overcome obstacles, conquer foreign lands and seas, exploit faraway resources etc. There are problematic aspects to the hero narrative, for instance the "winner takes it all" attitude, the limited good imagery ("whatever I have someone else cannot have") the purposeful ignoring of the fate of the "others" in the hero encounters, the hyper-individuality of many heroes, a rigid friend-foe distinction and the good/evil dichotomy, or the lack of any strategy of dealing productively with failure, unresolvable problems etc. What is worse, though, is that often the hero and his travels is considered the only possible way of designing the main role of characters in any game. By contrast, and comparatively speaking, the main character in much of human playful thought and practice is not necessarily a hero but more likely a trickster character.

Trickster figures and tricksterish behaviour are human universals, they are found on all continents and in many different constellations. A polythetic definition of tricksters include the following properties: Trickster are (1) switching identity, (2) tricking others, (3) shape shifting, (4) inverting and overturning rules (5) moving boundaries, (6) re-arranging culture (Hynes and Doty 1997). The definition is polythetic in that not all of these features need to be present for people to recognize a figure as a trickster. Given the high prevalence of the trickster across indigenous cultures across all continents it is rather surprising that this character does not dominate gaming, after all it is the ludic person par excellence. Yes, there is a lot of shape-shifting, especially in graphically sophisti-cated digital games, but other tricksterish features remain underexplored. Tricksters are morally ambivalent. They often transgress rules, often for selfish reasons (negative) but at the same time they also challenge self-appointed and imposing authorities and pro-vide weapons to the weak, if only through their (positive) example. This could become a key feature especially for various forms of serious games because they set out to allow users to learn about complexity and to train their tolerance for ambiguities. Bauer (2018) has shown how this tolerance towards ambiguity is at the heart of strategies to counter extremism and fundamentalism. Having more tricksterish figures (and actions) in games would not only introduce a greater social realism into games, it would also amplify the key message of many impact games, namely the need to train sociability, reasonability, an appreciation of complexity and adequacy of agency geared toward that complexity in dynamically changing situations.

Much more could be said in this context about the personality of play characters. I limit myself to only mention that comparatively speaking the individualistic person that is promoted by mainstream culture and entertainment is comparatively again a rather W.E.I.R.D. feature (see above). Characters need not have to have that monolithic and rather static personhood. Common other forms of personhood are the "dividual" (dominant in many Pacific cultures) but also "partible" personhood (described for India for example) but also other notions of "permeable" and relational persons (see Busby 1997, Fowler 2004). Instead of assuming that the characters of a game are by and large unchanging and come with a fixed set of properties, an orientation towards these other notions of personhood would mean that we recognize that persons can be made through ongoing social interaction, changing when relationships change and how the person itself can be seen as a bundle of relations with others (including non-human others) instead of a bundle of fixed features. Decolonizing our cast of characters in any one game does not only mean to diversify the characters but also to change the ways in which the characters shift their shape, their goals, their mindset, namely through social interactions. Many serious games have as their goal that players learn to change their lives (by being better informed, experienced etc.). Decolonizing the available roles in such games therefore seems to be a particularly promising path towards this goal.

4 Decolonized Play Actions

However, it is not only the shape of the play characters but also their actions that need decolonizing. Again, the dominant feature is that of accumulation. Play characters win a game by getting points, getting to higher levels, usually by outcompeting others, sometimes by pooling their forces and skills to jointly reach the points they need, for instance in escape games. In a decolonizing perspective this rather monomaniacal focus on accumulation needs to be challenged. The (over)exploitation of natural resources is inextricably linked to the colonial and imperial expansion (see Ghosh 2021). In other words, decolonizing also means realizing that there are limits to growth since there are social and environmental costs that make accumulation a maladaptive strategy. By implication, "the winner takes it all" and "to get as much out of this as possible" are goals that lead to colonial strategies and are in turn produced by them. Since they are not locally sustainable, an ever-increasing accumulation means expanding beyond one's own territory, enslaving or disappropriating others in order to be able to secure their assets for oneself, something that is deeply entrenched not only in the capitalist West but more fundamentally in the Abrahamic religions (see Brody 2000). To break up this link between non-sustainable accumulation and dominating others would presuppose a game setting in which the overall aim of the game is altered. There are at this stage no examples of games that could be given here but at our university we are currently developing *"The Fair Share Game"* which is based on the logic of sharing, here understood as "extending the circle of people who have access to what is valued" (see Widlok 2017: xvii). If we turn this into the goal of the game, the efforts of the players shift from accumulating goods (at the cost of others) to striving for a larger circle of others with access to what is valued. But again, it is not simply a maximization by those who exploit a resource. Resources in this setup are not unlimited but potentially demands for access can be unlimited and mutually exclusive. Hence, the strategy of the players would be to act appropriately according to the situation by distinguishing "humbug" demands, i.e. out of proportion demands by others, from appropriate demands for a fair share. It would also involve learning to dodge the inappropriate demands without jeopardizing or cutting off one's relationships to social partners. As we know from the ethnography of sharing (see Widlok 2017) this is by no means a banal problem. Indigenous Australians in precolonial and in contemporary settings spend quite some time discussing "humbug" demands and how to react to them (see Myers 1988). Among indigenous foragers in southern Africa, strategies of levelling outrageous demands without alienating others and without raising open conflict often involve a lot of talking, frequently moving away from others or hiding assets (Widlok 2017). Circumpolar ethnography suggests that it matters considerably what the assets (or "items of value") are that are subject to demand sharing. Some "bulky" items (whales, fishing boats) have different "affordances" of how they can be shared as compared to nuts, berries and other items that can be easily gathered individually (see Widlok 2017). And cultural conventions and evaluations differ: Foragers in tropical African forests are happy to share many of their material goods but they are, by contrast, eager to sell and own dances, spirits and ceremonies (see Lewis 2015). Serious games could easily explore the complexity of these situations and the challenge of players would be to develop an appropriate and socially acceptable strategy of dealing with the specificity of each situation, the types of resources that need to be shared, and the type of group structure that allows fair demands for a share by those in need. Strikingly, in "real life" situations documented by ethnography much of this challenge is responded to not by following hard and fast rules or static principles but rather by a high degree of playfulness of tentative and dialogical "trying things out" which involves learning from responses as one proceeds. There is, therefore, a considerable overlap between what goes on in gaming and what goes on in real-life situations of sharing which makes games a perfect place for learning about the logic of sharing. Conversely, gaming more generally could be a perfect training ground for acquiring skills of dealing with sharing as an alternative mode of transfer geared towards an alternative economy more appropriately suited to a finite planet.

There is not only room for alternatives to the accumulation efforts that dominate many games today. Rather, and more strongly put, there seems to be a prominent role for gaming in breaking with entrenched but counterproductive practices of accumulation and by acquainting and training players in alternative practices such as sharing. As ethnography suggests these practices are not simply a matter of gaining moral high ground (or even of intellectual understanding) but these practices can be trained under changing and challenging social conditions, e.g. through play.

5   Decolonized Play Environment and Resources

It is another big asset of games (both analogue and digital) that they can simulate an amazing spectrum of resources, assets, and environments. One should therefore imagine that this is an aspect in which a decolonizing agenda could easily be realized. In many other contexts, decolonizing also affects the epistemological and ontological standing of the entities that we are dealing with (see Braidotti and Gilroy 2016 on the ongoing debates on posthumanism). To put it more simply: Animals, spiritual beings, material objects need not be "things", as in the dominant "naturalist" Western discourse (see Candea and Alcayna-Stevens 2012) but all of these could become agents and social persons who can establish relationships with one another and who can interact with the players. And, of course, we already see this in many games, where animals and plants speak to humans, where things move and behave in an "animated" fashion and so forth. As a matter of fact, many games today already encompass different ontologies. Players are habitually being trained in learning about, and adapting to, different ontological environments, e.g. a world in which non-humans speak, have personalities, emotions and agency. This is, therefore, a very good starting point for decolonization. There is, however, still room for improvement because often the "alternative ontology" that players learn about in their game environment may be distinctly different from the everyday ontology they live in (e.g. with animals and plants speaking) but in mainstream commercial games that new environment typically demands the same rigorous acceptance and standardized "normality" that a naturalist or materialist environment demands. The crux of the decolonial challenge is not only that things, the universe at large, can be very different. Rather, it is realization that we are not dealing with a homogeneous universe but rather with a "pluriverse" (see Widlok forthcoming). The decolonial challenge for games in this context is therefore not only to train players to learn a different ontology, to find their way into a strange new environment. Rather, the players need to learn that there is a *plurality* of ontologies, that they cannot trust that everything they have learned at earlier levels is still valid at other levels they reach. In other words, players need to train their flexibility, and to maintain their alertness and their perceptiveness to expect the unexpected from the game environment as much as from other characters. While this can ideally be simulated in gaming environments, the decolonial agenda also means breaking with some established habits in the gaming industry where many players are encouraged (and rewarded) for taking on their new game environment as "second home", as a new normality. That new normality structurally often demands the same rigorousness in abiding to rules, conforming to values of the new world they are entering - including the habit to accumulate riches and to seek and gain status. Designing decolonized environments for games that can innovate the industry means nothing less than introducing new logics to gaming. Widlok and Stenning have discussed the role of different logics, in particular so-called non-monotonic logics (Widlok and Stenning 2018). Here it suffices to say that other logics exist that are unlike the inductive and deductive logics that dominate much of our problem-solving in games. Think of the "games of deduction" where the identity of the "werewolf" (or more conventionally "the murderer") has to be deductively established. By contrast, much of the established gaming life follows an "abductive" logic, for instance when dealing with misfortune through oracles (see Widlok and Stenning 2018, Widlok 2014). Abductive reasoning of the type "where there is smoke, there is also fire" (see Agar 2013) contradicts linear, monotonic logic, of textbooks but at the same time much of everyday reasoning is abductive. It requires being prepared to readjust premises instead of "monotonically" building on existing premises. It typically involves delving into the changing details of a situation instead of pursuing everlasting underlying principles (Widlok forthcoming). Recognizing abductive logic is therefore part of a decolonizing effort not only in the sense of plurification but also of upgrading practical knowledge that is not canonized in abstract principles. This upgrading is important for a re-evaluation of non-western epistemologies (Widlok 2014) but also of subaltern ontologies of practitioners in "the West". There is a final twist to this that has a particular relevance for gaming as a practice: While deductive and other monotonic logics privilege game designers and abstract planning, abduction underlines the skills and implicit embodied knowledge of the performers, the players themselves and the abductive reasoning skill that they develop through engaging with the game. To put it differently, the task of serious games, and impact games in particular, is not only to help unlearn standardized behaviour and to explore new forms of behaviour, it is also re-valueing the importance of performance of playful agency itself. It recognizes that problem solving can not only be improved through detached design but also by perfectionating the practices at hand.

6 Conclusion: Games Without Frontiers

Gaming has a great potential to playfully imagine and propagate "other worlds", worlds with less inequality and less marginalization of subaltern practices and ideas. Impact games can play an important role in undoing past injustices and breaking up structures of domination that have been produced through the imperialist colonialism of the past and that continues to have effects on living conditions today. However, this potential is not as yet fully realized, we need more games designed towards that goal. To the contrary, there are not only traces of colonialism in gaming practice but the gaming industry, together with many other parts of mainstream culture, tends to amplify tendencies that are implicated in the colonial project. As shown, there is evidence for this to be found with regard to the way in which role-play and game characters are conceptualized and in the way in which the main characters are considered "heroes" typically on their quest to riches. The actions of these characters often emulate that of colonial explorers and exploiters of raw materials in the colonies leading to disaster for the ecology of the environment as much as in the social life of the indigenous population. Many game environments and their resources have striking resemblances with the colonial backwaters exploited by colonial centers but also more generally with the imperial capitalism that created colonial and racist structures as an inevitable ingredient of exploiting the planet. These colonial vestiges are very rarely actively embraced, neither by game developers or players. However, such colonial traces are unlikely to simply disappear unless gamers actively re-design and re-orient the games they play. Serious games are the one branch of the game industry and of gaming culture more generally, that have a paramount role to play here. Giving more room to impact games in serious gaming can help to change the way in which we design and play games reaching out into the wider entertainment industry but also into teaching and learning about the world at large.

The good news is that the process of decolonizing games does not need to rely on moralizing narratives, on prohibitions, or strict rules of conduct. It also does not exclusively need to be fed by moral utopias. Rather, there is sufficient documentation of the ludic character of pre-colonial societies and also of ongoing subaltern resistance against colonialism that can serve as a shared cultural pool from which other types of games can be produced. As I have indicated in this contribution, there is a world-wide oral tradition of "tricksters" that can replace the monomaniacal narrative of the hero's quest. There are diverse forms of personhood in existence that can inspire new forms of agents in games. There is a detailed ethnographic record of sharing practices (and other forms of transfer such as pooling, commoning, gifting etc.) that can complement or replace the "accumulation" mode of practice that dominates much gaming to this day. And finally, alternative social and natural environments need not be invented from scratch since they are part of the social science and humanities record of the repertoire of what it means to be human. It is unlikely that mainstream entertainment gaming will pick up on these opportunities easily. Specialized impact games, on the other hand, are perfectly positioned to take on this role of a mediating device between the "serious" variability of human life and the playfulness of developing this life further.

Disclosure of Interests The author has no relevant competing interests to declare.

References

Agar, M.: The Lively Science. Publish Green, Minneapolis (2013)

Berland, M., Lee, V.: Collaborative strategic board games as a site for distributed computational thinking. International Journal of Game-Based Learning **1**(2), 65–81 (2011)

Bauer, T.: Die Vereindeutigung der Welt. Reclam, Ditzingen (2018)

Braidotti, R., Gilroy, P. (eds.): Conflicting Humanities. Bloomsbury, London (2016)

Brody, H.: The Other Side of Eden. Faber, London (2000)

Brosius, C., et al. (eds.): Ritual und Ritualdynamik. Vandenhoek, Heidelberg (2013)

Busby, C.: Permeable and partible persons. J. Royal Anthrop. Inst. **3**(2), 261–278 (1997)

Campbell, J.: The Hero with a Thousand Faces. Pantheon, New York (1949)

Candea, M., Alcayna-Stevens, L.: Internal Others: ethnographies of Naturalism. The Cambridge Journal of Anthropology **30**, 36–47 (2012)

Chaniotis, A. (ed.): Dynamics and the Science of Ritual. Harrassowitz, Wiesbaden (2010)

Drebenstedt, M.: Spiel gegen Kolonialismus. die Tageszeitung 22.8.25 https://taz.de/Spiel-gegen-Kolonialismus-/!6106060/ (2025)

Ferguson, J.: Expectations of Modernity. Univ. of California Press, Berkeley (2001)

Fowler, C.: The Archaeology of Personhood. Routledge, London (2004)

Freyermuth, G., Gotto, L., Wallenfels, F.: Serious Games, Exergames, Exerlearning. transcript. Bielefeld (2013)

Florida, R.: The world is spiky: globalization has changed the economic playing field, but hasn't leveled it. Atl. Mon. **2005**, 48–51 (2005)

Friedman, T.: The World is Flat. Allen Lane, London (2005)

Ghosh, A.: Nutmeg's Curse: Parables for a Planet in Crisis. U. of Chicago Pr, Chicago (2021)

Grimes, R., et al. (eds.): Ritual, Media and Conflict. Oxford Univ. Press, New York (2011)

Heinz, A.: Das kolonialisierte Gehirn und die Wege der Revolte. Suhrkamp, Berlin (2023)

Henrich, J., Heine, S., Norenzayan, A.: The weirdest people in the world? Behav. Sci. **33**, 61–135. https://doi.org/10.1017/S0140525X0999152X (2010)

Hutchins, E.: Cognition in the Wild. MIT Press, Cambridge (1986)

Hynes, W., Doty, W.: Mythical Trickster Figures. U. of Ala. Pr. Tuscaloosa (1997)

Lang, B.: Heiliges Spiel. Beck, München (1998)

Lewis, J.: Where goods are free but knowledge costs. Hunter Gatherer Res. **1**(1), 1–27 (2015)

Myers, F.: Burning the truck and holding the country. In: Riches, D., Woodburn, J., Ingold, T. (eds.) Hunters and gatherers, pp. 52–94. Berg. Oxford (1988)

Sahlins, M.: Stone Age Economics. Tavistock, London (1988)

Trammell, A.: Repairing Play. A Black Phenomenology. MIT Press, Cambridge (2023)

Widlok, T.: Agency, time, and causality. Front. Psychol. **5**, 1264 (2014)

Widlok, T.: Anthropology and the Economy of Sharing. Routledge, London (2017)

Widlok, T.: Lateral universalism in a decolonizing world. To appear. In: Mlambo, O., Chitando, E. (eds.) Palgrave Handbook of Decolonizing Knowledge in Africa (forthcoming)

Widlok, T., Stenning, K.: Seeking common cause between cognitive science and ethnography. J. Culture and Cognition **18**(1–2), 1–30 (2018)

Zagal, J., Rick, J., Hsi, I.: Collaborative games. Simul. Gaming **37**(1), 24–40 (2006)

Dragons in VR: Designing Visitor-Centered VR Exhibitions

Kevin Körner[✉][ID] and Rena Nagata[ID]

MA specialization Digital Humanities, University of Tübingen, Tübingen, Germany
kevin.koerner@uni-tuebingen.de, rena.nagata@student.uni-tuebingen.de

Abstract. The use of virtual reality (VR) applications for knowledge dissemination in museum exhibitions remains a relevant and evolving topic. As VR becomes more common as a medium in museum didactics, open-source alternatives have begun to emerge alongside high-budget, expert-developed applications. While these lower-cost solutions may not support every creative concept, they enable museums with limited budgets to independently create VR exhibitions that closely mimic real-world settings, including interactive showcases and embedded media such as text, audio, images, and (animated) 3D models. To investigate which media types are most effective within such VR environments, we conducted interviews with three museum curators from south-west Germany to gather insights into their experiences and expectations regarding real-world–mimicking VR exhibitions. Additionally, we carried out a field study, based on a prototype VR exhibition on the history of the dragon myth to collect quantitative data on visitor interaction preferences with different media types and user behavior patterns. In this paper, we present and analyze both datasets and offer practical recommendations for curators interested in developing VR exhibitions for their didactic portfolios.

Keywords: Virtual Reality Exhibitions · Museum Didactics · Visitor Behavior

1 Introduction

Virtual Reality (VR) is still increasingly being adopted as a medium in museum didactics. Owing to relatively novel character, VR serves as an engaging technology that can motivate visitors to actively participate in exhibitions and interact with artifacts and associated information in an immersive way. For museum professionals, it is essential to understand how different types of media are perceived by visitors within VR environments in order to determine the most effective ways of disseminating knowledge. This becomes particularly relevant as VR exhibitions are increasingly standardized: instead of relying solely on high-budget, custom-developed applications, more affordable solutions are emerging–such as open-source frameworks like ExPresS XR[1]–which enable the creation

---

[1] https://github.com/eisclimber/ExPresS-XR, last accessed 23.07.25.

© The Author(s), under exclusive license to Springer Nature Switzerland AG 2026
S. Bakkes et al. (Eds.): GALA 2025, LNCS 16307, pp. 247–256, 2026.
https://doi.org/10.1007/978-3-032-11043-5_24

of VR exhibits without the need for coding. These platforms typically replicate real-world exhibition settings using showcases and allow for the integration of diverse media types, including text, images, audio guides, videos, 3D models and animations, for the purpose of knowledge dissemination. While this approach is limited to creating VR experiences that imitate physical exhibitions, it is especially promising for smaller museums that often lack the financial resources for bespoke VR projects but still wish to offer immersive experiences to their audiences. In this paper, we present our research on media type preferences in real-world–mimicking VR exhibitions and offer design recommendations for curators to enhance the quality of future VR-based museum experiences. As a preparatory step for our study, we conducted qualitative interviews with curators from three local museums in southwestern Germany to gain insights into expert perspectives on exhibition design and their experiences with media use in VR. To compare these expert viewpoints with actual visitor behavior, we developed a compact, real-world-mimicking VR exhibition–*Dragons in VR: Depictions of Dragons from the Middle Ages to the present day*–focusing on the history of the Western European and East Asian dragon myth. This exhibition then served as the foundation for a field study in which we systematically examined visitor interactions with various media types.

2   Related Work

Our initial step in preparing this study was to identify best-practice recommendations for designing virtual reality (VR) exhibitions in museums, along with successful examples of such applications. Selected findings from this review are presented in this section. One foundational study was conducted by Hwei Teeng Chong et al. [1], who highlighted the growing significance of VR in cultural heritage over the past decade and provided a comprehensive overview of current trends in its application. The authors emphasize that *"the cultural heritage content determines the design and development of VR for cultural heritage before integrating it with specified VR tools"*. Accordingly, a didactic concept based on the heritage content and the associated knowledge should be developed first, and only then should the VR application be designed to reflect it. Additionally, the authors point out that *"VR interactivity refers to a high level of usability to meet users with low to no experience and may come from diverse backgrounds using VR technology to experience cultural heritage"*, and that *"this interactivity is unlike domains for education, automotive, medical, gaming or military training, which requires prior training on the usage of VR tools"*. These considerations are particularly relevant for museum contexts, where audiences are highly diverse in terms of technical experience, and where limited time is available to prepare or train visitors–many of whom engage spontaneously with exhibitions. Rodríguez-García et al. [2] outlined best practices for developing VR applications in the heritage sector. In terms of immersion, their work distinguishes between three degrees of freedom (3DoF) and six degrees of freedom (6DoF) movement in VR. While they note that 6DoF enhances visitor immersion, they also argue that 3DoF experiences may be preferable in certain didactic contexts–particularly when the goal is to guide user attention in a focused way. In our case, we chose a 6DoF setup to allow visitors the freedom to explore and engage with different media types at their own pace. This open-ended structure not only supported our aim of studying individual media preferences but also aligned with our concept of imitating a real-world exhibition environment. Relevant examples of successful VR exhibitions were also identified in Richardson's work [3], which reflects broadly on the role of VR in museums and presents a selection of prominent recent exhibitions. Notable among these are the Musée d'Orsay's *Van Gogh's Palette* (2023)[2] and the Louvre's *Mona Lisa: Beyond the Glass* (2019).[3] The former offered a 10-minute immersive exploration of Van Gogh's techniques and artwork, relying primarily on 2D visuals and audio guides. The latter allowed visitors to engage with a fully immersive 3D environment, offering an interactive encounter with the woman behind da Vinci's iconic painting. These examples demonstrated the importance of thoughtfully integrating 2D art, 3D environments, and audio narration for effective knowledge dissemination in VR. Other significant contributions in the field include the works of Cecotti [4] and Theodoropoulos and Antoniou [5], who analyzed a range of VR applications dedicated to cultural heritage preservation. Among the notable cases they discuss are The Dawn of Art,[4] which immerses users in the 36,000-year-old cave paintings of Chauvet, and Nefertari: Journey to Eternity,[5] a 15-minute VR experience offering detailed exploration of Queen Nefertari's tomb, complete with hieroglyphs and educational commentary on Egyptian mythology. In contrast to the art-focused examples presented by Richardson, these experiences provided valuable insights into how object- and site-based heritage can be communicated effectively through VR.

3   Study

3.1   Expert Interviews

To determine which aspects of a virtual reality (VR) exhibition are most relevant in a museum context, we conducted individual semi-structured interviews with three curators from regional museums in south-west Germany. All participants had prior experience implementing VR applications in their exhibitions. The interviews began with general questions about their experiences using VR and their resulting expectations for real-world-based VR exhibition design, followed by more specific questions on the use and perception of different media types.

---

[2] https://www.musee-orsay.fr/en/whats-on/exhibitions/virtual-reality-van-goghs-, palette, last accessed 23.07.25.

[3] https://www.louvre.fr/en/explore/life-at-the-museum/the-mona-lisa-in-virtual-reality-in-your-own-home, last accessed 23.07.25.

[4] https://store.steampowered.com/app/1236560/The_Dawn_of_Art/, last accessed 23.07.25.

[5] https://www.meta.com/de-de/experiences/pcvr/nefertari-journey-to-eternity/ 1491802884282318/, last accessed 23.07.25.

Although the sample size is too small to yield generalizable conclusions, we followed the qualitative content analysis approach proposed by Mayring and Frenzel [6], clustering curator responses to identify recurring themes and summarize expert perspectives. The feedback we received from the curators largely aligned with the findings of Shehade et al. [7]. Three core requirements for a successful VR experience were found: (1) ease of use, (2) appropriate duration, and (3) effective mitigation of motion sickness. In addition, several optional features were mentioned as beneficial: (4) highlighting of interactive elements, (5) the ability to stream gameplay, (6) multiplayer functionality, and (7) opportunities for active user participation. All Curators agreed that the ideal session length for spontaneous museum visitors should range between 10 and 20 minutes. However, they also emphasized the variability of user engagement: While some visitors remain immersed for extended periods, others remove the headset shortly after beginning. A consensus formed around 15 minutes as a balanced target duration. Regarding promising media types for knowledge communication in VR, all experts recommended combining multiple media types to enhance the visitor experience and accommodate heterogeneous preferences. Text was viewed critically by two of the curators, who observed that many visitors tend to avoid reading longer passages. As a result, they suggested using text sparingly. All curators agreed that images and videos are commonly used in VR exhibitions to incorporate real-world visual references. Visitors tend to engage with these media in VR as much as they do in physical exhibitions. However, one curator mentioned that users often skip images and videos when too many are presented, arguing that their passive nature can quickly lead to visual fatigue. Regarding 3D models, the curators agreed that these are the most engaging elements in VR exhibitions–particularly when they are interactive. Visitors frequently spend extended time interacting with manipulable objects. All three experts also noted that game-like elements can be highly motivating, especially for younger visitors. One curator cautioned that gameplay mechanics should remain simple due to the technological diversity of museum audiences, while another noted that formal mechanics are often unnecessary, as many visitors naturally engage in playful interaction with virtual objects. 3D scans and 360-degree images were also seen as valuable additions. Two curators emphasized that object quality and contextual integration play a key role in user acceptance.

3.2   Hypotheses

Based on the expert interviews, we formulated four hypotheses, which we aimed to qualitatively examine through a field study conducted in a museum setting. First, we hypothesized that *visitors prefer audio guides over text boxes within the VR environment* (H1). With regard to time spent, we assumed that *visitors engage most with 3D models compared to other media types such as text, images, and videos* (H2). Concerning the type of 3D content, we expected that *within a comic-style environment, visitors favor designed 3D objects representing present-day culture over photogrammetric 3D scans* (H3). Finally, we assumed that *it is possible to identify different player types among the visitors using the VR exhibition* (H4).

3.3   Study Design

To test our hypotheses in a setting that closely reflects everyday museum practice, we developed a VR exhibition on the topic "History of the European dragon myth in comparison with dragon mythology from East Asia": *Dragons in VR: Depictions of Dragons from the Middle Ages to the present day.* This subject was chosen due to its broad cultural familiarity and its recurring presence across various media over time. The application was built using the Unity game engine[6] in combination with the ExPresS XR framework for coding-free VR exhibition creation. As the setting, we opted for a simple, comic-style 3D room with white plaster walls and wooden parquet flooring, complemented by decorative plants to evoke the atmosphere of a real-world exhibition (Fig. 1a). The exhibition followed a linear structure, beginning with the medieval period, where primarily text and image sources were presented (e.g., depictions of Sigurd from Hylestad stave church (Fig 1b). This was followed by a section representing the early modern era, which featured images and 3D-scanned objects (e.g., a 3D scan of St. George slaying the dragon statue[7] (Fig 1c). The subsequent section showcased objects from the modern era, including video content such as an excerpt from Fritz Lang's 1924 film *Die Nibelungen.*[8] The final section focused on contemporary representations, featuring Creative Commons licensed 3D models of (animated) dragons from popular franchises such as Final Fantasy, Game of Thrones, and Pokémon (Fig. 1d) which we took from Sketchfab.[9] To mitigate motion sickness, we implemented teleportation-based movement, following the recommendations of Chang, Kim, and Yoo [8]. Each exhibition section was introduced via an audio guide that automatically played when visitors entered predefined areas. We also applied signaling techniques proposed by Albus, Vogt, and Seufert [9] to guide attention toward key interaction zones. In addition to using signaling, we intentionally omitted other automatically triggered, visually demanding elements to prevent cognitive overload, as suggested by Sari et al. [10]. Exhibits were displayed either as static images or as (interactive) 3D objects. Information could be accessed through virtual buttons, which users could activate by pointing and clicking. These buttons allowed access to audio guides, textual information, or video content. In the final section, additional buttons enabled playful interactions for the contemporary 3D dragon models, such as movement animations and fire-breathing effects.

---

[6] https://unity.com/, last accessed 23.07.25.
[7] https://skfb.ly/osWvO, last accessed 23.07.2025.
[8] https://smb.museum-digital.de/object/74785, last access 23.07.2025.
[9] https://sketchfab.com/, last accessed 23.07.2025.

Fig. 1. (a) Entrance to the exhibition (b) 2D images of Sigurd (c) 3D-scanned model of St. George statue (d) Interactive fire-breathing dragon

3.4 Methodology

The study was conducted as a field study in a local museum in southwestern Germany. We used Meta Quest 2 devices as the head-mounted VR hardware. Each visitor received a brief introduction to the VR controls, along with a short overview of the exhibition topic. Visitors then entered the VR environment while we observed their behavior through live streaming of their sessions. We recorded the total playtime for each participant, as well as their interaction time with different types of media within the exhibition. Based on these recordings, we calculated the percentage distribution of media usage for each visitor relative to their overall session duration. In addition, we observed how visitors interacted with the exhibition–whether their behavior was more playful, whether they attempted to engage thoroughly with all available information and interactions, and whether they interacted with peers outside the VR headset during their session. After completing the VR experience, visitors were asked to fill out a short survey. The survey aimed to gather further insights into their experience, including their overall impression of the exhibition, their perception of the media mix, their evaluation of each media type, and their assessment of the included audio guides and interactive elements.

3.5 Results

A total of 51 visitors participated in the VR exhibition. Playtimes ranged from 5 to 21 minutes, with a mean duration of 13.2 minutes (SD: 4.1, skew: −0.3). With respect to total playtime, visitors interacted most with the audio guide (left chart of Fig. 2), which accounted for a mean of 22.6% of their session time (SD: 7.2, skew: 0.2). This was followed by interactive elements (18.2%, SD: 4.2, skew: 0.4), 3D scans (17.6%, SD: 6.2, skew: 1.2), video content (16.4%, SD: 8.6, skew: −1.0), contemporary 3D models (13.5%, SD: 5.0, skew: 1.4), and lastly, text content, which received the least engagement (11.7%, SD: 3.9, skew: 0.9).

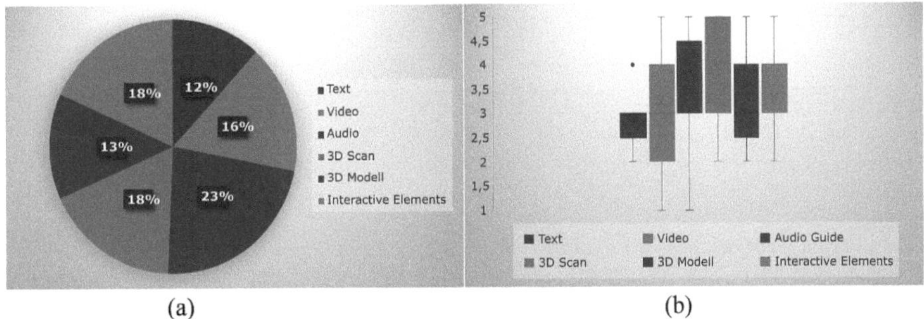

Fig. 2. (a) Distribution of average media interaction times (in %) (b) Visitor self-assessment of media preferences

Of the 51 observed participants, only 21 completed a post-experience questionnaire. All responses were recorded using a 5-point Likert scale (1 = very poor, 5 = very good). The overall exhibition was rated positively, with a mean score of 3.95 (SD: 1.1, skew: −1.0). The perceived media mix also received favorable ratings (mean: 3.9, SD: 1.0, skew: −1.0). Among individual media types, 3D scans were rated highest (mean: 3.9, SD: 0.9, skew: −0.3) (right chart of Fig. 2), followed by audio guides (mean: 3.4, SD: 1.1, skew: −0.1), interactive elements (mean: 3.3, SD: 0.85, skew: 0.31), and 3D models (mean: 3.3, SD: 0.96, skew: −0.02). Video content was rated slightly lower (mean: 3.2, SD: 1.09, skew: −0.26), with text receiving the lowest average score (mean: 2.9, SD: 0.6, skew: 0.05). Our observations during the sessions revealed a variety of play styles within the VR exhibition. Some visitors explored the exhibition thoroughly, activating nearly all available information buttons and engaging with each media type. Others focused primarily on 3D models and scans, avoiding the interactive buttons altogether. Almost all visitors, however, listened to the automatically triggered audio guide introductions at the beginning of each exhibition section. Notably, information buttons were used more frequently in the earlier parts of the exhibition than in the later sections. One exception to this trend were the buttons for interactive elements, which received significantly higher usage. These buttons appeared for the first time in the final section of the exhibition–dedicated to contemporary dragon representations–and may have stood out as a new and unfamiliar element, thus drawing particular attention. We also observed patterns of social interaction among visitors. Those who attended in groups often communicated with peers outside the headset, who were able to see the in-game view. While some of this interaction was casual small talk, a substantial number of visitors engaged in playful group dynamics. In several cases, people outside the VR headset gave humorous or exploratory instructions (e.g., "Go into the fire and let yourself burn!"), while the VR users responded by performing actions to entertain or provoke feedback, such as making the dragon bite their virtual hand. Other participants preferred to remain silent during their VR session but later explained the experience to their peers in detail. Several side observations added a funnier dimension to the study. For example, two visitors became deeply engaged with the examination of decorative plant models on the walls, speculating aloud about their realism. One participant "speedran" the exhibition, skipping all prior sections to reach the final area with the contemporary 3D dragons as quickly as possible. Another visitor commented that they particularly enjoyed "how clean the VR exhibition is compared to real-world museums".

4   Discussion and Outlook

Based on the expert feedback and the collected data, we consider our first hypothesis (H1) supported: both indicators–the average interaction time and the user rating–for the audio guides exceeded those for text content. However, it is important to note that interaction time may be a misleading metric in this comparison, as audio guides had a fixed duration and were sometimes triggered automatically when entering a new exhibition area, whereas text elements had to be activated manually and reading speed varied between users. Hypothesis (H2) is only partially supported. Visitors spent the most time with interactive elements and 3D scans. However, they spent less time on the contemporary 3D models than on the videos. This could again be attributed to the fixed length of the video content, while visitors may have quickly looked at the 3D models. Moreover, the 3D scans represented authentic cultural heritage artifacts, while the Sketchfab 3D models were drawn from pop and gaming culture and may have been perceived as less qualitative, relevant or impressive in a museum context. Thus, Hypothesis (H3) was not confirmed in our study setting. Nevertheless, this result offers a valuable insight: Future VR exhibitions may benefit from including 3D scans of relevant heritage objects or, alternatively, use more resources on the development of custom models. Regarding Hypothesis (H4), our observational data support the assumption that different types of users engage with VR exhibitions in distinct ways. We identified three informal player types that were roughly equally distributed and, in some cases, overlapping: (PT1) visitors who sought to consume as much information as possible and interacted with nearly all available content; (PT2) visitors who explored the environment in a playful and experimental manner; and (PT3) visitors who actively interacted with peers outside the VR headset during their session. These types correspond closely to Richard Bartle's classic player taxonomy [11]: the Achiever (PT1), the Explorer (PT2), and the Socialiser (PT3).[10] While Bartle's model dates back to 1996, it continues to serve as a foundation for modern research and offers a useful framework for understanding visitor engagement in VR exhibitions. Our

---

[10] Luckily we did not find Bartle's last player type in our setting: The Killer.

findings–both from user data and expert interviews–allow us to propose several suggestions for future VR-based museum exhibitions. First, the average time visitors are willing to spend in a VR exhibition appears to be around 15 minutes. This implies the need for a clearly defined didactic concept prior to development. In particular, it is essential to map the exhibition's intended knowledge content to the most suitable media type and to prioritize the most important content early in the experience, as some visitors may exit before reaching later sections. With regard to media types, our data suggest that textual content should be used sparingly. Text received the lowest average rating and the least interaction time. Based on curator input, we recommend that text be limited to short labels or brief contextual notes. Other media types should be chosen based on the exhibition topic. In our case, 3D scans were slightly preferred over custom-designed 3D models from contemporary media. However, since our study focused specifically on dragon representations and relied on pre-existing models from Sketchfab, these findings should be interpreted within a broader research context that includes a wider range of subjects and 3D models. Audio guides were generally well received and rated higher than text, indicating their value for conveying information. Nonetheless, since audio content can be time-consuming, it should focus on essential information, while additional visual context can be conveyed through images, 3D scans, or models. We also assume that it could be promising to research if combining audio guides with signaling techniques could help emphasize visual elements mentioned in the narration. However, our data should be viewed as an initial step toward identifying the media preferences of museum visitors in VR exhibitions, to be further explored through broader analyses. Regarding player types, while Bartle's taxonomy was useful for our initial classification, more recent models offer greater nuance. For example, Hamari and Tuunanen [12] present a meta-review that refines Bartle's model and incorporates aspects such as immersion. Similarly, Babić et al. [13] apply the Gamer Motivation Model developed by Quantic Foundry [14][11] to classify player types more precisely. These models provide promising directions for further research on museum visitor behavior in VR environments. Finally, we argue that further research is needed on interactive VR exhibitions that foster collaboration between visitors inside and outside the headset—for example, through socially cooperative tasks such as escape-room–style gameplay, where one participant must relay real-world information to the VR user, or vice versa.

5   Conclusion

The integration of virtual reality technology into museum exhibitions continues to be a relevant and evolving topic, especially since its entry into the consumer market in 2016. While many academic projects and high-budget VR exhibitions are still being developed, low-budget solutions that mimic real-world exhibitions are increasingly emerging-offering feasible options for museums with limited financial resources. With this study, we conducted a field experiment and,

---

[11] https://quanticfoundry.com/gamer-motivation-model, last accessed 23.07.2025.

based on our findings, aim to provide curators of such institutions with practical guidance for the design and implementation of VR exhibitions.

References

1. Chong, H.T., Lim, C.K., Rafi, A., Tan, K.L., Mokhtar, M.: Comprehensive systematic review on virtual reality for cultural heritage practices: coherent taxonomy and motivations. Multimedia Syst. , 1–16 (2021). https://doi.org/10.1007/s00530-021-00869-4
2. Rodriguez-Garcia, B., Guillen-Sanz, H., Checa, D., Bustillo, A.: A systematic review of virtual 3D reconstructions of Cultural Heritage in immersive Virtual Reality. In: Multimedia Tools and Applications Vol 83, April 2024. https://doi.org/10.1007/s11042-024-18700-3
3. Richardson, J.: Virtual Reality is a big trend in museums, but what are the best examples of museums using VR? In: museumnext, 10 Oktober 2024. https://www.museumnext.com/article/how-museums-are-using-virtual-reality
4. Cecotti, H.: Cultural Heritage in Fully Immersive Virtual Reality. In: Virtual Worlds Vol. 1, September 2002. https://doi.org/10.3390/virtualworlds1010006
5. Theodoropoulos, A., Antoniou, A.: VR Games in Cultural Heritage: A Systematic Review of the Emerging Fields of Virtual Reality and Culture Games in Applied Sciences Vol. 12, August 2022. https://doi.org/10.3390/app12178476
6. Mayring, P., Fenzl, T.: Qualitative Inhaltsanalyse. Presented at the (2019). https://doi.org/10.1007/978-3-658-21308-4_42
7. Shehade, M., Stylianou-Lambert, T.: Virtual Reality in Museums: Exploring the Experiences of Museum Professionals. In: Applied Sciences Vol. 10, 2020, ISSN 2076-3417, https://www.mdpi.com/2076-3417/10/11/4031,https://doi.org/10.3390/app10114031
8. Eunhee, C., Hyun, T.K., Byounghyun, Y.: Virtual Reality Sickness: A Review of Causes and Measurements. In: International Journal of Human–Computer Interaction, 2020, 36, 1658–1682. https://api.semanticscholar.org/CorpusID:221599965
9. Patrick, A., Andrea, V., Tina, S.: Signaling in virtual reality influences learning outcome and cognitive load. Computers & Education, Vol. 166, 2021, ISSN 0360-1315, https://doi.org/10.1016/j.compedu.2021.104154
10. Candra, S.R., Pranesti, A., Solikhatun, I., Nurbaiti, N., Yuniarti, N.: Cognitive overload in immersive virtual reality in education: More presence but less learnt?. In: Education and Information Technologies, Vol. 29, December 2023, https://doi.org/10.1007/s10639-023-12379-z
11. Bartle, R.: Hearts, Clubs, Diamonds, Spades: Players Who Suit MUDS (1996). http://www.mud.co.uk/richard/hcds.htm
12. Hamari, J., Tuunanen, J.: Player Types: A Meta-synthesis. Transactions of the Digital Games Research Association. 1, 29–53 (2014). https://doi.org/10.26503/todigra.v1i2.13
13. Babic, T., Vigato, M.: Research on Gamer Motivation Factors Based on the Gamer Motivation Model Framework (2021). https://doi.org/10.23919/MIPRO52101.2021.9596942
14. Yee, N.: The Gamer Motivation Profile: What We Learned From 250,000 Gamers, CHI PLAY '16, Association for Computing Machinery, 2016, ISBN: 9781450344562. https://doi.org/10.1145/2967934.2967937

Technology Track

Modeling Skill Progression in Children Through Novel Multidimensional Probabilistic DDA

Angela Pasqualotto[1,2](✉) , Marios Fanourakis[2] , Zeno Menestrina[2] , Mor Nahum[3] , and Daphne Bavelier[2]

[1] University of Applied Sciences and Arts of Southern Switzerland, Manno, Switzerland
`angela.pasqualotto@supsi.ch`
[2] University of Geneva, Geneva, Switzerland
`{marios.fanourakis,zeno.menestrina,daphne.bavelier}@unige.ch`
[3] Hebrew University of Jerusalem, Jerusalem, Israel
`mor.nahum@mail.huji.ac.il`

Abstract. Dynamic Difficulty Adjustment (DDA) systems are increasingly used in serious games to personalize challenge, sustain engagement, and optimize cognitive learning. This study presents a multi-dimensional, probabilistic DDA framework implemented in *Legends of Hoa'Manu*, a modular cognitive training game for children that targets core executive functions through distinct training modules, each featuring an independent DDA engine. We focus on the *Uka* module, which adapts a running memory span task to train working memory. Using gameplay data from 148 children, we evaluate how the DDA system adjusts difficulty across multiple parameters in response to real-time learner performance. Results show that gameplay difficulty rapidly converged to individually appropriate levels, aligning with players' Zone of Proximal Development (ZPD) within the first hour. The probabilistic adaptation strategy also maintained task variability after plateauing, preventing overfitting and sustaining learner engagement across diverse proficiency levels. These findings highlight the value of multi-dimensional, probabilistic adaptivity for game-based cognitive training.

Keywords: Dynamic difficulty adjustment · Cognitive training · Zone of proximal development · Personalization

1 Introduction

Video games are increasingly used to train cognitive functions [3,7]. Purpose-built cognitive games integrate engaging mechanics with training goals, enabling repeated practice while maintaining motivation and engagement [12]. A central challenge is aligning task difficulty to learner ability, commonly framed as the Zone of Proximal Development (ZPD), where tasks are difficult yet achievable

© The Author(s), under exclusive license to Springer Nature Switzerland AG 2026
S. Bakkes et al. (Eds.): GALA 2025, LNCS 16307, pp. 259–268, 2026.
https://doi.org/10.1007/978-3-032-11043-5_25

with support [25]. To operationalize this principle, Dynamic Difficulty Adjustment (DDA) systems modulate difficulty in real time to sustain challenge and engagement without causing frustration [15]. Most educational and cognitive training games adjust a single task parameter, limiting their ability to support complex, multi-component skills. Yet cognitive tasks often involve interacting demands that require more nuanced control.

We present a multi-dimensional DDA framework that adapts difficulty across several task parameters. We focus on a running memory span task designed to train working memory. Using gameplay data from 148 children, we show how the DDA system supports individualized challenge trajectories and maintains task variability after skill stabilization.

2   Related Work

Digital games are widely used for cognitive training. Two main approaches have emerged: gamified versions of lab-based tasks (e.g., N-back, flanker), and commercial action video games (AVGs). The former emphasize construct validity and isolate specific cognitive demands but often show limited transfer beyond the trained task [13,17]. This has led to growing interest in training designs that induce broader cognitive benefits. Commercial AVGs, despite not being designed for cognitive enhancement, engage diverse cognitive processes and have been linked to improvements in perception, spatial reasoning, attention, and flexibility [2]. Their task complexity and variability are believed to support broader transfer, though they offer limited control over task parameters, making it difficult to isolate the design features that foster broader cognitive gains.

Among design features associated with cognitive transfer, variability, adaptivity, and personalized progression are most frequently cited [21]. Task variability, or loading on a variety of cognitive constructs, has been proposed as one of the drivers of transfer [24]. Low variability games tend to yield minimal transfer [17], while cognitively rich, dynamic games (like AVGs) show broader effects [1]. Effective interventions combine repetition with structured variability to promote generalization.

Another key design principle is sustaining motivation by keeping difficulty within a learner's optimal challenge range [12,22]. DDA systems operationalize this principle, dynamically adapting game parameters based on real-time player performance to maintain a balanced cognitive load and consistent engagement [9,18]. Adaptive versions often outperform static ones in non-game contexts [10,11], although findings in game-based settings are more mixed [4,22]. This suggests that the success of adaptivity depends not only on its presence, but on how it is implemented. Most DDA systems used in educational and cognitive-training contexts still rely on one-dimensional adjustments, limiting their ability to accommodate the multi-faceted demands of cognitive skill development. In contrast, multi-dimensional DDA systems [8] allow for simultaneous adjustment of multiple task features, better aligning with the dynamic nature of real-world cognition [14]. For instance, Chrysafiadi et al. [6] introduced a fuzzy logic–based

DDA in a 3D educational game that adapts both content and environment. Other approaches employ reinforcement learning and probabilistic modeling to enable fine-grained personalization. Probabilistic DDA introduces controlled variability in difficulty progression [15]. This helps prevent over-dominant strategies, sustain engagement, and mirror the uncertain, non-linear conditions of real-world learning [14]. Multi-dimensional DDA enhances user experience and supports scalable, inclusive cognitive training by aligning task demands to abilities.

3   Methods

3.1   Study Context and Participants

148 typically developing children (mean age of 7 years–SD $= 0.4$; female, 54.1%), completed at least 13 game sessions, and up to 19 sessions (median gameplay hours, 8.85) as part of a registered study on cognitive training. The intervention was administered in school settings over approximately 6 weeks, with onboarding provided through brief introduction videos and in-game tutorials. All gameplay occurred under teacher supervision during scheduled sessions.

3.2   Game Architecture: Legends of Hoa'Manu

Legends of Hoa'Manu (developed in Unity3D) is a cognitive training video game that integrates AVG mechanics with targeted cognitive exercises. Its design addresses key challenges in educational game design, including the need for sustained engagement, structured variability, and individualized difficulty [20].

Players navigate a fantasy world through an AVG-style game ("Flight"), which connects to a set of standalone "satellite" modules. Each module is built around a core cognitive skill, such as working memory, response inhibition, or visual selective attention. A given play session calls for 3-4 min bouts on each satellite module, transitioning from one to the other via the AVG-style game. The modular structure eases implementation, while the switch between modules through AVG-play supports task and cognitive variability.

To maintain engagement between sessions, players periodically return to a central "Village" hub where they can customize avatars and access narrative-based rewards, supporting autonomy and intrinsic motivation. Gameplay thus alternates between action game play, cognitive mini-games and an exploratory rewarding world, balancing user-driven pacing with structured challenge.

A central innovation in Legends of Hoa'Manu is its multi-dimensional, probabilistic DDA system. Each satellite module independently implements a DDA engine that adjusts several task parameters in real-time based on player performance. These adaptive mechanisms are designed to help players operate within their individualized ZPD, limiting under- or over-challenge and sustaining motivation over time. We illustrate the DDA framework using the *Uka* module.

3.3 Running Memory Span (Uka) Module

The *Uka* module is an adaptation of the Running Memory Span task [5], designed to train updating in visual working memory. In each trial, players view a sequence of 2–9 symbols presented one at a time. After a brief delay, they are prompted to recall the final N symbols (N=1 to 5) in their correct order of presentation. A trial is successful only if all N target symbols are recalled in the correct sequence within the time limit. By requiring ordered recall from unpredictable sequence lengths, *Uka* exercises the continuous updating of working memory content. A short demo of the game module is available on this link.

3.4 Multi-dimensional DDA Implementation

Difficulty is structured across 5 main levels (N=1 to 5), each corresponding to the number of symbols to recall. Each main level contains 3 sub-levels for finer adjustments: (S1) sequence length, (S2) presentation duration, and (S3) response timeout. Player accuracy is evaluated every 4 trials to determine difficulty updates.

Sub-Level Difficulty Adaptation Difficulty changes if accuracy (computed every 4 trials) is above or below 50%; it remains unchanged at exactly 50% (2 correct responses among 4). Changes are probabilistic: 85% chance of a change, 15% of no change. The direction of change also depends on performance:

- if accuracy >50%, difficulty increases (70% probability) or decreases (15% probability);
- if accuracy <50%, difficulty decreases (70% probability) or increases (15% probability).

When increasing difficulty, the system prioritizes sub-levels at their easiest settings. When decreasing, any sub-level may be selected. An example of transition probabilities is shown in Fig. 1. Additionally, after four consecutive successes

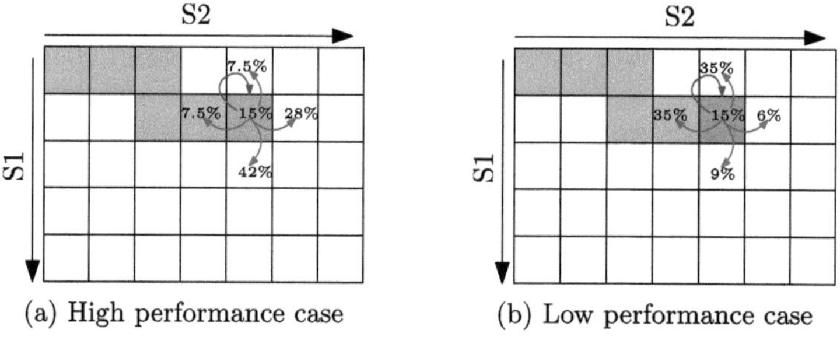

(a) High performance case   (b) Low performance case

Fig. 1. Transition probabilities after high performance **a** and low performance **b**, with two sub-levels. The upper-left cell is the easiest state. Previously visited states are shown in gray, while the current state is colored (green or red).(Color figure online)

or failures, the DDA applies two consecutive updates to accelerate difficulty tuning.

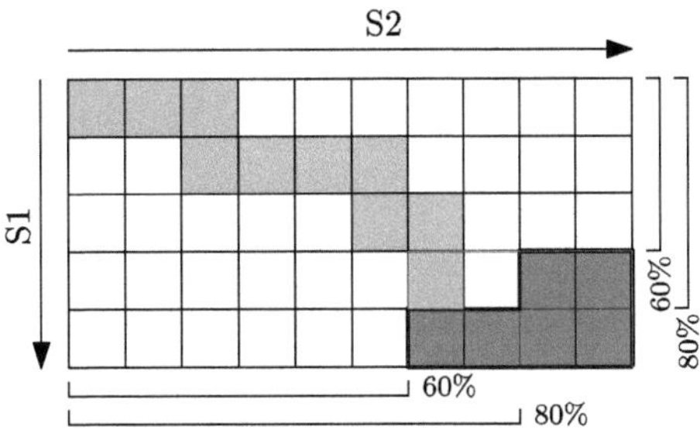

Fig. 2. Level-up region (highlighted in blue) for an example with two sub-level dimensions and level-up completion thresholds of 60% and 80%. Note these threshold values apply interchangeably across sub-level dimensions (Color figure online)

Main Level Difficulty Adaptation. Progression to a higher main level (e.g., going from 2 to 3 symbols to recall) is governed by a probabilistic rule, which is only activated when the player enters a designated "level-up" region. This region is not fixed but dynamically defined based on sub-level completion thresholds, allowing multiple paths to advance to the main level. For instance, assume two sub-levels (S1 and S2), with completion thresholds of 60% and 80%. The player qualifies for the level-up region once both thresholds are met: either 60% completion in S1 and 80% in S2, or vice versa (Fig. 2). While the player remains in this region, each new trial includes a 25% probability of triggering a main-level increase.

As players progress, level-up regions become narrower, given the typical learning pattern of rapid early gains followed by slower improvement near one's ZPD. In contrast, level-downs are triggered only when performance drops, while all sub-levels are already at their easiest.

Rollbacks Difficulty Adaptation. To mitigate fatigue and support confidence, the system occasionally triggers "rollbacks" to easier, previously unvisited sub-levels within cleared main levels. Rollbacks vary in depth (down 1-2-3 levels) and their likelihood increases at each trial. After 16 consecutive trials without a rollback, one is automatically triggered. The probability of a rollback is reset to 12.5% (1-level), 6.25% (2-levels), and 0% (3-levels), and increases incrementally with each trial until either a rollback occurs or the 16-trial threshold is reached.

3.5   Performance Logging and Engagement Rating

Trial-by-trial performance data are logged to inform the DDA and allow progression analysis. Full gameplay metrics are synchronized to a secure cloud for compliance monitoring and longitudinal analysis [19]. In addition to performance metrics, we collected subjective engagement data post-training. Children rated their enjoyment using the "Funometer," a 5-point Likert scale (1 = not fun; 5 = super fun) presented with a playful, child-friendly interface. This single-item measure was adapted from the Short Feedback Questionnaire [16].

4   Results

4.1   Training Exposure

The median *Uka* exposure per participant was 51 minutes (SD= 9.4), each completing over 150 trials (time: M=154; SD=33). Each Uka play bout lasted 3–4 minutes and was presented twice per session as part of the broader training protocol.

4.2   Progression to ZPD and Engagement Rating

To evaluate whether the *Uka* DDA system effectively guided players toward individualized challenge levels, we defined the ZPD convergence as the point at which performance reaches a plateau. In the *Uka* case, it was at moderately demanding levels (typically recalling 2-3 targets when the maximum level possible was 5). Across the 148 participants, most reached this stage within their first 10 *Uka* sessions or approximately 30-40 min of gameplay. During this period, the DDA applied an average of 20 (SD=2) difficulty updates to tailor the experience and guide players toward appropriate challenge levels.

Once the ZPD was reached, players' difficulty trajectories typically plateaued at a given number of symbols-to-remember or main level, but sub-level parameters (i.e., sequence length, presentation duration, and response timeout) continued to vary. This variability in gameplay was intended to maintain engagement and cognitive stimulation even in the absence of main level progression. Supporting this, children rated their enjoyment of the overall *Legends of Hoa'Manu* training experience highly on the Funometer scale (1–5), with an average score of 4.57 (SD=1.08), indicating that the program was engaging.

4.3   Difficulty Adjustment Behavior

The DDA system functioned reliably throughout training, with no technical failures or crashes. Across the first 13 sessions, difficulty increased during 36.1% of update periods, decreased in 33.3%, and remained unchanged in the rest, indicating balanced adaptation between challenge and accessibility. Extreme performances (four consecutive successes or failures) occurred in 25.8% of updates (12.5% perfect scores; 13.3% total misses), triggering double-step adjustments to rapidly correct mismatched difficulty. Rollback trials accounted for 22.4% of total trials.

To examine how challenge levels evolved over time, we compared early (sessions 1–6) and later (sessions 7–13) phases of training. Early sessions featured more difficulty decreases (42.5%) than increases (34.1%), along with 17.4% total misses and 12.8% perfect scores. In contrast, later sessions showed significantly fewer decreases (27.2%), while increases remained quite high (39.7%), as well as a clear drop in total misses (10.1%) and stable perfect scores (12.8%). This pattern signals excellent adaptation: the game became better calibrated to individual performance over time, reducing failure, and still supporting gameplay progression.

4.4   Example Progression Trajectories

To illustrate how multi-dimensional DDA supports diverse users, we examined two representative participants: one more and one less proficient–both of whom started at Level 2, the default entry point of the *Uka* module. The more proficient player (Fig. 3a) quickly reached Level 4 (recall of 4 symbols) by trial 85 (two thirds of their gameplay) and remained there for the rest of training. Although main-level progression plateaued, sub-level variation persisted, with continued exploration of unvisited parameter combinations via sub-levels exploration at level 4 and rollback trials. The less proficient player (Fig. 3b) initially dropped to Level 1 due to poor performance, then stabilized at Level 2 by trial 45. They subsequently continued to explore and advance in sub-levels of both Level 2 and Level 1; the latter, during rollback periods. These trajectories show how the system sustains variability in experience and challenge through probabilistic progression and sub-level exploration, even when learners stabilize at different performance levels.

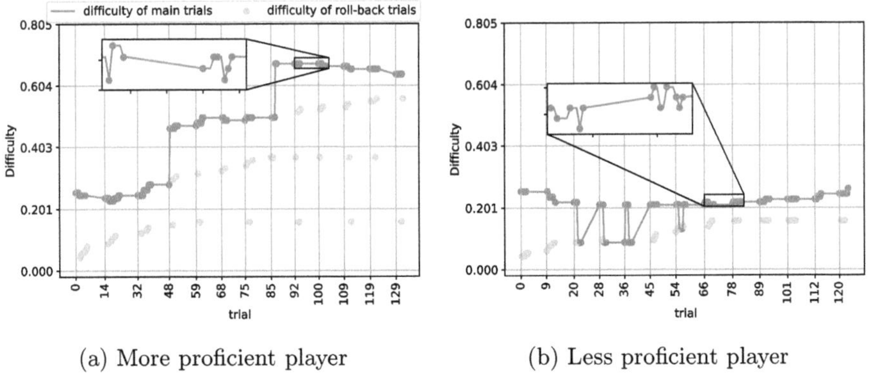

(a) More proficient player   (b) Less proficient player

Fig. 3. Difficulty trajectories for a more **(a)** and a less **(b)** proficient player. The start of each level is marked on the y-axis and the start of each 3-4min session on the x-axis.

5   Discussion

5.1   Multi-dimensional and Probabilistically-Driven Adaptivity

Unlike common DDA methods in cognitive training, our DDA adjusts multiple parameters simultaneously. This promotes exposure to diverse challenge states within levels, aligning with the ZPD framework [25]. Additionally, and unlike deterministic systems, our DDA employs a probabilistic adjustment algorithm, which introduces controlled variability and reduces predictability.

These two approaches combined help prevent overfitting or disengagement. Most players reached their ZPD within 30–45 min, after which difficulty continued to vary dynamically at the sub-level, maintaining challenge and interest. This approach builds on evidence that structured variability supports transfer [24].

5.2   Personalized Progression and Player Engagement

Our findings show that children in the study, with quite different levels of proficiency, benefited from individualized difficulty trajectories. More proficient players quickly advanced to higher difficulty levels. Once there, they continued to experience gameplay variation through the sub-level changes and rollback trials our DDA implements. Less proficient players stabilized at lower difficulty levels, but remained exposed to fine-grained sub-level variations within manageable challenges. This aligns with research on intrinsic motivation, which emphasizes the importance of perceivable progress and manageable difficulty in sustaining motivation [23].

The implementation of real-time, performance-based, multi-dimensional adaptation enhances user experience by aligning challenges with users' evolving capabilities. This design supports a sense of fairness, progression, and agency; factors shown to promote satisfaction and sustained engagement [21]. The rollback mechanic, which reintroduces easier and previously unvisited states, proved particularly valuable. It provided cognitively less demanding periods while at the same time enhancing gameplay variety. These trials not only reduced cognitive load but likely contributed to a sense of control and competence. Such mechanics may be especially important in long-term interventions, where the user is susceptible to fatigue or loss of motivation. The overall positive reception of the game, reflected in children's self-reported enjoyment, further supports the acceptability of this adaptive training approach.

6   Limitations and Future Directions

While the present study provides strong evidence of effective adaptation and engagement, it does not examine transfer to untrained tasks, a critical goal for cognitive training that remains to be addressed in future work. In addition, it does not compare the probabilistic DDA with simpler or static systems–an important benchmark for future studies and one that has rarely been reported in the literature. Finally, because only the *Uka* module was analyzed in detail, further work is needed to determine whether comparable adaptive dynamics occur in other modules targeting executive functions such as working memory and inhibition.

7   Conclusion

This study demonstrates the effectiveness of a novel DDA system in a cognitive training game. Thanks to its multi-dimensional and probabilistic nature, the implemented DDA rapidly guided players into their ZPD and continuously maintained variability in experience and appropriate cognitive challenge across sessions. Future work should examine the extent to which this novel framework facilitates cognitive transfer outcomes, can be adapted to other cognitive domains, and may accommodate an ever more diverse user populations, such as clinical ones.

Acknowledgments. This work was supported by the NCCR Evolving Language 51NF40_180888 , and the Klaus J. Jacobs Foundation to D.B. A.P. and M.F. equally contributed to this work.

Diclosure of Interests. A.P., M.N., Z.M., and D.B. are co-inventors on a patent application related to the DDA system used in Legends of Hoa'Manu.

References

1. Bavelier, D., Green, C.S.: Learning and Transfer: A Perspective From Action Video Game Play. Curr. Dir. Psychol. Sci. **34**(1), 43–50 (2025). https://doi.org/10.1177/09637214241287171
2. Bediou, B., Rodgers, M.A., Tipton, E., Mayer, R.E., Green, C.S., Bavelier, D.: Effects of action video game play on cognitive skills: A meta-analysis. Technology, Mind, and Behavior **4**(1) (Mar 2023). https://doi.org/10.1037/tmb0000102
3. Blumberg, F.C., et al.: Current state of play: children's learning in the context of digital games. J. Child. Media **18**(2), 293–299 (2024). https://doi.org/10.1080/17482798.2024.2335725
4. Blume, F., Pawar, S., Ninaus, M., Plass, J.L.: Individualisation in cognitive skills training: Essential or superfluous? Examining the effectiveness of an adaptive game for training executive functions in young adults. Learn. Individ. Differ. **114**, 102517 (2024). https://doi.org/10.1016/j.lindif.2024.102517
5. Broadway, J.M., Engle, R.W.: Validating running memory span: Measurement of working memory capacity and links with fluid intelligence. Behav. Res. Methods **42**(2), 563–570 (2010). https://doi.org/10.3758/BRM.42.2.563
6. Chrysafiadi, K., Kamitsios, M., Virvou, M.: Fuzzy-based dynamic difficulty adjustment of an educational 3D-game. Multimedia Tools Appl. **82**(18), 27525–27549 (2023). https://doi.org/10.1007/s11042-023-14515-w
7. De Freitas, S.: Are games effective learning tools? A review of educational games. J. Educ. Technol. Soc. **21**(2), 74–84 (2018)
8. Dziedzic, D., Włodarczyk, W.: Approaches to Measuring the Difficulty of Games in Dynamic Difficulty Adjustment Systems. Int. J. Human-Computer Int. **34**(8), 707–715 (2018). https://doi.org/10.1080/10447318.2018.1461764
9. Hunicke, R.: The case for dynamic difficulty adjustment in games. In: Proceedings of the 2005 ACM SIGCHI International Conference on Advances in Computer Entertainment Technology. pp. 429–433. ACM, Valencia Spain (2005). https://doi.org/10.1145/1178477.1178573

10. Jaeggi, S.M., Buschkuehl, M., Jonides, J., Perrig, W.J.: Improving fluid intelligence with training on working memory. Proc. Natl. Acad. Sci. **105**(19), 6829–6833 (2008). https://doi.org/10.1073/pnas.0801268105

11. Karbach, J., Kray, J.: How useful is executive control training? Age differences in near and far transfer of task-switching training. Dev. Sci. **12**(6), 978–990 (2009). https://doi.org/10.1111/j.1467-7687.2009.00846.x

12. Mayer, R.E.: Cognitive foundations of game-based learning. In: Handbook of Game-Based Learning, pp. 83–110. The MIT Press, Cambridge, MA, US (2020)

13. Melby-Lervåg, M., Hulme, C.: Is working memory training effective? A meta-analytic review. Developmental Psychology **49**(2), 270–291 (2013). https://doi.org/10.1037/a0028228

14. Mishra, J., Anguera, J.A., Gazzaley, A.: Video Games for Neuro-Cognitive Optimization. Neuron **90**(2), 214–218 (2016). https://doi.org/10.1016/j.neuron.2016.04.010

15. Mortazavi, F., Moradi, H., Vahabie, A.H.: Dynamic difficulty adjustment approaches in video games: A systematic literature review. Multimedia Tools Appl. **83**(35), 83227–83274 (2024). https://doi.org/10.1007/s11042-024-18768-x

16. Moser, C., Fuchsberger, V., Tscheligi, M.: Rapid assessment of game experiences in public settings. In: Proceedings of the 4th International Conference on Fun and Games. pp. 73–82. ACM, Toulouse France (2012). https://doi.org/10.1145/2367616.2367625

17. Owen, A.M., Hampshire, A., Grahn, J.A., Stenton, R., Dajani, S., Burns, A.S., Howard, R.J., Ballard, C.G.: Putting brain training to the test. Nature **465**(7299), 775–778 (2010). https://doi.org/10.1038/nature09042

18. Paraschos, P.D., Koulouriotis, D.E.: Game Difficulty Adaptation and Experience Personalization: A Literature Review. Int. J. Human-Computer Int. **39**(1), 1–22 (2023). https://doi.org/10.1080/10447318.2021.2020008

19. Pasqualotto, A., et al.: A Novel Multidimensional Dynamic Difficulty Adjustment Algorithm: Use Case in a Cognitive Training Video Game (Oct 2024). https://doi.org/10.31234/osf.io/r69eu

20. Pasqualotto, A., Parong, J., Green, C.S., Bavelier, D.: Video Game Design for Learning to Learn. Int. J. Human-Computer Int. **39**(11), 2211–2228 (2023). https://doi.org/10.1080/10447318.2022.2110684

21. Plass, J.L., Pawar, S.: Toward a taxonomy of adaptivity for learning. J. Res. Technol. Educ. **52**(3), 275–300 (2020). https://doi.org/10.1080/15391523.2020.1719943

22. Plass, J., Homer, B., Pawar, S., Brenner, C., MacNamara, A.: The effect of adaptive difficulty adjustment on the effectiveness of a game to develop executive function skills for learners of different ages. Cogn. Dev. **49**, 56–67 (2019). https://doi.org/10.1016/j.cogdev.2018.11.006

23. Sayalı, C., Heling, E., Cools, R.: Learning progress mediates the link between cognitive effort and task engagement. Cognition **236**, 105418 (2023). https://doi.org/10.1016/j.cognition.2023.105418

24. Schmidt, R.A., Bjork, R.A.: New Conceptualizations of Practice: Common Principles in Three Paradigms Suggest New Concepts for Training. Psychol. Sci. **3**(4), 207–218 (1992). https://doi.org/10.1111/j.1467-9280.1992.tb00029.x

25. Vygotsky, L.S., Cole, M.: Mind in Society: Development of Higher Psychological Processes. Harvard University Press (1978)

Formalizing Escape Game Mechanics: A Graph-Theoretical Framework for Modeling and Analyzing Puzzle-Based Environments

Gonzague Yernaux[✉][ID], Martin Verjans[ID], and Wim Vanhoof[ID]

Faculty of Computer Science, University of Namur, Namur, Belgium
`gonzague.yernaux@unamur.be`

Abstract. Escape games have become widely popular across entertainment, educational, and training domains, yet their underlying mechanics remain largely informal and under-theorized. In this work, we introduce a novel framework that provides a formal representation of both the structural and dynamic aspects of escape games. Our approach relies on the Static Graph, a directed graph that encodes the topological and logical organization of puzzles, clues, rooms, and player roles. Game progression and player interaction are modeled through the Dynamic Graph, capturing the live state of a session, as well as the Game Session Forest, which represents the set of possible traces under alternative player choices. This graph-based design can easily be manipulated by verification algorithms, and as such paves the way for automated reasoning over essential aspects of escape games, ranging from solvability and balance to determining the initial constraints on players and rooms. The framework is operationalized and illustrated in `GraphEG`, an open-source visualization tool that supports both the design of escape game scenarios and their simulation.

1 Introduction and Related Work

Escape games, also known as escape rooms, have rapidly transitioned from a niche form of entertainment to a widespread cultural and educational phenomenon. Since their emergence in the early 2000s in Japan and their international rise through commercial adaptations like *Real Escape Game* and *Escape the Room*, they have been adopted for various purposes, including team-building exercises, cognitive training, and formal education [14].

Their popularity stems from a compelling mix of immersive storytelling, collaborative problem-solving, and time-bound challenge dynamics. In pedagogical contexts, escape games have been shown to increase engagement, foster critical thinking, and improve knowledge retention through experiential learning [4,15]. Frameworks such as *EscapED* [2] and the *Star Model* [3] have offered conceptual and narrative guidelines for game-based learning.

The escape game genre has in fact been investigated through various disciplinary lenses, ranging from educational science to human-computer interaction

S. Bakkes et al. (Eds.): GALA 2025, LNCS 16307, pp. 269–279, 2026.
https://doi.org/10.1007/978-3-032-11043-5_26

and game design theory. Nicholson's foundational works [11] provided an early taxonomy of escape room principles such as narrative framing, collaborative puzzle-solving, and time-limited challenges. Wiemker et al. [17] also proposed classifications of puzzles and structural ideas for optimal player engagement.

Then, as the efficiency of escape games in active learning has been increasingly demonstrated in independent studies [5,14], several works proposed methodological guidelines for integrating educational objectives within game mechanics at the conception stage [3]. Meanwhile, in [13] and independently in [15], some authors insist on another crucial need, being the need to model the behavior of players during actual sessions of serious games. The existing approaches set on tackling this aspect relied on well-known mathematical objects such as Petri nets [1] and finite state machines [10].

However, such models tend to remain qualitative and lack expressivity when dealing with the layered dependencies, spatial configurations, and concurrent puzzle structures that characterize escape games. In that sense, Araújo and Roque caution that traditional modeling languages are limited when it comes to verifying and validating underlying game systems [1]; they then advocate for formalisms capable of handling more complex, concurrent interactions. In parallel, recent research in *serious games* (being games dedicated to serious outcomes such as learning) also tends to identify the need for formal models that support game design, since these can be used to enable simulation, complexity analysis, and Artificial Intelligence (AI)-driven design [13].

Attempts to formalize serious games in a more general way did emerge in the context of learning analytics and simulation [3]. But these apply poorly to escape games, which still suffer a lack of formal and computable representation. This limits their reproducibility, adaptability, and analytical potential. The internal mechanics of escape games thus remain to this day largely informal or heuristic.

In this context, this paper proposes a novel graph-theoretical framework for modeling escape games as dynamic, interactive systems; an endeavor that has, to the best of our knowledge, not been performed before, except in our own seminal work on the topic [18]. By abstracting escape games as directed graphs enriched with semantic constraints, we enable algorithmic reasoning over the structure and flow of gameplay. Our approach captures both the static configuration of an escape game (e.g., rooms, puzzles, clues) as well as the permanently evolving game state (e.g., player knowledge, progression or clues acquisition). As such, it allows for a range of formal validation checks that can shed light on the inner properties held by each of the modeled games.

To demonstrate the practical viability of our framework, we also introduce the latest version of a companion software tool called `GraphEG` that supports the creation, visualization, verification and simulation of escape games using the proposed formalism.

2   A Formal Framework for Modeling Escape Games

An Escape Game (EG) can be seen as a finite, rule-driven environment where a group of players collaborate to achieve a goal (often, "escape") by navigating through interconnected rooms, solving interdependent puzzles, and discovering clues. More formally, we define an EG as a triple $(\mathcal{G}, \mathcal{A}, \delta)$. Specifically, $\mathcal{G}$ refers to a Static Graph conforming with what we will further define in Sect. 2.1, $\mathcal{A}$ is a set of potential player actions, and δ an associated transition function that details which actions are possible in which game situations. The latter two concepts, $\mathcal{A}$ and δ, will be introduced in greater details in Sect. 2.2.

2.1 Blueprinting with the Static Graph (SG)

We start by defining a Static Graph (SG) as a directed graph $\mathcal{G} = (V,\ E)$ where:

- $V = R \cup Z \cup L \cup C \cup S \cup M$ is a finite set of *typed vertices*:
  - R: *room vertices*, representing spatial areas in the game;
  - Z: *puzzle vertices*, encoding the challenges to be solved;
  - C: *clue vertices*, items and bits of information helping to solve puzzles;
  - L: *role vertices*, modeling roles in puzzle solving or starting positions;
  - S: *skill vertices*, representing cognitive and physical abilities needed to solve puzzles (e.g. "trigonometry basics");
  - M: *meta-information vertices*, governing conditional branches, timers, game states, and win/loss conditions. We suppose the existence of at least one *victory* meta-information vertex in the set M.
- $E \subseteq V \times V$ is the set of directed edges representing logical dependencies and game mechanics between elements. The semantics of an edge is derived from the types of its origin and destination vertices, and some directed relations are prohibited, e.g. for r_1 and r_2 rooms and s_1 a skill, the edge $r_1 \to r_2$ represents a one-way path between the rooms, while $r_1 \to s_1$ is not allowed.

Each vertex type plays a specific role in the game logic. A puzzle $z \in Z$ *requires* at least one player to perform an action. This player is represented by a role $l \in L$ which may *require* a set of clues $\{c_1, \ldots, c_n\} \subseteq C$ and skills $\{s_1, \ldots, s_k\} \subseteq S$, and is *located* in a room $r \in R$. Solving a puzzle may *unlock* new room(s), *offer* new clue(s) or *unveil* new puzzle(s).

Now, the exact conditions on V and E that ensure that the SG is (semantically speaking) representing a valid EG are for now solely implemented in the companion proof-of-concept software (called GraphEG), and their formal study is left for future work. We refer the reader to GraphEG's documentation in regard with what is currently permitted (or not) in its underlying SG formalization, as well as more details regarding the rules that govern the direction of the edges.

Also note that, depending on the exact setting of each escape game, new vertex types could be incorporated in the model. This is left for future work; GraphEG should be seen as a first instantiation of the framework, and as such incorporates a collection of *usual* inherent mechanisms of escape games.

An example SG is given in graphical form in Fig. 1. Each different vertex type has received a different coloring and shape to ease the reader's comfort. For any given i, a **role** vertex of the form Li represents a starting position while Ri stands for a **room**. $L0$ is the standard starting position (to room $R1$) and $L1$ (to

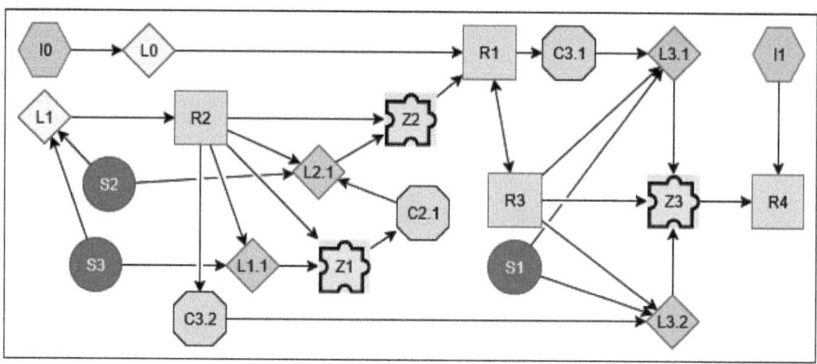

Fig. 1. An example Static Graph (SG).

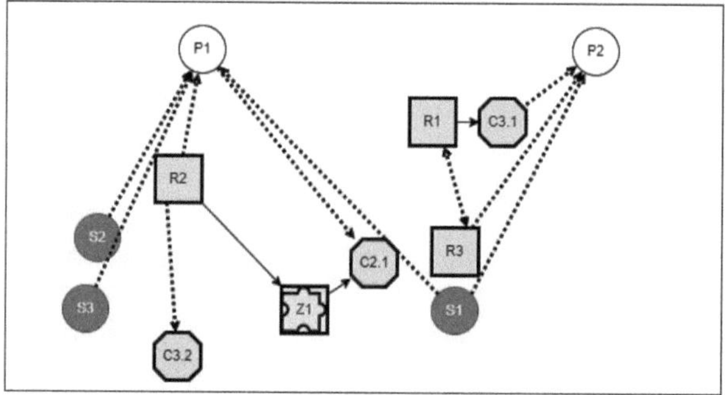

Fig. 2. A Dynamic Graph (DG) based on the Static Graph (SG) from Fig. 1

room $R2$) corresponds to a specific starting position for one of the players (so they are separated at game start). The player starting in $R2$ is supposed to solve the **puzzle** $Z1$ (by taking role $L1.1$) to obtain access to the **clue** $C2.1$. This, in turn, allows him to take on the role $L2.1$, required to solve the puzzle $Z2$, finally allowing this player to open the door and join the rest of the team in $R1$ and $R3$, two rooms with free circulation. Let us now consider the puzzle $Z3$: it is implied in the graph that two roles ($L3.1$ and $L3.2$) should be endorsed simultaneously in order to solve it. This might correspond to a situation where two players must communicate from inside the room $R3$ to, e.g., activate switches simultaneously. Si nodes correspond to **skills**; in the example, $S2$ is required to assume the role $L2.1$ (and therefore the starting position $L1$). Finally, the meta-informative nodes $I0$ (*victory*) and $I1$ (*exit*) respectively declare victory when no player is left and remove players from the game when they enter $R4$.

As we can see, the SG component of an escape game essentially constitutes its blueprint, conceptualizing a plan of how players can win in a step-by-step and chronological way. Thanks to this representation, automated static analyses can be performed. Examples include pre-computing the minimal number of different players required to solve the game (which amounts to 2 in the example above) as well as the detection of unreachable artifacts, dependency loops, and design inconsistencies; these checks are partially implemented in the application that will be introduced later on in the paper.

2.2 In-Game Modeling with the Dynamic Graph (DG)

To play the game, we add a set of players P. We can now define the Dynamic Graph (DG), given a Static Graph (SG) $\mathcal{G} = (V, E)$, as a directed graph $\mathcal{G}_d = (V_d, E_d)$, in which V_d is the vertex set V from SG to which we add *player vertices*; each vertex is then decorated with a *discovered* (boolean) attribute. $E_d \subseteq V_d \times V_d$ is the set of directed edges representing the players' (potential) progress.

Figure 2 illustrates an in-game snapshot based on the Static Graph from before. The nodes that have been *discovered* have a bold border. Player $P1$ is currently *located* in room $R2$ and *possesses* skills $S1$, $S2$ and $S3$. He *carries* clue $C2.1$. Clue $C3.2$ has been *discovered* but not *picked up*.[1] Puzzle $Z1$ has been *solved* (since it is *discovered* and no edge from $\mathcal{G}_d$ is pointing towards it anymore). Player $P2$ is *located* in room $R3$. He *carries* clue $C3.1$ and *possesses* skill $S1$. $Z2$ and $Z3$ have not been discovered yet; hence their absence from the DG.

From a given DG $\mathcal{G}_d$, it is possible to compute an action set $\mathcal{A}(\mathcal{G}_d)$ representing the possibilities that each player has in the situation described by $\mathcal{G}_d$); this particular computation is included in the GraphEG tool introduced in the next section; it allows to systematically generate the DG and to assess the validity of potential player actions. Resolving an action from this set would then update the graph according to the possibly newly discovered elements. For example, DG from Fig. 2 would generate the action set $\{Explore(P1), Pickup(P1, C3.2), Move(P2, R1), Explore(P2)\}$. The permissible actions also include actions of the form $Memorize(Px, Cy)$, $Enter(Px)$, $Drop(Px, Cy)$ and $Attempt(Px, Zy)$.

Now, operationally, one would typically need to *traverse* the (static and/or dynamic) graphs in order to perform formal property checks and verification. In this case, traversing the graph implies following dependencies whose semantics depend on the types of the connected vertices. More formally, a traversal step along an edge $(u, v) \in E \cup E_d$ is permitted if and only if some semantic conditions are satisfied with respect to the node types. For example, if $u \in Z$, then u must be solved for it to lead to some new element v in the DG; if $v \in R$ and the player is currently in room u, then there must exist an edge $(u \to v) \in E$. In the DG, traversing to a node v additionally triggers its activation (e.g., revealing all visible elements inside a room). Hence, a traversal of the graph corresponds to (the verification of) a sequence of valid state transitions, as defined by the third component of our definition of an EG.

The component in question is a transition function $\delta : \mathcal{A} \times \mathcal{G}_d \mapsto \mathcal{G}_d$, defining a sequence $\{\mathcal{G}_d^i\}_i \in 1..n$ such that $\mathcal{G}_d^{i+1} = \delta(a, \mathcal{G}_d^i)$ represents the DG obtained upon resolving the effect of a on $\mathcal{G}_d^i$. We can then consider the existence, at any moment in a game, of a succession of (past and present) DGs and actions, called

---

[1] We refer the reader to GraphEG's documentation for more information on this regard.

```
C:\Escape Game\Example>git log --oneline
08f63e6 (HEAD -> Example_2_GS, tag: Victory_InitialSession-2) Player P2 moved from Room R2 to Room R3
34c2490 Player P1 moved from Room R2 to Room R3
2cabbbe Players [P1, P2] solved Puzzle Z3 and found Room R3 as reward.
49ccf06 Player P1 moved from Room R0 to Room R2
30d4f66 Player P2 found a puzzle Z3.
76305ef Player P1 moved from Room R1 to Room R0
37cb9fe Player P1 memorized Clue C.3.2
7c1dcb1 Player P1 found a clue C.3.2.
f69a635 Players [P1] solved Puzzle Z2 and found Room R0 as reward.
9ba7ac0 Player P1 found a puzzle Z2.
732f255 Player P2 found a door to room R0.
1bead6a Player P2 moved from Room R0 to Room R2
ce313d1 Player P1 memorized Clue C.2.1
1ddeb94 Players [P1] solved Puzzle Z1 and found Clue C.2.1 as reward.
5885761 Player P1 found a puzzle Z1.
502c909 Player P2 found nothing.
03e914d Player P2 memorized Clue C.3.1
a7e99d0 Player P2 found a clue C.3.1.
ee0a344 Player P2 found a door to room R2.
a51e97d Player P2 started the game in room R0
162d3c4 Player P1 started the game in room R1
3587f2c P1:S1-S2-S3_P2:S1
bec2b0f (InitialSession) Game initialized
```

Fig. 3. A full Game Session visualization using Git native commands

the Game Session, and defined as $\langle G_d^0, a^0, \cdots, G_d^{n-1}, a^{n-1}, G_d^n \rangle$, where $\forall i \in 1..n$: $G_d^i = \delta(G_d^{i-1}, a^{i-1}) \wedge a^{i-1} \in \mathcal{A}(\mathcal{G}_d^{i-1})$.

2.3   Temporal Modeling with the Game Session Forest (GSF)

While a SG allows one to statically approximate some interesting properties regarding a given escape game, it cannot cover what occurs in practical runs of the games. A DG represents an in-game situation, but is only a snapshot of a practical game execution at a given point in time. Then, a Game Session is essentially the linkage of subsequent DG that unlocks the monitoring of the actions executed by the players from the start of the game until its resolution.

Now, to induce some properties that will or will not hold with respect to an EG, we are interested in capturing *all* of the potential player progressions. To do this, we define the **Game Session Forest (GSF)** as a set of trees $\mathcal{F}$. Each tree $T \in \mathcal{F}$ corresponds to the tree representation of a game session (essentially representing alternative decision policies). In practice, the GSF's size can be kept reasonable using ad hoc pruning techniques. As an illustration, in Fig. 1, one should only consider those game traces that attribute both skills $S2$ and $S3$ to the player entering $R2$ through $L1$, since all other traces would make the game impossible to win.

The GSF is mostly designed to allow subsequent analyses to identify solvable paths (i.e., the existence of a trace ending in a goal state corresponding to reaching the *victory* condition), but also to search for the most efficient such trace (according to some optimization criterion) and to perform redundancy and deadlock analysis. Additionally, it can be used to derive metrics regarding a game's average length or cognitive load, and to ensure e.g. that knowledge and item distribution remain balanced across players.

3   An Overview of the `GraphEG` Visualization Tool

`GraphEG` is an open source interactive tool written in C#[2] destined to be used by game designers for building, visualizing and simulating escape games based on the formalisms developed above. A first prototype version of the tool was introduced in [18]; however, it lacked several key features. In this section, we describe an updated version able to handle more situations and visualizations.

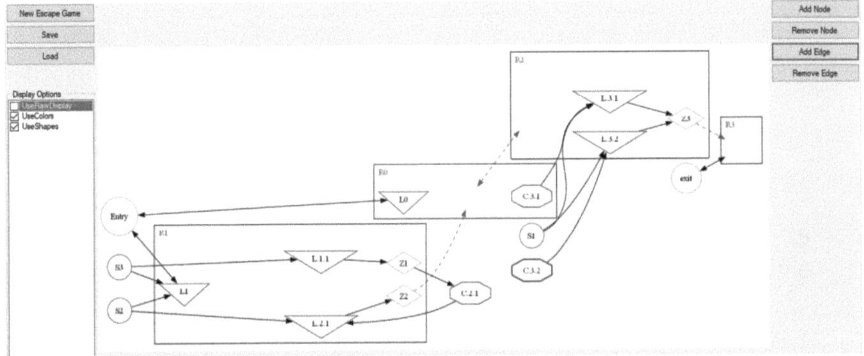

Fig. 4. A snapshot of the Designer interface corresponding to the `SG` from Fig. 1

The `GraphEG` software relies on the `QuikGraph` and `GraphViz` libraries to render `SGs` and `DGs` in the `DOT` graph description language [6]. To represent a Game Session Forest, the software leverages Git's native operations. Game sessions are represented by a branch in the repository; each commit then represents a `DG`, so that tracing a session is equivalent to requesting the log for the given session or branch. Then, the `GSF` can simply be retrieved as the full Git repository, including all of its branches. Note that this allows us to take advantage of Git's inner representation of repositories as being, essentially, trees, as well as its capabilities for comparing commits and pruning repository branches automatically. Figure 3 shows a command-line visualization of the whole `GSF` based on this. Next to the `GSF` integration, `GraphEG` offers two main user interfaces:

1. **The Designer** is the name given to the workspace that allows users to create and edit a `SG` by adding and removing nodes and edges. Figure 4 shows a screenshot of the Designer in which we recreated the example `SG` from Fig. 1. The Designer also provides basic formalism verification by preventing the creation of forbidden edges (e.g., connecting a room to a skill) and validating vertex consistency (e.g., a puzzle must be connected to at least one role). It is additionally possible to save the graph or to load one from a file.

---

2. **The Gameplay** is a second interface that first requests the user to pick an existing GSF (by selecting a Git repository) or to create a new one from a given SG file. Then, it will display the existing Game Sessions from the selected GSF or propose the creation of a new one. Finally, the user is allowed to simulate the game. GraphEG then displays the current game state (embodied by a DG) and details its corresponding action set. Upon selecting one of the available actions, the user triggers an update in the DG; in that case, a new Git commit is also created on the fly. A screenshot of the Gameplay view is given in Fig. 5; it corresponds to the example DG given earlier in Fig. 2.

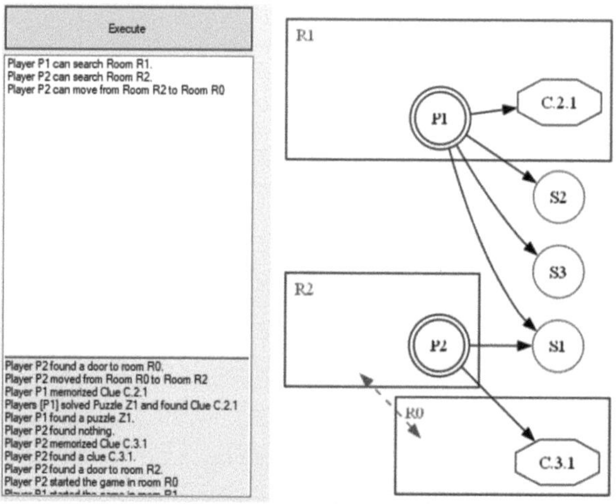

Fig. 5. A snapshot of the Gameplay interface corresponding to the DG from Fig. 2

In addition to these interfaces, GraphEG offers visualization features that facilitate the understanding of complex dependencies. For instance, different vertex types are distinguished by color and shape, and consistency checks are reported directly in the interface. Moreover, the possibility to display Static and Dynamic Graphs side by side helps designers follow the evolution of a session while preserving a clear overview of the underlying blueprint. Such visualization support is crucial to make the traversal semantics and player progress more transparent, especially for non-technical users such as educators and practitioners.

4   Discussion

This paper introduced a formal graph-theoretical framework for modeling, simulating, and analyzing escape games, treating them as structured, state-driven systems governed by interdependent puzzles, spatial progression, and player agency. Our layered representations offer a unified vocabulary for capturing both the design-time architecture and run-time unfolding of such experiences.

The model also enables automatic reasoning tasks such as solvability checking, dependency validation and balance assessment. This formalism was further operationalized through the development of a dedicated open-source application that allows designers to visualize, test, and iterate on game blueprints.

Despite its expressiveness and versatility, the proposed framework presents several limitations that merit discussion. First, while offering a robust formalization of structural and interactive components, it abstracts away the cognitive dimension of players. Aspects such as reasoning strategies, group coordination, intuition, and trial-and-error learning are not explicitly modeled, though they are often central to real-world escape room experiences. In the same vein, our model does not yet incorporate mechanisms for modeling evolving stories, character-driven events and branching dialogue systems. This could be tackled by incorporating e.g. logic-based storytelling structures or narrative graphs [12].

Secondly, the framework captures only discrete event sequencing, thus lacking the richness of continuous temporal modeling such as duration-based constraints, real-time pressure, and decay functions over time to represent more complex scenarios. From a practical standpoint, the creation of such scenarios involving dozens of interconnected (and timed) puzzles can become unwieldy without the aid of a higher-level domain-specific scripting interface. Incorporating such a feature in the **GraphEG** user interface, e.g. by leveraging Large Language Models (LLMs) able to generate adequate JSON files from a textual description of the game is an interesting avenue for further work.

Finally, while the theoretical underpinnings of the model are sound, its empirical validation is still pending. We plan to tackle this by including experimental validation and benchmarking, regarding both **GraphEG**'s runtime performances and effectiveness in real-life scenarios. To achieve such measures, one can, for example, draw upon existing structured evaluation frameworks tailored for (educational) escape games such as the methodologies developed in [9] and [16].

5   Future Work

The limitations above in fact pave the way for interesting avenues of further work. As a first example, following the trend of escape games used to train critical thinking, collaboration, and active learning in educational and corporate environments [5,7], **GraphEG**'s core mechanics have been chosen so that serious games could easily benefit from our models.

Of direct use in that regard is the dynamic tracking of player paths via our various graphs, which can straightforwardly be leveraged to extract learning analytics. This can help instructors and designers to, e.g., identify conceptual bottlenecks in their storytelling, or to adapt the content of their courses or games. Such efforts to evaluate the relevance of pedagogical escape games have been studied before (see e.g. [15]) and should benefit from the structured data collected during a **GraphEG**-monitored session. Even more, the **GraphEG** application naturally supports the integration of pedagogical objectives directly into the structural blueprint of a game. This is handled by the software's exhaustive listing of prerequisites of a given action, clue or puzzle, and by the possibility of encoding differentiated pathways for learners with varying skill sets.

Apart from these education-driven applications, `GraphEG` opens promising intersections with other research fields. For example, thanks to its manipulation of game traces, our framework may support the modeling of agents operating in multi-goal and/or constrained environments arising in plan recognition and automated reasoning, two important fields in the AI landscape [8]. Human-computer interaction may similarly benefit from our user-based modeling, which paves the way for more adaptive interfaces, especially in immersive contexts such as those explored in [16]. This is especially relevant in extended reality (XR) applications, where spatial reasoning and clarity are critical [14].

Additional future work includes the integration with automated solvers and AI assistants, as well as the development of metrics to evaluate graph complexity, educational efficacy, and player engagement for `GraphEG`-modeled games.

References

1. Araújo, M., Roque, L.: Modeling games with Petri nets. In: Digital Games Research Association Conference (2009)
2. Borrego, C., Fernández, C., Blanes, S., Robles, S.: Designing escape rooms for the classroom. In: ACM conference on innovation and technology in computer science education. pp. 331–331 (2017)
3. Botturi, L., Babazadeh, M.: Designing educational escape rooms: validating the star model. Int. J. Serious Games **7**, 41–57 (2020)
4. Clarke, S., Peel, D.: EscapED: A framework for creating educational escape room games. In: European Conference on Games Based Learning. pp. 111–118 (2017)
5. Delmas, G., Champagnat, R., George, S.: Structuring learning activities in escape games: A preliminary typology. In: International Conference on Human-Computer Interaction. pp. 121–139. Springer (2020)
6. Ellson, J., Gansner, E.R., Koutsofios, E., North, S.C., Woodhull, G.: Graphviz-open source graph drawing tools. Lect. Notes Comput. Sci. **2265**, 483–484 (2002)
7. Fotaris, P., Mastoras, T.: Escape rooms for learning: A systematic review. In: European Conference on Games Based Learning (2019)
8. Ghallab, M., Nau, D., Traverso, P.: Automated Planning: Theory and Practice. Elsevier (2004)
9. Kabimbi Ngoy, R., Yernaux, G., Vanhoof, W.: EvscApp: Evaluating the pedagogical relevance of educational escape games for computer science. In: International Conference on Computer Supported Education. pp. 241–251. SciTePress (2023)
10. Kebritchi, M., Hirumi, A., Bai, H.: What do we know about computer games and learning? Br. J. Edu. Technol. **41**(1), 18–38 (2010)
11. Nicholson, S.: Peeking behind the locked door: A survey of escape room facilities (2015), white paper
12. Riedl, M., Young, R.: From linear story generation to branching story graphs. IEEE Comput. Graphics Appl. **26**(3), 23–31 (2006)
13. Robison, B.: Games as models: Simulation, abstraction, and design. Simulation Gaming **52**(5), 558–575 (2021)
14. Romero, C., et al.: Escape rooms as innovative pedagogical tools for active learning: A systematic review. Educ. Res. Rev. **34**, 100404 (2021)

15. Taraldsen, L.H., Haara, F.O., Lysne, M.S., Jensen, P.R., Jenssen, E.S.: A review on use of escape rooms in education-touching the void. Educ. Inq. **13**(2), 169–184 (2022)
16. Veldkamp, A., Niese, J., Heuvelmans, M., Knippels, M.C., van Joolingen, W.: You escaped! How did you learn during gameplay? British Journal of Educational Technology **53** (2022)
17. Wiemker, M., Elumir, E., Clare, A.: Escape room games: Can you transform an unpleasant situation into a pleasant one? (2015)
18. Yernaux, G., Verjans, M., Vanhoof, W.: Towards a graph-theoretical framework for modeling and analyzing escape game mechanics. In: Geril, P. (ed.) 26th International Conference on Intelligent Games and Simulation. EUROSIS (2025)

Immersive Enhancement of Game Experience by Smell Sensing

David Widerberg, Chelsea Hong, Linus de Petris[(✉)], Markus Fiedler, and Siamak Khatibi

Department of Technology and Aesthetics, Blekinge Institute of Technology, Karlskrona, Sweden
{david.widerberg,chelsea.hong,linus.de.petris,markus.fiedler, siamak.khatibi}@bth.se

Abstract. Contemporary entertainment media, particularly games and films, primarily rely on visual and auditory stimuli to engage users. Although tactile feedback has become increasingly common through devices like vibrating controllers, olfactory stimulation remains largely unexplored in digital environments. Unlike passive media such as films, games offer interactive opportunities for users to both perceive and trigger smells, opening new possibilities for immersion. This paper presents the design and feasibility evaluation of a digital smell emission system aimed at enhancing immersion in gaming, particularly virtual reality (VR) experiences. We explore the mechanisms and key parameters for integrating scents into game mechanics and environmental storytelling. Testing across various scenarios reveals that smell can serve both as a supplemental sensory channel and a core interactive component. Our findings suggest that olfactory feedback, when contextually and spatially aligned, significantly enhances user immersion and has broad applicability across game genres.

Keywords: Virtual Reality · Smell · Scent · Digital Environments

1 Introduction

Modern entertainment experiences have evolved well beyond visual storytelling, incorporating advanced audio and haptic systems to enhance immersion. Devices such as surround sound speakers, haptic feedback controllers, and motion platforms exemplify this multisensory trend. Yet, despite its strong connection to memory and emotion, the sense of smell remains largely untapped in consumer-level digital entertainment. This paper explores the potential of olfactory feedback in enhancing interactive experiences, particularly within digital games and virtual reality (VR) environments.

Historically, attempts to introduce scent into media date back to the 19th century, such as Rimmel's fragrance diffusion at London's Alhambra Theatre in 1868 [2]. More recently, products like GameScent [1] have reintroduced this

S. Bakkes et al. (Eds.): GALA 2025, LNCS 16307, pp. 280–289, 2026.
https://doi.org/10.1007/978-3-032-11043-5_27

concept, using AI to pair scents with audio cues in real-time. Despite these advances, olfactory feedback is still rarely integrated into mainstream digital content.

Research has shown that scents not only evoke emotional responses but also enhance memory retention [3,4]. Unlike sound or visuals, smell has a direct pathway to the brain's limbic system, which governs emotion and memory. This paper investigates how olfactory stimuli can support game content both aesthetically—by enriching environmental realism—and functionally, as interactive game mechanics. The aim is to study the feasibility of hardware and software producing scent and how it can contribute meaningfully to the user experience and potentially become a staple in immersive digital media.

2 Related Work

To effectively integrate olfactory feedback into digital games, it is essential to understand how humans perceive and process smells. The olfactory system detects airborne molecules via receptors that encode these chemical signals into identifiable scents. Unlike visual or auditory stimuli, smells are often interpreted in association with objects or environments rather than as isolated signals [5]. Intensity plays a key role in perception: even familiar scents may be perceived differently depending on concentration [6].

Device design significantly influences user interaction with smell. Niedenthal et al. [7] developed a handheld scent device that enabled users to identify scents in a VR wine tasting simulation. While effective, the fan-based system caused distracting noise and inconsistent dispersion. Additionally, user background plays a role—Tortell et al. [8] found that experienced gamers were more receptive to olfactory feedback, perceiving it as novel and immersive, whereas casual players were less enthusiastic.

The material and construction of scent devices also affect usability and longevity. Materials like foam board and 3D-printed plastics offer durability and resistance to liquid damage compared to cardboard [9]. Moreover, research indicates that the timing of scent release must be precise; delays in emission or prolonged exposure can diminish effectiveness and even hinder user memory [10].

Overall, existing literature emphasizes the importance of synchronization, scent compatibility, and user expectations. These factors guided the development and testing of the prototypes presented in this paper.

3 Method

Design thinking is a user-centered and iterative problem-solving method utilized to develop practical and innovative solutions [12]. Our process followed four key phases: inception, ideation, prototyping, and test. After finding related research, primary interviews were conducted to better understand the design situation. We defined a problem statement and generated multiple creative ideas during the ideation phase. Selected ideas were then turned into low-fidelity prototypes, which were tested to gather feedback. This iterative approach allowed us to refine our prototypes incrementally to ensure that they were feasible and aligned with user experience expectations. During the design process, interviews and tests were conducted with university students and faculty. After finalizing the prototypes, an informal test with non-university persons was arranged.

Before constructing the first scent-diffusion prototype, initial experiments were conducted to explore how scent could interact with gameplay. This involved manually smelling everyday scented items—such as soap, deodorants, and perfumes—while playing computer games. This indicated that if the scent is thematically aligned with the in-game environment, it can enhance the gaming experience. When a scent did not match the visual and contextual elements of the game, it risked confusing the player. This observation supports findings by Tortell et al. [8], that incongruent scents can create a disorienting effect.

Just as audio cues are used to enhance user feedback in graphical user interfaces, scents were considered a potential complement to game elements that lie outside the visual environment. The tests also identified three primary factors that influenced a user's perception of scent intensity: the distance between the nose and the scent source, the duration of exposure, and the inherent strength of the scent.

None of the prototypes constructed included fans. The exclusion of fans was not primarily to avoid noise—although this had been a concern in previous experiments, such as those reported by Niedenthal et al. [7], but rather because fans were found to disperse the scent too broadly in the air, thereby weakening the olfactory impact. Additionally, fans did not noticeably accelerate the onset or dissipation of the scent, making them unnecessary for the intended use case.

3.1   Prototypes

Using the ultrasonic vaporizer *Grove–Water Atomization* (Seeed Studio, 2022), connected via jumper wires to a single-board microcontroller (Arduino Mega 2560 Rev3), it was possible to disperse scented liquids into the air. The vaporizer functions through a piezoelectric membrane that vibrates to release fine water particles, creating a visible mist. The microcontroller was connected to a computer running Unity game engine (Unity Technologies, 2022), which sent electrical signals to control the scent output.

The first prototype, named prototype V1 (Fig. 1), was initially inspired by *GameScent* (GameScent, 2023), particularly in its use of ultrasonic diffusion technology. Water was poured into small plastic containers. By adding concentrated oil-based aromas—specifically the Woody Essential Oils Set by Aeshory for forest scents and Nature Essential Oils by Salking for floral scents—the mist could carry distinct smells. To avoid spillage, the containers were filled using pipettes containing scented liquid.

To control the scent beam emitted by the vaporizer, the microcontroller delivered either high or low current through fixed signals or via hardware-supported pulse-width modulation (PWM). While both methods can switch the scent unit on or off, PWM also allows precise control over the intensity of scent dispersion.

Prototype V1 utilized a cotton wick to enhance liquid absorption into the vaporizer, resulting in a steady and stable mist output. Without the wick and its plastic casing, it was difficult to maintain consistent diffusion for more than a few minutes. The vaporizer ceased functioning if it was submerged below the waterline or if the water level dropped too low for the wick to absorb liquid effectively. The optimal liquid ratio for V1 was determined to be one drop of aroma oil per 40 milliliters of tap water. Too much oil led the cotton wick to absorb more oil than water, clogging the vaporizer and reducing its efficiency. Too little oil, on the other hand, failed to produce a noticeable scent. While Lei et al. [9] and Lukasiewicz et al. [10] used higher oil concentrations (up to 10 drops per milliliter), the lower concentration was chosen here to avoid clogging and maintain vaporizer performance.

Although scent dispersion began within milliseconds, a brief perceptible delay remained before the user noticed the aroma—consistent with findings by Lukasiewicz et al. [10]. One key takeaway from V1 was that distance from the nose was the most critical factor in how strongly a scent was perceived.

Prototype V1 occupied a flat surface measuring $300 \times 300 \times 50$mm ($W \times L \times H$). Users had to lean down toward the device to smell the scent beams, which did not naturally reach nose height from the tabletop. Additionally, the prototype took up valuable desk space, making it less practical alongside other equipment like keyboards and mice.

To address these issues, prototype V2 (Fig. 1) was developed with a smaller footprint ($150 \times 150 \times 170$mm). By raising the scent emitters, the need for users to lean forward was eliminated and, in addition, desk space was conserved. V2 focused on improving usability, refill convenience, aesthetics, and portability. It featured a detachable casing for easier maintenance, and its scent cartridges were arranged in a heptagon shape with one cartridge placed centrally—an improvement over the 2×4 grid layout of V1.

Prototypes V1 and V2 demonstrated what could be achieved with tabletop scent diffusion systems. These early designs highlighted proximity to the nose as the most influential factor in effective scent delivery.

3.2 VR Integration

Building on these findings, prototype VR-V1 was developed—the first scent diffusion system integrated with a VR headset (Fig. 1). By positioning scent emitters directly beneath the user's nose, the system reduced the distance to the olfactory receptors and allowed a more comfortable, upright posture. This placement also improved the angle of scent delivery.

VR-V1 used the same microcontroller as V1 and V2, allowing for identical control software. However, it remained wired to the computer. Initially, wooden mounts were used for attaching the scent units, but the wood emitted its own scent and eventually deteriorated due to moisture exposure. Plastic mounts were later used instead, offering durability and odor neutrality.

There were two major differences between the enclosed design of VR-V1 and the open design of desktop V2. In VR-V1, users could not avoid the scent simply by turning their head, resulting in a more immediate and consistent olfactory experience.

Due to limited space under the VR headset, only three scent emitters were used. They were positioned close to the user's face, with the nose as the focal point, allowing users to feel the mist and confirm whether the device was active.

Tests revealed that the cotton wick must be fully immersed in liquid to ensure optimal performance. Small refills using pipettes were insufficient for sustained output, as they only provided short bursts of scent. And, applying the lessons learned from V1 and V2, the VR-V1 prototype incorporated vertically mounted scent emitters positioned directly in front of the mouth. This design increased the vertical size of the VR unit and partially covered the user's mouth.

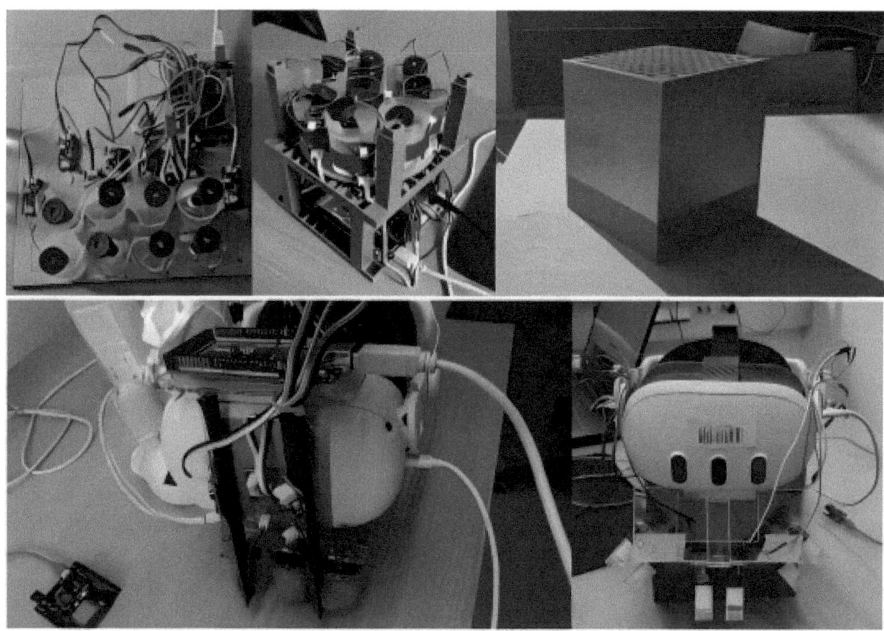

Fig. 1. Upper left: V1. Upper middle: the inside of V2. Upper right: the outside of V2. Lower left: VR-V1. Lower right: VR-V2

3.3   Prototype VR-V2

To address the limitations of VR-V1, particularly its limited number of scent emitters, a refined version VR-V2 was developed. This prototype was built upon the design principles of all previous models. VR-V2 was mounted on the Meta Quest 3 headset and featured six scent cartridges. It was fully wireless, with the onboard microcontroller (ESP32) receiving control signals via Bluetooth from a connected PC. VR-V2 also improved the weight distribution, thanks to a new mounting system that placed most hardware components behind the headset. The ultrasonic vaporizers were positioned so that each was equidistant from the nose, ensuring uniform scent delivery.

3.4   Test Environments—Application Development.

To prioritize rapid development over building custom software from scratch, pre-existing 3D environments were used for the gameplay scenarios. With the expansion of early-stage testing, the project relied on the *Hurricane VR* software package (Cloudwalkingames, 2025) to handle game mechanics. This gave users access to a variety of pre-built interactive systems, which were then enhanced with olfactory feedback.

These systems included mechanics such as archery with arrows, firearms with corresponding ammunition, operable doors, handle systems, and object penetration. They were selected, due to previous gaming experience, as common interactions and elements in many video games.

When the user performed an action, such as firing a weapon, they would immediately smell a corresponding scent as soon as the ultrasonic vaporizer dispersed it into the air. All prototypes in Fig. 1 use the same vaporizers, but the VR prototypes' vaporizers are always directed toward the user's nose, which leads to faster perception of scent, even though the dispersion rate is the same. While a more realistic approach would involve a slight delay—accounting for the time it takes for scent particles to travel through the air—immediate feedback was prioritized over strict realism to enhance the responsiveness and interactivity of the application.

In summary, fast and responsive scent feedback was chosen to improve user experience, even at the expense of physical realism in scent dispersal. A dispersal logic can be added to the software that calculates the required delays in the dispersal of the scents.

4   Results

The potential of scent to enhance immersion in virtual environments was demonstrated, especially when test users interacted with the environment. Figure 2 shows prototype VR-V2 worn by a user during the tests.

4.1   User Testing and Scent Integration.

After the first scent-diffusion prototype was constructed, it was tested in several interactive digital environments to evaluate its effect on immersion and player perception. For one of the first tests, a simple 2D computer game was created in which the player is supposed to move a white circle horizontally to avoid falling red circles and collecting green ones. When a green circle was hit, a perfume-like scent was emitted; when a red one was struck, the diffuser released a burst of 12-percent white vinegar. Players reported that the perfume scent triggered a

Fig. 2. Prototype VR-V2; a combination of VR-headset and scent-dispersion.

stronger reward response than the game's audio, while the vinegar was perceived as unpleasant but not aversive enough to change player behavior. A digital forest environment served as the primary testbed for evaluating scent diffusion in immersive settings. As users walked through different parts of the virtual forest, corresponding natural scents were released. For instance, a "mountain air" scent was triggered when the player reached higher elevations, while floral aromas were released near specific flowers. Some users felt that the vegetation had a realistic smell, while others thought it resembled synthetic perfume.

In further testing, mushrooms were added to the forest. Poisonous mushrooms were paired with an intended "toxic" scent, while edible mushrooms emitted a more pleasant aroma. However, one test substance—lime concentrate kept at room temperature—failed to deliver the intended toxic odor, leading players to misidentify poisonous mushrooms. In later iterations of the game, each mushroom type emitted a consistent scent throughout gameplay. Players learned to distinguish poisonous mushrooms by appearance after the initial olfactory cue, showing how visual memory quickly overtook scent cues in repeated interactions.

A virtual laboratory was used to explore how users perceived scent emission based on object positioning. When holding beakers directly in front of their faces, users found the scent dispersion unrealistic. Instead, they felt it was more natural when scents were released as the beaker approached just under the nose. These findings emphasized the importance of distance and orientation in triggering believable scent interactions.

In another VR experience, a perfume-sorting game was developed. The player received three different perfumes via a conveyor belt and had to place each one into a labeled box that matched its scent (e.g., "Wildflower"). Over time, players began identifying the perfumes not only by smell but also by the location on the nose where the scent fog landed, showing that spatial perception played a role in scent identification.

4.2   Digital Mechanics with Scent Integration

All scent-triggering systems were implemented using the Hurricane VR software package and programmed to include olfactory feedback:

1. Bow and Arrow System—The scent diffuser is activated when the player draws back the bowstring. The farther the string is pulled, the more frequently and intensely the diffuser releases mist. At full draw, the diffuser emits a continuous stream of scent, see Fig. 3.
2. Firearm System—When the trigger is pulled and a shot is fired, the diffuser emits a short burst of scent (approximately five milliseconds). This system supports both semi-automatic and fully automatic weapons.
3. Door System—Opening a virtual door triggers scent emission based on the degree of opening. The wider the door is opened, the longer and more frequently the scent is dispersed. When the door is fully open, the diffuser is active without pause.
4. Object Penetration System—When the player use an object to puncture another object, the depth of penetration determines the intensity and frequency of scent dispersion. At full depth, the diffuser emits the scent continuously.
5. Bottle Interaction, Direction & Rotation-Based Dispersion—When interacting with a bottle, the orientation of its lid relative to the player's nose controls the scent emission. As the lid is aligned towards and is close to the nose, the scent intensity increases accordingly, see Fig. 3.
6. Collision-Based Dispersion—Scents are also triggered when players walk near or into environmental objects such as trees or flowers. These objects have colliders that activate specific scents. For example, walking near a pine tree would release a pine forest aroma.

The results indicated that while scent recognition could reinforce player behavior and provide thematic cues, visual memory and spatial orientation often played an equally strong or stronger role. The findings underscore the importance of precise scent timing, directionality, and environmental context for delivering meaningful olfactory feedback in interactive media.

5   Discussion

Findings from our VR laboratory experiments highlight several nuanced design considerations for olfactory interaction. Notably, the most convincing scent interactions occurred when the virtual object was positioned just below the nose, rather than directly in front of the face. This spatial sensitivity emphasizes the importance of both orientation and distance for believable olfactory feedback.

Fig. 3. Two game scenes are shown from right to left: bottle interaction and bow and arrow game.

Game designers can manipulate these parameters to either reinforce realism or prioritize responsiveness, depending on gameplay goals.

In addition to the tests during the design process, an informal test was conducted with 18 participants consisting of children and adults. Participants were observed and feedback was collected for prototype V1 and prototype VR-V2 with the scent-triggering systems described above. Most participants liked the addition of scents to their virtual experience. Some participants complained about prototype VR-V2—"The beam goes directly into my nose", was one comment. Some participants stated that there was a discrepancy between the scents and the graphical environments, while others found the scents enriching the environments. Unexpected reactions also occurred, such as when one participant walked into a fence in the virtual environment, triggering the collision-based dispersion and stating "this smells like fence". This shows the potential of using scent for both pre-defined and emergent meaning making in virtual environments.

The broader integration of olfactory devices into consumer gaming remains limited. Challenges include the lack of standardized support in commercial games and the limited variety of scents available for real-time synthesis. Although artificial intelligence-driven systems can generate scents based on visual input [11], this compromises developer control and may introduce inconsistencies. Our findings suggest that the targeted, developer-controlled scent output provides a more reliable and engaging experience.

6   Conclusion

This paper has demonstrated the feasibility of integrating olfactory feedback into virtual environments through a series of custom-designed scent-dispersion devices. Our study shows that proximity, orientation, and contextual relevance of scent release significantly affect immersion and user perception. By embedding olfactory output into a Unity-based VR framework, we were able to deliver responsive and scenario-specific scent cues in various interactive settings.

The results underscore the viability of scent as an informative and engaging output modality in digital games. Participants expressed a preference for scent-enabled gameplay, noting enhanced realism and deeper engagement. The current market for consumer olfactory hardware is limited, but our findings point to a promising future for smell as a mainstream component of immersive media. Although this project focused on gaming, the implications extend to other domains such as education, therapy, and training simulations. Olfactory feedback could enrich learning experiences for fields such as wine tasting, emergency response training, or mental health.

Future work should include a more systematic evaluation of scents and user experience testing. As a feasibility study, our work was based on small-scale tests and a limited set of scents.

Acknowledgments. This study originates from a student project in the educational program Design of Digital and Immersive Experiences, Blekinge Institute of Technology.

Disclosure of Interests. The authors have no competing interests to declare that are relevant to the content of this article.

References

1. GameScent: GameScent, https://gamescent.com/, last accessed 2025/04/16
2. Early, A.: Smellie. Variety. **217**, 35 (1960)
3. Ehrlichman, H., Halpern, J.N.: Affect and memory: Effects of pleasant and unpleasant odors on retrieval of happy and unhappy memories. Journal of Per-sonality and Social Psychology. **55**, 769–779 (1988)
4. Herz, R.S.: Are Odors the Best Cues to Memory? A Cross-Modal Comparison of Associative Memory Stimuli. Annals of the New York Academy of Scienc-es. **855**, 670–674 (1998)
5. Wilson, D.A.: Learning to Smell: Olfactory Perception from Neurobiology to Behavior. Johns Hopkins University Press, Baltimore (2010)
6. Laing, D.G.: Relationship between Molecular Structure, Concentration and Odor Qualities of Oxygenated Aliphatic Molecules. Chem. Senses **28**, 57–69 (2003)
7. Niedenthal, S., Fredborg, W., Lundén, P., Ehrndal, M., Olofsson, J.K.: A graspable olfactory display for virtual reality. Int. J. Hum Comput Stud. **169**, 102928 (2023)
8. Tortell, R., Luigi, D.P., Dozois, A., Bouchard, S., Morie, J.F., Ilan, D.: The ef-fects of scent and game play experience on memory of a virtual environment. Virtual Reality **11**, 61–68 (2007)
9. Lei, Y., Lu, Q., Xu, Y.: O& O: A DIY toolkit for designing and rapid prototyp-ing olfactory interfaces. In: CHI Conference on Human Factors in Computing Systems. pp. 1–21. ACM, New Orleans LA USA (2022)
10. Lukasiewicz, M.S., Rossoni, M., Spadoni, E., Dozio, N., Carulli, M., Ferrise, F., Bordegoni, M.: An Open-Source Olfactory Display to Add the Sense of Smell to the Metaverse. Journal of Computing and Information Science in Engineer-ing. 24, 024501 (2024)
11. Al Luhaybi, A., Alqurashi, F., Tsaramirsis, G., Buhari, S.M.: Automatic Association of Scents Based on Visual Content. Appl. Sci. **9**, 1697 (2019)
12. Razzouk, R., Shute, V.: What is design thinking and why is it important? Rev. Educ. Res. **82**(3), 330–348 (2012)

An Adaptive Therapeutic Serious Game Using Connected Toys for Pediatric Cerebral Palsy Rehabilitation

Alexandre Isabelle[1]([✉]) [iD], Frédéric Muhla[2] [iD], Mehdi Ammi[3],
Yannick Francillette[1] [iD], Éric Desailly[2] [iD], and Bob-Antoine Menelas[1] [iD]

[1] Université du Québec à Chicoutimi, Chicoutimi, QC G7H 2B1, Canada
{aisabelle,yannick_francillette,bamenela}@uqac.ca
[2] Fondation Ellen Poidatz, Saint-Fargeau-Ponthierry 77310, France
{frederic.muhla,eric.desailly}@fondationpoidatz.com
[3] Université Paris 8, Saint-Denis 93200, France
mehdi.ammi@univ-paris8.fr

Abstract. This paper presents a therapeutic serious game integrating a commercial connected toy (LEGO Mario) to improve motor rehabilitation for children with cerebral palsy with unilateral upper limb disorder. By combining real-time sensor data, Bluetooth communication, a dynamic difficulty adjustment system implemented in Unreal Engine, and a progression system using pixel art as a motivation lever, the project offers a novel approach to maintaining engagement and personalizing rehabilitation. The research follows a clinically inspired methodology and introduces game prototypes validated by healthcare professionals and designed to be adaptable to individual patient profiles. The results show promising effects on engagement and motor participation.

Keywords: Serious Game · Pediatric Rehabilitation · Motivation · LEGO Mario · Dynamic Difficulty Adjustment · Connected Toys · Unreal Engine

1 Introduction

1.1 Context

The rapid advancement of embedded technologies over the past decade has significantly reshaped our interaction with everyday objects. These devices, miniaturized, portable and interactive, are now ubiquitous in domains such as home automation, agriculture, and healthcare [1]. In this technological landscape, Bluetooth Low Energy (BLE) [2] has emerged as a de facto standard for short-range wireless communication. BLE enables stable, low-power data exchange between connected objects and host devices such as smartphones or computers. The more recent Bluetooth Mesh protocol extends these capabilities by enabling many to many device communication within mesh networks, enhancing distributed sensor coordination at low energy cost [3].

S. Bakkes et al. (Eds.): GALA 2025, LNCS 16307, pp. 290–299, 2026.
https://doi.org/10.1007/978-3-032-11043-5_28

One notable BLE-enabled device is LEGO Mario, developed in partnership between LEGO and Nintendo. This interactive toy includes embedded sensors: accelerometer, color sensor, designed to respond to user manipulation. Through BLE connectivity, it becomes a dynamic interface capable of transmitting precise movement data in real time. This opens promising avenues beyond play, particularly in interactive health technologies as a low-cost non-invasive instrument.

1.2   Clinical Motivation

Cerebral palsy affects approximately 1.7 in 1000 live births [4] and may leads to impairments in fine and gross motor skills, complicating basic tasks such as reaching, grasping, or releasing objects [5]. Several rehabilitation strategies have been proven to be reliable in improving upper limb capacities and or functional performance through high intensity repetitive tasks. One widely used task that focuses on repetition is Reach-to-Grasp [6]. Despite being clinically validated, such a high number of repetitions, combined with the lack of interaction and the poorly contextualized nature, frequently result in patient disengagement [7].

Moreover, these exercises are typically applied uniformly, with little adaptation to real-time individual performance. Research in rehabilitation science suggests that maintaining a positive motivational state known as flow [8], requires dynamic regulation of task difficulty. Lack of adaptive feedback undermines both engagement and therapeutic personalization.

1.3   Research Question

In light of the shortcomings of conventional motor rehabilitation, often monotonous and unmotivating for children, emerging technologies that incorporate real-time sensors and adaptive environments hold promise for transforming therapy. The use of connected toys raises new questions. Can such tools improve engagement while respecting the clinical goals of structured protocols? The research question of this work is: *How can an interactive therapeutic application, leveraging the embedded sensors of LEGO Mario, dynamically adapt the difficulty of clinically inspired motor exercises to foster motivation and adherence in children with unilateral upper limb disorder?*

In line with current trends in digital rehabilitation, this work aims to explore the potential of connected toys in designing user-centered, intelligent, and playful therapeutic environments. Such solutions may support both supervised clinical interventions and autonomous use at home, tailored to the specific needs of young patients undergoing motor recovery.

2   Related Work

Recent studies have explored various implementations of dynamic difficulty adjustment (DDA) systems in serious games for motor rehabilitation. Pezzera et al. [9] proposed a clinically oriented fruit catching exergame that combines physical performance, emotional state, and in-game metrics to adapt difficulty. Their hybrid algorithm, based on fuzzy logic and linear adjustment, highlights the importance of maintaining an optimal challenge. However, the system lacks transparency in error detection and has not been validated with real patients.

Garcia and Crocomo [10] presented a Whac-A-Mole-inspired game using an evolutionary algorithm to adapt the target positions according to the user's spatial motor profile. While the simulated users validate the approach algorithmically, the study lacks clinical validation and does not incorporate motivational mechanisms critical for rehabilitation. Nonetheless, the simplification of motor profiles opens perspectives aligned with sensor-based systems like LEGO Mario.

Valencia et al. [11] developed Bug Catcher, a game inspired by the Box and Block Test, integrating fuzzy logic to dynamically modulate complexity factors such as timing, depth, and target motion. Although tested with only two patients, the protocol includes clinical supervision and functional measurement, making it a promising model despite limited generalizability.

Liao et al. [12] introduced a novel eye-tracking-based system that focuses on attentional engagement rather than motor performance. By modulating sensory feedback visibility based on gaze direction, the system fosters cognitive involvement. The results indicate that excessive assistance can reduce engagement. This study underlines the importance of maintaining attention, a key issue when designing child-focused experiences with interactive toys such as LEGO Mario.

Yang and Sun's [13] work on hyper-casual games demonstrates that DDA can improve engagement, tolerance to failure, and motivation even in short gameplay loops. Although not clinically focused, their findings are relevant for pediatric rehabilitation contexts where children require short, rewarding, and frustration-minimizing interactions.

Collectively, these studies support the integration of DDA to enhance engagement and personalized progression in rehabilitation games. However, common limitations include small or non-clinical populations, lack of pediatric focus, and reliance on complex or costly technologies. The need for simple, engaging, and clinically adaptable solutions remains, particularly for child-specific motor and cognitive dynamics.

3   Methodology

The development of the interactive rehabilitation solution was conducted within the PROGame framework [14], which promotes the participation of key stakeholders in game-based therapy, specifically children and therapists. This framework provides a structured approach to development that incorporates clinical evaluation of therapeutic outcomes. The participatory design process involved 3 occupational therapists, 2 physiotherapists, and 18 children aged 4 to 17 years old who presented unilateral disorder associated with motor impairments. Through the iterative testing phases, the technical feasibility of the game was verified, therapeutic requirements were addressed, and every aspect of the design was progressively refined to suit both long-term rehabilitation and motivational needs.

3.1 Hardware and Integration

LEGO Mario features embedded sensors, a Bluetooth Low Energy (BLE) module, and onboard firmware capable of broadcasting data. Integration with Unreal Engine was performed in part, using a third-party Python library that took care of the Bluetooth connection between LEGO and the computer and hook to LEGO events[1], which was converted into a running Windows application. This application was adapted to establish a dedicated local socket connection between each connected LEGO device and the Unreal Engine game instance, thus ensuring proper management of the different states of connection. Through this socket, sensor data, which are constant hexadecimal and binary strings, are continuously polled and translated through a dispatcher into actionable in-game events.

3.2 Prototype

Based on clinician feedback, a classic Whack-a-Mole inspired game (See Fig. 1a), was identified as having the highest potential for repetition and was deemed most suitable for Reach-to-Grasp rehabilitation therapy. In this game, the plates light up briefly (See Fig. 1b), and the player must quickly identify and place the corresponding LEGO on the matching physical color before the light disappears to score points. Following each attempt, the LEGO must be placed back on its tower represented by the green or red plates, regardless of success or failure. This step reinitializes the light-up mechanism. To promote full motor execution, the use of alternating LEGO Mario and Luigi was implemented to systematically elicit sequential reach-to-grasp and release actions.

(a) Whack-a-mole prototype idle state

(b) Whack-a-mole prototype light up state

Fig. 1. Representation of the Whack-a-mole prototype developed

---

[1] https://github.com/Jackomatrus/pyLegoMario.

3.3   Level Diversification

A total of 62 distinct levels were developed in collaboration with project researchers to create an initial layer of difficulty calibration based on the user's motor limitations. These levels are structured around eight postural variants targeting specific motor functions, including flat ground placement, variable elevation (10 or 20 cm), supination and extension movements at 45° and 90°, as well as their combinations (See Fig. 2). Special attention was paid to the physical layout design to avoid reaching constraints and ensure optimal legibility of the game board.

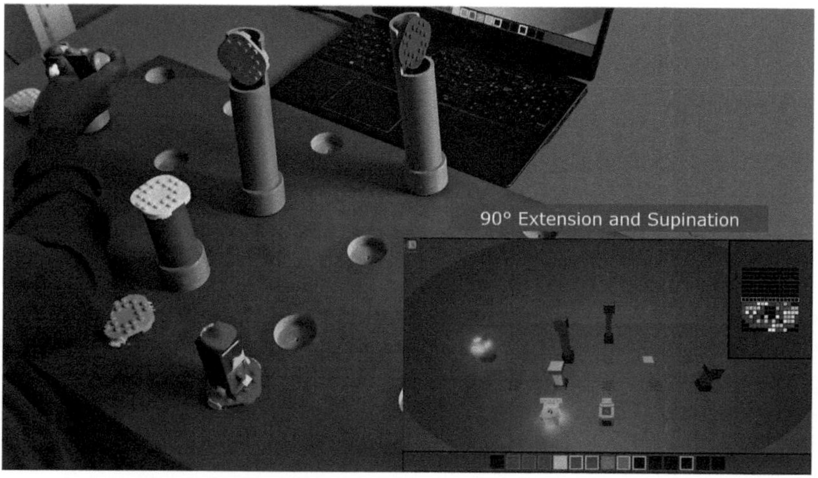

Fig. 2. Representation of a child playing the prototype

Each level configuration is encoded using a five-digit 'seed' that represents key parameters: grid position, angle of inclination, height of the tower and type of targeted movement. These seeds are dynamically loaded into a structured Unreal Engine data table, enabling flexible expansion and rapid deployment of new configurations. This modular architecture supports fine-grained control of difficulty. Levels may vary in spatial density (closer tower placement being easier) and can be tailored based on dominant laterality to either minimize effort or focus on targeted motor rehabilitation zones. A dedicated user interface was implemented to facilitate manual selection by therapists, exposing relevant parameters in an accessible format. The resulting infrastructure promotes high replayability, crucial for repeated therapy sessions, while offering clinicians a precise tool for task calibration. This customizable system supports a child-centered approach, accommodating motor needs.

3.4   Motivation Reinforcement

A visual reward system based on pixel art was designed to enhance emotional engagement and offer a tangible representation of progress. This system follows a stepwise structure, where each row of the pixel art corresponds to a stage within a level. For example, if the first row contains three pixels, the child must activate three colored plates in the game world to complete that row and unlock the next. This process continues seamlessly within a single level until the entire image is revealed, signaling full completion of the level (See Fig. 3a).

Each colored pixel directly reflects the hue of the activated plate (See Fig. 3b), forming a dynamic mosaic. This one-to-one correspondence anchors the child's in-game actions to the visual construction of an image, fostering curiosity and anticipation. The progressive unveiling of the artwork acts as an intrinsic motivational driver, grounded in positive visual reinforcement while avoiding cognitive overload or excessive gamification. Upon completion, the fully assembled mosaic reveals its true colors as a coherent artwork, providing a strong sense of accomplishment and enabling the child to discover the pixel art they have completed.

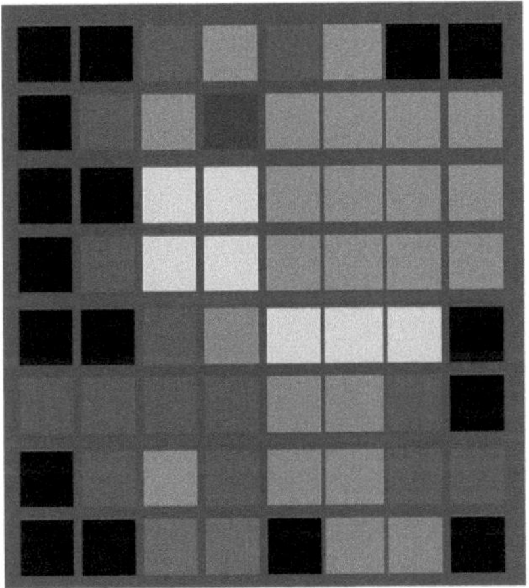

(a) Representation of a completed state pixel art

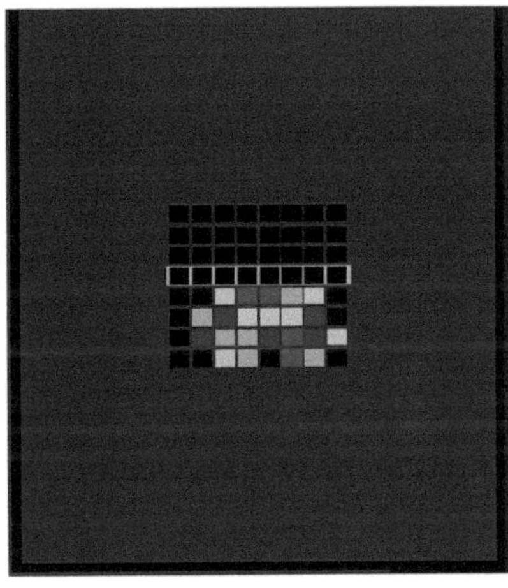

(b) Representation of an on-going pixel art

Fig. 3. Representation of an on-going pixel art progression and its full completion discovered state

3.5   Dynamic Difficulty Adjustment

A personalized, data-driven DDA system was introduced using user profiles to centralize performance tracking and continuity. Each profile records exposure times (duration a plate is illuminated), activation times (response latency), and success history. These metrics are explicitly linked to the encoded "seed" representing the level configuration, ensuring that performance data is contextualized according to spatial, postural, and motor parameters. Additionally, data is segregated by the LEGO figure used (Mario or Luigi) to account for lateral motor asymmetries. This multidimensional profiling ensures that difficulty scaling is tailored to the user's motor capabilities.

Among various adjustable parameters, exposure time was identified as the primary variable for dynamic modulation. A secondary variable, rest time between activations, remains under therapist control due to its sensitivity to fatigue and emotional state. To avoid frustration caused by rapid sequencing, a compensatory delay system was introduced following failed sequences. This system extends the exposure time of the first 40% of targets in the subsequent line, using a gradually decreasing timing scheme to restore pacing and confidence. To ensure smooth progression and avoid player frustration due to strict completion requirements, the next level is unlocked once 80% of the pixel art has been successfully filled. Players may return at any time to complete the level at 100% if desired, in which case the row is marked as fully completed, otherwise it is marked incompleted.

Core to the DDA system is a performance classification model that dynamically assigns players to one of four engagement states based on metrics such as win ratio, success streaks, and deviation from expected values:

- EDP_XBest: high, stable performance : difficulty is maintained at its maximum to preserve flow.
- $EDP\_Average$: balanced performance : difficulty remains stable to promote sustainable learning.
- EDP_XWorst: declining performance : difficulty is reduced slightly to prevent disengagement.
- EDP_Worst: recovery after repeated failures : difficulty is significantly reduced to restore confidence.

To avoid overreacting to isolated successes, a minimum of three data points is required before activating the DDA logic. Furthermore, difficulty is dynamically adapted using a logarithmic weighting function to avoid abrupt shifts between rows difficulty (See Fig. 4). This approach ensures that when the hit time closely matches the exposure time, the rate of difficulty increase is reduced, as the task is already near an optimal challenge level. Conversely, when there is a large discrepancy between the exposure time and the hit time, indicating that the task is relatively easy, the difficulty increases more rapidly to maintain engagement and prevent boredom.

- T_e Exposure time
- T_h Hit time
- $D = |T_e - T_h|$ Absolute difference between exposure and hit times
- W Weight factor controlling influence of T_e vs. T_h
- T_c Computed time for the next exposure time

$$W = \frac{1}{\ln(D+1)+1} \tag{1}$$

$$T_c = T_e \cdot W + T_o \cdot (1 - W) \tag{2}$$

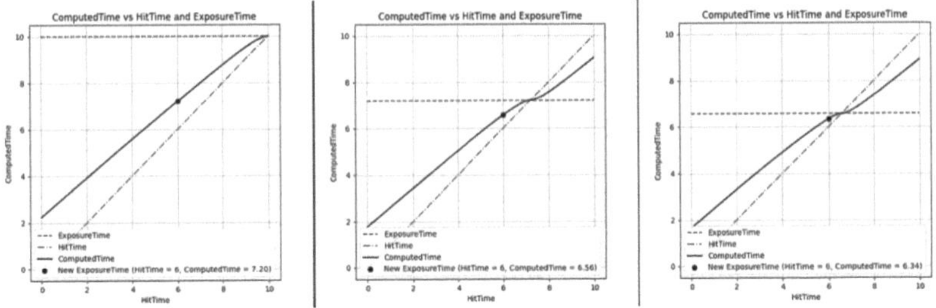

Fig. 4. Representation the new difficulty over 3 successfully completed rows.

4   Prototype Testing

The prototype was tested through a series of supervised sessions following a Single Case Experimental Design, conducted exclusively by the project's clinical partners, in accordance with ethical and institutional guidelines concerning pediatric participation in experimental activities. In total, six children aged from 6 to 11 were evaluated through three sessions of 20 min per week were conducted over 4 weeks resulting in more than 500 to 1900 movements for total of 4 h of intensive rehabilitation. The sessions aimed to assess both the functional aspects of the system in a rehabilitation context and the behavioral and motivational responses of children using the tool. Following the gameplay sessions, interviews were conducted with therapists to assess children engagement and perceptions of the intervention. Additionally, audiovideo recordings were collected to document relevant behaviors, verbal feedback, and motor performance throughout the sessions.

The therapeutic relevance of the prototype was confirmed by the participating therapists, who noted that the interactions effectively supported the intended motor engagement. They further reported that the system adjusted difficulty levels smoothly, without eliciting rejection or disengagement from the users. Although brief episodes of frustration were observed following repeated failures, these were frequently followed by renewed attempts to complete the pixel art. Such behavior was interpreted as a sign of perseverance and self-regulation, qualities regarded as highly beneficial in a rehabilitation context.

During the evaluation phase, pixel art exercises demonstrated a markedly strong motivational effect. Notably, many participants set personal goals, such as completing a specific number of lines or even an entire pixel art image within a single session. Achieving this required performing several hundred motor actions per session, sustained by high levels of focus and effort. These self-imposed objectives, which were not suggested by the therapist, provide evidence of strong intrinsic motivation, further reinforced by the game's progressive reward mechanism.

Beyond the clinical sessions, therapists reported indirect feedback from families, including spontaneous enthusiasm and sustained interest at home. Some children shared their experiences with parents and expressed a desire to return. The familiar and playful identity of the LEGO figurines appeared to contribute to this emotional attachment, with one therapist even being affectionately nicknamed "Mr. LEGO" by the children.

5   Discussion And Conclusion

This work introduces a modular and extensible interactive rehabilitation system that integrates pediatric motor therapy, serious gaming principles, and tangible interaction via LEGO Mario and Luigi figurines within the Unreal Engine 5 environment. The system was co-developed with clinical experts to ensure that gameplay mechanics are functionally aligned with therapeutic goals for children with unilateral upper limb disorder. The literature indicates that therapy efficacy is largely driven by intensity and repetition. However, these approaches can be perceived as monotonous, which may reduce adherence, particularly in pediatric populations. Our findings suggest that it is possible to preserve the effectiveness of these methods while enhancing engagement through more playful and enjoyable implementations for children.

Among the main contributions is a visual reward system based on progressive pixel art completion, designed to reinforce motivation and support repeated motor engagement. Additionally, a dynamic difficulty adjustment (DDA) mechanism, driven by individualized performance profiles and a weighted exposure time computation, adapts the challenge level to the child's evolving abilities without introducing punitive difficulty changes. The design includes a wide variety of level configurations, enabling both replayability and fine-grained adaptation to motor limitations. The architecture was conceived to support future scalability, including the integration of new level layouts and custom pixel art content.

In future works, patient metrics will be analyzed more comprehensively to assess motor recovery potential. Moreover, prototypes not retained in this paper suggest the potential for fine motor rehabilitation using LEGO as a joystick to control a character movements, leveraging the LEGO's accelerometer yaw and roll axes. Additionally, the integration of an online platform could allow therapists to remotely monitor therapy sessions. A multiplayer infrastructure offering social dynamics may further stimulate motivation and engagement among children.

In conclusion, this study demonstrates the potential of connected toys to serve as therapeutic instruments when integrated into serious games. The proposed system effectively supports motivation and engagement during repetitive motor rehabilitation, highlighting its relevance as a complementary tool for supervised clinical sessions and potentially integrating rehabilitation into everyday leisure activities.

References

1. Lohiya, R., Thakkar, A.: Application domains, evaluation data sets, and research challenges of IoT: a systematic review. IEEE Internet Things J. **8**(11), 8774–8798 (2021). https://doi.org/10.1109/JIOT.2020.3048439
2. Bluetooth SIG: Bluetooth technology website. https://www.bluetooth.com/ (2024)
3. Zhao, Y., et al.: A comprehensive evaluation of Bluetooth Low Energy mesh. In: Proceedings of the IEEE International Conference Parallel and Distributed Systems (ICPADS), pp. 544–551 (2024). https://doi.org/10.1109/ICPADS63350.2024.00077
4. S. McIntyre, S. Goldsmith, A. Webb, et al.: Global prevalence of cerebral palsy: a systematic analysis. Dev. Med. Child Neurol. *Dev. Med. Child Neurol.***64**(12), 1494–1506 (2022). https://doi.org/10.1111/dmcn.15346
5. Eliasson, A.-C., Gordon, A.M.: Impaired force coordination during object release in children with hemiplegic cerebral palsy. Dev. Med. Child Neurol. **42**(4), 228–234 (2000)
6. Kukke, S.N., Curatalo, L.A., de Campos, A.C., Hallett, M., Alter, K.E., Damiano, D.L.: Coordination of reach-to-grasp kinematics in individuals with childhood-onset dystonia due to hemiplegic cerebral palsy. IEEE Trans. Neural Syst. Rehabil. Eng. **24**(5), 582–590 (2016). https://doi.org/10.1109/TNSRE.2015.2458293
7. Li, W., et al.: The relationship between rehabilitation motivation and upper limb motor function in stroke patients. Frontiers in Neurology **15**, Article 1390811 (2024). https://doi.org/10.3389/fneur.2024.1390811
8. Csikszentmihalyi, M.: Flow: The Psychology of Optimal Experience. Harper & Row, New York (1990)
9. Pezzera, M., Borghese, N.A.: Dynamic difficulty adjustment in exer-games for rehabilitation: a mixed approach. In: Proceedings of the IEEE 8th International Conference Serious Games and Applications for Health (SeGAH), pp. 1–7 (2020). https://doi.org/10.1109/SeGAH49190.2020.9201871
10. Garcia, B.E.R., Crocomo, M.K., Andrade, K.O.: Dynamic difficulty adjustment in a Whac-a-Mole like game. In: Proceedings of the 17th Brazilian Symposium Computer Games and Digital Entertainment (SBGames), pp. 88–888 (2018). https://doi.org/10.1109/SBGAMES.2018.00020
11. Valencia, Y., Majin, J., Guzmán, D., Londoño, J.: Dynamic difficulty adjustment in virtual reality applications for upper limb rehabilitation. In: Proceedings of the IEEE 2nd Colombian Conference Robotics and Automation (CCRA), pp. 1–6 (2018). https://doi.org/10.1109/CCRA.2018.8588126
12. Liao, K.-L., Huang, M., Shi, J., Chen, M., Yang, R.: Focus-driven augmented feedback: enhancing focus and maintaining engagement in upper limb virtual reality rehabilitation. IEEE Trans. Visual Comput. Graphics **31**(5), 2653–2663 (2025). https://doi.org/10.1109/TVCG.2025.3549543
13. Yang, Z., Sun, B.: Hyper-casual endless game based dynamic difficulty adjustment system for players replay ability. In: Proceedings of the IEEE ISPA/BDCloud/SocialCom/SustainCom, pp. 860–866 (2020). https://doi.org/10.1109/ISPA-BDCloud-SocialCom-SustainCom51426.2020.00133
14. E. Amengual Alcover, A. Jaume-I-Capó, B. Moyà-Alcover: PROGame: A process framework for serious game development for motor rehabilitation therapy. *PLoS One***13**(5), e0197383 (2018). https://doi.org/10.1371/journal.pone.0197383

Application track

Are Narrative VR Games Effective in Promoting Positive Attitudes Embedded in Museum Educational Missions? Results from a Pilot Study

David Šosvald[1,2]([✉]) [iD], Lukáš Kolek[1,2] [iD], Christelle Dethy[3] [iD], Emilie Divoy[3] [iD], and Benjamin Wahl[4]

[1] Charles Games, Prague, Czech Republic
lukas.kolek@charlesgames.net
[2] Charles University, Prague, Czech Republic
sosvald@ksvi.mff.cuni.cz
[3] Le Bois du Cazier, Rue du Cazier, 80, B-6001, Marcinelle, Belgium
[4] Causa Creations, Vienna, Austria

Abstract. Narrative virtual reality (VR) games offer a powerful medium for learning and attitude change, which can be utilised to support the educational missions of museums. Grounded in the contact hypothesis and perspective-taking mechanism, this pilot study explores whether a narrative VR game can improve attitudes towards refugees. Conducted at the Le Bois du Cazier museum in Belgium, the study compares a VR game portraying the lives of Italian migrant workers in the 1940s and 1950s with a control group playing a PC game about climate change. Museum visitors participated in a pre-post experimental design measuring both explicit and implicit attitudes (N = 50). Results show a significant positive explicit attitude change in the VR group compared to control (d = 0.80, p = .005). The affective, cognitive, and behaviour attitude components are also investigated, with the cognitive showing the greatest change. Despite limitations such as small sample size and technical issues regarding implicit data collection, the findings bring methodological and empirical contributions to the field of serious VR games. This study lays the groundwork for a larger-scale experiment into how narrative VR could enhance museum-based education and reduce prejudice.

Keywords: Attitude change · Virtual reality · Contact hypothesis · Museum education · Video games

1 Introduction

Video games are increasingly being employed in museums to complement exhibitions. As virtual reality (VR) enables users to immerse themselves in simulated environments and interact with objects and people in historically inspired

---

D. Šosvald and L. Kolek—Contributed equally.

© The Author(s), under exclusive license to Springer Nature Switzerland AG 2026
S. Bakkes et al. (Eds.): GALA 2025, LNCS 16307, pp. 303–312, 2026.
https://doi.org/10.1007/978-3-032-11043-5_29

settings, such applications offer significant potential in the museum context. Drawing on the contact hypothesis, which suggests that even virtual contact can reduce prejudice and improve attitudes towards outgroup members, we present a methodological framework and a pilot study focused on the topic of migration, developed and tested in collaboration with the Le Bois du Cazier museum in Belgium. Our goal is to determine whether narrative VR games can truly support the educational missions of museums, especially in terms of influencing visitors' attitudes towards the topics that they depict.

2   Theory

2.1   Implicit and Explicit Attitudes and Attitude Change

Attitudes are summary evaluations that guide decision-making by simplifying complex information processing [20]. According to the Associative-Propositional Evaluation (APE) model [7], attitudes are shaped by two distinct processes, associative (implicit) and propositional (explicit). Implicit attitudes are activated from learned associations, without regard for their validity (how logically sound they are judged to be). In contrast, explicit attitudes result from deliberate reasoning that takes the perceived validity and structure of beliefs into account.

Because implicit and explicit attitudes stem from different processes, their mechanisms of change also differ. Implicit attitudes change through shifts in associative strength, most often via evaluative conditioning, which works by repeatedly pairing a conditioned (neutral) stimulus with unconditioned stimuli of positive or negative valence. With enough observed pairings, the valence of the unconditioned stimuli transfers to the conditioned stimulus [7]. Explicit attitudes may be subject to change when new information challenges existing beliefs, prompting a reassessment of their perceived validity [8].

2.2   Attitude Components and Perspective-Taking

Attitudes are shaped by various responses, including affective, cognitive, and behaviour ones [2]. Perspective-taking influences attitudes through affective mechanisms like parallel and reactive empathy, which foster empathic concern and impact explicit attitudes, and cognitive mechanisms such as shifts in attributional thinking and self-outgroup merging, which enhance explicit and implicit intergroup evaluations. Existing research suggests that perspective-taking influences affective responses more than cognitive or behaviour ones [18]. Our prior research [11] provided partial support for the idea that the affective component of an attitude is more affected by a perspective-taking intervention than cognitive and behaviour components, but this area still lacks sufficient empirical evidence, especially in the context of virtual reality.

2.3   Virtual Reality and Attitude Change

Although narrative video games can influence attitudes, existing meta-analyses have excluded studies using virtual reality (VR) games [10], leaving a gap in understanding its effectiveness. To address this, we adapted the methodology from Kolek et al. to include VR and screened Scopus for empirical studies on narrative VR games targeting attitudes or educational outcomes.[1]

The initial search yielded 120 results. We excluded studies lacking control groups, not using VR experimentally, or not involving interactive VR games focused on attitudes or education. Additional exploratory searches across Web of Science, Google Scholar, and APA databases brought the total to 15 studies, with nine identified through the Scopus search that met all inclusion criteria and six additional studies found through our exploratory search. While the identified studies addressed a wide range of topics, we focus on those examining social attitudes towards marginalized groups, specifically in relation to ethnicity, disability, and migration, given their relevance to our study on migration and refugees.

Two reviews explored the impact of VR on attitudes, showing promising effects, but without focusing on VR games. One found VR to promote altruism, reduce prejudice, and improve health behaviour [16]. The other showed VR to be more effective than non-immersive media in changing social attitudes [14].

Four empirical studies focused on social attitudes concerning immigrant, Black individuals, and persons with disabilities. A game on migration improved explicit attitudes when players embodied an outgroup avatar [4]. Another found that interacting with Black non-playable characters improved explicit but not implicit attitudes [3]. A 2024 study testing cooperative VR play to reduce bias against Black individuals reported improved explicit attitudes in one study, while the second lacked a pretest [17]. Another study found that immersive VR controls enhanced implicit attitude change and recall in disability education compared to a non-immersive version [5]. Overall, some studies support VR games' potential to improve explicit and implicit attitudes, but more research is needed, especially with proper control conditions unrelated to the intervention topic.

2.4 Contact Hypothesis

The contact hypothesis posits that intergroup prejudice can be reduced through equal-status contact in the pursuit of shared goals [1]. Meta-analyses support this, especially for rigorously designed studies [15]. Positive contact with immigrants has been linked to improved intergroup relations [19], with large-scale evidence confirming its relevance across diverse groups [12]. Studies focused on video games show that they can foster attitude change through virtual intergroup contact. One study found that higher-quality in-game contact with minorities improved explicit attitudes [13]. Another using *A Path Out* reduced explicit prejudice towards Syrian refugees [6] compared to a control game, but not implicit prejudice. VR-based parasocial contact shows similar results, as discussed in the previous paragraph [3,17].

---

[1] Search query used: TITLE-ABS-KEY ((attitude* OR stereotype*) AND (game*) AND (change OR effect OR significant* OR impact) AND (experiment* OR empirical* OR intervention) AND ("virtual reality" OR vr)).

3   Pilot Study

We have identified a research gap concerning whether narrative VR games in a museum setting influence players' attitudes towards the topics they depict. To address it, we compare a VR intervention with an active control condition (a non-VR game that does not depict the attitude topic) to filter out the general effects of video game playing. Further, we examine the effects on affective, cognitive, and behaviour components of attitudes. We have formulated the following hypotheses (those about implicit attitudes were excluded due to a technical error that prevented proper data collection).

Hypothesis 1 (H1). Participants in the experimental group will exhibit significantly greater positive change in explicit attitudes towards refugees following the intervention, compared to participants in the control group.

We expect H1 to hold, as it stems from the contact hypothesis and prior research showing that narrative video games can foster perspective-taking and improve explicit attitudes through virtual contact with outgroup members.

Hypothesis 2 (H2). The affective items of the explicit attitudes measurement will be more positively affected by the intervention in the experimental group than cognitive and behaviour items, compared to the control group.

Hypothesis 2 builds on our previous (non-VR) study [11] which showed that perspective-taking interventions had a strong effect on the affective component of explicit attitudes, an effect likely amplified by the immersive nature of VR.

4   Methodology

4.1   Participants

The participants of the study were 50 young adults recruited during March 2025 among the visitors of the museum of Le Bois du Cazier in Belgium. We used a quasi-experimental design, with participants sequentially assigned to experimental and control groups based on order of participation. Due to technical issues, explicit attitude data from two participants in each group, implicit attitude data from one experimental and two control participants, and one background questionnaire from the experimental group had to be excluded.

Descriptive statistics are shown in Table 1. There was no significant association between experiment group and gender, χ^2 (1, N = 49) = 0.98; p = .322. Further, there were no statistically significant differences in age, frequency of computer and smartphone use, and pretest explicit scores between the groups. There was a significant between-group difference regarding experience with VR ($d = 1.01$; $p = .001$). However, the intervention was primarily narrative in nature, and as such, it did not rely on complex mechanics or require VR expertise. Thus, differences in prior VR experience are unlikely to have had a substantial impact on the effectiveness of the intervention.

Table 1. Descriptive statistics for experimental and control group in pretest.

	Experimental group			Control group			Group Comparison				
	n	Male	Female	n	Male	Female	w	χ^2 stat		p	
Gender	24	12	12	25	9	16	0.141	0.980		.322	

	Experimental group			Control group			Group Comparison				
	n	M	SD	n	M	SD	M_{diff}	SD	d	t stat	p
Age	24	19.81	2.10	25	18.90	1.66	0.91	1.89	0.48	1.68	.097
Computer use	24	4.21	1.10	25	3.84	1.34	0.37	1.23	0.30	1.05	.301
Smartphone use	24	4.79	0.83	25	5.00	0.00	-0.21	0.58	-0.36	-1.23	.217
VR use	24	2.67	0.96	25	1.68	0.99	0.99	0.98	1.01	3.54	.001
Explicit pretest	23	18.09	7.04	23	17.48	5.08	0.61	6.14	0.10	0.34	.738

4.2   Measures

Single Category Implicit Association Test (SC-IAT). To measure implicit attitudes towards a single topic, we adopted the widely-recognised SC-IAT [9], a variant of the Implicit Association Test (IAT) which measures implicit bias in relation to two different topics. The testing procedure consists of the user sorting words to their corresponding categories, while their reaction time is measured. The difference in reaction times towards different category combinations is used to compute the implicit bias. Our categories included Positive adjectives (Just, Good, Fair, Right, Well-managed, Merciful, Moral), Negative adjectives (Wrong, Evil, Bad, Criminal, Humiliating, Unfair, Disgusting), and Refugees (Refugee, Diaspora, Movement, Fleeing, Displacement, Deportation, Relocation).

Explicit Attitude Questionnaire. Explicit attitudes towards refugees were measured using a six-question test with 5-point Likert scale, adopted from our previous study [11]. The achievable score range was from 6 up to 30 points, with higher values indicating more positive explicit attitudes towards refugees. Cronbach's alpha at both pretest ($\alpha = 0.889$) and posttest ($\alpha = 0.911$) indicated good internal consistency for the explicit measures. The questionnaire focused on the affective, cognitive, and behaviour aspects of participants' attitudes towards refugees, with the questions per category:

- **Affective:** Degree of (a) sympathy for and (b) likability of refugees (1 = Not at all, 5 = Very strongly).
- **Cognitive:** Perceived impact of refugees on (a) national values and society, and (b) national prosperity (1 = Threaten, 5 = Enrich).
- **Behaviour:** Agreement with (a) befriending or schooling with refugees; (b) accepting them as neighbours (1 = Strongly disagree, 5 = Strongly agree).

Background Demographic Questionnaire. We collected participant demographic information (age, gender) and technology use data (computer and smartphone use frequency, prior VR experience). Computer and smartphone usage frequency was rated on a 5-point scale (Never – Always), and VR experience on a 5-point scale (Never used – Used more than 10 times), coded 1-5.

4.3   Experimental Intervention

The experimental intervention involved playing the VR adventure game *Those From Below* (see Fig. 1) on the Meta Quest 3 headset. Developed by Causa Creations in collaboration with the museum Le Bois du Cazier, the game follows the lives of migrant workers in 1940 s and 1950 s Belgium, particularly those at the Le Bois du Cazier coal mine. Through narrative gameplay and perspective-taking mechanics, it presents the moments leading up to the 1956 mining disaster. The game is narrated by a son of a miner who died in the disaster. Taking on the role of a miner, the player moves through the digital world and experiences a day in the miner's life. This walkthrough is accompanied by small puzzles and VR interactions, during which the player performs simulated labour such as breaking rocks and loading carts; explores archival material and personal belongings; prepares a gift package for the miner's family; and explores the harsh working conditions of the mines and the difficult realities such as language barriers and poor housing in repurposed wartime barracks. The disaster scene, stylized to avoid psychological distress, and the symbolic signing of policy reforms conclude the experience. More details about the game can be found in this document.

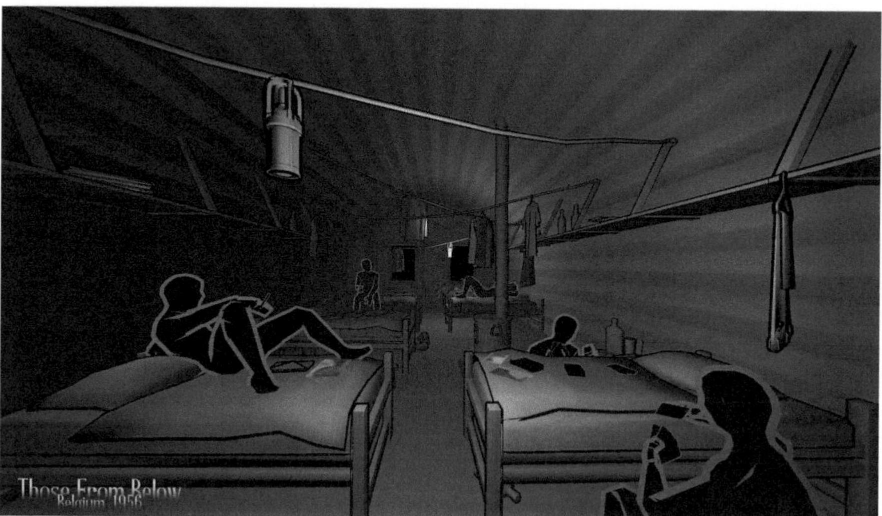

Fig. 1. The miners' living quarters, a repurposed wartime prison barrack, where the poor living conditions are depicted.

4.4   Control Intervention

The control group played the PC game *Beecarbonize*, a strategic card-based simulation with roguelike elements focused on climate change. The player takes on the role of a decision-maker balancing environmental sustainability, technological development, societal priorities, and resource management to mitigate the effects of global warming. With only peripheral references to migration, *Beecarbonize* serves as a suitable control condition for isolating the effects of a narrative VR game about refugees from the general effects of an educational video game.

4.5   Procedure

We designed a between-group experiment with an experimental and a control group, using the interventions described in previous sections. Before the intervention, we have gathered written consent from all participants. During the initial briefing, the experiment was introduced as research on the effects of multimedia in education, and the participants were informed that they will be exposed to video games. Both the experimental and the control group first took the pretest measures, including a SC-IAT, self-reported measurements using Likert scale, and a background demographic questionnaire. Demographic and explicit data were gathered using the EUSurvey platform, implicit data using our own Unity-based implementation of the SC-IAT test. All of these measures were taken on a desktop computer. After the intervention, which differed between the groups, the SC-IAT and self-reported questionnaires were repeated, and the session was concluded by debriefing. Both of the interventions took 15–20 minutes and the participants were instructed to free play, meaning no specific tasks were given.

5   Results

5.1   Data Analysis

Independent samples *t*-tests were used to examine potential group differences in baseline variables, including age, computer and smartphone use frequency, experiences with virtual reality, and pretest scores. Gender distribution between groups was assessed using a chi-square test of independence. To assess the impact of the intervention, we calculated difference scores (posttest minus pretest) for explicit attitudes towards refugees. These scores provided a direct measure of individual attitude change following the intervention. Group differences in mean change scores were analysed using independent samples *t*-tests, comparing participants exposed to *Those from Below* (experimental group) with those who played *Beecarbonize* (control group). Given the directional nature of our hypotheses, one-tailed *t*-tests were applied. Effect sizes are reported using Cohen's *d*. To test the hypothesis related to attitude components, group differences in mean change scores were calculated using the same method as for the overall explicit attitude scores, but conducted separately for the two affective, two cognitive, and two behaviour items, as described in Sect. 4.2. The results are shown in Table 2. For data availability, please see the acknowledgments.

Table 2. Pre-post changes in each group and between-group differences.

Experimental Group

	n	PRE M	PRE SD	POST M	POST SD	DIFF M	DIFF SD	d	p
Explicit	23	18.09	7.04	19.43	7.39	1.35	1.97	0.68	.002
Explicit aff.	23	6.52	2.39	6.74	2.40	0.22	0.42	0.52	.011
Explicit cog.	23	4.65	2.99	5.39	3.22	0.74	1.39	0.53	.009
Explicit beh.	23	6.91	2.25	7.30	2.20	0.39	0.84	0.47	.018

Control Group

	n	PRE M	PRE SD	POST M	POST SD	DIFF M	DIFF SD	d	p
Explicit	23	17.48	5.08	17.52	4.69	0.04	1.19	0.04	.431
Explicit aff.	23	6.61	1.62	6.65	1.53	0.04	0.47	0.09	.332
Explicit cog.	23	3.78	2.39	3.78	2.39	0.00	0.00	n/a	n/a
Explicit beh.	23	7.09	1.76	7.09	1.44	0.00	0.80	0.00	.500

Experimental vs. Control Comparison

	M_{diff}	SD	t stat	d	p
Explicit	1.30	1.74	2.72	0.80	.005
Explicit affective	0.17	0.45	1.31	0.39	.098
Explicit cognitive	0.74	1.04	2.55	0.75	.009
Explicit behaviour	0.39	0.83	1.62	0.48	.056

Because the scores of the cognitive component of explicit attitudes for the control group were identical before and after the intervention for every participant, there was no variation in the difference scores (SD = 0), thus neither the effect size nor the p value can be computed.

5.2 Hypotheses Evaluation

Hypothesis 1. We found a significant difference in the pre-post changes of explicit attitudes between the experimental and the control group, with a large effect size ($d = 0.80$; $p = .005$). Hypothesis 1 was supported.

Hypothesis 2. There was a significant difference in the effect size between the experimental and control group in the cognitive component ($d = 0.75$; $p = .009$). The differences for the affective and behaviour components did not reach statistical significance. Thus, Hypothesis 2 was not supported.

6 Discussion

This pilot study provides promising evidence that narrative VR games can support museums' educational missions by positively influencing explicit attitudes towards topics depicted and by reducing prejudice against outgroup members.

Participants who played *Those from Below*, a VR game that facilitates outgroup contact through perspective-taking, showed a significantly greater improvement in explicit attitudes towards refugees than a control group, aligning with prior findings on perspective-taking and the contact hypothesis. These findings, if supported by a larger study, suggest that narrative VR could drive positive social change. Still, more needs to be known about the specifics of the format in future media comparison studies. The cognitive component exhibited a large significant effect in pre-post comparisons between the experimental and control groups, which suggests that VR may influence how participants reason about outgroup members. There was also a trend within the experimental group that the affective and behaviour components improved, but this was not confirmed in the between-group comparison. Apart from small sample size (N = 50), the pilot study has several other limitations, including a lack of random participant group assignment, uneven prior VR experience, and potential participant selection bias among museum visitors. Further, technical issues prevented us from examining implicit attitude data. Despite these limitations, the experimental design proved feasible in the museum context. The insights gathered from the pilot study will help to improve the design of a planned larger-scale study. This future research will address the current limitations and provide more robust evidence on the role of VR in reducing prejudice through museum-based education.

Acknowledgments. This work has received funding from the European Union (GA no. 101061496). Views and opinions expressed are however those of the authors only and do not necessarily reflect those of the European Union or the Research Executive Agency. Neither the European Union nor the granting authority can be held responsible for them. The work was supported by the grant SVV2025260822. Human data were collected in accordance with APA ethical principles and all authors had full access to all data supporting the article. All supporting data will be shared upon request.

Disclosure of Interests. The authors have no competing interests to declare that are relevant to the content of this article.

References

1. Allport, G.W.: The Nature of Prejudice. Addison-Wesley (1954)
2. Bohner, G., Wänke, M.: Attitudes and attitude change, vol. 6 (02 2002). https://doi.org/10.4324/9781315784786
3. Breves, P.: Reducing outgroup bias through intergroup contact with non-playable video game characters in VR. Presence Teleop. Virt. **27**(3), 257–273 (2018). https://doi.org/10.1162/pres_a_00330
4. Chen, V., Ibasco, G., Leow, V., Lew, J.: The effect of VR avatar embodiment on improving attitudes and closeness toward immigrants. Front. Psychol. **12** (2021). https://doi.org/10.3389/fpsyg.2021.705574
5. Chowdhury, T.I., Shahnewaz Ferdous, S.M., Quarles, J.: VR Disability Simulation Reduces Implicit Bias Towards Persons With Disabilities. IEEE Trans. Visual. Comput. Graph. **PP**, 1–1 (2019). https://doi.org/10.1109/TVCG.2019.2958332

6. Cross, L., Atherton, G., Stiff, C.: A path out: using video games to reduce prejudice towards refugees. Behav. Sci. **15**(5) (2025). https://doi.org/10.3390/bs15050583
7. Gawronski, B., Bodenhausen, G.: Evaluative conditioning from the perspective of the associative-propositional evaluation model. Psychologia Społeczna **13**, e28024 (2018). https://doi.org/10.5964/spb.v13i3.28024
8. Gawronski, B., Brannon, S.: What Is Cognitive Consistency and Why Does It Matter?, pp. 91–116 (04 2019). https://doi.org/10.1037/0000135-005
9. Karpinski, A., Steinman, R.: The single category implicit association test as a measure of implicit social cognition. J. Pers. Soc. Psychol. **91**(1), 16–32 (2006)
10. Kolek, L., Ropovik, I., Šisler, V., van Oostendorp, H., Brom, C.: Video games and attitude change: A meta-analysis. Contemp. Educ. Psychol. **75**, 102225 (2023). https://doi.org/10.1016/j.cedpsych.2023.102225
11. Kolek, L., Šosvald, D., Flores, F., Halilovic, J.: Promoting Positive Attitudes Through Narrative-Driven Digital Heritage Games. In: Digital Heritage. The Eurographics Association (2025). https://doi.org/10.2312/dh.20253327
12. Lim, T., Neel, R., Hehman, E.: Intergroup contact is consistently associated with lower prejudice across group properties. Collabra: Psychol. **10**(1), 127426 (2024). https://doi.org/10.1525/collabra.127426
13. Mulak, A., Winiewski, M.H.: Virtual contact hypothesis: preliminary evidence for intergroup contact hypothesis in interactions with characters in video games. Cyberpsychol.: J. Psychos. Res. Cyberspace **15**(4), Article 6 (2021). https://doi.org/10.5817/CP2021-4-6
14. Nikolaou, A., Schwabe, A., Boomgaarden, H.: Changing social attitudes with virtual reality: a systematic review and meta-analysis. Ann. Int. Commun. Assoc. **46**(1), 30–61 (2022). https://doi.org/10.1080/23808985.2022.2064324
15. Pettigrew, T., Tropp, L.: A meta-analytic test of intergroup contact theory. J. Pers. Soc. Psychol. **90**, 751–783 (2006). https://doi.org/10.1037/0022-3514.90.5.751
16. Shriram, K., Oh, S.Y., Bailenson, J.: Virtual Reality and Prosocial Behavior, pp. 304–316. Cambridge University Press (2017)
17. Tassinari, M., Aulbach, M.B., Harjunen, V.J., Cocco, V.M., Vezzali, L., Jasinskaja-Lahti, I.: The effects of positive and negative intergroup contact in virtual reality on outgroup attitudes: testing the contact hypothesis and its mediators. Group Process. Intergroup Relations **27**(8), 1773–1798 (2024). https://doi.org/10.1177/13684302241237747
18. Todd, A.R., Galinsky, A.D.: Perspective-taking as a strategy for improving intergroup relations: evidence, mechanisms, and qualifications. Soc. Pers. Psychol. Compass **8**(7), 374–387 (2014). https://doi.org/10.1111/spc3.12116
19. Voci, A., Hewstone, M.: Intergroup contact and prejudice toward immigrants in Italy. Group Process. Intergroup Relations **6**(1), 37–54 (2003). https://doi.org/10.1177/1368430203006001011
20. Vogel, T., Wänke, M.: Attitudes and attitude change. Psychology Press (2016). https://doi.org/10.4324/9781315754185

Learning to Govern the Orbital Commons: A Serious Game on Incentivizing Debris Removal

Kenji Saito[1]([✉]) [iD], Shinji Hatta[2] [iD], Yasuhiro Yoshimura[3] [iD], and Toshiya Hanada[3] [iD]

[1] Graduate School of Business and Finance, Waseda University, Tokyo, Japan
`ks91@waseda.jp`
[2] MUSCAT Space Engineering Co., Ltd., Munakata, Japan
[3] Department of Aeronautics and Astronautics, Kyushu University, Fukuoka, Japan

Abstract. Active Debris Removal (ADR)—the task of extracting defunct satellites and fragments from orbit to ensure the long-term sustainability of space operations—raises a fundamental challenge of incentivization, as the effort produces global benefits but yields little direct return to individual actors. Prior work proposes a token-based reward for verified removals, yet its behavioral effects under competition, uncertainty, and limited coordination remain unexplored. We design and deploy a multiplayer serious game simulating an ADR economy with sequential investment, debris removal, and adaptive strategy. The gameplay reveals emergent behaviors such as strategic avoidance of high-value targets, informal coordination in the absence of communication protocols, and ethical tensions surrounding the removal of self-generated debris. Our findings suggest that serious games can function not only as institutional *crash-tests* but also as vehicles for public reasoning and critical reflection, offering insight into how novel governance mechanisms might succeed (or fail) when enacted by human agents.

Keywords: Serious Games · Policy Prototyping · Incentive Mechanisms · Orbital Commons Governance · Qualitative Game Analysis

1 Introduction

Orbital debris threatens the sustainability of space operations [5,8]. While active debris removal (ADR) is widely recognized as necessary, institutional and economic incentives remain underdeveloped despite technical progress [7]. This reflects a classic public goods problem [4]: benefits are shared, but costs fall on individual actors. A proposed solution is to issue digital tokens for verified debris removal, aligning private incentives with collective sustainability [11]. Yet this design remains untested in its behavioral consequences and public intelligibility.

S. Bakkes et al. (Eds.): GALA 2025, LNCS 16307, pp. 313–323, 2026.
https://doi.org/10.1007/978-3-032-11043-5_30

This paper therefore asks: *How might a token-based incentive for ADR shape strategic behavior, coordination, and ethical reasoning in a simulated orbital economy?* We frame the work as an *exploratory study,* aiming to surface emergent dynamics rather than generalizable results. To examine this, we prototype the ADR currency system through a multiplayer serious game.

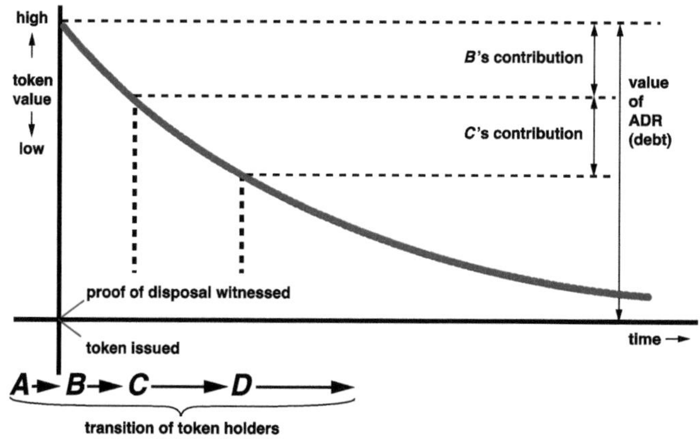

Fig. 1. Concept of the ADR currency. A is the issuer (the party that represents the space industry). The first token holder B has performed ADR. The value of the token (i.e., the value of the ADR) is the debt owed by A to B, and that debt is paid by the holders as the token circulates. (In reality, B would not like to hold the token, and would immediately spend it. Depreciation can be stepwise, such as yearly or monthly, and not as steep as shown in this diagram.)

We position serious games as dual-purpose tools: for institutional prototyping and for promoting public reasoning about complex planetary-scale challenges. This approach foregrounds qualitative inquiry as much as simulation, inviting participants not merely to play a game, but to *learn to govern* through it.

2   Background

2.1   Orbital Debris, ADR, and ADR Currency

The governance of orbital space is increasingly shaped by the problem of space debris, which poses long-term risks to satellite operations and planetary sustainability. As [13] argues, debris mitigation must be understood not only as a technical challenge, but as a pivotal element in shaping the institutional futures of the orbital commons.

Even under optimistic assumptions—no new launches, full compliance with post-mission disposal (PMD) guidelines, and no fragmentation events—modeling studies have shown that debris in low Earth orbit (LEO) continues to increase due to in-orbit collisions [8], leading to a potential cascade known as the *Kessler Syndrome* [6].

To address this, previous theoretical work [11] proposed a digital currency that rewards verifiable debris removal. Tokens are issued in proportion to estimated collision risk and depreciate over time, creating incentives for timely remediation (Fig. 1). This design, conceptualized as a form of *proof of disposal*, frames orbital debris as intergenerational debt, to be offset by present-day actions that reduce future risks.

2.2 Serious Games as Tools for Institutional Prototyping

The concept of serious games—games designed with explicit purposes beyond amusement—was first introduced as a form of structured decision-making within simplified models of reality [1]. Subsequent work formalized their application to policy contexts, enabling stakeholders to explore prospective institutional designs and anticipate unintended consequences [2]. One early example revealed systemic flaws in a proposed healthcare reform, demonstrating how such games can stress-test policies under realistic conditions.

Later studies introduced the idea of a *regulation crash-test*, in which draft policies are simulated through gameplay during the design phase [9]. This approach has shown how games can reveal hidden feedback loops, long-term effects, and design vulnerabilities that might be overlooked in conventional analysis.

This study extends these developments by applying serious game-based prototyping to the domain of orbital debris governance.

3 Game Design

To test a digital-currency incentive for ADR in practice, we developed a multiplayer serious game modeling strategic interactions among satellite operators. Implemented as a text-based system, the game resembles a tabletop role-playing game (RPG), where players describe actions in free form and the game master responds according to the rules. For example, a player may declare "I will remove the top-ranked debris," and at the end of the phase the AI game master reports whether the removal succeeded and what rewards were issued.

It reveals behavioral challenges left open by prior work—such as free-riding, coordination failures, and ambiguous reward attribution—within a simulated orbital economy. Technical challenges such as debris identification or capture of tumbling objects were abstracted to maintain playability, focusing instead on institutional dynamics.

The complete game rule script[1] is provided in the Appendix (Fig. 3). In brief, the game is turn-based (1 turn = 1 year) and follows six phases illustrated in Fig. 2. Players trade, operate, and remove debris using assets in USD and ADR tokens, with rewards for verified removals. ADR tokens depreciate each turn (Gesell-style demurrage [3]), creating time-sensitive incentives.

---

[1] The game script and the game log throughout this paper are originally in Japanese, and translated into English.

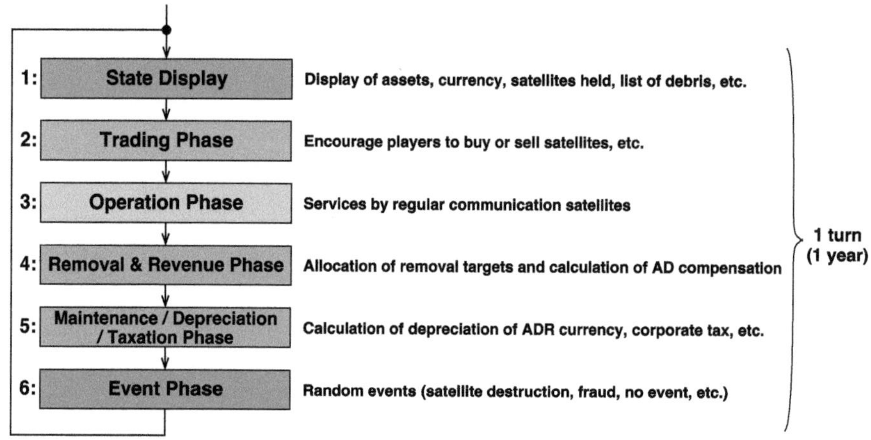

Fig. 2. Six phases in one turn (one year) in the ADR serious game.

4   Game Deployment

The game rule script can be played simply by providing it as a prompt to text-based generative AIs such as ChatGPT, Gemini, or Claude[2]. However, if one wishes to play alongside other human participants, a multi-user chat system (such as a chatbot on Discord) is required. Table 1 shows the availability of the game.

Table 1. Availability of the game. The GPT version is intended for single users; for multiplayer, one must use a system such as the Discord bot shown in this table. Though written in Japanese, one should be able to play the game in English as well.

Title	Type	URL
ADR Game	GPT	https://chatgpt.com/g/g-uKMdRDCBV-adrkemu
ADR (Active Debris Removal) Game	GitHub	https://github.com/ks91/adr-game
GPT Discord Bot *(our fork)*	GitHub	https://github.com/ks91/gpt-discord-bot

5   Observations and Findings

This study analyzes a single playthrough spanning 10 in-game years, conducted on a Discord thread with multiple human players and facilitated by an AI game

---

[2] Claude may start generating code for the game, which would undermine the flexibility of the game. To avoid this, your message to the generative AI should be like "Let's play without generating code for the game.".

master (GPT-4o[3] instructed by the game rule script), which managed turns and outputs in response to player inputs (all in text), using the Discord bot listed in Table 1.

Four human players (Table 2) participated as independent debris removal service providers. All players were also involved in the rule design process. Rather than viewing this as a limitation, we employ this as *reflection-in-action* methodology [12], where domain experts generate insights by critically examining institutional mechanisms while enacting them.

Table 2. Four human players.

Pseudonym	Disciplinary background
Player A	Aerospace Engineering
Player B	Aerospace Engineering
Player C	Space Industry Executive
Player D	Computer Science

5.1   Emergent Behavioral Patterns and Issues

Based on player utterances in the in-game chat log and video recording, several behavioral patterns and associated issues were identified through SCAT (Steps for Coding and Theorization) analysis [10]. Participants repeatedly verbalized the gap between theoretical rules and actual gameplay, which we rephrased, explained, and coded into emerging themes.

Competition Avoidance. When the possibility of overlap with other players arose, participants began to avoid targeting high-ranking debris (Table 3). This behavior reflects a questioning of strategic assumptions embedded in the reward structure. In the absence of explicit coordination mechanisms, players engaged in implicit coordination to reduce conflict risk and, at times, responded to perverse incentives by deliberately avoiding first place.

Immediate Consumption of ADR Tokens. The player who most effectively spent the AD (ADR tokens) earned through debris removal accumulated the greatest assets. Table 4 highlights how decaying token value induces time-sensitive spending behavior, demonstrating how institutional incentive design can shape player strategies under temporal pressure.

---

[3] This exhibited fidelity issues (e.g., skipping phases), but these are likely due to the language model itself. Preliminary trials with GPT-5 suggest that such problems are largely resolved. Since such issues can be corrected on the fly by asking the AI game master again, they do not pose a fundamental problem for this study anyway.

Table 3. Competition avoidance—steps for coding.

⟨1⟩Phrase	⟨2⟩Rephrasing	⟨3⟩Explanation	⟨4⟩Emerging theme
D: What is the reason why you all don't necessarily remove the higher-level debris? (Turn 2)	Why avoid high-value debris?	Recognition of unexpected player behavior contradicting reward- maximizing strategy	Questioning of strategic assumptions
C: Since Player D succeeded in removal and I failed, this essentially becomes an incentive not to aim for first place on purpose (Turn 2)	It's safer not to aim for top targets	Recognition that success by others imposes a cost on risk-takers; strategic behavior shaped by failure probability and zero-sum reward attribution	Perverse incentive under ambiguous competition rules
B: I will remove 2 debris that do not overlap with those targeted by other players (Turn 5)	I want to avoid conflict (I don't want to waste my effort)	Risk-averse behavior aimed at avoiding failure in the absence of explicit rules	Implicit coordination
D: As a strategy, that makes sense. We probably should have a rule—something like making declarations (Turn 5)	Maybe we need declaration rules	Recognition of structural ambiguity; call for procedural mechanisms to reduce coordination cost	Need for explicit coordination

Table 4. Immediate consumption—steps for coding.

⟨1⟩Phrase	⟨2⟩Rephrasing	⟨3⟩Explanation	⟨4⟩Emerging theme
A: I'll buy as many satellites as I can using ADR tokens (Turn 4)	I want to make the most of my available AD and avoid spending USD	Loss-averse, time-sensitive behavior in demurrage currency	Time-sensitive spending behavior under decaying token value

Self-Debris Removal. After a fragmentation event caused their own satellites to become debris, Player C chose to remove them. Table 5 reveals institutional contradictions regarding self-caused actions, where ethical behavior—such as cleaning up one's own debris—faces misaligned incentives and occurs only when explicitly rewarded.

This prompted suggestions for penalties (e.g., reduction in USD assets). Although ethically appropriate, self-debris removal risks becoming a profit opportunity, raising concerns about systemic fairness.

Table 5. Institutional contradiction—steps for coding.

⟨1⟩Phrase	⟨2⟩Rephrasing	⟨3⟩Explanation	⟨4⟩Emerging theme
C: I'll remove my 2 debris items using 2 removal satellites, and attempt to remove the top 3 ranked debris with the other 3 (Turn 10)	I'm cleaning up my own mess first	Tension between ethical responsibility and economic opportunity; self-generated externalities become a source of private gain	Institutional contradiction regarding self-caused actions
C: Getting more AD from removing your own debris… well, if your AD doesn't increase, you won't even try to remove it (Turn 10)	No gain, no cleanup	Institutional logic discourages ethical behavior without incentives; misaligning public good and private reward	Misaligned incentives for ethical behavior

Table 6. Research and educational nature—steps for coding.

⟨1⟩Phrase	⟨2⟩Rephrasing	⟨3⟩Explanation	⟨4⟩Emerging theme
D: Understanding those small details is the research value of trying out this game. Probably these conversations are important (Turn 2)	Reflective discussion adds research value	Recognition that experiential engagement and dialogic reflection generate insights that formal models may overlook	Serious games as platforms for situated learning and collaborative inquiry
D: I feel like I got a bit of a sense of what the satellite business might be like (After game)	I gained an intuitive feel for real-world space industry	Transfer of simulated experience into real-world conceptual understanding	Informal learning through embodied simulation

5.2   Post-Game Reflection

Research and Educational Nature of The Game. Table 6 shows how games can function as platforms for situated learning and collaborative inquiry. Through in-game experience and dialogue, participants developed research insights and intuitive understandings of the otherwise abstract domain of insti-

Table 7. Ethical reconstruction—steps for coding.

⟨1⟩Key words	⟨2⟩Rephrasing	⟨3⟩Explanation	⟨4⟩Emerging theme
Aluminum, ozone, evaporation, reentry, air pollution	Removal ≠ inherently good – it's not a simple equation	ADR so far does not incorporate the *environmental impacts after removal* into its design	Institutional blind spots toward less visible externalities
Resource recovery, on-orbit processing, reactivation, robotics	From *discarding* to *utilizing*	ADR should aim not only to remove risk but also to utilize resources	Emerging ideas for linking ADR institutions to the circular economy
Profit-making, launching recklessly, actually rare that debris removal proceeds smoothly	Is the system prioritizing short-term profits?	The system is designed to prioritize *scores and profits* over *sustainability*	Ethical reexamination of growth-oriented assumptions underlying the system

tutional and space system design. This highlights the game's potential not only as a prototyping tool, but also as a medium for embodied and informal learning.

Critique of Growth Models and Ethical Reconstruction of Institutions.
After the game, participants raised concerns about how PMD and ADR result in atmospheric reentry of satellites and aluminum release, highlighting institutional blind spots toward less visible externalities. They questioned whether resource recovery should be institutionalized as an alternative (Table 7).

The game began to shift from a mechanism for debris reduction to a platform for ethical reexamination of growth-oriented assumptions and imagining links between ADR and circular economy principles. In doing so, it served not only to test the institution, but to interrogate its underlying values.

6   Limitations

This study is exploratory in nature, and its findings are not generalizable. Several limitations qualify the results. First, the participant pool was small, consisting of only four players, which restricts the generalizability of the results. We emphasize, however, that the study was conceived as exploratory, with the aim of surfacing emergent dynamics rather than producing statistically representative outcomes.

Second, all four participants were also involved in the design of the game rules. This dual role may have introduced biases, such as a reduced likelihood of questioning underlying assumptions or a tendency to adapt quickly to the mechanics. While reflection-in-action provided valuable insights, future studies should recruit participants who are not directly connected to the rule design.

Finally, the study was based on a single playthrough of ten in-game years. Although rich in qualitative detail, a single session cannot reach data saturation, and additional playthroughs with diverse participants are needed to test the robustness of the observed patterns.

7   Discussion and Conclusion

This study used a serious game to prototype and critique a token-based incentive mechanism for active debris removal (ADR). Through a ten-in-game-year multiplayer session, we observed strategic behaviors shaped not only by the ADR token system but also by institutional ambiguities. Players avoided high-value targets due to competition risk, coordinated implicitly without formal rules, and at times (though unintentionally) exploited self-generated debris for private gain.

These behaviors reveal that monetary incentives alone are insufficient; procedural elements such as target declaration, transparency, and normative alignment are equally crucial. The use of a demurrage currency induced time-sensitive spending, while ethical dilemmas emerged around reward structures and unintended incentives. Such findings underscore the importance of integrating behavioral insight into the institutional design of ADR.

Beyond testing a mechanism, the game also served as a space for public reasoning. Participants reflected on the sustainability of current models, questioned growth-oriented assumptions, and imagined alternatives such as on-orbit resource recovery and circular economy principles. The game fostered intuitive understanding of orbital governance and exposed normative tensions not visible in static models. Even for non-experts, it offered educational value—for instance, Player D, a computer scientist, reported gaining an intuitive sense of the satellite business, suggesting relevance for students and policymakers.

Overall, this study demonstrates that serious games can function as both institutional crash-tests and platforms for ethical reflection. By enabling participants to enact and interrogate policy mechanisms, such games help bridge the gap between theoretical design and social complexity. In the case of orbital commons governance, they provide a way not only to simulate incentive structures, but also to question the values embedded within them.

Acknowledgments. We thank the developers of the Discord chatbot: Yuki Matsutani, Shiori Ueda, Jonah Egashira, and emeritus professor Naohito Okude (the first author of this work has also taken part in the development of the software).

Appendix

The full gameplay rules are detailed in Fig. 3, which serves as self-contained references defining the core mechanics and constraints. When used with an LLM,

[Serious Game for Space Debris Removal – Definitive Rule Script]

1. Turn-Based System

   - The game progresses in discrete turns (1 turn = 1 year).
   - Each turn consists of 1) State Display, 2) Trading Phase, 3) Operation Phase, 4) Removal & Revenue Phase, 5) Maintenance/Depreciation/Taxation Phase, and 6) Event Phase.
   - After each phase from the Trading Phase onward, a summary table of the players' and the market's state is displayed.
   - Before the game begins, the user specifies the number of players and their names, as well as the number of NPCs (Non-Player Characters). NPC names are generated automatically.

2. Player Assets and Currencies

   - Currencies used: USD (Fiat currency) and AD (ADR Currency, with demurrage).
   - ADR currency is issued only as a reward for debris removal. No other supply mechanism exists.
   - Initial USD balance: 200,000,000 per player.
   - Initial total assets: communication and debris removal satellites equivalent to USD 640,000,000.

3. Asset Prices and Maintenance Costs

   - Communication Satellite: USD 40,000,000 (maintenance: 2% per turn (USD 800,000))
   - Removal Satellite: USD 320,000,000 (maintenance: 2% per turn (USD 6,400,000))

4. Service Generation

   - Each communication satellite generates 1 unit of satellite service (sellable at USD 8,000,000).
   - Each removal satellite generates 1 unit of debris removal service (1 debris removed per turn).

5. Revenue from Debris Removal

   - Each use of a removal service yields an average of 80,000,000 AD, which is 25% of the cost of a removal satellite.

6. Removal & Revenue Phase Procedure

   - At the beginning of this phase, the current top 10 debris ranked by removal value are displayed.
   - Each player declares the number of removal services they will use that turn.
   - Once all declarations are made, debris are randomly assigned to removal actions.
   - Removed debris are eliminated from the market, and AD currency is issued accordingly.
   - After removal processing, the updated top 10 debris list is shown, reflecting the removal and shift-up from the long tail distribution (see Section 10).

7. AD Currency Demurrage

   - Each turn, AD currency depreciates by 2% (Gesell-style demurrage).

8. Corporate Tax Rule

   - At each turn's end, 20% of any USD gain is taxed.

9. Debt and Interest Rule

   - If a player's USD balance goes negative, it is treated as a loan.
   - Next turn, 4% interest is applied in the Maintenance/Depreciation/Taxation Phase.

10. Debris

   - Debris is managed by the market, but when a satellite is destroyed, the resulting debris is attributed to the corresponding player and tracked as a private asset.
   - Each player's personal debris holdings are displayed at every turn.
   - Immediately after the game begins, following the initial player and market setup, a ranked list displaying the removal value of 200 pieces of debris is shown.
   - The total removal value across all debris is 1,600,000,000 AD, following a long-tail distribution.

11. Random Events

   - Each turn includes one randomly selected event from the following list:
     - Satellite reaches end of life and PMD fails → 1 debris added
     - Micro-debris collision → 1 randomly selected satellite is destroyed (1 debris added)
     - Fragmentation event → 1 satellite destroyed and 3 debris added
     - Investment fraud → 10% of each player's assets disappear
     - Labor strike → Random player's satellites become non-operational for 1 turn
     - Quiet turn → No event occurs

12. Victory / Progression Conditions (Extensible)

   - The game is exploratory in nature. Goals may include reducing the global debris population, and observing whether ADR currency circulation can be sustained.

Fig. 3. ADR game full script.

the script should be accompanied by a short initiating prompt (e.g., "Let's play.")
to ensure that the session begins as a game rather than as a document analysis.

References

1. Abt, C.C.: Serious Games. Viking Press, New York (1970)
2. Duke, R.D., Geurts, J.A.M.: Policy Games for Strategic Management: Pathways into the Unknown. Dutch University Press, Amsterdam (2004)
3. Gesell, S.: The Natural Economic Order. Free Economy Publishing Company, London (1916). Translated by Philip Pye
4. Hardin, G.: The tragedy of the commons. Science **162** (1968)
5. Johnson, N., Krisko, P., Liou, J.C., Anz-Meador, P.: NASA's new breakup model of EVOLVE 4.0. Adv. Space Res. **28**(9) (2001)
6. Kessler, D.J., Cour-Palais, B.G.: Collision frequency of artificial satellites: the creation of a debris belt. J. Geophy. Res. **83**(A6) (June 1978)
7. Ledkov, A., Aslanov, V.: Review of contact and contactless active space debris removal approaches. Prog. Aerosp. Sci. **134** (2022). https://doi.org/10.1016/j.paerosci.2022.100858
8. Liou, J.C., et al.: Stability of the Future LEO Environment - An IADC Comparison Study. In: Proceedings of the 6th European Conference on Space Debris (2013)
9. Olejniczak, K., Wolański, M., Widawski, I.: Regulation crash-test: applying serious games to policy design. Policy Design Pract. **1**(3), 194–214 (2018). https://doi.org/10.1080/25741292.2018.1504372
10. Otani, T.: SCAT: steps for coding and theorization. J. Japan Soc. Kansei Eng. **10**(3), 155–160 (2011). https://doi.org/10.5057/kansei.10.3_155
11. Saito, K., Hatta, S., Hanada, T.: Digital currency design for sustainable active debris removal in space. IEEE Trans. Comput. Soc. Syst. **6**(1), 127–134 (2019). https://doi.org/10.1109/TCSS.2018.2890655
12. Schön, D.A.: The Reflective Practitioner: How Professionals Think in Action. Basic Books, New York (1983)
13. Yap, X.S., et al.: Four alternative scenarios of commons in space: prospects and challenges. Int. J. Commons (2023). https://doi.org/10.5334/ijc.1272

A Serious Gaming Schematic Design for Efficient and Application-Specific Chatbot Validation on the Example of Air Traffic Control

Dagh Zeppenfeld(✉) and Sebastian Schier-Morgenthal

German Aerospace Center (DLR), Lilienthalplatz, 738108 Braunschweig, Germany
`dagh.zeppenfeld@dlr.de`

Abstract. The prevalence of chatbot systems is on the rise globally. However, it remains challenging to conduct a comprehensive evaluation of their use cases outside of the domain of so-called service chatbots. This is particularly evident in the context of air traffic control, where safety concerns necessitate a high degree of reliability and accuracy. In this domain, the validation of a chatbot solely based on its performance is impractical and difficult to execute, given the limitations of current large language model technologies, which lack deterministic behavior. To address this challenge, this study proposes a novel approach to validate air traffic control chatbots through the use of serious gaming. By simplifying the real-world scenario, serious gaming offers cost-effective and safe means of testing unproven designs without the need for operational experts. To this end, a methodology integrating standard chatbot evaluation strategies with the european operational concept validation methodology is developed. This methodology was applied to assess the quality of a chatbot that assumes the role of a tower controller. It was found that a chatbot system could be validated with reduced effort using serious gaming. A total of 107 students took part in three distinct studies. The air traffic control chatbot was usable, achieving an above-average system usability score of 85 of 100 when tested with the latest version of the game designed for the proposed validation environment.

Keywords: Chatbot Validation Environment · Serious Gaming · Air Traffic Control

1 Motivation

In recent years, chatbots have been applied to various fields, such as customer service, where they are now a common feature in many industries [13]. Through the implementation of such chatbots, companies can streamline the delivery of information, reducing waiting times and costs simultaneously [11].

The development of the transformer neural network architecture [15] has enabled the implementation of much more competent large language models

S. Bakkes et al. (Eds.): GALA 2025, LNCS 16307, pp. 324–333, 2026.
https://doi.org/10.1007/978-3-032-11043-5_31

(LLMs). These models can now be used to develop advanced chatbots for the use in expert systems. A potential field of application is air traffic control (ATC), which is a highly specialized field based on airspace structures (e.g. waypoints, airways and sectors) and air traffic data (e.g. aircraft callsign, position and trajectory). The procedures to handle this system and coordinate with other air traffic controllers (ATCOs) require extensive training and education.

Current research aims on introducing automation like the digital ATCO [7] or a fully automated ground air traffic management [9]. However, an interface between the automation and human ATCO is needed, and chatbots are one technical possibility for providing a quick and natural information exchange. To realize this potential, a validation approach is required that proves the feasibility of chatbots in ATC. This work evaluates the principle of serious gaming to validate ATC chatbots and applies the developed validation environment (VE) to a specific chatbot assuming the role of a digital tower controller.

2   Existing Literature

Prior work has already been conducted on the development of expert chatbots for tasks within the air traffic system [12]. In order to identify whether a schematic design for a chatbot VE already exists, the existing work in this field was systematically reviewed in preparation of this work. The keywords "chatbot", "assessment", "evaluation" and "air traffic control" were applied within the survey. In total twenty papers were evaluated, with four deemed especially relevant for this work, as they address common chatbot validation practices. A brief summary of the most important findings will be provided below.

The evaluation of a chatbot can generally be divided into five different perspectives: user experience, information retrieval, linguistic, technology and business [10]. Peras proposed a chatbot evaluation framework based on these, where the perspectives themselves are again divided into 14 categories in total [10]. For each category there are suggested attributes and metrics. Furthermore, the metrics are classified into qualitative and quantitative measurements. Peras makes clear, that the evaluation process must be aligned to the field of chatbot application. In consequence, it is not always necessary to evaluate all five perspectives.

In a subsequent study, Casas et al. conducted a comprehensive review of a paper collection, with a particular focus on the usability attribute of chatbots [4]. The usability concept defined in ISO 9214 was employed, which distinguishes between effectiveness, efficiency and satisfaction of a system. The study's findings indicate that, when evaluating chatbots, only one of the three aforementioned methods is often employed, with efficiency being the most prevalent. However, this is merely a popular observation and not a rating in any sense.

Additionally, in 2020, research was conducted on the evaluation of airline service chatbots [14]. The research, while situated within the broader domain of aeronautics, is specifically focused on end-user chatbots. Nevertheless, insights regarding the assessment of chatbots via questionnaires are still highly relevant. It is demonstrated that an extensive range of question types, addressing diverse topics, can be employed. Examples of these include yes/no, multiple-choice, and Likert-scale questions. To ensure reliable results, the psychometric properties and internal consistency of the questionnaires must be assessed and evaluated.

Another work on service chatbots examines the most prevalent evaluation metrics utilized, given the absence of a definite standard [13]. Following the assessment of 25 distinct metrics, the paper identifies the accuracy, precision, recall, F1-score (which is given by the harmonic mean of precision and recall), and human evaluation as the most significant metrics. The chatbot VE follows this selection of metrics, but the terms objective and subjective measures are used, with a clear distinction being drawn between them. While objective measures provide unaffected values, subjective measures enable the consideration of human perception (e.g. helpfulness, appropriateness, and naturalness of the conversations). The chatbot VE will consider both objective and subjective measures to benefit from each strengths.

Additionally, there have been made efforts to harmonize air traffic management (ATM) concept validation. As Borkenhagen [1] outlines, changes to ATM systems affect five key reference points: capacity, safety, environment, economy, and operability. These reference points are based on the european operational concept validation methodology (E-OCVM) as published by EUROCONTROL [5]. A new ATM system should only be considered an improvement over the current state of the art if a systematic assessment across all reference points yields a net positive outcome. Moreover, a robust concept validation methodology must ensure transparency [1]. To support transparency and reproducibility, all evaluation scenarios and underlying assumptions should be publicly available and easily accessible.

3   Methodology

This chapter presents a scheme for the validation of chatbots in the ATC context. In order to achieve this, the methods and metrics typically employed for the validation of chatbots must be aligned with EUROCONTROL's five desired fields of enhancement. As none of the aforementioned fields can be assessed without validating the chatbot in practice, it is necessary to identify an appropriate VE. The deployment of the chatbot in operational ATC is precluded by the existence of numerous unsolvable safety considerations. Consequently, the conventional method of validating new ATC systems is to simulate real-world conditions with ATC experts and tools, specifically, in human-in-the-loop (HITL) simulations. Here, a new chatbot would be integrated and subjected to an extensive validation.

The primary drawback of a HITL based VE is the necessity of including ATC experts. Usually these ATC experts are required to own or having owned an ATCO license. Currently, the availability of ATCOs is reduced due to staff shortages in ATC [6].

In this paper we suggest to separate distinct design indicators and initially validate ATC chatbots using serious gaming. Serious gaming allows to prove the usability end efficiency of use without modelling complex and detailed air traffic systems. In consequence participants do not necessarily require full operational expertise to handle the system, which allows the use of students. The gaming session can be concentrated on the general working principles which shall be evaluated.

The following section presents a module overview defining the necessary functionalities for a chatbot VE using serious gaming, specifically adapted for utilization in ATC. In the subsequent step, the evaluation setup is explained in detail. Finally, the definition of chatbot evaluation metrics, which are necessary for validation in accordance with the E-OCVM framework, is provided.

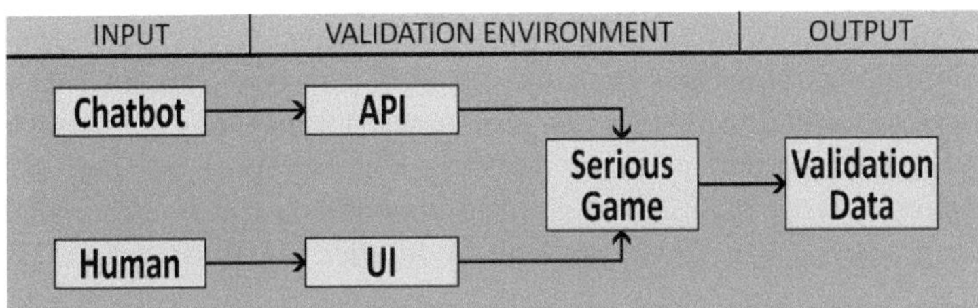

Fig. 1. Module Overview.

3.1 Module Overview

The validation modules can be divided into three categories, as illustrated in Fig. 1. The first category identifies the two main actors: the chatbot that is going to be validated and a human counterpart. These are the inputs into the VE itself. The second category comprises an arbitrary, but situationally fitting, serious game. This serves as the core of this category. While the chatbot is connected to it with a well-defined application programming interface (API), the human interacts with the game over some user interface (UI). The UI must be designed in a way that it does not hinder the validation of the chatbot itself. When selecting a serious game for this validation process, it is essential to carefully consider the desired complexity. If the situations are oversimplified, the results may be misleading. Conversely, if no simplification occurs, the benefit of a validation with serious games may be unexploited. While playing the serious game, it is crucial to collect and save the necessary validation data. As illustrated in Fig. 1, this singular output module represents the output of the system. A definition of the necessary metrics is provided below.

3.2 Experimental Setup

This section presents a specific and already proven experimental setup, which is depicted in Fig. 2 as an activity diagram. The trial should be executed with multiple human subjects, with the specific minimum number to be evaluated based on the given context. At the beginning of a trial run, it is essential that the subjects are introduced to the serious game, its objectives and the tasks they are expected to perform. The acquired knowledge should be reinforced through the help of a training round, with the option to utilize a standardized, pre-recorded video for this purpose.

After completion of the introduction and training round, subjects should be engaged in the serious game for a specified duration or number of rounds. A trial period that is too brief will prevent the evaluation of potential learning effects on subjects from being useful. If the trial is excessively lengthy, the subjects may become bored, the data points may become repetitive, and the costs may be unnecessarily high. This work proposes a total trial run duration of one hour as a rough guideline. One-half of the allotted time is designated for the provision of an explanation, a training round, and a debriefing.

The debriefing represents the final stage of the trial run. In this instance, the subjects are asked to respond to predefined surveys, engage in an interview conducted by the examiner, or otherwise provide a report on their experience. The selection of an appropriate setup also depends on the specific metrics to be measured in a given VE. This topic will be further discussed below.

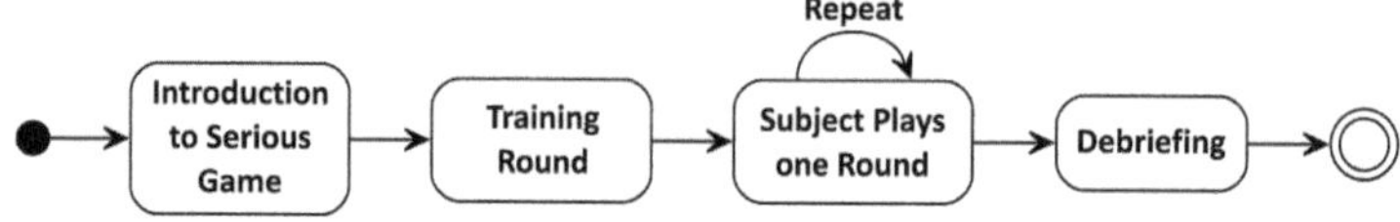

Fig. 2. Experimental setup, visualized as activity diagram.

3.3   Definition of Metrics

This section identifies appropriate validation areas for the five E-OCVM enhancement areas. Possible metrics are identified for each of the areas. Subsequent studies may use these as a guideline of possibilities, but are not required to use all of them, nor are they limited to them. Table 1 provides an overview of the areas and also metrics.

Table 1. Overview: Evaluation Metrics.

E-OCVM	Validation Area	Possible Metrics
Capacity	Game Performance	Time per decision, Quality of decisions
Safety	Game Performance, Chats	Security relevant failures, Precision, Accuracy, F1-score
Operability	Debriefing, Chats	SUS-Score, Precision, Accuracy, F1-score

Capacity enhancements cannot be measured directly in a gaming environment as it models a very simplified air traffic system. Nevertheless, the usage of a chatbot is expected to enhance the decision making process. As such the capacity of the ATCO should be increased in a way that decisions are taken faster or better decisions are taken.

The safety domain can also be measured by looking at the performance of the game. When simplifying the real-world use case into a serious game, at least one safety-relevant factor must be maintained. For example, this could be two aircraft getting in too close distance. After the trial, it can be evaluated, how many of these situations occurred. This quantitative measure can be used without a reference point, since none of these situations should occur. Additionally, an evaluation of historical chats can provide insights into the chatbots' capacity to comprehend human language within the context of the serious game. The evaluation of this metric is dependent upon the accurate classification of messages as either "understood" or "misunderstood". Precision, recall, and F1 score can be utilized to express this numerically. A worse score indicates a greater frequency of misunderstandings, which can result in safety-critical situations.

With the help of an appropriate serious game, a detailed analysis of the operability of the new system can be performed. A quantitative analysis of precision, recall, and F1 score can be conducted, analogous to the safety domain. In this context, the occurrence of misunderstandings at a higher frequency has the potential to induce frustration and dissatisfaction among human users. This is also directly related to the accessibility category defined by Peras, which means the ability to recognize meaning and intent in natural language [10]. The usability of a system can be further assessed by using a structured questionnaire during the debriefing. This can be done using the system usability score (SUS) [2].

The remaining two reference points, the environmental and economic impact of using the chatbot operationally, cannot be examined in detail using the evaluation metrics introduced by the VE. Further work could consider to define specific metrics for these reference points. For instance, in the context of a serious game simulating the management of runway operations at an airport by a human-chatbot team, the amount of fuel consumed by airplanes could serve as an indicator of the environmental impact of the team's performance. The feasibility of such metrics is dependent on the specific serious game and its goals.

4   Results

In the following section the developed VE is used to exemplary validate a tower control chatbot. First it is shown how the methodology was applied to the specific chatbot, then results of three conducted studies are given.

4.1   Applying the VE to a Tower Control Chatbot

Given a chatbot that acts as a digital controller for managing departures, a serious game was developed and connected via an API to the chatbot [8]. The chatbot is fully responsible for departing flights and is taking decisions autonomously.

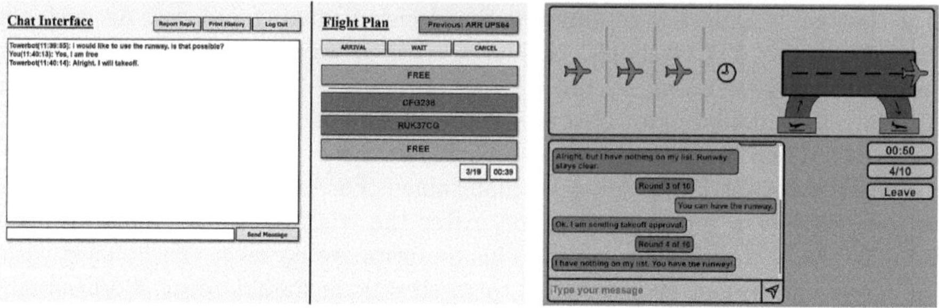

Fig. 3. The screenshots illustrate two distinct UI variants for the applied serious game. A text-based approach is given by the left UI as it was used in the study of Mutz et al. [8]. In contrast, Zeppenfeld (unpublished) used the UI given on the right which incorporates more graphical elements, animations and sounds. In a third study by Weber [16] the graphical UI was modified by adding a name and picture to the chatbot.

Together with a human player, who manages arrivals, the human-chatbot team must cooperatively try to achieve safe and efficient runway operations.

Interaction between players occurs solely through chat messages, utilizing simple first-person language for accessibility. However, this approach may be perceived as direct communication with pilots, potentially causing confusion. For chatting, the human player is presented with a specifically designed UI that includes a chatbox, flight backlog, and controls. The UI was adjusted to each of the conducted studies with two variants depicted in Fig. 3.

The serious game was meticulously designed and implemented to enable the seamless collection and extraction of validation data. Capacity is measured by logging all decisions and counting the number of flights delayed or canceled. Since there exists an optimal solution for these values in each scenario, the human-chatbot team's performance can be assessed in relation to the optimum. Safety is ensured if no crashes occur between two planes on the runway, which would immediately stop the game. Additionally, all chats between the chatbot and user are logged together with the game state at the time of occurrence. This enables a manual examination of whether the messages transmitted by the user were correctly categorized by the chatbot. This is imperative to calculate numerical metrics as outlined in Sect. 3.3. Combined with a questionnaire like SUS, this allows for a detailed but more complex evaluation of the chatbot's operability.

The experimental setup is adapted from Sect. 3.2 and is presented in detail by Mutz et al. [8]. More information on the definition of exact validation scenarios used can also be found in this source.

4.2   Findings from the Exemplar Application

A total of 107 participants successfully validated the chatbot using the serious game across three studies, two of which have been published ([8,16]) and one that remains unpublished. There were no break-ups, lost data or participants who were not able to conduct the trial. The effort to conduct the validation with the 107 participants was in average an hour per participant including introduction to the game, game play and structured debriefing. Open discussions in the aftermath are not encountered in this effort. All studies enabled evaluation of safety, operational feasibility and efficiency. For safety and operational feasibility, 11.900 decisions were recorded and analysed. Efficiency was examined on the basis of 595 landing/takeoff-sequences (solutions) that were compared with the optimum sequence.

While the game core and the chatbot were the same in all studies, the graphical user interface was adapted due to different research questions. The differences are for instance shown in Fig. 3. A text-based approach is given in the left screenshot (cf. [8]), while the interface in the right screenshot incorporates more graphical elements, animations and sounds. Among other metrics, Mutz et al. [8] and Zeppenfeld (unpublished) used the SUS questionnaire ([2,3]) to evaluate the user experience with the chatbot. In the study of Mutz 37 participants provided an average SUS-score of 71.2 while in the unpublished study by Zeppenfeld, 10 participants rated the system with an average SUS-score of 85. In the literature, a SUS-score of 85 corresponds to excellent usibility [3]. The influence of the presentation on the user experience is supported by a third study of Weber [16] who provided different names and pictures of the chatbot to 60 human participants without changing the functionality. Weber did not use the SUS, but showed that the human interaction with the chatbot is influenced significantly by the applied changes to the UI.

5   Discussion

The results show that the chatbot was successfully validated using the method of serious gaming. As another method for this purpose, EUROCONTROL suggests to use HITL simulations (cf. [5]) for operational feasibility evaluations. These simulations provide a close to reality working position, but as discussed in Chap. 3, they are dependent upon the availability of operational ATCOs. The serious game allows for a lower level of accessibility proven by the three studies which used participants without expert background. Moreover, the effort per participant for the gaming in comparison to the simulation is lower.

However, it is acknowledged that the VE primarily focuses on usability aspects, with simplified metrics being used for safety and capacity assessments. Additionally, in contrast to student participants, expert personnel are trained to work under stress and adhere to strict procedures, which might influence results for safety and capacity in a trial. The remaining two E-OCVM dimensions – environment and economy – are not addressed in this work, thereby confirming the emphasis on usability.

The study of Weber [16] and the differences in the studies of Mutz et al. [8] regarding user experience, show a deficiency of the serious gaming approach. The functionality of the chatbot cannot be evaluated independently from its presentation. As the presentation is not on an operational level like a HITL simulation requires, results of the game might not manifest completely in an operational environment.

A key finding by Mutz et al. [8] is that users developed their own phraseology, which is essential information when considering natural language for communication between digital and human controllers. This finding serves as a demonstration of the efficacy of the VEs early implementation.

Concluding the discussion, it was successfully shown that a serious game for a chatbot evaluation in the context of air traffic control can be applied. This approach owns the potential to reach a higher statistical validity in comparison to human in the loop simulations due to an increased availability of the participants and a lower effort per participant. Nevertheless, the external validity might be reduced as presentation and functionality cannot be divided and are not on an operational level in the gaming approach.

6 Summary and Outlook

The primary objective of this paper was to develop a validation environment for air traffic control chatbots. A serious gaming approach was proposed to depict real-world scenarios, where the game is played cooperatively by a human player and an air traffic control chatbot.

This work introduced metrics to assess chatbot performance in accordance with the five desired fields of future enhancements outlined by the european operational concept validation methodology. The application of the proposed validation environment demonstrated its potential for validating potential use cases for chatbots in air traffic control. One of the main strengths of the validation environment is its ability to assess a chatbot in a specific task in an inexpensive yet effective way, allowing for early evaluation during development without relying on human-in-the-loop simulations.

The validation environment was applied in three studies with a total of 107 students participating as human players. With the latest version of the game a system usability score of 85 of 100 was achieved, which corresponds to excellent usability. This result indicates that the proposed validation environment is effective in evaluating chatbot performance. The approach provides a novel and effective method for the validation of chatbots, contributing to the existing body of chatbot evaluation research.

In the future, the proposed validation environment of the present study enables exploration of the application of chatbots within the broader context of air traffic control, even considering more comprehensive validation metrics, addressing the current gaps in assessing chatbot performance in accordance with the dimensions of the european operational concept validation methodology.

References

1. Borkenhagen, U., Makins, N., Valmorisco, M.: The "European" operational concept validation methodology (E-OCVM). In: 2006 IEEE/AIAA 25TH Digital Avionics Systems Conference, pp. 1–10 (2006). https://doi.org/10.1109/DASC.2006.313764

2. Brooke, J.: SUS: A Quick and Dirty Usability Scale, pp. 189–194. Taylor & Francis Ltd (1996)
3. Brooke, J.: SUS: a retroperspective. J. Usability Stud. **8**(2), 29–40 (2013)
4. Casas, J., Tricot, M.O., Abou Khaled, O., Mugellini, E., Cudré-Mauroux, P.: Trends & methods in chatbot evaluation. In: Companion Publication of the 2020 International Conference on Multimodal Interaction, pp. 280–286. ICMI '20 Companion, Association for Computing Machinery, New York, NY, USA (2021). https://doi.org/10.1145/3395035.3425319
5. EUROCONTROL: European Operational Concept Validation Methodology (E-OCVM) (2010). https://www.eurocontrol.int/publication/european-operational-concept-validation-methodology-eocvm. Accessed 14 April 2025
6. EUROCONTROL: Think Paper #19 - 19 December 2022 (2022). https://www.eurocontrol.int/publication/eurocontrol-think-paper-19-atc-mobility-and-capacity-shortfalls. Accessed 08 June 2025
7. Jameel, M., Tyburzy, L., Gerdes, I., Pick, A., Hunger, R., Christoffels, L.: Enabling digital air traffic controller assistant through human-autonomy teaming design. In: 2023 IEEE/AIAA 42nd Digital Avionics Systems Conference (DASC), pp. 1–9 (2023). https://doi.org/10.1109/DASC58513.2023.10311220
8. Mutz, M., Oesen, G., Hasse, F., Zeppenfeld, D., Schier-Morgenthal, S.: How do you read? – Dynamics of future human-automation teams in air traffic control. ICRAT Technical Papers (2024)
9. Nöhren, L., Schaper, M., Tyburzy, L.: Towards full ATC automation for aircraft ground movement: a first step. In: 2024 AIAA DATC/IEEE 43rd Digital Avionics Systems Conference (DASC), pp. 1–9 (2024). https://doi.org/10.1109/DASC62030.2024.10749019
10. Peras, D.: Chatbot evaluation metrics: review paper. In: Veselica, R., Dukic, G., Hammes, K. (eds.) Economic and Social Development, pp. 89–97 (2018)
11. Sarol, S.D., Mohammad, M.F., Rahman, N.A.A.: Mobile technology application in aviation: chatbot for airline customer experience, pp. 59–72. Springer Nature Singapore, Singapore (2023). https://doi.org/10.1007/978-981-19-6619-4_5
12. Schier, S., Rosenau, L., Freese, M.: Trainieren mit CLAUDI: Das Potential kognitiver Agenten für Simulationen und Planspiele. Kognitive Systeme (2017). https://doi.org/10.17185/duepublico/44611
13. Suhaili, S.M., Salim, N., Jambli, M.N.: Service chatbots: a systematic review. Expert Syst. Appl. **184**,115461 (2021). https://doi.org/10.1016/j.eswa.2021.115461
14. Trapero, H., Ilao, J., Lacaza, R.: An integrated theory for chatbot use in air travel: questionnaire development and validation. In: 2020 IEEE Region 10 Conference (TENCON), pp. 652–657 (2020). https://doi.org/10.1109/TENCON50793.2020.9293710
15. Vaswani, A., et al.: Attention is all you need. In: Guyon, I., Luxburg, U.V., Bengio, S., Wallach, H., Fergus, R., Vishwanathan, S., Garnett, R. (eds.) Advances in Neural Information Processing Systems, vol. 30. Curran Associates, Inc. (2017). https://doi.org/10.48550/arXiv.1706.03762
16. Weber, J.: Der Einfluss von Anthropomorphismus auf die Akzeptanz und Vertrauenswürdigkeit eines virtuellen Agenten während einer kooperativen Flugüberwachungssaufgabe. Technische Universität Chemnitz (2025)

"Uuugh – False Play" – a Serious Game to Teach Detection and Prevention of Perpetrator Strategies

Janina Bittner[1]([✉]) [iD], Greta Hoffmann[2] [iD], Ulrike Hoffmann[1] [iD],
and Joerg M. Fegert[1] [iD]

[1] Department of Child and Adolescent Psychiatry, Psychosomatics and Psychotherapy,
University Hospital Ulm, Steinhövelstraße 5, 89075 Ulm, Germany
`janina.bittner@uniklinik-ulm.de`
[2] TH Köln, Gustav-Heinemann-Ufer 54, 50968 Köln, Germany

Abstract. Sexualized violence remains a pervasive issue in institutional settings, particularly voluntary organizations where children and adolescents are active. Despite increasing awareness, there is a lack of educational tools teaching about perpetrator strategies in such environments. This paper presents the pre-evaluation and design of a serious game developed within a federally funded German project to address this gap. The project challenges current didactical tools by using a simulation-based game design focused around the perpetrator. This approach was chosen to increase understanding among adolescents about grooming tactics and to empower players in terms of detection, prevention, and action opportunities. Extensive playtesting was conducted throughout the whole design process. It focused on usability, target-group acceptance, and knowledge retention and demonstrated promising results. Adolescents effectively learned complex perpetrator strategies and recognized parallels between gameplay and real-life experiences. While cognitive load challenges persist, user feedback affirms the game's potential as an accessible and engaging prevention tool. The game's implementation in group settings further enabled safe discussions around manipulative behavior. Our preliminary findings suggest that simulation-based serious games can be a valuable complement to traditional prevention methods and underscore the value of innovative approaches in serious game development for sensitive topics.

Keywords: Sexualized violence · serious game · perpetrator strategies · adolescents

1 Introduction/Problem Definition

Current representative, population-based studies show that sexual violence in institutions remains commonplace. Sexualized violence isn't just an issue that comes to light in the wake of high-profile scandals - it has always been part of institutions' everyday lives and can occur anywhere, including voluntary settings. Only a few studies have examined the prevalence of sexualized violence in voluntary institutions. A survey of 2,024 athletes

S. Bakkes et al. (Eds.): GALA 2025, LNCS 16307, pp. 334–343, 2026.
https://doi.org/10.1007/978-3-032-11043-5_32

revealed that 26% had experienced sexualized violence without physical contact and 19% had experienced sexualized violence involving physical contact in sports clubs [1]. Every voluntary organization, whether a sports club, altar society, orchestra, and so on, where children and adolescents are present, carries a potential risk of sexualized violence because of the inherent power imbalances that come with risks of and opportunities for misconduct. Institutional life is shaped through rules, attitudes, values, and routines. If violence is ignored, it will not disappear. However, addressing sexualized violence can reduce uncertainty and empower everyone in an organization to take action [2]. In 2019, 39.7% of people aged 14 and over did voluntary work. Children and adolescents are the main target group for voluntary work [3]. Given these facts, there is a need for preventive measures to protect children and adolescents from sexualized violence in voluntary institutions.

Major scandals have raised awareness that perpetrators exploit the characteristics of institutional systems for their purposes. Apart from encouraging the systematic implementation of prevention concepts in such institutions, educating children and adolescents about perpetrator strategies should be another important part of ensuring sustainable prevention strategies. It enables them to recognize warning signals more easily, strengthens their self-confidence, especially regarding their boundaries, feelings, and right to say no, and makes them less susceptible to manipulation [4], as perpetrators often exploit insecurity and lack of information [5]. Informed children are more resilient and more likely to protect one another, thereby contributing to a culture of awareness and mutual care.

2   Objective, Didactic Concept, and Theoretical Foundation

Despite numerous prevention efforts and awareness-raising campaigns carried out by organizations and ministries in recent years, there continues to be a need for innovative approaches to protect children and adolescents from sexualized violence through educational measures. To tackle this issue, we submitted a project application to a Federal Ministry for Education, Family Affairs, Senior Citizens, Women, and Youth that would include the creation of a web-based learning and information service to raise awareness of sexualized violence in general and impart specific knowledge on the development of prevention concepts in the voluntary sector. During the project, the following artifacts were created: an online information area, an online module to raise awareness of sexualized violence and risk factors, an online course on the creation of prevention concepts, and a serious game to impart knowledge and raise awareness of perpetrator strategies.

According to the literature, perpetrator strategies are particularly effective where insecurity, a lack of transparency, and a culture of silence prevail [6]. But it is crucial to not only understand the environments that foster perpetrating behavior but also exactly pinpoint how and where they emerge and the means perpetrators use. Tackling these specific issues can significantly contribute to raising awareness and promoting a greater willingness to develop and implement effective prevention concepts within organizations. Given their complexity and considering that the target audience for the information campaign is adolescents, we considered serious games as a suitable medium for communication. Active involvement of the participants generally means that the experiences gained in a game remain longer in the player's memory. The retention rate of what has been learned can therefore be higher compared to other learning methods [8].

This serious game aims to educate adolescents about perpetrator strategies in a safe and guided environment, to teach them how to recognize dangerous situations early on, and to react to them appropriately. It is based on knowledge conveyed through the project's two web-based learning programs. It is important to note that the game does not impart knowledge about specific offenses but creates an understanding of how perpetrator strategies emerge from seemingly normal/everyday club activities. After playing the game, the following questions should be clarified: *What steps do perpetrators take to achieve their goals? How can I recognize perpetrator strategies? What can I do to protect myself and others? How can I act, if I have a suspicion of a perpetrator's strategy being enacted?*

The game is currently in the final stages of its release process. From the beginning, the design process was accompanied by systematic user testing to ensure that the set goals were achieved and risks with this unusual perspective were hedged. This paper presents the results of the final study conducted before the last round of iterations before release. The focus of the study was to test matters of usability and target-group-oriented design (*do players understand how to navigate within the game? Do adolescents accept the game as a didactical asset? Do they consider its design appealing?*) and matters of expectable results (*do players effectively learn and remember grooming strategies? Does the game manage to raise awareness of the prevalence of the topic?*).

3 Game Design and Development of the Serious Game

The central design decisions for the game were made within the tension field of creating a game that is interesting and engaging enough for the target audience to interact with, while keeping the aforementioned learning outcomes at the core. We started with a review of serious games tackling this topic; however, all the games we found were either victim-centric [9] or bystander-centric [10] and focused on raising awareness more than actively teaching about specific detection or prevention strategies. Thus, the final game design significantly deviates from current state-of-the-art serious games on the topic, specifically in terms of its core gameplay (perpetrator perspective and simulation approach).

The game is designed as a 2D top-down mobile game, created in the game engine Unity, and will be published for Android and iOS. The output medium was chosen due to the widespread use and familiarity of mobile devices, enabling engagement with the learning content at youth centers as well as at home.

Target Audience: The serious game is aimed at teenagers and young adults aged 12 and over, especially in (voluntary) clubs where youth leaders, trainers, and club managers work on prevention concepts. Our age recommendation for the serious game is based on the German USK (Entertainment Software Self-Regulation). This is a voluntary self-regulation for the testing and age categorization of video games. The game is based on the USK 12 and therefore recommended for people aged 12 and over. The serious game can, however, be played independently by individuals without a club context or an association context. The intention is for adolescents to share and disseminate the game.

In contrast to existing serious games we found on the topic, we made two choices that fundamentally change the approach commonly taken.

Player Perspective: After heavy deliberation, we took the arguably radical approach of having players' in-game actions directly guided by a perpetrator. This is inspired by police procedure, where perpetration strategies are studied from the mind of the perpetrator, to be able to best discover and apprehend them (see, e.g., training methods like criminal mind/profiling expertise and curriculum-based simulations of the Behavioral Analysis Unit–5 (BAU-5) at the FBI Academy Quantico or the police profiling approach (operative Fallanalyse (OFA)) of the Bundeskriminalamt (BKA) and Landeskriminalämter (state detective departments) in Germany).

Research on the effect of avatars on self-perception and understanding indicates that players learn differently and more effectively if they are given an avatar embodying qualities that are different from themselves and immerse themselves in the roleplay of this character (Proteus Effect, [11]). This effect was highlighted in a study, where participants embodying a virtual Albert Einstein avatar in virtual reality showed improved performance on executive function tasks [12]. By having players roleplay from the perspective of a perpetrator, they take a perspective that highlights pattern detection on perpetration opportunities that were formerly hidden from them.

Among some early concerns with this design decision was the potential for misconstrual of this approach as a teaching game for perpetrator strategies. To ensure that the game achieves its actual learning outcomes, we took a multi-layered approach, where any perpetrator strategy players are prompted to use in the game is addressed and reflected. This is done via an extra-diegetic owl character that, after any briefing as well as at crucial moments in the game, breaks the fourth wall and directly communicates to the players and puts the in-game perpetrator's statements and actions into context. In addition to these measures, there are several extra-diegetic measures to frame the content of the game. There is a series of warnings and contextualization before the actual game as well as a help button, that takes players out of the game and offers a hotline and links to resources relating to the topic.

Game Type: The game is not a linear story with dialog options, but a fully designed simulation, where players are given full freedom of choice in terms of their in-game action. It is, however, not a sandbox game (like, e.g., Minecraft [13], where players can interact freely in the absence of a game goal or other rule- or story-based guidance). It is contentually structured. At the time of writing, two scenarios are implemented (tutorial and the "classic" scenario) and will be part of the initial release. The other scenarios are prepepared and are pending further funding. Each scenario is structured into phases that represent the phases in which perpetrators act: I) information gathering/boundary testing, II) group manipulation, III) target work, IV) normalization, and V) boundary crossing (this is an exemplary structure; the phases don't always appear in this exact order, nor are they always all present).

Core Gameplay: In the game, players act from the perspective of a trainer in a youth club setting where they can interact in various ways with their subordinate club members. Each turn, players can choose between various categories of actions that (in most cases) are or look normal to everyday youth-club life. The club members' reactions to these actions are based on a complex algorithm that factors in their own personalities (that are based on the OCEAN model [14]), as well as their self-esteem, motivation, current relationship to the trainer (in terms of trust, feeling special, and suspicion), and the general context (how normal the action is perceived by the club member).

Setting/Vibe/Style: The overall vibe was inspired by games like "Cult of the Lamb" [15], and "Persona 5" [16]. The color scheme was chosen to communicate a certain sense of danger and a subdued tone to fit the content theme. The style was chosen to combine edgy elements in the game UI to appeal to the target audience and softer elements in the character design to create empathy, especially with the club members. When designing the characters, an aesthetic in the sense of a „fable world" with animals and monsters was chosen (trainer (wolf), club members (gender-neutral figurines with animal masks), and guide/counselor (owl)), to avoid/circumvent focus on gender stereotypes and instead highlight the emergence of perpetrator strategies through the imbalance of power and manipulative relationships. Once players successfully complete the scenario, the end is not presented as a win but merely as a completion. Also, it is made clear that the perpetrator gets captured shortly after. The game never leaves any doubt that any act of perpetration has serious consequences.

The development of "Uuugh – False Play," the first simulation-based serious game about grooming strategies, was conducted in a collaboration between the "Greater Games" game studio with experience in serious games and the team of the working group "Knowledge Transfer, Dissemination, E-Learning" at the Clinic for Child and Adolescent Psychiatry, Psychosomatics, and Psychotherapy of the University Hospital Ulm in Germany.

4   Design Conduct and Initial Test Results

To obtain initial insights into how well our game will manage to achieve its goals within the target group and to identify any potential obstacles, we conducted systematic user testing from the very early stages of the project. After the design phase concluded, we assessed the risks of our choices in comparison to the potential gains. After a round of qualitative interviews with stakeholders, the common sentiment was that for the game to have its intended learning impact, certain unresolvable tensions concerning its content matter and approach will need to be endured but that the approach is not only recommended but "necessary."

After these promising preliminary results, we started working on an initial prototype for technical and creative experimentation. The goal of this phase was to work towards an immersive gaming experience that connects to the target audience, feels tonally correct, and is contentually grounded in extensive and solid research.

In the next phase, we conducted an in-house test, with participants from the youth club (Jugendmedienzentrum im Kölner Jugendpark). The study focused on usability and target group orientation as well as the effectiveness of the game. The feedback from the adolescent testers was generally positive, particularly regarding the atmosphere, graphic design, variety of characters, and user-friendliness. However, critical feedback was also provided: some players found the game difficult to understand and navigate. This issue was addressed, and the game was accordingly revised in the following development phase.

In another playtest at a youth center event (Jugendzentrum.digital Köln), feedback from the test subjects aged 12 to 20 showed a high level of acceptance of the serious game overall: the variety of characters, atmospheric mood, graphic design, and intuitive usability were particularly emphasized. The game was rated positively regardless of gender, and the central theme was recognized and understood by the majority of players. Notably, one youth who already had some experience as a group leader, immediately understood that the in-game characters had different personalities and needed to be approached differently. Fittingly, he focused his gameplay on being a good trainer instead of following the games' instructions. However, especially with younger participants, retention was low. Finally, once the game was at the release candidate stage, a big round of anonymized target group-oriented tests was conducted with youth clubs recruited from all over Germany (scouting, open youth clubs, church contexts, and the German Red Cross). The in-depth setup and results are discussed in the following chapters. This final evaluation focused on two major facets: user experience and target group suitability of the release candidate (particularly considering possible improvements before the final release) as well as the general acceptance of the content matter and the expected learning outcomes, specifically checking whether the game's intended effects can be manifested in real user behavior and awareness.

The overarching project was handed to the ethics commission of the university clinic. It was deemed not relevant for doctors in the region according to §15 of the professional code of conduct for physicians in Baden-Württemberg. Consent for participation in the study was handled via the youth organizations as follows: No children below the age of 16 were accepted for the questionnaire, and parents received an informational letter with an optional notice for their children to opt out of the playtest and evaluation.

5 Experimental Design:

To carry out the testing, youth leaders willing to try out the serious game as part of a group session with their adolescent club members aged 16 to 30 were recruited. Recruitment took place via the project's platform mailing list and during an accompanying project event. Interested individuals could register via email and then receive further information. Additional telephone appointments were arranged to answer any remaining questions. The project team then provided participants with a detailed implementation concept, access to the serious game, and links to the online questionnaires via email. The project team was available at all times to answer any queries. Before starting the testing, the youth leaders were instructed to study an accompanying brochure on the game's purpose and content in detail. The tests were carried out by the youth leaders on their own responsibility.

The total time of each session was ~ 90 min. After a brief introduction (~10 min) to the topic and the serious game, based on the content of the briefing and the brochure, the adolescents started testing the serious game independently for 45–60 min. During this phase, the youth leaders were available to provide support and answer questions. Afterward, the adolescents completed a seven-minute questionnaire to systematically record their experiences and impressions.

The questionnaire was a set of custom questions using a combination of a 6-point Likert scale (from one = "strongly disagree" to six = "strongly agree") and open questions. It was divided into four blocks: I) a short set of demographic questions, II) a section on the general reception of the game (if and how much they liked/disliked the game as well as its aesthetics and what they would change), III) a section about understanding the content of the game, being able to remember and play back some of the game's content, and prevalence of the game's content in their own lived experiences, as well as IV) a section on their emotional response to the game: if the game evoked fear or unwellness, and what parts of the game evoked these feelings. The session was concluded with a debriefing with the youth leaders that took around 20 min. At the end of the testing phase, the youth leaders were asked to complete a separate six-minute questionnaire to provide feedback on the testing procedure.

6   Results/Evaluation

A total of 39 adolescents took part in the playtests, of whom 14 were male (35.9%) and 25 were female (64.1%). The participants' average age was 21.5 years (SD = 5.2), ranging from 15 to 37 years. In addition, four youth leaders aged 24 to 45 years took part in the playtests with their groups. On average, the youth leaders were 30.3 years old (SD = 9.9). The participants came from the following areas of volunteering: Scouts, open youth centers, church institutions, and the German Red Cross. The results of the two online questionnaires are examined and categorized in more detail below.

To assess the game's user-friendliness and target-group-oriented design, the adolescents were asked about their overall satisfaction, their understanding of the content, and their satisfaction with the design. When asked how much the participants enjoyed the game overall, 14 people (35.9%) agreed with the statement that they liked the game. 19 people (48.8%) showed a neutral attitude, while 6 people (15.4%) stated that they did not like the game. 28 participants (71.8%) stated that they understood the content of the game well, while 15.4% answered neutrally and 12.8% tended not to agree or did not agree at all with the statement. The graphics and design of the game were rated positively by 51.3% of participants, while 33.3% gave a neutral assessment. In contrast, 15.4% rated the graphic design as less appealing. In addition, the extent to which the game promotes learning and recognition of perpetrator strategies to raise awareness of the topic was examined. Therefore, it was asked whether players knew which strategies perpetrators use and could recognize them after playing the game.

Participants were asked after the game if they could remember the perpetrator strategies that had been discussed. 29 people (74.4%) stated that they remembered several strategies and were able to name them afterward. The most frequently mentioned strategies included giving compliments and praise to gain trust, and isolating victims. In their assessment form, the youth leaders also agreed that the game could help adolescents recognize perpetrator strategies. Three out of four youth leaders (75%) agreed with this assessment, while one (25%) was neutral. The fact that many of the respondents were able to name several specific strategies indicates that the conveyed content has been mentally embedded, which is a hopeful initial result for the intended long-term retention. Some participants appreciated the opportunity to put themselves in the perpetrator's shoes, as this helped them to better understand their strategies and recognize perpetrator strategies in everyday life, as they indicated in the free text responses ("[I liked most about the game] To be the role of the perpetrator to have a more accurate empathy and understanding behind tactics").

We also investigated how the participants rated the impact of the game. 24 out of 39 people (61.5%) agreed with the statement that the game could help them to better recognize perpetrator strategies in everyday life. This was also emphasized by the responses of the youth leaders. Three out of four youth leaders (75%) agreed with the statement that adolescents can apply what they have learned to their everyday lives. The other youth leader (the same one that also remained neutral on the matter of adolescents being able to recognize perpetrator strategies) reported that the adolescents were not interested in reading, neither in perpetrator strategies nor in input from the Owl. This was one of the reasons why they found it difficult to recognize and understand the meaning of the game and the tasks. In his opinion, this affected both the game experience and the execution of the test. Regarding the relevance of the game scenarios, the respondents found the situations depicted in the game particularly realistic. 30 of the adolescents surveyed (76.9%) and three of the youth leaders (75%) considered it likely that such situations could occur in real club life. The possibility that such situations could also occur in their own club made 10 (25.6%) of the adolescents feel uncomfortable, and 6 adolescents (15.4%) stated that they had already experienced something similar, which again underlines the relevance of the topic. The playtests showed that the game was overall very well received. Both players and youth leaders particularly appreciated the innovative approach of learning about perpetrator strategies through play, perceiving it as an engaging alternative to conventional training formats.

Criticism was voiced in particular about the text-heavy nature and the sometimes uncomfortable feeling when playing. Addressing the first issue - the balance between necessary and excessive textual content - was discussed intensely within the team and readjusted throughout the whole development process and considered in the evaluation of the various playtests. The ratio the game is currently at is the result of these deliberations, and while not perfect - especially if it prevents actual engagement - we feel that any less would have taken away from a meaningful learning outcome on this complex matter. However, we acknowledge this as a drawback of the games' design. To the latter point, we see this effect as an actual positive resulting from deliberate choices we made for the game. This indicates that the game successfully walks the line between a distance that makes players comfortable enough to engage with this difficult topic without it becoming too demanding, while upholding the seriousness of this difficult topic.

Overall, the playtest results indicate a positive response to the game, especially regarding its realistic depiction of perpetrator strategies and its potential to help players recognize such behaviors in everyday life. The feedback received on the game and its design was taken on board and implemented in the latest iteration of the game during a two-week revision phase to improve accessibility and understanding for all users.

7 Summary and Outlook

Overall, given the combination of a target audience that can be difficult to engage for serious topics, as well as the general undesirability of the overall topic matter, the playtests have turned out very promising. The overall positive feedback from the playtests indicates that, despite the complexity of the content matter, the game has a realistic chance to not only effectively raise awareness of perpetration being an ongoing topic in youth clubs, but also help to prevent future disasters by imparting crucial knowledge relating to detection, protection, and potential courses of action. The playtesting highlighted valid criticisms, particularly pertaining to cognitive load, that, given our specific approach, are not fully solvable. This calls for even more new and different design approaches that should tackle these issues. But given the experimental nature of our design decisions and educative approach, we are satisfied with the preliminary results.

The successful retention of several complex perpetrator strategies within the target audience is of particular note and leaves us hopeful for the success of the game's agenda. Also, the participant's recognition that the situations portrayed in the game may also arise in real club settings, and that some had already faced similar experiences, showcased that the game's content was understood and perceived as relevant. The playtests showed that the playful approach provides an accessible introduction to a sensitive topic to the target audience. Using the game in a group setting within the youth clubs allowed for more in-depth discussions within a safe environment.

In terms of implications for research, the game can provide new insights into the effectiveness of digital prevention formats and the development of evidence-based approaches in the field of sexual violence prevention. In this context, the results of the evaluation have shown that the game can be used as tools for introducing and implementing further prevention measures. The playtests described in this manuscript were user tests to prepare the game for release in its near-final version. The results are therefore preliminary and do not yet allow for any definitive conclusions. Our objective for the phase following the release is to ensure that the game is widely used and has a lasting impact after its release, which will be assessed through continuous usage measurements in the future. Once released, the game will continue to undergo a thorough evaluation throughout the project, enabling conclusions about its long-term effectiveness and educational benefits.

Summarizing, we are satisfied with the (tentative) success of using the unconventional approach of a simulation-based serious game in this sensitive domain as an innovative method of engaging with younger target groups in a contemporary and effective way. We hope to inspire other collaborations of educators/target matter experts and medium-experts like game studios to build on the mutual expertise towards new, outstanding, and impactful artifacts. Finally, we hope to encourage readers of this manuscript to dare to conceptualize more controversial approaches in the domain of serious games. We believe that such courage can lead to particularly successful outcomes in raising awareness and inspiring action.

Acknowledgments. This study was funded by the German Federal Ministry for Education, Family Affairs, Senior Citizens, Women, and Youth as part of the project (Safeguarding Measures for Voluntary Work with Children and Adolescents). Additional support with the data analytics was provided by Marius Stickel, and further background research was provided by Anja Krauß.

Disclosure of Interests. The authors have no competing interests to declare that are relevant to the content of this article.

References

1. Rulofs , B., et al.: SicherImSport: Sexualisierte Grenzverletzungen, Belästigung und Gewalt im organisierten Sport – Häufigkeiten und Formen sowie der Status Quo der Prävention und Intervention. Deutsche Sporthochschule Köln & Universitätsklinikum Ulm. (2022)
2. Owczarzak, M., Sahle, D., Uhlmann, K.P., Schöber, S., Anderten, M.: Präventions- und Interventionskonzept zum Schutz vor interpersoneller Gewalt im Sport. Sport-Stiftung & Landessportbund NRW, Rheinland, Rhein-Ruhr, Westfalen
3. Simonson, J., et al.: Freiwilliges Engagement in Deutschland. Bundesministerium für Familie, Senioren, Frauen und Jugend (BMFSFJ) (2019)
4. Finkelhor, D.: The prevention of childhood sexual abuse. The Future of Children, pp. 169–194 (2009)
5. Enders, U.: Die Strategien der Täter und Täterinnen. In: Grenzen achten! Schutz vor sexuellem Missbrauch in Institutionen. Ein Handbuch für die Praxis. pp. 63–108. Kiepenheuer & Witsch, Köln (2012)
6. Wazlawik, M., Voß, H.-J., Retkowski, A., Henningsen, A., Dekker, A.: Sexuelle Gewalt in Pädagogischen Kontexten. Springer VS, Münster (2016)
7. Neuburger, R.: Serious Games: Kann Lernen Spaß machen? Wissensmanagement, pp. 24–26 (2022)
8. Wouters, P., Van Nimwegen, C., Van Oostendorp, H., Van Der Spek, E.D.: A meta-analysis of the cognitive and motivational effects of serious games. J. Educ. Psychol. **105**, 249 (2013)
9. Kikiyama: Yume Nikki (2004). https://store.steampowered.com/app/650700/Yume_Nikki/
10. ETC: Decisions that Matter (2015). https://www.cmu.edu/dietrich/news/news-stories/2015/may/decisions-that-matter.html
11. Yee, N., Bailenson, J.: The Proteus effect: the effect of transformed self-representation on behavior. Hum. Commun. Res. **33**, 271–290 (2007)
12. Banakou, D., Kishore, S., Slater, M.: Virtually being einstein results in an improvement in cognitive task performance and a decrease in age bias. Front. Psychol. **9**, 917 (2018). https://doi.org/10.3389/fpsyg.2018.00917
13. Mojang Studios: Minecraft (2011)
14. Costa, P., McCrae, R.: NEO five-factor inventory (NEO-FFI). Odessa, FL: Psychological Assessment Resources 3 (1989)
15. Massive Monster: Cult of the Lamb (2022)
16. Atlus: Persona 5 (2016)

Feeling an Itch: A Systematic Review of Games for Mental Health on Itch.io

Aquila Wessels⬤, Sander Bakkes⬤, and Julian Frommel⁽⊠⁾⬤

Utrecht University, Utrecht, Netherlands
`j.frommel@uu.nl`

Abstract. In this study, we systematically reviewed mental health-related games on the indie games platform itch.io. After initial screening and subsequent gameplay, we arrived at a dataset of 60 browser-playable games tagged with "mental health" on itch.io, which were reviewed and classified along a set of categories: targeted mental health topic, game type, player motivation type, method used, theoretical grounding, references to resources, itch.io genre, interaction style, single-player or multiplayer social presence, and playtime. Analyzing trends in this dataset, we found that anxiety and depression were the most commonly targeted issues, while the game experiences were commonly single-player interactive fictions and visual novels. Only 13.33% of the games mentioned a relevant theoretical grounding. In addition to these findings, the research produced a detailed dataset of classified games that assist game scholars and other individuals seeking accessible mental health-focused games. While, to our knowledge, these games have not been evaluated regarding their effects on mental health, this can be valuable for research and practice.

Keywords: Mental health · Serious games · Applied games · Games for health · Indie games · Itch.io · Gamification

1   Introduction

Serious games are increasingly recognized for their significance and effectiveness across a wide range of domains [5]. One particularly promising area of use for serious games is the healthcare domain, where their potential impact can be transformative. Indeed, mental health problems are widespread, with significant numbers of people experiencing anxiety and depressive disorders. In 2019, approximately 970 million people globally were living with a mental disorder, and this number significantly increased due to the COVID-19 pandemic [14]. While effective treatments exist, many individuals lack access to care [10], and stigma, discrimination, and human rights violations are also prevalent according to the World Health Organization (WHO) [14].

Potentially, some of these challenges can be alleviated with easily accessible *games for mental health*. That is, games that are specifically designed for therapeutic or emotional support goals may well serve as tools for increasing mental health awareness, offering support strategies, and training effective coping skills.

S. Bakkes et al. (Eds.): GALA 2025, LNCS 16307, pp. 344–354, 2026.
https://doi.org/10.1007/978-3-032-11043-5_33

Itch.io is a platform dedicated to publishing independent games (i.e., indie games), which are games created and released without the backing of major publishers. The platform allows creators to release their work without the constraints of the traditional gatekeeping found on mainstream platforms, and has become the key platform for independent developers [4].

Despite its popularity, itch.io has received limited attention in academic research [13]. Yet, its collection of over 200,000 games provides a wealth of content that may reasonably be expected to benefit academic investigations and individuals alike. Itch.io's diverse content is organized through a tagging system that helps users discover games based on specific themes or topics. The presence of the tag *"mental health"* – at present yielding 1,551 results – reveals an openness to addressing mental health issues through gaming on this platform. We explore itch.io as a platform because of the large number of free, browser-playable games.

Although there is growing interest in games that address mental health, most existing studies focus on specific games or targeted interventions rather than offering a broader overview of publicly available mental health games. In particular, there is a lack of systematic analyses that examine the scope and diversity of mental health games found on open-access platforms like Itch.io, which serves as a rich but underexplored resource. As such, this study aimed to conduct a structured, taxonomy-informed analysis of games for mental health on itch.io.

2   Related Work

Games for Mental Health. Games have increasingly found their way into healthcare and have been strategically used to affect a number of issues in health among patients. For example, Stapleton [12] illustrated that serious games can be used as a form of motivation and reward for patients undergoing some form of treatment, or as a means to help distract patients during certain procedures. Specifically in the context of mental health, serious games have successfully been applied for the treatment of phobias and anxieties [12], with participants generally indicating high levels of comfort in using video games as part of their treatment [2,12]. Scholars noted that games are a good platform to provide the motivation needed to persevere through treatment challenges [6,9], to serve as a distraction to ease the treatment experience, [5], and to address mental health challenges that are otherwise difficult to treat, such as impulsiveness, emotional regulation and frustration [2].

Indie Games. Most games for mental health are currently developed by large corporations, researchers or government entities [1]. However, small independent (i.e., indie) game developers are beginning to make their mark in creating these types of games as well, with their presence gradually growing in the field. Itch.io is a popular platform for indie developers, offering a diverse selection of games and a more accessible environment for smaller and beginner-friendly titles. The platform hosted over 1,000,000 products as of 2024, including over 200,000 games. Creators on itch.io can use specific tags and genres to categorize their games and highlight their themes. Searching the "mental health" tag on itch.io yielded 1,551 results as of writing, highlighting its relevance for this topic.

Classification of Serious Games. In the present research, we use existing taxonomies to classify serious games available on itch.io, focusing on their potential to support mental health. Regarding categorizing the *method used* for achieving health outcomes, Knöll & Moar adapted the "Games for Health Taxonomy" proposed by Sawyer and Smith [11], to create a usage-based taxonomy. The Knöll & Moar taxonomy consists of six categories: (1) exergames, (2) stress relief games, (3) rehabilitation games, (4) disease management games, (5) pain distraction games, and (6) learning games [7].

Regarding categorizing the *game type*, we adopt the categorization by Lau et al. [8], distinguishing between (1) goal oriented games, (2) problem-solving games, (3) cognition training, and (4) exergames – this final category is excluded from the present study. Regarding categorizing the *targeted mental health topic*, a systematic review by Lau distinguished between games focusing on depression, post-traumatic stress disorder (PTSD), autism spectrum disorder (ASD), attention deficit hyperactivity disorder (ADHD), cognitive functioning, and alcohol use disorder [8]. In addition to these topics, Fernández-Aranda et al. [2] observed a focus on obsessive-compulsive disorder (OCD), schizophre14nia, eating disorders, and anxiety disorders. As we expect various mental health topics in the dataset, we decided against deductive coding and instead intentionally coded these mental health topics inductively.

Regarding connecting to certain *player motivation types*, the influential meta-synthesis by Hamari and Tuunanen [3] is leveraged, categorizing player motivations into the categories (1) achievement, (2) exploration, (3) sociability, (4) domination, and (5) immersion. Further, we coded games for *interaction style, modality,* and as *single-player or multiplayer* (see Subsect. 3.2).

3   Methods

This study aimed to conduct a structured, taxonomy-informed analysis of games for mental health on itch.io. For that purpose, we conducted a systematic review of free browser-based games tagged with mental health on the platform. The overall review process was derived from systematic literature review methodologies and consisted of the following steps:

Data scraping Extraction of game metadata (title, description, link) for all browser-based games tagged with "mental health" on Itch.io.

Screening Title and description screening with predefined inclusion criteria.

Gameplay review Full gameplay of the remaining games to confirm inclusion criteria and collect classification data.

Classification Systematic coding of each game's characteristics using a structured framework.

Content analysis Examination of frequencies and patterns across the dataset.

3.1   Data Collection, Screening, and Review

As of March 1st, 2025, Itch.io listed 1,551 games tagged with "mental health". To narrow the scope and ensure accessibility for users, this study focused exclusively on games that are playable directly in the browser without download or additional software necessary to play the game. This reduced the pool to 742 games, which formed the initial dataset for screening. Each game underwent an initial systematic screening based on its title and description. To facilitate this, the Itch.io website was scraped using a Python script to collect key metadata, including the title, link, and description of each game. Games were included in the next phase of the study only if they met the following inclusion criteria:

1. Relevance to the theme of mental health (e.g., explicitly addressing mental health topics, such as depression, PTSD, or ADHD)
2. Availability to play for free in the browser
3. Relevance as a serious game (i.e., focus on mental health and excluding purely entertainment-focused games with minor mental health references)

After initial screening of titles and descriptions, we had 112 games remaining for gameplay review, in which the first author played the complete game. Before playing each game, the description was read to gain a general understanding of the game's premise. The descriptions were also checked for practical information, such as control instructions. We further check user comments in cases where inclusion was unclear based on the title and description alone.

Each game was played in full-screen mode and approached with the same intent: to experience its content as an ordinary player would. Observations were recorded after gameplay to minimize distraction during play. Before starting each game, a timer was set to record the duration of play. Every game was played in full until its end. When there was no clear ending, a single full session ended when the main idea of the game was clear. During the gameplay review, we excluded 52 games that did not meet the inclusion criteria after playing, despite passing the initial screening based on title and description alone, because they required a download that was not mentioned in the description, or technical issues that made the game unplayable. After this, we had a final list of 60 games included in the review.

3.2   Coding and Analysis

We coded the games both inductively for the targeted mental health topic (e.g., depression, PTSD, and ADHD) and deductively along a number of existing taxonomies, including (1) the game type (goal-oriented, problem-solving, cognition training), (2) method used (stress management games, rehabilitation games, pain distraction games, learning games), (3) player motivation type (achievement, sociability, exploration, domination, immersion), (4) Itch.io genre (e.g., action, interactive fiction, or platformer), (5) Itch.io tags (i.e., keywords chosen by developers to describe their game's themes, style and features), (6) interaction style (keyboard, mouse, gamepad, touchscreen, and point-and-click), (7) modality (visual, auditory, haptic), (8) single-player or multiplayer, (9) gameplay duration, (10) theoretical grounding (i.e., does the game mention relevant theoretical background), and (11) resources (does it refer players to resources that help them).

After initial coding, codes were reviewed and aligned for the inductive codes. This means that terms with similar meanings were standardized for the targeted mental health topic, e.g., combining 'low self-esteem' and 'low self-worth' into one label. Beyond this, we tallied up codes along categories to identify trends in the data. For some classifications, the games allowed for multiple codes (e.g., in the itch.io genres) that were kept separate.

4   Results

The results of this work are twofold. First, we created an extensive dataset of mental health games on itch.io (see project on osf.io) that serves as a valuable source for people looking for mental health-focused games, including researchers, students, and practitioners (see Sect. 5 for more details). Second, we examined the data set along a subset (due to space constraints) of coded categories to identify trends and gaps in the current state of mental health games on itch.io.

Table 1. List of the categories by the games.

Topic	n	Multiple topics	n	Genre	n
Anxiety	22	Anxiety and Depression	4	Interactive fiction	17
Depression	21	Depression and Loneliness	4	Visual Novel	11
Loneliness	5	Anxiety and Stress	1	No Genre	10
General mental health themes	3	Paranoia and Anxiety	1	Educational	9
Autism	2	**Method used**	**n**	Adventure	6
Feeling down	2	Learning games	35	Simulation	4
Trauma	2	Stress relief games	20	Puzzle	3
Low self-worth	2	Rehabilitation games	5	Role playing	3
Emotional literacy	2	Pain distraction games	0	Action	2
ADHD	1	Disease management	0	Rhythm	2
Procrastination	1	Exergames	0	**Playtime**	**n**
Verbalizing feelings	1	**Mental Health Resources**	**n**	5 min or less	25
Self-care	1	Yes	6	6–10 min	18
Anger issues	1	No	54	11–20 min	11
Paranoia	1	**Theoretical Grounding**	**n**	21–50 min	6
"Something on your mind"	1	Yes	8		
Academic pressure	1	No	52		
Exhaustion	1				
Burn-out	1				

4.1   Mental Health Topic

The first classification focused on the mental health topic targeted by the games. Table 1 provides an overview of the results. The most targeted topics were anxiety (36.07% of the dataset), depression (34.43%), and loneliness (8.20%). Beyond those, there is a wide range of different topics addressed by the games, for example, including ADHD or burnout. Some games targeted multiple mental health issues, such as anxiety and depression (n=4) and depression and loneliness (n=4).

4.2   Game for Health Type

We coded games based on Knöll & Moar's usage-based health game taxonomy [7]. Learning games were the most common, with over half of the games falling in this category. Learning games focus on educating users on topics like emotional intelligence, skill development, and coping mechanisms. An example of this method can be seen in the game *Rainy Day*[1] which is a short game about a family's struggle with and recovery from depression. By allowing the player to walk around the house and observe different interactions, the game shows how a family might deal with a member experiencing depression. This game highlights the primary objective of learning games, which is to provide players with meaningful insights and knowledge through interactive experiences. Stress relief games were also frequently used. These games' main objective is to support emotional regulation and relaxation. An example can be found in the game *Mind-OS*[2] which, through multiple rooms in the game, features breathing exercises and meditation methods as a means to reduce stress or anxiety. The rehabilitation games were not very common. These games aim to assist in cognitive or emotional rehabilitation, such as from trauma or depression. An example can be found in the game *Regain*[3] which is a clicker game centred on overcoming the darkness of depression. Players must muster their energy to have the courage to expand their surroundings. Although rehabilitation games share similarities with learning games in conveying important messages, their primary focus is on supporting players who are actively dealing with mental health challenges and aiding them in their recovery process. Regain is a small game, but it is designed to support players as they work on rehabilitation. Pain distraction games were not found in the mental health tagged games on itch.io, and neither were disease management and exergames.

4.3   Genres, Interaction, Gametime, and Number of Players

On itch.io, developers are encouraged to specify at least one genre for their games, making it easier for users to browse by broad game types. The data for game genres shows that the majority of games belong to interactive fiction and

---

[1] Rainy Day on itch.io: https://bee-tea.itch.io/rainyday.
[2] MindOS on itch.io: https://kirafarron.itch.io/mind-os.
[3] Regain on itch.io: https://sunie.itch.io/regain.

visual novels, which both fall in the same category of storytelling. These two genres together form almost half of all the games. Storytelling games seem to be useful in mental health aid because they allow players to engage at their own pace and encourage immersion and engagement. For some games, it would be even debatable if they qualify as games. For example, *Everything Is Awful and I'm Not Okay*[4] was a checklist people could go through before giving up, but contained no game elements beyond this static content.

The interaction style and modality are the most relevant classifications regarding accessibility. They can provide useful information for players who may want to know what input devices are needed, or those with hearing impairments who need to know whether sound is required. For the interaction style, 18 games could be played using only the keyboard, 28 required only the mouse, and 14 games required both.

We recorded the playtime for each game, as this is relevant for accessibility, appeal, and practical application (e.g., how it would be embedded in a therapy session or a class). As playtime may vary drastically between players, we used the playtime of our playthroughs as an estimate of the duration of each game. We assigned playtime into four categories. The games in the dataset varied considerably in length, ranging from just a few minutes to over half an hour. The longest game had playtime of 50 min. And the shortest playtime was under a minute per session, but encouraged daily check-ins over an extended period. Overall, the majority of games can be considered very short, with 71.77% of the dataset having a playtime under 10 min. Finally, we were interested in exploring whether games were singleplayer experiences or if there are multiplayer games. All games in our dataset were singleplayer games.

4.4   Theoretical Grounding and Mental Health Resources

Finally, we assessed the grounding of the games. Only 13.3% mentioned relevant theoretical background. For example, the game *Sword Of Meaning*[5] directly mentions a therapeutic method used in their game: *"This game was made to teach and celebrate CBT (Cognitive Behavioral Therapy)."* In the game, the player travels into their own mind to slay the demons that disturb their peace. This is done by answering three questions, of which the answers create a 'panel of hope' used to deal with difficult situations, illustrating core CBT principles. The description also mentions that the game was made in collaboration with an established psychologist, helping with the concept and science behind the game. In contrast, 10.0% of games referred players to resources. For example, *Hiraya*[6] is a game that offers access to mental health resources. The game explores unhealthy family traits, and in its description provides an extensive list titled *"Where to find mental help in the Philippines"*.

---

[4] Everything is awful and I'm not okay on itch.io: https://skal-ton.itch.io/everything-is-awful-and-im-not-okay-questions-to-ask-before-giving-up.
[5] Sword of Meaning on itch.io: https://magicdylen.itch.io/swordofmeaning.
[6] Hiraya on itch.io: https://unhappycats.itch.io/hiraya.

5   Discussion

The results of this study provide an overview of the mental health-focused games on itch.io. This offers insights into the specific issues they target and how they are designed. We discuss findings, implications, limitations, and future work.

5.1   Trends in Games for Mental Health on Itch.io

The results show depression and anxiety as the most targeted mental health issues on itch.io. This aligns with broader mental health research, which consistently identifies depression and anxiety as highly prevalent among young people today [14]. The attention these issues receive on itch.io suggests that many independent developers are similarly interested in the same topics and potentially even contributing to solving these global mental health challenges. While loneliness is less commonly targeted, it still appears as a notable theme.

Regarding the methods used, most games were categorized as learning games or stress relief games. Rehabilitation games were rare, and pain distraction games were not present in our dataset. This is not too surprising considering that pain distraction may more commonly focus on physical health rather than mental health. The largest portion of games were learning games, accounting for over half of all the games in the dataset. As previously defined, these games focus primarily on educating players about emotional intelligence, skill development, or coping strategies for conditions like anxiety or depression. Rather than aiming to directly change emotional states, learning games aim to inform and to build understanding. Considering that most developers are independent developers who may not have training in mental health practice, it is interesting to see that there are rehabilitation games on itch.io. In the few games that were categorized under this label, the developers made a clear attempt to have a positive direct impact on the players' mental health. While these games and their effectiveness are (to our knowledge) not evaluated, their intention to support mental well-being is evident. Stress relief games are also common in the dataset. These games usually focus on straightforward techniques, such as breathing exercises, rather than complex theories, making them more accessible for both developers and players.

Beyond the specific mental health categorization, we also coded the games based on game-related characteristics. First, all games were singleplayer experiences with an overwhelmingly short duration. This is not too surprising considering that these are indie games. Second, the majority of games were games from the interactive fiction, visual novel, and educational genres. These make intuitive sense for games focused on mental health that facilitate learning with empathy and immersion. However, this also points to a gap in the context of games for mental health. Not every player may enjoy such narrative-heavy games. There is potential for other types of genres for different players, like puzzles or action games, which are rare in our dataset.

5.2   A Dataset of Games for Mental Health on Itch.io

The created dataset (see osf.io) is valuable for people looking for mental health-focused games. Importantly, we do not recommend games to mental health professionals like therapists or individuals who are affected by mental health concerns themselves, because there is a lack of theoretical foundation and empirical validation of these games. However, the dataset can serve as a starting point for future efforts on research and validation of such games and thus be valuable for researchers, students, and practitioners who look for specific types of games. In the future, it would be valuable to have a comprehensive dataset with games for mental health, including itch.io but also other platforms, with detailed insights on their approaches and effectiveness. E.g., this would allow therapists interested in using games for mental health to quickly identify relevant games to use in their practice. It may also help individual users find games if they want to learn about specific mental health topics in a game-based approach. Future research that provides personalized recommendations could be a valuable direction.

5.3   Limitations

This research has limitations. First, while protocol and findings were discussed with multiple authors, the review and coding were conducted by a single coder. This means that there is some degree of subjectivity to the findings, and potential biases may have influenced how certain games were categorized. Second, constraints on paper length did not leave room to provide detailed explanations for individual classification decisions and why certain games were placed in one category rather than another. Third, some games used relevant theories in their games but we could not find any data on empirical evaluation of their effectiveness. While this is understandable considering that they may not even be developed for this purpose, this means that we cannot recommend these games as part of mental health support without further validation. Fourth, the quality of the games varied significantly. This research did not focus on assessing the quality or usability of the games, which are important factors when considering the potential impact they should have on users. Some games were aesthetically pleasing and thoughtfully designed, while others were clearly more experimental or earlier prototypes. Fifth, we focused only on a single platform and specifically on free browser-based games with a mental health tag. Due to this focus, we will have missed other relevant games on itch.io (e.g., without relevant tags) or other platforms. Future work with other search criteria or on other platforms would be valuable for comparison and extension of these results.

6   Conclusion

In this paper, we presented a systematic review of browser-based indie games on itch.io tagged with mental health. We categorized games based on their mental health focus and strategies and their game characteristics. Analyzing trends in the data, we found that anxiety, depression, and loneliness are the most common targeted mental health issues in the games, reflecting global trends in mental health prevalence, while their strategies commonly focused on learning and stress relief approaches. Considering their game characteristics, the majority of games are short singleplayer games, often from interactive fiction and visual novel genres. These findings provide an important overview of the state of mental health games on itch.io while also highlighting relevant gaps. Further, the dataset created through this review is available so that it can benefit people interested in such games, e.g., serious games instructors, researchers, or students interested in games for mental health. We hope that our study can help improve mental health games and make them more available so that they can help people.

Disclosure of Interests. The authors have no competing interests to declare that are relevant to the content of this article.

References

1. Dewhirst, A., Laugharne, R., Shankar, R.: Therapeutic use of serious games in mental health: scoping review. BJPsych open **8**(2), e37 (2022)
2. Fernández-Aranda, F., et al.: Video games as a complementary therapy tool in mental disorders: playmancer, a European multicentre study. J. Ment. Health **21**(4), 364–374 (2012)
3. Hamari, J., Tuunanen, J.: Player types: a meta-synthesis. Trans. Digit. Games Res. Assoc. **1**(2), 29–53(2014)
4. Hernandez, P.: The game store that outshines Steam by staying small and weird. The Verge (2018). https://www.theverge.com/2018/11/29/18118217/itchio-steam-leaf-corcoran-pc-games-indie. Accessed 22 July 2025
5. Kato, P.M.: Video games in health care: closing the gap. Rev. Gen. Psychol. **14**(2), 113–121 (2010). https://doi.org/10.1037/a0019441
6. Khazaal, Y., et al.: Impact of a board-game approach on current smokers: a randomized controlled trial. SATPP **8**(1), 3 (2013)
7. Knöll, M., Moar, M.: On the importance of locations in therapeutic serious games: review on current health games and how they make use of the urban landscape. In: International Conference on Pervasive Health, pp. 538–545. IEEE (2011)
8. Lau, H.M., Smit, J.H., Fleming, T.M., Riper, H.: Serious games for mental health: are they accessible, feasible, and effective? Front. Psych. **7**, 209 (2017)
9. Merry, S.N., Stasiak, K., Shepherd, M., Frampton, C., Fleming, T., Lucassen, M.F.: The effectiveness of SPARX, a computerised self help intervention for adolescents seeking help for depression. BMJ **344** (2012)
10. Phillips, L.: A closer look at the mental health provider shortage. American Counseling Association (2023). https://www.counseling.org/publications/counseling-today-magazine/article-archive/article/legacy/a-closer-look-at-the-mental-health-provider-shortage. Accessed 22 July 2025
11. Sawyer, B., Smith, P.: Serious games taxonomy. In: GDC Serious Games Summit, pp. 23–27 (2008)
12. Stapleton, A.J.: Serious games: serious opportunities. In: Australian Game Developers Conference, Academic Summit, Melbourne (2004)

13. Werning, S.: Itch. io and the one-dollar-game: how distribution platforms affect the ontology of (games as) a medium. Deutsche Nationalbibliothek (2019)
14. World Health Organization (WHO): Mental disorders — who.int. https://www.who.int/news-room/fact-sheets/detail/mental-disorders. Accessed 22 July 2025

# Short Papers

Learning to Navigate Polycrises Through Transformative Serious Games

Ronald Ivancic[(✉)] [iD] and Flavio De Bortoli [iD]

OST – Ostschweizer Fachhochschule, Rosenbergstrasse 59, 9000 St. Gallen, Switzerland
`lncs@springer.com, {ronald.ivancic,flavio.debortoli}@ost.ch`

Abstract. Navigating polycrises requires leadership strategies that integrate flexibility, resilience, and context-sensitive decision-making. Organizations must develop leadership approaches that balance operational efficiency with crisis adaptability. This paper explores the role of transformative serious games in fostering polydextric leadership, which enables leaders to seamlessly transition between management, leadership, and command functions. By leveraging immersive simulations, serious games provide structured environments for developing strategic planning, crisis response, and decision-making skills. This paper examines the application of serious games in various settings, including everyday business life, crisis situations, and leadership-by-example scenarios. While existing literature has primarily focused on serious games for knowledge acquisition and skill practice, it highlights the specific mechanisms through which transformative serious games can develop polydextric leadership competencies.

Keywords: Serious Games · Polydextry · Leadership Development

1 Fog Thickens and Danger Lurks

The days when the world could be described using the acronym SPOD (steady, predictable, ordinary, definite) are long gone. Instead, the abbreviation VUCA which labels a volatile, uncertain, complex, and ambiguous situation has become the accepted term for describing current developments. Various authors have postulated that the VUCA world is outdated and that current conditions should instead be described by the acronym BANI (brittle, anxious, non-linear, and incomprehensible). At the very least, there seems to be a consensus that the world is currently in a fundamental transition phase. This is the result of a multi-crisis that includes, among others, the escalated Middle East conflict, inflation, and fears of recession, but also developments in the areas of metaverse and artificial intelligence that are still difficult to predict. Both transformation and polycrises, understood as the occurrence of multiple, interlinked crises that amplify each other's effects, have become a permanent situation in today's world.

To succeed, organizations need resilience and the ability to switch between distinctive styles of behavior, what can be summed up as polydextry [1]. They often must make quick decisions to overcome crises, make daily processes more efficient and ensure openness to create opportunities. This can be successfully und sustainably trained by transformative

S. Bakkes et al. (Eds.): GALA 2025, LNCS 16307, pp. 357–362, 2026.
https://doi.org/10.1007/978-3-032-11043-5_34

serious games. VUCA and BANI are forcing us to overcome the traditional boundaries of academic and practical education and training. But not only that meanwhile games are a recognized method of developing leadership skills and competences [2], they are getting increasingly notable with a growth forecast to USD bn 34.08 in 2028 [3]. They help to overcome the current, complex, and paradoxical situation. For this reason, a polydextric leadership model will serve as the basis for the gamified development of skills in this paper, although several other models are of course conceivable [2]. Polydextry facilitates the simultaneous existence of contradictory directions. In this respect, serious games are aimed at specific behavioral changes in the mindset of managers. Especially transformative serious games are distinct from conventional simulation or educational games, as they are designed to foster long-term change in leadership competencies, not only short-term skill acquisition.

Breuer & Bente [4] conduct a thorough exploration of the terminology concerning serious games, delineating its differences from related concepts such as (digital) game-based learning, methods of entertainment education, and e-learning. Michael & Chen [5] define serious games along various categories, e.g., educational games, health games and persuasive games. The intention is to consider serious games approaches that have the potential to change the organization and culture and thus transform certain behaviors [6]. Consequently, as a further development of the taxonomy of Michael & Chen [5], a category for transformative serious games or serious games for transformative purposes is presented here.

2 Polydextric Leadership Skills

In addition to management and leadership, Grint [7] defines command as an independent function that gains importance within crises. This division of guidance is based on a taxonomy that differentiates between harmless, dangerous, and critical challenges. Harmless problems may seem complicated, but they can be solved using standardized management processes. On the other hand, dangerous issues are complex and cannot be managed directly. So, people-orientation in the leadership dimension is necessary. Crises, however, require rapid and clear action in the command dimension. To master the triad, leaders must identify with the organization's raison d'être and handle entrusted tasks with care. Switching between crises (3.2) and everyday business (3.1) ensures the flexibility required today. Leadership by example (3.3) and a culture of trust create a basis. The focus is therefore on constant work on one's own identity and the associated competences to develop the skills to implement leadership polydextry.

From a good five decades, serious games have developed from a niche in the military context, into a broader recognized phenomenon. In the context of efficient training of managers, serious games are becoming increasingly important. It is recognized that they can be expected to have positive outcomes for knowledge acquisition, skills development, affective, motivational, and physiological outcomes, and behavioral change [8]. They have proven their worth [9] and well-known companies use game mechanics [10], to bridge theory and practice.

3 Transformative Serious Games for Polydextric Leadership Skills

Serious games offer a targeted selection aimed at enhancing players' management, leadership, and crises management skills through simulated environments. The depth and variety of these games expose players to complex situations, preparing them for real-life scenarios. Furthermore, integrating additional, specific elements within serious games expands the scope of skill development, placing players in diverse management, leadership, and crisis management contexts. They activate and motivate the Homo Ludens accordingly and thus promote its development.

Some solutions in different fields of application can be identified in the development of leadership skills, such as games from Cypher Learning, Pacific or Kaos (by Gamelearn), Rising Star (Fabula Games), Evolution (SimVenture) or Moving tomorrow (ESCP Europe). As a matter of fact, currently most serious games do not focus on the development of polydextric leadership skills. Following explanations are intended to show how serious games can have a positive effect within the framework of leadership polydextry.

3.1 Transformative Serious Games for Managing Everyday Business

In everyday business the ability to communicate clearly is critical to clarify visions, missions, goals, and expectations. This goes along with building, leading, and motivating teams by recognizing strengths, resolving conflicts, and fostering positive team dynamics. Therefore, the competence to coach employees, provide feedback, create development opportunities and an environment that fosters ownership, creativity, and collaboration is necessary. Furthermore, it is essential to promote a culture of innovation and continuous improvement to ensure learning and long-term competitiveness. Some of the ways in which transformative serious games can be used to promote the above-mentioned skills are briefly described below as examples.

Gamification approaches that aim to develop team management skills allow players to analyze team roles, lead teams, resolve conflicts, motivate team members, and promote teamwork, collaboration, and effective communication. These games can offer both single-player and multiplayer modes to encourage collaboration and leadership and are intricately connected with serious games that aim at developing specific skills, such as the ability to motivate employees, communicate vision, make decisions, and resolve conflicts. Therefore, in addition to individual progress, cultural and team-building benefits are also possible through interactive collaboration of teams, which can be valuable for the entire organization. Players can try out different leadership styles and improve their understanding of effective leadership. Games that focus on conflict resolution offer the opportunity to experience different conflict scenarios and develop practical resolution strategies to find win-win solutions. Exercisers learn to identify, analyze, distinguish between several types of conflict, listen empathetically, find compromises, strengthen team relationships, and constructively resolve conflicts. Another possibility that utilizes game mechanics could be, that a player takes on the role of a mentor and support virtual team members in their professional development. Therefore, coaching skills, giving feedback, setting goals, and recognizing individual strengths and weaknesses of team members are required. Summing up, serious games encourage the development of emotional intelligence in several ways by challenging players differently. Possible fields of application or concrete implementations are solution clusters, tool libraries or problem-solving safe spaces.

3.2 Transformative Serious Games for Leading in Crisis

In crises situations quick decisions and rapid responses even under uncertainty, pressure, and limited resources are of immense importance to manage the situation effectively while minimizing damages and protect employees and stakeholders. This requires an analysis of the situation, weighing up risks and opportunities and the ability to make bold decisions and communicate them clearly to create trust and security while influencing public perception. Below are some examples that briefly describe how transformative serious games can be utilized to foster the skills mentioned above.

Serious games are very well suited to simulate crisis situations where players learn to react quickly, prioritize, assess risks, and make effective decisions under uncertainty and pressure by gathering, analyzing, and evaluating information. These games can depict distinct types of crises, including humanitarian crises, technical failures, security incidents and more, to prepare players for real-life situations. Others can confront players with various emergency scenarios, such as natural disasters and environmental crises as oil spills, forest fires or water shortages, terrorist attacks, pandemics or situations in which they must ensure the safety of employees, facilities, and data. They learn to plan preventative measures, respond appropriately to unforeseen events including coordination with external authorities and aid organizations and can be made aware of a wide variety of risks in a sustainable manner through a range of scenarios, often assessed under time pressure and decision making which determine different outcomes. Other scenarios might encourage players to take on the role of medical or safety staff as they have to deal with emergency setups such as heart attacks, accidents, or the like. They learn to take life-saving measures, prioritize medical care and act effectively under pressure. It is common that such situations are designed as team tasks in which the learners must lead an adventurous setting. Frequent applications can therefore be found in immersive (digital) experience and adventure worlds such as crises micro-learning, nightmare-competitor-, or worst-case-scenarios. Those measures require a clear understanding of oneself, the associated leadership by example and corresponding skills as well as a sense of team and organizational dynamics to maintain a holistic overview.

3.3 Transformative Serious Games for Leading by Example

Integrity is a fundamental quality for leaders who want to lead by example. They act ethically and morally correct and keep their promises and commitments. As confident humans they have a clear understanding of their strengths, weaknesses, and personality traits. They are aware of their impact on others and can reflect on their actions. Self-reflection enables them to continuously develop and improve, what goes hand in hand with an open mindset towards continuous learning and personal development. They actively seek new insights, skills, and perspectives to improve their leadership skills and adapt to challenges. Here are a few examples that briefly outline how transformative serious games can be employed to cultivate these skills.

By integrating case studies and scenarios, serious games can provide leaders with the opportunity to deal with specific situations where leadership by example is required. They can be confronted with challenges that real leaders face and must show how they can be a role model for their team through their behavior and decisions. Games can integrate feedback and evaluation options to provide players with continuous feedback on their leadership behavior. Some serious games deliberately integrate reflection phases or breaks in which players are asked to think about what has happened and organize their thoughts, e.g., using journaling or self-assessment tools that help defining their learning goals and tracking progress. This enables them to recognize their strengths and weaknesses and to develop further in a targeted manner. Such a behavior is also promoted by games that allow players to take on the role of different characters, look at a situation from diverse angles or even the integration of other persons via group discussions. This interactive form of reflection encourages players to share ideas and develop together. Narrative-based decision-making games allow to make decisions that affect the course of the storyline often referring to moral dilemmas. They must consider ethical principles while making decisions that can have an impact on their team, organization or even society, setting a positive example. Concrete implementations would therefore be role-playing games, any form of theatre and further performances, self-image/other-image comparisons, shadowing approaches and much more.

4 Discussion and Future Research

By awareness and active considering the three dimensions of leadership, organizations can become more flexible, adaptable, and resilient. This is crucial for success in both the constantly changing macro-environment and specific challenges and requires the development of polydextric leadership skills preferably through transformative play.

Regarding potential media-specific approaches to make game developments even more immersive for users and game experiences even more transformative, it is advisable to incorporate forms of social interaction, where (future) leaders can work together or give peer feedback and learn from each other to achieve an overarching goal. Leveraging gamification for social collaboration proves especially effective in collectively tackling challenges, facilitating decision-making, and fostering consensus-building. In addition, the approach must be equipped with effective basic gamification and reward elements. The fundamental motivation of players lies in the satisfaction of basic human needs and desires, including the desire for reward, self-expression, altruism, or competition. Accordingly, we believe it makes sense to combine serious games with further training approaches creating a dual skill development strategy. These can range from classic lessons to training, counseling, instruction, coaching, supervision, or mentoring. The form must therefore follow the content and objectives [11] of the transformative gamified training approach.

Gamification may be a useful strategy to utilize in teaching leadership; however, there is a lack of empirical validation for the theoretical models of leadership skills development using game-based learning. Accordingly, supplementary research, game development, application and evaluation are needed to further develop polydextric leadership skills that help to navigate polycrises in a gamified way. The chances of achieving success here are good, as the number of games and literature has increased substantially, and many are convinced of the effectiveness of game-based training.

Acknowledgments. The idea for this article was developed as part of an Innovation Cheque from Innosuisse in cooperation with the implementation partner Rotmont GmbH.

Disclosure of Interests. The authors have no competing interests to declare that are relevant to the content of this article.

References

1. Ivancic, R., Olbert-Bock, S., Oberholzer, B.: Leadership-Polydextrie – Zur besonderen Notwendigkeit kontextualer Führung innerhalb von Einsatzorganisationen. zfo – Zeitschrift für Führung + Organisation (under review)
2. Hao, T., Liu, Z., Bao, H., Chen, S., Llamas, J., Llamas, M.: Gamification as an effective method in developing leadership skills and competencies. The Scholarship Without Borders Journal **1**(2), 1–15 (2024)
3. Mordor Intelligence: Global Serious Games Market (2023–2028). https://www.mordorintell igence.com/industry-reports/serious-games-market. Accessed 29 Apr 2025
4. Breuer, J.S., Bente, G.: Why so serious? On the relation of serious games and learning. Eludamos. Journal for Computer Game Culture **1**(4), 7–24 (2010)
5. Michael, D.R., Chen, S.: Serious games: Games that Educate. Train and Inform. Muska & Lipman, Boston (2005)
6. Hammady, R., Arnab, S.: Serious gaming for behaviour change: a systematic review. Information **13**(142), 1–27 (2022)
7. Grint, K.: Leadership, management and command in the time of the coronavirus. Leadership **3**(16), 314–319 (2020)
8. Connolly, T.M., Boyle, E.A., MacArthur, E., Hainey, T., Boyle, T.M.: A systematic literature review of empirical evidence on computer games and serious games. Comput. Educ. **2**(59), 661–686 (2012)
9. Westera, W.: Why and how serious games can become far more effective: accommodating productive learning experiences, learner motivation and the monitoring of learning gains. Education, Technology & Society **1**(22), 56–69 (2019)
10. Ferreira, A.T., Araújo, A.M., Fernandes, S., Miguel, I.C.: Gamification in the workplace: a systematic literature review. In: Rocha, Á., Correia, A.M., Adeli, H., Reis, L.P., Costanzo, S. (eds.) WorldCIST 2017. AISC, vol. 571, pp. 283–292. Springer, Cham (2017). https://doi.org/10.1007/978-3-319-56541-5_29
11. Ivancic, R.: Zur notwendigkeit externer interventionen: supervision, coaching, mentoring und consulting als ansätze systemischer entwicklung. In: Laske, S., Orhety, A., Schmid, M.J. (eds.) PersonalEntwickeln: Das aktuelle Nachschlagewerk für Praktiker: 296. Erg.-Lfg. zum Loseblattwerk Dezember 2023, pp. 1–42. Deutscher Wirtschaftsdienst, Köln (2023)

Escape Game Chatbot: Co-designing Educational Games for Sustainability

Michael Louis Eulenstein[1] and Thorsten Schoormann[2(✉)]

[1] Universität Hildesheim, Universitätsplatz 1, 31141 Hildesheim, Germany
`eulensteinm@uni-hildesheim.de`
[2] Department of People and Technology, Roskilde University, Universitetsvej 1,
DK-4000 Roskilde, Denmark
`tschoormann@ruc.dk`

Abstract. The growing use of escape games in education has led to innovative digital tools that support learning and teaching. This paper introduces the *Escape Game Chatbot*, a ChatGPT-based tool that assists users in co-designing educational escape games through guided narrative planning, puzzle creation, and alignment with learning objectives focused on Sustainable Development Goals. The *Escape Game Chatbot* aims to lower design barriers for educators and game designers lacking expertise in this context. A formative evaluation with 15 university participants indicates positive impacts on design understanding, creativity support, and the likelihood of the *Escape Game Chatbot*'s reuse.

Keywords: Chatbot · AI-assisted pedagogy · Sustainability · Escape Games

1 Introduction

In the educational sector, a surge in interest for innovative learning formats is evident. Recent studies on playful learning demonstrate a positive effect on student motivation and engagement [1,2]. Digital Educational Escape Rooms (DEERs) stand out as collaborative and interactive learning activities [3,4], but their design demands a blend of pedagogical and game design skills [3] including narrative building, riddle crafting, and pedagogical alignment, which often requires significant time and scaffolding [3–6]. This complexity, combined with the urgent need to integrate sustainability education, highlights a gap: current literature reveals limited playful learning applications for the Sustainable Development Goals (SDGs), despite calls for immediate climate education [7,8]. Large language models such as ChatGPT have advanced chatbot capabilities beyond rule-based approaches [9], enabling context-aware, few-shot interactions that support personalized educational guidance and complex instructional design tasks [10,11].

This paper contributes the third iteration's design, implementation, and evaluation of the *Escape Game Chatbot*, a ChatGPT-based tool that guides users

S. Bakkes et al. (Eds.): GALA 2025, LNCS 16307, pp. 363–368, 2026.
https://doi.org/10.1007/978-3-032-11043-5_35

through narrative planning, puzzle creation, and SDG-aligned learning objectives to democratize DEER development for non-technical educators.

2   Research Background

AI-powered chatbots have emerged as promising design companions, providing structure and scaffolding in serious games [12,13]. Beyond content delivery, they can foster immersion and personalized learner experiences, serving as motivational tools aligned with self-determination theory [14,15] and have proven effective as design assistants in educational contexts, helping structure complex creative processes and providing scaffolding for non-technical users. However, overly complex designs risk overwhelming users, while simplified structures may hinder comprehensive design support [3]. Our approach builds upon the EscapED framework [5], which offers a six-step manual design methodology (Participants, Objectives, Theme, Puzzles, Equipment, Evaluation) for physical escape rooms, and Nicholson's classroom guidelines [4], transforming these traditional workflows into an AI-assisted digital process through the *Escape Game Chatbot*, which leverages a Design Canvas with eight building blocks such as theme, puzzles, and target group to support educators in DEER development [6].

3   Design and Evaluation

3.1   Practical Utility of the Escape Game Chatbot

To assess the practical utility of the second iteration of the *Escape Game Chatbot*, we surveyed 15 university educators, staff, and students in spring 2025 using Likert-scale items and open-ended questions. Overall, the evaluation demonstrated the chatbot's accessibility for educational game design, with most participants indicating they would recommend and reuse it. As summarized in Table 1, participants rated the chatbot's clarity of instructions highly (4.07), its support for understanding DEER design (3.73), creativity support (4.00), entertainment value (3.80), post-use confidence (3.60), and likelihood of reuse (3.87). Qualitative feedback highlighted its reliability (minor spelling and export issues) and its pedagogical value: *"The Chatbot helped me structure the storyline while aligning tasks with educational goals."* Users appreciated the *Escape Game Chatbot's* usability, noting: *"Versatile in use, quickly understandable... ideal for study and teaching"* and *"I would like to integrate escape rooms into my teaching. The chatbot makes it easier."*

3.2   Illustrating the Escape Game Chatbot

The feedback gathered during the evaluation led to enhancements for the third iteration (see Table 2). Based on participant feedback requesting improved memory retention, clearer prompt grouping, support for multimedia riddles, and downloadable PDF output, the third iteration employed established prompt

Table 1. Summary of Likert-Scale Evaluation Results (N = 15)

Evaluation Dimension	Mean Score (out of 5)
Clarity of Instructions	4.07
Understanding of DEER Design	3.73
Creativity Support	4.00
Entertainment Value	3.80
Confidence Post-Use	3.60
Likelihood of Reuse	3.87

engineering patterns [16,17] and implemented a dynamic Table of Contents for persistent memory across seven design blocks (see Fig. 1d). We added PDF export and flowchart generation (see Fig. 1b) using ChatGPT's API and Python, leveraging few-shot learning for adaptability [10]. The generated PDFs serve as implementation guides for educators, bridging the gap between digital design and physical DEER deployment. The system enables non-linear navigation through four intuitive entry prompts (see Fig. 1c) with one participant highlighting: *"Quickly implement creative ideas that would otherwise take a longer time to develop"*.

Table 2. Mapping User Feedback from Iteration 2

User Feedback	Implementation (Iteration 3)
Memory retention across design steps	Dynamic Table of Contents with progress tracking
Better cognitive flow	Thematically grouped prompts with established patterns [16,17]
Support for multimedia riddles	Flowchart generator for visual puzzle design
Downloadable output formats	PDF export functionality
Greater continuity	Persistent memory using ChatGPT's API

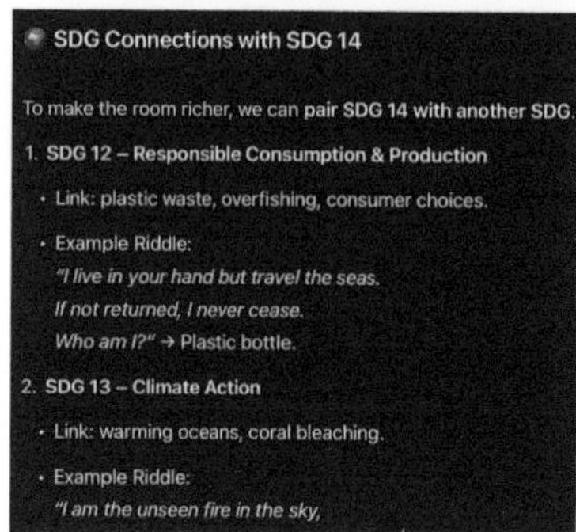

(a) SDG interconnection mapping for puzzle design

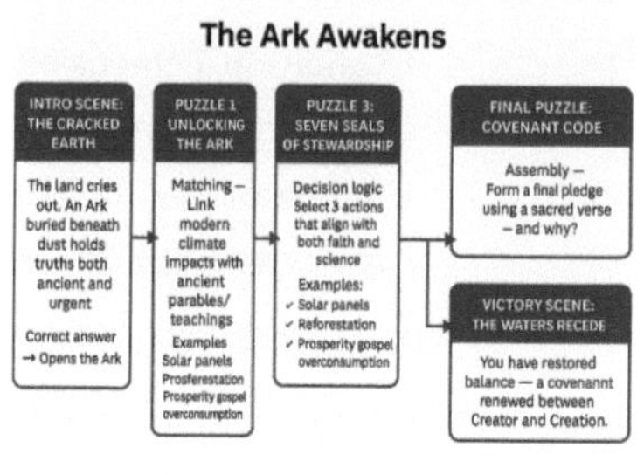

(b) Generated escape game flowchart structure

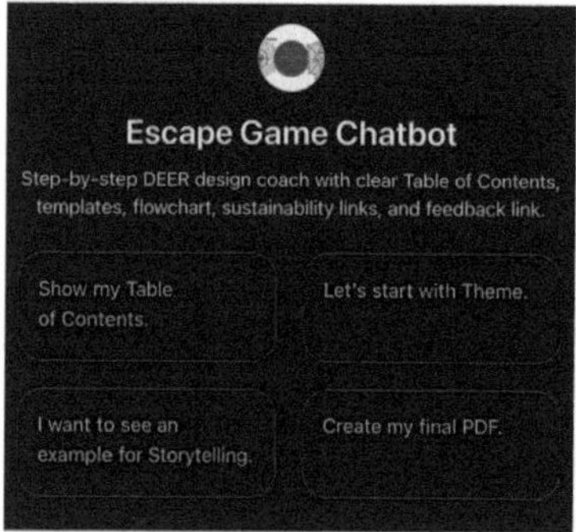

(c) Main chatbot interface with entry prompts

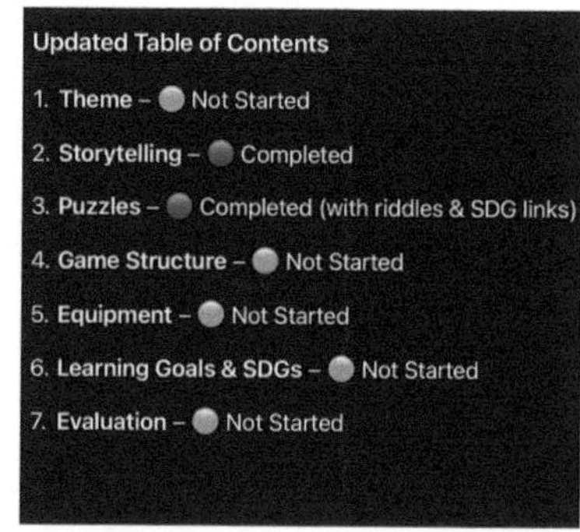

(d) Table of Contents with progress tracking

Fig. 1. Key features of the *Escape Game Chatbot*.

4   Discussion and Conclusion

While we already received promising findings, this study has limitations which open avenues for future research. The evaluation is constrained to the sample size that limits statistical power, while the absence of pre-post comparisons and control groups prevents causal claims about the *Escape Game Chatbot's* effectiveness. Although results show positive user feedback regarding clarity and creativity support, the tool's pedagogical impact requires further validation. Future evaluations will address these limitations through larger sample sizes, controlled designs, and assessment of actual DEERs produced using the system. Additionally, comparative studies with traditional design methods and integration with established platforms like Genial.ly will strengthen the evidence base. To support iterative improvement, the iteration features persistent feedback mechanisms that enable participatory design, allowing educators to continuously shape its capabilities based on practical use. In conclusion, the *Escape Game Chatbot* as a prototype exemplifies how LLMs like ChatGPT can serve as enablers in educational design processes, particularly for non-technical users aiming to create pedagogically grounded digital escape games. The tool offers guidance by translating complex instructional design processes into a structure. Positioned at the intersection of AI-assisted pedagogy and informal, game-based education, the *Escape Game Chatbot* also contributes to the discourse on responsible AI use in learning design [18].

Disclosure of Interests. The authors declare that they have no competing interests.

References

1. Alotaibi, M.S.: Game-based learning in early childhood education: a systematic review and meta-analysis. Front. Educ. 9 April 2024. https://doi.org/10.3389/feduc.2024.1362155. Systematic review showing game-based learning gained popularity with moderate to large effects on learning outcomes
2. Li, Y., et al.: The impact of digital educational games on student's motivation and learning engagement. Front. Psychol. 15 January 2024. https://doi.org/10.3389/fpsyg.2024.1287031
3. Veldkamp, A., van de Grint, L., Knippels, M.P.J., van Joolingen, W.R.: Escape education: a systematic review on escape rooms in education **31**, 100364. https://doi.org/10.1016/j.edurev.2020.100364
4. Nicholson, S.: Creating engaging escape rooms for the classroom. **94**(1), 44–49. https://doi.org/10.1080/00094056.2018.1420363
5. Clarke, S., et al.: Escaped: a framework for creating educational escape rooms and interactive games for higher/further education. Int. J. Serious Games 4(3), 18–32 (2017). https://doi.org/10.17083/ijsg.v4i3.180
6. Eulenstein, M.L., et al.: Learning through designing: a visual inquiry tool for digital educational escape games. In: Schönbohm, A., (eds.) Games and Learning Alliance, vol. 15348, pp. 394–400. Springer Nature Switzerland (2025). https://doi.org/10.1007/978-3-031-78269-5_41
7. Sabarwal, S., Marin, S.V., Spivack, M., Ambasz, D.: Choosing our future: education for climate action. technical report, world Bank, Washington, DC, September 2024. URL https://hdl.handle.net/10986/42098. License: CC BY 3.0 IGO
8. United Nations sustainable development solutions network. UN SDG Guide for Universities (2024). https://ap-unsdsn.org/wp-content/uploads/University-SDG-Guide_web.pdf Accessed 16 Sep 2025
9. Ray, P.P.: ChatGPT: a comprehensive review on background, applications, key challenges, bias, ethics, limitations and future scope. Internet Things Cyber-Physical Syst. **3**, 121–154 (2023). https://doi.org/10.1016/j.iotcps.2023.04.003
10. Brown, T., Mann, B., Ryder, N., et al.: Language models are few-shot learners. Adv. Neural. Inf. Process. Syst. **33**, 1877–1901 (2020)
11. Lund, B.D., et al.: ChatGPT and a new academic reality: artificial intelligence-written research papers and the ethics of the large language models in scholarly publishing. J. Assoc. Inf. Sci. Technol. (2023). https://doi.org/10.1002/asi.24750. Comprehensive review describing ChatGPT as OpenAI's generative pre-trained transformer with context-aware capabilities
12. Labadze, L., Grigolia, M., Machaidze, L.: Role of AI chatbots in education: systematic literature review. **20**(1), 56. https://doi.org/10.1186/s41239-023-00426-1

13. Aster, A., Lotz, A., Raupach, T.: Theoretical background of the game design element "chatbot" in serious games for medical education. Adv. Simul. **10** (2025). https://doi.org/10.1186/s41077-025-00341-7
14. Rosmalen, P.V., Eikelboom, J., Bloemers, E.: Towards a game-chatbot: extending the interaction in serious games. In: Proceedings of the European Conference on Games Based Learning (ECGBL) (2012)
15. Filippi, M., Dio, S.D., Schillaci, D., Malorni, S.: Conversation design for raising awareness on the responsible use of the internet: co-design of a chatbot game with secondary school students. In: International Conference on Design, Learning and Innovation (2022). https://doi.org/10.1007/978-3-031-49811-4_74
16. Giray, L.: Prompt engineering with ChatGPT: a guide for academic writers. Ann. Biomed. Eng. **51**(12), 2629–2633 (2023). https://doi.org/10.1007/s10439-023-03272-4
17. White, J., Fu, Q., Hays, S., Sandborn, M., et al.: A prompt pattern catalog to enhance prompt engineering with ChatGPT. arXiv preprint arXiv:2302.11382 (2023). URL https://arxiv.org/abs/2302.11382
18. Schoormann, T., Gupta, S., Möller, F., Kruse, L.C.: With great power comes great responsibility: responsible management of artificial intelligence in supporting design research activities. In: Proceedings of the 58th Annual Hawaii International Conference on System Sciences (HICSS-58), pp. 5405–5414, Maui, HI, 2025. Hawaii International Conference on System Sciences

Exploring Minecraft Education Edition's Effects on Motivation and Learning Strategies in STEM Subjects

Masiar Babazadeh[(✉)] [iD] and Jonathan Ferreras Ferreras [iD]

Department of Education and Learning/University of Teacher Education, University of Applied Sciences and Arts of Southern Switzerland (SUPSI), Locarno, Switzerland
masiar.babazadeh@supsi.ch, jonathan.ferreras@edu.ti.ch

Abstract. This case study investigates the impact of Minecraft Education Edition (MEE) on middle school students' motivation and learning strategies in science, technology, engineering, and math (STEM) subjects through a quasi-experimental mixed-method approach, combining qualitative and quantitative data analysis. The intervention was structured across two complementary settings: a voluntary after-school program and an integrated curricular activity. The after-school program involved two age groups (19 students aged 11–14), each participating in five sessions. The curricular integration occurred in third-grade science classes, with one small group of 7 students. Activities used predefined Minecraft worlds focused on biodiversity, space exploration, cybersecurity, and structural design. Data from the Motivated Strategies for Learning Questionnaire (MSLQ) and qualitative observations revealed a complex pattern of effects. While students showed high engagement, quantitative data revealed a significant decrease in metacognitive self-regulation and an increase in performance anxiety across both groups. The structured curricular setting, however, was associated with gains in cognitive strategies like elaboration. These results suggest that while MEE is a powerful tool for engagement, its effective implementation requires thoughtful pedagogical scaffolding to help students manage its cognitive and social challenges. Further investigation is warranted to optimize its integration into curricula.

Keywords: Game-Based Learning (GBL) · STEM Education · Self-Regulated Learning · Motivation · Cognitive Load · Minecraft

1 Introduction

Contemporary education faces the challenge of effectively engaging digital native students, particularly in Science, Technology, Engineering, and Mathematics (STEM) fields. These learners, immersed in technology from a young age, often exhibit a natural affinity for digital, three-dimensional spaces where exploration and experimentation feel less constrained than in traditional classroom settings [10]. Many middle school students hesitate to express ideas openly in class due to fear of judgment or error, hindering learning processes crucial in STEM disciplines where experimentation is key. Virtual environments like Minecraft Education Edition (MEE) offer a constructivist learning environment supporting exploration, creativity, and collaboration [10] to bridge this gap, yet despite the recognized potential of game-based learning [2, 5] a systematic understanding of their impact on motivation and learning strategies remains underdeveloped. The central problem addressed by this research is the gap between traditional teaching methodologies and the learning preferences of digital natives, specifically concerning motivation and the development of effective learning strategies in STEM. This short study tries to investigate in what way the use of MEE influences motivation and learning strategies in STEM subjects. Utilizing a mixed-methods approach, this study examines changes in motivational components and learning strategies as measured by the MSLQ [11]. Preliminary findings with small sample sizes suggest a complex interplay, including increased engagement and intrinsic motivation alongside unexpected decreases in metacognitive self-regulation and increases in test anxiety, highlighting the critical role of implementation context.

2 Theoretical Framework

This study is grounded in several theoretical perspectives relevant to game-based learning (GBL), motivation, and learning strategies in STEM education. GBL utilizes game mechanics and environments to achieve educational goals, including STEM [2] subjects. MEE as a didactic tool exemplifies the adaptation of a commercial game for educational purposes [11]. Its sandbox nature allows students to experiment with STEM concepts through direct construction and manipulation within a virtual world. Research indicates MEE can develop both disciplinary knowledge and transversal skills [8, 10]. The hypothesis behind Self-Determination Theory (SDT) suggests that intrinsic motivation arises when psychological needs for competence, autonomy, and relatedness are met [3]. Game environments often facilitate these needs. The concept of 'flow', a state of optimal concentration and engagement, is frequently observed in gaming and is linked to enhanced learning. Gamified elements in STEM contexts have been shown to significantly increase student motivation compared to traditional methods [6]. To these regards, MEE aligns well with Kolb's [9] experiential learning cycle and Vygotsky's social constructivism, emphasizing learning through social interaction, while Papert's constructionism is directly applicable to MEE's building mechanics. GBL environments facilitate collaborative knowledge co-construction, acting as virtual labs for authentic STEM practices [7], including planning, monitoring, and evaluating one's learning. MEE potentially supports self-regulation through its inherent cycles of planning, execution, and reflection, facilitated by immediate environmental feedback. Strategies developed in digital game environments may be transferable to other contexts [1].

3 Methodology

This study employed a quasi-experimental, mixed-methods design with a pre-post-test to investigate learning in authentic educational settings. Pre-test also measured a potential confounding variable related to the students' prior exposure with Minecraft. About half of the sample reported to be either occasional or regular players, while the others either had no experience or rarely played. The participants were 26 middle school students from Ticino, Switzerland, divided into two natural groups: an extracurricular after-school program (N = 19, grades 1–4, approx. 11–14 years old) and a curricular science class (N = 7, grade 3, approx. 13 years old). The intervention took place between February and March 2025, and received ethical approval from the relevant ethic committees, and written informed consent was obtained from all the parties involved. The after-school program consisted of five sessions of one class hour each using predefined MEE worlds focused on biodiversity and space exploration. The curricular integration involved two class hours where MEE activities were aligned with specific science curriculum objectives. The quantitative measure was collected through an adapted MSLQ (7-point Likert scale) pre- and post-intervention to assess motivational and learning strategy components. Based on the MSLQ's modular design [4], we omitted the 'peer learning' and 'help-seeking' subscales to focus on individual self-regulation. The teacher conducted systematic, semi-structured qualitative observations during all MEE sessions. Potential confounding variables were noted, including technical issues related to the hardware and the inherent social visibility of students' performance. While systematic controls for these factors were not part of the design, their influence was qualitatively monitored.

4   Results

The analysis of quantitative MSLQ data and qualitative observations revealed complex and context-dependent effects following the MEE intervention. Table 1 and Table 3 show the Motivational components results. We omitted the subscales focusing on Extrinsic Orientation, Task Value, and Control of Learning Beliefs to focus on the subscales that will help answer our research question. The same applies for Table 2 and Table 4, where we omitted the Critical Thinking and Time and Environment Management subscales. In the Tables, Cohen's d is indicated as "d".

Table1. Motivational components result for the after-school group (N = 19).

Subscale	Mean PRE	Mean POST	Diff.	t-value	p-value	d
Intrinsic Orientation	4.82 (0.79)	5.05 (1.01)	+ 0.24	0.91	0.38	0.21
Self-Efficacy	4.67 (0.77)	4.91 (0.64)	+ 0.24	1.04	0.31	0.24
Test Anxiety	3.79 (1.54)	4.99 (0.65)	+ 1.20	3.38	0.00	0.78

Table 1 and Table 2 (in the "Mean" column, the value in parentheses represents the standard deviation) show the results of the pre- and post-test with the MSLQ in the after-school group. Quantitatively, the after-school program (N = 19) showed statistically significant changes primarily in affective and regulatory domains, in fact test anxiety increased significantly, registering a medium to large effect size (Mean Diff = + 1.20, d = 0.78, p < 0.05). Conversely, students reported a decrease in metacognitive self-regulation, with a large negative effect size (Mean Diff = -0.98, d = 0.98, p < 0.001). A

Table 2. Learning strategies results for the after-school group (N = 19).

Subscale	Mean PRE	Mean POST	Diff.	t-value	p-value	d
Rehearsal	5.16 (1.06)	4.91 (0.94)	-0.25	-0.92	0.37	0.21
Elaboration	5.07 (0.87)	4.62 (1.14)	-0.45	-1.27	0.22	0.29
Organization	4.82 (1.49)	4.84 (1.19)	+ 0.03	0.07	0.95	0.02
Metacognitive Self-Regulation	4.86 (0.82)	3.88 (0.65)	-0.98	-4.28	0.00	0.98
Effort Regulation	5.16 (1.34)	4.05 (1.25)	-1.11	-2.30	0.03	0.53

significant decrease in effort regulation was also reported, showing a medium negative effect size (Mean Diff = -1.11, d = 0.53, p < 0.05).

Other motivational components like intrinsic orientation and self-efficacy showed slight, non-significant increases, while cognitive strategies like elaboration and rehearsal exhibited minor, non-significant decreases. Table 3 and Table 4 show the results of the pre- and post-test with the MSLQ in the single class. In this smaller curricular integration group (N = 7), the pattern differed.

Table 3. Motivational Components results for the single class (N = 7).

Subscale	Mean PRE	Mean POST	Diff.	t-value	p-value	d
Intrinsic Orientation	5.07 (0.84)	5.36 (0.80)	+ 0.29	0.56	0.60	0.21
Self-Efficacy	5.20 (1.02)	5.29 (0.99)	+ 0.08	0.16	0.88	0.06
Test Anxiety	3.19 (1.17)	4.18 (1.05)	+ 1.00	1.46	0.19	0.55

While metacognitive self-regulation also decreased almost significantly with a large negative effect size (Mean Diff = -0.45, d = 0.85, p = 0.07), other changes pointed towards potential cognitive benefits. Elaboration strategies showed an increase that approached statistical significance (Mean Diff = 0.50, d = 0.72, p = 0.10), and organization strategies also trended upwards with a small effect size (Mean Diff = 0.64, d = 0.38, p = 0.36). Intrinsic goal orientation increased with a not significant effect size (d = 0.21, p = 0.19), though statistical significance was not reached. Test anxiety also rose in this group, but the effect size was medium and not significant (d = 0.55, p = 0.19), and effort regulation showed minimal change (d = 0.10, p = 0.81). Qualitative observations provided rich context for these quantitative patterns. High levels of engagement and enthusiasm were consistently noted across both settings, particularly during collaborative building tasks where students often worked intensely, sometimes exhibiting "flow" states. This aligns with the trend towards increased intrinsic motivation seen in the MSLQ data. Collaboration itself was a dynamic process. While students were highly engaged, initial structured plans often deteriorated during execution, leading to conflicts but also spurring more synergistic collaboration. These observations explain the quantitative decreases in self-regulation: students engaged in planning but struggled to monitor and adhere to their plans amid technical or practical frustrations.

Table 4. Learning Strategies results for the single class (N = 7).

Subscale	Mean PRE	Mean POST	Diff.	t-value	p-value	d
Rehearsal	5.24 (0.90)	5.33 (0.92)	+ 0.10	0.18	0.87	0.07
Elaboration	5.00 (0.66)	5.50 (0.50)	+ 0.50	1.91	0.10	0.72
Organization	4.57 (0.84)	5.21 (1.07)	+ 0.64	1.00	0.36	0.38
Metacognitive Self-Regulation	4.71 (0.67)	4.26 (0.50)	-0.45	-2.24	0.07	0.85
Effort Regulation	4.60 (1.28)	4.30 (1.17)	-0.21	-0.25	0.81	0.10

This frustration often led to task abandonment, reflecting the decrease in reported effort regulation. Similarly, observed "novelty" and "performance" anxiety align with the increased test anxiety scores. Contextual differences mirrored quantitative findings: the less-structured after-school group showed more frustration, while the curricular group was more task-focused, likely supporting their development of elaboration strategies. Overall, MEE fostered creative problem-solving but also presented significant cognitive and affective challenges.

5 Discussion and Conclusion

In this paper we presented a mixed-methods case study investigating how MME influences student motivation and learning strategies in STEM subjects. The two observed case studies are not comparable (in size, population, context, exposure time), yet such study suggests context-dependency of the approach, the role of structure, and the importance of scaffolding. Our findings indicate that MEE is a powerful catalyst for engagement, yet it depends on the implementation context. MEE presents a significant cognitive load, causing a "temporary destabilization" of students' existing strategies. This emerged through a decrease in metacognitive self-regulation in both settings (curricular $p = 0.07$, $t = -2.24$, $d = 0.85$, after-school $p = 0.00$, $t = -4.28$, $d = 0.98$). This 'temporary destabilization' challenges the assumption that GBL environments are inherently self-regulatory and highlights the need for explicit pedagogical scaffolding, as suggested by constructionist learning theories. This challenge was accompanied by increased test anxiety, particularly in the after-school program ($d = 0.78$), which we could link to the social visibility of performance. This finding contrasts with studies that focus purely on the motivational benefits of GBL and suggests that the social pressures in collaborative virtual worlds can negatively impact affect, as predicted by SDT when perceived competence is threatened. The after-school group also showed decreased effort regulation when facing complexities without curricular pressure. Conversely, structure fostered cognitive benefits. The curricular group showed better elaboration ($p = 0.10$, $t = 1.91$, $d = 0.72$)

and organization (p = 0.36, t = 1.00, d = 0.38) strategies, an effect absent in the more exploratory after-school context. While MEE has educational potential, its implementation requires designs that help students adapt their regulation strategies to this complex, social environment; practitioners should support planning and reflection, foster a safe culture to reduce performance anxiety, and integrate MEE activities with clear curricular goals. This study's limitations include a small sample, short duration, and the unassessed reliability of the translated MSLQ, precluding causal claims and requiring future validation. Findings were also impacted by uncontrolled confounders: technical issues likely increased frustration and lowered effort regulation, while the social visibility of in-game work likely raised performance anxiety. Future research should use larger samples and longitudinal designs.

Disclosure of Interests. The authors have no competing interests to declare that are relevant to the content of this article.

References

1. Broadbent, J., Poon, W.L.: Self-regulated learning strategies & academic achievement in online higher education learning environments: a systematic review. The Internet and Higher Education **27**, 1–13 (2015)
2. Clark, D.B., Tanner-Smith, E.E., Killingsworth, S.S.: Digital games, design, and learning: a systematic review and meta-analysis. Rev. Educ. Res. **86**(1), 79–122 (2016)
3. Deci, E.L., Ryan, R.M.: The "what" and "why" of goal pursuits: human needs and the self-determination of behavior. Psychol. Inq. **11**(4), 227–268 (2000)
4. Duncan, T.G., McKeachie, W.J.: The making of the motivated strategies for learning questionnaire. Educational Psychologist **40**(2), 117–128 (2005)
5. Gee, J.P.: Good Video Games + Good Learning: Collected Essays on Video Games, Learning, and Literacy. Peter Lang (2007)
6. Hamari, J., Shernoff, D.J., Rowe, E., Coller, B., Asbell-Clarke, J., Edwards, T.: Challenging games help students learn: an empirical study on engagement, flow and immersion in game-based learning. Comput. Hum. Behav. **54**, 170–179 (2016)
7. Kafai, Y.B., Burke, Q.: Constructionist gaming: understanding the benefits of making games for learning. Educational Psychologist **50**(4), 313–334 (2015)
8. Karsenti, T., Bugmann, J., Gros, P.P.: Transforming education with Minecraft? Results of an exploratory study conducted with 118 elementary school students. CRIFPE (2017)
9. Kolb, D.A.: Experiential Learning: Experience as the Source of Learning and Development. Prentice-Hall (1984)
10. Nebel, S., Schneider, S., Rey, G.D.: Mining learning and crafting scientific experiments: a literature review on the use of Minecraft in education and research. J. Educ. Technol. Soc. **19**(2), 355–366 (2016)
11. Pintrich, P.R., Smith, D.A.F., Garcia, T., McKeachie, W.J.: A manual for the use of the Motivated Strategies for Learning Questionnaire (MSLQ). National Center for Research to Improve Postsecondary Teaching and Learning, University of Michigan (1991)

Avatar-Based Serious Game for Training Psychologists in Rorschach Test Administration: An Evaluation from Experts

Antonio Pio Facchino^(✉) ⓘ, Daniela Marchetti ⓘ, Maria Cristina Verrocchio ⓘ, and Piero Porcelli ⓘ

Department of Psychology, G. d'Annunzio University of Chieti-Pescara, Chieti, Italy
antoniopio.facchino@phd.unich.it

Abstract. The Rorschach Test, a personality assessment instrument, is notoriously challenging to master and use accurately due to the complexities of managing technical procedures and interpersonal dynamics. Serious games are a valuable opportunity to enhance training through flexibility, interactivity, and engagement. This study provides a preliminary evaluation of an avatar-based serious game for teaching the Rorschach Test administration process. The software features separate interfaces for students and teachers. Ten experts completed a survey on their Rorschach experience and participated in two sessions with the game, first as students and then as teachers. After the first session, they assessed the avatar's usability and their experience, and after the second session, they evaluated the software's usability, usefulness, and representativeness.

Results showed that both interfaces were rated positively for usability, and experts reported high efficacy in administering the Rorschach Test. The serious game was considered an accurate simulation and a valuable training tool. These preliminary findings support its potential as an effective resource for Rorschach Test training, highlighting areas for improvement for psychologists' training.

Keywords: Serious Game · Rorschach · Avatar

1 Introduction

The Rorschach Test is a psychological assessment tool constituted by ten inkblot cards (five multicolored and five in shades of gray), administered and coded following a standardized procedure. In the first "response phase" of administration, clients are asked what the inkblots might be. In the following "inquiry phase", the inkblots are resubmitted, and clients are asked to explain their perception in details. This task requires complex perceptual problem-solving, involving the identification and interpretation of meaningful elements within the inkblots [1]. Responses are then systematically coded according to variables such as location (where the perception occurs) and determinants (the features that shape perception, including form, color, shading, and movement) [2].

S. Bakkes et al. (Eds.): GALA 2025, LNCS 16307, pp. 375–380, 2026.
https://doi.org/10.1007/978-3-032-11043-5_37

The test is widely applied in mental health and forensic contexts and is included in more than half of psychology training programs, where students show strong interest and acknowledge its professional relevance [3]. However, mastering its administration and interpretation remains difficult, requiring structured supervision and targeted instructional methods to support procedural skills, investigative strategies, and emotional regulation in unfamiliar settings [3, 4]. Traditional methods, lacking interactivity and experiential learning, limit practice with real patients and realistic protocols, highlighting the need for a practical, time-efficient tool for consistent Rorschach administration.

In this context, serious games, defined as computer-based games designed within a pedagogical framework to support teaching and learning [5], have shown positive outcomes in psychology education and training [6].

Existing evidence shows that serious games, by immersing students in realistic simulated environments, actively engaging them, and providing a safe context for practice with efficient, unbiased feedback at reduced cost and time [7], significantly enhance professional skills, such as conducting investigative interviews with children [8].

Building on this background, the present study aimed to develop a serious game, designed according to the three-phase model [10] (a structured framework for best-practice serious game design), which simulates Rorschach clients to train psychologists in proper test administration, and to gather insights from experts on potential refinements and improvements in usability, effectiveness, and user experience.

2 Methods and Materials

2.1 Participants

Data were collected in September-December 2024 using an online self-administered survey. The study was approved by the Ethics Committee of the G. d'Annunzio University of Chieti-Pescara [Institutional Review Board of Psychology] and conducted in accordance with the Declaration of Helsinki [9] and APA guidelines [10].

The sample comprised 10 Rorschach experts (Mage = 38.9, SD = 8.5; 4 men, 6 women) from Italian universities, with professional experience (Myears = 12.2, SD = 8.2). All had postgraduate training and at least three years of experience with the Rorschach Test, using either the Comprehensive System (CS [1]; N = 6) or the Rorschach Performance Assessment System (R-PAS [11]; N = 3). Six experts had 3–5 years of experience, and four had more than five years. All used the test regularly, but only one had prior experience with both systems, and only one had experience with serious games.

2.2 Serious Game Design and Mechanics

AVAROR is an avatar-based serious game, delivered as a web application for desktop PCs, designed to train psychologists in Rorschach Test administration. It provides two modes: a standard full-test administration and a short mode allowing teachers to select specific cards. The mechanics were developed to align with educational goals and preserve authenticity. The system includes two interfaces (Fig. 1). In the student interface, an avatar simulates a test subject and interacts with the inkblot stimuli, providing responses based on real patient data during the response phase and adding localization and determinant information during inquiry. Facial expressions have been implemented to enhance realism.

The teacher interface features a control panel for responses, emotions, and card management (rotation, switching, restarting, or ending), with additional localization options during the inquiry phase. The system ensures that only correct administration produces interpretable protocols, with response complexity adapted to student expertise. Students must adjust to avatars that resist, avoid, or over-respond, fostering flexibility and diagnostic reasoning, while experiencing emotions such as satisfaction, frustration, and amusement, and practicing professional neutrality, simulating real Rorschach administration.

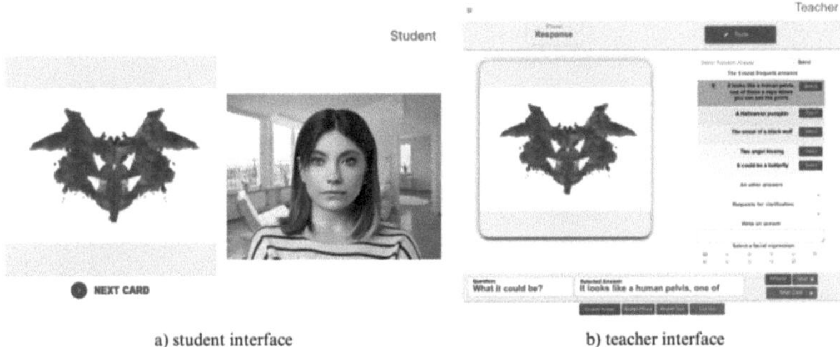

a) student interface   b) teacher interface

Fig. 1. Screenshots of AVAROR's student (a) and teacher (b) interfaces.

2.3 Procedure

After completing a pre-test survey on sociodemographic characteristics (age, gender), professional experience, Rorschach Test experience and system used (CS or R-PAS), and prior exposure to serious games, experts received training on AVAROR's student interface and directly administered the test to the avatar. They then completed a survey assessing usability and their Rorschach administration experience.

Usability was assessed with the Italian version of the System Usability Scale (SUS; [12, 13]) a 10-item questionnaire rated on a 5-point Likert scale with scores from 0 to 100, where higher values indicate greater perceived user satisfaction and usability of a system [14]. Experience in Rorschach administration was assessed with the 36-Item Questionnaire [4], rated on a 6-point Likert scale without a neutral option. It evaluates four domains: technical skills in administration, relational abilities in interpersonal dynamics, management of emotional experience, and perceived professional applicability. This last domain was omitted, as participants were already experienced. The instrument was translated into Italian by the authors through the back-translation process.

One week after using the student interface, experts participated in a second session, during which they received training on the teacher interface and directly operated the avatar controls while a researcher administered the Rorschach to the avatar. Afterwards, they completed a survey assessing system usability using the Italian SUS [12, 13] and evaluating the game's realism and usefulness for teaching Rorschach administration via ad hoc questions on a 10-point Likert-scale (1 = not at all; 10 = completely).

3   Results

Regarding the student interface, the usability was rated as good, indicating high perceived usability [14]. Experts reported low scores in the Rorschach administration process, reflecting a positive evaluation of their own experience [4]. Specifically, in terms of the technical aspects of the administration process, the task was considered easy, both in the response phase and in the inquiry phase. Similar results were found for interpersonal dynamics with the avatar and emotional experience.

Regarding the teacher interface, the usability was rated as good, indicating high perceived usability [14]. Moreover, experts reported that AVAROR is moderately representative of a real experience in Rorschach administration and declared a great utility for teaching the Rorschach administration process. Descriptive statistics are reported in Table 1.

Table 1. Descriptive statistics.

	M (SD)
Usability	
Student interface	81.25 (8.76)
Teacher interface	77 (8.39)
Experience in Rorschach's administration	
General technical aspects	1.19 (.59)
Response phase technical aspects	.67 (.47)
Inquiry phase technical aspects	1.34 (.90)
Interpersonal dynamics	1.08 (.64)
Emotional experience	1.32 (.35)
Rappresentativeness	5.60 (1.58)
Usefulness	7.30 (1.34)

4   Discussion

Psychologists' training poses significant challenges, including extensive preparation, ongoing feedback, and supervision, particularly for complex tests such as the widely used Rorschach [3, 4]. To address these challenges, there has been growing interest in using serious games in psychology. Supported by evidence in the literature [6], serious games appear to be a promising tool for psychologists and psychology students seeking to master Rorschach Test administration in a consistent, time-effective, and serviceable manner.

Therefore, the present study aimed to develop and provide a preliminary evaluation of AVAROR, an avatar-based serious game designed to support the learning of the Rorschach Test administration procedure. Following the three-phase model [15], the software was developed and evaluated by a panel of Rorschach administration experts.

The student interface of AVAROR received positive usability ratings, consistent with experts' assessments of the Rorschach administration experience, which indicated no technical, interpersonal, or emotional difficulties during interaction with the avatar. Analogous outcomes were identified for the teacher interface, which was rated favorably for usability, although slightly lower than the student interface. This difference is unsurprising, given the teacher interface's greater complexity and number of commands. Future improvements, such as a more organized response structure and a search feature, could further enhance the usability of teacher's interface. Overall, both interfaces were perceived as having good usability.

In accordance with these findings, the serious game was found to bear a moderate representativeness of a real Rorschach administration experience. In this regard, while the results appear promising, they were below our expectations. A possible technical explanation is that the avatar's lack of a signal while generating responses may have caused overlap with the examiner's question, reducing perceived representativeness. Additionally, experts may have rated the avatar as less representative due to their prior experience, consistent with the expertise-reversal effect [16], where methods effective for novices can be less beneficial or even detrimental for experts. Future versions, implementing further refinement like a signal when the avatar is generating a response may contribute to explain these results and increase representativeness.

Finally, all experts reported a high perceived utility of AVAROR for teaching the Rorschach administration process.

The present study is not free from limits. First, although sufficient for a preliminary evaluation, the sample size limits generalizability, and a larger sample could better clarify AVAROR's dynamics and effectiveness. Second, the use of questionnaires adapted from other languages warrants caution in interpreting the results.

Future research on AVAROR should include empirical trials with a larger sample of psychologists inexperienced in Rorschach administration. This would allow a more nuanced assessment of the interaction between software and interpersonal dynamics, as well as its impact on effectiveness. Comparing students' and experts' perceptions, and testing AVAROR against traditional methods, could highlight refinements and improve insights into usability, effectiveness and user experience.

Overall, these present findings highlight AVAROR's potential as an effective tool for teaching Rorschach administration. The serious game supports both technical and emotional aspects of Rorschach administration through its realistic design and usability. It allows immediate instructor feedback, enabling error correction without the drawbacks of traditional methods, and simplifies training by obviating the need to find suitable test subjects.

Acknowledgments. The authors acknowledge the experts of the study for their involvement and collaboration.

Disclosure of Interests. The authors have no competing interests to declare that are relevant to the content of this article.

References

1. Exner, J.E.: The Rorschach, Basic Foundations and Principles of Interpretation. Wiley, New York, NY (2003)
2. Abbate, L., Porcelli, P.: Rorschach Comprehensive System. Raffaello Cortina Editore (2017)
3. Villanueva van den Hurk, A.W., McCord, D.M., Görner, K.J., Jowers, C.E., Mihura, J.L.: New versions of the MMPI and Rorschach: how have training programs responded? J. Pers. Assess. **106**(4), 423–428 (2024)
4. Bangor, A.: Determining what individual SUS scores mean: Adding an adjective rating scale. J. User Exp. **4**(3) (2009)
5. Gentry, S.V., et al.: Serious gaming and gamification education in health professions: systematic review. J. Med. Internet Res. **21**(3), e12994 (2019)
6. Facchino, A.P., Marchetti, D., Colasanti, M., Fontanesi, L., Verrocchio, M.C.: The use of serious games for psychological education and training: a systematic review. Frontiers in Education **10** (2025)
7. Wouters, P., van Nimwegen, C., van Oostendorp, H., van der Spek, E.D.: A meta-analysis of the cognitive and motivational effects of serious games. J. Educ. Psychol. **105**(2), 249–265 (2013)
8. Pompedda, F., Zhang, Y., Haginoya, S., Santtila, P.: A mega-analysis of the effects of feedback on the quality of simulated child sexual abuse interviews with avatars. J. Police Crim. Psychol. **37**(3), 485–498 (2022)
9. World Medical Association.: World Medical Association Declaration of Helsinki. Ethical principles for medical research involving human subjects. Bulletin of the World Health Organization **79**(4), 373–374 (2001)
10. American Psychological Association: 2010 Amendments to the 2002 "Ethical principles of psychologists and code of conduct." American Psychologist **65**(5), 493 (2010)
11. Meyer, G.J., Viglione, D.J., Mihura, J.L., Erard, R.E., Erdberg, P.: Rorschach Performance Assessment System. Rorschach Performance Assessment System, LLC (2011)
12. Brooke, J.: SUS: A "Quick and Dirty" Usability Scale. In: . Usability Evaluation In Industry, pp. 189–194. CRC Press (1996)
13. Borsci, S., Federici, S., Lauriola, M.: On the dimensionality of the system usability scale: a test of alternative measurement models. Cogn. Process. **10**(3), 193–197 (2009)
14. Bangor, A.: Determining What Individual SUS Scores Mean: Adding an Adjective Rating Scale **4**(3) (2009)
15. Olszewski, A.E., Wolbrink, T.A.: Serious gaming in medical education: a proposed structured framework for game development. Simulation in Healthcare: Journal of the Society for Simulation in Healthcare **12**(4), 240–253 (2017)
16. Van Merriënboer, J.J.G., Sweller, J.: Cognitive load theory in health professional education: design principles and strategies. Med. Educ. **44**(1), 85–93 (2010)

Examining the Impact of Gamification on Utility Value and Learning Performance

Eva Boehlke[1]([⊠]) [iD], Stefan E. Huber[1] [iD], Kristian Kiili[2] [iD], and Manuel Ninaus[1,3] [iD]

[1] Department of Psychology, University of Graz, Graz, Austria
eva.boehlke@uni-graz.at
[2] Research Centre of Gameful Realities, Tampere University, Tampere, Finland
[3] LEAD Graduate School and Research Network, University of Tübingen, Tübingen, Germany

Abstract. Motivation is crucial for successful learning. Based on the Expectancy-Value Theory, this study investigated whether gamification enhances specific motivational constructs, particularly utility value, and how these relate to cognitive learning outcomes. We hypothesized that a gamified associative learning task would increase motivational aspects compared to a non-gamified version, and that higher motivation would predict better learning outcomes in adult learners. Contrary to our hypothesis, no significant group mean differences in motivation emerged. However, regression analyses revealed that self-concept and subcomponents of utility value significantly predicted cognitive learning outcomes. The minimal gamification elements and limited real-world relevance of the highly controlled learning task may partly explain the lack of motivational effects. We suggest future research explore gamification designs with stronger narrative connections, emphasizing real-life relevance or enhanced narrative transportation, and use more nuanced, context-sensitive measures of utility value to capture present-oriented utility.

Keywords: Gamified Learning · Utility Value · Expectancy-Value Theory

1 Introduction and Theoretical Background

Motivation plays a central role in successful learning and several theories address motivation in learning environments [1]. In this paper, our focus is on the Expectancy-Value Theory [2–4], which posits that motivation is primarily influenced by two key components: expectancies for success and subjective task values. Expectancies for success refer to an individual's belief about their ability to successfully complete a task and achieve a goal, reflecting one's self-concept of capability in that domain. Subjective task values refer to the perceived importance of a task and consist of four subcategories: intrinsic value (enjoyment a person gets from a task), attainment value (personal importance of doing well in the task), utility value (usefulness of a task for future goals) and cost (negative aspects of engaging in a task like time and effort) [2–4].

In educational settings, students often cannot choose their learning content or methods, which makes fostering motivation that is rooted in interest and future utility challenging. Therefore, many interventions have focused on increasing utility value by highlighting the relevance of the learning material to students' future goals [5, 6], which is

© The Author(s), under exclusive license to Springer Nature Switzerland AG 2026
S. Bakkes et al. (Eds.): GALA 2025, LNCS 16307, pp. 381–386, 2026.
https://doi.org/10.1007/978-3-032-11043-5_38

especially effective for students who were expected to perform low [6]. Another approach for increasing utility value could be gamified learning.

Gamification describes the application of game design elements in non-game contexts, such as points and badges [7, 8]. In contrast to game-based learning, in which complete (educational) games are used, gamified learning focuses on altering existing learning processes by adding some game elements to non-game contexts [9]. Meta-analyses have shown favorable effects of gamified learning on cognitive, affective, and motivational outcomes [7, 8, 10]. Explanations for the usefulness of gamification often refer to the "gamefulness" of the application, meaning that people tend to engage more deeply and for longer periods with the learning material because it feels more playful and enjoyable [9, 11]. While gamefulness primarily refers to the hedonic value of a learning task, some studies also examine the relationship between gamification and utility value [12, 13]. They found that specific gamification features (e.g., progress tracking and functional rewards) can enhance utilitarian value, thereby improving user experience, learning effectiveness, and intention to use the gamified system.

This study investigates whether gamification of an associative learning task can enhance specific aspects of motivation from the perspective of Expectancy-Value Theory. Previous studies, using the same learning task, have demonstrated its effectiveness in increasing motivation and affect [14, 15]. However, these studies assessed motivation primarily through the lens of self-determination theory or user experience. Drawing on findings from gamified learning, we propose that (i) a gamified learning task will increase perceived utility value compared to a non-gamified version, and (ii) a higher perceived utility value will be associated with better cognitive learning outcomes.

2 Methods

This study analyzes a dataset obtained over the course of a previous experimental investigation [16], focusing here on utility value, an aspect that has not yet been analyzed.

In total, 121 participants were included (90.9% university students; mean age 23.7, $SD = 5.45$; 61.2% female). The study was conducted on-site in a laboratory at an Austrian University, and data were collected from late April 2023 to early June 2024. Participants were recruited through university-wide email announcements, word-of-mouth, and social media advertisements. As compensation, they received course credits (for psychology students) and had the opportunity to participate in a raffle for five vouchers, each worth 50 EUR for an online retailer. Participants answered several questionnaires before and after the learning task.

The study employed an associative learning task, in which participants had to learn 20 symbol-number associations across five levels. At the start of the first level, a symbol appeared in the upper left corner of the screen. Participants had to guess the corresponding number displayed on a line at the bottom by moving a slider with the arrow keys and confirming the selected position with the spacebar. Corrective feedback followed each response. If no answer was given within 20 s, the correct solution was shown. The first level served as an instruction for all associations, while in subsequent levels, participants increasingly relied on recall supported by feedback. The aim of the task was to learn as many symbol-number pairings as possible across five levels.

Participants were randomly assigned to a gamified or non-gamified version of the learning task. The gamified version incorporated specific game elements, including enhanced visual aesthetics (e.g., an outdoor nature scene), a narrative about a dog searching for bones, and an incentive system (e.g., tallying the number of bones found). The slider's movement and placement were accompanied by an animation of a walking and digging dog. The non-gamified version served as a control without these game elements. Feedback also differed between the two versions: in the gamified version, correct answers showed the dog wagging its tail, incorrect answers showed the dog crying, whereas the non-gamified version displayed only a green check mark or red X.

To measure cognitive learning outcomes, we considered both learning efficacy (the knowledge acquired by the end of the task, i.e., number of correct responses in level 5) and efficiency (speed of learning, i.e., sum of correct responses across Levels 2–5).

To measure motivation based on the Expectancy-Value Theory, we used an adapted version of the Self-Concept and Attitude toward Programming Assessment (SCAPA) [20]. This questionnaire comprises six scales: two of these scales, *self-concept and intrinsic value*, are analyzed as total scales. The remaining four scales are further subdivided into subscales, which are used in the analysis: *attainment value (achievement* and *personal significance), utility value (daily life, future job, school* and *social utility value), cost beliefs (effort, emotional,* and *opportunity costs)* and *compliance and persistence (compliance* and *persistence)*. Items were rated on a 4-point Likert scale and, in contrast to the original questionnaire, were recoded so that higher scores indicate stronger agreement. One example of an item is "Being good at the learning task will help me in the rest of my studies" (subscale school utility value). Internal consistency was questionable for social utility value ($\alpha = 0.66$), opportunity cost ($\alpha = 0.69$), and persistence ($\alpha = 0.69$), but acceptable to excellent for all other subscales ($\alpha \geq 0.72$).

3   Results

Of 121 participants, 61 were in the non-gamified condition and 60 in the gamified condition. The conditions did not significantly differ in the gender composition ($p = .796$) and mean age ($p = .191$).

Motivation. Regarding the motivational constructs addressed by Expectancy-Value Theory, we found no significant differences between the gamified and non-gamified tasks for means of all assessed subscales of the adapted SCAPA questionnaire (all $p \geq .123$). Full descriptive statistics and test values are available on OSF [17].

Learning efficacy. Participants reached an average of 16.72 ($SD = 3.92$) correct symbol-number associations at level 5. Learning efficacy correlated positively with self-concept, intrinsic value, achievement (subscale of attainment value) and compliance ($r_s \geq 0.19, p \leq .039$). In contrast, all cost subscales (effort, emotional, and opportunity) were negatively correlated with efficacy ($r_s \leq -0.21, p \leq .023$).

The regression model that aimed to explain variance in learning efficacy with motivational constructs addressed by Expectancy-Value Theory was significant, $R^2 = .73$, $F(13,107) = 9.37, p < .001$, adjusted $R^2 = .48$. Self-concept was a significant positive predictor (std $\beta = 0.51, SE = 0.59, p < .001$). Future job utility value also showed a significant positive association (std $\beta = 0.31, SE = 0.50, p = .002$), whereas daily life utility value showed a significant negative association (std β = -0.24, SE = 0.49, p = .010). No other predictors were significant. Further details (regression coefficients, correlations) are available on OSF [17].

Learning efficiency. Participants reached an average of 49.29 correct symbol-number associations (SD = 16.95) across levels 2 to 5. Learning efficiency was positively correlated with self-concept, achievement (subscale of attainment value) and compliance ($r_s \geq 0.25, p \leq .007$) and negatively correlated with emotional cost and opportunity cost ($r_s \leq -0.26, p \leq .005$).

The regression model that aimed to explain variance in learning efficiency with motivational constructs addressed by Expectancy-Value Theory was significant, R^2 = .74, $F(13,107)$ = 9.87, $p < .001$, adjusted R^2 = .49. Self-concept was a strong positive predictor of performance (std β = 0.64, SE = 2.51, $p < .001$). Future job utility value showed a significant positive association (std β = 0.31, SE = 2.13, p = .002), while daily life utility value (std β = -0.24, SE = 2.07, p = .009) and opportunity cost (std β = -0.16, SE = 3.03, p = .045) showed a significant negative association. No other predictors were significant. Further details (regression coefficients, correlations) are available on OSF [17].

4 Discussion

This paper investigated whether gamification enhances specific aspects of motivation, such as utility value, and its relation to cognitive learning outcomes. Contrary to our hypothesis, no significant differences emerged between the gamified and non-gamified versions of the learning task in terms of any motivational constructs, including utility value. However, we did find some evidence that certain aspects of motivation, such as self-concept and specific subscales of utility value, were associated with learning.

In our learning task, the gamification elements seemed insufficient to improve utility value or other motivational aspects of the Expectancy-Value Theory [2–4]. Previous studies, including some using the same task [14, 15], and meta-analyses have shown that game elements can improve motivation, but these studies often used other theoretical frameworks, such as self-determination theory or user experience [7, 8, 10, 14, 15]. In contrast, many of the motivational aspects considered here, like utility value, refer to the learner's beliefs that the task is useful for long-term goals. Our task was intentionally designed to minimize the influence of dispositional interest and prior knowledge for a controlled investigation of gamification, but this limited its real-world relevance and may have reduced the potential impact of gamification.

Previous research on enhancing utility value with gamification has often used more instrumental incentives such as virtual currency that could be exchanged, for example, for deadline extensions in university courses, thereby offering a tangible, real-world benefit [12]. Another option might be to enhance gamification through an extended narrative that connects the learning task better to people's everyday lives. Previous interventions, without gamification, have increased performance by emphasizing such everyday and real-life relevance, thereby enhancing learners' perceived utility value [5, 6]. Stronger narratives or framing the task as meaningful in everyday or in-game contexts could enhance perceived utility. For instance, the task used in this study could be presented as a memory exercise or integrated into a narrative emphasizing its relevance within the game world.

Furthermore, using more differentiated measures of cost and utility could be useful: While utility value in Expectancy-Value Theory is future-oriented, more present-oriented measures could capture everyday relevance more effectively. For example, a study found that gamification can reduce perceived effort, measured through present- rather than future-focused items like "How difficult/effortful has the task been so far?", providing a complementary, non-future-related perspective on effort cost [18]. Future studies could use items like "Does this learning task provide knowledge or skills that I can use immediately?". Or, with respect to utility or relevance within the virtual/game world, "To what extent is the acquired skill/knowledge relevant within the game?".

Although we did not find significant mean differences in the considered motivational constructs between the gamified and non-gamified task versions, our regression analyses revealed that certain motivational factors were significantly associated with cognitive learning outcomes. Self-concept was a strong predictor of both learning efficacy and efficiency, consistent with prior research [19, 20]. Additionally, some aspects of utility value were also significant predictors for learning outcomes, but in opposite directions. Perceived utility for future job was a positive predictor, suggesting that participants who saw the task as useful for their future career goals tended to perform better. In contrast, perceived utility for daily life was a negative predictor, indicating that participants who saw the task as useful for their daily life tended to perform worse. The first result aligns with previous research, as higher perceived utility value should enhance performance [2–4]. The second result is more difficult to explain, as it contradicts expectations and literature, requiring further research to see if it can be reproduced. Lastly, higher perceived opportunity cost was a negative predictor for learning efficiency, indicating that higher perceived costs were linked to worse outcomes. This is also in line with expectations from the literature [2–4]. These results highlight that various motivational aspects influence learning, though further research is needed to clarify their interplay.

Disclosure of Interests. The authors have no competing interests to declare.

References

1. Urhahne, D., Wijnia, L.: Theories of motivation in education: an integrative framework. Educ. Psychol. Rev. **35** (2023)
2. Eccles, J.: Expectancies, values, and academic behaviors. In: Spence, J.T. (ed.) Achievement and achievement motives: Psychological and sociological approaches, pp. 75–146. W. H. Freeman, San Francisco, CA (1983)
3. Eccles, J.S., Wigfield, A.: Motivational beliefs, values, and goals. Annu. Rev. Psychol. **53**, 109–132 (2002)
4. Wigfield, A., Eccles, J.S.: Expectancy-value theory of achievement motivation. Contemp. Educ. Psychol. **25**, 68–81 (2000)
5. Harackiewicz, J.M., Rozek, C.S., Hulleman, C.S., Hyde, J.S.: Helping parents to motivate adolescents in mathematics and science: an experimental test of a utility-value intervention. Psychol. Sci. **23**, 899–906 (2012)
6. Hulleman, C.S., Godes, O., Hendricks, B.L., Harackiewicz, J.M.: Enhancing interest and performance with a utility value intervention. J. Educ. Psychol. **102**, 880–895 (2010)

7. Sailer, M., Homner, L.: The gamification of learning: a meta-analysis. Educ. Psychol. Rev. **32**, 77–112 (2020)

8. Looyestyn, J., Kernot, J., Boshoff, K., Ryan, J., Edney, S., Maher, C.: Does gamification increase engagement with online programs? A systematic review. PLOS ONE. **12**, e0173403 (2017)

9. Deterding, S., Dixon, D., Khaled, R., Nacke, L.: From game design elements to game-fulness: defining "gamification." In: Proceedings of the 15th International Academic MindTrek Conference: Envisioning Future Media Environments, pp. 9–15. ACM, Tampere Finland (2011)

10. Schlag, R., Sailer, M., Tolks, D., Ninaus, M., Sailer, M.: Effectiveness of gamification in education. In: Designing Effective Digital Learning Environments, pp. 143–159. Routledge, London (2024)

11. Huotari, K., Hamari, J.: A definition for gamification: anchoring gamification in the ser-vice marketing literature. Electron. Mark. **27**, 21–31 (2017)

12. Dicheva, D., Irwin, K., Dichev, C.: Exploring learners experience of gamified practicing: for learning or for fun? Int. J. Serious Games **6**, 5–21 (2019)

13. Luarn, P., Chen, C.-C., Chiu, Y.-P.: How does perceived value of gamification improve online learning effectiveness? The role of flow state. Interact. Learn. Environ. **33**, 3037–3051 (2025)

14. Huber, S.E., Cortez, R., Kiili, K., Lindstedt, A., Ninaus, M.: Game elements enhance engage-ment and mitigate attrition in online learning tasks. Comput. Hum. Behav. **149**, 107948 (2023)

15. Huber, S.E., Edlinger, M., Lindstedt, A., Kiili, K., Ninaus, M.: Game elements improve affect and motivation in a learning task. Int. J. Serious Games **11**, 103–126 (2024)

16. Huber, S., et al.: Addressing boundary conditions of cognitive and motivational effects of gamified learning. Frontline Learn. Res. **13**, 53–82 (2025)

17. Boehlke, E.: Examining the Impact of Gamification on Utility Value and Learning Per-formance: Complimentary Results (2025). https://osf.io/ft2cj/?view_only=b637dc7177d74f3 08ea099edf46731bb

18. Bernecker, K., Ninaus, M.: No Pain, no Gain? Investigating motivational mechanisms of game elements in cognitive tasks. Comput. Hum. Behav. **114**, 106542 (2021)

19. Kurniawan, A., Nastiti, D.: Fostering Lifelong Learning: Interplay of Self-Concept and Self-Regulation among Adolescents: Membangun Pembelajaran Seumur Hidup: Interaksi Antara Konsep Diri dan Regulasi Diri pada Remaja. Indones. J. Educ. Methods Dev. 21, (2023)

20. Mawardin, M., Adiansha, A.A., Mulyadin, M., Nurgufriani, A.: Correlation study: self-concept and mathematical disposition on learning outcomes of elementary school students. J. Insan Mulia Educ. **1**, 11–17 (2023)

Proposed Design Requirements for a Digital Knowledge Management Game for Nurses

Sinead Impey[1]([✉]) [iD], Gaye Stephens[2] [iD], and Declan O'Sullivan[2] [iD]

[1] School of Nursing and Midwifery, Trinity College Dublin, Dublin, Ireland
simpey@tcd.ie

[2] School of Computer Science and Statistics, Trinity College Dublin, Dublin, Ireland

Abstract. This paper outlines design requirements for a digital version of The Nurses' Knowledge Bank, a serious game for eliciting and evaluating nursing knowledge. While a low-fidelity prototype of the game was effective in capturing knowledge, it had limitations. These are presented across three themes: Facilitate personalisation, Reduce cognitive load for participants, and Improve feedback processes. It is proposed that a digital version could address these through elements such as open-ended play, avatar customisation, tailored prompts, task automation, and enhanced feedback. The proposed design requirements include unrestricted play time, and a points hierarchy for contributions.

Keywords: Knowledge management · Serious games · Nursing Knowledge

1 Introduction

1.1 Background

Serious games serve a dual objective; they aim to be both entertaining and educational [1]. Although nurses use serious games for education and training purposes [2], the use as knowledge management tools is underexplored. Managing nursing knowledge presents several challenges. Exploratory studies undertaken as part of one PhD research work identified 10 challenges related to managing nursing knowledge [3]. These challenges included tacit aspects of knowledge or how not all nursing tasks are documented or documented fully. While serious games were used to manage knowledge in other domains [5], no suitable game was found that addressed the challenges. In previous research, the authors of this paper, developed and evaluated the Nurses Knowledge Bank game [3]. While the game could manage nursing knowledge, limitations were evident including a lack of personalisation and the time required to engage with the game. This paper describes these limitations and proposes design requirements for a digital version of the game.

© The Author(s), under exclusive license to Springer Nature Switzerland AG 2026
S. Bakkes et al. (Eds.): GALA 2025, LNCS 16307, pp. 387–393, 2026.
https://doi.org/10.1007/978-3-032-11043-5_39

1.2 Methodology

An Elaborated Action Design Research (eADR) approach [6], was employed to develop the Nurse Knowledge Bank game [7]. As part of an eADR approach, a co-inquiry group (n = 11) was assembled - nursing education (n = 2), nurse experts (n = 7), and health informatics specialists (n = 2). The study site was a specialist Haematology/Oncology department in a large teaching hospital. eADR is an iterative process with continuous evaluation. This ensured the game was continuously improved based on end-user (participant) feedback. In total, three game cycles, each lasting 25 min, were performed. Following cycle, participants engaged in group discussions and a Post-Study System Usability Questionnaire (PSSUQ). Field notes taken during each game were reviewed at the end of each session as a validation exercise. A co-inquiry reflection activity reviewed the validated field notes.

2 The Nurses' Knowledge Bank

2.1 Knowledge Management Interactions

'The Nurses' Knowledge Bank' (Impey et al., 2023), created space for three types of knowledge management interactions: Elicitation, Evaluation Sharing. The game **elicited** knowledge from newly recruited nurses (n = 10) who were Knowledge Holders based at the study site. The nurses mentored an apprentice Knowledge Seeker (an avatar in the game) by sharing their knowledge with them. They did this by writing on Post-it notes and placing them on the game board (see Fig. 1). Knowledge Reviewers **evaluated** the elicited knowledge (on the game board). Reviewers were expert nurses (n = 8) based at the study site. To **share** the evaluated knowledge beyond the game, it was mapped to the SNOMED clinical terminology.

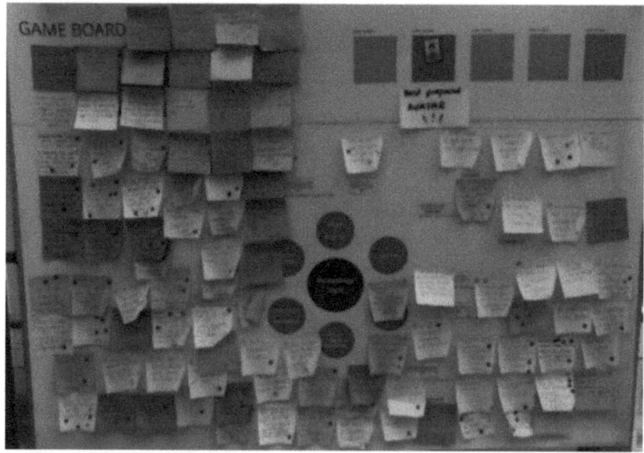

Fig. 1. Photograph of game board showing knowledge submissions on Post-it notes

2.2 Game Structure

The game has two parts: elicitation and evaluation. In part one, a clinical scenario regarding the discharge of a patient from an oncology day care setting was used to focus knowledge elicitation Knowledge Holders, Knowledge Seekers, and a Gatekeeper participated. Holders earn points for each piece of knowledge they share with the Seeker. At the end of each game, the Holder with the most points was declared the winner. The gatekeeper, who had clinical experience, managed the game and provided real-time feedback to players. The second part of the game focused on evaluating the knowledge elicited in Part One. Reviewers (experienced nurses) and a Gatekeeper participated were assigned knowledge to evaluate. After each evaluation, they advanced a set number of spaces on an evaluation board. The game ended when a player reached the 100th square or held the highest position after a set time.

2.3 Evaluation

Game enjoyment, utility, and usability were evaluated. Utility refers to whether the game could manage knowledge. Usability refers to how straightforward participants found the game to be. To assess enjoyment, players completed a PSSUQ. Findings noted that n = 10 Holders strongly agreed (n = 7) or agreed (n = 3) that they enjoyed playing the game and would play the game again. Of the 5 participants who completed the Reviewers PSSUQ, the results noted that they strongly agreed (n = 4) or agreed (n = 1) that they enjoyed playing the game and would play it again. To assess utility, the evaluated knowledge was mapped to a clinical terminology. In total, the game captured 112 evaluated knowledge submissions, 86 of which were mapped to SNOMED CT to produce a data reference set for adult oncology daycare nursing discharge (SNOMED CT refset ID 134791000220109). While this demonstrated the game's potential to manage nursing knowledge, 10 usability limitations were identified based on participant feedback. The co-inquiry group discussed the identified limitations and the potential impact of digitisation. The limitations and how they could be addressed digitally are shown in Table 1 and are further explored in the Discussion section.

3 Discussion

Based on co-inquiry discussions, limitations were grouped into thematic categories reflecting how a digital game could potentially address each issue. These themes are shown in Table 2. This Section uses these themes to explore how a digital format could overcome the limitations and proposes corresponding design requirements are presented in Table 3, Table 4 and Table 5.

Table 1. 10 Limitations identified and potential impact of digitisation.

Limitation	Description of limitation	A digital game could...
1. Length of game	*Game time was deemed too short, additional time was not possible*	*... remove set times and allow play on the participant's schedule*
2. Prompts to aid recall	*All participants received the same instructions, though needs varied*	*... allow participants to access instructions tailored to their needs*
3. Avatars	*Avatars could not be personalised due to time and technical limitations*	*... allow users to personalise their avatar*
4. Clinical scenario	*Some found the scenario too broad, others too specific*	*... allow participants to access a range of scenarios*
5. Community knowledge	*Due to the number of submissions (on post-it notes), the game board was difficult to navigate*	*... allow participants to search submissions based on participant tags or by topic*
6. Competition	*Keeping a running tally of the submissions captured was difficult*	*... allow tasks, if possible, to be automated*
7. Building consensus	*Awarding submissions was beneficial, but the readability of the game board impacted the fairness*	*... allow participants to search all submissions before allocating awards*
8. Onsite quality control	*Feedback was beneficial for participants, but it interrupted the flow of the game*	*... include a feedback function that users could access without interrupting the flow of their game*
9. Game components	*Reviewers would prefer to choose their topics to evaluate. Rather than have topics assigned*	*... allow Reviewers to select their preferred topics*
10. Providing rationale	*Providing a rationale (with knowledge submissions) should attract additional points*	*... allow for additional points to be awarded for different types of submissions*

Table 2. Limitations grouped by theme.

Theme proposed	Describes how a digital format could potentially…	Limitations addressed
1. Facilitate personalisation	*… enable participants to tailor the game to their own needs*	*1 (Length of game), 3 (Avatars),4 (Clinical scenario), 9 (Game components)*
2. Reduce cognitive load	*… automate routine tasks and help users navigate the game board*	*2 (Prompts to aid recall), 5 (Community knowledge)*
3. Improve feedback processes	*… provide a more effective means of providing feedback*	*6 (Competition), 7 (Building consensus), 8 (On-site quality control), 10 (Providing rationale)*

Theme 1: Facilitate Personalisation

As the game was played during an established educational session, this served as a stopping point. An open-ended digital version of the game could allow players to play at their own pace and in their own time. Participants indicated a preference for constructing their avatar, a digital system could facilitate this. Participants' feedback surrounding the clinical scenario was mixed: some found the scenario too broad, others too specific. Reviewers noted a preference to select relevant topics. It is proposed that a digital platform could allow participants to choose a scenario or topics to review.

Table 3. Facilitating personalisation: proposed design requirements.

Design requirement	Application of design requirements
1. Unrestricted game time	*Adopt an open-ended game that is not limited by time*
2. Promote personal choice	*Provide a broad selection of clinical scenarios to ensure players and evaluators can choose cases relevant to their interests or learning objectives*
3. Promote personalisation	*Allow players to design their avatar*

Theme 2: Reduce Cognitive Load for Participants

As participants become more familiar with the game, they require fewer instructions. However, in its current format, it was difficult to tailor instructions. A digital platform could address this by making information available when requested. Feedback (Holders group) noted that reviewing the community knowledge on the game board would be useful but challenging due to the lack of structure. A digital platform could potentially organise submissions and automate tasks, such as maintaining a tally of the submissions entered. This was a function of the Gatekeeper in the low-fidelity prototype.

Table 4. Reduce cognitive load for participants: Proposed design requirements.

Design requirement	Application of design requirements
4. Accessible information	*Ensure that relevant information is readily accessible and presented promptly when requested by participants*
5. Accessible knowledge	*Ensure that relevant knowledge is readily accessible through the use of tags, awards, or a search function (i.e. by topic)*
6. Automate where possible	*Minimise manual input by automating tasks where feasible, such as tracking the number of submissions*

Theme 3: Improve Feedback Processes

Participants enjoyed the competitive element of the game: a digital format could potentially build on this by including a real-time leaderboard. Awarding submissions was described as beneficial by participants, but the readability of the game board impacted the fairness of the award. A digital platform could allow awards to act as a form of feedback. The game also captured rationale for some submissions that provided context. All submissions received the same number of points. It is proposed that a digital game could potentially discriminate between the types of submissions.

Table 5. Reduce cognitive load for participants: Proposed design requirements.

Design requirement	Application of design requirement
7. Promote competition	*The game should have a competitive element*
8. Build consensus	*Awards can be used to build consensus*
9. Provide feedback	*The game should have a mechanism for providing feedback*
10. Hierarchy of points	*Award different points for different types of submissions*

4 Conclusion

While the game did elicit and evaluate knowledge, limitations were evident. These limitations were reviewed and how they could be addressed in a digital version of the game were explored. These are presented as design requirements in this paper. The proposed design requirements for a digital game have not been evaluated; therefore, they should be considered as proposed. A study is being designed to address this.

Acknowledgments. This research was partially supported by Research Ireland and co-funded by the European Regional Development Fund through the ADAPT Centre for Digital Content Technology (grant number 13/RC/2106_P2).

Disclosure of Interests. The author has no conflicts of interest to declare.

References

1. Abt, C.C.: Serious Games. The Viking Press, USA (1970)
2. Bayram, S.B., Caliskan, N.: Effect of a game-based virtual reality phone application on tracheostomy care education for nursing students: a randomized controlled trial. Nurse Educ. Today **79**, 25–31 (2019)
3. Impey, S., O'Sullivan, D., Stephens, G.: The nurse's knowledge bank: a serious knowledge elicitation and evaluation game. In: Dondio, P., et al. (eds.) GALA 2023. LNCS, vol. 14475, pp. 77–85. Springer, Cham (2024). https://doi.org/10.1007/978-3-031-49065-1_8
4. Impey, S., Stephens, G., O'Sullivan, D.: Capturing healthcare expert's knowledge digitally – a scoping review of current approaches. In: ICHIHIM 2021: 23rd International Conference on Health Informatics and Health Information Management, UK (2021)
5. Ahmed, A., Sutton, M.J.: Gamification, serious games, simulations, and immersive learning environments in knowledge management initiatives. World J. Sci. Technol. Sustain. Dev. **14**(2/3), 78–83 (2017)
6. Mullarkey, M.T., Hevner, A.R.: An elaborated action design research process model. Eur. J. Inf. Syst. **28**(1), 6–20 (2019)
7. Impey, S.: To what extent can a serious game elicit and evaluate nursing knowledge. School of Computer Science & Statistics. Trinity College Dublin, Dublin (2023)

Do Maths Anxiety and Gender Limit the Spontaneous Home Usage of an Educational Game? A Preliminary Study

Pierpaolo Dondio[(✉)]

School of Computer Science, Maynooth University, Co. Kildare, Ireland
`pierpaolo.dondio@mu.ie`

Abstract. In this study, we examined the spontaneous use of an educational game at home after pupils were exposed to it during a six-week game-based learning intervention in school. We investigated what influenced this decision, focusing on two factors—maths anxiety and gender—that are known to potentially act as barriers to both maths engagement and video game engagement. The game interactions of 1,900 primary school students were monitored for three months after the classroom intervention. We found that half of the students played the 7 Spells game at home. As expected, game performance and game enjoyment significantly predicted the decision to continue playing from home. Notably, however, maths anxiety did not limit home play, and no gender effect was found—girls played as much as boys. Our findings underscore the potential of educational games to foster spontaneous practice, making maths practice more inclusive and sustainable beyond the classroom.

Keywords: digital game-based learning · maths anxiety

1 Introduction

Regular practice is widely recognized as essential for developing and maintaining mathematical proficiency, improving both procedural fluency and conceptual understanding [17]. Practice is most effective when it is spontaneous and driven by intrinsic motivation [15], that is, the internal desire to engage with a subject for personal interest, enjoyment, or satisfaction rather than external rewards. However, motivation to learn maths tends to decrease with age, limited by cognitive, socio-economic, and emotional factors [4], such as maths anxiety [5] or gender stereotypes. Given these challenges, a key question remains: *how can educational systems stimulate spontaneous maths practice?*

Over the last two decades, digital game-based learning (DGBL) has gained visibility as an innovative learning tool, promising a stress-free environment with higher engagement levels. DGBL has been shown to support enjoyment, active learning, motivation, and engagement, with positive effects on learning

S. Bakkes et al. (Eds.): GALA 2025, LNCS 16307, pp. 394–400, 2026.
https://doi.org/10.1007/978-3-032-11043-5_40

[13], which can lead to better performance [8]. While the efficacy of DGBL has been extensively studied—typically through controlled pre-post experiments in schools—much less is known about the ability of educational games to trigger spontaneous maths practice at home without direct school obligations, and which profiles of students are more likely to engage in such practice.

If educational games can trigger spontaneous maths practice beyond the classroom, they could significantly expand their reach and impact, fostering sustained, self-directed learning combined with greater enjoyment—ultimately strengthening their learning effect over time. Educational games can be designed to be as appealing as entertainment games and, consequently, capable of triggering deep engagement. However, no studies have investigated how students interact with educational games once they are at home, voluntarily and outside mandatory educational activities such as homework. Moreover, there is a need to better understand student-related factors that influence the decision to engage with such games. This study provides a first contribution to this line of research.

Participants took part in *Happy Maths* [1], a six-week game-based learning project centered around *Seven Spells* [2], a digital card game designed to enhance strategic thinking and problem-solving. We monitored the gameplay of 1,900 primary school students for three months post-intervention to understand how students interacted with the game at home. We modeled students' profiles using demographic, cognitive, emotional, and game-related factors. The outcome variable was whether students played *7 Spells* at home after the intervention.

While previous studies suggest that motivation to play is supported by factors such as game performance and enjoyment [10], we focused on two potential barriers to home engagement—maths anxiety and gender—testing whether the game environment can mitigate their negative effects. We hypothesized that:

H1. *Maths anxiety (MA) is negatively associated with home playing.* It has been extensively observed that maths anxiety is associated with maths avoidance [6]: maths-anxious students are less likely to engage with mathematics tasks, especially when these tasks are optional. However, the playful nature of the task may mitigate the effects of maths anxiety, resulting in a weaker association.

H2. *Boys play the game more than girls.* This hypothesis is supported by a large body of work reporting that boys usually play and enjoy video games more than girls [11,14]. However, the age profile of the participants, the genre of the game used (a card game), and the educational context of the study might reduce the gender difference compared to what is typically reported in the literature.

2   Methods

Participants took part in the *Happy Maths* game-based learning intervention, which used the digital card game platform *Seven Spells* [2]. The intervention lasted six weeks, with weekly 1-hour sessions in class led by two researchers. *Seven Spells* (Fig. 1) is a digital card game designed to enhance mathematical skills and strategic thinking. It can be played in three different modes: SOLO, against a computer, or with another player. Players receive a deck containing Number cards (representing numbers) and Spell cards, which apply mathematical operations and concepts. The basic objective is to score points by capturing the opponent's number cards, which is done by matching cards strategically. The more cards a player captures, the higher their score. Successful play requires mental maths computation, manipulation of numbers, and application of concepts such as number sets, equality, inequality, intervals, tables, multiples, and prime numbers.

Several factors make *Seven Spells* suitable for this study. First, its game design: *Seven Spells* is a strategy-based, open-ended game that stimulates problem-solving skills and creativity. Its design follows the theory of intrinsic integration [12] and Malone's principles [16]. Second, it is a valid learning tool, as evidence shows the game positively impacts learning outcomes, measured by pre- and post-intervention maths tests [3,18,19]. Finally, extra practice with the game is important because game performance improves with continued play, and higher game performance is associated with better learning outcomes [18].

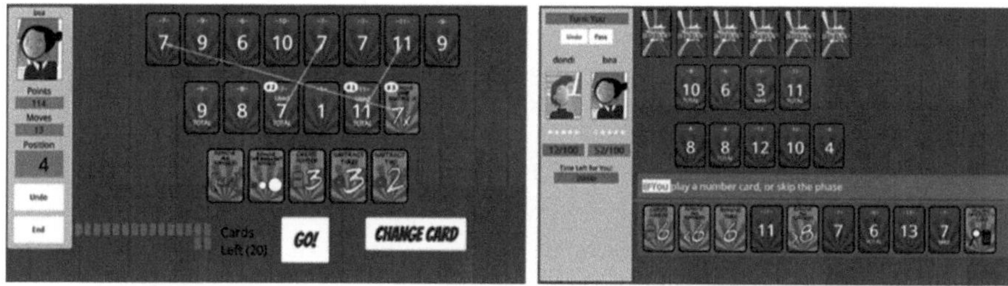

Fig. 1. Seven Spells played in single-player mode (left) and versus an opponent (right).

Data were collected between January 2022 and June 2024 in 88 classes participating in the *Happy Maths* program [1]. Before each intervention, teachers reported students' gender (binary), class grade (as a proxy for age), and maths proficiency (STEN scores from the Irish national mathematics test). Classes ranged from 3rd to 6th grade, corresponding to ages 8–11.

Students completed the Modified Abbreviated Maths Anxiety Scale [7], a validated tool for measuring maths anxiety (MA) in primary school children. We also collected data on students' gaming habits, including how much they enjoyed playing video games (1= *"I hate"* to 5= *"I love"*) and the typical daily time spent on video games. Gaming habits were key control variables to account for familiarity with video games, which could influence the decision to play the educational game at home.

Game logs were automatically saved to a relational database. From these logs, we extracted each student's game performance during the intervention. The average of their two highest SOLO game scores was used as an indicator of performance; other in-game metrics were excluded due to high correlation.

After the final game session, students rated *Seven Spells* on a scale from 1 (lowest) to 10. Access to home play was disabled throughout the in-class intervention. In the final week, students were informed they could continue playing at home using their existing accounts. Game logs were used to track timestamps of matches played from home for up to three months post-intervention.

Teachers were instructed not to use the game in class or for homework. After the intervention, teachers were contacted to verify whether they had encouraged home play. These responses were cross-referenced with game logs, resulting in the exclusion of nine classes that continued to play in class after the intervention. This ensured that home play reflected voluntary engagement and that all participants had equivalent exposure to the game.

3 Results

A total sample of 1,590 players from 79 classes was used for our analysis, out of an initial 1,930 players in 88 classes. Nine classes (245 students) were excluded because teachers used the game in class after the intervention, and an additional 95 players were excluded for not attending all six sessions. The dataset consisted of 55.1% boys and 44.9% girls. A total of 829 players (52.1%) played the game from home. The average number of home matches was 13.32, with an average total playtime of 4.3 h. Data were analyzed using a mixed-effects hierarchical logistic regression model, grouping students by class and school. Table 1 presents the central model of the study, which predicts the likelihood of playing from home while incorporating all predictors.

Table 1. Fully controlled model. Standardized coefficients were used.

Variable	β	z-value	p-value	CI 95%
MA	-0.011	0.11	0.91	[-0.18,0.21]
MS	**0.402**	**3.38**	**p<0.001*****	**[0.17,0.64]**
GE	**0.458**	**4.90**	**p<0.001*****	**[0.27,0.64]**
GP	**0.565**	**4.25**	**p<0.001*****	**[0.30,0.82]**
CYear	-0.182	-1.14	0.25	[-0.49,0.12]
LikeVG	**0.267**	**2.99**	**0.003****	**[0.09,0.45]**
TimeVG	-0.11	0.118	0.34	[-0.34,0.12]
Gender(Male)	-0.303	-1.56	0.12	[-0.68,0.08]
	R^2 marginal	0.27	R^2 conditional	0.445

Maths skills (MS) correspond to students' results in the national maths test, game enjoyment (GE) is the rating (from 1 to 10) assigned to the game by each player, and game performance (GP) is the average of the two best SOLO scores in the game. TimeVG represents the habitual daily time spent playing video games (ordinal variable with 4 levels: "I do not play", "<1hr.", "1–2hrs", ">2hrs."), and LikeVG indicates how much students generally like video games (Likert scale from 1 to 5).

Maths skills, game performance, and game enjoyment were the strongest predictors of home play. A weaker but still significant effect was observed for videogame liking: the more a player enjoyed video games in general, the higher the probability of playing *7 Spells* at home. Neither maths anxiety (MA) nor gender were significant factors. Therefore, both H1 and H2 were rejected.

4   Discussion

Our analysis showed that about half of the students played the game at home after trying it in class.

Maths anxiety was not significant in any of our models; therefore, H1 was rejected. MA did not explain additional variance beyond the other predictors, providing no evidence for a maths anxiety-specific effect. This suggests that the *Seven Spells* game environment, although potentially cognitively demanding, may have helped mitigate the avoidance behavior typically associated with maths anxiety, challenging previous research that linked maths anxiety to maths avoidance even after controlling for maths skills [6].

Both **maths skills** and **game performance** were significant predictors, as expected from previous studies. Maths skills had a moderate effect size ($\beta = 0.40$), while in-game performance was the strongest predictor ($\beta = 0.56$). Interestingly, the significance of both predictors also highlights the importance of **game enjoyment** (i.e., students' self-reported liking of the game) beyond performance. This indicates that the decision to play from home was not solely driven by performance. This finding aligns with previous research showing that enjoyment during maths learning positively affects interest and motivation to engage with the subject [10].

Regarding **gender**, this predictor was not significant in our models, suggesting that girls played as much as boys—contrary to most previous studies. Research [9,14] indicates that while girls do play video games, they typically invest less time and resources and take them less seriously than boys. We suggest that the nature of *Seven Spells* may explain this result. A study by [14] with 1,112 participants found that girls disliked games lacking meaningful social interaction, containing violent content, or featuring gender-stereotyped characters, and were less attracted to competitive elements, which boys typically value more. *Seven Spells* can be played solo, against AI, or with classmates, allowing players to choose between competitive and non-competitive play styles. The game is a card game that lacks violence and does not reinforce gender stereotypes, potentially making it equally attractive to both boys and girls.

5   Conclusions

In this paper, we investigated the spontaneous use of an educational game by primary school pupils after it had been used in the classroom as part of a game-based intervention. The results showed that half of the students played *7 Spells* at home. As expected, spontaneous practice was primarily driven by higher game performance and greater game enjoyment, measured by the ratings assigned by the players to their game experience. Maths anxiety did not significantly affect the likelihood of playing from home, indicating that the expected avoidance effect did not emerge in this game-based context. Gender was also not a significant factor—girls played as much as boys—contrary to the common trend observed in the literature. Overall, our findings support the use of educational games as a way to promote spontaneous, motivated, inclusive, and enjoyable maths practice.

References

1. The happy maths programme. www.happymaths.games Accessed 03 2025
2. Seven spells, the ancient art of number fighting. ellygames.com (2019)
3. Almo, A., Rocha, M., Brennan, A., Dondio, P.: Seven spells and peer tutoring: a collaborative mathematics game experience. In: 16th EGBL Conference. Academic Conferences and publishing limited (2022)
4. Amalina, I.K., Vidákovich, T.: Cognitive and socioeconomic factors that influencing students mathematical problem-solving skills. Heliyon **9**(9) (2023)
5. Ashcraft, M.H.: Math anxiety: personal, educational, and cognitive consequences. Curr. Dir. Psychol. Sci. **11**(5), 181–185 (2002)
6. Daker, R.J., Sokolowski, H.M., Lyons, I.M.: First-year students' math anxiety predicts stem avoidance and underperformance throughout university, independently of math ability. NPJ Sci. Learn. **6**(1), 17 (2021)
7. Carey, E., Hill, F., A.D., Szhucs, D.: The modified abbreviated math anxiety scale: a valid and reliable instrument for use with children. Front. Psychol. **8**, 11 (2017)
8. Castellar, E.N., A.A., Looy, J.V.: Cognitive abilities, digital games and arithmetic performance enhancement: a study comparing the effects of a math game and paper exercises. Comput. Educ. **85**, 123–133 (2015)
9. Ghețău, C., Rusu, D.O., Delcea, C.: Girls playing video games and their dedication towards games. Rom. J. Leg. Med. **30**, 297–301 (2022)
10. Giannakos, M.: Enjoy and learn with educational games: examining factors affecting learning performance. Comput. Educ. **68**, 429–439 (2013)
11. Gómez-Gonzalvo, F., Molina, P., Devís-Devís, J.: Which are the patterns of video game use in Spanish school adolescents? gender as a key factor. Entertainment Comput. **35**, 100366 (2020)
12. Habgood, M.P.J., Ainsworth, S.E.: Intrinsic integration: an approach to designing educational games that improve learning and player engagement. Comput. Hum. Behav. **29**(3), 1043–1052 (2013)
13. Hwa, S.: Pedagogical change in Mathematis learning: harnessing the power of game-based learning. J. Educ. Technol. **21**(4), 259–276 (2018)
14. Leonhardt, M., Overå, S.: Are there differences in video gaming and use of social media among boys and girls? a mixed methods approach. J. Environ. Res. Public Health **18**(11), 6085 (2021)
15. Lepper, M.R., Corpus, J.H., Iyengar, S.S.: Intrinsic and extrinsic motivational orientations in the classroom: age differences and academic correlates. J. Educ. Psychol. **97**(2), 184 (2005)
16. Malone, T.W.: Making learning fun: a taxonomic model of intrinsic motivations for learning. Conative and affective process analysis (1987)

17. Reder, S., Gauly, B., Lechner, C.: Practice makes perfect: practice engagement theory and the development of adult literacy and numeracy proficiency. Int. Rev. Educ. 267–288 (2020). https://doi.org/10.1007/s11159-020-09830-5
18. Rocha, M.: Gameplay performance as a predictor of adaptive expertise in primary school students. In: Gala Conference, pp. 14–24. Springer (2024)
19. Santos, F., Gomides, M., Rocha, M., et al.: Transforming mathematics education through digital games: insights from the arithmós project (2024)

Tangible Interfaces in Game Design Education: A Pilot Study on Learning 2D Level Design Through Physical and Digital Tools

Chloé Vigneau(✉)🆔 and Stéphanie Mader🆔

CEDRIC, CNAM, Paris, France
`chloe.vigneau@lecnam.net`

Abstract. This study examines how Tangible User Interfaces (TUIs) support learning level design for 2D platform games. In a workshop, participants built layouts with physical blocks that were later turned into playable levels. Observations of over 200 participants and questionnaires from 10% of them suggest that tangible interactions enhance intuitiveness, collaboration, and understanding of level-design principles, highlighting TUIs' potential in game-design education.

Keywords: Tangible User Interface · Level Design · Game-Development Based Learning

1 Introduction

Level design shapes how players interact with mechanics, challenges, and story, but professional tools can be daunting for novices. Tangible User Interfaces (TUIs), which link physical manipulation to digital outputs, offer a more intuitive, collaborative way to learn. Prior work shows tangible interaction enhances engagement and understanding (O'Malley and Stanton Fraser, 2007). To test this, we ran a pilot workshop with 200+ participants who built levels with blocks later digitized in a game engine; 25 completed a questionnaire on preferences and learning. This paper reports the workshop, findings, and the pedagogical value of TUIs for level-design education.

2 Background

2.1 Level Design: Building Blocks and Skills

This study builds on the thesis "Learning by Making Videogames" (Vigneau, 2024), which showed that Game-Development-based learning (GDBL) fosters skills such as problem-solving, communication, and collaboration. In our workshop, participants used tangible objects to explore level design, a key element

S. Bakkes et al. (Eds.): GALA 2025, LNCS 16307, pp. 401–406, 2026.
https://doi.org/10.1007/978-3-032-11043-5_41

of game development shaping player experience. Levels are arenas for gameplay (Byrne, 2004), "the virtual space where most interaction occurs" (Summerville et al., 2016). Engaging in level design fosters interdisciplinary skills: students develop geometry, spatial reasoning, and composition (Totten, 2014); apply physics concepts such as gravity and motion (Hämäläinen et al., 2015); and build higher-order abilities like analysis, evaluation, etc. (El-Nasr and Smith, 2006). Level design becomes meaningful for children when framed through constructivist, creative pedagogy (Lin, 2011).

Byrne outlines core level-design blocks: start and end zones, goals, obstacles, and rewards (Byrne, 2004). For 2D platformers, Smith and Whitehead (2008) add platforms, obstacles, movement aids, collectibles, and triggers, while Khalifa et al. (2019) describe patterns such as guidance, safe zones, foreshadowing, layering, branching, and pace breaking. Tools help novices learn level design: no-code engines (e.g., Scratch), apps like DrawYourGame, creation games (Mario Maker, Little Big Planet, Dreams), and sandboxes like Minecraft (Zhong et al., 2025). New systems add visual programming (Smith and Whitehead, 2010) or AI-generated levels (Galloata et al., 2024). Yet these tools often lack guidance, assume expertise, or limit collaboration (Zhong et al., 2025).

Tangible objects may offer a more accessible, structured path. A tangible object is a physical item linked to virtual content, enabling direct manipulation. Ishii and Ullmer (1997, 2000) introduced Tangible User Interfaces (TUIs) as "physically graspable" data representations, defined by binding, interaction, embodiment, and metaphor. TUIs have supported learning in programming (Wang et al., 2015) and interaction design (Cherek et al., 2018; Marco et al., 2010), but none target children designing 2D levels. Our pilot may be the first to apply TUIs to level design, using modular components to make abstract ideas tangible and engaging, especially for novices (O'Malley and Stanton Fraser, 2004; Marshall, 2007).

3   Designing a Level Design Workshop with Tangible Objects

This pilot study investigates how Tangible User Interfaces (TUIs) can support level-design learning. We hypothesize that TUIs (1) lower the entry barrier compared with traditional game engines, (2) foster understanding through hands-on, multimodal learning, and (3) promote collaboration.

In a workshop, participants built 2D platform levels with color-coded wooden blocks, which were photographed, detected via an OpenCV system, and reconstructed in the Godot engine for playtesting and refinement. The selection of blocks was informed by Smith and Whitehead's framework (2010), with each type representing a gameplay element (see Fig. 1): start point (blue), end goal (green), platform (orange), obstacle (brown), breakable platform (black), bouncing platform (blue), enemy (red), and collectible item (yellow). These elements supported safe zones, foreshadowing, layering, and branching paths. The setup used a 100×160 cm board for up to three users. Blocks were tracked with a webcam, producing a JSON file parsed by Godot to generate editable digital levels. This physical-to-digital workflow was central to engaging learners in both design and iteration.

Fig. 1. Board and blocks created for the workshop

4   Experimentation and Results

4.1   Experimental Protocol

The workshop took place at Digital Games, a free annual event in France organized by the Hauts-de-Seine department to showcase digital technology, game creation, and AI. Aimed at pupils and students (6–20) and their teachers or parents, the event helps participants explore innovative teaching methods and develop skills through digital activities. Over 200 people joined the level-design workshop, part of a stand that also featured animation and sound design. Sessions lasted 40 min, with up to 15 min devoted to level design. A facilitator introduced the tangible user interfaces (TUIs), explained the two mandatory bricks—start and finish—and invited participants to build levels with as many blocks as they wished. Finished layouts were photographed and digitized so participants could play them in the game engine. About 10% of attendees completed a post-workshop questionnaire assessing the first two hypotheses (accessibility and learning), while the third (collaboration) was evaluated through direct observation. The questionnaire collected demographics (age, platform-game experience, prior game creation) and feedback on TUI use. Because of limited mediators, not all participants could complete it.

4.2   Results

We collected 25 questionnaire responses. Each respondent built a level with the TUI, tested it in the game engine, and sometimes revised it. Although the sample limits generalization, several trends emerged. Participants ranged from children to adults (median age = 11, SD = 12.78): 14 were 9–11, 6 were 12–17, and 5 were over 29. 19 reported playing platformers occasionally or often, while 6 never played them. Half had no prior experience creating games.

Table 1. Clarity and User-Friendliness of Level Design Tools by Age Group

Age Group	Clarity Ratings			User-Friendliness		
	Clearer with TUIs	Clearer with Game Engine	No Preference	TUIs Easier	Engine Easier	No Preference
9–11	4	4	6	4	4	6
12–17	5	0	1	5	0	1
29+	4	1	0	4	1	0

When comparing physical and digital design, 13 participants found TUI-made levels clearer, and 14 found the TUI easier to manipulate than the game engine. Age influenced preferences: children were more open to the engine or had no preference, while teens and adults favored the TUI (Table 1). To examine the impact of prior experience, participants were grouped by familiarity with platformers and game creation: 4 had neither, 9 played but had not created games, 2 created without playing platformers, and 10 were both players and creators. Analysis of responses on the perceived clarity and usability of level design tools indicates a tendency among participants with no prior expertise to find the TUI clearer and more user-friendly (see Table 2), confirming the accessibility of this tangible objects.

Table 2. Clarity and User-Friendliness of Level Design Tools by Profile

Profile Group	Clarity Ratings			User-Friendliness		
	Clearer with TUIs	Clearer with Game Engine	No Preference	TUIs Easier	Engine Easier	No Preference
No expertise	3	1	0	4	0	0
Player only	3	2	4	3	5	1
Creator only	2	0	0	2	0	0
Player & creator	5	2	3	5	3	2

Participants rated their understanding of level design on a three-point scale (not at all, partially, totally). 14 fully grasped how to pace levels with calm and challenging phases; 13 understood obstacle placement; 11 felt confident about structuring difficulty; and 13 understood creating points of interest. These results are encouraging for a 15-minute workshop, with about half reporting solid learning. Collaboration was strong: participants gathered around the board and worked together. Two behaviors emerged—some placed blocks quickly then refined, others planned carefully. Many considered gameplay limits when building levels, such as the player's three-hole jump distance.

5 Discussions and Limitations

Tangible objects supported level design, especially for adolescents and adults. Participants aged 9–11 showed no clear preference between TUIs and the game engine, while those 12–17 and over 29 favored TUIs. TUIs were appreciated not only by beginners but also by expert users, suggesting value for advanced activities. Combining tangible interaction with digital tools encouraged collaboration and reflection: some participants designed through trial-and-error, others through discussion, often considering mechanics such as jump distance. Questionnaire data confirmed that many grasped core level-design concepts. The study faced limits: occasional detection errors, demanding questions for younger children, incomplete questionnaires, and a small sample ($n = 25$) due to limited facilitators. Future workshops should improve mediation, technical reliability, and data collection. Planned refinements include a better detection system, a revised questionnaire with "No opinion" to reduce bias, and an observation grid for analyzing design behaviors. Further research should examine why adolescents and adults show stronger TUI preferences and assess TUIs' pedagogical value at larger scale.

6 Conclusion

This pilot study examined the pedagogical value of Tangible User Interfaces (TUIs) for teaching 2D platformer level design. We hypothesized that TUIs lower barriers for novices, support conceptual understanding, and encourage collaboration. Observations of 200+ participants and questionnaires from 25 support these claims: adolescents and adults preferred TUIs over game engines, and both beginners and experienced players found them accessible. Participants showed collaborative, iterative design behaviors, and many reported understanding key level-design concepts. Limitations include technical issues with object detection, challenging questionnaire items for younger children, and a small sample size. Future work will refine technical and methodological aspects to improve data quality. Overall, TUIs appear to offer an effective way to engage learners in game design, combining hands-on interaction with digital tools to foster creativity and understanding.

References

O'Malley, C., Fraser, D.S.: Literature review in learning with tangible technologies. NESTA Futurelab Report 12 (2004). https://hal.science/hal-00190328

Vigneau, C.: Learning through video game creation : proposals for the design and production of pedagogical template. Thèse de doctorat. Informatique, HESAM Université (2024). https://theses.fr/2024HESAC013

Byrne, E.: Game Level Design. Charles River Media, Hingham, MA (2004)

Summerville, A.J., Snodgrass, S., Mateas, M., Ontañón, S.: The VGLC: the video game level corpus. In: 7th International Workshop on Procedural Content Generation (PCG), pp. 1–4. (2016). https://doi.org/10.48550/arXiv.1606.07487

Totten, C.W.: An Architectural Approach to Level Design, 1st edn. CRC Press, Boca Raton (2014)

Hämäläinen, P., Marshall, J., Kajastila, R., Byrne, R., Mueller, F.: Utilizing gravity in movement-based games and play. In: Mandryk, R.L., Johnson, D. (eds.) CHI PLAY 2015 – Proceedings of the Annual Symposium on Computer-Human Interaction in Play, pp. 67–77. ACM, New York (2015). https://doi.org/10.1145/2793107.2793110

El-Nasr, M.S., Smith, B.K.: Learning through game modding. Comput. Entertain. **4**(1), 1–20 (2006). https://doi.org/10.1145/1111293.1111301

Lin, Y.S.: Fostering creativity through education - a conceptual framework of creative pedagogy. Creat. Educ. **2**(3), 149–155 (2011). https://doi.org/10.4236/ce.2011.23021

Smith, G., Whitehead, J.: A Framework for Analysis of 2D Platformer Levels. In: Natkin, S., Dupire, J. (eds.) Entertainment Computing – ICEC 2010, LNCS, vol. 6243, pp. 212–217. Springer, Heidelberg (2010). https://doi.org/10.1145/1401843.1401858

Khalifa, A., de Mesentier Silva, F., Togelius, J.: Level design patterns in 2D games. In: IEEE Conference on Games (CoG) 2019, pp. 1–8. IEEE, London (2019). https://doi.org/10.1109/CIG.2019.8847953

Zhong, Y., Fryer, L.K., Zheng, S., Shum, A., Chu, S.K.W., et al.: The power of play: integrating competitive sandbox game for experiential learning to foster twenty-first century skills. Int. J. Educ. Technol. High. Educ. **22**(34), 1–17 (2025). https://doi.org/10.1186/s41239-025-00528-y

Gallotta, R., Liapis, A., Yannakakis, G.N.: LLMaker: a game level design interface using natural language. In: Proceedings of the IEEE Conference on Games (CoG 2024), pp. 1–2. IEEE, Milan, Italy (2024). https://doi.org/10.1109/CoG60054.2024.10645626

Ishii, H., Ullmer, B.: Tangible bits: towards seamless interfaces between people, bits and atoms. In: Proceedings of the ACM SIGCHI Conference on Human Factors in Computing Systems, pp. 234–241. ACM, New York (1997). https://doi.org/10.1145/258549.258715

Ullmer, B., Ishii, H.: Emerging frameworks for tangible user interfaces. IBM Syst. J. **39**(3–4), 915–931 (2000)

Wang, D., Qi, Y., Zhang, Y., Wang, T.: A TUI-based programming tool for children. In: Lee, S., Anderson, K. (eds.) Proceedings of the 2015 ACM SIGCHI Conference on Human Factors in Computing Systems, pp. 1234–1243. ACM, Seoul (2015). https://doi.org/10.1145/2729094.2742630

Cherek, C., Brocker, A., Voelker, S., Borchers, J.O.: Tangible Awareness: how tangibles on tabletops influence awareness of each other's actions. In: Proceedings of the 2018 CHI Conference on Human Factors in Computing Systems, pp. 298:1–298:7. ACM, New York (2018). https://doi.org/10.1145/3173574.3173872

Marco, J., Baldassarri, S., Cerezo, E., Xu, D.Y., Read, J.C.: Let the experts talk: an experience of tangible game design with children. In: Proceedings of the 2010 International Conference on Interaction Design and Children (IDC 2010), pp. 17–24. ACM, Barcelona (2010). https://doi.org/10.1145/1649475.1649490

Marshall, P.: Do tangible interfaces enhance learning? In: Proceedings of the 1st International Conference on Tangible and Embedded Interaction, pp. 163–170. ACM, New York (2007). https://doi.org/10.1145/1226969.1227004

Using Virtual Companions on Serious Games to Increase Knowledge and Immersion of Students

Cristiano França[1]([✉]) [iD], Genesis Betencourt[1] [iD], Beatriz Peres[1] [iD],
Pedros Campos[2] [iD], and Frederica Gonçalves[1] [iD]

[1] ITI/LARSyS, University of Madeira, Funchal, Portugal
`crisfranca@live.com.pt, beatriz.peres@iti.larsys.pt`
[2] ITI/LARSyS, University of Madeira, WowSystems, Funchal, Portugal

Abstract. Maintaining student focus is a key challenge in modern history classes. While serious games have shown potential to enhance engagement and learning, research on using virtual companions as the primary medium for delivering educational content remains limited. This study investigates whether a virtual companion guiding players through a serious game can increase motivation and knowledge acquisition. Twenty-one participants played the prototype and completed pre- and post-questionnaires. Results indicate that the companion fostered a strong emotional connection, supported learning, and, through interactions within detailed game environments, significantly enhanced immersion.

Keywords: Serious Games · Digital Storytelling · Non-Playable Characters · Virtual Companions · Immersion · Knowledge Retention

1 Introduction

Students often lose focus when lessons are dull or the environment is uncomfortable, reducing engagement and performance [1]. Technology, particularly educational games, can boost engagement, critical thinking, and historical understanding [2]. Immersive gameplay promotes deep absorption [3], while gamified elements enhance motivation, engagement, and knowledge retention [4].

Non-Playable Characters (NPCs) are used to convey story, guide players, and support gameplay [5]. Acting as companions or allies, they provide dialogue, hints, and dynamic learning opportunities [6], with research showing that their personality traits can enhance educational narratives [7].

Although serious games have been studied for engagement and learning, the role of virtual companions as primary educational tools remains underexplored. This study examines whether a virtual companion teaching Ancient Greece can improve student knowledge and motivation, offering insights for future research on NPCs in education.

S. Bakkes et al. (Eds.): GALA 2025, LNCS 16307, pp. 407–413, 2026.
https://doi.org/10.1007/978-3-032-11043-5_42

2   Related Work

2.1   Impact of Serious Games in Modern Education

Advances in technology have integrated digital resources into classrooms, transforming teaching and learning [8]. Serious educational games enhance this process by combining interactivity, engagement, and educational goals, fostering motivation and effective learning [9, 10]. Meta-analyses of Intelligent Tutoring Systems, Computer-Assisted Instruction, and technology-enhanced methods show that technology-supported approaches often outperform traditional instruction, underscoring the importance of integrating digital tools thoughtfully [11–13].

2.2   Influence of NPCs in the Learning Environments

In educational games, Non-Playable Characters (NPCs) support learning by guiding players, providing feedback, and fostering engagement. NPCs can offer emotional support, encouraging motivation and persistence, and act as social agents that influence knowledge acquisition, decision-making, and cooperation [14, 15]. By personalizing interactions, NPCs make learning more dynamic and learner-centered [16]. Studies show that NPCs in history games increase student interest, engagement, and learning outcomes, highlighting their role as both narrative and educational mediators [17].

3   Materials and Methods

This section describes the serious game prototype, its objectives, the role of the virtual companion, study design, data collection, participant involvement, and demographics.

3.1   Prototype

The prototype centers on Athens, chosen for its significance in Ancient Greek civilization, allowing students to explore its culture, architecture, and daily life to foster a dynamic understanding of the period. Development relied on three sources:

- Curriculum Content: to ensure alignment with history lessons.
- Scholarly Articles: to provide historical accuracy and depth.
- Expert Collaboration: from teachers to validate educational value (Fig. 1).

Narrative and Virtual Companion
The demo features five missions combining challenge and learning, where players progress with the help of a virtual companion. Acting as the main source of historical information, the virtual companion guides, assists, and delivers content, ensuring knowledge gains stem from gameplay.

Fig. 1. On the left, an image of the game world (Athens); on the right, the player's view, showing the controlled character at the center with the companion alongside.

3.2 Data Collection

Data was gathered through two questionnaires administered before and after the experiment, both assessing knowledge of Ancient Athens. The post-questionnaire also measured motivation.

1. Pre-questionnaire

Collected demographics (age, gender), prior gaming experience, technology proficiency, and baseline knowledge of Ancient Greece.

2. Post questionnaire

Reassessed knowledge and included open-ended questions on motivation and learning.

- Knowledge Questions: Both questionnaires used multiple-choice and written items on Ancient Athens to test the virtual companion's impact on retention.
- Engagement and Experience: Measured with the Immersion Scale (IS) [18] and the Game Experience Questionnaire (GEQ) [19], focusing on attention, flow, and emotional engagement.

3.3 Procedure

University students completed a lab study in three phases: (1) Pre-Questionnaire on demographics and prior knowledge; (2) individual gameplay of five missions; and (3) Post-Questionnaire, IS, and GEQ to assess learning and experience.

3.4 Participants

The study included 21 university students (12 males, 9 females) aged 19–43, recruited via convenience sampling from various departments to ensure diverse academic backgrounds. Participants' technology skills were recorded to confirm suitability for the computer-based experiment, and all provided informed consent.

4 Results

Findings are presented as quantitative (knowledge improvement, immersion) and qualitative data, with the latter coded and organized into themes to better interpret participants' experiences.

4.1 Quantitative Data

Knowledge

Table 1 presents the mean and standard deviation of correct answers. Despite some decline in individual scores, results show an average knowledge gain of 13.09% after playing the prototype.

Table 1. The mean and standard deviation results of knowledge.

	Pre-Questionnaire	Post Questionnaire
Mean	34,52%	47,61%
Standard Deviation	24,33	23,59

Immersion

Table 2 shows Immersion Scale results, with items like "I felt in control," "I felt immersed," and "My actions flowed." Scores range from 1.8 (very poor) to 18 (excellent). Results in the good–excellent range indicate high immersion during the experiment.

Table 2. Immersion Scale Results

Mean	Standard Deviation
12,99	2,38

Game Experience Questionnaire

Table 3 shows Game Experience Questionnaire results (subscales 1–5), indicating a generally enjoyable experience with moderate immersion.

Table 3. Game Experience Questionnaire Results. SD - Standard Deviation; C - Challenge; SII - Sensory and Imaginative Immersion; F – Flow; T – Tension; Cha – Challenge; NA – Negative Affect; PA – Positive Affect

	C	SII	F	T	Cha	NA	PA
Mean	3,73	3,66	3,03	1,81	1,89	2,06	3,71
SD	0,66	0,86	0,87	0,94	0,62	0,91	0,86

4.2 Qualitative Data

Most participants (85%) found NPCs—especially the companion—enhanced gameplay, guiding players, supporting learning, and enriching the storyline. Sixty percent noted its role in progression, 85% valued its historical content, and 35% relied on it in difficult tasks. Cutscenes, dialogue, and other NPCs also reinforced cultural understanding. Overall, the companion was seen as engaging, supportive, and central to both entertainment and educational values.

5 Discussion

The virtual companion increased knowledge of Ancient Greece by 13.09% and served as the primary source of narrative and educational content, enhancing engagement, motivation, and emotional investment. High immersion scores (Sensory & Imaginative: $M = 3.66$, $SD = 0.86$; Immersion Scale: $M = 12.99$, $SD = 2.38$) and positive GEQ subscales (Competence 3.73; Flow 3.03; Positive Affect 3.71; Tension 1.81) indicate an enjoyable experience. Participants valued the companion's guidance and educational content, though improvements to dialogue clarity and gameplay (e.g., subtitles) were recommended.

These results suggest that pairing a compelling narrative with a virtual companion effectively promotes immersion, motivation, and learning in historical educational games.

6 Conclusion

This study showed that a virtual companion enhanced player experience and learning about Ancient Greece by enriching the narrative, increasing immersion, and providing guidance and emotional support. Most participants felt connected to the companion, which boosted engagement, while accurate historical content and a compelling storyline reinforced educational value.

Limitations include a small sample size, technical issues affecting immersion, and dialogue comprehension challenges for non-native English speakers, suggesting the need for captions or localization. Future research should involve larger, more diverse samples to explore interactions with companions and examine whether knowledge gains transfer to academic performance.

Acknowledgments. This research was funded by the Portuguese Recovery and Resilience Program (PRR), IAPMEI/ANI/FCT under Agenda C645022399-00000057 (eGames-Lab).

References

1. Cicekci, M.A., Sadik, F.: Teachers' and students' opinions about students' attention problems during the lesson. J. Educ. Learn. **8**, 15–30 (2019)
2. Teaching History With Digital Historical Games: An Introduction to the Field and Best Practices - Jeremiah McCall (2016). https://jour-nals.sagepub.com/doi/abs/10.1177/1046878116646693
3. Jennett, C., et al.: Measuring and defining the experience of immersion in games. Int. J. Hum. Comput. Stud. **66**, 641–661 (2008). https://doi.org/10.1016/j.ijhcs.2008.04.004
4. Sailer, M., Homner, L.: The gamification of learning: a meta-analysis. Educ. Psychol. Rev. **32**, 77–112 (2020). https://doi.org/10.1007/s10648-019-09498-w
5. Paradeda, R.B., Freitas, G., Alves Filho, S.E., Abner Souza, A.: The influence of well-dressed NPCs on player perception, immersion and decision-making in gaming. In: 2023 IEEE Conference on Games (CoG), pp. 1–8 (2023)
6. Liew, T.W., Siradj, Y., Tan, S.-M., Roedavan, R., Khan, M.T.I., Pudjoatmodjo, B.: Game-changer NPCs: leveling-up technology acceptance and flow in a digital learning quest. Int. J. Hum. Comput. Interact., 1–22 (2024). https://doi.org/10.1080/10447318.2024.2344917
7. Liao, C.C.Y., Chen, Z.-H., Cheng, H.N.H., Chan, T.-W.: Unfolding learning behaviors: a sequential analysis approach in a game-based learning environment. Res. Pract. Technol. Enhanc. Learn. **7**, 25–44 (2012)
8. Peng, H., Ma, S., Spector, J.M.: Personalized adaptive learning: an emerging pedagogical approach enabled by a smart learning environment. Smart Learn. Environ. **6**, 9 (2019). https://doi.org/10.1186/s40561-019-0089-y
9. Barz, N., Benick, M., Dörrenbächer-Ulrich, L., Perels, F.: The effect of digital game-based learning interventions on cognitive, metacognitive, and affective-motivational learning outcomes in school: a meta-analysis (2024). https://jour-nals.sagepub.com/doi/abs/10.3102/00346543231167795
10. O'Doherty, E.: Educational Games in Higher Education: a case study in teaching recursive algorithms (2007)
11. Steenbergen-Hu, S., Cooper, H.: A meta-analysis of the effectiveness of intelligent tutoring systems on college students' academic learning. J. Educ. Psychol. **106**, 331–347 (2014). https://doi.org/10.1037/a0034752
12. Sosa, G.W., Berger, D.E., Saw, A.T., Mary, J.C.: Effectiveness of computer-assisted instruction in statistics: a meta-analysis. Rev. Educ. Res. **81**, 97–127 (2011). https://doi.org/10.3102/0034654310378174
13. Tamim, R.M., Lowerison, G., Schmid, R.F., Bernard, R.M., Abrami, P.C.: A multi-year investigation of the relationship between pedagogy, computer use and course effectiveness in post-secondary education. J. Comput. High. Educ. **23**, 1–14 (2011). https://doi.org/10.1007/s12528-010-9041-4
14. Yu, K., Wen, S., Xu, W., Caon, M., Baghaei, N., Liang, H.-N.: Cheer for me: effect of non-player character audience feedback on older adult users of virtual reality exergames. Virtual Real. **27**, 1887–1903 (2023). https://doi.org/10.1007/s10055-023-00780-5
15. Hong, T., Cabrera, J., Beaudoin, C.E.: Disentangling real-world and virtual-world social norms: the persuasive elements and social psychological effects of a serious game. Telemat. Informat. Rep. **9**, 100038 (2023). https://doi.org/10.1016/j.teler.2022.100038
16. Pretty, E.J., Fayek, H.M., Zambetta, F.: A case for personalized non-player character companion design. Int. J. Hum. Comput. Interact., 1–20 (2023). https://doi.org/10.1080/10447318.2023.2181125

17. Chan, H.-Y., Liu, S.-W., Hou, H.-T.: Interacting with real-person non-player characters to learn history: development and playing behavior pattern analysis of a remote scaffolding-based situated educational game. Interact. Learn. Environ., 1–21 (2023). https://doi.org/10.1080/10494820.2023.2192745
18. Ellis, G.D., Freeman, P.A., Jamal, T., Jiang, J.: A theory of structured experience. Ann. Leis. Res. **22**, 97–118 (2019). https://doi.org/10.1080/11745398.2017.1312468
19. IJsselsteijn, W.A., de Kort, Y.A.W., Poels, K.: The Game Experience Questionnaire. Technische Universiteit Eindhoven, Eindhoven (2013)

Towards Human-Game Interaction (HGI)

Brunella Botte[1,2](✉) [ID], Giada Marinensi[1] [ID], Francesca de Rosa[3] [ID],
and Alessandro Rizzi[4] [ID]

[1] Department of Human Sciences, Link Campus University, Rome, Italy
{b.botte,g.marinensi}@unilink.it
[2] Department of Information and Computer Science Utrecht University,
Utrecht, The Netherlands
[3] Center for Advanced Preparedness and Threat Response Simulation,
Austin, (TX), USA
francesca.derosa@captrs.org
[4] Department of Computer Science, University of Milan, Milan, Italy
alessandro.rizzi@unimi.it

Abstract. As serious games, as well as entertainment games, evolve along a continuum ranging from analog to digital, including hybrid solutions, the design and role of game interfaces have become increasingly complex and central to the player experience. This position paper proposes a conceptual shift, considering the interface not merely as a structural or aesthetic layer, but as a key mediator between game mechanics and the mental and emotional models formed by players during the game. Building on insights from previous research on interfaces and on player experience, we introduce the Human-Game Interaction (HGI) framework as a lens to systematically analyze how interfaces shape the player's experience both in serious games and in entertainment games. By referencing design heuristics, the tripartition of the mind, and Gestalt principles, we argue for a holistic understanding of the interface and we offer new perspectives for cross-disciplinary research and practical applications, particularly in the design of serious games where usability and meaningful engagement are essential.

Keywords: Human-Computer Interaction · Player's experience · Interface · Conceptual model · Human-Game Interaction

1 Introduction

What makes a game a game? Over the years both scholars and game designers have contributed to this ongoing debate, highlighting how games are complex systems which tend to be greater than the sum of their parts as players experience them [7,18,24]. In the conceptual transition from games as artifacts, to games as player experiences, a key role is played by the interface, defined by [22] as the point of contact between the player and the game system. This is particularly relevant in serious gaming, in which the impact of all elements of the game on the

S. Bakkes et al. (Eds.): GALA 2025, LNCS 16307, pp. 414–419, 2026.
https://doi.org/10.1007/978-3-032-11043-5_43

learning process or rigorous collection of data for analysis should be understood and carefully assessed.

The game interface shapes, layouts and structures are constantly evolving as a consequence of the growing variety of ludic artifacts. As a result of growing blend of analog and digital technologies, games are now categorized along a continuum ranging from purely analog to fully digital, and encompassing a wide array of hybrid games [5,12].

Wherever a game is situated in this continuum, it has its own interface, which connects players and their experience with the game mechanics. This work aims to present the interface not simply as a component, but rather as a fundamental element that connects the game mechanics with the mental and emotional model that players form during their entire gaming experience with the game. As a position paper, we want to present a formal point of view that can be used to describe, in a systematic way, practices often adopted by game designers, although through unconscious and fragmented approaches. This can bring several advantages. The immediate advantage is to have available, by simply remapping the domain, all the vast research activity developed over the years on Human-Computer Interaction (HCI). Additionally, it helps separating the complexity of the interface from the one related to the game itself, trying to reduce the former, while keeping intact the latter, which is the inner spirit of the game mechanics [18].

The objective of this paper is to pave the way towards a novel approach that can be referred to as Human-Game Interaction (HGI), which can serve as a foundation for the development of effective and intentional ludic interfaces across diverse design contexts and technologies.

2   Player Experience and Game Interface

In the last decades, we have observed the emergence of the term *player experience* (PE) to identify the application of user experience concepts mainly to digital games, which are interpreted as a sub-category of software [26]. Attention to game related aspects in the field of Human-Computer Interaction is demonstrated by the existence of dedicated conferences (e.g., HCI-Games [1]). However, it appears that the focus is mostly on player experience and to computerized games. Extensions of the concepts to the continuum between analog and digital games [21] and considerations on the interface as a medium are mostly overlooked.

As for human-computer interaction, which experienced a shift from usability to user experience, similarly, in game research a shift has occurred from the concept of *game experience* to PE [26]. In fact, the PE term is preferred over *game experience*, since the experience is made by the person who plays the game.

Several psychological models of PE have been proposed [26]. However, it appears that considerations regarding the game as an interface, mediating between humans and a system that aims to produce an intervention (i.e., learning and analytical serious game outputs), has been largely overlooked.

The term PE and *Human-Game Interaction* (HGI) are complementary, but not the same. In fact, the former refers to the overall experience lived by the player during gameplay, while the latter focuses on the interaction between the player and the game. Similarly to the definition of human-computer interaction of a multi-disciplinary field dealing with the interaction of a human and a task through a computer [9], we refer to Human-Game Interaction as the interaction between a human and a task through a game (see Fig. 1(A)). For serious games, such tasks can be either a learning or an analytical one.

In this paper, we focus on design considerations complementary to the ones reported in PE research, in recognition of the game as an interface that plays a key role on the *effectiveness* [18] [20] of the game design in the intended context (e.g., learning, awareness raising or analysis).

3   The Proposed Framework

Figure 1(B) shows the scheme of the proposed approach. It reproduces in a schematic way how the game interface is positioned between the game mechanics and players. In fact, the game is composed, in a simplified way, of internal mechanics and an interface for accessing these mechanics. Players cannot directly access the mechanics, but must use the interface for this purpose. In doing this, the interface allows players to form a mental model of what the game mechanics are. If the interface changes, the players' perception and idea regarding the game changes. In other words, a different interface will create a different game, in a similar way to what McLuhan intended, stating that "the medium is the message" [15]. Through the mental model formed as a result of the interface, combined with players' own experience and with the purpose for which they are using the game, the players form their situation awareness related to the specific game session. The combination of these aspects leads to that particular players experience that is lived in that moment.

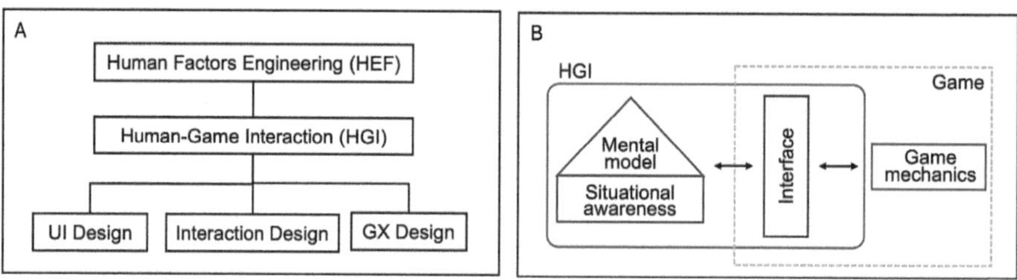

Fig. 1. (A) HGI hierachy; (B) A scheme of the HGI framework.

This high-level scheme, which might resemble other high-level models, highlights the pivotal role of the interface. Through this design perspective, we could adapt and re-purpose many research results on interfaces developed in other domains. Next sections present a non-exhaustive explanation of some of the prominent ones.

3.1   The Theoretical Underpinnings of the Proposed Framework

Human-Game Interaction (HGI) is characterized by a multifaceted nature, due to aspects concerning both the players' experience when interacting with the game and the interface as the medium between players and game mechanics. Therefore, to theoretically frame HGI we suggest to refer to three main domains: (1) Tripartition of the mind; (2) Heuristics as support for experience design; (3) The Gestalt approach.

Tripartition of the Mind. The tripartition of the human mental activities has its roots far back in time [10]. According to this approach, the way a phenomenon is perceived depends on the impact it has on cognition, i.e., the intellect, on affection, i.e. feelings, and on conation, i.e., the desire to act. In the case of games we could define the three areas as follows: cognition concerns the game's ability to be perceived and understood and, consequently, the ability to develop strategies while respecting its rules; affection concerns the way in which the game as a whole impacts the player's emotions; conation (or volition) concerns the player's actions within the game system, and is closely dependent on the affordances that the game offers.

Furthermore, this classic tripartition finds a clear parallel in [6] model of student engagement, which distinguishes between cognitive, emotional, and behavioral engagement. This is particularly relevant when designing serious games, because they can only fulfill their educational, training or awareness raising purpose, if they successfully engages players across all three dimensions.

Heuristics as Support for Experience Design. The artifact "game" is *de-facto* an interface. As such it can be structured and analyzed following the heuristics proposed by Nielsen [16].

Human-Computer Interaction research looking at video games has a long tradition [8, 11, 16, 23]. Even if those heuristics were designed thinking of digital interfaces design, some attempts were made to apply them to the study of video games as interactive artifacts. Special attention was given to Nielsen's Heuristics [13]. The results showed that, for studying video games, it would have been better to rely on heuristics specifically designed for this purpose [2–4, 17, 19].

Additionally, in recent years the bond between digital and analog games has grown stronger underscoring the need for a more holistic approach to Human-Game Interaction.

The Gestalt Approach. Finally, to bring together heuristics, affordances and domains of experience, we can refer to the principles of Gestalt psychology [25].

What we would like to suggest is to consider the whole set of visual features that make a game easier to use and more immediate in its interaction and in forming a relative mental model in the players. Gestalt laws are a valid tool for this analysis, but also alternative assessment methods of the visual features can be used to foster the formation of a robust mental model of the game [14, 18].

This concept is fundamental and also helps us to understand how the gaming experience can change (or not) when, for example, a game is transposed from digital to analog and vice versa.

4   Conclusion

This position paper proposes a paradigm shift in how we conceptualize the game interface as a central actor in the construction of player experience. By introducing the Human-Game Interaction (HGI) framework, we aim to formally recognize the game interface as a dynamic element that shapes the player's mental model of the game itself and mediates the experience, both in entertainment games and serious games. Drawing from established traditions in Human-Computer Interaction, and expanding it through the tripartition of the mind and the principles of Gestalt psychology, the HGI perspective offers a unified lens through which study and design game interfaces across the digital-analog continuum. In fact, every game, independently from its nature, relies on the interface to translate mechanics into meaningful experiences. Furthermore, HGI opens a path for cross-disciplinary insights to inform the design of more usable, engaging, and impactful games. Looking ahead, further work is needed to empirically validate the HGI framework, by applying it in the analysis of existing games, be them analog, digital or hybrid.

References

1. International Conference on HCI in Games (HCI-Games). https://2025.hci.international/hci-games Accessed 03 July 2025
2. Desurvire, H., Caplan, M., Toth, J.A.: Using heuristics to evaluate the playability of games. In: CHI '04 Extended Abstracts on Human Factors in Computing Systems, pp. 1509–1512. ACM, New York, NY, USA (2004). https://doi.org/10.1145/985921.986102
3. Desurvire, H., Wiberg, C.: Game Usability heuristics (PLAY) for evaluating and designing better games: the next iteration. In: Ozok, A.A., Zaphiris, P. (eds.) OCSC 2009. LNCS, vol. 5621, pp. 557–566. Springer, Heidelberg (2009). https://doi.org/10.1007/978-3-642-02774-1_60
4. Desurvire, H., Wixon, D.: Heuristics uncovered for games user researchers and game designers. In: Drachen, A., Mirza-Babaei, P., Nacke, L.E. (eds.) Games User Research, chap. 14, pp. 217–256. Oxford University Press (2018)
5. Fassone, R., Salvador, M., Vanetti, M.: Turno Extra – Estensioni digitali del gioco da tavolo. In: Mostra a cura di Riccardo Fassone, Mauro Salvador e Mauro Vanetti. Play – Festival del Gioco, Bologna (2025)
6. Fredricks, J.A., Blumenfeld, P.C., Paris, A.H.: School engagement: potential of the concept, state of the evidence. Rev. Educ. Res. **74**(1), 59–109 (2004). https://doi.org/10.3102/00346543074001059
7. Fullerton, T.: Game design workshop: a playcentric approach to creating innovative games. Elsevier Inc., Burlington, MA, second edi edn. (2008)

8. Gerhardt-Powals, J.: Cognitive engineering principles for enhancing human-computer performance. Int. J. Hum. Comput. Interact. **8**(2), 189–211 (1996). https://doi.org/10.1080/10447319609526147

9. Helander, M.G., Landauer, T.K., Prabhu, P.V.: Handbook of human-computer interaction, 2nd edn. Elsevier Science Inc., USA (1997)

10. Hilgard, E.R.: The trilogy of mind: cognition, affection, and conation. J. Hist. Behavioral Sci. **16**(2), 107–117 (1980). https://doi.org/10.1002/1520-6696(198004)16:2<107::AID-JHBS2300160202>3.0.CO;2-Y

11. Kamper, R.J.: Extending the usability of heuristics for design and evaluation: lead, follow, and get out of the way. Int. J. Hum. Comput. Interac. **14**(3-4), 447–462 (2002). https://doi.org/10.1080/10447318.2002.9669129

12. Kankainen, V., Arjoranta, J., Nummenmaa, T.: Games as blends: understanding hybrid games. J. Virtual Reality Broadcast. **14**(4) (2017). https://doi.org/10.20385/1860-2037/14.2017.4

13. Laitinen, S.: Do usability expert evaluation and test provide novel and useful data for game development? J. Usability Stud. **1**(2), 64–75 (2006)

14. Lecca, M., Rizzi, A., Serapioni, R.P.: An image contrast measure based on retinex principles. IEEE Trans. Image Process. **30**, 3543–3554 (2021)

15. McLuhan, M.: Understanding media: the extensions of man. MIT press (1994)

16. Molich, R., Nielsen, J.: Improving a human-computer dialogue. Commun. ACM **33**(3), 338–348 (1990)

17. Mylly, S., Rajanen, M., Iivari, N.: Usable usability heuristics for game developers. In: Proceedings of the 28th International Conference on Information Systems Development (ISD 2019) (2019)

18. Passarelli, M., Masini, M., Piccinno, T.F., Rizzi, A.: Don't flip the table yet: a framework for the analysis of visual and cognitive ergonomics in board games. Games Culture, 1–26 (2024). https://doi.org/10.1177/15554120241248487

19. Pinelle, D., Wong, N., Stach, T.: Heuristic evaluation for games. In: Proceedings of the SIGCHI Conference on Human Factors in Computing Systems, pp. 1453–1462. ACM, New York, NY, USA (2008). https://doi.org/10.1145/1357054.1357282

20. Procci, K., Chao, A., Bohnsack, J., Olsen, T., Bowers, C.: Usability in serious games: a model for small development teams. Comput. Technol. Appl. **3**(4) (2012)

21. de Rosa, F.: Knowledge acquisition analytical games: games for cognitive system design. Ph.D. thesis, University of Genoa, Italy (2020)

22. Salen, K., Zimmerman, E.: Rules of play: game design fundamentals. The MIT Press (2003)

23. Shneiderman, B., Plaisant, C., Cohen, M., Jacobs, S.: Designing the User interface: strategies for effective human-computer interaction, 5th edn. Pearson Education, London, UK (2013)

24. Sicart, M.: Play matters. The MIT Press (2014)

25. Wertheimer, M.: Gestalt theory. (1938)

26. Wiemeyer, J., Nacke, L., Moser, C., Floyd' Mueller, F.: Player Experience. In: Dörner, R., Göbel, S., Effelsberg, W., Wiemeyer, J. (eds.) Serious Games. LNCS, pp. 243–271. Springer, Cham (2016). https://doi.org/10.1007/978-3-319-40612-1_9

Gamification in International Supply Chain Management: Impact on Students' Engagement and Performance

Frazen Tolentino-Zondervan$^{(\boxtimes)}$, Margarita Bagamanova , Raul Casado Linares , Casper Draijer , Erik van den Thillart, Habiba Khan , Maarten van Amerom, and Teresa Sanchez Rico

Amsterdam School of International Business (AMSIB), Amsterdam University of Applied Sciences, Fraijlemaborg 133, Amsterdam, The Netherlands
`{f.t.zondervan,m.bagamanova2,r.casado.linares,c.t.draijer,`
`e.p.a.van.den.thillart,h.khan,j.m.van.amerom,`
`m.t.sanchez.rico}@hva.nl`

Abstract. This study evaluates the effect of gamification on the engagement and performance of first-year students in the International Supply Chain Management course at a University of Applied Sciences. Several students were exposed to the pilot of The Fresh Connection compact, a simulation game which was implemented between May to June 2025. Based on 350 observations, students are categorized as control group (without exposure to game, n = 217) and treatment group (with exposure to game, n = 133). These groups were further divided based on individual's final grade: pass (grade $\geq$ 5.5) or fail (grade <5.5). The dataset is supplemented by a survey of students that played the game. Results show significant difference between students who participate in the game and took both exams (78%) versus 44% of students who do not participate in the game (p-value = 9.39e−10), as well as between students' participation in the game and their exam performance (p-value = 7.17e−13). Overall, the survey shows significant satisfaction of students in using TFC game (71%), although some students would like to see tighter integration of the game in course assessment. Learnings from this pilot will be used to improve student engagement and passing rate.

Keywords: Digital simulation · Experiential learning · Gamification · Higher education · Supply chain management

1 Introduction

Digitalization has rapidly transformed the delivery of courses and learning of students. Although traditional teacher-led style that focuses on imparting theoretical knowledge to students can be effective, they are nowadays seen as insufficient to facilitate engagement and learning process of students [1]. Thus, traditional learning style requires merging with modern methods to optimize the development of knowledge, abilities, and values of students. The emergence of student-centered learning is linked to effective classroom practices and has shown high level of student development and satisfaction [2]. The didactics for facilitating student-centered learning include problem-based learning using scenarios and cases, experiential-based learning that includes gamification, and feedback approach to students [3]. Gamification as part of experiential-based learning can help students develop deeper understanding and master core theories in a practical setting [4]. The application of game elements in education enhances students' participation in class, promotes higher information retention and problem-solving abilities, as well as fosters emotional benefits [5].

This paper focuses on the application of gamification in supply chain management (SCM). SCM is about managing the flows of products, information, and finances from suppliers up to the end consumers, to optimize operations, ensure customer satisfaction and mitigate risks. The objective of this paper is to evaluate the relationship between the use of a simulation game in SCM and students' engagement and learning performance, based on a pilot of The Fresh Connection (TFC) compact implemented in the International Supply Chain Management 1 (ISCM1) course at a University of Applied Sciences in the Netherlands. Conducting this study is important for assessing the effects of adopting gamification in ISCM1 and potentially in other SCM courses. Using two main groups of students – with and without exposure to SCM simulation game, this study uses quantitative methods supported by qualitative feedback from students. This study contributes to literature by extending knowledge on the effectiveness of gamification in students' learning engagement and performance. On practical level, this study provides insights on considerations when integrating gamification in a course.

2 Literature Review

2.1 Gamification in SCM

Gamification focuses on incorporating elements of a game such as challenges, rankings and score system, with traditional teaching methods to enhance students' motivation and learning [6]. In SCM, several gamification tools have emerged to aid educators in teaching. First is Beergame, which exposes students to real life challenges of managing supply chains and the impact of bullwhip effect. Second is DISASTER, a blockchain enabled platform that evaluates the effect of information sharing on supply chain based on ordering strategies and behavioral traits of players. Third is Inchainge simulation game, which focuses on making decisions in four business roles namely Purchasing, Operations, SCM, and Sales, as well as on evaluating the effects of each decision on the supply chain and Return on Investment (ROI). This study focuses on gamification using Inchainge's TFC compact game for two reasons. First, the introduction of TFC compact game is done in conjunction with traditional teaching methods. Second, the use of TFC compact game is at pilot stage and will serve as a learning for the course.

2.2 Impact of Gamification on Students' Engagement and Performance

The impact of gamification on the engagement and performance of students has been studied with mixed outcomes. In terms of engagement, evidence shows on one hand that gamification positively influences the experiences of students based on their level of interest, intellectual concentration, and intrinsic motivation due to their independence and skills developed through the games [7, 8]. Other studies on the other hand reported negative impact of gamification on students' engagement due to discouraging effect of ranking system, unreadiness for independence, perceived unusefulness, as well as unclear linkage of the games with exam preparations [9, 10]. Other studies are inconclusive since the effect of gamification on students' engagement can be attributed to the motivational elements, continuous financial and time investment in the implementation stage, and the need for capable and dedicated teaching staff [11, 12].

When it comes to performance, gamification is associated with increased passing rate of students as well as with reducing the gap in grade between the lowest and top performers [8]. Meanwhile, the study of Toda et al. [9] found that based on 71% of the literature that they reviewed, gamification can have negative effect on performance when gamification hinders the learning process when a) students do not understand the rules b) focus too much on game mechanics or c) when the game is too difficult.

3   Methodology

3.1   The Fresh Connection (TFC) Compact Pilot

This study uses the TFC compact as a pilot delivered among first-year ISCM1 students. This game provides hands-on experience in managing supply chain and making decisions across four business functions of a virtual fresh juice company, by allowing students to play each role individually weekly and to generate positive ROI for the company. In preparation for the pilot, eight (8) SCM lecturers did educator's training as a requirement for teaching TFC compact game. The pilot was delivered to nine (9) out of 11 ISCM1 classes from May to June 2025. Participating in the game is voluntary.

3.2   Experiment Set-Ups and Data Analysis

To examine the effects of gamification on both students' engagement and performance, we prepared two experiments set-ups using the data collected after students took the midterm and final exams. Experiment set-up 1 consists of 350 students' observations, which are divided into two groups: (1) control (no exposure to TFC game, n = 217) and (2) treatment (with exposure to TFC game, n = 133). These groups are used for measuring the effect of gamification on students' performance in the exam. We first plotted the data via histogram and boxplot to see the distribution of the data set (refer to Fig. 1 left). Based on the plots, the data for both groups do not look normally distributed. Therefore, we tested the dataset for normality using Shapiro-Wilk test (W = 0.81, p-value = 1.83e−15) as well as on uni-modality/multi-modality using Hartigans' dip test (D = 0.077, p-value <2.2e−16). This means our data is not normally distributed and at least bimodal. Therefore, we used Welch 2-sample t-test, which is suitable for non-normally distributed data, to see if there is significant difference on the mean final mark of students between control and treatment groups. To test the relationship between the game and student's engagement, measured by students being able to take either none or both

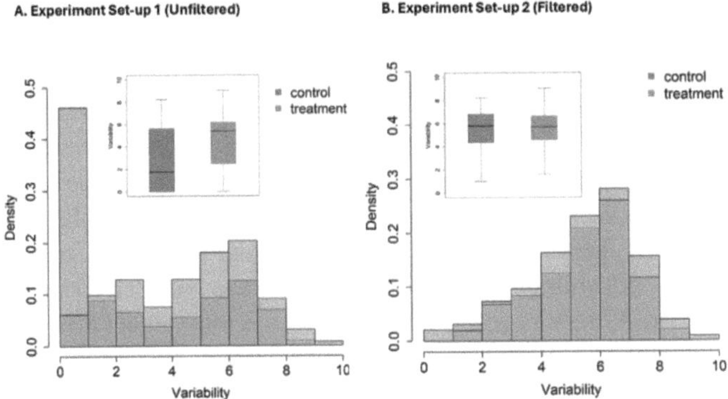

Fig. 1. The left figure shows the histogram and boxplot comparing control and treatment groups without excluding students missing exams, while the right figure shows them after excluding students who took none.

exams, we further divided the groups into students participating and not participating in both exams. We used Pearson's Chi-squared test to examine this relationship.

Experiment Set-up 2 tests the effect of TFC game on students' who participated in both exams (n = 200 observations). We divided these observations into two main groups: (1) control (no exposure to TFC game, n = 95) and (2) treatment (with exposure to TFC game, n = 105). The histogram and boxplot were first plotted (refer to Fig. 1 right). Each group was then further divided into two categorical groups based on final grades: fail (grade <5.5) and pass (score $\geq$5.5). Pearson's Chi-squared test between two categorical variables was conducted to test the effect of gamification on students' performance. In addition to Experiment Set-ups 1 and 2, a survey was conducted (n = 34) to measure students' level of satisfaction and the linkage of TFC game in the ISCM1 course.

4 Results and Discussion

4.1 Effects of Gamification on Students' Engagement

For Experiment set-up 1, the result of Pearson's chi-squared test shows a very significant correlation (p-value = 9.39e−10) between students participating both in the game and in two exams. It appears that a higher percentage of students (78%) remain actively engaged and participate in taking the exams in the treatment group compared to control group (44%). This implies that students who participate in the game have a much higher chance to participate in both exams and achieve their learning objectives. To validate the engagement of students in ISCM1 course, the survey shows that 71% of students scored highly positive on the overall experience, hence are satisfied with the simulation game. In addition, 71% also recommends using TFC game for future students. In the period that the game was introduced, there is overall higher student satisfaction score for the course. This might mean that there is a higher satisfaction in the learning experience. This result also indicates that further adoption and integration of TFC game is recommended for ISCM1 and other SCM courses for increased engagement and exam participation of students.

4.2 Effects of Gamification on Students' Performance in the Exam

Experiment Set-up 1 shows a significant effect of gamification on the performance of students in the exam based on the outcome of Welch 2-sample t-test (p-value $= 7.17e{-}13$). In addition, the mark distribution in Fig. 1 (left) appears to show two subpopulations of students, which can be called as low- and high-performing based on the bimodal distribution of data for both control and treatment groups. In control group, the low-performing category is very left skewed with many students scored between 0–1, while treatment group shows low-performing students scored on average between 2–3 in the exam that they participated in. Next, we see that control group has most students in low-performing category, while treatment group has most students in high-performing category, which suggests that treatment group has higher student engagement. This becomes even more apparent when we look at the boxplot in Fig. 1, which shows a much higher median final grade for the treatment group than for the control group.

The outcome of Experiment Set-up 2 shows no significant difference in the performance of students in the exam with exposure versus non-exposure to the game (two sample t-test p-value $= 0.23$). The same insignificant result appears after conducting a Pearson's chi-squared test (p-value $= 0.99$). The average student mark is higher, especially among low-performing students compared to Experiment Set-up 1. In line with literature on gamification, the difference between low-performing and high-performing student groups is smaller. Although no conclusion on causality can be made, gamification in our data shows a higher percentage of students achieving the learning objectives of ISCM1 measured by them passing the course.

When it comes to validation of these results via survey, some students' feedback mentioned that they enjoyed playing the game, but they wanted to see tight and explicit integration of the game in the course content and assessment. Respondents indicated 59% level of agreement in understanding better the content of the course and 65% found the game useful for their learning. For the rest, they want to see how the game can help them pass the exam and enable them to benefit in the long-term.

5 Conclusions

This study found that student engagement in the ISCM1 course increased when students used the TFC game, as shown by higher exam participation and high satisfaction reported in surveys. While gamification had a positive effect on exam participation and passing rates, there was no significant difference in final marks when excluding students who did not participate in both exams. Additionally, gamification narrowed the gap between the median grades of low- and high-performing students. These results indicate that participation in the game appears to increase engagement and passing rates.

The limitation of this study is that the samples are based on voluntary participation of students. Most teachers are first time users of the game which may have impacted the outcome. Since it is only a pilot, there needs to be proper integration of the game with the didactics of the course. Other factors that may have influence the outcome of this study include the exam timing, students' motivation and goal, and other personal factors. Future research should explore these unaccounted factors in gamification and exam performance, and how gamification can be tightly integrated into the SCM course to enhance learning outcomes and exam performance.

References

1. Wang, Y.: A comparative study on the effectiveness of traditional and modern teaching methods. Presented at the (2022). https://doi.org/10.2991/978-2-494069-89-3_32
2. Dong, Y., Wu, S.X., Wang, W., Peng, S.: Is the student-centered learning style more effective than the teacher-student double-centered learning style in improving reading performance? Front. Psychol. **10** (2019). https://doi.org/10.3389/fpsyg.2019.02630
3. Tang, K.H.D.: Student-centered approach in teaching and learning: what does it really mean? Acta Pedagogia Asiana **2**, 72–83 (2023). https://doi.org/10.53623/apga.v2i2.218
4. Jonathan, L.Y., Laik, M.N.: Using experiential learning theory to improve teaching and learning in higher education. Eur. J. Educ. **7**, 18–33 (2024)
5. Serice, L.: Prisms of neuroscience: frameworks for thinking about educational gamification. AI Comput. Sci. Robot. Technol. **2** (2023). https://doi.org/10.5772/acrt.13
6. Aguiar-Castillo, L., Clavijo-Rodriguez, A., Hernández-López, L., De Saa-Pérez, P., Pérez-Jiménez, R.: Gamification and deep learning approaches in higher education. J. Hosp. Leis. Sport Tour. Educ. **29**, 100290 (2021). https://doi.org/10.1016/j.jhlste.2020.100290
7. Anderson, A., Huttenlocher, D., Kleinberg, J., Leskovec, J.: Engaging with massive online courses. In: Proceedings of the 23rd International Conference on World Wide Web, New York, NY, USA, pp. 687–698. ACM (2014). https://doi.org/10.1145/2566486.2568042
8. Barata, G., Gama, S., Jorge, J., Gonçalves, D.: Improving participation and learning with gamification. In: Proceedings of the First International Conference on Gameful Design, Research, and Applications, New York, NY, USA, pp. 10–17. ACM (2013). https://doi.org/10.1145/2583008.2583010
9. Toda, A.M., Valle, P.H.D., Isotani, S.: The dark side of gamification: an overview of negative effects of gamification in education. Presented at the (2018). https://doi.org/10.1007/978-3-319-97934-2_9
10. Berkling, K., Thomas, C.: Gamification of a software engineering course and a detailed analysis of the factors that lead to it's failure. In: 2013 International Conference on Interactive Collaborative Learning (ICL), pp. 525–530. IEEE (2013). https://doi.org/10.1109/ICL.2013.6644642
11. Morrison, B.B., DiSalvo, B.: Khan academy gamifies computer science. In: Proceedings of the 45th ACM Technical Symposium on Computer Science Education, New York, NY, USA, pp. 39–44. ACM (2014). https://doi.org/10.1145/2538862.2538946
12. O'Donovan, S., Gain, J., Marais, P.: A case study in the gamification of a university-level games development course. In: Proceedings of the South African Institute for Computer Scientists and Information Technologists Conference, New York, NY, USA, pp. 242–251. ACM (2013). https://doi.org/10.1145/2513456.2513469

Clinical Avatar for Nerve Diagnosis and Instruction (CANDi): A Serious Game for Cranial Nerve Examination Training

Aye Chan Zay Hta[1]([envelope]) [iD], Simon Campion[1] [iD], Georg Meyer[1] [iD], Craig Rothwell[1] [iD], and Anthony Smith[2] [iD]

[1] Virtual Engineering Centre, University of Liverpool, Liverpool, UK
ayechan@liverpool.ac.uk
[2] School of Medicine, University of Liverpool, Liverpool, UK

Abstract. In medical education, it is often challenging to ensure that students encounter patients with specific clinical conditions during their placements. This study examines the use of a digital human patient simulator designed to replicate cranial nerve conditions, providing students with repeated and consistent opportunities to develop their skills in clinical identification and diagnosis for further management. The simulator enhances students' understanding of cranial nerve anatomy and enables them to perform virtual examinations to assess potential nerve damage. As a fully accessible tool, the digital patient allows for unlimited, self-paced practice within a supportive and non-judgemental learning environment, facilitating both formative learning and assessment.

Keywords: Virtual Patient · Clinical Avatar · Serious Games · Simulation · Medical Education · Clinical Examination · Cranial Nerves

1 Introduction

Medical education faces persistent challenges, including limited access to diverse patient cases, the need for safe practice environments, and consistent feedback. Serious Games (SGs) offer a promising solution, providing interactive platforms that enhance cognitive and practical skills in medical training [1–3]. This paper introduces CANDi, a serious game designed to teach cranial nerve examinations. By simulating patient interactions in a controlled digital environment, CANDi enables repeated, structured practice that fosters understanding, diagnostic accuracy, and learner confidence. We present its design, key functionalities, and pedagogical alignment, highlighting its potential contribution to digitally enhanced medical education.

2 Background: Serious Games in Medical Education

Serious Games are designed to achieve educational objectives beyond entertainment, delivering experiential learning opportunities and safe environments for practice [4]. In medical education, they help overcome challenges such as limited patient diversity

S. Bakkes et al. (Eds.): GALA 2025, LNCS 16307, pp. 426–431, 2026.
https://doi.org/10.1007/978-3-032-11043-5_45

during placements [5, 6], and virtual patient simulations are linked to improved learning outcomes when combined with traditional methods [5, 7–9]. A notable example is NERVE [10], which provides standardized cranial nerve examination practice. While effective, it offers limited customisation focusing on standardised experiences. In contrast, CANDi emphasizes fully configurable patients, significantly higher graphic fidelity through Unreal Engine's Metahumans, and dynamic loading of examination tools tailored to each cranial nerve. Other health-related serious games, such as the Orthoptics VR Tool [11], demonstrate the potential of immersive VR for training. However, VR often faces accessibility barriers, making screen-based designs more suitable for flexible, self-paced learning [12]. By adopting a screen-based approach, CANDi balances fidelity, accessibility, and repeatability to support medical education.

3 Pedagogical Alignment and Expected Learning Outcomes

CANDi was developed in collaboration with clinical academics and refined through iterative prototyping to ensure alignment with existing study guides and clinical skills modules. Its design integrates proven strategies in game-based learning, with features tailored to the needs of medical education.

- **Experiential learning:** CANDi places students in a virtual examination room with configurable patients, where they can practice all twelve cranial nerve tests step by step. This "learning by doing" provides hands-on exposure that is often limited in clinical placements.
- **Active engagement and motivation:** Interactive checklists, dynamic toolboxes, and real-time feedback transform examinations into active tasks rather than passive observation, keeping learners engaged.
- **Adaptable and personalized learning:** Lecturers can customize patient cases and examination complexity, enabling tailored scenarios that match learners' progression and provide opportunities for remediation or advanced practice.
- **Structured practice and skill development:** Guided checklists reinforce proper sequencing of clinical protocols, while repetition across multiple patient profiles strengthens diagnostic accuracy.
- **Feedback and reflection:** Immediate verbal and visual cues highlight errors (e.g., failing to ask a patient to close their eyes during olfactory testing), encouraging self-correction and reflective practice.

The learning objectives are to (1) enhance recognition of cranial nerve dysfunction, (2) develop systematic examination techniques, and (3) build diagnostic confidence prior to patient contact.

4 System Overview

This section will outline CANDi's architecture and design, specifying its main functionalities and technical elements.

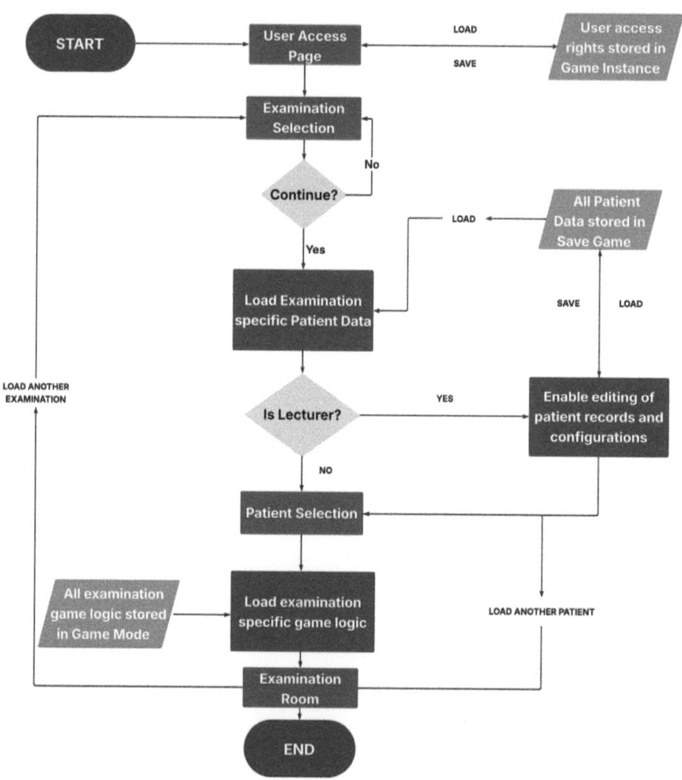

Fig. 1. Systems flowchart. Labels: Game Levels (Pink), Game Data/Logic (Green), Validation checks (Yellow), Processes (Blue)

4.1 System Design

As shown in Fig. 1. CANDi's architecture was designed to provide a structured yet flexible learning experience. Users select their role (student or lecturer), the cranial nerve to examine, and a virtual patient from a diverse set of profiles. Lecturers are granted additional privileges, such as editing patient records and configuring nerve-specific settings, allowing customized pathways and assessments. Following role selection, the application transitions to the examination selection level, which presents relevant information for each cranial nerve highlighted by the cranial nerve view of the brain anatomy, allowing users to select the specific nerve they wish to examine. This design supports a focused learning approach, enabling users to concentrate on particular areas of knowledge or skill development. Once a patient is selected, the application transitions into a 3D examination room where the virtual patient sits opposite the user, simulating a clinical setup. A dynamic toolbox on the right provides only the relevant instruments for the chosen examination, while a checklist of tasks and patient prompts is displayed on the left. To support learners, contextual hints can be toggled on or off, and certain examinations trigger verbal cues when steps are missed (e.g., reminding the user to ask a patient to close their eyes before an olfactory test). These features ensure a systematic approach to practice while offering immediate feedback, promoting reflection and reinforcing correct methodology. By combining structured scenarios with flexible lecturer configurations, CANDi supports both individualized learning and scalable instruction (Fig. 2).

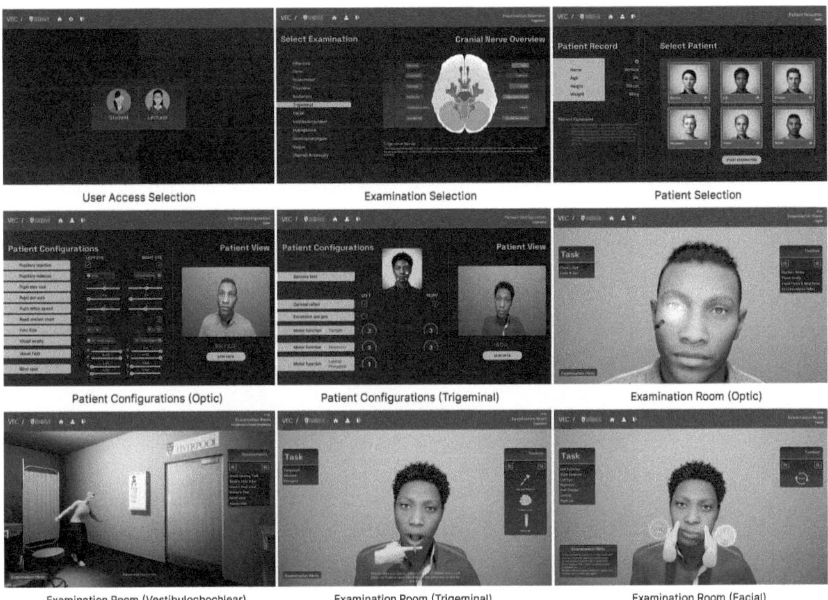

User Access Selection	Examination Selection	Patient Selection
Patient Configurations (Optic)	Patient Configurations (Trigeminal)	Examination Room (Optic)
Examination Room (Vestibulochochlear)	Examination Room (Trigeminal)	Examination Room (Facial)

Fig. 2. Screenshot of different pages in the application with removed logos

4.2 Game Mechanics and Visualisation

The core concept of CANDi lies in fully configurable virtual patients, enabling lecturers to design tailored learning scenarios without external tools. To prevent cognitive overload, configuration options are displayed contextually depending on the nerve and examination mode. While virtual reality offers natural depth perception and immersion, 2D interfaces can feel less intuitive. This perspective facilitates direct interaction through familiar actions like dragging tools onto the patient to conduct examinations.

The first-person interface places students directly in the examiner's role. This perspective facilitates direct interaction through familiar actions like dragging tools onto the patient for interaction. For tasks requiring tactile input, such as trigeminal and facial nerve muscle strength assessment, substitute cues are provided through directional colour-coded arrows, particle effects, and audio signals to represent resistance levels. This method of adding substitute sensory cues was found to be particularly effective in a previous study conducted by Cooper et al. [13].

4.3 Accessibility and Pixel Streaming

A key advantage of screen-based simulations over immersive VR solutions lies in their broader accessibility, particularly for students with limited hardware capabilities. Furthermore, CANDi includes adjustable graphics settings for use on lower-end machines and supports pixel streaming from high-performance servers as shown in Fig. 3. This allows learners to run the simulation directly in a web browser on laptops, tablets, or smartphones, without requiring installations or specialized hardware. The system can also be integrated into platforms such as Moodle or Canvas, lowering technical barriers and expanding availability. In addition to hardware accessibility, there were some considerations for inclusive design such as subtitles, support for both mouse and touch screen inputs. Additionally, to reduce cognitive load, the interface offers a list of tasks, optional hints, and tooltips to guide the user.

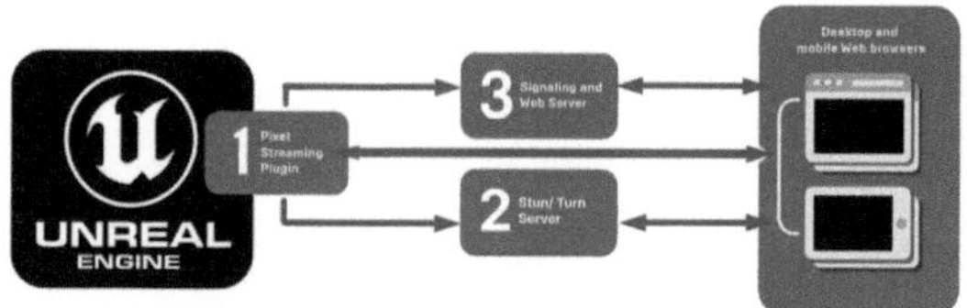

Fig. 3. Pixel streaming architecture [14]

5 Conclusion and Future Works

CANDi is a screen-based serious game that supports cranial nerve examination training through repeated, self-paced practice with configurable virtual patients. It fosters experiential learning, active engagement, and confidence in a safe digital environment.

Future work will focus on (1) integrating AI-driven virtual patients to enable dynamic communication and history-taking while supporting development of soft skills such as empathy and clinical reasoning, (2) conducting user studies with medical students and lecturers to evaluate usability, engagement, and learning outcomes, and (3) exploring evolving patient conditions across multiple sessions to simulate continuity of care.

References

1. Ricciardi, F., De Paolis, L.T.: A Comprehensive review of serious games in health professions. Int. J. Comput. Games Technol. **2014**(1), 787968 (2014). https://doi.org/10.1155/2014/787968
2. Laamarti, F., Eid, M., El Saddik, A.: An overview of serious games. Int. J. Comput. Games Technol. **2014**(1), 358152 (2014). https://doi.org/10.1155/2014/358152
3. Hammady, R., Arnab, S.: Serious gaming for behaviour change: a systematic review. Information **13**(3), 142 (2022). https://www.mdpi.com/2078-2489/13/3/142
4. Gouveia, D., Lopes, D., Carvalho, C.V.d.: Serious gaming for experiential learning. In: 2011 Frontiers in Education Conference (FIE), 12–15 October 2011, pp. T2G–1–T2G–6 (2011). https://doi.org/10.1109/FIE.2011.6142778

5. Cook, D.A., Triola, M.M.: Virtual patients: a critical literature review and proposed next steps. Med. Educ. **43**(4), 303–311 (2009). https://doi.org/10.1111/j.1365-2923.2008.03286.x

6. Okuda, Y., et al.: The utility of simulation in medical education: what is the evidence? Mount Sinai J. Med. J. Transl. Pers. Med. **76**(4), 330–343 (2009). https://doi.org/10.1002/msj.20127

7. Haoran, G., Bazakidi, E., Zary, N.: Serious games in health professions education: review of trends and learning efficacy. Yearb Med. Inform. **28**(01), 240–248 (2019). (in En.). https://doi.org/10.1055/s-0039-1677904

8. Berman, N.B., Durning, S.J., Fischer, M.R., Huwendiek, S., Triola, M.M.: The role for virtual patients in the future of medical education. Acad. Med. **91**(9), 1217–1222 (2016). https://doi.org/10.1097/acm.0000000000001146

9. Cook, D.A., Erwin, P.J., Triola, M.M.: Computerized virtual patients in health professions education: a systematic review and meta-analysis. Acad. Med. **85**(10), 1589–1602 (2010). https://doi.org/10.1097/ACM.0b013e3181edfe13

10. Hirumi, A.., et al.: Advancing virtual patient simulations through design research and inter-PLAY: Part I: design and development. Educ. Technol. Res. Dev. **64**(4), 763–785 (2016). https://doi.org/10.1007/s11423-016-9429-6

11. Meyer, G., Mehta, J., Newsham, D., Ward, R., Campion, S.: Evaluation of a high-fidelity orthoptic learning simulation using unreal MetaHumans. In: EuroXR 2023, Rotterdam, Netherlands (2023)

12. Dong, C., Shin, C., McDonagh, J., Champ-Gibson, E.: Immersive virtual reality simulation versus screen-based virtual simulation: an examination of learning outcomes in nursing education. Clin. Simul. Nurs. **102**, 101710 (2025). https://doi.org/10.1016/j.ecns.2025.101710

13. Cooper, N., Milella, F., Pinto, C., Cant, I., White, M., Meyer, G.: The effects of substitute multisensory feedback on task performance and the sense of presence in a virtual reality environment. PLoS ONE **13**(2), e0191846 (2018). https://doi.org/10.1371/journal.pone.0191846

14. E. G. D. Documentation: Hosting and Networking Guide for Pixel Streaming in Unreal Engine. https://dev.epicgames.com/documentation/en-us/unreal-engine/hosting-and-networking-guide-for-pixel-streaming-in-unreal-engine. Accessed 21 July 2025

How Puzzles and Emojis Impact Engagement in Gamified Text Annotation

Fatima Althani[(✉)] , Chris Madge , and Massimo Poesio

Queen Mary University of London, London, UK
{f.althani,c.j.madge,m.poesio}@qmul.ac.uk

Abstract. Games With A Purpose (GWAPs) for linguistic annotation often struggle to sustain engagement. We investigate whether puzzles and emojis enhance engagement in a word-sense disambiguation (WSD) task. Participants completed three within-subject conditions: (1) puzzles with emojis, (2) puzzles, and (3) annotation alone. Novices found visual cues motivating; experts preferred streamlined tasks. A reflexive thematic analysis revealed distinct preferences regarding puzzle complexity, visual aids, and perceived cognitive load.

Keywords: GWAPs · Player Engagement · Cognitive Load · Visual Cues

1 Introduction

Games With A Purpose (GWAPs) were originally designed to harness human effort to solve computational problems through play [1]. They have since been applied to linguistic data collection [8], offering advantages over crowdsourcing [15]. However, text-labelling GWAPs have struggled to match the success of visual GWAPs (e.g., the ESP Game [2], Foldit [4]). Engagement remains a challenge, as text annotation tasks are often more cognitively demanding and less intrinsically entertaining. This work investigates a gamified annotation interface designed to support Word Sense Disambiguation (WSD)-the task of identifying a word's intended meaning in context, which has been described as one of the hardest tasks to gamify [6].

Puzzles promote problem-solving and engagement through interactive challenge. To evaluate their role in WSD tasks, we integrated puzzles and emoji cues into a simplified annotation interface. While GWAPs are typically full-fledged games, our approach deliberately simplifies the game layer. Rather than building a complete game, we designed a streamlined annotation task with puzzles as a gamified mechanic and emojis as supportive visual cues. This allowed us to isolate their effects on engagement.

This study addresses the research question: *How do puzzles and emojis within a word sense annotation GWAP influence player engagement?* We developed three versions of a gamified WSD task: (1) with puzzles and emoji support, (2)

S. Bakkes et al. (Eds.): GALA 2025, LNCS 16307, pp. 432–438, 2026.
https://doi.org/10.1007/978-3-032-11043-5_46

with puzzles, and (3) with the annotation task alone. Using a within-subject design, we explore how these elements influence engagement, particularly across novice and expert users. Engagement was assessed via semi-structured interviews and analyzed using reflexive thematic analysis; which was informed by Dual Coding Theory [14], Cognitive Load Theory [19], and Self-Determination Theory [5].

2   Related Work

While many games exist for NLP annotation, we focus here on those targeting our chosen task: **GWAPs for Word Sense Disambiguation (WSD)**. *Jinx* [18] is a two-player WSD game where players volunteer substitutions and are scored based on agreement. In *Puzzle Racer* [6], word senses are linked to images, though this is used for labeling rather than as a motivational mechanic. *Wordrobe* bears some resemblance to our approach, as it uses a multi-choice selection interface [21] similar to our annotation phase. These games demonstrate the potential for embedding annotation tasks into playful interfaces.

Puzzles. have a longstanding role in educational games, offering intrinsic rewards through problem-solving and fostering engagement. In *Wormingo* [7], gameplay alternated between motivational puzzles and annotation tasks, mitigating fatigue and cognitive burden. Our work builds on the motivation–annotation paradigm by examining whether adding visual aids, such as emojis, can further sustain engagement and reduce cognitive burden. **Emojis** are widely recognized as effective visual representations for conveying emotions and clarifying textual meaning, reducing ambiguity and enhancing comprehension [13].

Theoretical Frameworks. Our study is informed by three key theories: *Dual Coding Theory (DCT)*, *Cognitive Load Theory (CLT)*, and *Self-Determination Theory (SDT)*. DCT suggests that information is processed through verbal and visual channels, and combining them can improve comprehension and retention by forming richer mental models [14]. This supports our use of emojis as contextually relevant visual cues in annotation puzzles. CLT posits that learning is shaped by the mental effort required to process information, distinguishing between intrinsic, extraneous, and germane load [20]. The goal is to maximize germane load while minimizing extraneous load, as excessive difficulty can cause frustration and disengagement [16]. SDT explains intrinsic motivation in terms of autonomy, competence, and relatedness [5]. Many works have explored how gamification can leverage SDT [17], including *Foldit*, which integrated both CLT and SDT to improve motivation and task performance [12].

3   Materials

We developed the WSD task as a web application with an interface aimed to enhance engagement and support effective annotation through gamified elements, consisting of two primary phases for each word requiring annotation: a **hangman-style puzzle phase** followed by a **definition selection phase**.

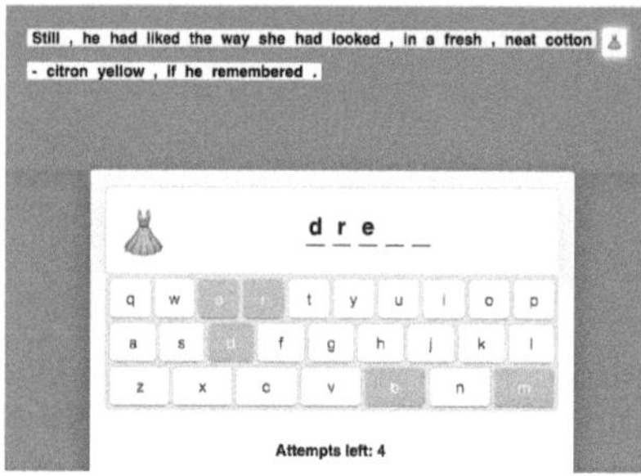

Fig. 1. The puzzle phase.

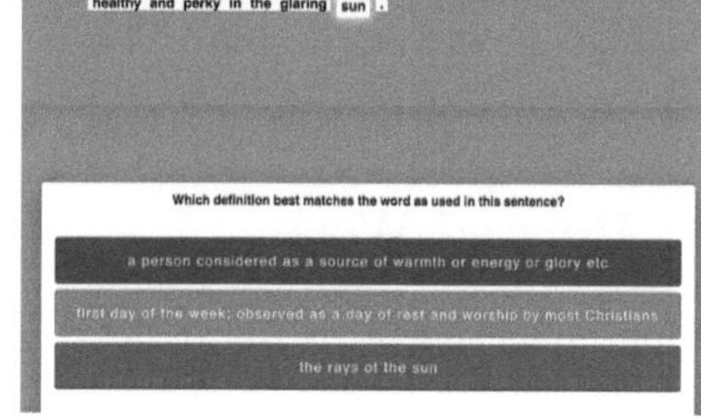

Fig. 2. The definition selection phase.

In the initial **hangman-style puzzle phase** (see Fig. 1), Players encounter a sentence with a missing word, which they have to guess by selecting letters. An emoji clue is displayed above the blank space, acting as a visual aid to support their guesses. Players have a limited number of attempts, introducing a light strategic challenge. Once a player identifies the correct word, they move on to the **definition selection phase** (see Fig. 2), where they select the appropriate meaning from a set of definitions. This core annotation task was deliberately kept clear and uncluttered, with minimal visual distraction. The goal here is to reduce extraneous cognitive load, aligning with CLT. By separating the puzzle and annotation steps, we aim to support mental focus and avoid overwhelming working memory. Definitions were sourced from SemCor [11] (for the correct sense) and WordNet (for distractors) [10], This phase required players to apply contextual understanding by reading the provided sentence and selecting the appropriate sense for the word.

4   Method

We employed a within-subjects study design where participants experienced the gamified WSD task conditions in a randomized order: (1) with puzzles and emoji support, (2) with puzzles, and (3) with the annotation task alone.

Participants. We recruited 9 participants (4 Female, 4 Male, 1 Non-binary, $M_{age} = 44$, $SD = 15.2$). Novice players were selected via a screener survey targeting individuals interested in linguistic and language-learning games. While expert players were participants who had previously ranked highly on the leaderboards of at least one of our GWAPs: Phrase Detectives [15], TileAttack [9], or Wormingo [7]. All participants received a £30 voucher. Ethics approval was granted by the Queen Mary University of London ethics board. Each session began with informed consent, demographics, and task instructions, followed by a semi-structured interview. Sessions were audio-recorded and anonymized.

Analysis. We analyzed 531.46 min of gameplay transcripts to address our research question. We followed Braun and Clarke's reflexive thematic analysis [3]. The first author, experienced in both qualitative analysis and game design, led the process. Initial codes were broad and theory-informed (e.g., engagement, emoji use, interface), with sub-codes refined through iterative review, allowing both deductive and inductive insights. Inter-rater reliability was not calculated, in line with the method's reflexive approach. Reflexivity was maintained through memos and positionality awareness, as the analyst was also the designer.

5   Results

Our thematic analysis revealed that participants navigated a balance between playful engagement and efficient annotation. While novice players (P1–P6, hereafter NPs) often leaned on playful features like visual aids and puzzle-based variety to sustain motivation, expert players (P7–P9, hereafter EPs) generally preferred a cleaner, annotation-focused approach.

Theme 1: Puzzles as Playful Breaks. For NPs, puzzle elements were often described as a motivating break from repetitive annotation (P1, P4) and were sometimes tackled first, suggesting they actively prioritized playful engagement. Several remarked that although puzzles could be harder than annotation, they were more fun and satisfying to complete. Some suggested combining puzzles with emojis to create a more seamless experience (P4). However, both NPs and EPs sometimes shifted to efficiency-oriented strategies when puzzles felt overly complex (P7, P9), increasing *extraneous load* and occasionally disrupting *flow*. EPs often questioned the need for puzzles, preferring annotation-only for efficiency, though a few noted that puzzle variety could help reduce monotony during longer sessions.

Theme 2: Role of Emojis as Visual Cues. Many NPs described emojis as visual cues (P2, P5), consistent with DCT, by providing a parallel verbal-visual channel. Some found mismatches playful and "game-like" (P1, P4, P6), boosting confidence and making guessing more engaging. EPs frequently saw emojis as superfluous or "too easy" (P7, P9), with mismatches creating extraneous load (P8) and, in some cases, visual clutter that disrupted focus. One EP (P5) raised cultural clarity concerns, noting that unfamiliar icons (e.g., the sake emoji) could confuse players. Both groups agreed that emoji helpfulness varied with task complexity and word ambiguity, underscoring the need for careful emoji selection.

Theme 3: Cognitive Overload in Word Guessing. Across both groups, short words and specialized text often exacerbated intrinsic load [19]. NPs frequently requested hint or skip features (P1, P4), consistent with CLT's emphasis on scaffolding and worked examples. Some NPs still enjoyed puzzle complexity, citing a sense of accomplishment when solving difficult words (P3, P6). EPs (P7, P9) advocated removing puzzle elements entirely. Task-switching between guessing and annotation was also cited as load-inducing (P4, P7), with several participants resorting to trial-and-error strategies or pattern guessing to cope.

Theme 4: Game vs. Test Experience. NPs often viewed puzzle/emoji conditions as "game-like" and enjoyable, breaking up monotony, whereas annotation-only felt more "test-like." Some appreciated points or celebratory pop-ups as extrinsic motivators (P1, P2), though puzzles themselves were often described as more rewarding (P6). EPs appreciated annotation-only clarity, sometimes labeling puzzles "unnecessary add-ons," but noted that variety could help reduce fatigue over long sessions. EPs typically dismissed point systems (P9), caring more about correctness than rewards.

Theme 5: Balancing Player Control, Feedback, and Task Flow. Participants valued streamlined workflows, clear instructions, and immediate feedback on correctness. NPs leaned on hints and skips to stay motivated, which acted as scaffolding to reduce intrinsic load. EPs sought efficient navigation and layout, often recommending that puzzle steps be optional or removed when unnecessary. Across groups, autonomy emerged as a critical factor, aligning with SDT's emphasis on player choice and self-directed engagement [5], suggesting that adaptive complexity—allowing players to adjust hints, skips, or puzzle difficulty— could further enhance engagement.

Accuracy. Annotation accuracy was comparable across conditions (with puzzles and emoji support: 76%, with puzzles: 76%, annotation task alone: 81%). A Shapiro–Wilk test showed two conditions were non-normal ($p < .05$), so we ran a Kruskal–Wallis test, which was non-significant ($H = 1.08$, $p = .58$), indicating no difference in accuracy scores.

6   Discussion and Conclusion

Our findings suggest that puzzles and emojis can either motivate or strain players depending on expertise and task demands, without affecting annotation accuracy. Visual aids supported NPs' guessing but distracted EPs, who preferred text-only for clarity. These results indicate that gamification elements should remain optional, allowing players to engage when beneficial and bypass when distracting to minimize extraneous load. Prioritizing usability and autonomy— through clear instructions, immediate feedback, and optional hints/skips— can help players tailor task flow to their preferences. This study is limited by its small, niche sample ($n{=}9$) and single-session engagement, so findings should be interpreted as exploratory rather than generalizable. Future work should involve larger, more diverse samples, explore between-subjects designs, and assess longitudinal effects to refine puzzle-based annotation strategies for education and crowdsourcing. It should also examine cross-cultural interpretations of emojis, as cultural familiarity and iconography may shape their effectiveness as visual aids.

References

1. von Ahn, L.: Games with a purpose. Computer **39**(6), 92–94 (2006)
2. von Ahn, L., Dabbish, L.: Labeling images with a computer game. In: Proceedings of the SIGCHI Conference on Human Factors in Computing Systems, pp. 319–326 (2004)
3. Braun, V., Clarke, V.: One size fits all? what counts as quality practice in (reflexive) thematic analysis? Qual. Res. Psychol. **18**(3), 328–352 (2021)
4. Cooper, S., et al.: Predicting protein structures with a multiplayer online game. Nature **466**(7307), 756–760 (2010)
5. Deci, E.L., Ryan, R.M.: Intrinsic motivation and self-determination in human behavior. Springer (1985)
6. Jurgens, D., Navigli, R.: It's all fun and games until someone annotates: video games with a purpose for linguistic annotation. Trans. Assoc. Comput. Linguistics **2**, 449–464 (2014)
7. Kicikoglu, D., Bartle, R., Chamberlain, J., Poesio, M.: Wormingo: a'true gamification'approach to anaphoric annotation. In: Proceedings of the 14th International Conference on the Foundations of Digital Games, pp. 1–7 (2019)
8. Lafourcade, M., Joubert, A., Le Brun, N.: Games with a purpose (GWAPS). John Wiley and Sons (2015)
9. Madge, C., Chamberlain, J., Kruschwitz, U., Poesio, M.: Experiment-driven development of a gwap for marking segments in text. In: Extended Abstracts Publication of the Annual Symposium on Computer-Human Interaction in Play, pp. 397–404 (2017)
10. Miller, G.A.: Wordnet: a lexical database for english. Commun. ACM **38**(11), 39–41 (1995)
11. Miller, G.A., Leacock, C., Tengi, R., Bunker, R.T.: A semantic concordance. In: Human Language Technology: Proceedings of a Workshop Held at Plainsboro, New Jersey, March 21-24, 1993 (1993). https://aclanthology.org/H93-1061/
12. Miller, J.A., Narayan, U., Hantsbarger, M., Cooper, S., El-Nasr, M.S.: Expertise and engagement: re-designing citizen science games with players' minds in mind. In: Proceedings of the 14th International Conference on the Foundations of Digital Games. FDG '19, Association for Computing Machinery, New York, NY, USA (2019). https://doi.org/10.1145/3337722.3337735
13. Novak, P.K., Smailović, J., Sluban, B., Mozetič, I.: Sentiment of emojis. PloS one **10**(12), e0144296 (2015)
14. Paivio, A.: Mental representations: a dual coding approach. Oxford University Press (1986)
15. Poesio, M., Chamberlain, J., Kruschwitz, U.: Phrase detectives: utilizing collective intelligence for linguistic annotation. ACM Trans. Int. Intell. Syst. **3**(1), 3 (2013)
16. Schoenau-Fog, H.: The player engagement process–an exploration of continuation desire in digital games. In: Proceedings of DiGRA 2011 Conference: Think Design Play (2011)
17. Seaborn, K., Fels, D.I.: Gamification in theory and action: a survey. Int. J. Hum Comput Stud. **74**, 14–31 (2015)
18. Seemakurty, N., Chu, J., Von Ahn, L., Tomasic, A.: Word sense disambiguation via human computation. In: Proceedings of the acm sigkdd workshop on human computation, pp. 60–63 (2010)
19. Sweller, J.: Cognitive load during problem solving: Effects on learning. Cogn. Sci. **12**(2), 257–285 (1988)

20. Sweller, J.: Element interactivity and intrinsic, extraneous, and germane cognitive load. Educ. Psychol. Rev. **22**(2), 123–138 (2010)
21. Venhuizen, N.J., Basile, V., Evang, K., Bos, J.: Gamification for word sense labeling. In: Koller, A., Erk, K. (eds.) Proceedings of the 10th International Conference on Computational Semantics (IWCS), pp. 397–403. Association for Computational Linguistics, Potsdam, Germany (2013). https://aclanthology.org/W13-0215/

User Experience of Simulated Reality in Museums

Iulia Adina Zaha[1]([✉])(iD) and Hanna Hauptmann[2](iD)

[1] Dimenco B.V. and Utrecht University, Utrecht, The Netherlands
iulia.adina.zaha@gmail.com
[2] Utrecht University, Utrecht, The Netherlands
h.j.hauptmann@uu.nl

Abstract. In today's fast-paced world, museums must evolve to meet the growing demand for immersive and interactive visitor experiences. This study explores how touchscreen kiosks and Simulated Reality (SR) technology support user experience in museums. Through a user study with 104 visitors we identify the strengths and limitations of both technologies. Our findings show, for example, that touchscreens offer more control whereas SR offers more enjoyment. Adopting adequate technologies can make museum experiences more engaging.

Keywords: Simulated Reality · Touchscreen Kiosk · User Experience

1 Introduction

Traditional museum formats struggle to attract attention with as passive viewing of untouchable artifacts. Museum visitors increasingly seek engaging, multimodal experiences [11]. Previous efforts to evolve technologically include the integration of Augmented Reality (AR) and Virtual Reality (VR). However, these approaches fall short in conveying the full value of real artifacts and may disrupt the contemplative atmosphere associated with museums [11]. Touchscreen kiosks offer contextual information, yet pose hygiene concerns and may hinder engagement due to their static interaction mode. Similarly, video content often fails to sustain visitor attention due to its length.

To address these challenges, this paper investigates an alternative approach: using Simulated Reality devices - autostereoscopic (glasses-free 3D) monitors with eye- and hand-tracking integration. These devices allow for interactive, immersive experiences without requiring physical contact or wearable devices, offering a more intuitive and hygienic alternative. The study compares user experience and engagement between touchscreen kiosks and autostereoscopic displays via a cross-platform serious game, focusing not on artifact reproduction but on presenting contextual and procedural content. Our key metrics include sense of presence, agency, engagement, and participants' opinions.

The full materials and results of this study are available at in the master's thesis of the first author at https://studenttheses.uu.nl/handle/20.500.12932/44581.

S. Bakkes et al. (Eds.): GALA 2025, LNCS 16307, pp. 439–445, 2026.
https://doi.org/10.1007/978-3-032-11043-5_47

2 Related Work

The perception of museum visits has evolved over the centuries. In the twenty-first century, there is a renewed focus on sensory experience, with museums increasingly integrating didactic, multimodal approaches and encouraging emotional involvement [1]. **Touchscreen kiosks** are among the most commonly used interaction tools in modern museums. As Burmistrov notes [2], their use aims to boost visitor engagement and attendance. However, touchscreen kiosks also come with limitations, such as issues related to accessibility, physical reach, visibility, interface design, and feedback [2].

Virtual Reality (VR). is increasingly adopted in museums to align with technological trends and appeal to younger audiences [9]. While VR can attract visitors and enhance learning through custom experiences, Shehade and Stylianou-Lambert [11] identify that it can also cause distractions, reduce social interaction, increase costs (for high-quality graphics), disrupt exhibit flow, and require additional staff and training. Accessibility issues, particularly for younger children and disabled visitors, also limit its universal application.

Simulated Reality (SR). refers to a convincingly interactive form of "reality" experienced without the need for headsets or controllers [3]. When paired with gesture-based controls, such as Ultraleap hand tracking, autostereoscopic displays provide an intuitive and immersive interaction without the need for headgear or external controllers. Developed by Dimenco, SR relies on autostereoscopic 3D monitors with eye and hand tracking [3]. This technology produces unique parallel images using motion parallax, allowing users to interact with 3D content directly on-screen in a more comfortable, glasses-free manner.

SR may offer similar benefits to VR, without many of its limitations. In this study, we compare SR devices to touchscreen kiosks. We chose touchscreen kiosks as a baseline due to their popularity in museum contexts.

3 Game Design

This study follows the Serious Games Design and Development (SGDD) cycle [5]. First, an open-question survey was conducted with a 3D model expert to understand what makes a 3D game application engaging in museum environments. First, the visualization of objects that can't be displayed due to scale, sensitivity, or damage is essential. Second, maintaining an object's reality and style enhances credibility and user experience. Finally, an adapted story and object presentation should reflect the museum's goals and its audience.

The outcome of the design and prototyping cycles is a cross-platform serious game. Its objective is to collect and assemble three spacecraft parts to complete a space mission while studying and learning about the objects in the levels. In Level 1, players assemble a pulsar by connecting three pieces using their fist to drag and two hands to zoom or rotate the final model. Visual and audio feedback is given after each successful connection. In Level 2, players rotate Saturn with a flat hand and "smash" it with a fist to reveal its interior, which can also be explored through rotation. In Level 3, players assemble the spacecraft using the same gestures as in Level 1; each part is unlocked after completing a level. Upon final assembly, the spacecraft launches with confetti and applause. Transitions between levels are marked by a countdown when the system loses hand tracking.

A pilot study has been run to review the audiovisual appeal of the application, the controls, and the content. Feedback revealed that certain hand gestures were not intuitive or failed due to tracking issues. Participants also noted that overly bright level designs caused visual issues like cross-talk. Further suggestions included extending the level-transition countdown and slowing down the animated tutorials. These changes aimed to reduce cognitive overload and improve clarity. The feedback and the observations have been translated into game improvements. All improvements have also been implemented for the touchscreen, to maintain an identical application for the comparison.

4   User Study

An A/B evaluation was conducted at the Beeld & Geluid Media Museum in Hilversum, on the "Wonder" floor. A total of 104 participants participated in a between-subject experiment (54 male, 49 female, 1 anonymous).

4.1   Experiment Setup

Participants were split to use one of the two devices (44 touchscreen, 60 SR) for 5 min, followed by a questionnaire covering background information as well as CAMIL [7] and miniPXI [6] constructs.

The Cognitive Affective Model of Immersive Learning (CAMIL) is a theory-based model of learning in Immersive Virtual Reality (IVR) that synthesizes existing research to explain the learning process in IVR [7]. CAMIL emphasizes presence and agency as key psychological affordances of IVR learning [7]. These are influenced by immersion, sense of control, and representational fidelity. We use the CAMIL questions on the constructs of *Sense of Presence* and *Agency*.

The miniPXI is an 11-item abbreviated version of the original PXI using one item per construct [6]. Since this study was conducted in a time-limited field setting, the miniPXI was deemed suitable despite the lower validity than the original PXI [6]. The miniPXI covers the following constructs: *Audiovisual Appeal, Challenge, Ease of Control, Clarity of Goals, Progress Feedback, Enjoyment, Autonomy, Curiosity, Immersion, Mastery*, and *Meaning*.

4.2   Quantitative Results

Since the current experiment is a comparative study based on an AB testing approach with questionnaires that are measured on a Likert scale, Mann-Whitney U tests were performed for both device conditions (Touchscreen application, SR monitor) for the miniPXI constructs. Since CAMIL question constructs (sense of presence, agency) are designed for numerical scales, we performed independent T-tests. Below we describe the significant differences between the two systems.

Audio-visual appeal. Judging by the Mean Rank (MR), the SR application received overall higher ranks (p=0.026, MR=57,55, U=1623.000, Z=2.219) than the Touchscreen application in the audiovisual appeal construct. Although the application was identical for both devices in terms of audio and visuals, it was still expected that a novel technology would impact the audiovisual perception.

Enjoyment. The observed mean rank implies that the SR application received overall higher ranks (p=0.003, MR = 59,45, U = 1737.000, Z = 2.999) on the enjoyment construct than the touchscreen application, which means that participants enjoyed the SR application more than the touchscreen application.

Mastery. The Mean Rank suggests that the SR application received overall higher ranks (p=0.001, MR=60.18, U=1780.500, Z=3.420) than the Touchscreen application. This shows that SR participants had a stronger feeling of performing well, which might be one reason for enjoying the SR application more.

Sense of Presence. With regard to the sense of Presence construct, the SR application ranked significantly higher (p=0.042), showing that there is an increase in the sense of presence for individuals who played the SR game.

Immersion. Judging by the Mean Rank, the SR application received overall lower ranks (p=0.02, M=46.86, U=981.500, Z=-2.332) than the Touchscreen. This contrasts the sense of presence results and needs to be explored further.

Intuitive Controls. Judging by the Mean Rank, the SR application received overall lower ranks(p=0.009, MR=46.13, U=938.000, Z=-2.626) than the Touchscreen. This might be the case due to high familiarity with touch gestures among participants, while SR technology and hand gestures are less ubiquitous. This may also be one reason for the lower immersion in the SR application.

4.3   Qualitative Results of the User Study

To gain a qualitative perspective on visitors' reasoning, the questionnaire also included open questions. Regarding the use of SR technology most people were positive (43/55), some neutral (7/55), and only few negative (5/55). Regarding user experience, the most common topic among the SR participants were the 3D visual effect without the need for glasses and hand gesture interactions that controlled the game. On another note, 2 participants indicated tiring eyes after the performance, but they did not want to stop the experiment. For the touchscreen applications, the most common topics were the game effects (visual and audio). Visitors' generally reported positive attitudes for both technologies in museums. Participants who performed on the touchscreen application responded: *"Technology is very important in the current digital age"*, *"I enjoy it when it is easy to use, interactive, and adds value to the exhibit. No need to overuse."*, *"It is more than just delivery. Interaction, action, reaction - is nicer to discover things."*. SR application users responded: *"It's useful because it helps you understand things better", "Has a lot of potential to make the experience more interesting if applied in the right way", "Interaction makes the museum visit more enjoyable".*

5   Discussion

After conducting the experiment, we found that the SR application was significantly more enjoyable and audio-visually appealing than the touchscreen one. Participants also experienced a greater sense of mastery while using the SR application. This may be due to the novelty of the technology, which likely stimulated interest, motivation, and curiosity through bare-hand interaction and glasses-free 3D visuals. SR participants also reported a stronger sense of presence compared to those using the touchscreen, likely due to the 3D effect. According to the CAMIL framework [7], presence activates cognitive and emotional engagement, suggesting museum visitors may show increased interest and motivation. Prior research defines presence as awareness of being in a specific place or time [10], while immersion refers to how well the virtual world replaces the real one [4]. Since some participants described the SR DevKit as a "3D bubble," it appears to have triggered presence. However, it doesn't fully cover the visual field, which may explain why visitors familiar with VR didn't report high immersion.

Interviews with museum staff revealed that visitors appreciated the SR monitor's glasses-free 3D and natural gestures. Younger visitors seemed more eager to explore and learn through new technology, while older generations often preferred touchscreens. Participants differed across age groups in how natural the control felt to them. It was noted that the touchscreen should offer more text, while the SR monitor should focus on visualizing 3D objects for learning. Finally, the touchscreen was considered more intuitive due to the widespread familiarity with this technology. Younger users found the SR application's controls intuitive, but older users did not. One participant remarked, "You have to learn the movements," contrasting with the ease of touchscreen use. Overall, younger visitors may be more engaged and motivated throughout the experience.

Limitations: Conducted in a museum setting, the experiment was limited to five minutes, requiring the use of single-item PXI questions [6] and a 5-point Likert scale to reduce participant effort. These choices may affect the reliability of responses. The specific SR DevKit was prone to overheating, which may have negatively impacted the experience for some users. The difference in screen sizes between the 32" SR display and the 10.5" tablet may also have influenced perception and interaction. Finally, since the study was conducted in a Dutch museum with mostly Dutch-speaking visitors, the results may have cultural bias.

6   Practical Guidelines

While touchscreen kiosks are widely used in museums, Simulated Reality (SR) is a novel technology that can enhance visitor engagement, especially among younger audiences, by boosting enjoyment, engagement, and curiosity. The SR

DevKit offers a noticeable 3D effect and sense of depth, resulting in greater visual realism and presence compared to touchscreen tablets, which lack these features. This absence of depth contributed to a lower perceived sense of presence with the tablet. As supported by previous studies [8], autostereoscopic displays like the SR DevKit improve 3D visualization, object manipulation, and analysis. However, to avoid cognitive overload, SR content included less text. This can be both a benefit and a drawback, depending on the museum's design goals and audience. The touchscreen device included the same amount of text, but some participants expected more, suggesting different content expectations. In terms of interaction, touchscreen controls felt intuitive and offered users a strong sense of agency. SR controls were rated lower overall, but younger users found them natural, indicating that SR may appeal more to younger generations, while touchscreen kiosks remain accessible to a broader age range.

7   Conclusion and Future Work

This study introduces simulated reality (SR) monitors as an alternative to touchscreen kiosks. Emphasizing user-centered design, accessibility, and hygiene, SR monitors offer touch-free interaction and a stronger sense of presence. Results suggest SR monitors enhance the museum experience, particularly for younger visitors who reported higher levels of engagement and control. However, touchscreen kiosks generally offered higher perceived control and immersion to users. Future research should explore how to make SR monitor controls more accessible to broader audiences, particularly older generations. Investigating hand meshes that mimic real gestures may improve control familiarity and immersion.

References

1. Howes, D.: Introduction to sensory museology. The Senses and Society.https://doi. org/10.2752/174589314X14023847039917
2. Burmistrov, I.: Touchscreen kiosks in museums. Tallinn. interUX (2015)
3. B.V., D.: (2023). https://www.dimenco.eu/
4. Cummings, J.J., Bailenson, J.N.: How immersive is enough? a meta-analysis of the effect of immersive technology on user presence. Media psychology (2016)
5. Dörner, R., Göbel, S., Effelsberg, W.e.a.: Serious games. Springer (2016)
6. Haider, A., Harteveld, C., Johnson, D.a.: minipxi: development and validation of an eleven-item measure of the player experience inventory. In: Proceedings of the ACM on Human-Computer Interaction (2022)
7. Makransky, G., Petersen, G. B: CAMIL: a theoretical research-based model of learning in immersive virtual reality. Educational Psychology Review (2021)
8. Melmoth, D.R., Grant, S.: Advantages of binocular vision for the control of reaching and grasping. Exp. Brain Res. **171**, 371–388 (2006)
9. Mohd Noor Shah, N.F., Ghazali, M.: A systematic review on digital technology for enhancing user experience in museums. In: User Science and Engineering: 5th International Conference, i-USER 2018, Puchong, Malaysia, August 28–30, 2018, Proceedings 5 (2018)

10. Riva, G., Davide, F., IJsselsteijn, W.: Being there : concepts, effects and measurements of user presence in synthetic environments. Emerging communication : studies in new technologies and practices in communication (2003)
11. Shehade, M., Stylianou-Lambert, T.: Virtual reality in museums: exploring the experiences of museum professionals. Appl. sci. (2020)

Elucidating Learning Gains of Educational Games by Comparing Statistical and Structural Analyses

Michael D. Kickmeier-Rust[(⊠)] [iD] and Katharina Richter [iD]

St.Gallen University of Teacher Education, St.Gallen, Switzerland
`michael.kickmeier@phsg.ch`

Abstract. This study examines the learning app Basketball Challenge, designed to teach ballistic trajectory concepts at the secondary school level. The app incorporates competencies such as force, angle, mass, and resistance. A comparison between a gamified and a standard version was conducted, assessing learning effects through pre- and post-tests. While statistical analyses did not yield conclusive results regarding learning performance, a significant gender difference in game performance measures was observed. To deepen the analysis, Knowledge Space Theory was applied, offering a structural competence-based approach to data analyses. This method identified a well-fitting model for knowledge tests and game levels. Additionally, a slight increase in participants' competencies from pre- to post-test was noted, though no distinct gender differences emerged in this aspect. These findings highlight the potential of gamification in educational applications while emphasizing the need for further exploration of gender-related learning effects.

Keywords: Gamification · Physics Education · Gender Differences · Performance · Competence · Knowledge Space Theory

1 Gamification in Education: Benefits, Challenges

Gamification—the integration of game elements into education—has gained traction as a tool to enhance motivation and engagement. Meta-analyses highlight positive effects on motivation, whereas findings on actual learning outcomes remain mixed and context-dependent [1–5, 15]. While extrinsic rewards such as points and badges can sustain engagement, they may also undermine intrinsic motivation [3, 7, 8], and competitive mechanics may disadvantage less proficient learners [2]. Ethical concerns also arise, including data privacy issues and psychological effects of ranking-based systems [9]. Despite these challenges, gamification can foster knowledge transfer when grounded in cognitive and instructional principles [10–14], whereas poorly aligned designs risk cognitive overload and disengagement.

In this study, we address two gaps. First, prior work suggests that males and females may respond differently to gamification in STEM contexts, yet systematic evidence

S. Bakkes et al. (Eds.): GALA 2025, LNCS 16307, pp. 446–451, 2026.
https://doi.org/10.1007/978-3-032-11043-5_48

remains scarce. Second, conventional pre/post tests capture learning only partially. We therefore complement standard statistics with Knowledge Space Theory (KST) and its competence-based extension (CbKST) to model structured learning states alongside observable performance.

2 The Basketball Challenge

The Basketball Challenge is an educational app designed for secondary school students, focusing on physics concepts related to ballistic trajectories. Players adjust angle and force (sliders) and launch balls of different materials into the hoop. The app is available in two versions: a standard version and a gamified version (accessible at *chimeo.ch/BasketballChallenge*). The content aligns with Switzerland's *Lehrplan 21* and addresses core competencies such as force, angle, mass, resistance, gravity, buoyancy, and magnetism. Difficulty increases gradually to sustain engagement and scaffold conceptual understanding. Before gameplay, users enter personal data and complete a pre-test; a post-test follows to measure knowledge gains. After an open-ended practice level, structured levels present specific objectives. Each level offers two hints, and players get three attempts per ball within five minutes. The gamified version adds visual upgrades, robot-guided instructions, a countdown timer, and scoring: higher points for first-attempt successes.

3 Method

Although the app is publicly available, data for this study were collected in classroom settings to ensure controlled conditions and compliance with pre- and post-testing. In total, 170 students from nine Swiss secondary school classes participated (71 male, 73 female, 26 unspecified; $M = 13.66$ years, $SD = 0.79$, range 11–16). Students were randomly assigned to either the gamified ($n = 89$) or the standard version ($n = 81$). The knowledge test comprised eight multiple-choice questions (four options each) aligned with the competencies targeted in the app (see Fig. 2). These items covered, for example, force, angle, mass, and resistance, corresponding to the design of the game levels.

The intervention was conducted within a single lesson. Students first entered demographic data and completed the pre-test, then played one practice level followed by the eight structured game levels (five-minute limit per level, up to three attempts per ball). After finishing the final level, they completed the post-test. Both conditions were presented as learning tasks, not as competitions, and the app itself does not promote competitive behavior.

4 Results

In the practice level, no significant differences emerged for any dependent variables. For the eight structured levels, a MANOVA revealed significant main effects of grade level on hits ($F(2,141) = 5.84$, $p < .001$, $\eta2 = .12$), points ($F(2,141) = 7.71$, $p < .001$, $\eta2 = .16$), and time ($F(2,141) = 6.87$, $p = .002$, $\eta2 = .10$). Post-hoc (Scheffé) tests showed that ninth graders outperformed seventh- and eighth-graders, who did not differ significantly from each other. No main effects of condition or gender were observed.

More importantly, a significant interaction of gender and condition was found. For attempts, no significant interaction occurred ($F(2,141) = 3.51$, $p = .063$, $\eta 2 = .03$). For hits, males performed better in the gamified (M = 14.06, SD = 3.44) than in the standard condition (M = 13.10, SD = 3.64), whereas females showed the opposite pattern (gamified: M = 12.23, SD = 2.67; standard: M = 13.56, SD = 3.84), $F(2,141) = 4.71$, $p = .032$, $\eta 2 = .04$. A similar trend appeared for points: males scored higher in the gamified (M = 1382.12, SD = 454.57) than in the standard version (M = 1222.41, SD = 408.94), while females scored higher in the standard (M = 1247.94, SD = 451.15) than in the gamified version (M = 1077.14, SD = 261.09), $F(2,141) = 6.74$, $p = .011$, $\eta 2 = .05$. For time, males spent more in the gamified (M = 1047.15, SD = 370.65) than in the standard condition (M = 1010.45, SD = 216.74), whereas females spent more in the standard (M = 1109.88, SD = 279.58) than in the gamified version (M = 1046.86, SD = 257.67), $F(2,141) = 4.09$, $p = .045$, $\eta 2 = .03$. No further significant interactions were found.

In the knowledge tests, no significant differences were found at pretest ($p = .796$). Scores averaged 4.91 (SD = 1.87) in the gamified and 4.46 (SD = 1.90) in the standard condition. No gender differences were observed ($p = .308$; males: M = 5.15, SD = 1.77; females: M = 4.73, SD = 1.95). At posttest, scores again did not differ by condition ($p = .599$; gamified: M = 4.54, SD = 2.08; standard: M = 4.38, SD = 1.73). Across all groups, mean performance decreased slightly from pre- to posttest (–0.45, SD = 1.85). Only 101 participants (59%) completed both tests, suggesting limited test motivation. Pre- and posttest scores correlated moderately ($r = .554$).

Combinatorial structural analyses provide insights into learning processes that conventional statistics often miss. Knowledge Space Theory (KST) [16–18], part of the Cognitive Diagnostic Models family, conceptualizes learning domains as structured sets of tasks with prerequisite relations. In this framework, a learner's *knowledge state* is the subset of tasks they can solve, constrained by the assumption that more complex tasks require mastery of simpler ones.

In the present study, the design of the *Basketball Challenge* implied such prerequisites among game levels. For example, mastering Level 3 presupposes the competencies required for Level 2 (Fig. 1). This surmise relation reflects the intended increase in difficulty across levels, where later levels build upon competencies acquired in earlier ones. From this relation we can derive the knowledge space, i.e., the set of all feasible performance patterns. In our case, the model yielded 11 admissible knowledge states, compared to a theoretical maximum of $2^8 = 256$ possible states. The reduced set illustrates how structural dependencies substantially limit the number of meaningful learning trajectories.

To evaluate the empirical adequacy of this structure, we applied the minimal symmetric set difference (MSSD) [19]. The dataset produced an average MSSD of 1.264 (SD = 0.932; range 0–4). Such deviations typically reflect occasional errors (failing a level despite having the necessary skills) or lucky guesses (succeeding by chance). To account for the size–fit trade-off [20], we compared the observed fit with chance expectation. With 11 of 256 possible states ($= 4.29\%$), a random model would predict only ~7.3 exact matches. Our model explained 40 zero-distance patterns (23.53%), $\chi 2(1, N = 170)$

$= 138.45$, $p < .001$. This provides strong evidence that the hypothesized competence structure is a good representation of actual performance data.

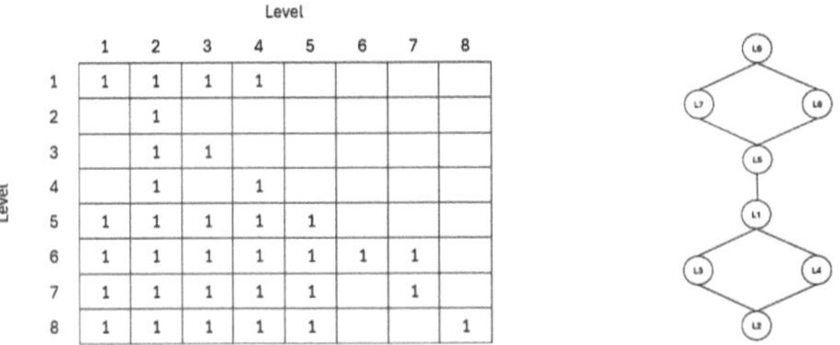

Level	1	2	3	4	5	6	7	8
1	1	1	1	1				
2		1						
3		1	1					
4		1		1				
5	1	1	1	1	1			
6	1	1	1	1	1	1	1	
7	1	1	1	1	1		1	
8	1	1	1	1	1			1

Fig. 1. *Left:* surmise relation (binary matrix). *Right:* Hasse diagram of prerequisite relations between game levels (bottom → top); e.g., mastering L3 implies L2.

From a diagnostic perspective, however, it is equally important to identify which competencies individual learners hold. We therefore applied Competence-based Knowledge Space Theory (CbKST) [17], which adds a latent layer of competencies to the observable performance data. Figure 5 illustrates the prerequisite relations among competencies (left) and their mapping to game levels and test items (right). This mapping does not require a one-to-one relation but reflects the didactic design of the app.

The analysis yielded 22 distinct competence states. Game levels alone translated into 8 states, the pre-test into 9, which together produced 13 unique states because several overlapped. This partial overlap is consistent with the observed weak correlations between game and test scores and highlights that both measures capture complementary aspects of competence. Compared to raw score comparisons, the CbKST analysis produced more consistent and interpretable results. The median difference in competence state cardinality (i.e., number of competencies per participant) between game and pre-test was 2 ($M = 3.32$, $SD = 2.61$). For pre- vs. post-test, the median difference dropped to 1 ($M = 2.44$, $SD = 2.70$), indicating closer agreement and a more stable representation of learner knowledge.

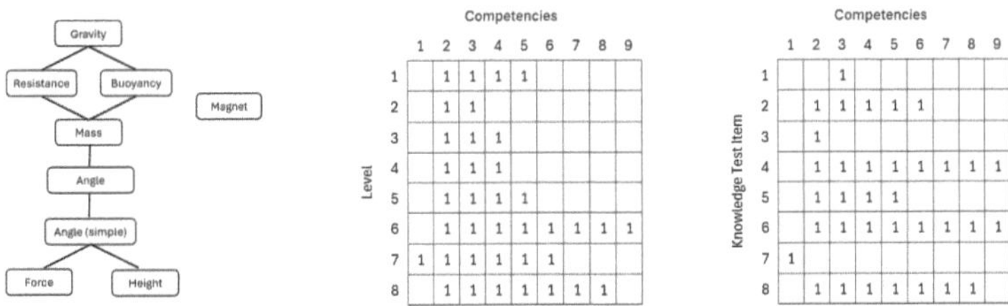

Left table (Level × Competencies):

Level	1	2	3	4	5	6	7	8	9
1		1	1	1	1				
2		1	1						
3		1	1	1					
4		1	1	1					
5		1	1	1	1				
6		1	1	1	1	1	1	1	1
7	1	1	1	1	1	1			
8		1	1	1	1	1	1		

Right table (Knowledge Test Item × Competencies):

Knowledge Test Item	1	2	3	4	5	6	7	8	9
1			1						
2		1	1	1	1	1			
3		1							
4		1	1	1	1	1	1	1	1
5		1	1	1	1				
6		1	1	1	1	1	1	1	1
7	1								
8		1	1	1	1	1	1	1	

Fig. 2. Left: prerequisite (Hasse) diagram of competencies (bottom → top). Right: mapping of competencies to game levels and test items.

Finally, we examined learning gains in competence cardinality. While raw test scores decreased slightly, CbKST suggested a small increase in the gamification condition

(+0.64, SD = 3.13) and no change in the standard condition (−0.02, SD = 4.12). This difference was not statistically significant, $t(100) = 0.92$, $p = .180$. Most participants showed no change, a few gained or lost multiple competencies, and extreme shifts (e.g., from all to none) are likely artefacts of low test motivation. Overall, the structural approach revealed subtle differences not visible in conventional analyses and provided a richer picture of learners' competence development.

5 Discussion

A main finding is that performance did not differ significantly between gamified and standard conditions, indicating that gamification alone does not guarantee performance or learning benefits (cf. [21]). However, we observed a gender × condition interaction in game performance: boys performed better in the gamified condition, girls in the standard condition, with no differences in knowledge tests (cf. [22]). Such results caution against competition-oriented mechanics that may favor certain groups; prior work similarly reports stronger engagement of boys in competitive formats and advantages for girls in content-driven tasks [25]. Policy documents stress avoiding instructional biases that risk widening gender gaps [26]. A second observation is the weak relationship between pre- and post-test scores, likely due to limited test motivation (cf. [23]); raw game metrics also showed little connection with test outcomes, consistent with trial-and-error strategies (cf. [24]). To address these limits, we combined conventional analyses with KST/CbKST. The structural model fit the data well and revealed competence patterns not visible in scores. Although gains in competence cardinality were modest and not significant, structural diagnostics provided a richer account of learners' knowledge and complement standard statistics in game-based learning.

Acknowledgments. The research presented in this paper was funded by the Swiss National Fund (SNF) under grant number 100014_207864.

References

1. Slamet, T.I., Meng, C.: Gamification in collaborative learning: synthesizing evidence through meta-analysis. J. Comput. Educ. (2025)
2. Fernández-Velásquez, J.D.R., López-Regalado, O., Fernández-Hurtado, G.A.: Educational dualism in action: systematic review of gamification and flipped classrooms' effects on young learners. Contemp. Educ. Technol. **17**(1), 557 (2025)
3. Galan-Elvira, J., Palau-Irisarri, P.: Who's who in zoology: transversal application of gamification and new technologies in university teaching. Front. Vet. Sci. **12**, 1596906 (2025)
4. Sounthornwiboon, P., Sriprasertpap, K., Nilsook, P.: Simulation game-based learning for cognitive apprenticeship development: a focus on processing speed. Cogent Educ. **12**(1), 2449280 (2025)
5. Mushtaq, N., Nazeer, N., Fayaz, I., Gulzar, F.: Next-gen learning: gamification's impact on higher education. Educ. Inf. Technol. (2025)
6. Dymek, M., Zackariasson, P.: The Business of Gamification: A Critical Analysis. Routledge (2016)

7. Kohn, A.: Punished by Rewards: The Trouble with Gold Stars, Incentive Plans, A's, Praise, and Other Bribes, 25th edn. Houghton Mifflin Harcourt (2018)

8. Bogost, I.: Why gamification is bullshit. In: Walz, S.P., Deterding, S. (eds.) The Gameful World: Approaches, Issues, Applications, pp. 65–79. MIT Press, Cambridge (2015)

9. Nadi-Ravandi, M., Batooli, Z.: Exploring gamification in digital education: a bibliometric analysis. Libr. Hi Tech 42(2), 381–391 (2024)

10. Perkins, D.N., Salomon, G.: Rocky roads to transfer: rethinking mechanisms of a neglected phenomenon. Educ. Psychol. 24(2), 113–142 (1989)

11. Perkins, D.N., Salomon, G.: Knowledge to go: a motivational and dispositional view of transfer. Educ. Psychol. 47(3), 248–258 (2012)

12. Garris, R., Ahlers, R., Driskell, J.E.: Games, motivation, and learning: a research and practice model. Simul. Gaming 33(4), 441–467 (2002)

13. Wouters, P., van Oostendorp, H., van der Spek, E.D.: A meta-analysis of the cognitive and motivational effects of serious games. J. Educ. Psychol. 105(2), 249–265 (2013)

14. Mayer, R.E.: Computer games in education. Annu. Rev. Psychol. 70, 531–549 (2019)

15. Gris, G., Bengtson, C.: Assessment measures in game-based learning research: a systematic review. Int. J. Serious Games 8(1), 3–26 (2021)

16. Doignon, J.-P., Falmagne, J.-C.: Spaces for the assessment of knowledge. Int. J. Man Mach. Stud. 23(2), 175–196 (1985)

17. Albert, D., Lukas, J. (eds.): Knowledge Spaces: Theories, Empirical Research, and Applications. Lawrence Erlbaum Associates Publishers (1999)

18. Stefanutti, L., Anselmi, P., de Chiusole, D., Spoto, A.: On the polytomous generalization of knowledge space theory. J. Math. Psychol. 94, Article no. 102306 (2020)

19. gnon, J.-P., Falmagne, J.-C.: Knowledge Spaces. Springer, Heidelberg (1999). https://doi.org/10.1007/978-3-642-58625-5

20. Albert, D., Kickmeier-Rust, M.D., Matsuda, F.: A formal framework for modelling the developmental course of competence and performance in the distance, speed, and time domain. Dev. Rev. 28, 401–420 (2008)

21. Diaz, A.F., Estoque-Loñez, H.: A meta-analysis on the effectiveness of gamification on student learning achievement. Int. J. Educ. Math. Sci. Technol. 12(5), 1236–1253 (2024)

22. Li, M., Ma, S., Shi, Y.: Examining the effectiveness of gamification as a tool promoting teaching and learning in educational settings: a meta-analysis. Front. Psychol. 14, Article no. 1253549 (2023)

23. Plass, J.L., Homer, B.D., Kinzer, C.K.: Foundations of game-based learning. Educ. Psychol. 50(4), 258–283 (2015)

24. Shute, V.J., Ventura, M.: Stealth Assessment: Measuring and Supporting Learning in Video Games. MIT Press, Cambridge (2013)

25. Chung, L., Chang, R.: The effect of gender on motivation and student achievement in digital game-based learning: a case study of a content-based classroom. EURASIA J. Math. Sci. Technol. Educ. 13(6) (2017)

26. European Parliament: Report on promoting gender equality in science, technology, engineering and mathematics (STEM) education and careers (A9-0163/2021) (2021)

Excellium: Designing a Psychological Visual Novel to Foster Reflection on University Students Mental Health

Filipe Tomé[1,2](✉) ⓘ, Carla Ponte[3] ⓘ, Carlos Coelho[3] ⓘ, Pedro Ferreira[3] ⓘ, Rúben Campos[3] ⓘ, Ana Pires[1,4] ⓘ, and Pedros Campos[1,4,5] ⓘ

[1] ITI/LARSyS - Interactive Technologies Institute, Funchal, Portugal
tome.filipep@gmail.com
[2] University of Beira Interior, Funchal, Portugal
[3] University of Madeira, Funchal, Portugal
[4] Instituto Superior Técnico, University of Lisbon, Funchal, Portugal
[5] Wow! Systems, Funchal, Portugal

Abstract. *Excellium* is a psychological visual novel designed to foster reflection and raise awareness about mental health challenges faced by university students. Inspired by Squid Game, our game explores positive discomfort as a narrative strategy to provoke reflection around issues such as anxiety, burnout, and isolation. In this short paper, we describe the game's design process and report findings from a pilot study with twelve university students using the Mini Player Experience Inventory (Mini-PXI). Participants reported high levels of immersion, curiosity, and ease of control. Open-ended responses indicated that players interpreted the game's themes as relevant to student life and mental health struggles, highlighting *Excellium*'s potential as a meaningful tool for emotional engagement and reflection.

Keywords: Visual Novel Game · Digital Games · Mental Health Awareness

1 Introduction

Mental health has emerged as a global priority, especially in the wake of the COVID-19 pandemic, which underscored how isolation, academic uncertainty, and burnout can deeply impact student well-being [21]. These challenges renewed attention to stigma and misinformation surrounding mental health, highlighting the role of inclusive public communication in fostering empathy and reducing discrimination [21]. Among youth populations, university students are particularly vulnerable to psychological distress — a trend confirmed by recent studies on Portuguese higher education, which report rising levels of anxiety, depression, and emotional exhaustion [2,13,14].

Interactive media, particularly digital games, are potential tools for mental health awareness, combining emotional engagement with experiential learning

[8,16]. However, few games have been deliberately designed around positive discomfort or morally complex narratives to provoke player's reflection. This missed opportunity led to the development of *Excellium* — a game based on psychological visual novels, specifically inspired by the cultural resonance of *Squid Game*, with a narrative that is based on recent mental health research on university students in Portugal [1,2,10,12–14].

In this short paper, we present our design approach for *Excellium* and report our findings from a pilot study conducted with twelve university students. Results indicate strong engagement and narrative immersion, suggesting *Excellium*'s potential as a meaningful tool for mental health dialogue and awareness for university students.

2   Background and Motivation

Digital games have been used as tools for mental health education and stigma reduction [18]. Immersing players in emotionally challenging scenarios can prompt reflection on mental health [19,20]. Previous studies have shown that games addressing themes such as death, illness, grief, and depression can foster engagement, self-reflection, and even catharsis [3,6,19,20]. This constructive use of discomfort, often described as positive discomfort, shows how negative emotions can lead to meaningful reflection [9]. Jørgensen [9] demonstrated this in *Spec Ops: The Line* [22], where techniques such as fabrication and reversal created complicity and resulted in what players described as a "positive negative experience".

Most existing studies examine discomfort broadly, without focusing on its role in fostering reflection on mental health among young adults. University students are especially vulnerable to anxiety, depression, and emotional exhaustion [2,13,14], yet few games address these challenges directly. To address this, we created *Excellium*, a psychological visual novel that combines a narrative-driven experience with moments of positive discomfort to encourage players to reflect on mental health challenges relevant to university student life.

3   Game Concept and Narrative Design

Excellium is a psychological visual novel inspired by the first season of *Squid Game* [17]. The series demonstrates how morally uncomfortable scenarios can provoke global reflection on issues such as capitalism, inequality, and mortality [4,11,15]. This ability to blend high-stakes tension with social critique inspired us to use *Squid Game* as the foundation for the game's narrative. While *Squid Game* features hundreds of participants, *Excellium* focuses on a cast of eight university students as the characters—a deliberate choice to enable deeper character development and foster player empathy.

The game features eight student characters, each facing financial hardship and mental health challenges, reflecting research on university students in Portugal, including burnout [1], emotional exhaustion [5], substance use [14], and post-pandemic isolation [10]. Players embody Lourenço, a male psychology student in debt after losing his scholarship, experiencing the narrative from his first-person perspective. This perspective allows players to make dialogue choices that shape Lourenço's interactions with the other students, fostering direct engagement with the financial and mental health challenges central to his experience.

Originally, we set the game in a university, but it was unrealistic for students to vanish unnoticed for years. Instead, they are confined in a secret, luxurious mansion, where completing psychological games is required to graduate and escape. Failure erases memories, heightening the stakes and narrative tension.

In this version of the game, players can experience the prologue and the first game—a modified version of "Two Truths and a Lie" (see Fig. 1)—where they must identify the falsehood in each character's statements to gain points. If the player chooses incorrectly, they lose points. Throughout the game, the player is given clues and insights into the characters' backstories, which are crucial for advancing in the narrative. Depending on their score, the story culminates in a moral dilemma: the player must decide which of two characters will retain their memories. An alternate ending exists in which both can be saved—but only if the player chooses to lose.

Fig. 1. In this mini game, the player has to identify which character statement is a lie.

4   Pilot Study and Findings

The goal of this study was to examine whether *Excellium* could foster mental health reflection through the discomfort elements of the game's narrative. For this purpose, we conducted a pilot study with 12 participants to evaluate player engagement and gather preliminary feedback. Participants provided assent and signed consent forms. Nine were aged 25-34, and three were 18-24. Gender distribution was balanced, with six female and six male participants. Each played the game individually and completed a post-play questionnaire, which included the

Mini Player Experience Inventory (Mini-PXI) [7] to assess emotional and cognitive responses. The Mini-PXI is a concise, validated 11-item scale, answered on a 7-point Likert scale ranging from 1 ("strongly disagree") to 7 ("strongly agree"), measuring key aspects of player experience across cognitive, emotional, and social dimensions, including Ease of Control, Clarity of Goals, Immersion, Enjoyment, Curiosity, Autonomy, Challenge, Meaning, Mastery, Progress Feedback, and Audiovisual Appeal. These constructs capture how intuitive, engaging, and meaningful the gameplay is from the player's perspective.

Table 1 presents the descriptive statistics for all Mini-PXI constructs. Participants rated Ease of Control (M = 6.58, SD = 0.67), Clarity of Goals (M = 6.33, SD = 0.78), and Immersion (M = 6.33, 0.65) highest, suggesting that the game was intuitive, engaging, and easy to navigate. Enjoyment (M = 6.00, SD = 0.60), Curiosity (M = 6.08, SD = 0.90), and Autonomy (M = 5.83, SD = 0.83) also scored positively, reflecting a strong sense of agency and sustained interest. Challenge showed greater variability (M = 5.75, 1.14), while Meaning received the lowest average score (M = 5.25, 1.06), indicating potential for further narrative refinement. However, the positive scoring suggests that many players did have an overall positive experience.

To complement the quantitative data, we asked participants to describe in their own words what they believed the game was about. Their responses revealed three recurring themes: shared academic struggle, mental health in early adulthood, and societal pressure.

"For me, this game is about a group of students who, despite following different courses, paths, and personal histories, unknowingly share a common struggle: the difficulty of completing their studies." - P9

Table 1. Descriptive statistics for player experience constructs (Mini-PXI)

Construct	M	SD	Min	Max
Audiovisual Appeal	5.75	0.62	5	7
Challenge	5.75	1.14	4	7
Ease of Control	6.58	0.67	5	7
Clarity of Goals	6.33	0.78	5	7
Progress Feedback	6.00	1.04	4	7
Autonomy	5.83	0.83	4	7
Curiosity	6.08	0.90	4	7
Immersion	6.33	0.65	5	7
Mastery	6.00	0.60	5	7
Meaning	5.25	1.06	3	7
Enjoyment	6.00	0.60	5	7

"I think the game was about a second chance at a more positive academic experience, as well as providing the opportunity to complete the program. Moreover, I believe it was also a way to bring together a group of people who had gone through the same thing and could support each other by sharing their experiences." - P1

5   Implications and Future Work

Excellium. is a psychological visual novel that fosters reflection on mental health in university students through a narrative-driven experience with moments of positive discomfort. Pilot study findings suggest this approach is promising: participants reported high enjoyment, immersion, and curiosity, and qualitative feedback indicated reflection on academic stress, mental health, and shared struggles. Given the small sample size, these results are preliminary but offer insights for future iterations and broader testing.

Excellium. contributes to the GALA community by demonstrating how a narrative-driven visual novel can integrate positive discomfort to foster mental health reflection. It combines narrative, emotional challenges, and preliminary evaluation to explore design strategies that promote meaningful reflection.

We recognize that emotionally challenging games can foster empathy [3,6, 19,20] but may also elicit distress. To address this, *Excellium* includes a content warning and an in-game QR code linking to mental health resources.

Although initial testing involved Portuguese university students, *Excellium* addresses globally relevant themes such as time pressure, identity, and psychological well-being. Future testing will include international participants to explore cultural influences on reflection and engagement.

Future iterations will refine character development and portrayals of mental health challenges. By blending positive discomfort with narrative agency, *Excellium* aims to create space for empathy, dialogue, and change.

Acknowledgments. This research was funded by the Portuguese Recovery and Resilience Program (PRR), IAPMEI/ANI/FCT under Agenda no.26, C645022399-00000057 (eGamesLab). The authors would also like to acknowledge the Portuguese Foundation for Science and Technology, for projects 10.54499/LA/P/0083/2020; 10.54499/UIDP/50009/2020; 10.54499/UIDB/50009/2020.

Disclosure of Interests. The authors have no competing interests to declare that are relevant to the content of this article.

References

1. Almeida, T., Kadhum, M., Farrell, S.M., Ventriglio, A., Molodynski, A.: A descriptive study of mental health and wellbeing among medical students in Portugal. Int. Rev. Psychiatry **31**(7–8), 574–578 (2019)
2. Amaro, P., et al.: Depression and anxiety of Portuguese university students: a cross-sectional study about prevalence and associated factors. Depress. Anxiety **2024**(1), 5528350 (2024)
3. Bopp, J.A., Opwis, K., Mekler, E.D.: An odd kind of pleasure: differentiating emotional challenge in digital games. In: Proceeding CHI '18, pp. 1–12. ACM (2018). https://doi.org/10.1145/3173574.3173615
4. Beaunoyer, E.: Commodified death as the ultimate outcome of social inequalities: an analysis of the Squid Game discourse. Leis. Sci. **46**(6), 883–899 (2024)
5. Durão, M., Carvalho, C., Soromenho, G.: Psychological well-being of young Portuguese university students. [Publication information unavailable] (2021)
6. Gowler, C.P.R., Iacovides, I.: Horror, guilt and shame – uncomfortable experiences in digital games. In: Proceedings CHI PLAY '19, pp. 325–337. ACM (2019). https://doi.org/10.1145/3311350.3347179
7. Haider, A., et al.: MiniPXI: development and validation of an eleven-item measure of the player experience inventory. In: Proceedings of the ACM on Human-Computer Interaction, vol. 6, CHI PLAY, Article 244, 26 pages (2022). https://doi.org/10.1145/3549507
8. Isbister, K.: How games move us: emotion by design. MIT Press, Cambridge (2016)
9. Jørgensen, K.: The positive discomfort of Spec Ops: the Line. Game Studies **16**(2), 12 (2016)
10. Laranjeira, C., Dixe, M.A., Valentim, O., Charepe, Z., Querido, A.: Mental health and psychological impact during COVID-19 pandemic: an online survey of Portuguese higher education students. Int. J. Environ. Res. Public Health **19**(1), 337 (2021)
11. Nan, M.M.: Squid game: the hall of screens in the age of platform cosmopolitanism. Global Storytelling: J. Digital and Moving Images **3**(1) (2023)
12. Reis, M., de Matos, M.G., Ramiro, L.: Worries, mental and emotional health difficulties of Portuguese university students. Adv. Soc. Sci. Res. J. **6**(7), 558–569 (2019)
13. Reis, M., Ramiro, L., Paiva, T., Gaspar-de-Matos, M.: National survey on the importance of sleep in the quality of academic life and mental health of college students in Portugal. Sleep Science **14**(S 02), pp. 125–132 (2021)
14. Rodrigues, A., et al.: Saúde mental dos estudantes do ensino superior e o consumo de substâncias psicoativas: revisão integrativa da literatura. Gestão e Desenvolvimento **31**, 33–52 (2023). https://journals.ucp.pt/index.php/gestaoedesenvolvimento/article/view/11842
15. Sani, F.H., Syarif, H.: The analysis of using deixis references on Netflix series "Squid Game" as an awareness of social issues. In: Conference on English Language Teaching, pp. 1096–1104 (2023)
16. Schlote, E., Major, A.: Playing with mental issues: entertaining video games as a means for mental health education? Digital Culture Educ. **13**(2), 94–110 (2021)
17. Squid Game, TV series, Season 1. Netflix (2021)
18. Sousa, J.P.V., Campos, P., Bala, P.: College tales: pilot study on large language models generated narratives for mental health literacy. In: Proceedings of the 27th International Academic Mindtrek Conference (Mindtrek '24), pp. 270–275. ACM, New York, NY, USA (2024). https://doi.org/10.1145/3681716.3689447

19. Tomé, F., Pires, A., Jiskrová, A., Saial, A., Campos, P.F.: "I found it cathartic": Exploring empathy and mental health awareness in psychological horror video games. Proc. ACM Hum.-Comput. Interact.**8**(CHI PLAY) ,1–2, (2024). https://doi.org/10.1145/3677083
20. Tomé, F.P., Pires, A.C., Vasconcelos, F., Campos, P.F.: Eidolon: exploring the complexities of prolonged grief disorder through a digital game. In: Proceedings Extended Abstracts CHI '25, pp. 1–4 (2025)
21. World health organization: guidance on mental health policy and strategic action plans: module 2. key reform areas, directives, strategies, and actions for mental health policy and strategic action plans. Geneva: World Health Organization (2025). ISBN 978-92-4-010681-9
22. Yager Development: Spec Ops: The Line. 2K Games (2012)

Integrating Participatory Design and Reuse in Serious Game Development

Barbara Göbl[1]([✉]) [iD], Jannicke Baalsrud Hauge[2,3] [iD], and Heiko Duin[2] [iD]

[1] Centre for Teacher Education, University of Vienna, 1090 Vienna, Austria
barbara.goebl@univie.ac.at
[2] BIBA – Bremer Institut für Produktion und Logistik GmbH, 28359 Bremen, Germany
{baa,du}@biba.uni-bremen.de, jmbh@kth.se
[3] KTH-Royal Institute of Technology, 15181 Södertälje, Sweden

Abstract. Reusing existing serious game concepts and components can reduce cost and shorten time to market. However, the process is complex, and best practices such as participatory design (PD) may be impacted. This paper presents a case study exploring this impact. We outline the development of the "Coop game", which aims to raise awareness for benefits and pitfalls in interorganisational cooperations. We describe the process that integrates stakeholder participation and reuse of game components and take a look at the frictions between these two practices. Data from preliminary evaluations suggests that participants' felt they could contribute well despite the limitations of reusing game components. Finally, we discuss how stakeholder input may be coupled with expertise and interests.

Keywords: Serious Game Design · Reuse · Participatory Design

1 Introduction

Digital serious games (SGs) are defined through the integration of so-called characterizing goals, e.g. learning or awareness raising, next to entertainment purposes [1]. SG design needs to align domain and game design expertise and, thus, often invites relevant stakeholders to join a participatory design process (see e.g. [2, 3]). Accordingly, the overall development process poses a costly endeavor in terms of time and budget [4, 5]. As a means to reduce cost, practices such as the reuse of serious games and their components have been explored but reuse may impact flexibility in design. This paper presents a case study that integrates these two practices and explores the research question: "How does the integration of participatory design and reuse impact participants' perception of their contributions and the outcome of serious game development?".

Below, we outline our approach and lessons learned from the case study of the "Coop game", a serious game aimed at displaying the intricacies of international research cooperation and discuss how a design and analysis framework can be used to facilitate design decisions in the context of reuse and stakeholder participation.

S. Bakkes et al. (Eds.): GALA 2025, LNCS 16307, pp. 459–464, 2026.
https://doi.org/10.1007/978-3-032-11043-5_50

2   Background

Two different practices in SG design constitute the pillars of this case study: reuse as a means for efficient development and participatory design (PD) for stakeholder involvement.

Reuse refers to the adoption and adaptation of serious games and their components. Various assets, including and going beyond actual game software, are considered as reusable items, e.g. audiovisual assets, architecture design, design patterns, narratives, or test cases [6–8]. Reusable games and assets need to be scrutinized properly, especially in regard to their fit for the characterizing goal of the serious game [9, 10], as reuse is facilitated by deeper understanding of underlying educational, technical and game design aspects.

Participatory design may involve stakeholders to various degrees. As *testers*, participants provide feedback on prototypes, as *informants*, participants engage in dialogue with other stakeholders and designers. As *design partners*, participants engage in dialogue with designers and have a more direct say in the process (to different extents) [11]. A high level of participation, limited time and budget, pre-determined (e.g. project- or research-related) development goals, or a lack of expertise of participants may lead to issues in participatory development processes [12, 13].

3   Methodology and Research Approach

The presented case study of the "Coop game" is part of the DigiLab4You project that aims to connect scientific organizations through the shared use of remote laboratory equipment. Prospective collaborators can use the "Coop game" to explore benefits and challenges of resource sharing in a multiplayer setting. The game was designed in a participatory process led by the authors of this paper ("dev team"). Different, partly overlapping, groups of DigiLab4You project team members ("participants") took part in the iterative design process outlined below. Participants consisted of scientific staff from doctoral students to professorial level from institutions across Germany, Italy and Austria with varying experience (none to several years) in the use and development of serious games. The Activity Theory-Based Model for Serious Game Analysis (ATMSG) [14] was used to support the process. The ATMSG can analyze and design educational games from the perspectives of instructor, player and learner (the latter two refer to different viewpoints of the same person). It allows us to describe and link the different perspectives' actions, tools, and goals and provides an extensive taxonomy of serious game components that lists examples for each of the three categories.

Requirement Elicitation and Choice of Game Components. In the initial stage of the design process, 20 participants gathered requirements in a brainwriting session as part of a kick-off workshop. This included topics and learning goals (LGs) (see first column of Table 1) that the game should address, i.e. a first overview of the instructor and learner perspective. After the kick-off workshop, the dev team used the ATMSG taxonomy to define a list of suitable gaming tools, actions and goals matching the gathered topics and learning goals (second column of Table 1). Next, serious games with available source code were analyzed with the ATMSG to see which games already featured some of the game components identified as suitable. A small game engine for developing scenario-based browser games based on PHP, HTML and JavaScript was identified as the best fit (features listed in third column of Table 1). The game engines' functionality, code, design tools (e.g. documents to sketch scenarios), and user interface elements were adapted and expanded to match the requirements of the "Coop game".

Table 1. Topics initially identified by participants, suitable components (analyzed by the dev team), and the features in the game components that were reused

Topics/LGs	Suitable Game Components	Features in Reused Game Components
Cooperation	Multiplayer, Interdependency	Multiplayer, player roles, interdependent steps, player actions
Costs and benefits	Resource management, limited resources, player abilities	Individual key performance indicators (KPI), player actions
Hidden information	Resource visibility, individual win condition	Scenario description, role description
Uncertainty, risks	Randomizers, individual win conditions	Events impact game resources, scenario description, role descriptions

Participatory Scenario Description. Based on the initially gathered topics and LGs and the reused game engine's features, the dev team roughly sketched scenario and role description and devised templates for further participant input. Seventeen participants received instructions and documents as part of a webinar. Participants built teams of 2–4 people and devised detailed role/character descriptions, game events and described game characters' individual as well as common goals based on the provided template. This included information on how these events impacted costs and benefits and what hidden goals and information each character had that could lead to uncertainty and risks (see topics/LGs in Table 1).

Preliminary Evaluation of a New Game Scenario. Subsequently, the dev team implemented one of these scenarios and it was played and evaluated by 18 participants. Each of the scenario's three roles was played by a team of 6 participants. Subsequently, online questionnaires were filled in separately by each participant. The aim of the survey was to evaluate whether participants were content that the implemented game elements were suitable for the LGs they identified in the kick-off workshop and whether they felt their input was sufficiently acknowledged in the game (ratings on a 5-point scale ($1 =$ strongly disagree to $5 =$ strongly agree)). Questions on acknowledgment of input were only answered by participants that were previously involved in developing the roles and events of the evaluated scenario ($n = 10$).

Feedback on suitability of game elements was largely positive, as Fig. 1 shows. Regarding each of the seven core mechanics of the new game, a majority considered them either somewhat or very suitable to support the game's purpose. Participants reported that, despite the restrictions posed by the reuse (i.e. mechanics were pre-determined), they did not feel that the method was too restrictive. Additionally, 5 out of 10 felt their contributions were helpful for the game. Half of the participants felt their contributions were considered properly in the evaluated game prototype while 5 stated that they did not know whether this was the case (see Fig. 2).

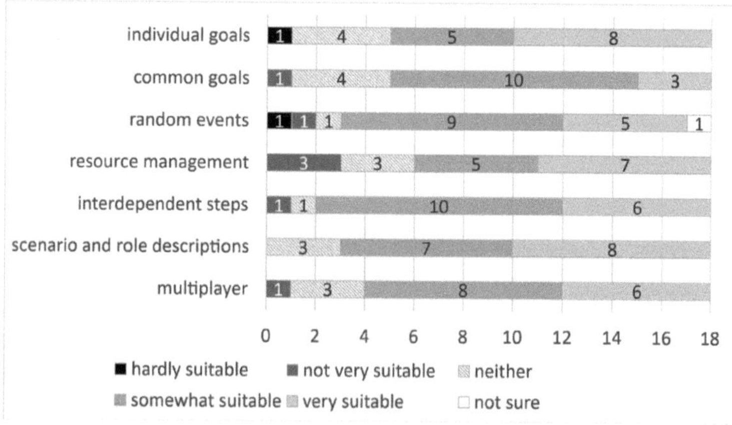

Fig. 1. Reports on suitability of game mechanics

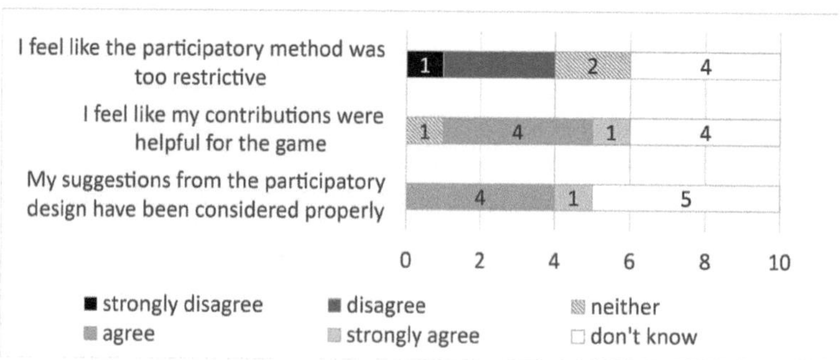

Fig. 2. Reports on the participatory design aspects of the process

4 Discussion and Conclusion

This study discusses the integration of reuse and participatory design in serious game design. Reuse and PD may seem contradictory at first glance as reusing existing games and components may limit participants' means to contribute. Nevertheless, participants largely felt their input was well integrated in the game and, while some were unsure, reports largely indicated that they did not feel restricted by the PD approach practiced. These results suggest that participants may feel heard even if some design decisions were made without direct participation. Participants' feedback in the case study suggests that the mapping of requirements by the dev team - derived from earlier participatory sessions - on concrete game mechanics has been well received.

Considering the ATMSG's differentiation between instructor, learner and player, it becomes clear that in our case study, these perspectives were designed with different levels of participation. The instructor/learner perspective, in terms of what topics would be necessary to address and what should be learned, was a collaborative endeavor where all participant input was gathered and summarized together, matching the concept of design partners as suggested by Druin [11] (see Sect. 2). Similarly, role descriptions and narrative of the game were contributed by participants with little to no adaptation of the dev team – acknowledging the domain expertise of our participants (all scientific staff) regarding the benefits and challenges in scientific cooperation. In their work with youth, Khaled and Vasalou [12] noticed that – depending on related expertise, participants in co-design processes tend to suggest unsuitable game elements or instructional/learner elements, depending on their previous experiences and knowledge. Similarly, other works find that what aspect young participants focus on when contributing to game design in open settings may still depend on their expertise and interests: well-versed gamers rather develop game mechanics while people familiar with the topic rather focus on narrative and content-related aspects [15]. This may suggest that to a certain extent, the perspective on which the participants can contribute, and potentially the level of participation, may also be matched to participants' expertise and interests.

Summing up, the paper outlines theory and practices in SG development focussing on the integration of participatory design into processes limited by the reuse of games and their components. The presented findings suggest that despite this restriction, participants feel they can contribute meaningfully to the design process. Involving participants on different levels for different aspects, depending on expertise and interest, may help to resolve some friction in this process. To explore this further, more in-depth, qualitative data gathering through e.g. interviews or focus groups, including explicit elaboration of participants' pre-existing knowledge, interests and experience with the topic and the methods, is necessary.

Acknowledgments. Barbara Göbl's work was supported by a DOC-Team scholarship of the Austrian Academy of Sciences. The project DigiLab4U (No. 16DHB2112/3) was funded by the German Federal Ministry of Education and Research (BMBF).

References

1. Dörner, R., Göbel, S., Effelsberg, W., Wiemeyer, J.: Introduction. In: Dörner, R., Göbel, S., Effelsberg, W., Wiemeyer, J. (eds.) Serious Games, pp. 1–34. Springer, Cham (2016). https://doi.org/10.1007/978-3-319-40612-1_1

2. Kayali, F., et al.: Participatory game design for the INTERACCT serious game for health. In: Göbel, S., Ma, M., Baalsrud Hauge, J., Oliveira, M., Wiemeyer, J., Wendel, V. (eds.) JCSG 2015. LNCS, vol. 9090, pp. 13–25. Springer, Cham (2015). https://doi.org/10.1007/978-3-319-19126-3_2

3. Göbl, B., Hristova, D., Jovicic, S., Chevron, M.-F., Slunecko, T., Hlavacs, H.: Fostering social media literacy through a participatory mixed-methods approach: discussion of workshop findings. In: 2019 IEEE 7th International Conference on Serious Games and Applications for Health (SeGAH), pp. 1–8. IEEE (2019)

4. Baalsrud Hauge, J., Bellotti, F., Nadolski, R., Berta, R., Carvalho, M.B.: Deploying serious games for management in higher education: lessons learned and good practices. EAI Endorsed Trans. Game Based Learn. 1, e4 (2014). https://doi.org/10.4108/sg.1.3.e4

5. Carmosino, I., Bellotti, F., Berta, R., De Gloria, A., Secco, N.: A game engine plug-in for efficient development of investigation mechanics in serious games. Entertain. Comput. 19, 1–11 (2017). https://doi.org/10.1016/j.entcom.2016.11.002

6. Lim, T., et al.: Narrative serious game mechanics (NSGM) – insights into the narrative-pedagogical mechanism. In: Göbel, S., Wiemeyer, J. (eds.) GameDays 2014. LNCS, vol. 8395, pp. 23–34. Springer, Cham (2014). https://doi.org/10.1007/978-3-319-05972-3_4

7. Protopsaltis, A., et al.: Scenario-based serious games repurposing. In: Proceedings of the 29th ACM International Conference on Design of Communication, Pisa, Italy, pp. 37–44. ACM (2011). https://doi.org/10.1145/2038476.2038484

8. Stefan, I.A., Lim, T., Baalsrud Hauge, J., Wendrich, R., Gabriela, N., Bellotti, F.: Strategies and tools to enable reuse in serious games ecosystems and beyond. In: Proceedings of the 10th International Scientific Conference eLearning and software for Education, Bucharest, Romania (2014)

9. Stanescu, I.A., Baalsrud Hauge, J., Stefan, A., Lim, T.: Towards modding and reengineering digital games for education. In: De Gloria, A., Veltkamp, R. (eds.) GALA 2015. LNCS, vol. 9599, pp. 550–559. Springer, Cham (2016). https://doi.org/10.1007/978-3-319-40216-1_59

10. Hauge, B., et al.: Serious game mechanics and opportunities for reuse. In: eLearning & Software for Education, Bucharest, Romania, pp. 19–27 (2015). https://doi.org/10.12753/2066-026X-15-094

11. Druin, A.: The role of children in the design of new technology. Behav. Inf. Technol. 21, 1–25 (2002)

12. Khaled, R., Vasalou, A.: Bridging serious games and participatory design. Int. J. Child Comput. Interact. 2, 93–100 (2014)

13. Jovicic, S., Göbl, B., Verstappen, S., Kayali, F.: Designing amidst uncertainty: drifting and byproducts in the intersection of anthropology and computer science. CoDesign, 1–16 (2024). https://doi.org/10.1080/15710882.2024.2396945

14. Carvalho, M.B., et al.: An activity theory-based model for serious games analysis and conceptual design. Comput. Educ. 87, 166–181 (2015). https://doi.org/10.1016/j.compedu.2015.03.023

15. Göbl, B., Hristova, D., Jovicic, S., Kriglstein, S., Hlavacs, H.: OutSmart! Evaluation of a serious game and its conversational interface for reflective social media use. In: Veloso, A., Mealha, Ó., and Costa, L. (eds.) 22nd International Conference on Intelligent Games and Simulation (GAME-ON 2021), Ostend, Belgium. EUROSIS-ETI (2021)

Social Anxiety in VR-CBT: Insights for College Students

Élton Camacho[1,2(✉)] [iD], Pedros Campos[1,3] [iD], and Paulo Bala[2,4] [iD]

[1] Universidade da Madeira, Funchal,Madeira, Portugal
[2] ITI/LARSyS, Lisbon, Portugal
`elton8@live.com.pt`
[3] WowSystems, Funchal, Portugal
[4] ARDITI - Regional Agency for the Development of Research, Technology and Innovation, Madeira, Portugal

Abstract. Mental health issues are a major challenge for college students, with social anxiety disorder being common, leading to avoidance and fear of negative judgment. Digital interventions using virtual reality (VR) show promise by providing immersive and controlled environments. This work explores how a VR-CBT (Virtual Reality Cognitive Behavioral Therapy) game can effectively convey CBT concepts while addressing design challenges. Twelve college students aged 18âĂŞ25 tested the artifact, completing pre and post-intervention questionnaires and a semi-structured interview. Findings indicate positive experiences, improved CBT knowledge, and increased mental health literacy. While refinements and long-term evaluation are needed, this study highlights the potential of VR-CBT as a tool for social anxiety in college contexts.

Keywords: Virtual Reality · Cognitive Behavioral Therapy · Games · Mental Health · Social Anxiety

1 Introduction

Mental health issues are highly prevalent in college students, with a significant 35% of college students claiming to have at least one mental disorder [3]. In particular, social anxiety disorder (SAD) stands out as one of the leading mental disorders [15], often beginning early on and can persist into adulthood, affecting academic and social functioning. Access to professional care is often challenging due to time constraints, stigma and insufficient campus support [5,8]. Digital interventions offer flexibility [11], with computerized cognitive behavioural therapy (CBT) found to be especially effective on college students [17]. Gamification can further increase their effectiveness [1], while virtual reality (VR) offers immersive, controllable environments suitable for addressing specific social anxiety scenarios [9].

Despite the promise of VR and games in CBT interventions for social anxiety, we identify a lack of research in combining these two approaches within a

S. Bakkes et al. (Eds.): GALA 2025, LNCS 16307, pp. 465–470, 2026.
https://doi.org/10.1007/978-3-032-11043-5_51

college context. In this work, we designed and developed a VR-CBT game aimed at conveying CBT concepts about social anxiety for college students. Through a user study (n=12), we evaluate its impact on CBT knowledge, mental health literacy, user experience and design feedback. For this work, we posit two central research questions: **RQ1:** *Can CBT concepts and practices be effectively integrated into a VR-CBT game?* **RQ2:** *Does a VR-CBT game effectively support college students' understanding of CBT concepts?*

2   Related Work

Anxiety disorders are the most common mental health condition among college students, affecting around 12% and often leading to depression, low self-esteem, and reduced academic performance [15,16]. Cognitive behavioural therapy (CBT) is a form of psychological treatment widely used for anxiety disorders, showing long-term symptom reduction and increase coping skills [2].

Previous work [17] has shown that VR has the potential to reduce stress, anxiety and depression, while improving engagement. For instance, games like AweDyssey and VR-based social exposure interventions show how immersive environments can elicit emotional and therapeutic responses [12,18].

Serious games that integrate CBT elements have shown to be effective in reducing anxiety, using mechanics like story-drive scenarios and gamification to enhance engagement [1,4,10]. The combination of VR and CBT offers controlled and scalable environments that enhance exposure and increased engagement, showing effectiveness for social anxiety [6,19].

3   Game Design

The design of our VR-CBT game was guided by Culyba's Transformational Framework [7], which emphasizes purpose, audience, barriers and assessment in creating transformative games. Such games often face tensions between interaction/enjoyment and content delivery, requiring a balance of hedonic (fun) and eudaimonic (meaningful) experiences, as well as clear mechanics to support immersion without causing confusion [13]. Our game places students in a lively party-themed environment. To integrate multiple CBT concepts effectively, we adopted a modular approach with individual mini-games, each focused on a specific CBT concept. This structure allows players to choose which mini-game to play, simplifies testing and supports scalability. The game contains two mini-games, illustrated and explained in Fig. 1.

4   User Study

To evaluate the effectiveness of our VR-CBT game, we conducted an experimental study using the Meta Quest 3 platform. Through convenience sampling, we recruited 12 Portuguese college students (ages 18–25, 67% male, 33% female).

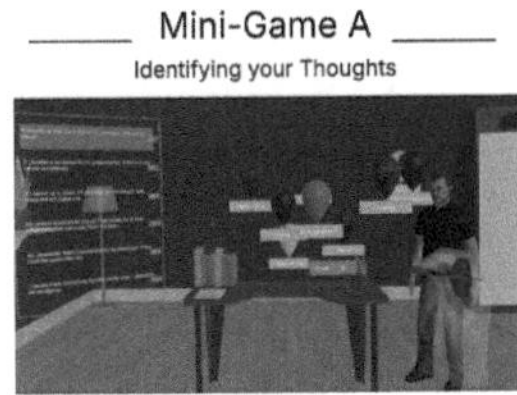

Mini-Game A focuses on the concept of **Identifying your Thoughts**, where players learn to recognize negative automatic thoughts (NATs) by popping balloons labelled with cognitive distortions, such as "Mind Reading". When the player pops the balloon corresponding to the highlighted NAT, it transforms into a healthier alternative.

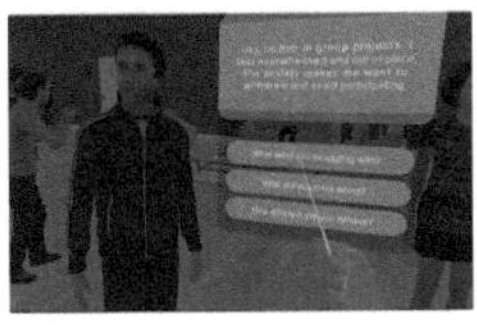

Mini-Game B addresses the concept of **Normalization**, where players interact with NPCs spread out in the party, and get to know about their struggles with social anxiety by asking them questions. Then, players complete a matching puzzle using fragmented pieces of information from each NPC's story, aiming to reduce stigma and feeling of isolation by reinforcing the idea that such experiences are common and manageable.

Fig. 1. Illustration of each mini-game

Social anxiety was not an inclusion criteria, as the study focused more on CBT concept understanding, rather than treatment. Additionally, the ethical approval was obtained from the local university. The artifact and study were developed in english to ensure a broader accessibility and replicability of the intervention, and since Portuguese college students are proficient in English, language was not expected to be a problem.

We adopted a mixed-method, pretest-posttest design. After informed consent, participants completed baseline questionnaires: demographic, mental health literacy (MHLS [14], with one item omitted due to an oversight) and CBT knowledge. The CBT knowledge is a custom questionnaire based on CBT practices [2], divided into two sections: (1) a quiz for factual knowledge of eight multiple choice questions (mainly on mini-Game A); (2) a cognitive section with five Likert items (from "Strongly Disagree" to "Strongly Agree") – *"It's important to identify negative/irrational thoughts"*, *"I'm confident in identifying my negative/irrational thoughts"*, *"I'm wiling to challenge my negative/irrational thoughts"*, *"Changing negative/irrational thoughts can have a positive impact in life"*, *"It's helpful to know that other people share the same thoughts/feelings"*. Then, participants played mini-games A and B, for a maximum of 10 mins each, using Meta Quest 3. Each session ended with a semi-structured interview, consisting of eight open-ended questions designed to collect qualitative feedback.

5   Results

5.1   Quantitative Results

We conducted paired t-tests after verifying normality, which revealed significant improvements in Mental Health Literacy (p=0.04, Cohen's d=0.41, small-to-moderate effect) and CBT-Cognitive (p=0.043, Cohen's d=0.57, moderate effect) questionnaires, but not in the CBT-Quiz scores (p=1, Cohen's d=0, no effect).

The increase in MHLS mean score (see Table 1) indicates a mental health literacy gain from the participants with more consistent responses, though item 12 was omitted. CBT results were mixed: the CBT-Cognitive improved, while the CBT-Quiz mean value remained unchanged. GEQ components has the following scores: Competence (M=2.77, SD=0.86), Sensory and Imaginative Immersion (M=3.21, SD=0.48), Flow (M=2.95, SD=0.86), Tension/Annoyance (M=0.42, SD=0.59), Challenge (M=1.03, SD=0.65), Negative affect (M=0.40, SD=0.47),

Positive affect (M=3.53, SD=0.63), Positive Experience (M=2.38, SD=1.04), Negative experience (M=0.38, SD=0.62), Tiredness (M=0.58, SD=0.63), and Returning to Reality (M=1.36, SD=0.66). The GEQ scores revealed high mean scores in components such as *Flow, Competence* and *Positive Experience*, and with low scores in *Negative Affect, Tension* and *Negative Experience*, indicating an overall enjoyable and immersive player experience.

Table 1. Mean and Standard Deviation results for each Questionnaire.

	Pre Intervention		Post Intervention	
	M	SD	M	SD
MHLS	128.42	12.72	133.33	11.08
CBT-Quiz	6.0	1.28	6.0	1.70
CBT-Cognitive	20.67	2.06	22	2.55

5.2 Qualitative Results

We structured our qualitative data around three distinct themes. First, participants' preferences were split: Mini-game A was fun but lacked content clarity, while mini-game B was more meaningful but lacked interactivity. Second, participants reported that the artifact effectively conveyed CBT concepts, especially through their personal experiences such as presentation anxiety. Finally, VR was highlighted as a high contributor to immersion and connection with the NPCs, though a few noted issues with comfort and accessibility. Suggestions included clearer instructions, voice-guided tutorials, smoother balloon movement, refining Mini-game A's content, and adding more gamification to Mini-game B.

6 Discussion

The modular mini-game design aimed to convey CBT concepts through an engaging and educational experience (RQ1). However, preferences were split: Mini-game A was fun but lacked conceptual depth, while mini-game B felt meaningful but less interactive. This contrast reflects a tension between balancing hedonic and eudaimonic experiences, a challenge explored in previous research on serious game design [13], suggesting that both mini-games require a design rework. GEQ scores reported high levels of immersion and engagement, though the novelty of VR may have biased results.

Understanding whether the artifact was able to support understanding of CBT concepts is essential in determining its educational and therapeutic value (RQ2). Our findings suggest that the artifact improved both mental health literacy and CBT-related knowledge. However, results from the CBT-Quiz section showed no clear improvement in theoretical knowledge, likely due to the observed ambiguous content in mini-game A. This aligns with Natucci and Borges' observation where complex content can affect comprehension [13]. In contrast, mini-game B fostered empathy and relatability, through relatable narratives such as public speaking, aligning with prior work showing the importance of relatable scenarios in helping people understand and internalize CBT concepts [4].

6.1 Limitations and Future Work

This study is limited by its small sample size, the omission of one MHLS item, and the reliance on a custom made CBT questionnaire, which affects comparability. The short-term nature of the study also prevents conclusions on a long-term scale. Future work should include larger and more diverse samples, long-term follow-ups, and design refinements such as additional mini-games, voice-guided tutorials and possibly, adaptive content through LLMs.

7 Conclusion

This study aimed to assess whether a VR-CBT based game was capable of conveying social anxiety CBT concepts in a clear and effective way to college students. Findings suggest that this type of intervention can provide engaging learning experiences and convey knowledge of CBT practices, though design improvements are necessary to balance interactivity and content. While preliminary, these results highlight the potential of gamified VR-CBT based interventions as complementary tools for mental health education to college students.

Acknowledgments. This research was funded by the Portuguese Recovery and Resilience Program (PRR), IAPMEI/ANI/FCT under Agenda no.26, C645022399-00000057 (eGamesLab) and the Portuguese Foundation for Science and Technology for projects 10.54499/LA/P/0083/2020; 10.54499/UIDP/50009/2020 & 10.54499/UIDB/50009/2020. The last author would also like to acknowledge the contract program signed between the Autonomous Region of Madeira and ARDITI.

References

1. Abd-alrazaq, A., et al.: The effectiveness of serious games in alleviating anxiety: systematic review and meta-analysis. JMIR Serious Games **10**(1) (2022). https://doi.org/10.2196/29137
2. American psychological association: what is cognitive behavioral therapy? https://www.apa.org/ptsd-guideline/patients-and-families/cognitive-behavioral
3. Auerbach, R.P., et al.: The WHO world mental health surveys international college student project: prevalence and distribution of mental disorders. J. Abnorm. Psychol. **127**(7), 623–638 (2018). https://doi.org/10.1037/abn0000362
4. Báldy, I.D., et al.: How to design and evaluate a serious game aiming at awareness of therapy skills associated with social anxiety disorder. In: Proceedings of the 6th EAI International Conference on Smart Objects and Technologies for Social Good. ACM, Antwerp Belgium (2020). https://doi.org/10.1145/3411170.3411249

5. Balon, R., et al.: College mental health: a vulnerable population in an environment with systemic deficiencies. Acad. Psychiatry **39**(5), 495–497 (2015). https://doi.org/10.1007/s40596-015-0390-1

6. Bouchard, S., et al.: Virtual reality compared with in vivo exposure in the treatment of social anxiety disorder. Br. J. Psychiatry **210**(4), 276–283 (2017). https://doi.org/10.1192/bjp.bp.116.184234

7. Culyba, S.: The transformational framework: a process tool for the development of transformational games. CMU (2018). https://doi.org/10.1184/R1/7130594.v1

8. Czyz, E.K., et al.: Self-reported Barriers to Professional Help Seeking Among College Students at Elevated Risk for Suicide. J. Am. Coll. Health **61**(7), 398–406 (2013). https://doi.org/10.1080/07448481.2013.820731

9. Geraets, C.N., et al.: Virtual reality-based cognitive behavioural therapy for patients with generalized social anxiety disorder: a pilot study. Behav. Cogn. Psychother. **47**(6), 745–750 (2019). https://doi.org/10.1017/S1352465819000225

10. Heng, Y.K., Liew, J.S.Y., Abdullah, M.F.I.L., Tang, Y., Prestopnik, N.: ReWIND: a CBT-Based Serious Game to Improve Cognitive Emotion Regulation and Anxiety Disorder. Int. J. Serious Games **10**(3), 43–65 (2023). https://doi.org/10.17083/ijsg.v10i3.603, https://journal.seriousgamessociety.org/index.php/IJSG/article/view/603

11. Lattie, E.G., et al.: Digital mental health interventions for depression, anxiety, and enhancement of psychological well-being among college students: systematic review. J. Med. Internet Res. **21**(7) (2019). https://doi.org/10.2196/12869

12. Miller, N., et al.: Awedyssey: design tensions in eliciting self-transcendent emotions in virtual reality to support mental well-being and connection. In: Proceedings of the 2023 ACM Designing Interactive Systems Conference, pp. 189–211. ACM, Pittsburgh PA USA (2023). https://doi.org/10.1145/3563657.3595998

13. Natucci, G.C., Borges, M.A.F.: Balancing pedagogy, emotions and game design in serious game development. In: Anais Estendidos do XX Simpósio Brasileiro de Jogos e Entretenimento Digital, pp. 1013–1016. Sociedade Brasileira de Computação, Brasil (2021). https://doi.org/10.5753/sbgames_estendido.2021.19749

14. O'Connor, M., Casey, L.: The mental health literacy scale (mhls): a new scale-based measure of mental health literacy. Psychiatry Res. **229**(1–2), 511–516 (2015). https://doi.org/10.1016/j.psychres.2015.05.064

15. Pedrelli, P., et al.: College students: mental health problems and treatment considerations. Acad. Psychiatry **39**(5), 503–511 (2015). https://doi.org/10.1007/s40596-014-0205-9

16. Perch, T.C.: Social anxiety in college students (2021)

17. Philippe, T.J., et al.: Digital health interventions for delivery of mental health care: systematic and comprehensive meta-review. JMIR Ment Health **9**(5), e35159 (2022). https://doi.org/10.2196/35159

18. Sun, A., Conde, S., Elor, A.: Increasing sociability in a virtual world: a serious game for social anxiety disorder. In: 2021 IEEE 9th International Conference on Serious Games and Applications for Health(SeGAH), pp. 1–5. IEEE, Dubai, United Arab Emirates (2021). https://doi.org/10.1109/SEGAH52098.2021.9551867

19. Wu, J., et al.: Virtual reality-assisted cognitive behavioral therapy for anxiety disorders: a systematic review and meta-analysis. Front. Psychiatry **12**, 575094 (2021). https://doi.org/10.3389/fpsyt.2021.575094

Parental Mediation and Children's Digital Game Use: A Ludo Literacy Perspective on Playful Learning

Aslihan Istanbullu[1] , Şirin Küçük-Avcı[2] , and Murat Topal[3]($\boxtimes$)

[1] Amasya University, Amasya 05100, Turkey
[2] Akdeniz University, Antalya 07070, Turkey
[3] Sakarya University, Sakarya 54050, Turkey
mtopal@sakarya.edu.tr

Abstract. This qualitative study explores Turkish parents' perspectives on their children's digital gaming behaviors, focusing on evaluation criteria, mediation strategies, and ludo literacy levels. Guided by the Parental Mediation framework, responses from 147 parents were analyzed using content analysis. Findings reveal children predominantly favor racing and sports games, indicating preference for dynamic and competitive gameplay. Parents demonstrate predominantly risk-focused and restrictive mediation approaches, with primary concerns centered on violence, inappropriate content, and addiction potential. Positive perceptions of games' cognitive, social, or creative benefits remained secondary. Parents with higher educational backgrounds exhibited more advanced ludo literacy, evidenced by greater sensitivity to game mechanics and educational potential. Single-child households applied stricter monitoring and content control. The study underscores limited use of active mediation strategies and the need for balanced parental approaches recognizing both risks and educational affordances of digital games, suggesting importance of developing ludo literacy-based parent education programs.

Keywords: Digital Games · Parental Mediation · Ludo Literacy · Media Literacy · Turkish Parents · Playful Learning

1 Introduction

The increasing integration of digital games into children's daily lives has fundamentally transformed their gaming practices, social interactions, and media consumption habits. As digital games have become dominant entertainment among children, parents face new responsibilities regarding regulation and guidance of children's gaming experiences. Parental decisions concerning appropriate games, necessary rules, and gaming effects interpretation critically shape children's digital habits. This process relates to parental attitudes, digital skills, and cultural context [1]. The interactive and social structures of digital games complicate parents' evaluation of positive and negative effects,

S. Bakkes et al. (Eds.): GALA 2025, LNCS 16307, pp. 471–477, 2026.
https://doi.org/10.1007/978-3-032-11043-5_52

making examination of parents' perspectives significant at theoretical and practical levels. Parental mediation refers to strategies employed by parents to guide, monitor, and make sense of children's media use. These strategies are classified under four categories: restrictive mediation (time and content limitations), active mediation (discussion and guidance about content), co-using (playing together without commentary), and participatory learning (interactive media use between parent and child) [1, 3]. Parents with high digital skills prefer more guiding and participatory strategies, while those distancing themselves from technology exhibit more restrictive approaches [2]. Since most strategies focus on risk reduction, they may overlook opportunities from children's experiences. Current studies argue for balanced approaches including educational and social aspects of games [3]. Parents' attitudes toward digital games directly affect children's access and supervision strategies. These attitudes have contradictory structure: games support learning and creativity, while risks such as addiction, violent content, and excessive screen time create anxiety [4]. Parents with positive attitudes engage through interactive means, while negative attitudes bring limitation-oriented strategies [5]. However, restrictive approaches can result in secretive use or parent-child conflict [6]. Media literacy and ludo literacy emerge as fundamental frameworks shaping parents' attitudes toward digital games. Media literacy encompasses skills in accessing, evaluating, analyzing, and producing digital content [7], while ludo literacy refers to comprehending structures, rules, narratives, and cultural contexts of digital games [8]. Parents with high media literacy analyze cognitive, social, and emotional effects critically [9]. Ludo literacy enables parents to evaluate games as social, cultural, and pedagogical domains [10]. Digital games function as socio-technical learning environments fostering participation, design thinking, and critical reflection [19, 23]. Research shows games broaden learners' literacies, while mediation studies highlight how strategies shape learning opportunities [21, 22]. Studies considering digital games' increasing place in family life remain limited [11]. This study examines parents' perspectives through three questions: (1) What digital games do children prefer? (2) What criteria do parents use when evaluating games? (3) How do parents perceive positive and negative effects? These answers will contribute to developing strategic approaches for improving children's digital gaming experiences.

2   Method

This qualitative study employed case study methodology, utilizing open-ended questions via Google forms as the primary online data collection platform, offering advantages including accessibility, cost-effectiveness, and enhanced anonymity that encourages honest responses [12, 13]. The research sample was selected using snowball sampling and criterion sampling techniques to ensure participants met specific inclusion criteria: Turkish parents with at least one child over seven years old, having at least one child who plays digital games minimum 2–3 times per week for at least 3–4 h weekly, and individuals who lived their entire lifetime in Turkey to reflect authentic Turkish family perspectives [14, 15]. This sampling approach aligned with case study methodology's flexibility while maintaining qualitative inquiry depth within the specific cultural context [15]. The data collection form was developed through a systematic four-stage process. Following literature review of digital game and media habits research, an initial question pool was created targeting four key domains: gaming preferences, parental evaluation criteria, perceived effects, and monitoring strategies. The draft instrument underwent expert validation by four PhD-qualified specialists in educational technology, psychology, digital media research, and digital game studies to ensure content validity. The instrument was refined to its final form comprising four open-ended questions and demographic items, targeting: (1) children's game preferences, (2) parental evaluation criteria, (3) perceived benefits and risks, and (4) supervision strategies. A total of 147 Turkish parents participated. Most participants (n = 85) were aged 36–45 years, followed by those aged 25–35 years (n = 32) and participants aged 46+ years (n = 30). Regarding educational attainment, participants with four-year university degrees comprised the largest group (n = 49), followed by high school graduates (n = 37) and those with graduate degrees (n = 30). The sample demonstrated highly educated profile, with 53.7% holding university level or higher qualifications. Two-child families represented the majority (n = 91), while single-child and three-child families each comprised 17.7% (n = 26 each). Professional backgrounds varied, with education sector employees forming the largest occupational group (n = 35), followed by homemakers (n = 38). Thematic analysis was conducted following Braun and Clarke's six-phase framework [12], using inductive coding approach. All authors independently coded initial 20% of responses. Intercoder reliability assessment resulted in Cohen's Kappa coefficient of 0.82, indicating strong agreement. The full dataset was then coded, and emerging codes were iteratively refined into broader categories and themes through collaborative discussion, ensuring themes accurately reflected participants' perspectives while maintaining analytical rigor and trustworthiness [15].

3   Results

Analysis of children's gaming preferences reveals a clear hierarchy favoring active, skill-based gaming experiences. Racing games emerged as most preferred (n = 24), followed by sports games (n = 23) and action/adventure games (n = 23), indicating children's attraction to competitive, dynamic, and physically simulating digital experiences. Creative games featuring construction mechanics ranked fourth (n = 20), demonstrating interest in open-ended, user-generated content. Educational games and puzzle/brain games showed moderate appeal (n = 15 each), suggesting learning-oriented content requires integration with engaging gameplay mechanics. Music/rhythm games (n = 8) and social/online games (n = 6) received limited preference, with minimal social gaming adoption likely reflecting parental mediation prioritizing safety.

Thematic analysis of parental evaluation criteria revealed four primary content domains and corresponding mediation approaches (Table 1). Content control emerged as the predominant evaluation criterion, with violence prevention being mentioned by 89 participants, followed by age-appropriateness considerations (n = 72) and sexual content concerns (n = 34).

Analysis of mediation strategies revealed restrictive mediation was most prevalent, with gaming time limitations mentioned by 78 participants, content restrictions by 65 participants, and age-based rules by 59 participants. Active mediation showed lower adoption rates, with game discussions reported by 41 participants and collaborative evaluation by 33 participants. Co-using strategies demonstrated moderate adoption through

Table 1. Parental Evaluation Criteria and Mediation Strategies

Parental Evaluation Criteria by Themes			Distribution of Parental Mediation Strategies		
Main Theme	Sub-theme	n	Main Theme	Strategy	n
Content Control	Violence Content	89	Restrictive Mediation	Game time limits	78
	Age Appropriateness	72		Content restrictions	65
	Sexual Content	34		Age limit rules	59
Educational Value	Learning Potential	45	Active Mediation	Discussion about games	41
	Skill Development	38		Joint evaluation	33
Safety	Online Safety	56	Co-using	Playing together	47
	Personal Information Protection	29		Game monitoring	52
Time Management	Time Limitation	78	Technical Mediation	Parental Control	31
	Addiction Prevention	42		Device settings	24

joint gaming (n = 47) and game monitoring (n = 52). Technical mediation showed limited implementation via parental control software (n = 31) and device settings (n = 24). Ludo literacy was demonstrated by participants in game mechanics comprehension (n = 34), educational value recognition (n = 45), age-appropriateness evaluation (n = 72), and online risk awareness (n = 56).

Analysis of parents' perceptions regarding digital gaming effects, combining responses from two related survey items, revealed distinct patterns of positive and negative attributions (Tables 2).

Positive effects included Cognitive Development (problem solving n = 67, quick thinking n = 54, concentration n = 48), Technological Skills (digital literacy n = 71, coordination n = 42), Social Skills (teamwork n = 29, communication n = 23), and Creativity (imagination n = 38, design thinking n = 31). Technological skill acquisition was highly recognized, with digital literacy benefits cited by 71 participants and coordination improvement by 42 participants. Negative effects dominated perceptions, including Addiction Risk (excessive use n = 89, time waste n = 76), Health Problems (eye strain n = 68, physical inactivity n = 54), Behavioral Changes (increased aggression n = 43, social isolation n = 41), and Academic Impact (decline in grades n = 37, attention distraction n = 52). Addiction risks dominated concerns, with excessive usage mentioned by 89 participants.

Table 2. Positive and Negative Effects of Digital Games by Perspective of Parents

Positive Effects of Digital Games			Negative Effects of Digital Games		
Main Theme	Sub-theme	n	Main Theme	Sub-theme	n
Cognitive Development	Problem solving	67	Addiction Risk	Excessive use	89
	Quick thinking	54		Time waste	76
	Concentration	48			
Technological Skills	Digital literacy	71	Health Problems	Eye strain	68
	Coordination	42		Physical inactivity	54
Social Skills	Teamwork	29	Behavioral Changes	Increased aggression	43
	Communication	23		Social isolation	41
Creativity	Imagination	38	Academic Impact	Decline in grades	37
	Design thinking	31		Attention distraction	52

4   Discussion, Conclusion and Limitations

Children in this study most often preferred racing, sports, and action/adventure games, emphasizing competition, skill, and rapid progression, reflecting interest in agency and cultural values around speed and individual success [8]. Parents typically approached these genres from risk-focused perspective, emphasizing concerns about violence, age appropriateness, and online safety, explaining relatively low preference for social/online games [16]. Parents with higher education levels demonstrated greater ludo literacy, recognizing not only risks but also potential benefits such as learning, skill development, and creativity—consistent with literature on active mediation [17]. Parental evaluations were shaped by media literacy, parenting self-efficacy, and family communication dynamics. Common strategies included setting age restrictions, limiting playtime, and emphasizing educational benefits, though restrictive and technical controls often dominated [17]. While such approaches may create false security, evidence shows active guidance and open communication more effectively support children's healthy engagement with games [18]. From ludo literacy perspective, games cultivate narrative, procedural, and collaborative skills, underscoring need to view them as pedagogical tools. Parents' perceptions were primarily risk-oriented, highlighting concerns such as addiction, excessive use, declining academic performance, health issues, and behavioral changes. Benefits such as cognitive development, problem-solving, imagination, and digital literacy were acknowledged less frequently, usually by parents with stronger ludo literacy [19, 20]. This imbalance reflects limited awareness of games' educational affordances. Findings indicate Turkish parents primarily adopt risk-focused, restrictive, and technical mediation strategies, while approaches acknowledging games' pedagogical potential remain limited [8]. Expanding media literacy and ludo literacy-based programs could help parents view games as cultural tools supporting children's cognitive, social, and creative development. This study has limitations: findings rely solely on parental reports, and sample did not focus on single child age group. Future research should include children's perspectives and examine specific developmental stages.

References

1. Livingstone, S.M., Blum-Ross, A.: Parenting for a Digital Future: How Hopes and Fears about Technology Shape Children's Lives. Oxford University Press, Oxford (2020)
2. Nikken, P., Opree, S.J.: Guiding young children's digital media use: ses-differences in mediation concerns and competence. J. Child Fam. Stud. **27**(6), 1844–1857 (2018)
3. Meeus, A., Beullens, K., Eggermont, S.: Like me (please?): connecting online self-presentation to pre-and early adolescents' self-esteem. New Media Soc. **21**(11–12), 2386–2403 (2019)
4. Clemente-Suárez, V.J., et al.: Digital device usage and childhood cognitive development: exploring effects on cognitive abilities. Children **11**, 1299 (2024)
5. Liu, J., Wu, L., Sun, X., Bai, X., Duan, C.: Active parental mediation and adolescent problematic internet use: the mediating role of parent–child relationships and hiding online behavior. Behav. Sci. **13**(8), 679 (2023)
6. Beyens, I., Beullens, K.: Parent–child conflict about children's tablet use: the role of parental mediation. New Media Soc. **19**(12), 2075–2093 (2017)
7. Hobbs, R.: Create to Learn: Introduction to Digital Literacy. John Wiley & Sons, Hoboken (2017)
8. Apperley, T., Walsh, C.: What digital games and literacy have in common: a heuristic for understanding pupils' gaming literacy. Literacy **46**(3), 115–122 (2012)
9. Lauricella, A.R., Blackwell, C.K., Wartella, E.: The "New" technology environment: the role of content and context on learning and development from mobile media. In: Barr, R., Linebarger, D. (eds.) Media Exposure during Infancy and Early Childhood, pp. 1–23. Springer, Cham (2017). https://doi.org/10.1007/978-3-319-45102-2_1
10. Lin, T.J., Duh, H.B.L., Li, N., Wang, H.Y., Tsai, C.C.: An investigation of learners' collaborative knowledge construction performances and behavior patterns in an augmented reality simulation. Comput. Educ. **68**, 314–321 (2013)
11. Pérez-Escoda, A., Castro-Zubizarreta, A., Fandos-Igado, M.: Digital skills in the Z generation: key questions for a curricular introduction in primary school. Comunicar **24**(49), 71–80 (2016)
12. Braun, V., Clarke, V.: Thematic Analysis: A Practical Guide. Sage, London (2021)
13. Dillman, D.A., Smyth, J.D., Christian, L.M.: Internet, Phone, Mail, and Mixed-mode Surveys: The Tailored Design Method. John Wiley & Sons, Hoboken (2014)
14. Patton, M.Q.: Qualitative research & Evaluation Methods: Integrating Theory and Practice. Sage Publications, London (2014)
15. Creswell, J.W., Poth, C.N.: Qualitative Inquiry and Research Design: Choosing Among Five Approaches. Sage Publications, London (2016)
16. Görgülü, Z., Özer, A.: Conditional role of parental controlling mediation on the relationship between escape, daily game time, and gaming disorder. Curr. Psychol. **43**(4), 3821–3829 (2024)
17. Lou, J., et al.: The association between family socio-demographic factors, parental mediation and adolescents' digital literacy: a cross-sectional study. BMC Public Health **23**(1), 2932 (2024)
18. Commodari, E., Consiglio, A., Cannata, M., La Rosa, V.L.: Influence of parental mediation and social skills on adolescents' use of online video games for escapism: a cross-sectional study. J. Res. Adolesc. **34**(4), 1668–1678 (2024)

19. Gee, J.P.: What Video Games Have to Teach Us about Learning and Literacy. Palgrave Macmillan, London (2003)
20. Steinkuehler, C.: Massively multiplayer online gaming as a constellation of literacy practices. E-Learn. Digit. Media 4(3), 297–318 (2007)
21. Livingstone, S., Helsper, E.J.: Parental mediation of children's internet use. J. Broadcast. Electron. Media **52**(4), 581–599 (2008)
22. Nikken, P.: Parental mediation of children's video game playing: a similar construct as television mediation. In: Proceedings of DiGRA (Digital Games Research Conference) Conference: Level Up. (2003)
23. Zagal, J.P.: Ludoliteracy: Defining, Understanding, and Supporting Games Education. ETC Press, Pittsburgh, PA (2010)

An Integrative Process for Making Serious Games

Daniela De Angeli[1]([✉]) [iD], Daniel J. Finnegan[2] [iD], and Lee Scott[3] [iD]

[1] University of Applied Sciences St. Pölten, St. Pölten, Austria
`Daniela.De-Angeli@fhstp.ac.at`
[2] Cardiff University, Wales, UK
[3] Echo Games CIC, Keynsham, England, UK

Abstract. Serious games – games designed for purposes beyond recreation – rely on input from experts, stakeholders, and target audiences to ensure they meet their objectives in an accurate, authentic, and sensitive manner. These objectives may range from education to encouraging social change. Yet existing frameworks, while offering sound guidance on design principles and practices, are often unclear about how and when to involve key stakeholders, risking underutilising domain-specific experience and expertise. To address this gap, we propose an integrative design process for creating "seriously fun games" that applies an iterative, multi-stakeholder approach across three phases: Co-discovery, Co-design, and Co-evaluation. We illustrate the process through case studies (e.g. *Built from Beneath*, *T Cell Titans*) where sustained stakeholder engagement was critical in defining game purpose, shaping impactful narratives, aligning mechanics with objectives, and anticipating audience interpretations. This work contributes a replicable, stakeholder-driven methodology for designers seeking to create entertaining titles that support learning and address complex societal issues.

Keywords: design · method · process · integrative · co-design · serious games

1 Introduction

Designing serious games presents distinct challenges. Unlike commercial games, which often pursue broad entertainment goals, serious games are driven by specific objectives such as education, raising awareness, or promoting social change [3, 6, 8]. These goals can be difficult to define and must be carefully tailored to audiences and contexts. To achieve this, it is crucial to involve experts, stakeholders, and members of the target audience throughout the game's design process [6]. Without such engagement, a serious game can risk missing its objectives, losing focus, being perceived as inauthentic or even trivialising sensitive issues [7]. A co-creative approach, on the other hand, can help ensure the game remains relevant, respectful, and meaningful to those it seeks to engage or support.

Drawing from years of experience designing '*seriously fun games*' as Echo Games CIC, we have adapted an integrative design process. Rooted in participatory design

S. Bakkes et al. (Eds.): GALA 2025, LNCS 16307, pp. 478–483, 2026.
https://doi.org/10.1007/978-3-032-11043-5_53

principles, this iterative, multi-stakeholder approach is especially effective for addressing issues that require diverse perspectives and adaptable solutions. Additionally, it helps clarify the purpose of the game and guides how that purpose can be effectively evaluated. Through selected case studies, this paper presents how we use an integrative design process to create serious games, following three phases: Co-discovery, Co-design, and Co-evaluation.

2   Background

Designing Serious Games (SGs) is a complex, multidisciplinary process that requires careful consideration of both pedagogical objectives and engaging gameplay [1, 4]. A key challenge is ensuring effective collaboration among various experts, such as project managers, cognitive specialists, domain experts, storyboard writers, artistic directors, pedagogical experts, and programmers [2]. To address this, several methodologies, frameworks, and tools have been proposed to guide the design process, including co.LAB [10], iPlus [4], Marne et al.'s Six Facets of SGs Design [11], and Yusoff's 12 attributes of educational games [14]. These frameworks often start by identifying objectives and move to designing and testing mechanics, scripts, and content. Many of those methodologies also explicitly incorporate **iterative** cycles, allowing for continuous refinement and adaptation based on feedback and evaluation [10, 11].

However, the need for multidisciplinary teams often leads to difficulties in **communication and mutual understanding** [2, 11, 13]. Experts from different fields (e.g., design, pedagogy) may use different vocabularies and have conflicting objectives, hindering efficient collaboration [2]. And although user and stakeholder involvement is widely encouraged, it often remains limited to feedback on later stages of development, rather than active **participation** in early ideation and co-design [5, 13]. This highlights the need for more inclusive and collaborative design approaches that promote engagement and shared understanding among different stakeholders from the outset.

Table 1. Overview phases of the Integrative process.

Phase	Aim	Examples activities
Co-Discovery	Explore purpose, needs, values, design brief	Iterative conversations, focus groups, game modding, mini games (storytelling, RPG)
Playtest & interpret		
Co-Design	Define tone, narrative, aesthetics, mechanics	Brainstorming, concept testing, iterative interview rounds, paper prototypes
Playtest & interpret		
Co-Evaluate	Validate narrative and gameplay; Test usability	Digital evaluation platforms (e.g. Miro), visual tools (e.g. interactive PDF), usability testing

3 The Integrative Process

The integrative design process is collaborative, iterative, and inclusive. It values communication, collaboration, and critical reflection, so it is particularly well-suited to address "wicked problems" such as climate change, healthcare, and social inequality [9, 12]. It is grounded in critical inquiry, inherently tied to political and economic contexts [12]. It also involve multiple stakeholders such as citizens, entrepreneurs, policymakers, and researchers, all contributing to socially innovative solutions [9, 12]. We realised this type of collaborative design approach was ideally suited for complex projects, like 'seriously fun games'. Thus, we have adapted it to the development of our games and found it to be an effective approach because it involves stakeholders (e.g. professionals, researchers, and students) through the full design process, which is made of **three consecutive phases**: Co-discovery, Co-design, and Co-evaluation (Table 1).

3.1 Co-discover the Game's Purpose

The *Co-discover* phase initiates the process by bringing together all stakeholders to define the game's purpose. This stage is essential for establishing a common vision and ensuring that the game addresses real-world needs and values. For example, with the digital escape room *Built from Beneath*, we wanted to tell the story of the city of Bath from different perspectives, from its prehistoric beginnings to the technological and societal developments of the modern era. To this end we brought together stories and objects from five museums in and around Bath - Bath Royal Literary and Scientific Institution (BRLSI), Radstock Museum, the Museum of Bath at Work, the Museum of Bath Stone, and Bath Medical Museum. These museums have distinct missions and collections. Our goal was to include each institution equitably, creating a shared message that resonates with all. Thus, we had multiple conversations with professionals from each institution to find a common purpose for the game. We took the information we collected during these co-discovery conversations to identify a shared goal.

In another project, we worked with a youth justice team, young offenders, and academics to design a game that supports reflection and future-oriented thinking. We began with a co-discovery phase using games to facilitate conversations. For example, young offenders modified existing tabletop games to explore themes relevant to their lives. We also created a storytelling game where they played as students at a superhero academy—an allegorical setting that allowed them to express challenges and needs without sharing personal details. This Co-discovery process helps define the game's purpose, concept, and an initial design brief that will guide the development of the game. The design brief is key to ensure stability and coherence, so that the development team has a solid foundation through what is a very flexible and iterative process.

3.2 Co-design Narrative and Core Mechanics

During the *Co-design* phase, the game's theme, narrative and core mechanics are developed in close collaboration with stakeholders. This phase is highly iterative, with continuous feedback loops ensuring that the design remains aligned with stakeholder values and needs. For example, we worked closely with museum professionals to determine which stories to tell and which objects to feature in the digital escape room *Built from Beneath.* We organised a one-day workshop during which representatives from each museum could share their stories and values. This was a truly collaborative effort that offered a rare opportunity to bring regional museums together to share their insights and experiences. The event included two main activities. Firstly, a group brainstorming guided by us where museums could discuss which stories and artefacts we could include in the game together. Secondly, we held individual interviews with each museum where a creative writer helped the five institutions to express the stories they wanted to tell and how these could be sequenced to express a shared narrative. The workshop was complemented by a series of site visits and online interactions where historical information, images, and representations of key artefacts were exchanged. Through this iterative process, a multidisciplinary team—comprising developers, artists, and researchers—translated all these inputs into a coherent narrative and a playable experience.

In other cases, we used concept testing sessions to share early ideas with stakeholders, collecting feedback via email or surveys. For more detailed input, especially from domain experts, we preferred iterative interviews - online or in person - with one or two participants at a time to refine game elements like narrative, characters, and puzzles. This method was central to *Immersed in Conservation,* a digital escape room exploring deforestation in Malaysia and the impact of global purchasing habits. We collaborated with Dr. Cedric Tan, an expert on the Malaysian rainforest, through a series of online interviews. His insights shaped a unique shopping mechanic where players made purchasing decisions based on environmental and economic factors. These choices influenced how many trees were cut down in a visual representation of the rainforest, reinforcing the connection between consumer behaviour and environmental impact.

3.3 Co-evaluate to Ensure Authenticity and Alignment

The *Co-evaluation* phase focuses on validating the game's content and narrative but also tests its playability. For example, stakeholders may assess full prototypes and narratives, as well as specific game mechanics and aesthetics. We often use digital co-evaluation platforms - like Miro or Figma- or other visual tools - like interactive PDFs - that allow for remote evaluation such as rating aspects of the experience. For example, after we storyboarded the whole narrative for *Built from Beneath* based on inputs from the co-creation phase, we shared interactive PDFs via email with museum professionals. The PDF presented the storyboard and the related artefacts, with space for comments. In this way, stakeholders could review the storyboard of the narrative and the game objects at their own pace, providing clear guidelines to ensure authenticity and representation of each institution's voice.

We also often engage with the target audience to ensure that the experience is not only authentic but also engaging and easy to play. This was the case with *T Cell Titans,* a game we created for Great Ormond Street Hospital (GOSH) to help young patients understand what happens in their bodies when undergoing CAR-T therapy. We invited a group of young patients to playtest a beta version of the game and provide detailed deconstructions and feedback on the game's mechanics and narrative during online interviews. During these semi-structured interviews, the young players helped shape its look, tone, and gameplay style. They also contributed with their own creative ideas on how to increase the game engagement and appeal. For example, based on this input, we added a final boss in the last level of the game. Their feedback was invaluable to enhance the final product.

3.4 An Iterative Process

Although co-evaluation is the final phase of this integrative process, development is iterative, continuous, and bidirectional. After each phase, teams interpret stakeholder input and may return to Co-design or Co-discovery if revisions are needed. Regular brainstorming helps not only to make sense of findings but also to decide on the next steps. In game design, early and repeated playtesting is essential - especially when addressing complex topics like war and conflict. This can begin even before technical development, using low-fidelity methods such as paper prototypes.

This approach was central to our collaboration with the Ruhr Museum in developing the Agonistic Games *Umschlagplatz '43* and *Endless Blitz* for the Ruhr Museum in Essen [6]. Agonistic Games reject an antagonistic 'us' vs 'them' way of remembering in favour of a multi-perspective approach to contextualising and learning from war and conflict [6]. In this project, there were (to the best of our knowledge) no examples of practice available indicating that Agonistic Games were a new concept. With no existing models to draw from, we worked closely with researchers and curators to iteratively test and refine narrative and gameplay elements. The result was two games that embodied the principles of agonistic memory, encouraging players to engage with World War II through a multi-perspective lens.

4 Conclusion

This paper has presented the potential of an integrative approach for the design of serious games to address complex societal challenges. Through iterative phases of Co-discovery, Co-design, and Co-evaluation, we ensure the creation of games that are meaningful, authentic in their purpose, and impactful. In a digital era where technology shapes human experience, integrative design offers an inclusive and socially innovative framework for developing transformative digital tools. Importantly, this approach can extend beyond the evaluation of design to the evaluation of impact – a challenge that remains significant in the field of serious games. Although games may be engaging, assessing their impact on knowledge, attitudes, or behaviour is complex. A parallel line of work is therefore examining how co-evaluation methods can be refined to better capture long-term effects, involving stakeholders not only in validating content but also in defining relevant metrics and longitudinal strategies. In addition, ongoing research is investigating how other serious game designers apply the integrative framework in their own projects, to assess its practical benefits and adaptability across contexts.

References

1. Barbosa, A.F.S., Pereira, P.N.M., Dias, J.A.F.F., Silva, F.G.M.: A new methodology of design and development of serious games. Int. J. Comput. Games Technol. **2014**(1), 817167 (2014). https://doi.org/10.1155/2014/817167

2. Bellotti, F., et al.: Designing serious games for education: from pedagogical principles to game mechanisms. In: Proceedings of the 5th European Conference on Games Based Learning, 2011. University of Athens Greece, pp. 26–34 (2011)

3. Bunt, L., Greeff, J., Taylor, E.: Enhancing serious game design: expert-reviewed, stakeholder-centered framework. JMIR Serious Games **12**(1), e48099 (2024). https://doi.org/10.2196/48099

4. Carrión-Toro, M., Santorum, M., Acosta-Vargas, P., Aguilar, J., Pérez, M.: iPlus a user-centered methodology for serious games design. Appl. Sci. **10**(24), 9007 (2020). https://doi.org/10.3390/app10249007

5. Castillo, J.F.V., et al.: Design of virtual reality exergames for upper limb stroke rehabilitation following iterative design methods: usability study. JMIR Serious Games **12**(1), e48900 (2024). https://doi.org/10.2196/48900

6. De Angeli, D., Finnegan, D.J., Scott, L., O'Neill, E.: Unsettling play. J. Comput. Cult. Herit. (JOCCH) **14**(2) (2021). https://doi.org/10.1145/3431925

7. De Groot, L., Demeijer, F.A., Zweekhorst, M., Urias, E.: Multi-stakeholder networks in the higher education context: a configurative literature review of university-community interactions. J. High. Educ. Policy Manag. **47**(4), 490–508 (2025). https://doi.org/10.1080/1360080X.2025.2451445

8. Djaouti, D., Alvarez, J., Jessel, J.-P.: Classifying serious games: the G/P/S model. In: Felicia, P. (ed.) Handbook of Research on Improving Learning and Motivation through Educational Games: Multidisciplinary Approaches. IGI Global (2011). http://www.ludoscience.com/EN/diffusion/537-Classifying-Serious-Games-The-GPS-Model.html. Accessed 3 Dec 2019

9. Emerson, K., Nabatchi, T., Balogh, S.: An integrated framework for collaborative governance. J. Public Adm. Res. Theory **22**(1) (2012). https://doi.org/10.1093/jopart/mur011

10. Jaccard, D., Suppan, L., Sanchez, E., Huguenin, A., Laurent, M.: The co.LAB generic framework for collaborative design of serious games: development study. JMIR Serious Games **9**(3), e28674 (2021). https://doi.org/10.2196/28674

11. Marne, B., Wisdom, J., Huynh-Kim-Bang, B., Labat, J.M.: The six facets of serious game design: a methodology enhanced by our design pattern library. In: Ravenscroft, A., Lindstaedt, S., Kloos, C.D., Hernández-Leo, D. (eds.) EC-TEL 2012. LNCS, vol. 7563, pp. 208–221. Springer, Heidelberg (2012). https://doi.org/10.1007/978-3-642-33263-0_17

12. Michel, R.: Integrative Design. De Gruyter, Berlin, Boston (2019.) https://doi.org/10.1515/9783038215318

13. Pacheco-Velazquez, E., Rodes-Paragarino, V., Mayer, L.R., Bester, A.: How to create serious games? Proposal for a participatory methodology. Int. J. Serious Games **10**(4), 55–73 (2023). https://doi.org/10.17083/ijsg.v10i4.642

14. Yusoff, A.: A conceptual framework for serious games and its validation. phd. University of Southampton (2010). https://eprints.soton.ac.uk/171663/. Accessed 9 Sept 2025

HLDD STRIDES: A Conceptual Framework for Instructional Serious Games

Oguz Orkun Doma[✉][iD], Vanissa Wanick[iD], and Yuanyuan Yin[iD]

Winchester School of Art, University of Southampton, Southampton, UK
{oguz.doma,vwv1n12,Y.Yin}@soton.ac.uk

Abstract. Serious games (SGs) integrate pedagogical design with game development. Yet, current practices often rely on abstract frameworks that rarely provide production-ready artefacts, and static Game Design Documents (GDDs) that soon become outdated and clash with Agile workflows. As a result, teams adopt ad hoc processes and fragmented documentation, causing drift between design and implementation, increased rework, and limited traceability from learning objectives to gameplay. It also limits timely input from subject-matter experts (SMEs) and industry stakeholders, undermining instructional alignment and compliance assurance. This paper introduces HLDD-STRIDES, a two-layer framework addressing these challenges: a High-Level Design Document (HLDD) that captures core instructional intent and compliance anchors, and a STRIDES table that expresses instructional steps in a structured, runtime-aligned format. This combination enables SME authoring, rapid CSV re-import, and optional LMS integration (SCORM/xAPI). Deployed in six projects across mining, healthcare and creative sectors, HLDD-STRIDES illustrates how data-oriented documentation can link pedagogy to production while supporting Agile development in SG contexts.

Keywords: Serious games · Instructional design · Design documentation

1 Introduction

Serious games (SGs) combine pedagogical frameworks with game design and development practices, operating in a hybrid space between learning theory and interactive media. This duality makes SG documentation more complex than in entertainment game projects. Conventional Game Design Documents (GDDs) work in Waterfall pipelines, but their static and text-heavy nature conflicts with Agile workflows, leading to drift, obsolescence and rework [1,19].

Existing SG frameworks, such as RETAIN [10], LM GM [2], and SGDDEdu [13], map learning outcomes to mechanics but overlook runtime constraints and iterative production. Model-driven approaches improve flexibility [11,18], yet

S. Bakkes et al. (Eds.): GALA 2025, LNCS 16307, pp. 484–490, 2026.
https://doi.org/10.1007/978-3-032-11043-5_54

still stop short of producing executable artefacts that support rapid iteration or subject-matter expert (SME) authoring. No current method unifies instructional intent, SME collaboration, Agile iteration, and engine-ready implementation.

We address this gap with HLDD STRIDES, a two-layer framework that combines: (1) a High-Level Design Document (HLDD) for stable, auditable instructional intent; and (2) a STRIDES table for structured, runtime-aligned, SME-editable content with optional LMS integration (SCORM/xAPI). Developed through industrial practice and applied in several SG projects, HLDD STRIDES demonstrates an engine-agnostic documentation pipeline that links pedagogy with production.

This paper contributes: (1) a synthesis of current documentation challenges in SG development, and (2) the HLDD STRIDES framework, grounded in literature and illustrated through early applications.

2   Background and Related Work

As no universal GDD format exists, studios customise templates for efficiency across genres and pipelines [3]. Critics have long labelled the monolithic GDD dead, citing rigidity and upkeep costs [15]. Current views emphasise that a GDD is only useful if it functions as a live, Agile-supporting artefact [7]. Modern practice treats it not as a fixed design bible but as a lean, project-specific structure negotiated per project [16]. These challenges are amplified in SGs, where documentation must also satisfy instructional and compliance requirements.

Current GDD approaches in SG development are mostly model-driven [5], with numerous frameworks proposed over the past two decades [4]. Early work adapted instructional models for game contexts, such as SG-ISD [12] and DOD-DEL [14], while later models bridged gameplay and learning outcomes (e.g., RETAIN [10], Four-Dimensional Framework [9], LM–GM [2]). More recent efforts included instructional engineering methods such as MISA [17], lightweight documentation (e.g., SGDDEdu [13]), knowledge elicitation (e.g., ACTA [20]), or modular collaboration (e.g., co.Lab [11], SGDA-IE [5]).

Across these approaches, recurring challenges persist: (1) static formats drift and rarely reference compliance; (2) instructional models remain abstract, rarely addressing runtime needs; (3) weak mapping exists between learning objectives and mechanics, leaving SMEs and developers in separate spaces; (4) Agile alternatives (wikis, spreadsheets) lack formalisation; (5) SCORM/xAPI alignment and evaluation logic are seldom explicit; and (6) most validations are small-scale or tool-specific.

Despite valuable progress, no current method provides a data-driven, engine-ready pipeline that enables SME authoring, Agile iteration and pedagogical integrity. This paper addresses this gap with the HLDD STRIDES framework.

3   HLDD STRIDES Conceptual Framework

High-Level Design Document (HLDD). The HLDD serves as a concise, central hub across the project lifecycle, capturing essentials without exhaustive detail. Typical sections include:

- *High Concept:* core idea, audience, purpose, features.
- *Gameplay:* mechanics, loops, progression, rewards.
- *Design Basics:* environment, characters, controls, audiovisual style.
- *Instructional Layer:* learning outcomes mapped to standards (e.g., Bloom, RETAIN), assessment, replayability.

The HLDD is version-controlled and updated only when intent or compliance changes. Granular production details remain in live tools (e.g., Confluence, Notion, Jira) and link back for traceability.

STRIDES. The STRIDES table structures instructional steps into a runtime-ready format. Each row captures: (1) Step ID, (2) Task Intro, (3) Request, (4) If Fails, (5) Dynamic Hint, (6) End Info, (7) Success condition. Both *If Fails* and *Success* may redirect to other steps for progression or simple branching.

SMEs can edit the spreadsheet directly and add contextual comments, but only the defined columns are parsed into the engine (e.g. as CSV for Unreal DataTables). A lightweight syntax keeps entries both readable and engine-compatible. Optional LMS fields (e.g. SCORM/xAPI IDs, weights) can also be included.

Workflow. HLDD STRIDES is applied through a four-step workflow (Fig. 1):

1. **HLDD creation** designers and instructional leads capture core goals and compliance anchors.
2. **STRIDES authoring** SMEs populate the structured spreadsheet (Task Intro, Request, If Fails, Hint, End Info, Success), using simple markup for assets.
3. **STRIDES refinement** designers review logic, add details (e.g., audio, animations, LMS IDs), and align with engine data structures.
4. **Runtime integration** the CSV is imported into the engine (e.g., Unreal DataTables + Blueprint manager).

Edits require only CSV re-import and a data/asset rebuild as needed, not re-implementation of mechanics. This pipeline shortens the gap between instructional authoring and execution, increases SME transparency, and supports traceable compliance.

3.1   Case Studies

HLDD STRIDES has been applied in six projects across mining, healthcare, AEC and creative sectors, using both CryEngine and Unreal Engine.

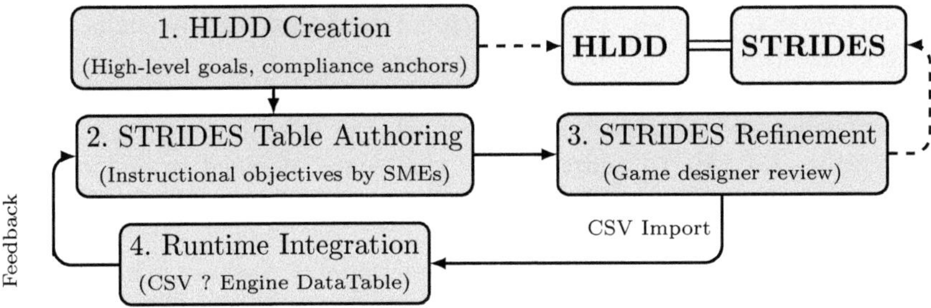

Fig. 1. HLDD–STRIDES workflow from documentation to engine integration.

In the early CryEngine implementation, a spreadsheet-to-FlowGraph pipeline was used: STRIDES rows defining steps, dependencies and outcomes were automatically converted into FlowGraph nodes and connections, reducing manual scripting effort. The current Unreal Engine 5 workflow adopts a CSV-to-DataTable approach. STRIDES exports populate a DataTable. A tutorial manager Blueprint parses each row at runtime, presenting instructional panels (Intro → Request → Hint → End Info) and handling branching through success and failure callbacks. Because all instructional content resides in the STRIDES spreadsheet, SMEs can revise text, timings or branching flags; developers then re-import the updated file into the engine, which updates data and assets without re-implementing mechanics, enabling faster iteration and reducing developer overhead.

These deployments show that HLDD–STRIDES is not only a conceptual model but an operational pipeline that balances stability with Agile iteration, improves SME engagement, and ensures compliance-ready traceability.

4   Discussion

HLDD STRIDES addresses the tension between instructional rigour and iterative workflows noted in SG literature [2,8]. It functions both as a reference model and as a practical method, having been exercised in six industry projects.

Conceptual Contribution. HLDD anchors instructional intent and compliance in a stable document, while STRIDES expresses interaction steps in a runtime-ready table. Together they close the pedagogy production gap of monolithic GDDs [6], while off-loading dynamic details to collaborative tools (e.g., Notion, Confluence, Jira).

Empirical Signals. The framework has so far been exercised in projects across mining, healthcare, AEC and creative sectors. These early deployments suggest that SME-authored spreadsheet updates can accelerate iteration and support compliance traceability, though systematic validation remains future work.

Implications. For practitioners, HLDD STRIDES shortens feedback loops, embeds compliance tags at design time, and increases confidence through auditable version histories. The approach is transferable to any engine supporting CSV ingestion.

Limitations and Outlook. Current spreadsheet schemas struggle with complex branching and adaptive sequencing, echoing prior limitations reported in the literature [11,18]. To address these challenges, planned work includes the development of a node-based editor, a more extensible schema, and broader empirical studies.

HLDD records learning objectives and compliance anchors, while STRIDES encodes the corresponding runtime success checks, preserving traceability from intent to execution.

5   Conclusion

HLDD STRIDES aligns learning objectives, SME input and runtime logic in a traceable, data-driven form. It offers a practical alternative to static GDDs while supporting Agile workflows. Future work will expand validation, develop visual authoring tools, and extend interoperability through JSON and SCORM/xAPI connectors.

Acknowledgments. This research was supported by Innovate UK through a Knowledge Transfer Partnership project between Stewart Signs Ltd and the University of Southampton, Winchester School of Art *(KTP Project ID: 13577; UKRI GtR Ref: 10063400)*. The authors thank the project partners. Special thanks to Petar Kotevski and Burak Furkan Aksahin for their valuable contributions to the development of early iterations of the STRIDES framework in the serious game projects in which we worked together.

Disclosure of Interests. The authors declare that they have no conflicts of interest relevant to the content of this paper.

References

1. Aleem, S., Capretz, L.F., Ahmed, F.: Critical Success Factors to improve the game development process from a developer's perspective. J. Comput. Sci. Technol. **31**(5), 925–950 (2016). https://doi.org/10.1007/s11390-016-1673-z
2. Arnab, S., et al.: Mapping learning and game mechanics for serious games analysis. Br. J. Educ. Tech. **46**(2), 391–411 (2015). https://doi.org/10.1111/bjet.12113
3. Atmaja, P.W., Siahaan, D.O., Kuswardayan, I.: Game design document format for video games with passive dynamic difficulty adjustment. Register: Jurnal Ilmiah Teknologi Sistem Informasi **2**(2), 86 (2016). https://doi.org/10.26594/register.v2i2.551
4. Ávila-Pesántez, D., Rivera, L.A., Alban, M.S.: Approaches for serious game design: a systematic literature review. Comput. Educ. J. **8**(3), 1–11 (2017), https://coed.asee.org/wp-content/uploads/2020/08/9-Approaches-for-Serious-Game-Design-A-Systematic-Literature-Review.pdf

5. Ben Amara, B., Mhiri Sellami, H., Ben Said, L.: An approach for serious game design and development based on iterative evaluation. J. Softw. Evol. Process **36**(10), e2680 (2024). https://doi.org/10.1002/SMR.2680

6. Colby, R., Shultz Colby, R.: Game design documentation: four perspectives from independent game studios. Commun. Des. Quart. **7**(3), 5–15 (2019). https://doi.org/10.1145/3321388.3321389

7. Ellison, G.: From GDD graveyard to living document: a lean approach to game design (2025), https://www.wayline.io/blog/lean-gdd-game-design-documentation

8. Engström, H., Backlund, P.: Serious games design knowledge: experiences from a decade (+) of serious games development. EAI Endorsed Trans. Serious Games **6**(1), 1–13 (2022)

9. de Freitas, S., Rebolledo-Mendez, G., Liarokapis, F., Magoulas, G., Poulovassilis, A.: Developing an evaluation methodology for immersive learning experiences in a virtual world. In: Proceedings of the 2009 Conference in Games and Virtual Worlds for Serious Applications, VS-GAMES 2009, pp. 43–50 (2009). https://doi.org/10.1109/VS-GAMES.2009.41

10. Gunter, G.A., Kenny, R.F., Vick, E.H.: Taking educational games seriously: using the RETAIN model to design endogenous fantasy into standalone educational games. Educ. Technol. Res. Dev. **56**(5-6), 511–537 (2008). https://doi.org/10.1007/s11423-007-9073-2

11. Jaccard, D., Suppan, L., Sanchez, E., Huguenin, A., Laurent, M.: The co.LAB generic framework for collaborative design of serious games: development study. JMIR Ser. Games **9**(3), e28674 (2021). https://doi.org/10.2196/28674

12. Kirkley, S.E., Tomblin, S., Kirkley, J.: Instructional design authoring support for the development of serious games and mixed reality training. In: Interservice/Industry Training, Simulation and Education Conference (I/ITSEC), pp. 6–9. Citeseer (2005)

13. Martins, R.S., Raulino, F., Burlamaqui, A., Burlamaqui, A.: SGDDEdu: a model of short game design document for digital educational games. Int. J. Innov. Educ. Res. **7**(2), 167–180 (2019). https://doi.org/10.31686/ijier.vol7.iss2.1335

14. McMahon, M.: The DODDEL model: a flexible document-oriented model for the design of serious games. Research outputs pre 2011, pp. 98–118, January 2009. https://doi.org/10.4018/978-1-60566-360-9.ch007

15. MCV: death of the game design document (2014), https://mcvuk.com/development-news/death-of-the-game-design-document/

16. de Oliveira, P.H.R.L., de Miranda, C.A.S., Gomide, J.V.B.: Applied alternative tools and methods in the replacement of the game design document. In: Research Anthology on Game Design, Development, Usage, and Social Impact, pp. 585–598. IGI Global, October 2022. https://doi.org/10.4018/978-1-6684-7589-8.ch028

17. Paquette, G., de la Teja, I., L onard, M., Lundgren-Cayrol, K., Marino, O.: An instructional engineering method and tool for the design of units of learning, pp. 161–184. Springer, Berlin Heidelberg (2005). https://doi.org/10.1007/3-540-27360-3_9, http://link.springer.com/10.1007/3-540-27360-3_9

18. Roungas, B.: A model-driven framework for educational game design. Int. J. Ser. Games **3**(3) (2016). https://doi.org/10.17083/ijsg.v3i3.126

19. Salazar, M.G., Mitre, H.A., Olalde, C.L., Sanchez, J.L.G.: Proposal of game design document from software engineering requirements perspective. In: 2012 17th International Conference on Computer Games (CGAMES), pp. 81–85. IEEE, July 2012. https://doi.org/10.1109/CGames.2012.6314556
20. Seager, W., Ruskov, M., Sasse, M.A., Oliveira, M.: Eliciting and modelling expertise for serious games in project management. Entertainment Comput. $2(2)$, 75–80 (2011). https://doi.org/10.1016/J.ENTCOM.2011.01.002

Design and Pilot Study of a Digital Gamified Assessment for Computational Creativity

Katerina Tsarava[1,2]([envelope]) [iD], Johannes A. Schubert[1], Manuel Ninaus[2,3] [iD], Mathias Benedek[3] [iD], Korbinian Moeller[2,4] [iD], and Ann-Kathrin Jaggy[1,2] [iD]

[1] Hector Research Institute of Education Sciences and Psychology, University of Tübingen, Tübingen, Germany
`katerina.tsarava@uni-tuebingen.de`
[2] LEAD Graduate School and Research Network, University of Tübingen, Tübingen, Germany
[3] Department of Psychology, University of Graz, Graz, Austria
[4] Centre for Mathematical Cognition, School of Science, Loughborough University, Loughborough, UK

Abstract. Computational thinking (CT), as an overarching problem-solving skill, and creativity, as a drive for innovation are both considered essential 21st-century skills and recommended to be acquired early on in education. However, tools to assess their relationship still remain limited. This pilot study ($N = 125$) presents the development and piloting of a new gamified assessment tool, the Computational Creativity and Computational Thinking test (CCCT), for primary school children. Results show that the CCCT is feasible to measure domain-specific creativity in the context of CT and provide initial insights into their relationship. Our findings support the CCCT as a promising instrument for holistically assessing the complex and synergistic relationship between CT and creativity.

Keywords: Computational Thinking · Creativity · Computational Creativity · Gamified Digital Assessment Tool

1 Introduction

In a world increasingly shaped by technology, competencies such as CT and creativity are essential for navigating and contributing to the current environment. Their relationship in educational contexts, however, remains underexplored and challenging to assess. Building on the existing concept of computational creativity (CC), this study introduces a gamified digital tool that evaluates creative thinking within CT tasks.

K. Tsarava and J. Schubert—Equal contribution.

© The Author(s), under exclusive license to Springer Nature Switzerland AG 2026
S. Bakkes et al. (Eds.): GALA 2025, LNCS 16307, pp. 491–497, 2026.
https://doi.org/10.1007/978-3-032-11043-5_55

1.1 Computational Thinking, Creativity and Computational Creativity

CT is widely recognized as a key competence in modern education. Shute et al. [1, p. 151] describe CT as "the conceptual foundation required to solve problems effectively and efficiently," emphasizing problem-solving beyond programming. Similarly, Barr and Stephenson [2], define it as a process grounded in logical reasoning and abstraction, reflecting its broad relevance across disciplines. Despite this importance, no consensus exists CT's definition or assessment, resulting in varied approaches [1]. Tang et al. [3] identify four main assessment types: selected-response tests, portfolio assessments, surveys or self-reports, and interviews. Instruments like the Computational Thinking test (CTt) [4] target specific CT components (e.g., sequences, loops), whereas others like the Computational Thinking Scales (CTS) [5] assess broader competencies including problem-solving, critical thinking, and creativity, but most assessment tools still overlook these broader competencies, but most assessment tools still overlook these broader competencies. There remains a clear need for more comprehensive and accessible classroom-suitable assessment tools.

Creativity is the ability to produce ideas that are both novel and valuable [17], important for innovation and complex problem-solving. It is often described as a process involving two phases: divergent thinking, which involves generating many diverse ideas (fluency, flexibility, originality), and convergent thinking, the critical evaluation and selection of the most promising idea [6, 7]. Convergent thinking can involve insight, a process of restructuring to overcome mental impasses. Despite this framework, many assessments often focus only on divergent thinking. Creativity correlates with cognitive abilities such as executive functions, fluid and crystallized intelligence [8–10], linking creativity to problem-solving and suggesting shared cognitive foundations with CT [11]. Debate persists on whether creativity is domain-general or domain-specific [12], with growing evidence for domain-specificity, making CT a relevant context for its study (Fig. 1).

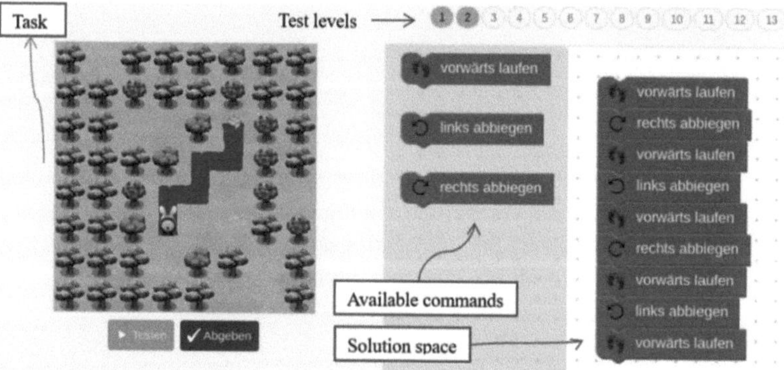

Fig. 1. Screenshot of the CCCT interface. The available commands for this item are *move forward* (feet graphic), *turn left* (left arrow graphic), and *turn right* (right arrow graphic).

At this intersection lies computational creativity (CC), defined as creative processes that support algorithmic problem-solving, artifact creation, and knowledge generation within computational contexts [13]. Both CT [1] and creativity [14] emphasize effective, novel problem-solving, reinforcing this conceptual link. However, empirical research on CC is scarce and existing studies often assess only narrow facets, particularly divergent thinking (e.g., originality) [15, 16]. Therefore, more comprehensive tools are needed to capture the multidimensional relationship between creativity and CT in domain-specific contexts.

1.2 Aim of the Study

This study presents the development of a gamified, domain-specific creativity assessment tailored to the CT context, designed to measure both phases (divergent and convergent thinking) and multiple facets of divergent thinking (fluency, flexibility, and originality) of creativity. The aim is to provide first insights into the pilot of the Computational Creativity and Computational Thinking test (CCCT), examine its feasibility and investigate the relationship between CT and creativity in young learners.

2 Method

All data, analysis codes, methodological and design details, and other research materials are available at the OSF repository of the project: https://osf.io/zebfw/. The study was not preregistered. Ethical approval was obtained from the Faculty of Economics and Social Sciences Ethics Committee, at the University of Tübingen.

2.1 Participants and Procedure

The study was conducted with children from grades 1 to 4 across eight classes of a single elementary school in Germany. After obtaining informed consent from students and their legal guardians, a total of 136 children participated in the study. Due to incomplete data from the CCCT assessment, 11 children were excluded from the analysis. The final sample consisted of $n = 63$ first- and second-grade students ($M_{age} = 7.0$ years, $SD_{age} = 1.0$), 44.4% of whom were girls, and $n = 62$ third- and fourth-grade students ($M_{age} = 9.04$ years, $SD_{age} = 0.79$), with 45.6% girls. Data collection was conducted in a group setting within regular classroom environments. The CCCT assessment was administered digitally on tablets. The assessment took 40 min and was administered by trained university student assistants.

2.2 Instrument Design, Development and Scoring

The CCCT was conceptually modelled after the research-proven Kodetu.org platform [13, 15, 16] and adapted from the Google's Blockly open-source code to create a gamified, developmentally appropriate tool for assessing CC while addressing constraints such as language and proprietary issues. Two age-specific versions were developed for first-second graders and third-fourth graders, with task completion indicated by brief character animations (technical details available on the OSF repository of the project). Items were reviewed in two rounds by six experts in computer science education, didactics, psychology, developmental psychology, and creativity research, providing face and content validation.

The CCCT comprises 13 levels across five modules, each assessing different aspects of CT and CC, by requiring participants to construct block-based code guiding a character through a maze to a predefined goal. Module 0 (Training, Levels 1–4) introduces the interface and basic CT concepts with guided solutions. Module 1 (CT Assessment, Levels 5–6) evaluates basic CT skills independently. Module 2 (Divergent Thinking – CC-D, Levels 7–11) encourages multiple solutions per task to assess fluency, flexibility, and originality. Module 3 (Convergent Thinking – CC-C, Level 12) measures participants' ability to select the most efficient solution from their previous attempts. Module 4 (Creative Insight – CC-I, Level 13) assesses insight-based problem-solving by requiring creative navigation of maze constraints. Full module descriptions, levels, and screenshots are available on the OSF repository of the project.

Modules 1 and 4 were scored dichotomously (1 point for each correct solutions, 0 otherwise), while Modules 2 and 3 required manual scoring. In Module 2, participants were encouraged to submit multiple correct solutions, allowing assessment of divergent thinking across fluency, flexibility, and originality [13, 14]. Fluency was measured as the number of unique solutions (max. 5 points), flexibility as the range of conceptual categories covered—defined by task direction, command type, and path complexity— and originality as the inverse frequency of each solution among participants, averaged across submissions [13]. Elaboration was not scored due to testing constraints [16]. In Module 3, convergent thinking was assessed by having participants select the most efficient solution among their previous submissions (1 point if optimal, 0 otherwise) [7]. Additional information on scoring procedures is available on the OSF repository.

3 Results

Table 1 presents descriptive statistics for the CCCT across the two age groups. As expected, older children scored higher across most indicators, while convergent thinking and creative insight scores (CC-C/I) were comparably low in both groups.

Table 1. Descriptives of CCCT variables.

Mod.	Indicators	Grades 1 and 2			Grades 3 and 4		
		M (SD)	Range	n	M (SD)	Range	n
1	CT	0.79 (0.77)	0–2	63	1.60 (0.61)	0–2	62
2	CC-D-Fluency	1.43 (1.46)	0–5	63	3.85 (1.21)	0–5	62
2	CC-D-Flexibility	1.30 (1.27)	0–5	63	2.94 (0.97)	0–5	62
2	CC-D-Originality	64.14 (16.34)	50.00–99.22	63	75.01 (11.67)	50.00–98.96	62
3	CC-C	0.33 (0.47)	0–1	55	0.35 (0.48)	0–1	62
4	CC-I	0.21 (0.41)	0–1	58	0.62 (0.49)	0–1	60

Note. Sample sizes (*n*) vary due to missing data in later modules. Originality = 100 – % of participants with the same correct solution; higher values indicate greater originality.

Table 2 presents the correlations between CT and all other creativity indicators and gender, grouped by age. Overall, divergent thinking components were closely linked to CT skills, whereas convergent thinking and insight-based problem-solving appear more distinct and less integrated with other constructs.

The CCCT demonstrated strong feasibility in a classroom setting. The application was technically stable, and qualitative observations confirmed that the gamified interface was engaging and usable for this age group. High completion rates for the younger (92.1%) and older (96.8%) groups further support its suitability as an assessment tool.

Table 2. Correlations between CT and Creativity Indicators by age group.

Indicators	1.	2.	3.	4.	5.	6.	7.
1. CT		.53**	.58**	.32*	.33*	.49**	−.14
2. CC-D-Fluency	.67**		.96**	.42**	.13	.16	−.09
3. CC-D-Flexibility	.59**	.80**		.42**	.19	.18	−.11
4. CC-D-Originality	.26*	.28*	.46**		.34**	.08	0.02
5. CC-C	.08	.06	.08	.01		.07	−.12
6. CC-I	.36*	.43*	.29*	.05	.10		−.10
7. Gender	−.12	−.37*	−.20	.01	.10	.00	

Note. Gender: 0 for male and 1 for female. Above diagonal: grades 1–2; Below diagonal: grades 3–4.

4 Discussion

This study introduced the CCCT, a gamified digital assessment of CT and domain-specific creativity in primary school children, providing initial evidence of feasibility and insights into CC in young learners. A key finding is the strong correlation between CT skills and all facets of divergent thinking measured, indicating CT as a scaffold for creative exploration and aligning with theories on domain-specific knowledge [12, 17]. The high correlation between fluency and flexibility, however, questions their distinction for novices. In contrast, the link between CT and convergent thinking was notably weaker, suggesting that generating and evaluating creative solutions represent separable skills, with the latter reflecting a distinct metacognitive process. Creative insight also correlated with CT, showing stronger links to divergent thinking in older children, positioning it as a measure of problem-solving that combines systematic thinking with cognitive flexibility.

Gender differences were minimal, limited to higher fluency scores in older boys, possibly reflecting the gamified design's ability to engage all participants equally and reduce stereotype effects in computer science education. The strong link between CT and creativity highlights the potential value of open-ended CT activities that foster exploration rather than single-solution outcomes. The CCCT could be adapted as both a formative and diagnostic tool, capturing process data and illustrating that creative solutions are possible within constrained rulesets, helping children view computer-based systems as spaces for innovation.

Limitations include the single-school sample and the focus on internal structure without external validation. Future studies should replicate findings with broader samples and validate CCCT against established measures of creativity and achievement. Taken together, the CCCT offers a novel, open-access tool for assessing creativity within CT, revealing the synergy between CT and divergent thinking, the multidimensionality of CC, and the relevance of foundational CT skills for digital problem-solving.

References

1. Shute, V.J., Sun, C., Asbell-Clarke, J.: Demystifying computational thinking. Educ. Res. Rev. **22**, 142–158 (2017). https://doi.org/10.1016/j.edurev.2017.09.003
2. Barr, V., Stephenson, C.: Bringing computational thinking to K–12. ACM Inroads 2(1), 48–54 (201). https://doi.org/10.1145/1929887.1929905
3. Tang, X., Yin, Y., Lin, Q., Hadad, R., Zhai, X.: Assessing computational thinking: a systematic review of empirical studies. Comput. Educ. **148**, 103798 (2020). https://doi.org/10.1016/j.compedu.2019.103798
4. Román-González, M., Pérez-González, J.C., Jiménez-Fernández, C.: Which cognitive abilities underlie computational thinking? Criterion validity of the computational thinking test. Comput. Hum. Behav. **72**, 678–691 (2017). https://doi.org/10.1016/j.chb.2016.08.047
5. Korkmaz, Ö., Çakir, R., Özden, M.Y.: A validity and reliability study of the computational thinking scales (CTS). Comput. Hum. Behav. **72**, 558–569 (2017). https://doi.org/10.1016/j.chb.2017.01.005
6. Guilford, J.P.: The Nature of Human Intelligence. McGraw-Hill, New York (1967)
7. Cropley, A.J.: In praise of convergent thinking. Creat. Res. J. **18**(3), 391–404 (2006). https://doi.org/10.1207/s15326934crj1803_13

8. Benedek, M., Neubauer, A.C.: Intelligence, creativity, and cognitive control: the common and differential roles of executive functions in intelligence and creativity. Intelligence **46**, 73–83 (2014). https://doi.org/10.1016/j.intell.2014.05.007

9. Batey, M., Chamorro-Premuzic, T., Furnham, A.: Intelligence and personality as predictors of divergent thinking: the role of general, fluid and crystallised intelligence. Think. Skills Creat. **4**(1), 60–69 (2009). https://doi.org/10.1016/j.tsc.2008.09.001

10. Nusbaum, E.C., Silvia, P.J.: Are intelligence and creativity really so different? Fluid intelligence, executive processes, and strategy use in divergent thinking. Intelligence **39**(1), 36–45 (2011). https://doi.org/10.1016/j.intell.2010.11.002

11. Wang, J., Yang, W., Yeung, M.K.: Cognitive foundations in the interplay between computational thinking and creativity: a scoping review. Think. Skills Creat. **56**, 101729 (2025). https://doi.org/10.1016/j.tsc.2024.101729

12. Baer, J.: The importance of domain-specific expertise in creativity. Roeper Rev. **37**(3), 165–178 (2015). https://doi.org/10.1080/02783193.2015.1047480

13. Hershkovitz, A., Sitman, R., Israel-Fishelson, R., Eguíluz, A., Garaizar, P., Guenaga, M.: Creativity in the acquisition of computational thinking. Interact. Learn. Environ. **27**(5–6), 628–644 (2019). https://doi.org/10.1080/10494820.2019.1610451

14. Runco, M.A., Jaeger, G.J.: The standard definition of creativity. Creat. Res. J. **24**(1), 92–96 (2012). https://doi.org/10.1080/10400419.2012.650092

15. Israel-Fishelson, R., Hershkovitz, A., Eguíluz, A., Garaizar, P., Guenaga, M.: A log-based analysis of the associations between creativity and computational thinking. J. Educ. Comput. Res. **59**(5), 926–959 (2021). https://doi.org/10.1177/0735633120973429

16. Israel-Fishelson, R., Hershkovitz, A., Eguíluz, A., Garaizar, P., Guenaga, M.: The associations between computational thinking and creativity: the role of personal characteristics. J. Educ. Comput. Res. **58**(8), 1415–1447 (2021). https://doi.org/10.1177/0735633120940954

17. Eguiluz, A., Guenaga, M., Garaizar, P., Olivares-Rodriguez, C.: Exploring the progression of early programmers in a set of computational thinking challenges via clickstream analysis. IEEE Trans. Emerg. Top. Comput. **8**(1), 256–261 (2020). https://doi.org/10.1109/TETC.2017.2768550

When Does Gamification Help? Exploring Item-Level Effects on Physics Misconceptions

Katharina Richter$^{(\boxtimes)}$ ⓘ and Michael D. Kickmeier-Rust ⓘ

St.Gallen University of Teacher Education, St.Gallen, Switzerland
`{katharina.richter,michael.kickmeier}@phsg.ch`

Abstract. Misconceptions in physics are persistent and resistant to conventional instruction. This study investigated whether a gamified digital environment facilitates conceptual change compared to a structurally equivalent non-gamified version. Ninety-four secondary school students (Mage = 13.5) completed pre- and post-tests while engaging with eight levels, each targeting a common physics misconception. No overall learning gains were observed. Item-level analyses, however, revealed heterogeneous effects: some misconceptions appeared more responsive to gamified features, particularly when perceptually grounded, whereas others benefited more from the non-gamified format. Correlational trends suggested potential interactions between task complexity and instructional design, though estimates were imprecise due to the small item pool. The findings indicate that gamification is not inherently beneficial, but contingent on the alignment of game mechanics with the epistemic structure of specific misconceptions.

Keywords: game-based- learning · conceptual change · gamification · physics misconceptions

1 Introduction

Misconceptions in physics are persistent and often resistant to conventional instruction. Students frequently enter classrooms with scientifically inaccurate yet coherent beliefs, such as that continuous force is needed to sustain motion or that heavier objects fall faster than lighter ones [1–3]. These are not mere gaps in knowledge but alternative conceptual frameworks requiring active restructuring for meaningful learning [4, 5].

Game-based learning environments (GBLEs) may support this process by combining motivational features with cognitively demanding tasks [6, 7]. They can model dynamic systems, visualize invisible forces, and trigger conceptual conflict through immediate feedback [8, 9]. Yet it remains unclear which types of misconceptions are most responsive to gamified interventions and how specific design elements shape learning.

This study addresses that gap by contrasting gamified and non-gamified versions of the same digital environment, each targeting eight common misconceptions in domains such as projectile motion, gravity, and magnetism. Beyond overall outcomes, we analyze item-level sensitivity to identify conditions under which gamification fosters—or hinders—conceptual change, thereby contributing a nuanced perspective on the alignment between game mechanics and cognitive demands.

S. Bakkes et al. (Eds.): GALA 2025, LNCS 16307, pp. 498–503, 2026.
https://doi.org/10.1007/978-3-032-11043-5_56

2 Theoretical Framework

2.1 Persistent Misconceptions in Physics Learning

Recent literature supports the claim that gamified learning environments (GLEs) can foster conceptual understanding in physics education by enhancing student engagement and promoting active exploration. For instance, [10] provide evidence that interactive and feedback-rich learning contexts improve learners' engagement and inquiry behavior—key precursors to conceptual change. While studies such as [11] suggest that digital interventions may support the correction of misconceptions, empirical demonstrations of large-scale conceptual shifts remain limited. Notably, misconceptions grounded in everyday intuitions appear especially resistant, requiring carefully scaffolded instructional design. Emerging research highlights the role of visual feedback and cognitive conflict as mediating mechanisms in successful gamified interventions [12].

2.2 Conceptual Change Through Gamified Learning

Gamification in STEM, particularly physics, is considered a promising means of fostering conceptual change. Gamified learning environments (GLEs) can enhance engagement, encourage active knowledge construction, and support the revision of misconceptions through cognitive conflict and feedback [13, 14]. A meta-analysis showed that gamification improves both motivation and learning outcomes, especially when elements are aligned with instructional goals and deliver sustained feedback [13]. GLEs can further trigger productive dissonance by confronting learners with intuitive but incorrect ideas, thereby fostering refinement of prior conceptions [14]. Such effects depend on learners' ability to interpret and act on feedback, which is shaped by autonomy and perceived competence [15]. Longitudinal findings indicate that repeated engagement with feedback-rich environments strengthens both immediate comprehension and long-term retention [14]. Taken together, gamified approaches appear most effective when feedback, cognitive challenge, and motivational support are meaningfully integrated.

2.3 Cognitive Alignment and Instructional Fit

The instructional effectiveness of gamified learning environments depends on aligning game mechanics with cognitive demands. Cognitive Load Theory stresses that learning improves when extraneous load is minimized [16]. Well-integrated gamification can achieve this by structuring challenges, clarifying goals, and offering adaptive feedback [17]. From an embodied cognition perspective, simulations with dynamic visualizations and manipulable representations make abstract concepts (e.g., force, motion, magnetism) perceptually accessible and support revision when paired with feedback [18, 19]. However, surface elements such as points or leaderboards may distract from conceptual processing if poorly integrated [13]. Thus, mechanics should amplify rather than dilute the epistemic core of the content.

3 Method

3.1 Participants and Recruitment

170 Swiss secondary students (ages 11–16) from nine school classes were recruited. Participation was organized by class to standardize administration; each class received 300 CHF compensation. 94 students completed both pre- and post-tests and all eight game levels and were included in the analysis (Mage = 13.48, SD = 1.01; 52 female, 39 male, 3 diverse/unspecified). Participants were randomly assigned to either the gamified (n = 49) or standard (n = 45) condition (Fig. 1).

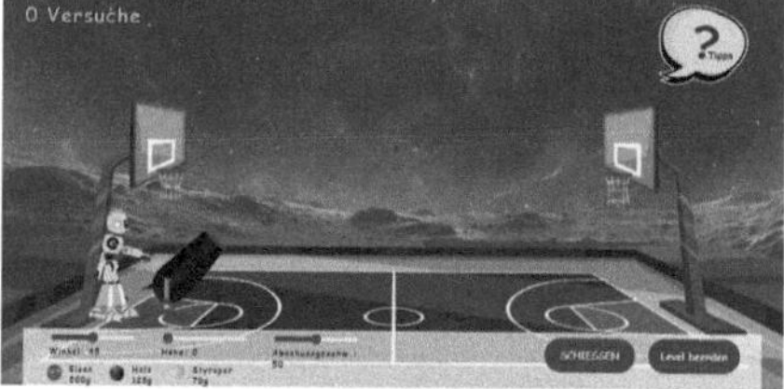

Fig. 1. Physics learning game 'Basketball Challenge'. The left image shows level 5 (moon) in the gamified version, the right image shows the standard version.

3.2 Research Design and Hypotheses

We employed a 2 (Group: gamified vs. standard) × 2 (Time: pre vs. post) mixed design with random assignment at the individual level. The intervention comprised a pre-test, gameplay across eight levels, and a post-test. Both conditions used identical tasks; only the gamified version added points, animations, and progression cues.

The study examined whether gamification leads to stronger learning gains, whether different misconceptions vary in susceptibility to change, and how specific mechanics (e.g., visual feedback, task complexity) interact with outcomes. We hypothesized (*H1*) greater overall gains for gamified instruction, (*H2*) lower susceptibility for intuitively grounded misconceptions (e.g., "heavier means faster"), and (*H3*) stronger effects when mechanics align with the conceptual structure of the targeted principle.

3.3 Intervention and Measures

The *Basketball Physics Challenge* comprised eight levels: Levels 1–4 focused on procedural aspects of projectile motion (e.g., angle, height, position), while Levels 5–8 targeted conceptual misconceptions such as impetus, mass–weight confusions, lunar gravity, magnetism, and fluid resistance. The gamified version included UI elements like points and animations, whereas the standard version presented the same tasks without them. Conceptual understanding was measured with an 8-item multiple-choice quiz administered before and after the intervention. Each item corresponded to one level and misconception, was reviewed by a physics education expert, and scored dichotomously (0/1; max = 8). Internal consistency was moderate (α = .61). Item-level learning gains were defined as Δ = Post – Pre. Only participants with complete data were included.

4   Results

Across all participants (N = 94), the mean pre-test score was 5.13 (SD = 1.93), while the post-test average was slightly lower at 4.98 (SD = 2.00). A paired-sample t-test indicated that this difference was not statistically significant, $t(93) = 0.86$, $p = .39$, suggesting no overall learning gain across the sample (Fig. 2).

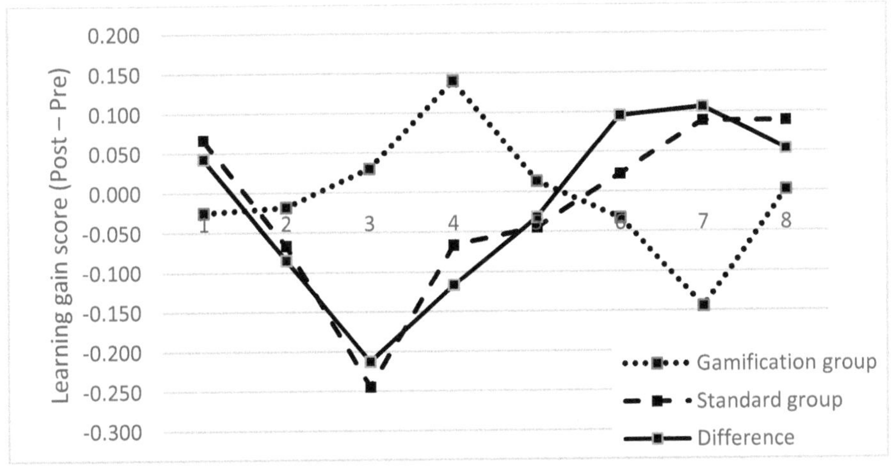

Fig. 2. Item-wise learning gains (Post–Pre) for gamified and standard conditions.

Group-wise analyses revealed a slight decrease in mean scores in both conditions. In the gamified group (n = 49), scores declined from $M = 5.04$ (SD = 1.87) to $M = 4.90$ (SD = 2.00), while the standard group (n = 45) dropped from $M = 5.22$ (SD = 2.02) to $M = 5.07$ (SD = 2.02). Neither change reached statistical significance. A 2 (Group) × 2 (Time) mixed ANOVA confirmed these results: no main effect of Time, $F(1,92) = 0.24$, $p = .62$; no main effect of Group, $F(1,92) = 0.47$, $p = .49$; and no interaction effect, $F(1,92) = 0.21$, $p = .65$. While neither group showed a statistically significant gain in overall performance, a more fine-grained, item-level analysis reveals heterogeneous learning effects that vary by question content and instructional format. In the gamified condition, Level 4 exhibited the most pronounced gain (+0.14), suggesting that visual or interactive scaffolds may have supported conceptual integration in this domain. In contrast, the standard condition showed a notable decline in Level 3 (-0.244), which may indicate that abstract or counterintuitive content posed challenges without additional game-based support. These findings point toward a differentiated effect of instructional design based on content complexity and conceptual structure.

4.1   Relationship Between Cognitive Level and Learning Gain

To examine whether learning gains varied with conceptual complexity, Pearson correlations were calculated between item level (1–8) and mean gain scores (Δ = Post – Pre).

Across all items, a significant positive correlation emerged ($r = .74, p < .05$), suggesting that more complex tasks were associated with greater gains. Separate analyses by condition revealed divergent patterns: in the standard group, a strong positive correlation was found ($r = .85, p < .01$), whereas the gamified group showed a small negative, non-significant trend ($r = -.26, p > .50$). Confidence intervals were wide (e.g., gamified: $-.80$ to $.51$; standard: $-.34$ to $.97$), reflecting the limited precision of these estimates with only eight items and underscoring their exploratory nature.

A regression model on the item-level dataset ($N = 752$) confirmed that task complexity predicted gains overall ($B = 0.039, p = .017$), but the interaction with instructional format was not significant ($B = 0.013, p = .588$). Thus, while more complex tasks tended to elicit higher gains, this effect was not moderated by gamification.

5 Discussion and Conclusion

The intervention did not yield significant group-level learning gains. Nonetheless, exploratory item-level analyses revealed heterogeneous response patterns, with some misconceptions more sensitive to instructional format than others. Items embedded in perceptually salient contexts—such as lunar gravity or underwater dynamics—tended to show stronger gains in the gamified condition, whereas abstract concepts lacking perceptual anchors improved more in the standard format. This suggests that visual affordances and embodied simulations can scaffold conceptual change, but only when feedback is interpretable and triggers cognitive conflict.

A positive correlation between task complexity and learning gain appeared only in the standard version, possibly because reduced visual load preserved attentional resources for analytical processing. In the gamified group, motivational elements may have introduced extraneous load [16]. These findings highlight that gamification is not inherently beneficial; its value depends on aligning mechanics with the epistemic demands of the targeted concept. Several limitations constrain these conclusions. The short intervention and the small 8-item test ($\alpha = .61$) limit statistical power and make item-level effects exploratory. Gamification was implemented as a bundled UI package (points, animations, progression cues), which prevents identification of active components and contrasts with mechanic-driven design. In addition, no process data (e.g., logs, eye tracking) were analyzed, restricting insights into learner strategies.

Despite these constraints, the study offers initial evidence that the effectiveness of gamification depends on the epistemic nature of the concept addressed. Perceptually grounded misconceptions may profit from dynamic feedback and simulation, whereas theory-laden concepts require cognitive clarity and minimal interference. Future research should isolate specific mechanics and employ richer measurements to clarify when and how gamification can best support conceptual change in STEM education.

References

1. McCloskey, M.: Naïve theories of motion. In: Gentner, D., Stevens, A.L. (eds.) Mental Models, pp. 299–324. Lawrence Erlbaum, Hillsdale (1983)

2. Halloun, I.A., Hestenes, D.: The initial knowledge state of college physics students. Am. J. Phys. **53**(11), 1043–1055 (1985)
3. diSessa, A.A.: Toward an epistemology of physics. Cogn. Instr. **10**(2–3), 105–225 (1993)
4. Vosniadou, S.: Capturing and modeling the process of conceptual change. Learn. Instr. **4**(1), 45–69 (1994)
5. Chi, M.T.H.: Commonsense conceptions of emergent processes: why some misconceptions are robust. J. Learn. Sci. **14**(2), 161–199 (2005)
6. Wouters, P., van Nimwegen, C., van Oostendorp, H., van der Spek, E.D.: A meta-analysis of the cognitive and motivational effects of serious games. J. Educ. Psychol. **105**(2), 249–265 (2013)
7. Hamari, J., Koivisto, J., Sarsa, H.: Does gamification work? A literature review of empirical studies on gamification. In: 47th Hawaii International Conference on System Sciences (HICSS), Waikoloa, pp. 3025–3034. IEEE (2014)
8. Mayer, R.E.: Thirty years of research on online learning. Appl. Cogn. Psychol. **33**(2), 152–159 (2019)
9. Plass, J.L., Homer, B.D., Kinzer, C.K.: Foundations of game-based learning. Educ. Psychol. **50**(4), 258–283 (2015)
10. Schwichow, M., Osterhaus, C., Edelsbrunner, P.A.: The relation between the control-of-variables strategy and content knowledge in physics in secondary school. Contemp. Educ. Psychol. **63**, 101923 (2020)
11. Uden, L., et al.: Integrated STEM project-based learning for physics from neuroscience perspectives. Front. Psychol. **14**, 1136246 (2023)
12. Korlat, S., et al.: Phylab – a VR laboratory for experiments in physics: intervention effectiveness and gender differences. Front. Psychol. **15**, 1284597 (2024)
13. Sailer, M., Homner, L.: The gamification of learning: a meta-analysis. Educ. Psychol. Rev. **32**(1), 77–112 (2019)
14. Thacker, I., Sinatra, G.M.: Supporting climate change understanding with data, estimation, and epistemic prompts. J. Educ. Psychol. **114**(5), 910–927 (2022)
15. De Graaf, J.: Inquiry-based learning and conceptual change in balance beam understanding. Front. Psychol. **11**, 1621 (2020)
16. Sweller, J., Ayres, P., Kalyuga, S.: Cognitive Load Theory. Springer, New York (2011). https://doi.org/10.1007/978-1-4419-8126-4
17. Wang, Z., et al.: How to make computer-based feedback more productive: the power of erroneous solutions. J. Educ. Comput. Res. **62**(6), 1199–1219 (2024)
18. Wirth, J., et al.: An interactive layers model of self-regulated learning and cognitive load. Educ. Psychol. Rev. **32**(4), 1127–1149 (2020)
19. García Marquez, C., Bauer, K.N.: An extension of gamified learning theory: goal orientation as moderator. Simul. Gaming **52**(4), 407–434 (2020)

Fuelling Creativity with Brainrot as a Theme: Game Design Interdisciplinary Week

Bárbara Barroso[1]([⊠]) [iD], Inês Barbedo[2]([⊠]) [iD], Rita Costa[2] [iD],
and Cláudio Gonçalves[3] [iD]

[1] CEDRI, Bragança Polytechnic University, Bragança, Portugal
bbarroso@ipb.pt
[2] CITED, Bragança Polytechnic University, Bragança, Portugal
{inesb,rita.costa}@ipb.pt
[3] Bragança Polytechnic University, Bragança, Portugal

Abstract. This paper explores how the culturally saturated and generationally marked theme of *brainrot* was interpreted, developed, and expressed by students during the 13th edition of the Interdisciplinary Week in a Game Design undergraduate program. Drawing on project documentation, facilitator observations, and selected student outputs, the study investigates how this theme, rooted in digital overstimulation and meme culture, functioned as both constraint and provocation within a five-day, project-based learning format. Through a qualitative case study approach, we examine how students mobilized interdisciplinary competencies in design, programming, and visual arts to produce aesthetic, narrative, and ludic responses. The theme prompted diverse emotional and generational reactions, often requiring teams to navigate irony, critique, and discomfort. We argue that culturally dense and ambiguous concepts like *brainrot*, when framed critically, can serve as powerful catalysts for reflective storytelling, collaborative negotiation, and media literacy. The findings reinforce the pedagogical value of integrating emotionally charged themes into game design education to foster creative experimentation and interdisciplinary dialogue.

Keywords: Game Design · Interdisciplinary Learning · Brainrot · Digital Culture · Collaborative Creativity

1 Introduction

In recent years, game design education has increasingly embraced interdisciplinary and project-based learning approaches to respond to the evolving demands of creative industries. The Interdisciplinary Week (IW) at the Game Design bachelor's program of Bragança Polytechnic University, now in its 13th edition, offers a unique curricular space where students from different academic years collaborate to address a theme through the lenses of game design, computer science, and visual arts [2]. Over the years, themes such as Post-Humanism, Doppelgänger, and Futures have served as conceptual anchors to stimulate ideation, critical analysis, and creative production. In April 2025, IW adopted

S. Bakkes et al. (Eds.): GALA 2025, LNCS 16307, pp. 504–514, 2026.
https://doi.org/10.1007/978-3-032-11043-5_57

brainrot as its theme, a meme-culture term describing cognitive overload and cultural decay, encapsulating critical issues of digital life. Framed as both a cultural diagnosis and a creative resource, the theme invited student exploration through visual glitch, narrative absurdity, and aesthetic repetition. Drawing on selected cognitive and socio-cultural perspectives (e.g., Baudrillard [3], Han [8], and Sweller [17, 18]), *brainrot* was presented as both a symptom of the digital age and a tool for critical, interdisciplinary creation. We report an exploratory pedagogical case study that analyses how *brainrot* was received, interpreted, and expressed by students during IW. Using project documentation, coordination notes, and selected outputs, we examine the pedagogical affordances of a culturally saturated, generationally marked theme in game design education, arguing that – when critically framed – it can catalyse reflective storytelling, aesthetic experimentation, and cognitive awareness for meaningful design.

2   Theoretical Background

Game creation demands the integration of diverse knowledge areas – from programming logic to narrative design, from visual semiotics to player psychology. Educational models such as IW exemplify this approach by assigning unstructured and complex challenges that must be approached collaboratively across the fields of visual arts, computer science, and game design. Perspectives on interdisciplinary learning emphasize the capacity to synthesize multiple forms of knowledge and methodologies [17], to develop both analytical and creative skills in response to real-world or speculative problems [4], and to foster transversal competencies such as teamwork, self-management, and communication [2]. This context also aligns with game design-based learning, where learning emerges through the act of designing games. Recent studies highlight its potential to enhance digital competence [14], creativity [5], social perspective-taking [20], and computational thinking [6, 21]. Such skills are increasingly vital for both creative industries and the broader context of digital innovation. Within IW, a project-based learning framework [13] requires students to iteratively define, develop, and present a prototype in just five days, emphasizing collaboration under time constraints.

In 2025, the semester theme was *brainrot*. Originating in meme culture, the term refers to cognitive overload and cultural decline associated with excessive media consumption. At first glance, it signals a reduction in intellectual engagement driven by the algorithmic repetition of memes and short-form videos, yet it also reflects generational identity, affective alienation, and socio-technological critique. Cognitive Load Theory explains how constant stimuli can undermine deep learning [18, 19], while recent neuropsychological studies demonstrate how overstimulation affects memory, attention, and emotion regulation [7]. Research on digital addiction further underscores the risks of continuous exposure, linking overuse of digital media to psychosocial, emotional, and cognitive disruption [9, 11, 16]. From a sociocultural standpoint, *brainrot* resonates with Baudrillard's concept of simulacra, in which signs become untethered from their referents [3]; with Han's critique of hyperperformance under neoliberalism, which produces exhaustion and loss of relationality [6]; and with Nietzsche's reflections on nihilism as the erosion of shared values [15]. These perspectives situate *brainrot* not only as a symptom of overstimulation but also as a critical lens for interrogating digital culture. Rather than treating the theme as decline alone, IW framed *brainrot* as a cultural mirror. Students were invited to interrogate the platforms they use daily not only as consumers but as critics and creators. In this way, *brainrot* became both critique and playground, enabling projects that translated lived media experience into irony, absurdism, and experimental design.

3   Methodology

This study adopts a qualitative case study approach to examine how the theme *brainrot* was implemented and interpreted during the 13th IW in the Game Design degree at Bragança Polytechnic University. The methodology is framed within an educational design research perspective, focusing on reflective practice, situated learning, and cultural interpretation within a project-based learning environment.

3.1   Context and Participants

IW is a structured educational intervention embedded within the undergraduate curriculum of Game Design. The 13th IW took place from April 7–11, 2025, involving all students enrolled in the program. Participants were organized into inter-year teams (4–6 students each), ensuring diversity of experience and skill levels across the three core disciplinary areas of the program: game design, computer science, and visual arts [2]. A total of 94 students participated, distributed across 20 interdisciplinary teams. Faculty members from each area were involved as facilitators providing structured feedback throughout the week.

The week followed a five-day project-based learning cycle, with defined daily goals and deliverables:

- *Day 1 – Ideation and Problem Definition:* Teams brainstormed within the theme *brainrot*, generating guiding questions and framing conceptual or gameplay challenges.
- *Day 2 – Executive Summary and Draft Proposal:* Teams submitted a one-page outline of their planned solution (e.g., game concept, interactive prototype, artistic experiment).
- *Day 3 – Prototype Development:* Low-fidelity digital or analogue prototypes were created, with emphasis on core mechanics and thematic coherence.
- *Day 4 – Refinement and Poster Creation:* Visual identity and communication materials were produced; feedback loops were reinforced.
- *Day 5 – Final Pitch and Collective Evaluation:* Teams delivered pitches in a demo fair setting and engaged in peer review through structured feedback forms and open voting.

The theme *brainrot* was introduced during the opening session, accompanied by a theoretical and historical framing referencing meme culture, cognitive overload, aesthetic excess, and philosophical commentary. Students received visual and textual prompts and were encouraged to explore the theme through satire, irony, glitch aesthetics, or critique of overstimulation. These suggested approaches were not prescriptive or closed off—students were free to interpret and expand upon them, drawing from their own media experiences, aesthetic references, or conceptual frameworks to develop original and personally resonant responses.

3.2 Data Collection, Data Analysis and Ethical Considerations

The data corpus includes: Reflective documents (group summaries, logs, self-assessments, peer reviews); Digital artifacts (posters, screenshots, project descriptions, prototypes); Facilitator observations collected throughout the week (field notes, oral feedback, Discord exchanges); Pitch documentation and voting feedback. In addition, insights from the opening session presentation were incorporated to contextualize student interpretations of the theme. Data were analyzed using a combination of thematic content analysis and interpretive synthesis. The research team (comprising faculty coordinators) reviewed all documentation, grouped artifacts into categories based on the forms of engagement with the theme (aesthetic exaggeration, media critique, absurdist gameplay, etc.), and identified emergent patterns. Analytical focus areas included: a) How the theme influenced project ideation and tone; b) The relationship between thematic interpretation and interdisciplinary collaboration; c) The extent to which students used irony, excess, or subversion as design strategies; d) Reflections on creativity, attention, and overstimulation within digital culture. All analyzed student work was produced within the scope of the Game Design degree program and evaluated as part of regular coursework. Participants were informed of the research purposes and provided consent for the anonymous use of their outputs and reflections. No identifying personal data is disclosed in this paper.

4 Brainrot in Practice: Creative Engagement During the Interdisciplinary Week

The 13th IW invited students to reflect critically on their own digital culture by confronting *brainrot* as both constraint and provocation. Rather than treating it as a superficial joke or derogatory label, students transformed the concept into creative design direction, aesthetic language, and narrative metaphor. Their projects spanned narrative games, visual experiments, and interactive prototypes, collectively showing how *brainrot* became a fertile space for exploration. Three broad interpretive axes emerged. **Cultural Satire and Irony**: some groups parodied algorithmic content, meme formats, or influencer culture, often through chaotic interfaces or exaggerated tropes. **Aesthetic Excess and Glitch**: others leaned into overload, drawing on glitch art, vaporwave, and dada to experiment with fragmentation, broken navigation, and layered noise. **Cognitive and Emotional Metaphors**: a third set used *brainrot* as metaphor for burnout, attention fragmentation, or derealization, often through surreal or minimalist experiences. These responses were not mutually exclusive; many projects combined elements of all three, demonstrating nuanced reflection and playful experimentation.

4.1 Representative Projects

Five representative projects were selected – *The Epic Experience of Being Human, W.G.O.T.Y. (Worst Games of the Year), Brain Beasties, Let it Rot,* and *Delirium Mentis* – based on the diversity of their core concepts, the variety of primary media employed, and the results as recognized through peer evaluation. These projects were analyzed according to the set of parameters described in Table 1.

Table 1. Set of analytical parameters applied to each student project developed during 13th IW.

Parameter	Description
Project Title	Title
Format	Game, narrative experience, visual piece, card game, prototype, etc.
Primary Medium	Digital (2D/3D), analogue (cards/board), audiovisual, hybrid
Disciplinary Contribution	Specific roles of design, programming, and visual arts within the project
Core Concept	Brief description of the project's central idea or metaphor
Interpretative Axis	One or more of: satire/irony, aesthetic excess/glitch, cognitive metaphor
Thematic Relevance	How directly and reflectively the project engages with *brainrot*
Narrative Style	Fragmented, absurdist, introspective, humorous, critical, etc.
Aesthetic Strategy	Use of glitch, noise, visual overload, meme formats, minimalist contrast
Gameplay or Interaction	Key mechanics, interactions, or rule structures (if applicable)
Notable Features	Any particularly innovative or surprising elements

Individually, these projects mobilize distinct artistic, technological, and ludic strategies to reflect on the cultural condition of *brainrot*. Rather than uniform critiques, they offer divergent modalities of interaction – recursive self-chase, disorientation-as-gameplay, digital intimacy, or empty repetition. This diversity highlights both the multiplicity of the phenomenon and the potential of digital and analogue games as critical, affectively complex media. To analyze these strategies, we draw on the MDA framework (Mechanics, Dynamics, Aesthetics) [10], which distinguishes formal components (mechanics), interactive behaviors (dynamics), and the responses they evoke (aesthetics). This lens helps unpack how meaning emerges from play, especially in games that aim to provoke reflection or discomfort as much as entertainment. Humor, irony, and tension operate not only to amuse but to disrupt passive consumption. Finally, interdisciplinary innovations – from 3D asset production to AR integration and analogue surrealism – demonstrate awareness of both technological possibility and conceptual depth. Together, these projects converge experimental game design with critical media theory, showcasing the potential of games as reflective and subversive mediums.

The Epic Experience of Being Human places the player in a recursive loop where they design an avatar only to be pursued by it, transforming the typically empowering act of creation into entrapment. This mechanic literalizes digital self-destruction and auto-surveillance, turning agency into pathology. The claustrophobic, glitched aesthetic mirrors the density of online stimuli, while the arcade loop reinforces compulsive inter-action as both challenge and critique. Humor, inflected with "cringe," provides no real relief; instead, it functions as structural irony, disarming the player while exposing the absurdity of desensitization. The project thus succeeds in converting aesthetic excess and recursive design into a metaphor for overexposure and self-recognition.

W.G.O.T.Y. (Worst Games of the Year) employs parodic pastiche to critique the logic of gamified spectacle. By appropriating the format of a reality-show contest, it simu-lates the commodification of humiliation and confusion, revealing how reward systems operate within sensory chaos. The mechanics – disruptive pop-ups, deliberately unsta-ble menus, and rapid feedback loops – generate dynamics of frustration, confusion, and fragmented attention. Aesthetically, low-resolution meme textures, garish color schemes, and constant interruptions transform the interface into an obstacle. The act of "clicking away" unwanted content mirrors the player's daily resistance to digital noise, making overload an aesthetic effect rather than just a theme. What stands out is the game's abil-ity to translate critical media theory into visceral engagement: meaning is not delivered through exposition but emerges through resistance, confusion, and failure, aligning ludic experience with the overstimulation it critiques.

Brain Beasties departs from screen-locked logic by integrating augmented reality, collapsing the barrier between digital detritus and physical presence. Mechanics such as scanning QR codes, capturing memes as virtual creatures, and performing daily care tasks recall *Pokémon Go* and *Tamagotchi*, yet their associations are deliberately distorted. These mechanics generate dynamics of repetition, attachment, and obligation, turning simple interactions into acts of emotional labor. Players sustain absurd digital entities, mimicking the rituals of engaging with superficial online content. The game implicates the player in a care economy without meaningful payoff, critiquing the performative intimacy fostered by digital platforms. Aesthetically, it emphasizes affect, ambiguity, and dissonance, drawing players into the emotional economies of digital waste and asking what it means to feel responsibility toward shallow or algorithmically engineered content. This shift from attention mechanics to affective metaphors makes *Brain Beasties* a compelling case of aesthetic critique through ludic immersion.

Let It Rot adopts the clicker genre's minimalist form to invert its conventions. Mechanics such as single-tap input, incremental decay, and constant micro-interactions simulate a futile care economy in which players sustain a digital plant through repetitive actions with no real reward. These mechanics generate dynamics of compulsive main-tenance, low-stakes urgency, and emotional detachment, keeping the player in a state of perpetual non-progress. The tension between the organic object of care (a plant) and the mechanical form of interaction (clicks) reinforces this critique. Aesthetically, the game embraces banality, entropy, and numbness: no escalation, flourish, or clear goals, only ambient erosion. Its stark minimalism and anti-reward loop resist gratification, offering intentional dissatisfaction. By stripping away excess, *Let It Rot* demonstrates how even minimal systems can reproduce the inertia underpinning overstimulated media environments.

Delirium Mentis is a team-based board game that uses surreal aesthetics and rotating mini-games to simulate the destabilizing effects of *brainrot*. Its mechanics – randomized rules, bizarre objectives, and distorted mini-games with conflicting instructions or ambiguous scoring – subvert the clarity typical of analogue games. These rules create dynamics of confusion, contradiction, and negotiation, as players adapt to shifting expectations. The interplay of collaboration and competition within unstable logic mirrors the fragmented attention and emotional swings of overstimulated digital media. Gameplay unfolds in cognitive imbalance, requiring players not only to act but to constantly reinterpret what the game demands. Aesthetically, it produces disorientation, absurdity, and low-level fatigue – a tactile enactment of digital overload. By reclaiming analogue space to stage digital anxieties, *Delirium Mentis* bridges the clarity of board games with the chaotic ethos of brainrot, transforming familiar mechanics into experiential critique (Table 2).

Table 2. Comparative Overview of Mechanics, Dynamics, and Aesthetics in the Selected Projects.

Project	Mechanics	Dynamics	Aesthetics
The Epic Experience of Being Human	Avatar creation and self-pursuit loop; glitched interface	Auto-surveillance, loss of agency, recursive tension	Irony, disorientation, self- reflection
W.G.O.T.Y. (Worst Games of the Year)	Pop-up interruptions; disorienting UI; parodic reward system	Frustration, resistance, confusion under sensory overload	Absurdity, satire, media critique
Brain Beasties	Meme capture via AR; care loops; digital creature maintenance	Emotional attachment, ritualized maintenance, ambivalent responsibility	Affective unease, corrupted nostalgia, ironic intimacy
Let It Rot	Repetitive clicking; decay prevention loop; anti-progression system	Compulsion, futility, ambient inertia	Banality, entropy, intentional dissatisfaction
Delirium Mentis	Rotating mini-games; inconsistent rules; surreal board setup	Confusion, forced adaptation, cooperative tension	Disorientation, absurdity, analogue enactment of overload

Visually, the games range from glitch-heavy maximalism (*The Epic Experience, W.G.O.T.Y.*) to intentional minimalism (*Let It Rot*), using aesthetic friction to provoke discomfort, irony, or reflection. Memes, low-res textures, and pop-up chaos are not simply stylistic — it's through these visual disturbances that the games articulate overload, decay, and detachment. Meanwhile, *Brain Beasties* uses augmented reality and nostalgic aesthetics to play with emotional investment in trivial digital icons, offering a softer but no less critical commentary. On the other hand, *Delirium Mentis*, the only analogue game, employs surreal illustrations, physical noise elements, and rotating mini-games to simulate digital chaos in a tactile format. Its unstable rule system and unpredictable pacing recreate the affective instability of digital saturation – but in shared, co-present space. Narratively, all projects resist traditional structure. They rely on fragmentation, recursive loops, and conceptual metaphors, placing the player in unstable roles – creator, caretaker, contestant. Humor often appears, but it is dry, self-aware, and laced with unease. These narratives are less about progression and more about performing saturation, forcing the player to feel disoriented, complicit, or fatigued. *Delirium Mentis*, in particular, transforms narrative coherence into absurd game logic, inviting players to collectively interpret and reinterpret their own confusion.

5   Outcomes and Reflections

The projects developed during the 13th IW required students to integrate disciplinary skills such as game design, visual communication, programming, and narrative design in a collaborative environment, with interdisciplinary processes evident in both ideation and prototyping phases, where iterative discussions and critiques facilitated knowledge transfer and concept refinement [1]. The open-ended theme added complexity, requiring teams to align diverse interpretations, emotional responses, and aesthetic strategies, highlighting the importance of well-managed transactive activities like communication and coordination, as outlined by Collaborative Cognitive Load Theory (CCLT) [12]. Observations revealed that mastering interdisciplinary design demands not only technical and conceptual skills but also emotional literacy and meta-awareness, with CCLT emphasizing the role of team composition, prior experience, and structured guidance in reducing cognitive load and fostering meaningful learning [1, 12]. Differences in how students processed the theme, both cognitively and emotionally, influenced the distribution and management of cognitive load within teams.

Brainrot inspired a diverse range of creative and critical responses, fostering interdisciplinary collaboration and experimentation. Students engaged deeply with the theme, developing critical thinking by exploring media consumption, identity, and digital overstimulation; taking creative risks through unconventional aesthetics like chaotic interfaces and absurdist logic; and enhancing collaboration and self-awareness through discussions, peer assessments, and reflections on their own media habits. While the theme encouraged meaningful conversations about digital overload and design ethics, it also posed challenges, such as superficial interpretations, difficulties in assessing unconventional projects, and emotional fatigue linked to the theme's focus on cognitive overload. These outcomes highlight the potential of thematic framing to drive creativity and metacognitive growth, while also emphasizing the need for structured prompts, balanced framing, and emotional support in future editions.

6   Limitations

The 13th IW generated a wide range of creative and critical responses but revealed limitations related to the theme, process, and analysis of outcomes. The theme *brainrot* while provocative and idea-generating, proved ambiguous, making it challenging for some teams, who at times resorted to superficial references such as memes or internet slang without deeper conceptual integration. The open-ended nature of the theme, with its multiple meanings (medical, metaphorical, cultural, generational), contributed to this disparity, highlighting the need for more structured guidance in future editions. The participatory evaluation process, which included self-assessment, peer evaluation, and open voting, promoted autonomy but complicated the assessment of unconventional projects, such as those adopting glitch aesthetics or absurd logic. The coordination team had to carefully moderate feedback to ensure fairness, particularly for works that challenged traditional norms. Despite the richness of the collected data (process documentation, informal observations, and project outputs), the absence of individual interviews or directed post-event surveys limits the comprehension of internal dynamics, emotional nuances and reflective impact on the teams, thus our understanding of student experiences remains partially inferred.

7   Conclusion and Future Work

The 13th Interdisciplinary Week (IW) in the Game Design degree program showcased how a culturally dense and emotionally charged theme like *brainrot* can act as a powerful catalyst for interdisciplinary creativity. Rather than being dismissed as unserious, the theme allowed students to critically engage with the aesthetics, logic, and emotional states of digital culture through satire, fragmentation, and overload, while reflecting on their dual roles as creators and consumers within algorithmic ecosystems. The ambiguity of the theme encouraged students to confront their own media habits and experiment with expressive forms of resistance, irony, and reflection, fostering critical engagement and interdisciplinary dialogue. This experience highlighted the value of integrating thematically charged concepts into design education, not only as stimuli for creative production but also as tools for deeper cognitive, emotional, and collaborative learning.

Looking ahead, the success of this edition suggests several opportunities for future development in both pedagogy and research methodology. The deliberate use of an ambiguous and culturally relevant theme proved effective in encouraging critical engagement and experimentation, particularly when students drew upon their own media habits and generational identities. Future strategies could include tools like autobiographical mapping or media journaling to deepen this connection. Methodologically, the need for more structured data collection was evident, with reflective surveys, interviews, and ongoing documentation offering potential for richer insights. Additionally, co-developing a template for interdisciplinary reflection with students could help capture the often-invisible dynamics of collaboration, such as emotional tensions and role shifts, while fostering metacognitive skills essential for design education.

References

1. Arthars, N., Markauskaite, L., Goodyear, P.: Constructing shared understanding of complex interdisciplinary problems: epistemic games in interdisciplinary teamwork. J. Learn. Sci. (2024). https://doi.org/10.1080/10508406.2024.2341390
2. Barroso, B., Barbedo, I.: Interdisciplinary week in game design: a learning experience. In: 9th International Conference on Higher Education Advances (HEAd 2023). Universitat Politècnica de València (2023). https://doi.org/10.4995/HEAd23.2023.16375
3. Baudrillard, J.: Simulacra and Simulation. (S. F. Glaser, Trans.). University of Michigan Press (1994). https://press.umich.edu/Books/S/Simulacra-and-Simulation2
4. Boix Mansilla, V., Miller, W.C., Gardner, H.: On Disciplinary Lenses and Interdisciplinary Work. In: Wineburg, S., Grossman, P. (eds.) Interdisciplinary Curriculum: Challenges of Implementation, pp. 17–38. Teachers College Press (2000)
5. Bulut, D., Samur, Y., Cömert, Z.: The effect of educational game design process on students' creativity. Smart Learn. Environ. **9**, 8 (2022). https://doi.org/10.1186/s40561-022-00188-9
6. Cafarella, L., Vasconcelos, L.: Computational thinking with game design: an action research study with middle school students. Educ. Inf. Technol. (2024/2025). https://doi.org/10.1007/s10639-024-12430-1
7. Firth, J., et al.: The "online brain": how the Internet may be changing our cognition. World Psychiatry **18**(2), 119–129 (2019). https://doi.org/10.1002/wps.20617
8. Han, B.-C.: The Burnout Society (E. Butler, Trans.). Stanford University Press (2015). https://www.sup.org/books/title/?id=24010
9. Hopper, J.W., Spinazzola, J., Simpson, W.B., van der Kolk, B.A.: How processing of sensory information from the internal and external worlds shapes perception and engagement with the world in the aftermath of trauma: implications for PTSD. Front. Neurosci. **15**, 625490 (2021). https://doi.org/10.3389/fnins.2021.625490
10. Hunicke, R., LeBlanc, M., Zubek, R.: MDA: a formal approach to game design and game research. In: Proceedings of the AAAI Workshop on Challenges in Game AI, San Jose, pp. 1–5. AAAI Press (2004)
11. Karakose, T., Tülübaş, T., Papadakis, S.: Revealing the intellectual structure and evolution of digital addiction research: an integrated bibliometric and science mapping approach. Int. J. Environ. Res. Public Health **19**(22), 14883 (2022).. https://doi.org/10.3390/ijerph192214883
12. Kirschner, P.A., Sweller, J., Kirschner, F., Zambrano R.: From cognitive load theory to collaborative cognitive load theory. Int. J. Comput. Support. Collab. Learn. **13**, 213–233 (2018). https://doi.org/10.1007/s11412-018-9277-y
13. Krajcik, J.S., Shin, N.: Project-based learning. In: Sawyer, R.K. (ed.) The Cambridge Handbook of the Learning Sciences, 2nd edn., pp. 275–297. Cambridge University Press (2014). https://doi.org/10.1017/CBO9781139519526.018
14. Laakso, N.L., et al.: Developing students' digital competences through collaborative design of digital games. Comput. Educ. **173**, 104287 (2021). https://doi.org/10.1016/j.compedu.2021.104287
15. Nietzsche, F.: On the Genealogy of Morality (K. Ansell-Pearson & C. Diethe, Eds. and Trans.). Cambridge University Press (2006). https://doi.org/10.1017/CBO9780511812071
16. Radzilowski, S.: Overstimulation: Symptoms, causes, and how to manage it. Therapist.com (2024). https://therapist.com/anxiety/overstimulation/
17. Repko, A.F., Szostak, R., Buchberger, M.P.: Introduction to Interdisciplinary Studies, 3rd edn. SAGE Publications (2019). https://us.sagepub.com/en-us/nam/introduction-to-interdisciplinary-studies/book257777
18. Sweller, J.: Cognitive load during problem solving: effects on learning. Cogn. Sci. **12**(2), 257–285 (1988). https://doi.org/10.1207/s15516709cog1202_4

19. Sweller, J.: Cognitive load theory and individual differences. Learn. Individ. Differ. **110**, 102423 (2024). https://doi.org/10.1016/j.lindif.2024.102423
20. van Vught, J., et al.: Facilitating social perspective taking in class through (co)design game-methodology. Imaginations **15**(2), 1–19 (2024). https://doi.org/10.17742/IMAGE.SPECTA CLE.15.2.3
21. Wu, C.H., et al.: Integrating computational thinking, game design, and design thinking. Humanit. Soc. Sci. Commun. **12**, 150 (2025). https://doi.org/10.1057/s41599-025-04502-x

Correction to: Games and Learning Alliance

Sander Bakkes⬤, Francesco Bellotti⬤, Pierpaolo Dondio⬤, Manuel Ninaus⬤, Vanissa Wanick⬤, and Antonio Bucchiarone⬤

Correction to:
S. Bakkes et al. (Eds.): *Games and Learning Alliance*, **LNCS 16307,**
https://doi.org/10.1007/978-3-032-11043-5

In the original version of this book, one of the editor's name has typo in the surname. This has been corrected. Correctly it should read as name: "Vanissa Wanick".

The updated version of this book can be found at
https://doi.org/10.1007/978-3-032-11043-5

Author Index